49.95

ADULPHE DELEGORGUE'S

TRAVELS
IN SOUTHERN AFRICA

VOLUME I

Killie Campbell Africana Library Publications

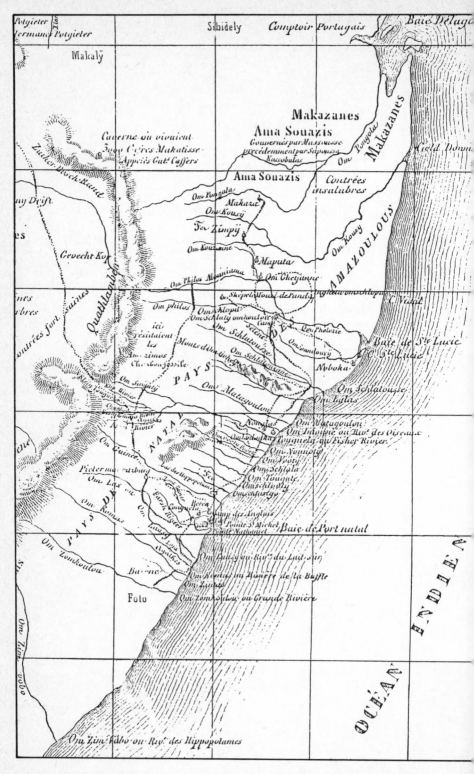

DELEGORGUE'S TRAVELS IN NATAL AND ZULULAND.

ADULPHE DELEGORGUE'S

TRAVELS
IN SOUTHERN AFRICA

VOLUME I

Translated by
FLEUR WEBB

Introduced and indexed by
STEPHANIE J. ALEXANDER
and
COLIN DE B. WEBB

Killie Campbell Africana Library
Durban
University of Natal Press
Pietermaritzburg
1990

ISBN 0 86980 727 7
ISBN 0 86980 529 0 (Set)

Typeset in the University of Natal Press
Pietermaritzburg
Printed by Kohler Carton and Print
Box 955, Pinetown, 3600 South Africa

CONTENTS

Travels in Southern Africa

ILLUSTRATIONS

The illustrations are all reproduced from the 1847 edition of *Voyage dans l'Afrique Australe*. The cover picture is from George French Angas's *The Kafirs Illustrated* (1849) and shows the mouth of the Om Nonnoty River.

GENERAL INTRODUCTION

The publishing history of Adulphe Delegorgue's two-volume *Voyage dans l'Afrique Australe* has never been fully unravelled. In recent years, a further twist in the skein has been brought to light through the endeavours of two dedicated Africana authorities, the late Mr Ronald Butcher and Mr R.E. Levitt, who in succession have ensured the survival of a unique hand-written document bearing Delegorgue's signature. Produced in June 1848 – just one year after the publication of the *Voyage* – it is the rough draft of a pamphlet, prepared by Delegorgue to promote the sale of his book. The name of the agent to whom this advertising copy was addressed is difficult to decipher. It would appear to be 'M Guerin'. But even if that is incorrect, one thing is certain: neither the agent's name nor his address (Rue Bourbon le Chateau, No 1) bear any resemblance to the names and addresses of firms known to have been associated with the production of the book.

The initial printing and publishing in 1847 was undertaken by A. René et cie, whose address was Rue de Seine, 32, Paris. There was, however, at least one further issue of the work. This was undated, and differed in certain important respects from the first. In the second issue, the printed format of the text is indistinguishable from that in the issue put out by A. René et cie. Indeed, the two issues appear to derive from a single print-run. The points on which they differ are all to be found on the preliminary pages, where dissimilar type-faces and other anomalies occur. Most notably, there is in the second issue no mention whatsoever of the printing and publishing house of A. René. Instead, the printer is identified as

W. Remquet et cie
Successeurs de Paul Renouard
Rue Garancière, 5, Derrière Saint-Sulpice

and, at the foot of the title-page, where the name of the publishing house is conventionally given, the following appears instead:

Paris
Au Dépot de Librairie, Rue des Moulins, 8
Près la rue Thérèse
Addresser les demandes et mandats a Mme Croissant.

It would appear that, by the time of the second issue, a breach of some sort had occurred in Delegorgue's working relationship with René et cie, and that as a consequence he had removed the remaining unbound copies of the original print-run from that firm, and had handed them over to the agency served by the worthy Mme Cròissant. These agents had then presumably arranged for the printing of new preliminary pages by W. Remquet et cie in order to be able to market the work in their own name. A complicated story! And one which, if correct, still leaves unresolved the question why it was that Delegorgue went to yet another agency for the printing of the pamphlet he had prepared for the promotion of his work.

However, the draft pamphlet derives its interest not simply from its bearing upon the tangle of business relationships into which Delegorgue was drawn through his book. It is interesting, too, because of what it reflects of the man himself. Modesty, whether false or sincere, was not the distinguishing characteristic of his draft. The virtues of author and book are presented as virtually inseparable, and the puff which is given to the work derives much of its strength from the puff which Delegorgue gives to himself.

His credentials are listed in the draft pamphlet as 'membre de la Société de Géographie de Paris, membre de la Société Ethnologique de Paris, membre correspondence de la Société Orientale de Paris etc., etc., Chevalier de l'Ordre de la Légion d'honneur'. These were unusual attainments for a young man of 33 years; and, since they are not mentioned anywhere in the prefatory pages of the two issues of his work, one is left wondering when it was that he was admitted to these august fraternities, particularly to the highly distinguished and exclusive Légion d'honneur.

Whatever the answer to that question, there can be no doubt that he had made himself deserving of high recognition. His was an account of travel, exploration, hunting and scientific observation unlike any that had been published before: and it was based on a range of interests and a sharpness of observation that set him apart from the ordinary run of adventurers and hunters whose tales found their way into print in the nineteenth century.

Delegorgue believed that, as a record of hunting, his book was rivalled, in the whole of Europe, by only one other work, *The Wild Sports of Southern Africa* by Sir William Cornwallis Harris. But, as he also makes clear in the draft pamphlet, his book, unlike that of Cornwallis Harris, is much more than an account of African hunting. It is, he points out, of interest to 'the botanist, the geologist, the ornithologist, the entomologist, the hunter, the linguist, the philosopher and the colonist'. It deals not only 'with animals and their habits', but also with 'the history of the country . . . the customs of its various inhabitants . . . and the produce of the land'; and it offers 'a complete vocabulary of the Caffre

Zoulou language which is the first ever to appear'. All these claims are, in a measure, true. In somewhat varying strengths, the elements identified by Delegorgue are all present in his book, from the philosophy (which liberally garnishes his observations on the human and natural worlds) to the Zulu vocabulary (which appears at the end of the second volume, and which, if a little less complete than he liked to believe, was nevertheless a remarkable achievement, pre-dating by ten years the pioneering *Zulu-Kafir Dictionary* of J L Döhne).

Today, the information which Delegorgue assembled has been massively superceded by advances in knowledge in all the fields he mentions. But, for other reasons, the wide appeal of his work remains. It has the romance of a nineteenth century tale of adventure; it has scientific interest as a reflection of European attitudes towards, and knowledge of, the natural world in the first half of the nineteenth century; and it has historical value as a unique record of people, environment and events at a critical moment in the development of South Africa.

When Delegorgue arrived in the country in 1838 events were in train which were to be of transforming significance for its future. In the preceding decades, the African societies of south-east Africa, in response to a complex of economic and social pressures, had moved into a phase of conflict and political restructuring. Powerful new polities had emerged such as the Zulu and Ndebele kingdoms, and far-reaching adjustments had taken place in the location and distribution of people. In the later phases of these upheavals, two further population shifts of major significance had occurred. First, in 1820, large numbers of British immigrants had been brought to South Africa, and had been settled along the Cape-Xhosa frontier, whence bands of English-speaking hunters and adventurers, lured by the trade in ivory and skins, had begun to make their way to Natal from 1824 onwards. Next, in the mid-1830s, Dutch-speaking colonists from the Cape had broken out of the confines of the colony in large numbers, and with their families, servants and herds had moved into the interior, occupying lands in the territories that came to be known as the Orange Free State, the Transvaal and Natal.

Thus, a new society was in the making – a society in which, from the Atlantic in the south to the Limpopo in the north, the destinies of indigenous Africans and intrusive whites were becoming inextricably intertwined. During his relatively short initial sojourn at the Cape, Delegorgue observed some of the consequences for the colony of the great Boer emigration; and when he reached Port Natal in May 1839 he found himself at the epicentre of cross-cutting pressures and tensions between Boers, Britons and Blacks.

Just a little over a year prior to his arrival at the Port, in February 1838, a Boer delegation under the leadership of Pieter Retief had been massacred at Mgungundlovu, the capital of the Zulu king, Dingane, and shortly thereafter Boer encampments south of the upper reaches of the Thukela (Tugela) river had sustained heavy losses when attacked by Dingane's forces. In the hope of restraining conflict between the emigrant Boers and their black neighbours to north and south, a British occupation force was sent to Natal; but when it arrived, on 4 December 1838, a Boer commando was already on its way to wreak vengeance on the Zulu for the February massacres. The resulting defeat which the Zulu suffered at the iNcome (Blood) river on 16 December 1838 did not destroy Dingane's kingdom, but left it gravely weakened.

It was into this unstable situation that Delegorgue moved in May 1839. Four months after his arrival, the Zulu king's half-brother, Mpande, seceded south of the Thukela, and in October was visited by a Boer delegation at the Thongathi river, where an alliance against Dingane was formed. This alliance, followed by the withdrawal of the costly and largely ineffectual British occupation force in December 1839, opened the way for a new phase in the politics of the region. The Boers proclaimed the Republic of Natalia, and shortly thereafter, Mpande's forces, with the Boers trailing some way behind, inflicted a crushing defeat on Dingane's armies at the battle of Maqongqo in January 1840. Dingane fled his kingdom, only to be put to death by the neighbouring Nyawo people, and Mpande was recognised as Zulu king.

Delegorgue accompanied both the Boer delegation to the Thongathi and the Boer expedition in support of Mpande. He also spent long periods hunting and exploring in Natal, and in the Zulu kingdom after Mpande's succession. This volume is thus an important documentary source about Boer-Zulu relations in the critical years 1839–40, about life in the Zulu kingdom during the early years of Mpande's reign, about Boer-British relations in the late 1830s and early 1840s, and about life in the short-lived Republic of Natalia, whose independence was extinguished by Britain in 1843 after the Boers had mounted armed resistance against a second occupation force sent to the Port in 1842.

Unconsciously, Delegorgue's work also reflects upon something more profound: the impoverishment of the indigenous people as land was taken from them, as game was destroyed in great orgies of blood-letting, and as ivory and cattle were traded out of the region to satisfy demand in the markets of the mercantile world.

Delegorgue's own record of animal slaughter was not inconsiderable, and one finds him pausing at moments to cogitate upon the implications of what he was doing. But these interludes of reflection did not last long. A great continent stretched out beyond his immediate field of action – a continent holding seemingly limitless quantities of the game he was destroying; and his exuberant delight in being young and alive amidst the challenges and dangers of the African wilds turned him back to the chase without any lasting perturbation of conscience.

His lust for adventure, and his scientific curiosity have been seen as twin facets of the questing spirit of post-Enlightenment Europe; and his adulation of the Zulu has been linked to nineteenth century romanticism and the cult of 'the noble savage'. Doubtless, there is truth in both these observations. It would have been surprising had Delegorgue not been influenced by the intellectual climate of his time. But he was also his own man, with a view of people and things not quite like any-one else's. Notwithstanding his admiration for the Zulu, there were individual Blacks whom he disliked, and aspects of Zulu life which he spurned. Although his general attitude to the emigrant Boers was one of disdain, there were individuals whom he befriended, and there were things which he found to admire amongst the Dutch-speaking colonists of the Cape. Moreover, his scarcely-concealed conviction that the French were blessed with superiority over other European nations, did not diminish his delight in the company of lively and interesting non-French fellow-Europeans; nor did it deter him from applying some of his sharpest strictures to the Frenchman, François Le Vaillant, whose purportedly scientific observations he found to be flawed by inaccuracy and fancifulness.

Had he been older, Delegorgue might have been more cautious about the risks of self-righteousness criticism of others. He himself was not beyond error; nor was he beyond exaggeration. A story which he relates about gaining access to the royal quarters at the Thongathi river, while Mpande and his maidens were sleeping, is inconsistent with all the other surviving evidence about the impenetrable security that usually surrounded high-ranking personages of the Zulu royal house. If the account is true, as it may indeed be, the manner in which he presents his experience is more than a little embellished.

That there should be error and distortion in his work is hardly surprising. Few, if any, historical documents can be accepted at face value; and Delegorgue's record, like any other, has to be evaluated in the context of the full corpus of surviving evidence. Its uniqueness lies in the richness and sharpness of his observations, in the enthusiasm and energy with which he participated in the events of his time, and in the good-humour and courage with which he handled strange people and unfamiliar situations.

His was a short life, but he packed a great deal into it. Born in the village of Courcelles, near Douai, Picardy, on 14 November 1814, he was orphaned at the age of four, and was brought up in the home of his grandfather, who was a judicial official in the court at Douai. It was in that home that he was introduced to natural science, and it was there that his curiosity about the world beyond Europe was honed to a sharp edge. His decision at the age of 16 to enrol in the merchant navy instead of pursuing the traditional family calling of the law was perhaps to be expected, therefore, as was his decision five years later to commit himself to science and to undertake a great journey of exploration in southern Africa. His choice of destination was determined by his awareness of the wealth of South Africa's zoological and botanical resources; but it is possible that there was also a secondary consideration concealed behind that choice. Douai lies close to Flanders; and if in his youth Delegorgue had picked up some Flemish, which is not unlikely, he may well have been attracted by the prospect of working in a field where language would not be a barrier to the gathering of valuable primary information. Certainly he seems to have possessed a remarkable facility to communicate with the Dutch-speaking colonists of the Cape and the emigrant Boers, and there can be no doubt that his scientific work benefited as a consequence.

The years spanned by his southern African expedition are the best-documented phase of his life. After his return to France via St. Helena, in February 1844, his time was taken up with the preparation and publication of the book, and he then began to plan another expedition. This time his destination was West Africa, and he set sail again early in 1850. He was not to attain his purpose, however. He developed fever on board, and died between Gorée and Grand Bassam on 30 May 1850.

We are fortunate that more than five years of Delegorgue's short life were spent in South Africa. He was not yet twenty-four when he arrived in the country, and he was just rising twenty-nine when he left. His sojourn has given us a young man's record of the fascination and excitement of being present at a juncture in history when part of the veil that had shrouded old Africa from Europe was being torn open by colonists, missionaries and the agents of mercantile capitalism.

It is our hope that with the assistance of the annotated indexes that accompany this translation, the world which Delegorgue explored will become accessible to English-speaking readers more than a century and a half after his time.

*   *   *   *   *

Certain people have responded without hesitation to appeals for help when editorial problems have arisen. In particular, I wish to thank Dr Frank Bradlow, Mr Robert Levitt and my colleagues Dr John Wright and Professor Anthony Davies of the University of Natal, Pietermaritzburg.

What goes before the public in this volume is the product of team endeavour. Three members of the team are readily identifiable; the fourth is not. This is Margery Moberly of the University of Natal Press.

Although she gets no title-page credit, she has been more than our publisher; from early on, she has been closely involved in advising and assisting in the planning of this volume. To these three partners – to my wife Fleur, and to Stephanie Alexander and Margery Moberly – I wish to record thanks for holding the venture together over many long years and through some trying and difficult times.

COLIN DE B. WEBB

Pietermaritzburg, May 1990

WORKS CONSULTED

BIBLIOGRAPHIES, GUIDES AND WORKS OF REFERENCE

Botha, C.G.   *Place names in the Cape Province*. Cape Town, 1926.

Botha, T.J.R.   *Watername in Natal*. Pretoria, 1977.

Bryant, A.T., comp.   *Zulu-English Dictionary*. Pietermaritzburg, 1905.

Cope, A.T.   *A Select bibliography relating to the Zulu people of Natal and Zululand*. Durban, 1974.

Dictionary of South African biography. Cape Town, Durban, 1968–81. 4v.

Dent, G.R. and Nyembezi, C.L.S., comps.   *Scholar's Zulu Dictionary*. Pietermaritzburg, 1969.

Doke, C.M., Malcolm, D. McK. and Sikakana, J.M.A., comps.   *English-Zulu Dictionary*. Johannesburg, 1985.

Doke, C.M. and Vilakazi, B.W., comps.   *Zulu-English Dictionary*. Johannesburg, 1972.

Encyclopaedia Britannica, 15th ed. Chicago, 1974. 30v.

Lugg, H.C.   *Zulu place names in Natal*, revised by A.T. Cope, Durban, 1968.

Merrett, C.E.   *Index to the 1:50 000 map series. Part 1, Natal*. Pietermaritzburg, 1977.

Merrett, C.E.   *A Selected bibliography of Natal maps, 1800–1977*. Boston, 1979.

Müller, C.F.J., ed.   *South African history and historians: a bibliography*, ed. by C.F.J. Müller and others. Pretoria, 1979.

Pettman, C.   *South African place names*. Rivonia, 1985.

Raper, P.E.   *Dictionary of South African place names*. Rivonia, 1987.

A South African bibliography to the year 1925: being a revision and continuation of Sidney Mendelssohn's 'South African bibliography' (1910). London, 1979. 4v.

Stayt, D. *Where on earth? A guide to the place names of Natal and Zululand.* Durban, 1971.

Standard Encyclopaedia of Southern Africa. Cape Town, 1970–76. 12v.

Thompson, L. *Southern African history before 1900: a select bibliography of articles*, by L. Thompson, R. Elphick and I. Jarrick. Stanford, 1971.

Webb's guide to the official records of the Colony of Natal: an expanded and revised edition together with indexes, comp. by J. Verbeek, M. Nathanson and E. Peel. Pietermaritzburg, 1984.

PUBLISHED SOURCES

Agar-Hamilton, J.A.I. *The Native policy of the Voortrekkers.* Cape Town, 1928.

Axelson, E. *Portuguese in south-east Africa, 1600–1700.* Johannesburg, 1960.

Bell, K.N. and Morrell, W.P. *Select documents on British colonial policy, 1830–1860.* Oxford, 1928.

Bird, J. *The Annals of Natal.* Pietermaritzburg, 1888. 2v.

Brookes, E.H. and Webb, C. de B. *A History of Natal.* Pietermaritzburg, 1987.

Bryant, A.T. *Olden times in Zululand and Natal.* London, 1929.

The Cambridge history of the British empire. v.VIII. *South Africa*, ed. by the late E.A. Benians, Sir J. Butler, P.N.S. Mansergh and E.A. Walker. Cambridge, 1963.

Chase, J.C. *The Natal papers, a reprint of all notices and public documents, 1488–1843.* 2 pts. Grahamstown, 1843.

Cloete, H. *Five lectures on the emigration of the Dutch farmers from . . .the Cape . . . and their settlement in . . . Natal, until their formal submission to Her Majesty's authority in . . . 1843.* Cape Town, 1856.

Cory, Sir G.E., Preller, G. and Blommaert, W. *Die Retief-Dingaan ooreenkoms.* In *Annale van die Universiteit van Stellenbosch*, Serie B, No.1. Cape Town, 1924.

Du Plessis, A.J. *Die Republiek Natalia.* Archives Year Book for South African History, 1942, Part I. Cape Town, 1943.

Francois Le Vaillant: traveller in South Africa. Cape Town, 1973. 2v.

Galbraith, J.S. *Reluctant empire: British policy on the South African frontier, 1834–1854.* Berkely, 1963,

Gibson, J.Y. *The Story of the Zulus.* Pietermaritzburg, 1903.

Hammond-Tooke, W.D., ed. *The Bantu-speaking peoples of Southern Africa.* 2nd ed. London, 1974.

Harris, W.C. *The Wild sports of southern Africa.* London, 1852.

Holden, W.C. *History of the colony of Natal.* London, 1855.

Hugo, M. *Piet Retief.* Johannesburg, 1961.

Hummel, H.C. 'Adulphe Delegorgue: an enlightenment view of nineteenth century South African'. Acta Academica, 22 (1), March 1990.

Jansen, E.G. *Die Voortrekkers in Natal.* Cape Town, 1938.

Knaplund, P. *James Stephen and the British colonial system, 1813–1847*. Madison, 1953.

Krauss, F. *Travel journal / Cape to Zululand: observations by a collector and naturalist*, ed. by O.H. Spohr. Cape Town, 1973.

Lugg, H.C. *Historic Natal and Zululand*. Pietermaritzburg, 1948.

Mackeurtan, G. *The Cradle days of Natal, 1497–1845*. London, 1931.

Müller, C.J.F. *Die Britse owerheid en die groot trek*. Cape Town, 1947.

Nathan, M. *The Voortrekkers of South Africa . . .* London, 1937.

Notule Natalse Volksraad (met bylae), 1838–1845. South African Archival Records, Natal No.1. Cape Town, 1953.

Preller, G.S. *Andries Pretorius . . .* Johannesburg, 1937.

Preller, G.S. *Historiese opstelle*. Pretoria, 1925.

Preller, G.S. *Piet Retief . . .* Pretoria, 1908.

Preller, G.S. *Sketse en opstelle*. Pretoria, 1928.

Preller, G.S. *Voortrekkermense*. Cape Town, 1918–38.

Samuelson, R.C.A. *Long, long ago*. Durban, 1929.

Shooter, J. *The Kafirs of Natal and the Zulu country*. London, 1857.

Smail, J.L. *Historical monuments and battlefields in Natal and Zululand*. Cape Town, 1965.

Smail, J.L. *Monuments and trails of the Voortrekkers*. Cape Town, 1968.

Smith, A. *Andrew Smith and Natal: documents relating to the early history of the province*, ed. by P.R. Kirby. Van Riebeeck Society, No.36. Cape Town, 1955.

Smith, E. *The Life and times of Daniel Lindley (1801–1880). Missionary to the Zulus. Pastor of the Voortrekkers . . .* London, 1949.

Tabler, E.C. *Pioneers of Natal and South-eastern Africa, 1552–1878*. Cape Town, 1977.

Theal, G. McC. *History of the Boers in South Africa*. London, 1887.

Thompson, G. *Travels and adventures in South Africa*. London, 1827. 2v.

Voigt, J.C. *Fifty years of the history of the republic in South Africa, 1795–1845*. London, 1899. 2 v.

Walker, E.A. *The Great Trek*. London, 1934.

Watt, E.P. *Febana: the true story of Farewell*. London, 1962.

Webb, C. de B., 'Great Britain and "Die Republiek Natalia"'. *Theoria*, 37, 1971.

Webb, C. de B. and Wright, J.B., eds. *The James Stuart archive of recorded oral evidence relating to the history of the Zulu and neighbouring peoples*. Pietermaritzburg, 1976, 1979, 1982, 1986. 4v.

Webb, C. de B. and Wright, J.B., eds., *A Zulu king speaks*. Pietermaritzburg, 1978.

Wilson, H.C. *The Two scapegoats: a few remarks on Piet Retief in defence of Captain Allen Gardiner and the Rev. F. Owen*. Pietermaritzburg, 1914.

Wood, W. *Statements respecting Dingaan, king of the Zoolahs, with some particulars relative to the massacres of Messrs. Retief and Biggars, and their parties*. Cape Town, 1840.

UNPUBLISHED SOURCES

Berman, E.M. 'How far was the breakdown of the Republic of Natal due to inherent weaknesses in its native policy?' M.A. Cape Town, 1933.

Grieve, C.S. 'The Policy of His Majesty's government towards Europeans beyond the colonial borders, 1830–1840'. M.A., Cape Town, 1924.

Shiels, R. 'Newton Adams, 1835–1851'. B.A. Hons. Natal, 1963.

Vietzen, S. The Rev. James Archbell: a study in missionary activity'. B.A. Hons. Natal, 1962.

ADULPHE DELEGORGUE – SCIENTIST

Adulphe Delegorgue would think it proper that he be presented to posterity as a scientist. In his day the natural historian was not, as now, regarded as a mere dabbler on the fringe of *real* science. Natural historians *were* scientists, for 'natural history' then was synonymous with our own 'biology' and simply meant the study of living things. There were illustrious museums of natural history – some still exist – and at universities there were departments and chairs in the subject. There were many respected amateur natural historians whose pioneering work provided information that is of fundamental importance to the biological sciences today.

Strangely, though Delegorgue's southern African travels are known to historians, the biological aspects that he himself considered the most interesting part of his travel memoir are unfamiliar to modern biologists, except, perhaps, to some ornithologists and entomologists. In Natal, both amateur and professional birdwatchers have seen or read about *Columba delegorguei*, the shy bird of coastal forests whose common name is Delegorgue's pigeon (also called the bronze-naped pigeon). These readers will, alas, be disappointed that *C. delegorguei* is not mentioned in the present volume: it is described (and quite improperly named by Delegorgue for himself) in an appendix to Volume Two. His catalogue of insects, too, is placed at the end of that volume.

The other zoologists and the botanists for whom Delegorgue intended so much of his book may also be disappointed at first, for this is, clearly, a record made by a very young man (Delegorgue arrived at the Cape at the age of 23), and, apparently, an irresponsible one. One gains a swift impression of a youthful eye, caught by the large, the colourful, the spectacular and, when necessary, the edible; an eye unwilling (or unable) to see the inconspicuous. Loud in his protestations of dedication to science and love of natural beauty, Delegorgue rushes over the southern African landscape, systematically destroying as much of its fauna as possible. Similarly, his claims to scientific professionalism (and to various highminded attitudes) appear to be belied by erratic and carelessly used terminology, by unsatisfactory recording of data and by zoological arguments which often seem uninformed and naïve.

Although these criticisms are to a certain extent valid they do Delegorgue an injustice. They do not take into account the period in which he lived, for example, or his educational, social and cultural background. They ignore, too, his remarkable personal qualities – his eager, enquiring mind, his determination, his intelligence, his integrity, his obvious charm. This book is far from the usual dry travel journal or log of hunting and collecting statistics, and if there are omissions and inconsistencies that is, surely, a small price to pay for vivid descriptions and anecdotes and a sense, always, of delight in discovery.

Delegorgue's youthfulness was not, in fact, exceptional. It had long been fashionable for young Europeans and Scandinavians to travel intrepidly to wild parts of the globe and indeed, if they joined formal expeditions of exploration, as did Jacques Arago, they might embark while still in their teens. Solitary travellers who came south for the sake of a career as hunter or scholar were usually older than this, but often not by much. The 18th century Swedish travellers, Sparrman and Thunberg, were aged 24 and 28 respectively, while Delegorgue's contemporaries, Krauss (German) and Wahlberg (Swedish), were 25 and 28. Each of these four returned home to write works that have had a lasting influence on several scientific fields. Perhaps the best known example of a biologist whose youthful travels had a profound influence upon him (and upon the science of biology as a whole) was Charles Darwin. He was 23 when he was appointed to the post of naturalist on the research vessel HMS *Beagle* in 1831.

What makes Delegorgue different from these other travellers is his lack of a formal scientific education. However, while this does affect his presentation of scientific material, it allows him the latitude to explore and to set down anything that takes his fancy. The result is as rich and varied as, we may conclude, had been his earlier life.

He was born in Courcelles-les-Sens, in northern France. Soon orphaned, he spent his childhood in the home of his grandfather, a 'royal court judge' of Douai. The elder Delegorgue took his grandson's education in hand himself, rewarding good behaviour by allowing him access to his own fine private collection of natural history specimens, among which were doubtless items from many parts of the world, including Africa and South America. How had the judge acquired this collection? Probably he had bought specimens from professional hunter-travellers who made a living by selling them to well-to-do amateur naturalists and to museums. Adulphe Delegorgue himself indicates that he was collecting for this same purpose, presumably to finance these and later travels.

The judge took natural history seriously and would certainly have owned a good library, in which Adulphe read the works of at least one ancient but still important scientific author (Aristotle), as well as many more recent French works of classical zoology, often in numerous volumes (Belon, Buffon, Cuvier, Lesson). Travel memoirs were popular, and he knew the respected writings of Tavernier and the later – rather lighter, if not downright sensational – accounts of such as Arago. His great inspiration was, of course, Le Vaillant's celebrated *Travels*, and his references to this in the present text indicate an intimate knowledge of Le Vaillant's southern African sojourn gained by careful study, perhaps over a period of years.

It is probable that the grandfather supplied little more than the stimulus, in the form of studious example, specimens and literature, and that with a minimum of tuition the boy, imagination caught, was virtually able to educate himself. His lack of a university education, therefore, was not a great handicap, the more so because he possessed qualities which, had he been more singleminded, might even have helped turn him into a considerable scientist. One was a freshness, an innocence; the other was insatiable curiosity. These qualities kept him 'tenacious and steadfast' at boring or unpleasant tasks (for the first time in his life, as he says), and they gave him the energy to spring from his sickbed at the least suggestion that he might see something new and strange. This innocence, this perpetual questioning, this openness, tends to be belittled in our own jaded times, but the combination – which can be as ruthless as it is engaging – has often been one of the hallmarks of scientific greatness, from Darwin to Einstein; from Rutherford to Watson and Crick. Delegorgue fell short of greatness, not because he lacked the wit, but because he dispersed, joyfully, his energies in so many directions and because, hardly pausing to consolidate work and thoughts, he was planning or undertaking further travels – and so, finally, died of fever en route to West Africa at the age of 35.

Delegorgue's self-education must surely have continued after he left home in his late teens, when he went to sea for four years. It was, after all, not so much the process of travel that enchanted him as the wonders awaiting his arrival, and we know that he found sea voyages tedious. It is likely that nights afloat spent wakefully smoking, as he describes, were also spent reading. There is no doubt that his experiences in those years whetted his appetite for more and it can be assumed that the two years of enforced recuperative idleness back at home must have included study. This would have entailed more than the reading of works of science and travel. Somehow, during this period, he acquired the practical skills essential to his chosen career and to his southern African destination.

For, by the time he reached the Cape, he possessed a fairly solid knowledge of southern African birds and larger mammals (gained mainly from Le Vaillant and, perhaps, from Burchell, whose *Travels*, published in 1822 and 1824, he may have read in English or in French translation). Further, he was equipped to kill cleanly anything from an insect to the largest mammals. He knew, also, how to skin, to clean, to preserve chemically, to mount or otherwise prepare a whole range of specimens, and he seems to have been a good taxidermist. He understood the importance of keeping records and was also a practised illustrator. He had, in short, become the equivalent of a versatile museum technician, able to prepare his material out of doors when necessary, and in the most difficult climatic conditions. As he returned to France with very large numbers of specimens of all kinds, many to be used for further study and some reportedly still in existence, we can be sure that much of his work was excellent.

When notes made on the spot are later used in chronological order to build a memoir it may be possible to follow the author's intellectual – and even emotional – development over the period covered by the book. Thus, it is easy to see that Delegorgue maintained his habit of assimilating and at once using new information throughout his stay in southern Africa. Exclusively French common names for animals recorded on the southward voyage are supplemented almost immediately after arrival at the Cape by Dutch and vernacular names. As very few in southern Africa would have been able to communicate with him in French, and as he was always urgently wishing to know things, Delegorgue must have set himself to learn some basic Dutch and the rudiments of the vernacular wherever he happened to be. A willingness on the part of foreigners to learn and use one's language is attractive, and may partly account for his ready acceptance by disparate persons and communities in southern Africa – and the ease with which people seem to have co-operated with him. He had a good ear and probably an agile tongue, as can be deduced from his French phonetic spellings, of Zulu words in particular. These, if pronounced aloud with French intonation, have an auditory authenticity that no English-based transliteration provides. His renderings of Dutch words are less satisfactory. Although some are ingenious (e.g. 'Paerde' for 'perde'), some are strange. 'Book', for example (as in spring-book, riet-book, plural –booken), will not sound like bock or bok, no matter how it is pronounced. A possible explanation for this oddity is that Delegorgue was influenced in his pronunciation of some Dutch words by the German accent of his friend Krauss, who included 'Springböcken' in the brief but quite comprehensive survey of fauna and flora in the introduction to his 1843 paper (on southern African Crustacea). Incidentally, one could wish that Krauss had had more of a scientific influence on Delegorgue: his grasp of taxonomy and use of nomenclature is assured. By contrast with his Teutonic thoroughness Delegorgue's approach looks very casual – or perhaps one might say debonairly Gallic.

Still, his various renderings of common and vernacular names, though often baffling at first, are almost all traceable and it is the scientific names that sometimes give trouble. Eccentric usages, such as more than one generic name for an animal, the species name used alone to denote the genus, unconventional abbreviations and names of Delegorgue's own invention which never appear again, may all be laid at the door of his want of drilling in the rules of taxonomy, as also can the scant attention he gives to higher levels of classification. However, variability in nomenclature may reflect also his wide and unselective reading in zoology and, perhaps, a tendency to accord equal taxonomic weight to every publication, recent or obsolete. It must be remembered that one traveller after another was 'discovering' the same animal over and over again, naming and renaming (and creating, by the way, labyrinthine confusion for 20th century taxonomists). Seen in this light, Delegorgue's errors are understandable, and it is then surprising that he is correct as often as he is.

Difficulties with names mean that the identities of plants and animals in this book often have to be arrived at by a process of deduction, elimination, educated guesswork or all three. The reader wishing to establish a locality or date may also need to apply these methods, and may not always be successful. This kind of detective work, too, has had to be undertaken in the identification of diseases, both human and of stock, mentioned in the text. Sometimes identification, as with malaria, necessitates the collection of symptoms scattered almost idly over many pages: Delegorgue had not realised that together they presented an identifying syndrome. Occasionally the symptoms described are so severe – because of ignorance and neglect – that they seem to be those of some mediaeval scourge (e.g., Natal sores). Where symptoms are not given, as with the disease of horses, they have to be arrived at by arguing backwards from the assortment of remedies listed in the text.

Delegorgue's attitude towards disease and injury was individual and yet in keeping with the time. He was a stoical fellow with a robust constitution, able to walk long distances fasting when ill with malaria and to lead a very active life despite months of bone-deep leg ulceration. At the same time he took the trouble to discover and list Boer remedies and, to some extent, those of the indigenous people – and not as mere curiosities, for he tried (or considered trying) some of them just in case – while heartily scoffing at anything that seemed to him super-stitious or primitive. On the whole he accepted illness in a subtropical climate as an occupational hazard (lamenting only the absence of the Frenchman's panacea, the medicinal leech), and his only real fear was of the unknown.

Into this category fell the spectre of dread miasmata and effluvia – the odour of decay which, in itself, carried 'foul contagion' – and he refers to this several times in different contexts. Human corpses released gases so evil-smelling that they must be poisonous, he believed, as did mounds of dead locusts, while noxious vapours hung over marshes at night.

With hindsight it is easy to dismiss this as unscientific nonsense, but we should realise that Delegorgue was writing, not only long before the discovery of bacteria and all microscopic pathogens, but even before John Snow's 1849 discovery that cholera could be eradicated if drinking water was not contaminated by infected persons – i.e., if adequate sanitation was provided. The discovery and use of such basic rules of cleanliness gradually paved the way for an understanding of aspects of disease transmission, although improved hygiene would, of course, have little effect on the transmission of some insect-borne diseases. Malaria, known in English until 1827 as 'marsh miasm', 'marsh fever', 'ague', etc., was not known to be caused by a blood parasite until 1880, and it was almost 20 years before the life history of the parasite had been worked out and the stages passed in the primary (human) host and secondary (mosquito) vector were understood. It is no wonder, then, that even in the late 19th century everyone, including the greatest scientific and medical intellects, tended to invoke malign influences to explain infection and the spread of disease. We need not, therefore, shake our heads at Delegorgue's failure to link mosquito bites to his own infection, nor condemn the amusement he derived from recalling his first encounter with mosquito swarms in Natal.

Not all of Delegorgue's scientific thinking is antique, however, and at times it is startlingly modern: '. . . it is showing too much respect for our forefathers,' he says, 'if we do not attempt to go beyond the frontiers of knowledge which they have reached.'

This is wholesome and progressive, but his first attempts to 'go beyond the frontiers' lack refinement. Early in the book he is led into the kind of argument common in undergraduates keen to impress with a display of erudition. He tries, in jumbled and inconclusive fashion, to compare the brown hyaena of the Cape with the beaver ('*latax*') referred to by Aristotle (slily omitting a contradictory fragment of the Aristotle quotation) and the enigmatic 'sea wolf' of Belon – with a few words about the Canadian otter thrown in. The argument is zoologically worthless, but it tells us a great deal about Delegorgue's belief in his ability – and right – to break new ground and rethink older work. Fortunately he was intelligent and honest enough to abandon such juvenilities thereafter, and although his arguments about hornbills and toucans, ticks and leeches, are naïve, they show a pleasing aptitude for the kind of topsy-turvy, speculative thinking that can sometimes lead to advances, especially in the biological sciences.

He soon discovered, and kept rediscovering, that there is no sub-stitute for personal observation and experience and that accuracy is important if one's writings are to endure. It may be that, in a quite unexpected way, Le Vaillant's '*Travels*' helped develop this awareness. It was, as already mentioned, Le Vaillant who had been Delegorgue's inspiration, in both destination and style of work. Hardly had he arrived in Africa, though, than he began finding Le Vaillant in error: the inaccuracies he cites, geographical and zoological, are astonishing. As later scholars have agreed, Le Vaillant would not, for some reason, be content with the truth of what he saw and did and, having tainted his work with invention and embellishment, lost the chance of honour and a lasting reputation.

The point here is not the extent – or even the fact – of Le Vaillant's weaknesses, but rather Delegorgue's discovery that the great are not infallible. In this particular context the discovery must have been a great disappointment, but it may well have had the effect of increasing Delegorgue's confidence in himself and in the worth of his own observations. If his observations did not coincide with those of earlier workers, he need not feel anxious or intimidated. Indeed, far from evincing signs of anxiety, his upstaging of past authorities usually has an air of half-suppressed glee. Fortunately, he tries always to support his arguments with evidence, which is usually clear. The factual information he gives is on the whole accurate, and faults or omissions are due to misinterpretation or else reflect the state of zoological knowledge at the time.

Invertebrate zoologists will regret Delegorgue's neglect of a wealth of southern African material, much of which is now depleted. His lopsided education is probably partly to blame for his ignorance of and lack of interest in the so-called 'lower' animals: apart from ticks, leeches and insect pests he mentions only snails (vaguely) and a pill millipede, which he misidentifies as a woodlouse. Also, unlike Krauss, who could satisfy his own enthusiasms (which happened to be for two groups of invertebrates: crustaceans and coelenterates), Delegorgue was collecting to sell and had tailored his practical and theoretical preparations for the work accordingly. 'Big game' was exciting to Europeans, who might pay well for skins, horns and so on; also, amateur or professional entomologists would probably be glad to buy his collections of preserved insects such as butterflies and beetles.

Botanists, too, may be sorry that Delegorgue, who seems to have been making some sort of plant collection, gives plants such a thin and scrappy treatment in the book. These things are a pity, but like any other lone worker, Delegorgue had to make choices. His choices were in keeping with his own flamboyance: he loved what was splendid and showy, in plants, in animals, in people. While this emphasis sometimes makes the scientific aspects irritatingly patchy, it also makes the book as a whole a thoroughly good read.

The most difficult chapters for the modern, conservation-conscious reader are those describing hunting, especially of hippopotamus and elephant. Here, Delegorgue kills and kills again; maimed creatures bleed and die, not to be eaten, not, even, as trophies or specimens, but simply because they are there. It seems almost, both when he kills and when he writes of it later, that reason deserts him, as when, in chapter

12, he compares the figures for hippo killed in the Tugela River from 1839 to 1843 and fails to make the connection between numbers killed and numbers left alive to be killed (the monthly kill in 1839 had been 30–36; by 1843 it was less than four). His implied suggestion is that harrassment by huntsmen has caused the animals to move away, and if this is not disingenuous it must indicate one of those mental cut-offs people often use to divide destructive pleasures from their consequences and thus avoid the pain of guilt. That some such cut-off mechanism was at work in him is suggested further by the final chapter in which an apparent relish for the slaughter of elephants sits side by side with sensitive and affectionate comments on their biology.

There was, of course, at the time and continuing well into the present century, a tendency to glorify hunting as a noble sport – and a proper profession – for a gentlemen. By extension, killing had become generally equated with manliness and, as the supply of game in Africa (and in Asia and the Americas) seemed limitless, the most appalling bloodthirstiness masqueraded as sport. Bloodlust did seize Delegorgue, and much of the killing he did was unjustifiable, but he did, also, have a scientific purpose, and on the whole his aim was to obtain a wide variety of specimens and not mere statistics. Sometimes, indeed, he seems to take his role as specimen collector too far, as when he is sorry not to be able to collect the heads of human battle casualties – though this is doubtless bravado: he would surely have changed his tune had his companion relented and agreed to transport the heads.

For he was not, despite his tough talk and tougher actions, a callous person. Natural beauty moved him, and he was conscious of the despoiling and corrupting effects of civilisation upon it. He was able, too, to turn an ironical eye on himself and see himself, now the artistic and romantic worshipper of lovely living things, now the 'pitiless' hunter, killing in order to be able to gloat over his 'gorgeous' hoard of skins and feathers. We may wonder if this self-appraisal is sincere, so extravagant and self-conscious are his condemnations of killing as a 'futile desecration' of nature, and the like. Perhaps it isn't quite sincere and yet, one feels, there must be at least an element of honest regret and shame as he looks back on 'the madness of collecting'.

In this, as in so much else, he is unusual for his time. This blend of modernity and archaism, of sang-froid and humanity, accompanies a mingling of boyishness and wisdom, the whole contributing to the complexity which makes Delegorgue and his writing so interesting. In one sense he is not a good scientist, because so much of his personality intrudes when he should be coolly recording facts. From another point of view, however, he is the best kind of scientist, because (unlike Le Vaillant) he is a realist who writes of what he himself has seen and done, and who pays special attention to what he most enjoys. And, in search of aesthetic or intellectual enjoyment, he is bold, both mentally and physically. 'Accept danger calmly,' he says. 'A man who takes flight is a lost man.'

The biological sciences, now, could do with an injection of this spirit. Perhaps Adulphe Delegorgue's free and open mind and his treatment of science as an adventure can provide a little inspiration.

*   *   *   *   *

My first thanks go to Fleur Webb, whose translation brought Adulphe Delegorgue alive for me, so that the compilation of the natural history index, though demanding, was never drudgery – and was often great fun. I thank, too, the University Publisher, Margery Moberly, a gentle guide to the ways of indexes and, when necessary, a patient and encouraging editor.

Special thanks are due to Dr K.D. Gordon-Gray and Professor B.H. Fivaz. Dr Gordon-Gray took pains to show me that even the most enigmatic of Delegorgue's plants might yield to informed botanical thinking. Professor Fivaz responded eloquently to a request for information about South African ticks. As eloquent at different times during the course of the work were Dr D.W. Ewer's replies to queries about locusts, elephants and various historical figures. His efforts are but the latest of many debts I have owed him over the years and he has, as always, my affectionate gratitude.

Several friends and former colleagues were generous with their time and expertise, and some kindly loaned me literature. I thank in particular T.E. Edwards, A. Koopman, B.H. Lamoral, J.A.J. Meester, N. Ndlovu, M.R. Perrin and P.F. Tempest.

Finally, for his unflagging interest and support, for hunting down research material, for willingly reading and rereading, for valuable discussions and criticism, I am grateful to L.R. Alexander, for whom science has always been a great adventure.

STEPHANIE J. ALEXANDER

Pietermaritzburg, May 1990

WORKS CONSULTED

Allaby, M. (ed.) (1985). *The Oxford dictionary of natural history*. Oxford: OUP.

Aristotle. *Historia Animalium*, Book VIII: 6, 594^b–595^a. (The works of Aristotle, IV: D'A.W. Thompson transl., D. Ross ed., 1910) Oxford: Clarendon.

Attwater, D. (1965). *The Penguin dictionary of saints*. Harmondsworth: Penguin.

Baker, J.R. (1969). *Parasitic Protozoa*. London: Hutchinson.

Batten, A. and Bokelman, H. (1966). *Wild flowers of the eastern Cape Province*. Cape Town: Books of Africa.

Best, P.B. (1970). Exploitation and recovery of right whales *Eubalaena australis* off the Cape Province. Investigational Reports of the Division of Sea Fisheries of South Africa **80**, 1–15.

Bolus, F. (1926–1928). Various short ornithological articles, *In* Nature Notes (a bulletin issued under the auspices of the Wild Flower Protection Society). Wynberg, Cape: Specialty Press.

Burton, M. and Burton, R. (eds) (1968). *Purnell's encyclopaedia of animal life* Vols. 1–6. London: Purnell.

Cassell's French-English, English-French dictionary (E.A. Baker ed.). (1920). London: Cassell.

Chambers Encyclopaedia. (1950). New Edition. Vols 1–15. London: Newnes.

Coates Palgrave, K., Coates Palgrave, P. and Coates Palgrave, M. (1985). *Everyone's guide to trees of South Africa*. Johannesburg: CNA.

Coates Palgrave, K. and Drummond, R.B. (1977). *Trees of southern Africa*. (E.J. Moll, ed.) Cape Town, Johannesburg: Struik.

Coe, M. (ed.) (1985). *Oxford illustrated encyclopaedia*. Vol.2. *The Natural world*. Oxford: OUP.

Corner, E.J.H. (1966). *The natural history of palms*. London: Weidenfeld and Nicolson.

Ellerman, J.R., Morrison-Scott, T.C.S. and Hayman, R.W. (1953) *Southern African mammals 1758 to 1951: a reclassification*. London: British Museum (Nat. Hist.).

Encyclopaedia Britannica (1926). 13th Standard Edition, Vols 1–32. London & New York: Encyclopaedia Britannica Co., Ltd.

FitzSimons, F.W. (1910). *The snakes of South Africa: their venom and the treatment of snakebite*. Port Elizabeth: Walton.

FitzSimons, V.F.M. (1970). *A field guide to the snakes of southern Africa*. London: Collins.

Forbes, V.S. (1945). Sparrman's travels. The South African Geographical Journal **27**, 39–64.

Forbes, V.S. (1946). Thunberg's travels. The South African Geographical Journal **28**, 39–63.

Forbes, V.S. (1950). Le Vaillant's travels. The South African Geographical Journal **32**, 32–51.

Fox, F.W. and Norwood Young, M.E. (1982). *Food from the veld: edible wild plants of southern Africa*. Johannesburg: Delta Books.

Frade, F. (1955). *Ordre des proboscidiens*. In P.-P. Grassé (ed.): *Traité de Zoologie: anatomie, systématique, biologie*. Tome XVII: *Mammifères*. *1° Fasc.*, 715–783. Paris: Masson.

Grassé, P.-P. and Devilliers, C. (1965). *Zoologie .II: Vertébrés. Précis de sciences biologiques* (P.-P. Grassé ed.). Paris: Masson.

Harrap's shorter French and English dictionary (1940). London: Harrap.

Howse, P.E. (1970). *Termites: a study in social behaviour*. London: Hutchinson.

Isemonger, R.M. (1968). *Snakes of Africa*. Cape Town: Books of Africa.

Jaeger, E.C. (1955). *A source-book of biological names and terms* (3rd ed.). Springfield, Illinois: Thomas.

Kaestner, A. (1968). *Invertebrate zoology*. Vol.2: *Arthropod relatives, Chelicerata, Myriapoda*. (H.W. and L.R. Levi transl. and adap.) New York: Wiley Interscience.

Krauss, F. (1843). *Die südafrikanischen Crustaceen. Eine Zusammenstellung aller bekannten Malacostraca*. 1–68, Pls I–IV. Stuttgart: E. Schweizerbart'sche *Verlagsbuchhandlung*.

Langenscheidt's standard dictionary of the French and English languages (1968) (K. Urwin, ed.). London: Hodder & Stoughton.

Lurker, M. (1987). *Dictionary of gods and goddesses, devils and demons*. London: Routledge.

Mackworth-Praed, C.W. and Grant, H.B. (1962). *The African handbook of birds*, Series II, Vol.I.: *Birds of the southern third of Africa*. London: Longmans.

Maclean, G.L. (1985). *Roberts' birds of southern Africa*. Cape Town: John Voelcker Bird Book Fund.

Meredith, D. (ed.) (1955). *The grasses and pastures of South Africa*. Part 1: *A guide to the identification of grasses in South Africa*, by L.K.A. Chippindall. Part 2: *Pasture management in South Africa*, by J.D. Scott, J.J. Theron and D. Meredith. Johannesburg: CNA.

Partington, J.R. (1937). *A text-book of inorganic chemistry* (5th ed.). London: Macmillan.

Patterson, R. and Meakin, P. (1986). *Snakes*. Johannesburg: Struik.

Patton, W.S. and Evans, A.M. (1929). *Insects, ticks, mites and venomous animals of medical and veterinary importance*. Croydon: Grubb.

Phillips. E.P. (1951). *The genera of South African flowering plants* (2nd ed.) Mem. Bot. Surv. *25*. South Africa: Department of Agriculture.

Rousseau, F. (1970). *Proteaceae of South Africa*. Cape Town: Purnell.

Sikes, S. (1971). *The natural history of the African elephant*. London: Weidenfeld and Nicolson.

Skead, C.J. (1980). *Historical mammal incidence in the Cape Province*. Vol.I. *The western and northern Cape*. Cape Town: Cape Department of Nature and Environmental Conservation.

Skaife, S.H. (1953). *African insect life*. London, Longmans.

Smith, A. (1836).* *Report of the expedition for exploring central Africa, from the Cape of Good Hope . . . 1834 . . .* Cape Town: Government Gazette Office.

Smith, A. (1840).* *Illustrations of the zoology of South Africa –Mammalia,* Part 12. London: Smith and Elder.

Smith, C.A. (1966). *Common names of South African plants.* (E.P. Phillips and E. van Hoepen, eds). Pretoria: Government Printer.

Smithers, R.H.N. (1983). *The mammals of the southern African subregion.* Pretoria: University of Pretoria.

Smithers, R.H.N. (1986). *Land mammals of southern Africa: a field guide.* Johannesburg: Macmillan.

Standard Encyclopaedia of Southern Africa (1970). Cape Town: Nasou.

Stark, A.C. and Sclater, W.L. (1900–1906). *The birds of South Africa* Vols I–IV. (*The fauna of South Africa*, W.L. Sclater, gen. ed.). London: R.H. Porter.

Stutley, M. (1985). *Hinduism: the eternal law.* Wellingborough: Aquarian Press.

Tabler, E.C. (1977) *Pioneers of Natal and south-east Africa, 1652–1878.* Cape Town: Balkema.

Visser, J. and Chapman, D.S. (1978). *Snakes and snakebite.* Cape Town: Purnell.

Watt, J.M. and Breyer-Brandwijk, M.G. (1962). *The medicinal and poisonous plants of southern and eastern Africa* (2nd ed.). Edinburgh: Livingstone.

Wingate, P. (1972). *The Penguin medical encyclopaedia.* Harmondsworth: Penguin.

Young, J.Z. (1950). *The life of vertebrates.* Oxford: OUP.

*Not seen in the original.

TRANSLATOR'S NOTE

'This book,' writes Adulphe Delegorgue in the draft of an announcement of his *Voyage dans L'Afrique Australe*, 'is as good to read and as useful as a classic, while it is as agreeable as any novel'. The challenge facing me as translator has been to convey the book's classic qualities as well as its readability.

The young author was from a worthy bourgeois family and had the privilege of growing up in a cultivated provincial home. He had quite considerable literary talent and wrote in the style of his time when taste was nurtured on the contemporary romanticism. He is inclined to show off sometimes and to indulge in elaborate descriptions and philosophizing, but always apparent are the intelligence, the perceptiveness, the exuberance and the humour of a lively young mind. I have tried to capture these qualities. While abbreviating some of the unnecessarily lengthy passages which might have deterred the impatient modern reader (and have made the book less agreeable than a novel!), I have not reduced the text to a spare précis of the original.

With some exceptions, his unique and amusing spelling of Zulu and Dutch words, and of place-names, has been retained. The exceptions are some of his own variant forms of these words where their retention might have confused the reader, and well-known place-names like St. Lucia and Constantia. To have modernised his orthography would have deprived the book of some of its nineteenth century flavour and would have denied the reader the satisfaction of discovering how well his renderings work phonetically.

Often it has been necessary to revise punçtuation and sometimes even paragraphing. I have also exercised translator's discretion in retaining the soft French 'cafre' rather than the harsh, emotive 'kaffir', and have preferred certain South African words to their English counterparts e.g., 'bush' rather than 'woods' for *bois* in the original. It has been my aim throughout to avoid using words and expressions which would have sounded unfamiliar to a mid-nineteenth century ear.

All parentheses within the text are Delegorgue's. I have added a few of my own explanations in brief translator's notes. These are clearly identified to distinguish them from the author's footnotes which have been retained.

I have throughout endeavoured to remain faithful to the spirit, if not always to the absolute letter, of Delegorgue's text.

FLEUR WEBB

Pietermaritzburg, May 1990

WORKS CONSULTED

Cassell's French-English / English-French Dictionary. London etc., 1955.

Collins-Robert French Dictionary. Glasgow, 1983.

Encyclopaedia Britannica, 15th ed. Chicago etc., 1974. 30 v.

Gill, L.   *A First Guide to South African Birds*. Cape Town, 1970.

Harrap's Shorter French and English Dictionary. London, 1970.

Labuschgne, R. J. and Van der Merwe, N. J.   *Mammals of the Kruger and other national parks*. National Parks Board, 1966.

Maclean, G. L.   *Roberts' Birds of Southern Africa*. Cape Town, 1985.

Nouveau Petit Larousse Illustré. Paris, 1931.

Reader's Digest Great Encyclopaedic Dictionary. London etc., 1962. 3 v.

Webster's New International Dictionary. Cambridge Massachusetts, 1913.

VOYAGE

DANS

L'AFRIQUE AUSTRALE.

F. Grenier

A. DELEGORGUE.

VOYAGE

DANS

L'AFRIQUE AUSTRALE

NOTAMMENT

dans le territoire de Natal
dans celui des Cafres Amazoulous et Makatisses
et jusqu'au tropique du Capricorne

Durant les années 1838, 1839, 1840, 1841, 1842, 1843 & 1844

Avec Dessins et Cartes

PAR

M. Adulphe DELEGORGUE

(DE DOUAI)

TOME PREMIER.

PARIS

AU DÉPOT DE LIBRAIRIE, RUE DES MOULINS, 8.
PRÈS LA RUE THÉRÈSE.
Adresser les demandes et mandats à Mme CROISSANT.

A Monsieur

Monsieur le Comte **de Salvandy**,

GRAND MAITRE DE L'UNIVERSITÉ,

MINISTRE DE L'INSTRUCTION PUBLIQUE,

Cette Relation est offerte
En témoignage de respect & de reconnaissance,

Par son très-humble & très-obéissant
serviteur,

ADULPHE DELEGORGUE.

INTRODUCTION

At the southernmost tip of Africa lies a vast expanse of territory known as the Colony of the Cape of Good Hope, which is today one of the most profitable of British possessions, its capital town providing an invaluable port of call for vessels plying the route to India.

The Cape Colony, situated between 34° 50′ and 29° 50′ south latitude, and 15° 20′ and 25° 10′ east longitude, is bordered by a coastline more than 450 leagues long. From west to east the colony measures more than 200 leagues; the greatest width in the western part exceeds 120 leagues; at its narrowest, in the centre, it measures about 70 leagues. It is estimated that the surface area is no less than 15 000 to 16 000 square leagues and that the population numbers 160 000 to 200 000 inhabitants of which 60 000 are white, or free men of colour, 30 000 are Hottentots, 40 000 negroes and the remainder Cafres and Boschjesmans (or men of the bush).

Bounded to the north by independent Hottentot country which extends as far as the Tropic of Capricorn, to the west by the Atlantic Ocean, to the south by the great southern ocean and to the east by Cafrerie, the Cape Colony possesses several notable rivers, namely the Orange, the two Elephant rivers, and the Fish or Groote Vish Rivier. It is spanned by several ranges of high mountains and there is more than one desert or *karrou*, where the soil is impregnated with salt. The climate, which is generally rather warm, divides the year into two equal seasons, the dry and the rainy. The first of these seasons occurs when the sun is in the northern hemisphere, and the second when it moves into the southern hemisphere. The first constitutes the winter and the second the summer in these parts; the winter lasts from March to September, and the summer from September until March.

The colony is rich in abundant natural products of all kinds; delicious fruit, trees and plants, and even excellent vineyards. Among the domestic animals, cattle, sheep and horses are to be seen; as for the wild animals, they are retreating further and further northwards as civilization advances. There are swarms of flies and the fields are infested with white ants. Partridges and bustards abound but unfortunately so do reptiles. In this land of contrasts, one encounters not only the tall ostrich but also the little tree-creeper, the elephant as well as the mouse, the monstrous hippopotamus and the dainty gazelle, the great wild buffalo and the timid hare.

To complete this brief description of the Cape Colony, we should add that it is divided into two provinces, one in the west where the capital, called Cape Town by the English, is situated, and one in the east, whose principal town is called Graham's Town. This town has already surpassed in size Uitenhagen, which is situated 20 miles from Port Elisabeth, the only good anchorage on Algoa Bay. The western province produces grain and wines, the eastern province, cattle and pastures. Cape Town, where the produce of the colony is landed and stored, now has about 25 000 inhabitants, while Graham's Town, which is barely twenty-six years old, can already lay claim to almost 16 000. Other towns are also springing up and increasing in population in the eleven districts of the colony, five of which are in the western province and six in the eastern province; among these is the district of Graaf-Reynett which borders on Cafrerie.

Having mentioned these generalities about the country which at present engages our interest, let us now try to recall briefly the journeys and the principal events of the history which has been enacted upon this stage from the time of its first discovery until the present day.

Three more or less influential maritime powers, Portugal, Holland and England, have in turn hoisted their flag on this tip of Africa, which was first known as the Cape of Storms because of the perilous seas which threatened to dash ships on to the rocky coastline. The first man to round this dangerous peninsula was the intrepid Portuguese, Vasco de Gama, who opened up the Indian Ocean to European navigation and had the name Cape of Storms changed to Cape of Good Hope, thus presaging the future successes of the noble sons of the Tagus. This memorable event took place in 1497. But the Lusitanian ships declined for some time to put into these waters which they regarded as inhospitable; the Portuguese sailors did no more than skirmish briefly with the natives; the government in Lisbon did not wish to establish even a temporary settlement there.

The Dutch, who had followed closely in the wake of their rivals through the maze of the Asiatic archipelagos began, from about 1600, to have thoughts of calling at the Cape; it was, however, not until forty-eight years later that they laid the foundations of a colony which took shape only two or three years afterwards when the first of their governors, Van Riebeek, who arrived in April 1652, established the beginnings of a permanent settlement. The Batavian domination of these distant lands was to be consolidated and extended for almost a century and a half, which is to say until 1795, the year in which England surreptitiously took possession of the Cape. In fact she restored it seven years later at the Peace of Amiens, only to take it back again three years afterwards, thenceforth to retain it, having ensured that it would be ceded to her with a semblance of legality by the Treaty of Vienna.

Let us now examine the principal journeys of exploration which were undertaken when these lands were under Dutch and English rule. The first traveller of note was Lopez, the account of whose journey, published by Pigafetta in 1591, provides the first available information on the interior of Cafrerie. This name was unknown at the time, at least to Lopez, who gives to the lands in which he journeyed the title 'Countries situated between the Congo, the Cape of Good Hope and the river Nile'. The author also mentions the Land of Natal which, he says, was discovered on the day of the Nativity of our Lord; he mentions a river, Magnice.[1] At about this time, the Dutch were making contact with the natives, and the English were also beginning to appear upon the scene.

A second traveller, Ten Rhyne, explored the Cape and the Hottentot country in 1673; the account of his travels was published in Latin at Schaffouse in 1686. Ten Rhyne begins by describing Saldanha Bay, situated 18 leagues to the north of Cape Town and then gives a rather inaccurate picture of Table Bay. The remainder of his work deals briefly with the Hottentots.

Next comes the *landdroost*, or magistrate, Kupt, to whom the Dutch company gave the charge of collecting young cattle in the interior. He left the Cape in October 1705, visited several kraals or villages, and forty-two days later brought back 179 cattle for which he had offered in exchange only glass beads and copper necklaces.

Kolbe, a conscientious but credulous writer, remained eight years at the Cape from 1705 to 1713. This author describes the territory which then formed part of the colony, the system of government and the customs of the natives. In his three-volume work he mentions the singular ceremony of sprinkling newly-wed couples with urine, a procedure which has been contradicted by more recent travellers who have made merry at good Kolbe's expense.

The mountains which surround the Cape, namely the Table, the Head and the Rump of the Lion, and the Devil, are carefully des-

1 This river is apparently the Oury or Limpopo, at the source of which M. Delegorgue hunted for some time.

scribed by Kolbe. However, he reckons the height of Table Mountain to be only 1 857 feet, whereas in reality it is 3 600 feet high. The surface appears from a distance to be as flat as a table but is in fact very uneven and rough. From the top of Lion Mountain, which is very steep, one can distinguish the smallest boat as far as twelve miles out to sea.

Devil's Mountain is separated from Table Mountain only by a narrow declivity. It owes its name to the terrible effect of the south-easterly winds which rush down this gorge and buffet the town with unparalleled violence. This mountain is not as high and not as wide as Table Mountain and the Lion, but unlike them, it reaches down to the seashore.

Kolbe also describes the rivers of the Cape and the town itself, but this is beyond our scope. We confine ourselves to brief general remarks about each of the travellers whose works are mentioned here, and will not comment on his description of Table Bay or False Bay, both of which provide shelter for vessels lying at anchor. Table Bay offers protection from the southeaster, while False Bay is a haven when westerly and north-westerly winds blow.

I shall mention in passing the Abbé de La Caille, whose visit to the Cape from 1751 to 1752 was concerned only with astronomy. I note also the travels of Hop and Brink in 1761 and 1762, which were fairly important to the history of exploration. I do no more than record that the dreamer, Bernardin de Saint-Pierre, visited the Cape in 1771, before I come to the travels of Sparmann, between the years 1772 and 1776. His account contains much natural history as well as curious details about the Hottentots, the Boschjesmans and the Cafres.

At about the same time an equally distinguished naturalist, Thunberg, appears on the scene. He carefully explored the environs of the Cape as well as the interior, particularly from a botanical point of view. The next traveller was Paterson who made his way north beyond the Orange River and east as far as the land of the Cafres, beyond the Great Fish River.

Then comes Levaillant, born in Surinam, Dutch Guyana, of a family which originated from Lorraine. The account of his travels, which lasted from 1780 until 1785, is particularly attractive because of the ornithology and the zoology. This account, which was edited by a young writer of the time called Varon, should be read judiciously as it frequently savours of the novel; its interest lies in the ingenious-ness of his interpretations, the aptness of his remarks and the charm of his descriptions.

In 1796, the American captain, Stout, visited Cafrerie, while the French captain, Degrandpré, made studies of navigation along the Cape coast, and the Hollander, Cornelius Jong, explored the interior.

That same year, 1796, saw the colony fall into the hands of the English and the traveller, Percival, published his observations, which only appeared three months after the first volume of the travels of Barrow which took place between 1797 and 1799.

Two years later Semple published the story of his fairly lengthy stay at the Cape. At the same time, there appeared a report by Truter and Somerville who had just crossed the Snowy Mountains (Sneuwbergen) to discover fertile lands beyond the deserts, whose existence had hitherto escaped the notice of the Europeans.

From 1803 to 1806, a period when by virtue of the Treaty of Amiens the Cape was returned to Batavian rule, a travelling scholar, Henri de Lichtenstein, journeyed throughout the country and later published a report which was rich in scientific facts and observations of local customs and practices, which the confines of this Introduction do not permit me even to remark upon briefly.

After the Cape Colony had fallen once more beneath the British yoke, other travellers came to explore the country, a notable example being the missionary, Campbell, who from 1812 to 1815 ventured into the northern and eastern parts and visited the land of the Griquas and the Namaquas. He reappeared in 1820, accompanied by another missionary called Philip who in 1825 penetrated as far as Lattakou. This preacher of the Gospel was determined to prove that the missionaries in southern Africa had helped to maintain peace between the colonists and the natives on the frontiers, a claim which is contested by M. Delegorgue, whose sojourn of almost seven years amongst these peoples has enabled him to appreciate the true facts of the matter.

At the same time as the envoys of the London Missionary Society were investigating the countries and the peoples of southern Africa, the traveller, Burchell, was making his own enquiries into natural history in the heart of these distant lands, and was assembling an immense collection of botanical and zoological specimens. Although his journey was made between 1810 and 1812, the report of it was only published in 1842, which deprived it of the merit of novelty.

Thompson, from 1821 until 1824, followed in the footsteps of Burchell, concentrating his attentions on tracing the progress of emigrants from the mother country. While Thompson was ordering his scientific material, Cowper Rose, from 1824 to 1828, went off to observe more closely the movement of populations as far as the territorial limits of the colony, while the missionary, Hallbeck, in 1827, visited the country of the Tamboukis and the Cafres, and two English colonists from the Cape, Cowie and Green, reached Algoa Bay. Closer to our own times, Doctor Smith, in 1836 made contact with some Cafre tribes and advanced as far as the Tropic of Capricorn, although he did not follow exactly the same route as our compatriot,

M. Delegorgue, who took a direction unknown to any European before him.

The last of our travellers, Captain Harris of the English army in Bombay, published in London in 1841 the account, in one volume, of his hunting expeditions into the land of the Cafre chief, Moselekatse, an account which includes geographical references to Graham's Town, Graaf-Reynett and the Snowy Mountains and mentions the Dutch farmers or Boers. These details about Captain Harris's hunting experiences are of some interest, but the works of M. Delegorgue, and we say this without flattery, are much more exact and are infinitely more animated; they have the added advantage of providing a summary of the journey of the unfortunate travellers, Cowie and Green, to the Amazoulou country, the visits of various missionaries to the land of the Makatisses, as well as those of Messrs Smith and Harris to Massilicatzi's country. In addition, he provides us with information about the territory of Natal which none before him has previously given.

Captain Harris is grossly unjust towards the Boers who preferred the adventurous life and the freedom of the desert to the vexatious despotism of those in power at the Cape. M. Delegorgue nobly exonerates them from the accusations and the false judgments which instruments of the English have presumed to raise against these men, whose only crime is to have cherished in the depth of their souls the memory of their national origin, and to have desired that their dignity as citizens should be respected.

The French traveller's judgment is revealed as all the more impartial in that he does not spare his reproaches when he believes that they are merited and, on several occasions, he has reason for serious complaint against these selfsame Boers.

It is probable that henceforth journeys to the Cape of Good Hope will become less frequent than they formerly were, for the preferred route to India seems more and more to lead via the Red Sea. This prediction will be further proved correct if the project of cutting through the isthmus of Suez is realised. If this should come to pass, the account of M. Delegorgue's travels will be of even greater value to us as it will mark the end of an era of travel to the countries of southern Africa; unless of course, and this appears to be his intention, the author decides to return there himself some day.

Paris, 24 June 1847   ALBERT-MONTÉMONT

TRAVELS

IN

SOUTHERN AFRICA

CHAPTER I

Reasons for the journey — The voyage — Arrival at the Cape of Good Hope — A glimpse of Cape Town — Table Mountain — Departure for Verlooren Valley — Mode of transport — Different types of oxen — Arrival at Verlooren Valley — I begin my investigations into natural history — The striped hyaena — Flamingo hunting — Behaviour of these birds.

The interest which my fellow countrymen have been kind enough to express and my own wish to make known the findings of explorations, lasting almost seven years, which I made into the south-eastern countries of Africa, have together determined me on publishing this account of my travels. It will contain no more than the facts, for I leave to my readers the task of adding whatever comment and of drawing whatever conclusions they may please. Should the interests of science be furthered by my investigations, some uncertainty resolved perhaps, or some theory confirmed, well and good; the pride of having been, however modestly, of service to my country must be my sweetest reward.

People have sometimes enquired the reasons why I travelled; they could not understand how it was possible for a man to prefer a life of adventure to a life of peace, or that he might choose to live in a country other than the one where he was born. I account for it in the following manner.

1

I lost my parents in infancy and went to live with my grandfather, Monsieur Delegorgue, a judge at the royal court in Douai, who decided to take personal charge of my early education. Whenever he was pleased with me, he would reward me with objects of natural history drawn from his private collection. Gradually, my young imagination was fired by the brilliant colours and the singular shapes. These early impressions, which were later confirmed, left me with a passionate and abiding interest in all that is curious in nature. When eventually I arrived at an age when the mind is, in general, exploring new ideas, I read the interesting voyages of Levaillant and became more and more inspired by thoughts of the liberty which may be discovered only in the heart of the deserts of Africa.

Unfortunately, I was destined to practise the law, either at the bar or on the bench, a decision which I believed at the time to be immutable. Although reconciled to my fate, I remained unwavering in my true interests without daring even to hope that one day I would be borne along on the winds of fortune towards a wonderland. However, circumstances arose which enabled me to escape from the nightmare of an enforced vocation. Obliged immediately to choose another profession, I joyfully resolved upon becoming a sailor. Five years at sea in the waters of northern Europe, as well as off Senegal, and in the Antilles, left me with a loathing of the restrictive shipboard life but with no distaste for travel.

A tenacious fever contracted in Guadeloupe compelled me to take serious stock of my situation and I returned to France. My state of health necessitated a long rest, but the inactive life was more tedious even than the fever and, as I progressed in convalescence, I began to recall all the delightful things that I had seen on the beautiful coasts of Gambia and Sierra Leone, where the vegetation is rich and luxuriant. I had not the will to resist my strongest inclinations; the contemplation of the bewitching pictures which my memory painted and presented continually before my mind's eye, gave rise to plans which, without further delay, I put into execution.

On 10 May 1838, with the good wishes of my friends ringing in my ears, I left Douai, my native town, for Paris where I was to make preparations for a long voyage. These preparations completed, I boarded the Bordeaux coach. Having arrived at the port, I impatiently awaited the moment when we would set sail, but this was not to be for eighteen days. It is difficult to imagine the irksomeness and the tedium of this period of waiting, the cruel state of being always on the eve of departure, and above all the torment of farewells repeated each evening, farewells which are renewed of necessity and which become ridiculous by their very repetition. 'Ah, how I suffer', a friend said to me. 'Leave! Be done with it, so that we shall no longer be obliged to exchange farewells. Farewells are the death of me!'

And if he who remained behind thus appreciated the poignancy of the matter, what should my feelings have been? For, after all, those who remain take leave only of the friends who are departing; others still surround them, all does not change about them. But do not those who are departing enter as it were into a field of death? For what is there at sea, if not the total absence of all that the land offers? All is contrary. There the weary soul must find its rest in the billowing wave, a kind of watery hell, a sort of oblivion into which it sinks. Indeed, is not all that one loves left behind? On every side lies the unknown and ahead uncertainty looms, wide as the horizon, which continually shapes and reshapes itself. An important goal becomes necessary, a well-defined objective towards which one may reach out at every moment, such as a land to be conquered or a motherland to be regained. And so I set sail for the Cape of Good Hope, the land which was conquered for science by the famous Levaillant, whose writings on natural history had decided my vocation.

Le Télégraphe, a charming little brig of 175 tons, was not a ship with spacious accommodation for passengers, but on the other hand, its slender lines and the bold set of its masts, enabled it to cut through the waves rapidly, and Heaven knows how those on board appreciate such an advantage. Thanks to the superiority of the vessel and to the agreeable society of a man as amiable as the supercargo,[1] fifty-four days seemed to pass rapidly enough.

To begin with, the Gulf of Gascony shook us roughly. We had almost put it behind us when we found ourselves obliged to heave to. We spent three days off Cape Ortegal, time enough to appreciate the excellent qualities of Bordeaux's finest vessel which, like a seagull, rode the swell without shipping a drop. The standards achieved by modern navigators compel one to admiration. Confident in the precision of their calculations, they remain calm amidst the storm. Heaving to in heavy seas is no longer what it used to be. In such a situation, our fathers prayed for they believed themselves lost; but in our day, hardly has the ship hove to, when the crew goes to sleep, only to re-awaken when the fine weather returns.

As soon as the sea had ceased its fruitless endeavours against our graceful ship, a full breeze drove us round Cape Finistère. It bore us rapidly towards the south, and it was not long before we felt a rise in the temperature which predicted that within a few days we should pass the Tropic.

I had on previous voyages been baptised according to seafaring rites and I had even found myself transformed into the principal

1 M. Geraud of Bordeaux.

actor aboard a French warship. Though only a simple sailor 'on 24',[1] my ephemeral rank as Neptune entitled me to the command of the schooner *La Mutine*. I had therefore been initiated into all the mysteries of the ceremony of the crossing and the Tropic held for me only the charms of recollection. However, I must confess that all things eventually grow stale, old customs are lost, and if a ceremony is to take place these days, it has become necessary that a large number of passengers should be assembled on board. It is essential that the initiates should be presumed to be generous enough to meet the expense and bear the inconvenience. The wastage in tow transformed into beards, wigs and cloaks is immense. The hail which Old Man Tropic casts down, had its origins in the fields — beans and peas innundate the deck; the quantity of tar required to fix the angels' wings to the naked bodies of the cabin boys is unlimited, and when it becomes necessary to relieve these little creatures of all their romance, this can only be achieved with the aid of an astonishing quantity of fat or butter. In addition to the expense, the preliminary labour is considerable, everything being prepared in the crew's quarters as if unbeknown to the captain, so that the newcomers should be filled with amazement. All this requires some recompense, and Old Man Tropic disdains to descend from the heavens for an insignificant reward.

True to his mercenary nature, this omniscient inhabitant of high places watched the *Télégraphe* pass by without even taking the trouble to hail her. The Tropic of Cancer is definitely behind us, the first stage is over. Before us lies the Line, then comes the Tropic of Capricorn, and finally the first sight of the land of our destination. There remains still much of the journey to be done, but the sailing is so easy and the days so fine that they slip by, one very much like another.

Here then are the islands of Cape Verde. San Antonio rises steeply on our left, only ten hours' sailing separates us, but the dusk prevents us from seeing it clearly. The breeze stiffens, reinforced by a few squalls which are due to the proximity of the land. We sail swiftly on, the coast is left behind, it melts imperceptibly into the sky and, by evening, San Antonio has disappeared like the sun beneath the horizon.

Our progress continues, unremitting. The Line is already passed and shoals of flying fish distract the idle passenger who endeavours to kill time as best he can. Sometimes dolphins are caught, which distinguishes those days from the rest; or else if it is calm, a shark is hauled on board and tortured on the deck by every sailor who

---

1 On 24 francs a month which is a 3rd class sailor; the 2nd is on 30 francs and the 1st on 36 francs.

has lost a father, a brother or a friend at sea.

The appearance of a phaeton, that bird of heaven, is hailed by the watchful helmsman, who calls it twenty times by name. This event is discussed for hours on end.

However, a more interesting incident awaits us. A topman, who is repairing the rigging of a topgallant mast, cries 'Ship ahoy!' and takes the bearings of her course. Half an hour later the tips of her masts, like needles, show on the horizon. Slowly they rise, and soon the topgallant sails, and then the topsails appear. The attention of everyone is directed towards the vessel, for this time we know that human beings are out there, with news from the ends of the earth. But are these men friends? Opinion is divided; some say that they are English, others that they are American. It is entirely a matter of supposition, based on the method of rigging, and at a distance, mistakes are common. One man thinks that he notices the absence of bowlines, and for him the ship is English. Another, because of the lightness of certain iron standing rigging, believes he can declare the vessel to be American.

The captain does not remain indifferent; with his eye to his telescope, he is better informed than the rest of us. He does not immediately express his opinion, but at last he pronounces it loudly and, at his suggestion, bets are laid. 'Let us see,' he says. 'Who maintains that it is an Englishman?' 'I do captain. I pray you determine the wager.' 'Good. I claim the opposite; a dinner on land.' 'Agreed.'

The two ships are pursuing a course which will bring them athwart; they are close enough to recognise each other's colours. We French venture to be the first to make the courteous gesture. Our flag climbs to the masthead, seems to hesitate and then streams out. Time passes; our signal remains unacknowledged and gradually indignation takes the place of curiosity. Already the captain repents having revealed himself so openly; he chews on his tobacco, and from time to time he kicks the bulwarks. He says nothing, although he appears to be muttering to himself. He would like the helmsman to go off course so that he might vent his seething ill-humour on him. He says to the cabin-boy, clinging to the yard rope like a cleat, 'Come my boy, prepare to lower.' Then, as if in an aside, 'English pigs! Look here! Who said so? Who wagered that it was an Englishman?' 'I did captain.' 'Right. Do not let us speak of it again. I lost. Half an hour already and nothing up there. They are trifling with us. Boy, lower the flag!'

The flag comes down and only then does something red climb to the masthead of the other ship; it stops, and as it unfurls, it reveals the cross of St. George in the upper corner. 'Well that's it,' growls the captain, 'I am sure of it. Pigs of Englishmen. There's nobody else at sea these days.' The captain will be consumed by ill-humour until tomorrow; the very idea of an Englishman turns his bile. Out of

5

sheer compassion I accost him, hoping to help him to a better mood. I gently try to make him admit his injustice, for I admire the greatness, and above all the bold enterprise of the English nation, in spite of condemning its ways. But he calls me a traitor, or at the very least, the son of an Englishman, for daring to speak in this way. In short, the storm rages on in the captain's mind, and the most prudent move which I can make is to leave him to himself. But you see, this man's fault is excusable. In infancy he was suckled by a woman whose sailor-husband had been a prisoner at Chatham. As a boy, he was told by his father of the suffering and the torture and, above all, of the inhumanity of these English, these people who pride themselves on being unique in their nobility. He is of the finest clay from which a man may be formed; never has he cuffed a cabin-boy, which is the least sin a captain can commit; but the sight of an Englishman almost turns him into a man-eater, He would devour ten or twenty of them with pleasure, however old and tough they were — or so he said! I reckoned that my words would have little effect on a mind so prejudiced.

The south-easterly wind has forced us to begin tacking. The captain prowls alone like a bear in his pit on the port afterdeck. His jaws are clenched, his features are contorted, his glance moves rapidly up and down, his fiery eyes roll in their sockets: he is dreaming, and his favourite dream is of battle. His enemies are the English. At every step that he takes, he fells one or two of them in imagination. He is attacked from all sides and wounded, but his wild imagination has so inflamed his blood that he feels nothing. Let us leave him alone then. When he has massacred enough English and lost enough blood, the captain will again become a man like any other.

Evening comes. A voice rings out: 'Stand by for four bells.' It comes from the quarterdeck, and four bells are rung in answer from the foot of the mizen-mast. It is six o'clock and time for supper. The mess tins appear, and the ship's cook, armed with his fork and his ladle, emerges from his dark smoky den and prepares to distribute the steaming treasures of his cauldron to the crew, who are soon gathered and sitting about on the hatches, or on heaps of spars and yards, or on the deck, clutching their iron-banded wooden bowls. All of them eat except for the helmsman, who is busy at his post, the cook who considers himself too fine to associate with the sailors, and the cabin-boy who is setting the table for the officers and the passengers.

A quarter of an hour is sufficient for the crew. The helmsman has been relieved. Now comes the turn of the passengers. 'Captain,' says the cabin-boy, 'supper is served.' Good. We sit down to table, we wait, but in vain; the captain does not appear, and nobody, out of respect, wishes to begin the meal without him. 'Boy, call the captain.' 'Captain, you are awaited for supper.' And the king of the vessel returns the invitation with a resounding oath, fit to crack the heavens. Then he adds, 'Let them sup without me this evening.' You see, the anger aroused by the hated English would require an entire night to abate. But at least this day, unlike all the others, has not passed uneventfully; it has been one of the most memorable of the journey; it has provided a subject for discussion; the idle spirit has found nourishment and, thanks to the unusual character of the captain, time has dragged less heavily for all.

May this serve to give some conception of the boredom of life at sea, a boredom which is not of the ordinary sort, for there is a total impossibility of escape. But the greater the boredom, the more easily one is diverted by even the slightest distraction.

Now we have reached the twenty-fifth degree of south latitude. Creatures which are not of the waves come to cheer our thoughts, to remind us of the gentle terrestrial doves, of the Holy Spirit, if our ideas tend that way; or of the chequer board, if we are gamblers. These pretty, checkered seabirds, the Cape petrels,[1] *Procellaria capensis*, fearlessly fly in the wake of the vessel. They are capable of great speed, and in order not to overtake the ship they change their 'trim', as if they were tacking. They extend their wings and expose their pure white breasts, they glide, they swoop and skim the stern almost without moving their wings; they fly off suddenly and then return slowly, describing a thousand rounded zigzags so that one might almost take them for kites or flying machines rather than for birds as we know them.

But if some good-hearted soul, who is used to keeping chickens, or perhaps the cajoling helmsman, or even a heedless topman — if any of these throws or drops a little piece of tallow into the sea — the behaviour of the birds will change, and immediately the thoughtful passenger will guess the etymology of the word 'petrel'. The bait falls, spins in an eddy, then, having been drawn in by opposing forces, finishes by floating upwards, whereupon the first petrel to see it, drops to the surface of the moving water. Four or five feet separate it from the object which it covets; it hovers on its half-closed wings, walks on the water, seizes in its beak the fragment, gives a beat of its wings and rises again. 'Here is a bird,' a Dutch sailor might have said to his friend during one of the first voyages to these parts, 'which walks on the water. What man in the world can do the same?' 'If the Bible does not lie,' the other might have replied, 'I know of one.' 'Who is he then?' 'Saint Peter the Fisherman.' 'These then are little Peters' — whence comes 'petrel,' little Peter. Scholars

---

1 The French word is *damier* which also means chequer board. *Translator's note*

have not disdained to perpetuate this nautical nickname which refers now to those seabirds that have a disproportionately small, feathery body, webbed feet, a very compressed beak with the upper part curved, and prominent nostrils.

Unfortunately for those who love to handle the beautiful creatures of nature, these birds, which are so pretty, so graceful, and so attractive in flight, once they are caught with a fish hook and brought down to the deck, discharge an oil so fetid, that one is tempted to cast them away. The odour of this oil is very penetrating and clings most tenaciously.

Now there begin to appear more petrels of the sort which are encountered in the northern hemisphere, and which mingle with the Cape petrels; these are the *Procellaria pelagica*, so small of body and so covered in feathers that they are the hunter's despair, for he brings them down very rarely. The sailors sometimes call them 'birds of Satan' and sometimes 'damned souls'.

Because of their lightness, these birds perform a very remarkable feat which, until now, has not been reported by any traveller that I know of. I was a child when first I observed it, and I believe it worth mentioning here.

It was in 1832 on board the brig *le Commerce de Dunkerque*, master Captain Collet. We were returning from the Antilles. A shark had been caught and part of the remains were being thrown into the sea. Pieces of the entrails, cut very small, were being cast overboard by the cabin-boy. As they were light, they sank slowly. At that time, some 'birds of Satan' were flying in our wake. From the taffrail, where I was sitting, I was at liberty to observe the flight and the manoeuvres of these voracious birds. While I watched them, I did not lose sight of their quarry, which disappeared too quickly. They made great efforts to reach their objective, but all their attempts were fruitless. However, as a few pieces of the shark were floating at a depth of about eight inches, some of the petrels dropped down on them from a height of two or three feet. They did not succeed in their endeavours, as they touched the water feet first. A second and a third attempt were no more successful; the weight of the birds was too slight and their method of attack too unsuitable, although their determination was undiminished. A moment later a 'Satanique' took aim at a piece of submerged debris; he glided above it and came down to touch the water. At the same moment another 'Satanique' hovered above its comrade and dropped down on to its back. Thus weighed down, the first bird was able to plunge deeply enough to seize the coveted object. This manoeuvre was too rapidly performed for me to be able to tell how the food was seized; but I think that the petrel brought it to the surface with the aid of its webbed feet. The favour appeared later to be reciprocated, which proves a certain intelligence among these birds. However, I must mention that we had been for some days in absolutely calm seas, which made it difficult for the petrels to find food. Although at that time I was very little occupied with observations of natural history, I did not fail to observe this incident, which I am particularly happy to report as it was the first such opportunity which presented itself to me on these vast seas, where so many men have passed heedlessly by.

Next to arrive were the brown *shoemakers*, those great travellers. I killed a few, which, falling into the wake, were lost to sight. Then there were the different varieties of albatross, the *mouton du Cap*, with their narrow wings so long that they cannot fold them to their bodies when they float on the water. I have particular regrets about one of these, which I killed with a rifle-shot at more than a cable's length; however, as everyone knows, there is not a captain obliging enough to lower a boat under such circumstances. I had to sacrifice my albatross as well as hundreds of Cape petrels, which I had cruelly shot down without any hope of retrieval.

But the diversion provided by the birds is limited; at sea those who are happiest are the ones who can dispense with company and pursue long mental conversations with themselves, without feeling the compulsion to transmit the outcome of their reflections. In addition, the use of tobacco, which stirs the imagination and conjures up dreams in which we may isolate ourselves, is a powerful resource against the boredom of life at sea. How many nights, which might otherwise have proved so long, passed by only too briefly for me as I savoured the charm of the poetic tropical darkness through the clouds of my pipe smoke. How many dark nights have seemed wonderful to me, as much in the contemplation of the coppery stem of the vessel cutting through the swell and the stern curling back the phosphorescent waves, as in the fancies born of the smoke of the companionable weed. But it is not everyone who is able to inhale tobacco smoke and to delight in this occupation; these I pity sincerely for if they have not the society of other passengers, I know of nobody on board with whom they might exchange even a few insignificant words; reading, alone, can bring them solace.

The captain keeps watch all night; he rests during the day, or is occupied with observations and calculations; he is beset by anxieties which he alone comprehends; thus the captain is a man apart, and not in the least amiable. The officer of the watch has his duties; besides, he would be unable to sustain a conversation, and it is all he can do to give half his attention to his questioner. The helmsman is a deaf-mute machine with regard to all but his prime functions. The cabin-boy is a little creature whom one frequently encounters, but to whom one speaks only in gestures. The apprentices are aloft, suspended along a topmast which they are scraping, or making fast

9

a studding sail at the tip of a yard. They sing, these offspring of the devil, some monotonous refrain which sets one longing to hear the sirens of old; and when they come down at last, they must do the bidding of the sailors, their masters; thus they never have a minute to themselves.

The sailors make spun-yarn, blocks, reef-points, trim the rigging, splice ropes, mend sails. They are expert workers, speak of nothing but their profession, and are determined to prove how well they know it, although they never cease to curse it. Their style is picturesque, their appearance singular, their speech of the greatest originality. The passenger feels a strong desire to exchange a few ideas with them, to sound the depth of their tarry souls, which are destined to reap their reward in another world. Let him but approach them, however, and he is forced by their language to retreat to the quarterdeck. For no man is more caustic than a sailor, no man more embarrassed than a ship's passenger. And if the passenger is a priest or a magistrate, and the sailor a veteran of the hold or the topmast, looks are exchanged, a witty remark is passed, and war is declared, an innocent enough and harmless war but one which will not cease until the anchor is cast when the journey is done.

At last the trade winds, especially those from the south-east, which drove us fifty leagues from Fernanbouc have moved due east, then north-east, and then into the north. We have reached the variable winds, and we continue on a straight course. The sea remains calm, and in a fortnight, God willing, we will be at the Cape of Good Hope.

As we draw nearer, the days seem longer: each one of us feels an urgent need to see land; and, to hasten the happy moment, a man is constantly on look-out. This is done solely for the benefit of the passengers, however, for with the aid of a well regulated chronometer, a captain, these days, is always able to ascertain the exact time at which land should appear above the horizon.

'Tomorrow morning,' our captain had said, 'if the breeze does not slacken, we shall be off-shore.' I was hardly able to sleep, and in the early dawn, my eyes were straining towards the east.

'Land, land!' cried the look-out. 'Table Mountain!' Indeed, so it was, but the breeze was so slight that we were obliged to be patient.

At long last we touched land at the Cape of Storms, which was rounded for the first time by the illustrious Gama three and a half centuries ago.[1] My heart was brimming with hope, and fancies crowded my brain.

---

1 Everyone knows that the Cape of Good Hope, first called the Cape of Storms, was discovered by the Portuguese navigator, Vasco de Gama in 1486. But Portugal, too much preoccupied with the riches of India, appeared disdainful

The town at the Cape, so neatly established by the Dutch, and which today bears the name Cape Town since the English have made themselves masters of it, is distinguished by long, perfectly straight streets, which intersect each other at right angles, and by houses of uniform height, with flat roofs and whitewashed facades. The streets are not paved; instead they are covered in hard, well-beaten gravel. As rain is infrequent there, this gravel is as good as any paving. A pleasing air of cleanliness is everywhere apparent, and recalls the origins of this settlement, for cleanliness is the rule in Holland.

Today the population numbers 25 000 inhabitants of all colours. The white population is made up of Dutch and English; the coloured comprises Hottentots, Cafres, Negroes, Malays, with mulattos originating from a mixture of all these races. Thus, there are shades of every colour from white to black, which produces an unusually varied and picturesque effect.

of the seemingly sterile lands at the tip of Africa, where no wealthy peoples were to be found whom the conquerors might plunder; and so, in the eyes of the Portuguese, the southern tip of Africa had no importance beyond that of a port of call, suitable, it is true, for the revictualling of ships, but, as there was then no competition to be feared, the establishment of a station was postponed. The Portuguese went to India simply as conquerors, heedless of the future, and established nothing en route. When afterwards the Dutch, those parsimonious merchants, came to dispute the Portuguese possessions, they were not content merely to conquer, but founded settlements, and Riebeck, a simple surgeon on board a Company ship, was given a sympathetic hearing when he indicated the need for a station which would divide the length of the voyage to India — a measure destined to save the lives of a great number of men, especially at that time when navigation was so slow, a measure which was to prove useful to all in time of peace, and particularly advantageous to the Dutch themselves in time of war. Riebeck was charged with the execution of his own plan, and soon afterwards Kaapstaadt lay at the foot of Table Mountain, with the bay as its northern boundary, while it was bordered on the left by the Rump and the Head of the Lion, and on the right by Devil's Mountain. From that time forth, this place became the meeting point of people of many races. The first inhabitants were sailors of the Company, joined soon by poor peasants from Holland and Germany. There was, from the earliest times, some assimilation with the Hottentots, and later, following the revocation of the Edict of Nantes, French immigrants arrived bringing, it is said, the first vines, and reintroducing the use of bread, which the Dutch colonists had forgotten. Gradually, the kernel of a town, although still very insignificant, began to grow. Cafres from the east, negroes brought from Guinea or from Mozambique, Malays expelled from Batavia, Lascars taken from the banks of the Ganges, now mingled with the Hottentots who, seduced by the tobacco and the brandy of the Dutch, had no thought of opposing the activities of those who provided these new delights. An ox, say the travellers of those days, was the price of a pipe of tobacco and a glass of brandy; and when the Hottentots no longer had any oxen to pay for these wonders, they sold themselves to whoever would provide them with

11

The situation of the town is perfect to the eye; it rests on a long gentle slope; at its back stand Devil's Mountain, Table Mountain, and the Head and the Rump of the Lion; these elevations forming behind the town a wide segment of a circle. In the foreground lies the bay which they call Table Bay, crowded during the season with ships en route to the East Indies or returning home. This anchorage was chosen of necessity because of the protection it affords against the south-easter; in the north-west, where the bay is too open, the sea is so strong that it drags the anchors or breaks the chains; each year this results in shipwrecks when lives and possessions are lost. The necessity of avoiding such grave disadvantages has latterly inspired the notion of building the foundations of a breakwater to withstand the effect of the sea from the west. This gigantic task will be undertaken at the Colony's expense.

Cape Town is generally thought to be very healthy, except for all the maladies produced by a too sudden transition from heat to cold, an alteration effected in a few minutes by a change in the wind. Should it come from the north, the weather is very hot; if it moves to the south-east, it rushes down from Table Mountain upon the town, accompanied by icy cold. It is for this reason that one frequently sees all the inhabitants with colds in the head on the same day. In spite of these slight inconveniences, the Indians, or rather the English employed in India, always consider the Cape as the most

these goods. In their society, the land belonged to everybody, as it still does today among the Cafres. The Dutch made offers for certain lands which they intended should belong to them exclusively. These dealings appeared strange to the Hottentot chiefs, who saw a value, which they did not comprehend, assigned to the land. Too impatient for their rewards, and considering only the present, they readily accepted, and thenceforth the Dutch became their masters. Whether there was dissension among them over what had been done, or whether the Hottentots had seen the danger and recognised that they had been duped, they tried to reconquer by arms that part of the land which they had in fact conceded. The Dutch resisted; the superiority of their arms dispersed the Hottentots, and to indemnify themselves, they extended their boundaries, so that after each attack the natives were forced to retreat further into the interior. In this way the Dutch slowly advanced, always retaining the territories which they invaded. Today they are replaced by the English, and we will see later how the latter profited by the Boer colonization of Natal, how Cafre Land is at present isolated between two of their possessions and on the eve of being incorporated into the ever-growing colony of the Cape of Good Hope. There remains today only one reminder of the founder Riebeck, whom I have just mentioned. It is a mountain situated towards the north, fifteen leagues from Cape Town, known by the name of Riebeck Kaastel because Riebeck had built there for his private use a villa which was probably very modest and which must only later have been called 'castle'.

favourable situation for regaining their health; it is here that they come to spend their leave. They are very well off here on their enormous emoluments.

Fine public buildings once made of the Cape a most agreeable town; frank and cordial manners gave a pleasant impression of the society. I have not seen all this myself, but old inhabitants have spoken a great deal to me about it. The rich and enormous Company garden where all the products, both of the temperate and of the torrid zones, were gathered together; the nursery where the plants of Batavia were acclimatised slowly on their way to Holland, whence they benefited all Europe — all this has disappeared! A third of the land has been converted into a cabbage-patch for the sole use of the governor; the rest serves as a pasture for his cows! The menagerie has met with the same fate. The theatre has just been transformed into a church by the philanthropist party; the museum has been relegated to no one knows where, to make way for a church which is being built; and another church, the largest of them all, was completed at great expense while I was there.

A certain section of this missionary society which has a strong influence on the government, is known at the Cape as the Philip party, the name of the reverend doctor who is its founder and protector. It is this party which calls itself the propagator of civilization, of Christianity, and of temperance, in order to spread its philosophy to the ends of the earth. Unfortunately the civilization which it spreads only results in the corruption of the natives; the Christianity is merely superficial for it only makes hypocrites; and when temperance is so much preached it does not cure drunkenness. In a word, the fruit of their endeavours hardly disguises the self-interested intentions of these good missionaries. It is particularly to this party that is owed the destruction of edifices where the spirit of man was able to imbibe useful knowledge and cultivate a taste for beauty. These people were not content merely to attack *things* — every individual had now to bow beneath the yoke. Thus, Sunday was struck from the days which belong to man; all the shops were obliged to close, including those public gathering places where the Dutch loved to give vent to their frank and noisy enjoyment; the victor wished the vanquished to be as bored as he himself was.

During my stay at the Cape, my whole time was given to preparations for my projected journey to the north, except for one day which was devoted to visiting Table Mountain — a visit which I shall briefly describe. Our party numbered three, and as we had no guide, we lost our way and wandered for more than two hours in search of the place called Plaat Klip, flat rock, over which a stream flows, before falling in a cascade on its way down to the town. Here we rested a moment, before beginning the laborious climb up the ravine which is the only access in the north. We were soon aware of a delightful freshness; it was a fine rain which was falling upon us like mist, and which was produced by the water seeping through the rocky fissures and trickling down from the upper rocks. This diversion renewed our energies, and in spite of our guns, which were more cumbersome than heavy, in an hour and a half we had emerged from the ravine, having climbed 1 200 metres. The first thing which struck us was the great number of names written on the rocks, each visitor having been determined to leave behind him in this remote place a mark of his visit. There were women's names among them, which seemed rather extraordinary to me, considering all the difficulties which small feet might encounter in ascending to such a height by a path so rough and steep and covered with loose stones.

We separated and each of us went off in a different direction in pursuit of our own interests. We did not walk far because, except for a few plants growing in deposits of earth loosely lodged between the stones, there was nothing to interest us. Three partridges were the only birds that we saw; not an eagle, not a baboon, not even a vulture, although Levaillant had found a fair number there.

Reassembled once more, and sitting together on the edge of the precipice, we gazed at the adjoining mountains which seemed infinitely smaller than our own. The white town at our feet looked rather like a game of dominoes turned upside down and arranged symmetrically. Further away lay the rounded bay, its shores edged with shining sand, and the anchorage where the ships appeared like drowned insects floating on the surface. In the distance was the sea with, here and there, the suggestion of a sail. On the horizon nothing was visible, for there the sky and the sea were one. And we, who were so insignificant, had the temerity to judge these great things as small in comparison with ourselves. What opinion would we have had of our own consequence had it been granted us to see ourselves at this distance! Ah yes, there you have it: from contemplation of the spectacle of nature, man's thoughts turn inward to consider himself. He is astonished and humbled when he pictures himself reflected in the distance, no bigger than an atom in the empty spaces of the air. The magnitude of all about him compels him to recognize his insignificance. I presume that it is his pride which has flattered him, saying to him: 'Man, all the grandeur which you see at your feet is at your disposal — it is you who are king of it all.' What reflections must arise in him if he will first consider that he is not in the least the creator of this kingdom, which is simply conceded to him for a short time by the Creator of all things. And yet, although this truth is so apparent, there are still many who continue to doubt.

When we had taken our fill of this immense view, we went down again by the same way, and soon arrived at a knoll covered with trees

14

that gleamed with a silvery lustre. These trees, from which I gathered a few branches, were the *Protea argentea* which apparently exist only on the slopes of these mountains lying at the tip of Africa, between the town and the Cape of Good Hope. The leaves underneath are covered with hairs which have the soft sheen of satin. The fruit is similar to that of the pine. The trees are used for firewood in some of the neighbouring districts and, towards Constantia, they have been planted over fairly large areas of ground, probably because they succeed better there than trees brought from Europe.

We returned from our little excursion at about five in the evening, glad to have made this pilgrimage which European visitors rarely miss.

I lost precious time in preparations which were interminable for various reasons, all of them beyond my control. The first of these was the Retief[1] emigration, for which there were scarcely sufficient wagons available, so that it was with difficulty I found what I wanted. For this same reason oxen were rare, thin, and exorbitantly expensive, and the sale of gunpowder was prohibited. The second reason was a difficulty raised by the Collector of Customs at the Cape. I had brought ashore at Simon's Town[2] twenty-four French guns, declared their value, and paid the duty; the customs officials had accepted my money. I did not know that foreign firearms were prohibited in all the English colonies. The Collector at Simon's Town, although he ought to have known these rules better than I, was unaware of this or pretended to be.

Some days later, finding me at the Cape, the Collector General informed me through the ship's forwarding agent that he regretted the mistake made by his representative; that he expected me to re-export my arms and to sign an undertaking to that effect the same day. I felt myself to be too much within my rights to make the least concession, especially as they were confidently depending on my doing so: I refused absolutely. They pleaded with me, adding that the official ran the risk of losing his situation. Sure of my advantage, and taking into consideration the false position in which this person had voluntarily placed himself, I proposed this solution: Return to me the duty I have paid and I will sign the undertaking of re-exportation; that is all I can do. They declared that it was imposs-

---

1 There will be further mention of this extraordinary man who, wishing to remove from English domination over the Dutch population of the Cape of Good Hope, sought asylum in the interior among the Cafres, where he was later assassinated in a cowardly manner.
2 It is perhaps necessary to mention here that the underwriters do not pay out the value of a ship which, on its way to India, is lost in port, if it has contravened the regulation which states that Table Bay should be used for six months of the year only and Simon's Bay, or False Bay, for the other six months. The distance between these two points, which are separated by the Cape of Good Hope itself, is about seven leagues.

ible to refund my money, and I retracted my offer.

The next day, realising that they could not succeed by persuasion, they had recourse to intimidation. I was threatened with a raid on my lodgings and with the seizure of my arms. I replied to these gentlemen, 'Come on then.' They did not come; instead they threatened to bring a case against me so that my obstinacy should be punished. I replied, 'Proceed'. Finally, after several days, I left the Cape and although I returned there a number of times, they let me alone. The Collector's endeavours nevertheless detained me for some time; for had I left as soon as I was ready, it might have been assumed that I was in the wrong. I considered my presence necessary simply as a matter of propriety.

A difficulty which I should have mentioned earlier was that of procuring hired oxen to serve me on the journey from the Cape to Verlooren Valley, the Lost Lake, the first place which I wished to explore and which is situated 45 leagues to the north of the Cape of Good Hope. This lake has a small outlet or drainage into the Atlantic. There was, at the time, a scarcity of oxen in the vicinity of the Cape.

A man, taking advantage of the circumstances, presented himself to me as a driver, with a boy to lead and fourteen oxen. He undertook to drive my wagon to the required spot and back again, although I wanted simply to get there and not to return. He estimated the journey at fourteen days, asking £3.10 sterling for each day. These terms were too expensive and I refused them. The next day the same driver returned. I offered him £12 sterling for the whole journey and he accepted, asking to be paid in advance. Only too happy to be off, I did not try to discover whether this was excessive but when I arrived at Verlooren Valley, some farmers questioned me as to what I had paid, and told me that a price of £3 sterling would have been reasonable.

I shall now describe the method of transport employed in these regions of southern Africa. I take the trouble to do so for the guidance of travellers, as it is the only means used on long journeys and is not lacking in originality.

The vehicle is nothing but a great wagon with four wheels bound with iron, and robust enough for any encounter. The bodywork is one metre wide, and five and a half metres long; it is composed of what the Boers, or farmers, call a *buik-plank*, that is to say a bottom board, and of two *leer* or ladders. These three pieces are simply placed upon a back section which is fixed, and a front section which pivots on a strong bolt; pegs and straps, passing through clamps, hold them firmly in position. This swivel system is preferred by the Boers, as the wagons often capsize and the principal parts would be broken each time if they were linked by screws. The necessity of frequent dismantling, to cross rivers, ravines or difficult gorges, or for any other purpose, gives this vehicle every advantage. Hoops of pliable wood, fifteen in number, linked by longitudinal crossbars of bamboo or Spanish reed, support a painted waterproof canvas, covered by a second white canvas, which is lashed to the ladders a third of the way along. In front and behind are extensions which fasten and which are called *klappje*.

A complete wagon is furnished with four boxes. The one in front serves as a seat for the driver; the one at the back prevents things from falling off; the other two run along the outside against the ladders, between the two pairs of wheels; they are very useful for storing goods which are constantly needed on the journey, such as powder, crockery, and light provisions like sugar and coffee.

Behind the wagon, underneath the projecting portion, hangs a *trappe*, constructed in the manner of a grid, and which, by reason of its proximity to the ground, serves as a step for boarding the wagon from behind as it moves along. This extension is very useful; the iron pots, saucepans, frying-pans, gridirons, kettles, and all the other cooking utensils which are blackened by smoke, and cannot be stored inside, are attached to it. In spite of these encumbrances, there is room to store a supply of dry wood, which it is essential should be carried for use on wet days while crossing the bare plains.

These peasants, whether they are out hunting or whether they are emigrating with their families, travel only with the barest essentials. There is almost always, within the wagon, a wooden frame of the same width as the bodywork, squarely hung on a level with the ladders, and across which leather thongs are stretched. This forms a resilient bed, the necessity for which is particularly felt as the Boers habitually use only sheepskins and palliasses stuffed with feathers as mattresses.

In spite of the widespread acceptance of this arrangement, a naturalist encumbered with all sorts of objects, would not sacrifice precious space in the frivolous pursuit of comfort; thus my wagon was stripped of this bed, called *kaartel* by the Boers.

Underneath, the wagon is almost the same as its European counterpart, except that the method of articulation between the front section and the back is even simpler. Two drag chains attached to the front gear are hooked to the ladders, a short distance from the back wheels. On the same hook hangs a skid made of iron or wood for use on the long descents. A pot of tar must be firmly attached to the shaft for it is customary, every second day, to grease the axle boxes which are reached by raising the side of the wagon with the aid of a nine foot lever. This precaution is considered indispensable, not only in order to lessen the friction, but also to allay fears of fire.

Now, this great machine, capable of carrying three or four thousand pounds, must be made to travel across country where roads do not exist; it will be required to climb steep mountains and descend slopes crumbling with loose stones: it must cross river-beds, and hills of shifting sand. There is thus no possibility of using only two, or four, or even six oxen. A team of six would be a mockery in the face of such difficulties; the minimum therefore is ten; the usual maximum is eighteen. But, however great the strength of nine pairs of oxen, I have found it insufficient in certain circumstances and I have been obliged to resort to using twenty-four of these animals.

This is the arrangement: a long trace, *trek-touw*, made of buffalo hide, is attached to the end of the shaft, where the first yoke is fixed — that of the two *agter-os*, the after-oxen, the most intelligent of the team, who know how to hold back in case of too rapid descent. This is the manner in which the yoke is made: a piece of rounded wood, 1,60 metres long, has a clamp fixed in the middle, dividing it into two equal parts. Each of the parts is pierced by two longitudinal holes, allowing between them sufficient space to accomodate the neck of the ox, and intended to hold two flat little pieces of wood fifty centimetres long and notched on the outer edge. These notches are cut to hold the strap which passes under the animal's neck and prevents the yoke, against which the withers press, from lifting. But, as this strap could slip, leaving the ox free to escape, the heads of the animals are tied with a thong known as an *os-riem*. The *riem* on the right-hand ox is attached to the left-hand ox, whose horns are used as a kind of cleat, round which the slack is twisted; in this way each pair is too firmly held to pull apart.

This method of harnessing is much more simple and practical than that of attaching the yoke to the horns, which is practised in Bordeaux, and which I consider detestable. This way the ox retains much more liberty of movement; he tires less easily and his strength is much greater because the yoke is nearer to his centre of gravity. It is true that there is friction, that the hair is sometimes rubbed off, the skin is grazed and the ox avoids making efforts which are painful to him. But this happens only when the animals are put to work after a long rest. Among those which habitually work, the skin is so thickened that they feel none of these effects. The withers of an ox which has not worked are like the hands of a sailor who puts to sea after three months of idleness.

Two men are required to drive, lead, and encourage these long spans. One takes the head-thong of the two *voor-os*, and guides the first pair, which are followed by all the other pairs. The second man, sitting on the box, is armed with an *agter-os chambok*[1] as well as

1 Short whip used on after-oxen.

18

with the great whip whose handle measures eighteen feet and whose thong is twenty-seven feet long. His occupation is constantly to maintain a balance between the yokes; he shouts the name of any ox which is slowing down, and reinforces his words with the whip, thereby encouraging the ox to obey the voice alone. Frequently the driver jumps down from his seat to chastise the farthest oxen; he moves from right to left at the risk of being crushed, and all the while he calls out to the stragglers in time-honoured phrases. This exercise requires much skill, agility and courage; it is most tiring work, which would be very boring to a European. But to the South African Boers it is a matter of honour to be able to drive a wagon well; they love to prove their skill and I have never known them to consider this activity a chore. In their eyes, to take the box and the whip is equivalent to the sailor's taking the wheel of a ship.

These wagons, which are purposely dislocated for greater resilience, are not very pleasant to travel in; but when a halt is made on a long journey, they enable the traveller to feel quite at home wherever he may be, and because of their elevation above the ground, they are far preferable to live in than a tent. Snakes find their way into a tent without impediment and spend the night side by side with man. Besides, a tent has too great a surface area; it is invariably not sufficiently supported; the wind whisks it away from over the sleeper's head and tears it up. It is true that once I had to tie even my wagon to some trees to prevent the wind from blowing it over; but it was on high ground and my vehicle was empty at the time. Such circumstances are rare.

This is the slowest means of travel known to man and a journey will take months which camels could do in a matter of weeks. More often than not with wagons, it is necessary to explore the way in advance, to make great detours in order to reach practicable fords, to skirt mountains which are too high or too steep, or where the passes are too narrow, to cut paths through the woods, to fill gullies. And yet, in spite of all these precautions, damage still occurs. I have always regretted the absence of camels in this part of Africa, where without a doubt, they could be better maintained than in the north.

I have already said that oxen draw these wagons; but for those who might have read Jacques Arago, it is perhaps necessary that I repeat myself. These are true oxen. Those which have very long divergent horns with points that are six, or even eight, and sometimes nine feet apart, belong to the variety which the Boers call *Afrikaander*. Large and long-legged, they move fast and their gait astonishes newly arrived Europeans. Their colour — red, white, blue, yellow — is rarely pure and even; and the scrotum is well-muscled.[1]

1 Presumably, one should read 'sacrum' for 'scrotum'. *Translator's note*

Those whose horns are moderately long, sharply pointed and form half an elipse, are distinguished from those just mentioned by their smaller size, their colour, which is almost always red, the roundness of their hind quarters, their spiritedness and their irritability. These are the *Zoulah*, Zoulou oxen. They were introduced into the Colony in March 1840.

Those whose horns are short, that is, not exceeding six or eight inches, are distinguished by their black colouring which is sometimes marked with white, either on the ridge of the back or on the stomach. The body is very long, and proportionately the legs are very short. Their leanness contrasts unpleasantly with the rounded shapes of other oxen; in fact the bones of the pelvis, those of the scrotum and even the ribs, can be seen protruding; one would think that these animals were ill. They are very submissive and docile and appear to have known discipline for longer than the others. It would seem at first that one should not expect too much of them, but that is a mistake, for they are in fact, heavy and muscular, and withstand fatigue better than the more high-spirited oxen. These are the *Vaader- landers*, oxen from Holland.

Those which result from a mixture of *Afrikaanders* and *Vaader- landers* are called *Bastaard-Vaaderlanders*. They have more of the characteristics of the *Vaaderlanders* and are the best animals I know. There are many other cross-breeds which are less worthy of interest. However, among all these varieties, not one resembles the buffalo, whether it be the Italian, the Asiatic or the African variety. Never has a harnessed buffalo, of any breed whatsoever, walked in the streets of Cape Town, and yet a Frenchman, Jacques Arago, who ought to be able to discriminate since he is a writer, speaks of wagons drawn by buffaloes. Furthermore, according to him, these buffaloes drew his wagon to the eastern shores of False Bay, where he, in the company of Rouvières, engaged in that famous lion hunt which is so much admired by our Parisian sportsmen.

I have never been able to understand how anyone, after having travelled the world, should find it necessary to lie. Harnessed buffa- loes at the Cape! I suppose he means, *Bos cafer*,[1] a terrible animal, mastered by the Boers, who have no more use for it than they do for the gentler varieties like the *Boselaphus oreas*. Wild lions killed at False Bay, indeed! And with the aid of a pair of pocket pistols! Lions at False Bay, where for more than a hundred and fifty years not one has dared to imprint his paw upon the earth! These rash assertions startle me more than the actual sight of a buffalo or a lion. Jacques Arago is not, I know, the only traveller who has com-

1 Cafre buffalo.

mitted the serious error of mistaking oxen for buffaloes; there are others whom the celebrated Cuvier has consulted, and who have misled this father of modern science into stating that the herds of the Hottentots consist in general of buffaloes. This is the manner in which errors are frequently perpetuated, and the matter is the more regrettable in that a host of false assertions is daily reprinted, the briefest refutation of which would fill thousands of volumes.

On 1 September 1838, having finally succeeded in leaving Cape Town, I crossed the Zout Rivier, the salty river, and made my way towards the north. This day, like those that followed, was not distinguished by any remarkable event. On the 5th, at about two o'clock in the afternoon, we came to Berg Rivier where the water was eight feet deep and barred our way. Fortunately there was a boat which was put at our disposal for the price of 5 rixdollars. It served to transport ourselves and our goods, while the wagon, laden with an enormous, empty, well-secured cask was hauled across by the fourteen oxen, swimming behind their leaders attached to a towline. With the assistance of a handful of men, we effected in only two hours, a crossing which might have delayed us for several weeks or even months, as befell me later once or twice, simply for want of a wretched little boat.

We continued in the same direction until the 8th, across a country of burning sand, into which the wheels of the wagon sank eight or ten inches. The going was constantly heavy, the heat was unbearable and we breathed in more dust than air. There was no means of distraction; the bushes which covered the land stood isolated, a few feet apart, providing no protection for game; and always there was the incessant grinding of the sand beneath the wheels, a dreary sound, accompanied only by the insipid call of a dove, poor bird, the only one perhaps, to be heard there, repeating the same thing, the same sound, over and over. A few ostriches appeared and then disappeared again almost immediately. The sight of them, out of reach at 600 or 800 paces, contributed to our feeling of desperation.

When we descended into the valley, I was greatly cheered by the sight of a lake bordered by thick reeds from which a cool freshness emanated. This oasis promised good water, baths and a great abundance of water-birds. We crossed over at a point between the dwellings of Henderick Kotze and Henderick Facolin Gous in the eastern reaches, where the want of width and depth of water provides the only practicable ford for wagons.

On the 9th we travelled along the northern shore and outspanned a mile and a half from the sea. My intention was to make my camp there for some time, to form an opinion of the country and to decide where next to proceed. The situation was favourable; camped 200 paces from the lake, we had within our reach a great quantity of coot, duck and other birds which were doomed to fill our cooking pots. Behind us, the country was exactly as it had been all the way from the Cape; there were dreary, monotonous bushes, eight to twelve feet high, with here and there a duyker, a steenbook or an ostrich.

Opposite us, on the other side of the lake stretched a ridge of rocky mountains, 400 to 500 feet high, the eastern section of which is called Elands Berg, Mountain of the Cannas, and the western section, Bawians Berg, Mountain of the Baboons. Only the latter still has a right to its name. We found this species of ape fairly numerous there; but the cannas had disappeared from the other mountain and the old people hardly remembered having seen any. What one does still find there however, is the leopard, as one does in other mountainous places where enormous rocks stand precariously balanced, leaning perilously one against another, propped up sometimes on a slender overhang in perfect disorder and interspersed by ravines and caves; as I was saying, one does find the leopard, which is attracted by the presence of rock-rabbits, *klip-dassen*, an easy prey, and by baboons, the older and larger of which sometimes successfully resist the attack, which generally occurs every other day, two hours after sunset. It will also take *klip-springers* which, in spite of their agility, do not always escape. These regions suit the leopard for several reasons; it is undisturbed there, as man comes that way less frequently than he does in the plains; it can conveniently make its lair there, hide its prey and leave no visible tracks; and hearing man's approach from afar, it can more easily escape pursuit.

Because of all the advantages which these surroundings offer, the leopard often lives in close proximity to the dwellings of man and preys upon his flocks. Goats and sheep are carried off without difficulty and even calves are sometimes snatched from the mother. All its skill however and all its muscular strength, are ineffectual against the ox. Infinitely more dangerous to man than the hyaena, the leopard has the advantage of claws, but it lacks the strength of the hyaena's teeth and neck.

I intended to avail myself of every opportunity to hunt the leopard, and I accepted with pleasure a number of proposals which were made to me. Unfortunately we had not the luck to flush out a single one, which was probably due to excessive precautions. A small number of dogs might have been very useful; but the twenty or thirty which noisily preceded us by a hundred paces, must have frightened off our quarry from a mile away. I soon learnt that in this African-Dutch type of hunt, the dogs usually accomplish the business all alone. Those in front are torn to pieces and disembowelled; the rest, attacking in a mass, bite at whatever they can grasp — the leopard is overpowered by numbers. To expose to certain death several undoubtedly useful animals in order to destroy one single noxious creature, which could so easily be dispatched by surer and nobler means, seemed to me quite unworthy, and repelled me to such an extent that I politely declined the offers of those who believed they were doing me a favour by inviting me on these expeditions.

This method however is not generally adopted; it is principally practised by the inhabitants of the western part of the Colony. Those from the east, and especially those from Port Natal, who are more seasoned hunters, behave differently. I had, several years later, the opportunity of discovering among them men of strong character, brave hunters of lion and elephant, who would allow a leopard to escape without firing a shot, claiming that one could use one's powder more usefully and more nobly. For them, the hunt is not merely recreation; their whole existence depends upon it, and I have known young men who intended to make it their life's work.

We also observed in this part of the country, the animal which the Boers call *strand-wolf*, and which naturalists know by the name of *Hyaena fusca*. In spite of all its similarities to the *Hyaena crocuta*, this hyaena is quite different in its habits, which are not encountered among other carnivores of the same type. The function of the *Hyaena crocuta* is to dispose of the remains of animals which the lion has killed in the bush or on the plains. The duty of the *Hyaena fusca* is to clear from the shore the refuse left by the sea, debris of all kinds which is cast up from the depths, and particularly those heaps of dead crustaceans whose carapaces form a sort of dyke, four to six feet high in certain parts of southern Africa. The *Hyaena fusca*, although without the ability to catch its food in the water, is thus a fish eater. Indeed, its tracks intersect all over the shore; each night it haunts the beaches; it roams amid the heaped debris and it finds its food like any other beach-comber. The Boers do not fear for their cattle, at its approach, for they regard it as perfectly harmless. *Hyaena fusca* is a large animal, shaped like the spotted hyaena; the body is covered in long hair and banded with dark perpendicular stripes. The strength of its jaws is remarkable and this has attracted the particular attention of naturalists.

Two accounts, one by Aristotle, the other by Belon, offer different descriptions which could apply to this animal, and which Buffon mistakenly attributes to *Lutra canadensis*. Aristotle singles out from among the amphibians an animal which he calls *latax*. This is what he says about it:

Quae latior lutre est, dentesque habet robustos, quippe quae

*noctu plerumque egrediens; virgulta proxima suis dentibus ut
ferro praecidat: lataci pilus durus specie inter pilum vituli
marini et cervi.*[1]

Aristotle compares the size with that of the otter, and this would
naturally have led the scholar Buffon to think of the Canadian otter,
which is bigger. Buffon has apparently not taken sufficient account
of the action of the teeth, which Aristotle describes so well, nor of
the nature of the coat, which the ancient naturalist describes as being
very rough.

Belon has this to say:

> Since the English have no wolf within their land, nature has pro-
> vided them, on their sea-shores, with an animal which so closely
> approaches in appearance our wolf that, were it not that he
> feeds upon fish rather than flocks, one would say that he re-
> sembles, in all things, our rapacious beast; his stoutness, his
> coat, his head, which is very large, and his tail, much resemble
> those of the land wolf; but, although he feeds only on fish, so
> they say, and was quite unknown to the ancients, he seems to
> me not less noteworthy than the animals quoted above, which
> lead a double life.

Buffon has shown evidence of much ingenuity in likening the *latax*
of Aristotle to Belon's sea-wolf, which seems perfectly acceptable to
me. But because Aristotle, in choosing to use the European otter as
an illustration of size, and the seal to convey an idea of the nature
of the coat, appeared to be preoccupied with amphibious animals, so
also did Buffon choose to concentrate his researches on this type of
animal.

Belon, having established the habitat of his sea-wolf in England,
which I believe to be a mistake, influenced Buffon to do the same.
Nevertheless, this is an excusable mistake, for what could be more
natural than to think that an animal which feeds on fish, should be
a swimmer, and above all a skilful diver! If Belon had been better
acquainted with the animal he was describing, he would have said
that it was primarily fish-eating, but unlike the otter, it does not
catch fish; it simply grazes on dead fish and crustaceans cast up by
the sea.

Supposing that the Canadian otter were also to be found in

1 The beaver is flatter than the otter and has strong teeth; often at night-time it
   emerges from the water and goes nibbling at the bark of aspens that fringe the
   riversides . . . The hair of the beaver is rough, indeterminate in appearance
   between the hair of the seal and the hair of the deer. (Aristotle: *Historia
   Animalium*, VIII:, 594[b]—595[a], translated by D.A.W. Thompson)

northern Europe, and taking into consideration the fact that, at the same latitude, the cold is much more intense in Canada than in Europe, this otter would have been confined to the northern regions of Scandinavia, and Aristotle could not have known it. It is unlikely that it ever existed in England; moreover, no kind of otter can be compared with the common wolf either in the shape and the size of the body or the tail.

As the most salient characteristics of these two descriptions apply particularly to the *Hyaena fusca*, I tend to the belief that the ancients knew the African species, or if they did not, at least they were familiar with an animal of the same appearance and behaviour.

One must not be led to believe that the *Hyaena fusca* would spurn the flesh of mammals, were he to encounter their remains; he is in this respect like the otter, which frequently takes a brooding hen from the nest, although his fish-eating requirements ensure that he is never far from the littoral.

I soon had in my possession specimens of most of the birds which inhabit or frequent this stretch of water, which I estimate to be fourteen kilometres long. I found nothing particularly remarkable — several species are common in Europe. We had the purple and grey herons, the night herons, the stilt and other types of plover, the godwit, the snipe, the seagull, sea swallows, pelicans. We also had the caruncular coot, the reed-hen, several kinds of ducks, the little egret, the river cormorant, the snake bird, the Cape penguin, the water rail, the horned grebe, etc.

I was already anticipating further acquisitions, when a circumstance, although in itself disagreeable, led to my witnessing an astonishing and dazzlingly beautiful sight. I had set out quite early and had just visited the mouth of the lake, where there was a barrier of pebbles over which the waters at certain times flowed into the sea, and the high tide washed back into the lake. I was walking along the bank in a northerly direction when a male ostrich suddenly appeared, emerging from between the dunes, and making for the water barely 150 paces away. I immediately lay down flat, hoping that it would take me for a body cast up by the sea, as often happens; but it was not deceived and made off. All I could do was to follow its tracks, and for more than four hours I did so, with stubborn determination. At last, weary and so thirsty that my tongue seemed on fire, I changed my mind. I must have been a long way from my camp; to return to it was hardly possible — the heat was too great, my thirst too unbearable. I had heard tell of a dwelling situated somewhere in the direction in which I was already going, but I was not sure of the distance. I thought it nearer than in fact it was and I went painfully on, expecting to glimpse it from the top of every incline, but neither cultivated fields nor flocks met my eye. My torments became intolerable so I sat down under a bush without any shade, on sand much hotter than the sun, as perplexed as any European newly arrived in these parts, and I considered my situation. The more I reflected, the more I was convinced that I was very hot and very thirsty. It did not occur to me to dig a hole two feet deep, which would provide me with some coolness; I thought only of killing a dove and sucking the flesh to replenish my saliva, a wretched solution, but in fact more efficacious than one might think. So I went on walking and at about six o'clock in the evening I came upon the fields of Abraham Lauw, who lived on the banks of the Salt Lake at Lange Valley. Realising that I was close to the house I began to walk rapidly. I soon arrived, and had the indescribable pleasure of quenching my thirst from a large bucket of buttermilk which I drained to the last drop.

The owners were away, and so I had no choice but to deal with the manager and his wife. I had arrived inopportunely, as these sorts of managers are even more parsimonious than their masters. Although I was completely unknown to them, and did not speak their language, I had nevertheless to oblige them by telling my story and listening in turn to theirs. I would have abstained from these pleasures had I been able to sup and sleep elsewhere. Finally, when the time came to bid each other goodnight, I was shown an open door; I went in and found myself in a spacious room containing eight or ten beds. Engelbrecht, the manager, showed me mine, and then, only three paces away, stretched himself out beside his better half. I lay down also, astonished to see that in these happy lands, people share a bedroom as they might share a meal. For the rest, there was nothing untoward; the bed was a frame supported on four legs; crossed leather thongs took the place of springs; several sheepskins replaced the usual covers; one lay down completely clothed as if one were at table. But the difference was that at table I had eaten my fill, while in bed I was unable to sleep. Myriads of insects kept me constantly awake. I did not wait for dawn before going out to take the air. It was then that I noticed my linen was literally red with blood — while my neighbours, the fortunate creatures, had slept most peacefully. How true it is to say that eventually one may grow accustomed to anything.

But I was destined to receive compensation for my unexpected pains. Engelbrecht arrived armed with a long gun; he had promised the night before to take me to a lake near the farmhouse to show me the flamingoes, whose number would astonish me he said. We set out and within a quarter of an hour we were at the lake. 'Now, do you see a great flock of flamingoes?' he asked. 'Where?' I said. 'Over there at the end of the lake; that white line.' Indeed I was able to make out some white, but I could see no birds. Enjoying my disbelief

26

and anticipating my surprise, he took aim with his long gun and fired a bullet which ricocheted at 700 or 800 paces. Immediately the white line turned to flame; an unbelievable uproar was heard and then, gone was the white line, gone the flame, and the day was darkened by a canopy overhead formed of a hundred thousand flying crosses. I suddenly understood the meaning of the name flamingo — flaming. Never was a name so apt.

My guide lost no time in taking leave of me. I thanked him for his hospitality, and then set out to gain possession of some of these birds, which I was now seeing for the first time. After several attempts, I broke the wing of one of them with a charge of buckshot fired at 200 paces; my bitch tracked it down for some time without success, but gained the advantage when the flamingo was obliged to resort to swimming, whereupon she seized it and brought it back intact: a perfect adult specimen. I subsequently had further opportunities of hunting these creatures and of learning to know them. As they rank among the most distinctive of birds, I believe that it will be worth recounting what I know of them, although many naturalists have already described them at length.

The flamingo stands in the same relationship to the web-footed birds as the secretary bird does to the predators; one is indeed web-footed and the other a bird of prey, but they differ from those with which they have most in common by an exceptionately long tarsus: therefore they should form a separate genus. There are three kinds of flamingo which inhabit southern Africa, not to mention others originating either from America or from New Holland. The type of which I am speaking is the biggest, the most beautiful, and also the most numerous. It is the one which was so much sought after in ancient times in Rome. Wanton nature seems sometimes to play tricks with her creatures; she does not always make the limbs in proportion to the body, as one would expect them to be.

Beauty has been her yardstick, but she sometimes gives good measure and sometimes short; she has created thick bodies and slim bodies, the brilliant and the dull and, among the ranks of the aquatic birds, she has made the penguin very plump and the flamingo very slender. Seeing this bird in flight, one can hardly distinguish the body, which is no greater than that of a domestic duck; it has a long neck, long feet, long, very narrow wings. It forms a perfect cross of four feet nine inches to five feet long: thus, the least accident which disturbs its balance in flight, results in a fall; a lead pellet is sufficient to break the tarsus and bring the flamingo down, unable to fly or to run. It is more effective to strike the tarsus than the wing, because generally the bird runs faster than a man.

In the adult, white feathers predominate and pink tinges the upper surface of the wings; the wing tips are black. In the young, the wing tips are only brownish; the beak and the feet are either grey or yellow, but always with a light pink tinge. Amongst almost all birds, the upper jaw, which is fixed, is larger and deeper than the lower — the reverse is true in this case. It is perhaps this which had led some authors[1] to believe that the upper jaw was mobile and the lower fixed; or perhaps the reason is the manner in which the creature takes its food, with its beak upside down, and the upper jaw beneath the lower. I, who have had the opportunity of examining this structure, dare to confirm that the lower is the mobile portion in the flamingo, as in other birds. If the flamingo had not received from nature a beak of this shape, with which to dabble upside-down, and had been armed with, let us suppose, the beak of a swan, a goose or a duck, it would have been impossible for him to seek out and grasp his food, because, in this operation, the position of the beak having to be horizontal, the neck would have to describe a curve tangental to the surface of the water, and in order to do that, the already long neck of the flamingo would need to be six inches longer. The neck differs essentially in shape from that of the geese, the ducks, the herons, the storks, the bitterns, which all have two folds by means of which they can retract their necks between the shoulders, some of them during flight, others while swimming. The flamingo, not having this advantage of flexibility, is burdened by the whole length of its neck, whether in flight or in repose. In spite of this constraint, it is far from ungraceful in its usual attitudes; only when it is in flight is one tempted to remark on the excessive length of these parts, but as there is perfect harmony between them, the eye is soon accustomed to them, and the more so because of the attractive colour. The pink colour is unique and is found all over the body, not only on the upper and under parts of the wing; if one lifts the white plumage of the neck, the stomach and the back, one sees this shade quite strongly pronounced. The beak, the feet, the eye, even the flesh, the blood and the tongue, all share this colour.

I believe that I am not wrong in saying that the flamingo is very closely related to the goose, in that the beak is edged with a thousand blunt ridges, a characteristic which distinguishes the geese, and also because of its trumpeting cry which leads one to believe that there is a certain similarity in the organ structure. It flies in the same formation as the goose, and feeds in the same way, which means that its stomach contains not fish, but grit and a small quanity of masticated grass.

Travellers do not agree upon the excellence of the flesh; this is because it is subject to variations according to the locality which the bird frequents. When the bird is killed on the coast, at Saldanah bay,

1 Rondelet, Wormius, Cardan and Charleton, cited by Buffon.

the flesh has, I imagine, an oily taste, which is disagreeable to a refined palate; while at the salt lakes, where the water is merely brackish, the flesh is often quite good, even delicate. The tongue deserves the great reputation it has acquired from having been considered a delicacy by several Roman emperors; it appears to contain only melting fat which tastes exquisite. It is as much prized by the African hunters as are the marrow bones of the buffalo, the eland and the giraffe.

The month of September is the time when the birds display their most brilliant plumage. In January the flocks include many strongly flying birds, and it is at that time particularly that they are hunted for their flesh. According to the colonists, their breeding ground is unknown, and this leads me to believe that they do not raise their young on the mainland, but rather on the numerous little islands just off the coast.

Domestication seems not to suit this bird at all; one undeniable reason is its preferance for the salt marshes. I have never seen flamingoes on the banks of rivers or on fresh water lakes; when they are encountered there, it is only as birds of passage.

CHAPTER II

Three months had already gone by in exploring the banks and the environs of Verlooren Valley and yet I had failed to enrich my collection. I was intending, without more ado, to investigate the possibility of proceeding further afield, when an opportunity arose of establishing immediately whether there was any truth in the unfavourable accounts I had heard of that country.

Henderick Kotze, the field-cornet of the district, invited me to accompany him on horseback to Hantam, the northern-most limit of the colony, about 110 leagues from the Cape. It was rather a long rough journey for anyone who was not in the habit of riding — the prospect of twenty-two days spent almost constantly in the saddle ought to have caused me to hesitate; however I was far from doing so, and accepted with alacrity.

As is usual on these occasions, we set out before dawn. A friend of the field-cornet accompanied us, and an *agter-ruyter* rode behind with the light baggage and a spare horse on a lead rein. The roads, which were at first tolerable, led across sandy countryside, bristling with rocky outcrops. It was 14 December. The sun generously poured forth its burning rays; the hot dust, rising from the trodden sand, clung to the sweat on our hands and faces, and darkened the colour of our sodden clothing.

At about three o'clock we left the sand behind, but only to enter rocky gorges, so steep that we were obliged to lead the horses. The poor creatures often hesitated; we needed to be patient and, above all to have confidence in their unshod hoofs. If the animal were to lose his footing, he would plunge to the depths, dragging with him the rider who was leading him by the bridle. The time spent in these repeated climbs and descents, and the resultant fatigue to us and to our horses, ensured that we would not reach Clanwilliam that day. We were obliged to put up for the night at the Smett homestead, whose owners, excellent people, welcomed us in true patriarchal fashion.

This farm, which was situated in the heart of a deep, green valley where pure, fresh water was abundant, appeared to be very well maintained. The house, built of stone and embellished with a moulded white gable, was perched on a perron, six feet high and twenty feet long, and contained those cool rooms which provide a delightful haven on hot days. The view was limited and consisted of a well-kept vegetable garden, bordered by a huge orange grove which was watered by a murmuring stream — the source of life in these regions.

I was soon recovered from my fatigue and as I began to consider my present situation, my thoughts travelled the 2 000 leagues which separated me from my homeland. This inward contemplation stirs the soul, and produces as much pain as pleasures. We see, as it were on the same page, the past with its nostalgia, and the future which charms us with uncertain hopes, glimpsed through a fresh light haze, whose beauty we clutch at like children.

The sun was setting and the air was cooling slightly when a thousand cries, emanating from somewhere above my head, attracted my attention. A fast-gathering flock of bee-eaters, *Apiaster*, was fluttering and wheeling about the tops of my orange trees, their resting place for the night, and the choice spot for a league around. As their numbers were great, they showed much determination in their squabbles over the temporary possession of the tip of a branch. Their twittering and fluttering lasted a good three-quarters of an hour; then all was silent, each one having found a roosting place. Until then I had seen these birds only in daylight, soaring high as the swifts, and like them, flying low before a storm. The colonists call them *berg-swaluwe*.

On the 15th, after travelling for an hour an a half, we crossed the Olyphant's Rivier which is two-thirds the width of the Seine in Paris, and where the water, at the time, was three feet deep. Sand banks were visible and, judging by the reeds, branches and roots which were entangled in the bushes at the edge, the water had not risen above six feet during the rains.

Clanwilliam is a ten minute ride from the river. The little town, consisting of about thirty dwellings, is noteworthy only for its very fine gardens, the fruit of which is quite famous. We passed through without making a stop and climbed the mountain on the other side, the Cedar Berg, cedar mountains, at the top of which we dismounted and allowed our horses to graze. Twenty paces away on our left, was the cave called Klip Huys, stone house, formed by an enormous block of loose granite resting on top of two other blocks. This cave, open to the north, is twenty paces long and twelve paces wide. We lunched there and each one of us, with a piece of coal, wrote his name on the rock, as visitors are wont to do. An adage, which I wrote in Latin, was no longer there on my return. It had probably been effaced by a peasant who, not understanding the meaning, might have imagined that it contained some epigram, or else an insult to his compatriots.

We continued on our way beneath a sun as burning hot as it had been the previous day, but we did not feel it as much. We were now on high stony ground. We had just covered a stretch of six miles when, to our right on a hillside, a great number of rocks came into view; squarely cut and alike in shape though not in size, they reminded me of Paris seen from the observation tower of the Jardin-des-Plantes. After riding for a long while through stony country, we came upon a pretty valley, covered in superb pink and white amaryllis, which led us soon by way of a deep crevice in the mountains, down to the Biedow Valley. Many clumps of indigenous trees grew there and a few planted poplars which sheltered a multitude of bee-eaters.

Two miles further on, this valley opens up suddenly to reveal a beautiful plain where the river is artificially channelled for human use. At the head of the valley stands the home of Mr Francois Lubbe, the richest and most beautiful farm that I looked upon during the whole of my stay in Africa. The best of our European fruit flourished there. Peaches, apricots, apples, pears, figs, grapes, melons, watermelons, cucumbers, pumpkins, calabashes, almonds, mulberries, guavas, bananas, oranges, lemons, grapefruit, all prospered there, planted by the hand of an octogenarian, the father of a numerous and wealthy family, the true patriarch of a type to be met with only in these remote parts. I admired this exceptional man with an admiration quite different from that which a great soldier or orator inspires. I took pleasure in judging him according to his works, which were all profitable to his fellow men. How pure his life must have been. His eighty years had not bowed him, and his old age was sweet with the satisfaction of having done good for so long and for having provided for the generations to come.

After a sojourn of two days with this rustic Nestor, we took our leave in the afternoon and slept that night at Matjes Fonteyn, the spring of rushes, which we left again at dawn the following day. After having crossed the Doorn Rivier, the thorn river, at its confluence with the Biedow Rivier, we painfully pursued our course across the Hantam Karroo.

The effect of the sun, combined with that of the red saline dust, had inflamed my eyes to such an extent that I dared not keep them open. Six hours of slow travel brought us to Zout Pan, salt spring. We found in this area of scrawny vegetation a family of poor but honest people. As the water was too brackish for drinking, they offered us tea without sugar. Taken hot, this drink, which tasted to me like medicine, quenched the thirst very well.

When we had had dinner and an hour's siesta, we set off again and soon crossed the dry bed of the Wolf Rivier, after which we called at the Visagie farm. At least we could breathe there: the Karroo was behind us and the water which was offered us to drink was fresh and cool. The master, Visagie, whose original name was Visage, was descended from some Frenchman who had emigrated after the revocation of the Edict of Nantes; he told me this himself.

I subsequently met such people many times. They were remarkable for their black hair, and they always greeted me with the words 'Ah, here is a Frenchman! Frenchman, my grandfather (or my great-grandfather) was one of your compatriots.' These people differed from the others in that they were more vivacious, more forthcoming and perhaps also more patriotic.

From the Hantam Karroo, my companion pointed out Spions Berg, the mountain of spies, which forms a boundary between these lands and the country of the *boschjesmanes*.[1] The following day not once, but two or three times, we crossed the meandering course of the Oorlogs Kloof Rivier, river of the valley of war; there was no water in it, and on its banks only the *Carée-Boom*[2] grew.

We slept the night at Tiger Howek, the home of Mr Burgher, whose first concern was to show me a presentation gun, given him by the English government as a reward for having punished the Koranas in 1835, after various thefts and massacres in the colony. From here we went on the next day to watch a cattle sale, where there were far fewer buyers than parasites, attracted from twenty-five leagues around by the generous libations of brandy which it is the custom to offer to visitors, with the purpose of exciting them into paying excessive prices for the stock. We spent that night at a new farm where there lived a widow and her two daughters. The next day we found ourselves on an immense plain covered with stunted, succulent plants interspersed with wretched dry bushes that were little more than sticks. The earth was red, the dust flew up and formed thick clouds in every direction; sometimes it arose in swirling columns 100 or 200 feet high which had the appearance of whirlwinds, but which gave me no cause for alarm, for it did not take long to realise that these seeming whirlwinds were raised by numerous herds of *springbooken*. It was the first time that I had witnessed such a spectacle, and I admit that the sight astonished me so much that I had constantly to reassure myself that it was not a vision. Great herds, 3 000 to 10 000 strong, crossed each others' paths as they swept over the plain. Other herds were resting, while still others quietly grazed. In repose, they had a tawny look which was replaced, immediately they took flight, by a flash of snowy white as they presented their hind-

1 This word which means men of the bush, is of Dutch origin.
2 The only large tree which grows in the country of the Karroo or Karrou. This is the name given to the great expanses of those elevated plains where the earth is laden with saline particles and supports only fleshy plants of dreary aspect, among which euphorbias are particularly in evidence.

quarters to reveal their long-haired pouches. This is the leaping gazelle, sometimes called by the colonists *pronk-book*, the show-off, the pouched gazelle, which scholars have agreed to call *euchore*.

Individually, these graceful animals are very interesting; they are even more so in great numbers, surpassing anything the imagination can conceive. Round about November and December, which is to say at the beginning of summer when the grazing is good, these animals, coming down from the north, move into the Colony. They come from beyond the Tropic where they have spent the winter and they are driven south by the drought. They find food on the way but the herds, although advancing over a very wide area, are so numerous that only the vanguard effects this migration without loss. Since even the smallest shoots are eaten, and all the rest is trampled underfoot, the rearguard arrives much diminished in numbers.

The African hunters sometimes succeed in distinguishing these inferior herds and spare them; for an animal whose flesh is of the tastiest when he is in good health, yields only insipid and repulsive meat when he is thin. The flesh of the *spring-book* is the best of all the small game. The farmer in the Hantam rarely kills an ox or a sheep; the meat of the *spring-book* almost invariably supplies his needs. He makes *beulton*[1] by hanging the meat up to dry after it has been lightly salted. It may then be eaten without further preparation. Europeans find the flavour delicious.

The skins of these animals are used as mats of different kinds; the Hottentots and the Cafres use them as *kros*;[2] the colonists work them into blankets, floor mats and table covers. I have sometimes even seen them draped over a sofa. But these articles are less prized than the ones made up by the Cafres from the skins of fox, genet, leopard or cheetah, as the carnivore's fur is always the best and the thickest. When they are stripped or tanned, the skins are used to make trousers for the men, and in several remote places, I even saw women transform them into petticoats. Luxury for a man consisted in having the legs of his trousers wide enough to conceal a child.

These buck are hunted, not only for their flesh and their skin, which would be reason enough, but also to protect the grazing adjacent to the dwellings. If this precaution were neglected, even for a short while, the colonists would be obliged to move their cattle to new pastures, as sometimes happens in a drought, or when every blade of vegetation has been shaved to the ground by locusts.

On our right, the great expanse of the plain stretched away to a line of mountains on the distant horizon. I asked their name, and

---

1 This is obviously biltong! *Translator's note*
2 *Kaross*: a skin cloak or blanket. *Translator's note*

Hendrick Kotze, after satisfying my curiosity, said, laughing, 'If you want to know the name of every mountain and to write it down, the work will be long. The more you see, the more there is to see. However, continue to ask me, I shall tell you the name of each one.'

It was only a few minutes later, at ten o'clock in the morning, that I saw, lying in the same direction, mountains of a different shape, long, level, and flattened on top. My guide called them *taffel-bergen*; table mountains. This great change in appearance in so short a time seemed very singular to me. I looked at them once more and saw, this time, nothing but a single mountain, four times higher than the others, and shaped like a square tower.

'What name do you give to that one?' I asked him, already suspecting an illusion.

'Tooren Berg, the tower mountain,' he replied, trying to keep a straight face. Then, after we had ridden another 300 metres, the mountain appeared to stretch upward, rising to an enormous height, and isolated completely from the horizon by a wide sheet of what seemed like water, so convincing that one would have wagered on its authenticity.

'This time,' I said to my guide, 'I very well recognise Robben Eyland, the seal island, so I shall not ask you the name.' This man, who had restrained his mirth all the while, now laughed heartily at my mystification. The illusion was so complete, and the idea of a mirage so far from my thoughts, that I had to see the complete metamorphosis to be convinced.

This optical illusion, produced by refraction, occurs particularly in warm climates; the determining causes seem to vary according to the time of day. In this case for example it was caused by heat condensed by the sun's rays; but during the course of several journeys that I made to Guadeloupe, I witnessed similar effects before sunrise: some buoys which, at a distance of a mile and a half, appeared enormous and seemed to be floating right out of the water, when the sun came up, resumed their normal place or even disappeared completely. Later on at Port Natal, I had occasion to observe similar, and even stranger cases, from the place called Conguela. From there, the headland and the point which form the entrance to the bay, appear to merge and prevent one from seeing the sea. However, when a ship comes in over the bar before sunrise, the mirage gives the impression that it is floating well above the land. This illusion seems to me to be produced in two different ways, depending on the place and the time. At sea, it occurs before sunrise, while on land, it happens at nine or ten in the morning. Whatever the time of day, the same effect is produced on my gunbarrel when it is heated by the sun until it burns: the shining gun-sight looks like a candle flame fluttering elusively in the wind. This is why the colonists prefer sights made of ivory.

At about eleven o'clock, we crossed the Rhenoster Rivier, the rhinoceros river, which contained only a little stagnant water. An hour later, we entered the mountain gorges, and went down to the Vandermerwe place, where we were served *spring-book* in abundance. That same evening, we arrived at Gemerkte-Carrée-Hout-Boom, or Out-Boom, the home of Mr Redelinghuys, the field commandant of Hantam. He was a dignified man, who was distinguished from his neighbours by his pleasant appearance, and manners which he had acquired during a long stay at the Cape.

Mr Redelinghuys was a Freemason, a rare thing among the inhabitants of the interior; we recognised each other immediately and this bond, added to the fact that I was French, which pleased him greatly, assured me of a warm welcome. I felt then very strongly how cleverly contrived and how humane the fundamental idea of Masonry is. Far from remaining an empty unprofitable theory, it is a practice strictly followed and religiously observed by all its adherents; a practice whose aim is simple virtue without ostentation or arrogance. The only enemies of this association, which has ramifications throughout the world, are the Jesuits. As the secret enemies of good, wherever it exists, their attitude towards the association is not surprising, for their first object is to follow the teachings of Loyola. Be that as it may, I had reason to congratulate myself on being a Freemason, and the more so, as the observance of Masonic practices appears stricter among foreigners than among ourselves. I cannot too much impress upon the traveller that he should affiliate himself to this society before undertaking voyages to distant parts, where a thousand perils await him against which he might need to seek protection. Although this was not my position, I cannot adequately express how comforted I was by the knowledge that I had a brother in these outposts of civilisation.

A hunt was arranged for the next day. As it was harvest time, we wanted for trackers. There were seven of us on horseback, and we brought back only eleven *spring-booken* after three hours of relentless pursuit. In fact one needs perfectly trained horses, which will follow the game on sight and stop immediately they feel the bridle on their necks. If these conditions are not fulfilled, one must resign oneself to returning empty-handed, which is what happened to me, as well as to three others whose horses were not trained hunters. I noticed that the head was cut off each of the animals that was killed and the blood used to smear the horse's muzzles. They told me that the object was to refresh the horse, while inspiring him with renewed vigour. The heads were then abandoned to the vultures. In these plains of the Karroo, apart from *spring-booken*, I saw only hares, which were abundant because the farmers disdained to shoot them. I saw also two kinds of bustard, and the birds which the Dutch call *witte kraai*, the white crow, and the Namaquois *ourigourap*.

The Hantam produces good wheat, excellent grapes, passable wine; but its distinct advantage over the rest of the colony lies in the excellence of its pasturages and its healthy climate, two factors which are essential to the breeding of horses. The ones I saw were, without a doubt, the finest in southern Africa, beautiful horses, full of fire, and resistant to fatigue. Smaller and sturdier than the English breed found in Europe, they are better suited to this country. The malady referred to in the Colony as *paerde sickt*, horse sickness, is not prevalent in the Hantam. This allows the inhabitants to breed horses without the fear of losing them all within a space of a few weeks. The Colonial government has offered substantial rewards for a cure for this malady, but none has yet been found. Losses from horse sickness were enormous during the first year of my stay, yet it does not appear that great preventive efforts were made. In this respect the farmers are indifferent and negligent. They seem convinced that sickness of this sort is incurable and will remain so because no remedy has yet been found. They consider that if something has never been done, it is impossible that it will ever be done. I believe that it is showing too much respect for our forefathers if we do not attempt to go beyond the frontiers of knowledge which they have reached. In any event, the farmers treat their horses themselves. Sometimes they make incisions in the palate to stimulate the appetite, or they perform a blood-letting operation; sometimes they administer sea-salt or castor oil. With so few resources, often ill-applied, it is not surprising that they lose so many animals, particularly as not one of them has any real knowledge of the veterinary arts.

The inhabitants of the Hantam live in fairly easy circumstances which they owe more to the peace that they enjoy than to the fertility of the land, which is questionable. If they cultivate at all, it is on too limited a scale, although sufficient for the needs of the population, which is very sparse and scattered over a large area. These people are simple and kind and more hospitable than those who live in the east. A little education would become them, but there, as in the whole of the Cape Colony, each household possesses only one book, the Bible, several copies perhaps, but never anything else. The Bible is to them as the Koran is to the sons of Omar.

Children aged from ten to twenty, the older ones sometimes already married, are put to read according to an American system. They repeat the lesson in a confused fashion, the sole object being to read the Bible. More often than not it is impossible for them even to read a letter which is directed to them, though it is written by the sweat of the author's brow. Thus, it is customary to inform the messenger of the contents; his assistance is called upon, and this, combined with some guesswork, makes it possible for the recipient to understand, more or less, why the letter was written. As a result, some very strange misconceptions occur which have on occasion caused me much amusement.

The Hantam yielded no additions to my collections; this dry country of sparse vegetation produces nothing but the *spring-booken* which tread it into dust. Their great numbers astonished me, but for every naturalist, endless repetition of the same species produces satiety; one needs the variety of many species to stimulate new ideas. And so I hastened to remind my companions that we must prepare for the return journey, considering myself fortunate to have made the expedition on horseback, rather than with wagon and oxen, which would have proved to be of no advantage and would have occasioned much loss of time.

Beyond Spionsberg, the deserted plains of the Karroo are immense, devoid of water and passable only in the rainy season. Because of the uncertainty of the location, experienced guides are necessary to lead one to the brackish muddy springs, where one dares spend no more than a night, as the water is soon exhausted. The abundance of salt in the earth appears to be the principal cause of the lack of vegetation; one encounters virtually nothing but fleshy plants which are rarely useful either to man or beast; however a few scrawny bushes do grow there, the tips of the branches being avidly sought out by sheep and goats. This Karroo grazing is more beneficial to them than that of places where the grass is abundant, just as the brackish water has, for a long time, been recognised as healthier and more fortifying to the sheep than water that runs clear and fresh.

The brackish water seems to have an advantageous effect, not only on animals, but on men too. I have seen Dutch peasants who, in order to have fat flocks, have been obliged to live on the banks of some great stretch of abominably insipid water; these men soon became accustomed to it and seemed to enjoy more robust health than their neighbours.

The fact remains that these waters are never harmful, while those in the east, which are also stagnant but lack salt, harbour dangerous fevers that are a threat to natives and Europeans alike.

CHAPTER III

Return to the Verlooren Valley and Cape Town — Visit to Groen Kloof —
The Moravian Brothers — Plans for a voyage to Port Natal.

On 4 January 1839, I arrived at the Verlooren Valley where I continued with my work until the 25th, the day fixed for my departure for the Cape, which I eventually reached on 30th. I spent the month of February there, and left again on 7 March, travelling by way of Coeberg Karamelck-Fontyn, Mr Bester's farm, Mr Melck's place at Berg Rivier, and on past St Helena Fontyn and Kruys Fontyn. I visited Groen Kloof, the Moravian Brothers' settlement, where several hundred Hottentots and mulattos were being taught a variety of useful trades. Perfect order reigned there and the Brothers I saw seemed happy that peace prevailed. I am inclined to believe that of all the missionaries, of whatever religion or sect, these latter have achieved the most favourable results.

They have chosen to work within the Cape Colony without endeavouring to extend their influence beyond its borders. They are neither trouble-makers nor intriguers, nor speculators and, so far, have taken no part in politics. However, although they enjoy general esteem, they are not, for various reasons, universally loved. I have noticed that most of their colonial neighbours complain of the scarcity of Hottentots, who leave their old masters to go to Groen Kloof, where they enjoy the rewards of less rigorous and demanding labour; this is the reason why the extent of the fields under cultivation is reduced and, far from providing luxuries, the harvests barely support basic needs.

The missionaries on this station, who do not set themselves up as pioneers of civilization, appear to be quite self-supporting. The English government does not afford them the official protection which it gives to the protestants, the Welleyens,[1] and the thousand and one sects which have come from England. The Moravian Brothers, when they have attended to their religious duties, instil in their pupils a love of industry. They train their Hottentots as skilled workers, capable of turning to good account the local products, without first having to send the raw material to the metropolis to be manufactured into articles of daily use, which would then be sold back at great cost. A certain rivalry between settlement and metropolis has arisen from this practice. The government realises this and

1 Obviously Wesleyans. *Translator's note*

can do nothing except to grant or withhold protection; and it is quite clear that in this matter, the Moravians are not as favoured as the other missionaries, who have all become more or less political, and even commercial, agents.

Except for the Moravians, all the missionaries I have seen, met, or heard of in southern Africa, belong to the reformed religion. There is not a single Catholic. They are English, German, American or French and all enjoy equal protection from the British authorities to whom they are all equally loyal in return. They are generally involved in petty politics for their own benefit, and, in larger issues, often take the part of the government which protects them. They appear not to be very scrupulous as to the means they employ to gain their ends. Others will confirm this. I have reasons for reserve, however, and will confine myself to my subject, which is to collect and collate scientific material. I shall just mention two or three incidents which will be sufficient to make it clear that the good pastors ought to be grateful to me for keeping silent.

The names of the Reverend Doctor Owen and of Captain Gardiner, turned missionary, appear in the history of Port Natal at the time of the massacres of Unkunglove[1] or Ungunkunklove, and of Bosch-jesmans Rivier. The Reverend G. Champion, one of their colleagues, has divulged particulars of their conduct; and information collected from the Cafres at the time of the peace, has confirmed what he has said.

Four years later, the Reverend Doctor Adams spread the word among the Cafres of the proclamation of Lieutenant-Colonel Cloete, which urged them to seize and make off with the cattle and horses belonging to the farmers; this was, since truth must be told, simply an order to pillage which was to lead to blood-shed. Was this the act of a preacher of the Gospel?

Dr Grout, whom Panda, chief of the Amazoulous, had welcomed to his country, built a very fine dwelling on the banks of the lake of Om-Schlatousse. This reverend gentleman had, by his actions, deprived the chief of some of his influence. Indeed the people of Om-Schlatousse, Om-Goey and Om-Lalas were already according *him* the respect due to a chief. Panda discovered this and said, 'The country of the Amazoulous is not made for two kings.' The doctor was asked to leave.

To return to the Moravian Brothers at Groen Kloof, I commend them for the good they do and the good they intend doing. Their simple life, their simple methods, and the happy results for the Hottentots of these methods must win the approbation of every

1 This massacre of P. Retief and of fifty-nine others took place on Tuesday 6 February 1838.

visitor. I am little concerned with grand schemes, I do not care if the metropolis is the loser; the true philanthropist does not stop to consider these things. I can envisage only the goal and I see here its attainment. Those people to whom the Moravians have devoted their care have profited by it. Their position is improved, their intelligence is developed and cultivated, and the efforts of this intelligence are directed towards virtue.

I also visited another place which I expected to find agreeable in a different sense. Often in my youth, I had been transported there by Levaillant, to enjoy with him the patriarchal life. Through him I had formed a most picturesque impression of this place which came back to me when I saw the roof of the farmhouse at Tea-Fontyn. But I soon wondered whether I had come to the right place. On entering, I looked for the Slaber family; a fruitless task, for I found only the Brandts. I wondered then if perhaps, more recently, some other farm had been named Tea-Fontyn. I made enquiries and learnt that this really *had* been the Slaber's home, but that the family had dispersed. I was greatly disappointed. I had pictured such beautiful things, and had found only a wretched house, ill-situated on sandy plains covered with stunted bushes. To prevent myself from feeling too resentful towards Levaillant, I tried to recall the circumstances which had brought him here, and the comfort which he had found, particularly on his return from the Namaquoi country.

Places appear beautiful or ugly to us according to the pleasant or painful associations we have with them. I realised this long ago, and I have always tried to remain detached, so as to be able to judge more clearly. When I got back to the Verlooren Valley, I decided that I must leave this part of the country, where there was nothing worthy of the attention of a naturalist. I left on 11 April, arriving at the Cape on the 18th, and immediately began making arrangements for my departure for Port Natal, although various circumstances had arisen there of a nature to deter exploration in that quarter. I had, however, heard talk of the natural riches which abounded there, of the great forests of giant trees, the tall grasses, the deep lakes and limpid rivers. It was impossible that all this should not yield numerous animals, birds and insects, especially as the heat at 30 degrees latitude is much more intense than at the Cape. In addition, the descriptions I had been given, so closely resembled my recollections of Senegal, Gambia and Sierra Leone, that it was impossible I should hesitate another moment. I was encouraged by meeting the Swedish naturalist, Wahlberg, who was also preparing to leave for Natal. We were not long in becoming acquainted and in forming a friendship which, in spite of our diametrically opposed personalities, was firmly enough founded on a similarity of tastes.

CHAPTER IV

Departure from the Cape for Port Natal — Putting in at Port Elisabeth —
Arrival at Port Natal — Danger of the bar, 500 metres from the point — The
ship grounds and threatens to lose her masts — Fortunate circumstances set her
up again.

On 5 May we set sail from the Cape on board the *Mazeppa*
in the company of several merchants and a few English officers. The
ship, an excellent craft, bore us in four days to Port Elisabeth, which
is situated on Algoa Bay. A week spent in port enabled me to make
some acquaintance with the town and its environs.

The establishment of Graham's Town, situated 60 miles away, has
brought Port Elisabeth into being. These two towns which are
already of some importance, date back only twenty-five years. All
Graham's Town's trade must pass through Port Elisabeth. This place,
however, offers nothing of interest. Seen from the sea, the coast-line
on which the town stands, is dominated by a pyramid erected to an
English lady. It is a monument which, from afar, creates some effect,
but which at close quarters, is unimpressive. The hotel Scorey is, I
believe, the only one to be found there, and one pays a great deal to
be very uncomfortable. The charge of 200 francs a week is not considered excessive, although the service is worse than in the cheapest
eating house in France.

However, there are other resources in Port Elisabeth, as there are
at the Cape: a number of people make a profession of hospitality;
that is to say, they take in strangers to the town as boarders. The
cost is less, and one is infinitely better off. The usual charge is 5 rixdollars, or 9 francs 35 cents a day which includes board as well as
lodging.

From the few walks which I took in the vicinity I realised that
birds were very rare there, probably because the forests were composed chiefly of *stinck out*, that is to say trees with strong-smelling
wood. These trees, garlanded with five or six foot strands of moss,
have a very strange bearded look; this moss seems to hinder them in
their growth, for beneath it the branches are twisted as if in agony.
The few leaves they have turn mouldy while still alive. The humidity
is great in these forests; grass is rare and ferns abundant. Several
naturalists have made use of this parasitic moss-like plant, which
they first dry in the oven, and then use to stuff birds. Because of its

lightness, it is used for all sorts of packing; it does not attract insects and has the advantage of being economical. I particularly recommend it, and if I have used it very little myself, this is because I did not remain long in those parts where it is to be found.

The plains of this country are remarkable for their sour pasturage, *suren vlaacke*, as the Dutch say. They are beautiful to the eye, bad for cattle and only fair for horses. I saw secretary birds there, which I hunted for hours without coming within reach of them. Although this bird, when it walks, seems hardly to hurry, it runs faster than a man and will not condescend to fly in order to escape the hunter. Furthermore one hesitates to shoot it for there is a law which fines a man 500 rixdollars if he kills a secretary bird. It is not surprising that this bird is protected; its well deserved reputation is founded on the service that it renders by destroying large numbers of reptiles.

This law also extends its protection to a number of animals which do a great deal of damage to crops. Their species were dying out and it was feared that they would disappear. As their presence was considered to contribute to the natural beauty of the Colony, they were added to the list of useful animals. Some examples of these protected animals are: the *bonte-book*,[1] *Gazella pygarga*, the hippopotamus and the ostrich. I am prepared to admit that the *bonte-book* is not very destructive, but I cannot say the same for the hippopotamus which, if it finds its way into a wheatfield at night, does a great deal of damage and eats as much wheat as would feed a man for a whole year. As the stalks crushed by its enormous feet never revive, it is undoubtedly destructive to farming. But fortunately, it has become very rare in the Colony; I have seen only two specimens, and they were at Mr Melck's place at Berg Rivier; they were quite wild but never left the farm.

The ostrich, on the other hand, never destroys by trampling, but in satisfying its huge appetite. As its numbers are abundant and its capacity for ripening wheat enormous, the damage it causes is very significant. To protect it is, in a way, to sacrifice the useful to the decorative. However, it is not impossible to obtain permission to hunt these protected animals. Provided that one gives acceptable reasons to the government — that one is a naturalist or an explorer for example — a licence is rarely refused.

A mile and a half to the west of the town, near the dunes beside the sea, Mr Wahlberg and I found a fossil, uncovered by a rock-fall. We had reason to believe that it was a hyaena, either *Hyaena crocuta* or *Hyaena fusca*. We left it. We were shown a semi-woody plant with white flowers, whose round green seed is used in a singular manner; the pulp combined with tallow serves to make domestic candles;

1 Antelope with white markings.

this vegetable wax can also be used to make soap; the colonists call it *kaarsh-boschjes*, candle bush.

We hoped to find *rhee-book*,[1] *Redunca capreolus*; *spring has*,[2] the Cape jerboa; *aarde vark*,[3] *orycterope*, but we found none, the reason being that as the human population increases, so the wild animals diminish in number. This change has taken place since Levaillant travelled through these parts where previously game abounded; today the land is almost completely depleted.

It was at Algoa Bay, between the Cape and Port Natal, that I saw the first Cafres. They were Fingous, remarkable for their tall stature, which exceeds that of the average European; their limbs are excessively long, which deprives them of all grace, and gives no promise of strength. Yet, since they do all the heavy work, the loading and unloading of goods at the port, the hauling in of ships etc., they are apparently far from feeble. They are for the most part naked, the only garment which they consider indispensable being a bit of rag or skin which covers the tip of the genitals, as one would wrap up a sore finger.

These Fingous come from thirty leagues distant to work for money, which they lose no time in converting into cattle. As the goal which attracts them is soon attained, they rarely remain longer than six months. I saw the village to which they retire at night; it is a collection of wretched huts suggesting, by the lack of comfort, that their intention is not to stay.

It seemed to me that these Cafres differed in the shape of their bodies from those whom I subsequently met; they have the same hair, the same skin-colour, and something of the physiognomy of the other Cafres, but their bearing is essentially different. For the rest, their customs are very nearly the same. Their tribe, which lives some distance from the coast, is not very numerous. They are peaceful men who perform great services in this part of the Colony.

Algoa Bay is large and wide, which means that the anchorage although tolerable, is not very safe. It is nothing but an open roadstead, where the disembarkation of goods is carried out by means of lighters. When there is a tide-race, the sea pounds the coast with such force that all communication between ship and shore is suspended. If, in these circumstances, it happens that a passenger is obliged to return to his ship, which must put to sea immediately, the hired boatmen do not fail to exploit him to the utmost. I recall seeing an English botanist en route for Ceylon, who could not resist going ashore to gather plants, which he did for four hours in the driving

1 Species of Cape chamois.
2 Leaping hare.
3 Earth pig.

44

rain. On his return to the hotel, they gave him no time to change his clothes or to take any refreshment. He was obliged to go aboard immediately, as the sea was growing rough and the ship was about to sail. A boat was put at his disposal, and for this transport, which usually costs five francs, he was asked 15 pounds sterling, or 375 francs. Although the price was excessive, there was no alternative, and the Englishman paid.

At Port Elisabeth, as at the Cape, one finds boats equipped for whale-catching. A look-out, constantly posted on high ground, gives the signal when he sights the cetacean blowing. The crews, who are always at the ready within reach of their boats, leap aboard and give chase, either sailing or rowing. When they have succeeded in killing the whale, they tow it back towards a point which they call the Fishery, where the cutting up and melting is done. Whole carcasses and enormous skeletons litter this unhealthy place, the haunt of seagulls, terns and crows, until some farmer collects the ribs to make fences for his fields. This whale-catching is quite lucrative, as long as there are not too many boats in competition. The crews must be composed of *British-born-subjects* which means that foreign sailors are excluded.

I think I should point out here a geographical error made by Levaillant, either due to carelessness or because of faulty information obtained from an inferior map. On reaching Plettenbergs Bay, Levaillant is amazed at the caprice of the governor who planted his *baaken* (beacon) there, and imposed his own name on a place which had no need of it, as it already had one, Algoa Bay, given it by the Portuguese who had been the first to discover it, and by which name it had long been designated on all the maps. I can state categorically that the Dutch governor did not change the name Algoa Bay to Plettenbergs Bay. If one consults any map whatsoever, whether ancient or modern, one will see that Algoa Bay is situated at 27° of longitude east of the Greenwich meridian, and that it is separated from Plettenbergs Bay which lies at 24° 15′, by another bay called Kromme Rivier Baay, lying at 26° 5′. The error of longitude made by Levaillant is therefore 2° 45′ — an enormous mistake when one considers that he set sail from 18° 25′ and, having arrived at 24° 15′, he believed himself to be at 27°.

As this error was perpetuated, I am not surprised that his map takes us into the land of Natal, when he was in fact still a long way off. He was only four days' journey north of the Groote Vish Rivier, which today forms the eastern frontier of the Colony. There are other errors to be found in his observations. For example, with reference to Caiman-Gat,[1] he says that he never saw, or heard talk of

1 Caiman hole. A Dutch expression.

caimans or crocodiles in southern Africa, where they are unknown. One is inclined to believe, after such an assertion, that Levaillant never even ventured into the territory of Natal, where the rivers swarm with these hideous animals.

After a week's stay at Port Elisabeth, our ship was preparing to set sail and I went on board to find an addition in the number of passengers. Already I rejoiced in the advantages of a more numerous society, already I imagined the usually slow, tedious voyage becoming lively and full of incident — our days at sea would be agreeable. I depended upon it. But, as it so often happens that one is disappointed in one's expectations, my calculations proved erroneous. A doctor of theology came on board with another doctor of theology, and soon afterwards, came a doctor of philosophy. Certainly nothing can be more out of place than a moralist on board ship; the mind has no need of such a presence to incline it to reflect on human misery.

I found distraction in the society of the young and learned naturalist Wahlberg, always an agreeable companion, who was determinted to succeed in his task of discovery and research. Despite his modesty, such distinguished qualities were apparent in him, that he inspired in me not only friendship, but respect. Seated together at the stern, we watched the flight of the bold seabirds, whose long narrow wings seemed to cleave through the air, or else we gazed at the vast forests of Cafrerie, which were clearly visible from the ship. Already exploring them in anticipation, we found the time weighing heavily. These fascinating glimpses of the land, seen from afar, so inflamed our ardour, that to distract ourselves, we turned our attention to minute sea objects which we endeavoured to define; we particularly admired the tiny transparent animalcules which were so numerous that the water seemed half full of them.

These occupations served to divert us from the monotony of life at sea and enabled us to overcome the vexation caused by the adverse currents. These currents, originating in the Mozambique channel, combined with the tide to force our vessel, sailing at six knots an hour, to lose way. We confirmed this repeatedly by taking bearings on the coast.

Nevertheless, within five days we reached the headland of Natal, at the foot of which lies the bay channel. As the tide was already going out, we crowded on all sail to enable us to cross the bar and enter the bay. In my opinion this bar appeared threatening. It was red-brown with sand churned up from the bottom, and seething with foam from the waves which rose up and broke thunderously against it. We drew nine feet, and I sensed that there was not enough water to carry us over. In order to establish the depth for myself, I climbed into the spars of the topgallant mast. Hardly had I got there, when I realised that we would certainly ground. I climbed hastily down and seeing Messrs Kraus and Wahlberg in conversation at the foot of the mizen-mast, I warned them of the danger, urging them to go to the stern. Mr Wahlberg took heed, but Mr Kraus began to laugh at this advice, saying that the captain should know his business infinitely better than I. Hardly had I spoken, when the ship struck bottom, rebounded and struck again with a sickening jolt. The ribs of the poor ship cracked in an agonising manner; it seemed that the hull must be destroyed, as each section threatened to come adrift under the impact. The captain, who had declined to heed my observations, had changed countenance. His face had turned a livid white; his eyes, round and protruding like a lobster's, were sufficient proof that his composure had abandoned him at the first moment of confusion. He leapt about as though he were on burning coals, shouted, yelled and stormed like a madman. As his contradictory orders came in quick succession, the crew knew not which way to turn. The passengers were concerned only with themselves. Dr Adams's wife was left forgotten in her cabin by her husband, who had time to think only of himself. Dr Kraus, who began to realise the danger, believed it to be greater than it really was, for he had already removed his coat to facilitate swimming ashore — a foolhardy endeavour in which even the best of swimmers nearly always perish, an action deplored by sailors, who know that it is safest to remain aboard as long as there is a beam afloat.

Although the faces of the other passengers showed signs of great anxiety, nobody behaved rashly, everyone clung on tightly to avoid being carried away by the waves which swept over the deck, taking with them many articles which we, who were in danger of losing all our possessions, made no effort to save. Each one of us seemed silently preoccupied in calculating the combined force of the wind and the waves. Each one inwardly staked his fate on one wave or the next, praying that the mass of green water, which was breaking over us and threatening to swallow us up, would be strong enough to lift us clear of the obstacle on which we were grounded. At last we were over, thanks to the valiant helmsman Douglas, an excellent English sailor who, paying no attention to the captain's confused orders, got us out of our difficulties at the very moment that we were considering lowering the boats. We entered the channel and rounded the sandy point, sailing very close to the left hand shore where there was more water. Then, as the tide was now appreciably lower, the ship ran aground again, but without any danger, as the harbour is so well barred and the entrance so narrow, that one never feels any movement of the sea beyond.

CHAPTER V

The harbour at Port Natal is wide, beautiful, and circular in shape. The water is not very deep, and in the centre there are two little green islands. A channel, which is quite visible at low tide, leads from the point to Conguela, a village three miles distant. Ships may be drawn up there as in a dock. It would not be difficult to turn the whole harbour into a floating dock, and to build tidelocks which would operate at low tide to open a deep channel across the bar. The population is too small at present, and the trade not important enough to warrant such undertakings. Nevertheless, I dare to predict that this harbour, because of its shape and its situation, is destined to become the safest and the most important in southern Africa.

The two points of land which form the entrance lie at right angles to each other. The southern-most point which rises like a cape to a height of 200 feet, stretches from west to east. The northern point extends southward in the shape of a tongue of sand, flattened at the end and covered with full-grown trees. It was on this point that we found the obliging and worthy Captain Jarvis, in command of a detachment of a hundred English soldiers. This company was formerly commanded by Major Charter.[1] The governor of the Cape, Sir George Napier, had sent the company on the benevolent pretext of preventing clashes between the emigrant farmers and the Cafres, to prevent bloodshed, and even to protect the Boers against Cafre invasions. But one soon realised that the real intention of the English governor was very different, since he was in fact throwing these hundred men into the balance on the side of the Cafres, with the purpose of thwarting the Boers in their plans for revenge against the odious acts of Dingaan. These English soldiers were at first received with enthusiasm, but relations soon became strained. The farmers were annoyed at the seizure of their powder magazine, which was indispensable to their daily needs. In addition, this deprivation exposed them without defences to Cafre attack. Captain Jarvis was asked to leave, but he was a cautious man who knew well enough how to handle his adversaries in order to gain time to inform the governor and to await his orders. He was quite determined to defend

---

1 Major Charter arrived in Natal on 5 December 1838.

VIEW OF THE BAY OF PORT NATAL AND CONGUELA
First Boer encampment of 1837

1 Entrance to the Port
2 English fort
3 Anchorage
4 Cape Nathaniel, the top of
  which is inhabited by
  Ogle's Cafres

5 Camp at Conguela
6 Road
7 Direction of compass needle
8 Sand banks drying at low
  tide
9 Islets covered with coastal
  forest

his position, which he had skilfully fortified, profiting by the natural advantages of the terrain; but he was able to appreciate and recognise his numerical weakness. Although he was opposed by inexperienced men, he knew quite well that they were clever marksmen, and that he would not kill many of them. On the other hand, he knew that his own losses would be heavy, and that it would hardly be possible for him to hold out long enough for reinforcements to arrive. Taking all this into consideration, he was resolved to risk nothing. An order soon came from the government, directing that the observation corps should leave Natal on the arrival of the ship *Vectis*, which was placed at its disposal.

In order to create the impression that this measure was not dictated by exigency, the rumour was spread about that the conduct of Sir George Napier had been censured by Lord Stanley and that England had no interest in Port Natal and its territories and never would have. Everything possible was done to save face. In short, the English departed, saluted by fifty guns. From the mast at the fort there fluttered a new and unfamiliar flag, a fusion of the French and Dutch colours.

But I am anticipating these events, for I arrived at Port Natal at the end of May 1839, and the departure of the English troops took place on the 24th of the following December.

My immediate concern was to go ashore to explore the great tangled forests which border the entire coastline. I was welcomed at Conguela by Mr F. Roos, an old man of seventy, born at the Cape and educated in Holland, whose ability to speak French was not only extremely agreeable to me but also very useful. On his invitation I moved into his house without any formality. A few days sufficed to make me completely one of the family. From the very first, I devoted my time to combing the woods and to preparing my specimens. When I was out hunting, it sometimes happened that I was too intent on the pursuit of my prey and lost my way completely. Sometimes I was caught up by twisted, thorny, impenetrable bush, from which I could extricate myself only by lying flat on the ground and crawling. There was always the risk of having to spend the night out in the open, an infinitely disagreeable situation to be in, particularly in those parts which were frequented by leopards.

A number of people took me to task, intending to make me aware of the danger to which I was exposing myself by venturing forth alone. It must happen sooner or later, they said, that I would be found dead in the depths of the woods. I had no intention of following their advice. To prove to me how frequently accidents occurred, they told me a number of stories which I afterwards discovered to be true. Among these was the account of a very recent event which had occurred on the eve of my arrival at Port Natal. This concerned a troop of elephants, five or six strong I believe, which, having crossed the upper part of the bay during the night, had advanced on to the land of the Englishman, Ogle. These elephants had followed the first little path they came upon which led into the bush and up a hillside. At the end of the path stood a *mouzi*[1] consisting of about ten or so huts inhabited by Cafre families who were fast asleep at the time. Unfortunately, these huts were not protected by the usual hedge of dry thorns. The leading elephant, probably quite unintentionally, crushed one of the huts; the inhabitants cried out, whereupon the elephant charged. All the others followed, stampeding through the little *mouzi* where four people were trampled underfoot. I saw near the bay, the footprints of one of these elephants in the clay; they were three feet six inches deep and were so wide that I was able to conceal myself completely in them.

Be this as it may; if one were to take account of all that people say, if one were to be forearmed against every accident, it would be best to stay at home, for I can see no possibility of guarding against every eventuality. It is a fact that tropical virgin lands teem with destructive forces. In the absence of man this is necessary, for otherwise the creatures of nature become too numerous. Man arrives, discovers rivals and disposes of them by superior force, but at first there is a struggle and the human species, for a while, loses numerous individuals, although there can be no doubt as to the final result.

It is best to accept calmly the danger that threatens. Sometimes, there is a sort of unexpected duel, a challenge which one must decide rapidly to accept or to reject. Sometimes, retreat is easy. If one keeps calm, the threat of danger will point the way to safety and lend fleetness of foot to those who need it. It inspires us to find resources of cunning which we had no idea we possessed. I say this because it has happened, in the most critical circumstances, that I have resorted to the horizontal position, which I had never before thought of assuming, but which saved my life.

It seems to me hardly worth mentioning that a man who takes fright is a lost man. Fear, by contracting certain muscles and relaxing others, permits neither flight nor resistance. I therefore advise those who are endowed with great sensitivity not to leave their firesides, and not to attempt the adventurous life.

A fortnight after my arrival at Port Natal, a sickness peculiar to this locality, deprived me of the use of my legs. This malady is called by the Boers *port-natal-sickt*, or *port-natal-seurven*, Port Natal scurvy or sickness. Large ulcers, violet rimmed, and coated with white scales, covered my legs and punctured my flesh right down to the bone, so as to leave permanent marks. Men, women, children, every-

---

1 Cafre village called *Kraal* by all the colonists.

body except the old people, were more or less affected by this disgusting malady, which they all endeavoured to hide. Some people attributed it to the bad water at Conguela, but I was not of this opinion, because, at the furthest limits of the bay of Port Natal, at Om-Las and at Om-Guinée, the inhabitants are no more immune than are those at Conguela.

From the day I disembarked, I had relentlessly explored the long dry grass and combed the bush, and I had noticed that after each excursion, my clothes were covered with several thousands of reddish ticks of infinitely small proportions. This resulted in terrible itchings all over my body, but especially on my legs. At first, numerous blisters appeared, containing a clear liquid, and round the edges the flesh swelled up and became red. All these inflamed spots eventually merged, until there were few parts of my body that were not afflicted. I am of the opinion that general inflammation of the blood on the surface was the real cause of this unsightly malady. All sorts of medicaments were tried, although they were very costly to these poor people who had not even enough to eat. These remedies brought no improvement, because the only solution lay in a change of situation. However, I think it is worth mentioning that some years later, lead acetate applied in a lotion brought about several cures and, without any doubt, purges, purification of the blood and baths, added to this method of treatment, produce excellent results. But as, in those early days of my stay, we suffered from privation even of the necessities of life, we could only wait for time to heal; so much was this the case that during the second year of my stay I suffered cruelly for six successive months, and many a time I was obliged to give up my hunting, not only because of the pain, which is of the acutest kind, but because the least scratch developed into new ulcers which turned first red and then violet.

My belief that ticks alone cause *port-natal-sickt*, is based on the fact that beyond the first row of hills, on the other side of the Berea, where ticks are comparatively rare, the malady affected no one. Since 1842, the time when the population began to grow and the grass was burnt more carefully, ticks have become less common, and today few people complain of *port-natal-sickt* which was so prevalent when I arrived in 1839.

Apart from this common small tick which produces the Port Natal sickness among whites, there are others of larger proportions, more than twenty varieties of which I brought back with me. Certain species attach themselves in great numbers to both wild and domestic animals, and do not fear even to thrust their probosces into the flesh of a man. At first it was impossible to protect the horses whose bodies become virtually one large wound laden with pus; these animals were exhausted by the sheer numbers of ticks which clung to them. I have seen horses, while yet alive, infecting the air more foully than a carcass. The tendons were exposed, and in this condition the animal could no longer stand. The flies, attracted by the smell, took advantage of the raw live flesh and covered it with maggots. Many oxen and cows were lost in this manner also, but they resisted longer than the horses. When a man was bitten by these large ticks, he often hastily pulled them off without sufficient care, so that the proboscis remained implanted in the flesh along with the head of the creature. On more than one occasion, this gave rise to very unpleasant wounds, and in one case even the amputation of a limb was considered necessary.

Then there are also very large ticks with yellow markings which attach themselves to the groin of the rhinoceros, but I found them only in the country of the Amazoulous and beyond Makali's Bergen where these pachyderms are common. These blood-sucking parasites live in the grasses; they attach themselves to the ends of the stalks in such a way that the animal, in passing, carries them off on his body, particularly on those parts where the skin is least thick.

Ticks adhere not only to man and mammals but also to the birds which seek their food in the grasses. I have often killed larks with ticks around their eyes and throats. They are also found between the scales of reptiles, on the necks of tortoises, and in the outer ear of the hippopotamus. The smallest kinds of tick, unlike the larger, do not cling singly to the heads of the grasses. I have often seen clusters of several hundred, forming a sort of ball on the leaves of a plant which grows to a height of seven or eight feet in the heart of the Natal bush.

The Boers have given them the name *bosch-luys*, bush lice, but to the naturalist they are tracheal arachnids, *G.acharus*. Serious attention should be given to these creatures, which are a plague in certain parts of southern Africa. Attempts should be made to find a means of destroying them, since nature, so it seems to me, has not provided one. The *Ardea bubulcus* and two species of *Buphaga* seek them out avidly, but only on the bodies of animals when they are already swollen with blood, like bladders full of air, and ready to drop. I do not know that many insectivores search them out in the grasses and on the edge of the bush where they are extremely abundant. It appears that in India certain forests are also infested with great numbers of similar arachnids; at least it seems to me that this is what Tavernier means when he talks of leeches attaching themselves to his body as he made his way through the forests. This traveller claims that to be free of them, he was obliged to spend the night on a sandy island which was probably devoid of vegetation. This seems to suggest that the leeches were nothing but ticks.

My first researches at Port Natal were principally concerned with ornithology. These promised to be fruitful as there were many colourful species to be found there including rare birds of brilliant plumage. Natal, in this respect, was superior to anything I had yet seen and indeed, to the naturalist, the west coast seemed insipid by comparison. The vegetation here was quite different: thick and incredibly tall, it sheltered many fine varieties of birds, such as the *Touraco porphyroelopha*, the loury, the shrike, pigeons, the souimanga, the barbet, the bee-eater, the golden-green cuckoo, the Diderick cuckoo, the Klaas cuckoo, the white-breasted blackbird, the widows, the waxbills. All these richly coloured birds were brilliantly set off against the green background of the woods and the grasslands, which they illuminated with flashes of colour, ranging from the very light to those of deepest intensity. Some, like the blackbird, *Leucogaster*, left behind a long trail of fire in which blue deepened to violet, warmed to purple, and then burst into flame as it caught the sun's rays. More than once, lost in admiration of this magical effect, I merely gazed and forgot to fire. Love of beauty seemed to forbid me the use of arms. I was afraid to desecrate nature by taking from her such beautiful creatures, with the futile intention of offering them up dead to the admiration of European collectors. It was this very object, however, which had brought me so far; it was to accomplish this that I had left behind me, 3 000 leagues away, family, friends, motherland, everything that may attach a man to life; security, the affections of the heart, so sweet and dear, everything that a man could desire for happiness.

I had left everything for this; I was obliged therefore to relinquish the part of an adorer for that of a sacrificer; this is what reason made me do. Pitiless, I made my resolve, and the most beautiful, the most graceful, the most innocent creatures of nature fell beneath my murderous bullets. My collection of sumptuous feathers grew rapidly. I was soon gloating over my treasures, which I often visited at night, when the sheer joy of possessing them would awaken me. I was then like a miser, who finds happiness in seeing and touching, and who assures himself of possession by holding his treasure in his hands. Let this surprise no one. By concentrating our thoughts and our desires on any object, of whatever value, which we have obtained at enormous sacrifice, great privation and fatigue, this object acquires in our eyes inestimable value, which mere monetary price cannot reflect. Collectors of objects of art, antiquities and specimens of natural history, are affected in this way. In the eyes of other men, it is a sort of madness. The collector believes himself to be the only one endowed with reason; he believes others to be fools, when they are but ignorant of the value of the riches which he possesses.

Oh, how many times was I not obliged to bear with the ironical laughter of the Dutch farmers when they saw my prepared specimens.

How many times did I not shrug my shoulders, disdaining to reply to their ridiculous questions. They were simple-minded questions, and I found them stupid! Convinced as I was of the contribution which a naturalist working in these parts could make to science, it seemed to me that their crude minds should have been capable of understanding the aims of an explorer, but this was not so. These obstinate people insisted that my intention was to make my fortune. The birds I was preparing were intended for a destination in Europe which was quite incomprehensible to them. They were persuaded that the feathers were to adorn either the head of a pretty woman or the altar of a temple. Tired of their conjectures, I showed them my great ugly vultures, ignoble birds in their opinion. They were silent, as if half convinced; then they said to each other in low voices, 'Friend, or cousin, don't believe it; this is just to put us off the scent.' All in all, they regarded me with pity. He is nothing but a *voogel obstroper* they said, a stuffer of birds, a *bloemsoeker*, a collector of flowers, what they call a *botanicus*, a naturalist. But this pity which they bestowed on me, I returned with interest; never have I shrugged my shoulders as often as I did at that time.

Of all the species of birds which lived in the bush, one of the first which I noticed was the hornbill, *Buceros buccinator*. The enormous horned excrescence which surmounts his beak gives to the cry of this bird a loud nasal reverberation. The hunter is alerted to the presence of the hornbill, from a great distance away. Living in flocks of twenty to forty, they appear to be the enemy of silence. You will understand how easy it is to come upon them if you will imagine, in a large fig tree, a gathering of these carnival characters, giving forth confused sounds like those of a wooden or a tin trumpet, which shatter the stillness of the air and are repeated by the distant echoes. Then they fly away noisily in a mass or straggling one behind the other, beating the air with uneven, jerky movements, their heavy beaks tending to droop and drag the rest of the body downwards, while all their efforts are directed towards keeping themselves in the air. Poor birds, born of a whim of nature, how offensive they appeared to my eyes. What a great hollow beak, graceless and ill-fitting and lacking in strength! What a great container for a tongue so small, flat, dry and horny! Why this lack of proportion, what can be the purpose? If they fed on grasshoppers, centipedes and reptiles like the *Buceros abyssinicus*, one could see the disproportionate beak as a useful implement; but this bird is purely a fruit eater, he feeds mainly on the little figs of the immense *bosch touw boom*[1] whose branches hang down on one side, the tips burying themselves in the earth, to be converted into roots which form picturesque hoops.

1 Rope tree.

However ugly these calaos might be, they are nonetheless well made for the intentions of nature. They combine all the qualities necessary for existence and for reproduction too, for they are numerous. Their modest, though slightly lustrous, plumage is marked by two distinct colours; the stomach, the breast, the rump, the tips of the wings and the tail are white; all the rest is greenish black. The young bird is distinguished by eight or ten russet feathers near the nostrils. The prominence of the beak is not as pronounced as in the adult bird.

Among the hornbills which I prepared, I noticed that the skin adhered to the flesh only by means of fine muscles, which were capable of extension. Although there was no apparent cellular tissue beneath, as in the pelican, this peculiarity seemed to me to exist in both birds for the same purpose. Differing needs require different adaptations. This bird, burdened as he is with a long beak which obliges him to lean forward in flight, and supported only by two short, concave, feeble wings, must augment the volume of his body by inflating it in fulfillment of the law which states that, of two bodies of equal weight, the more voluminous comes last to earth.

I leave it to the scholars to determine the reason; as for myself their humble servant, I have only the right to provide them with the facts. For after all, a traveller, a hunter, an explorer is a man who ventures forth, *Deo adjuvante*, he kills when he can, and observes when he has the leisure to do so; he notices a thousand details many of which preoccupy him to no purpose; these in particular he records and delivers over to be discussed by men of more acute insight who are able to judge from afar. For what applies to the mechanical arts, applies also to science; in the first case the primary matter must pass through more than one hand, in the other, through more than one head. To each his own speciality; to depart from my own and to aspire to debate would be folly indeed.

A fairly close similarity exists between the toucans of America and the hornbills of the old continent, and this similarity has led a famous naturalist to construct a whole theory that the toucans are the counterpart of our hornbills, from which the uninformed concluded that the hornbills and the toucans were brothers. In Natal, more than one Englishman has told me of having killed toucans, a confusion arising from the similarity with which scholars are well acquainted. I beg to point out the difference.

Firstly, the toucans live exclusively in trees; they have two claws in front and two behind; they are climbers. Half of our hornbills, which have three claws in front and one behind, also live in trees, but the other half finds its food in the grass: it lives on insects, even reptiles. All the large varieties belong to the second half, but even among the small ones I have noted this behaviour. One may see in the hornbill that the nostrils, situated in front of the eye, are round and large, while in the toucan they are rather small, oval in shape, situated above the eyes, not far apart and oddly enough, slanting backwards. The nature of the feathers is also quite different. In the toucan the wattles are separate, fine, long and silky, while almost without exception in the hornbill, they are close, short, rounded and form distinct scales. For the rest there is the same general formation; long, light, notched beak, long tail, feet covered with scales, claws and wings similarly curved.

The classifiers have understood these differences so well that they have separated the two species. My observations will not profit the scholar, but will be of interest to the layman. Scholars are rare and laymen numerous. In the circumstances one cannot please both.

Shall I tell of the *addidas*,[1] the first birds which interest the visitor to Port Natal? In the morning before daybreak, in flocks, they silently leave the mangroves on the island or at the mouth of the Salt River where they have spent the night, and make their way towards the forests where the great dead trees entwine their gaunt white branches. Here they settle for an hour or two. The dew is too heavy on the grass, and they are obliged to wait until it has completely evaporated. At one time I was reduced to hunting them for the pot. I would station myself to advantage, without arousing their suspicions, at the very foot of the tree where two hundred of them came regularly to perch every morning. I had thus every opportunity of observing them arrive, settle lightly and silently, pause, then look to left and right beneath them, smooth their feathers with their long beaks and remove the formidable parasites which feed upon them. All was quiet at this early hour, only the loud cry of the francolin, shrill, staccato, urgent, could be heard. But just as the sound of a familiar bell passes unnoticed, so the inhabitants of the wood are heedless of the noise. It was left to me to break the silence and rudely awaken every creature in the vicinity.

A clap of the hand would have sufficed to produce magical effects which I alone would have witnessed. However as it was infinitely more important to me to bring down a couple of *addidas* which invariably provided the basis of my meagre meal, it was almost always one or two gunshots which determined the noisy departure of the flock. The contrast with the silence was most amusing, the uproar surpassed that of all the tin kettle bands in the world. Once again, man must learn from the animals if he wishes to attain perfection, even in this sphere. They all flew off, chose another place to settle, or sometimes returned to their original perches. Often other flocks, or even isolated individuals, arrived to join them. From my

1 Ibis of the bush.

vantage point, I killed in less than an hour seven, eight, ten or even thirteen, whose combined weight was too much for me to carry away all at once. I had a kind of monopoly of these birds, and became rather sought after as a result. More than one housewife today must miss those famous *addida karries*[1] which surpassed all the other *karries* in the world, Indian or otherwise.

This bird, which is an ibis, feeds on insects, principally one which is shaped rather like a large woodlouse, has a multitiude of legs, and rolls up in a ball. Shortly after sunset, the *addida* flies off again on his way to the mangroves; but this time he makes a lot of noise. In fine weather he flies rather high; in stormy weather he is obliged to lower his altitude. Even though very common around the bay of Natal, the *addida* ibis is none the less a fine collector's piece; the head, the neck, the stomach are of a rather uniform dirty grey; the back is olive green turning to coppery green; the wings and the tail feathers are bluish, on the top of the wings there is a mixture of green and purple, with the metallic gleam of rose copper; the feet are reddish black, the beak is black, ridged with red.

The three species of ibis which I collected, the *addidas*, the sacred and the bald, are all about exactly equal in size and in weight. Although their habitat remains unchanged throughout the year, I saw no nests. Moreover I have never heard of their eggs being discovered; they must lay them in the forests, probably on the ground, but I have never been able to discover anything.

Besides it is very rarely that one comes upon the nests of the more interesting birds; the only ones that are to be found everywhere are the enormous nests belonging to the birds of prey — the fish eagle, the bateleurs etc.; those belonging to the umbretta, *Ardea ombretta*, which are enormous for so small a bird and are remarkable also for the square opening, those belonging to the sparrows, *Oryx, Ignicolor*[2] etc. and those of the weaver birds, swaying on the heads of the reeds or hanging on the ends of flexible branches which bow beneath the gentle weight. Gathered together in great numbers on the same tree, they appeared to me in my ignorance like fruit; this is only one of the deceptions that await the explorer in these parts. In spite of the present interest in nests and in eggs, it is not surprising that I was unable to bring back anything of this nature. Certain enthusiasts have gone so far as to reproach me for this; in my place these worthy people would have earned the same reproaches.

---

1 Or *Kurrie*, an Indian stew.
2 The *oryx* is a yellow and black hawfinch, the *Oryx capensis*.
  The *ignicolor* is a finch, generic name of the sparrow.

CHAPTER VI

First hippopotamus hunt — Mosquitoes — Failure — The crocodile, its astonishing usefulness — Range of vision of the natives.

In the early days of my stay at the bay, there was complete harmony between the inhabitants and the English troops; a harmony which probably had its origins in the fact that both sides were far from home.

From the outset the whites, who lived widely dispersed, either alone or in isolated groups, all called each other brother. *Old brother* was the greeting heard at every encounter; first upon meeting, and again when taking leave; even those who had scarcely met, exchanged the term freely and heartily; the very day after their arrival, newcomers were greeted as *old brother*. There was something odd about this salutation and the more so as it was sincerely intended. Spoken originally from the heart, frequent usage had made it customary. I reflected upon this and discovered the cause. In all difficult circumstances, men instinctively gather together like animals; unity is strength, all differences are forgotten for a time, only to reappear again when danger is past. When circumstances are difficult, this sense of unity is so strong, even among individuals of differing background and origin, that the tendency is to fraternise. Thus the Boers and the English, astonished to find themselves thrown together in a new land, surrounded by the same dangers, extended the hand of friendship to each other without gritting their teeth. And so I made the acquaintance of the English lieutenant, Harding, an excellent young man disposed to hunting and with a positive taste for the freedom of the bush as well as for the thrill and the danger of the chase. He sought this excitement as a spice to season the monotony, the overwhelming dullness, of the duties of an officer on the sandy point of Nathaniel. Our tastes were so similar that it was impossible we should be incompatible; the hippopotamus were so close that it was inevitable that we should be tempted. I was free; he was dependant upon his superiors, who fortunately granted him leave of absence. As excited as two schoolboys on holiday, we set off on a wagon belonging to David Stellar, hired for the occasion. We climbed Berea and then followed a tortuous path which lies like a great snake along the top of the ridge that separates the valleys of Natal and the Omguinée. Eventually we began the long descent, passing on our left a recently abandoned Boer encampment. After we had crossed the sandy bed and forded the beautiful river, another challenge faced us in the guise of a steep and difficult ascent on the other side. Without benefit of roads, we reached the summit of this hill and then skidded down towards a pretty peninsula surrounded by a deep lake, where the large heads of hippopotamus could be seen here and there on the surface of the water.

'There they are! one, two, three, eight, twelve, fifteen! Fine hunting Mr Harding. We'll get them, my friend! We'll not leave this place until we have killed them all!' As we looked down upon the scene, it seemed that nothing could be more simple. There was the lake bordered with reeds, there were the heads of the peaceful monsters, a stone's throw away, or so it seemed.

A Hottentot mulatto, our *drywer*[1] Henderick, when applied to, said, 'Yes, yes, master,' in apparent agreement, yet laughing to himself all the while. Without the aid of figures, the only one of us who was capable of calculating the distance was this mulatto born in a wretched hut, this savage, this child of the land, who was accustomed to the sun and its magical effects. While *we* attempted to calculate angles, Henderick, aided only by his bright experienced eye, judged the distance rapidly and correctly. We Europeans, who were deceived by the unfamiliar circumstances, had quite misjudged the situation.

Whenever one outspans, the immediate concern is to find dry wood and light a fire to boil water for the inevitable cup of coffee. If the master would only agree to it there would be at least six stops a day, with coffee on each occasion. While this ritual was being performed, we pitched our tent on the inviting green promontory which seemed to have been placed there on purpose to tempt us. Ignorant and weak, we fell immediately into the trap. The slope was so gentle, the grass so short, the top of the little hill so well placed between the crocodiles and the hippopotamus! What a delightful situation for two Europeans, an Englishman and a Frenchman, one still fresh from London, the other from Paris! What a desirable situation for hunters to be in, surrounded by our quarry; our dreams of success would be but a prelude to the real triumphs of the following day. Alas! there was no opportunity even for disappointment; there were no dreams that night! What? Our situation was completely reversed. We who came to hunt, to kill enormous animals, were quite unexpectedly hunted ourselves; cruelly, relentlessly, noisily, not by hippopotamus, which have better things to do than to feed on human flesh, nor by alligators which are quick and bold in the water but cowardly on land. By what then, the impatient reader hastens to ask. Forgive me; I encroach upon your time and try your patience; I should have told you sooner. But you will readily agree that there is

1 Driver.

60

always some shame in acknowledging defeat, particularly when the enemy is weak and contemptible.

I admit today to the greatest respect for this once despised foe, a force to be reckoned with in countries where the climate is hot, where the mud and the reeds on the banks of lakes and rivers nourish him and protect him from the heat of the sun. It was mosquitoes which attacked us in their millions, finding their way under the bedclothes which gave no protection, invading our noses, our ears, our eyebrows and our beards. They were for the most part of the very small variety and were particularly disagreeable for they flew into our mouths when we attempted to breathe.

We withstood the first onslaught, but tried in vain to hold our ground; after half an hour of indescribable torment, we were obliged to retreat, swathed in our bedclothes like a pair of ghosts. Even this measure was to no avail for, having once become their prey, we were assailed on all sides by clouds of these insects, which battened upon us mercilessly.

Can you imagine then, that lovely night and all the beautiful dreams transformed into hideous reality; those swarms thirsting after our blood, relentlessly pursuing us wherever we fled? What a strange sight! A distant observer might have witnessed what seemed to be an unusual dance. Draped in white bedclothes, like phantoms dancing on a green carpet beside the waters of the lake, we flitted endlessly to and fro as if engaged in an interminable game of prisoner's base. You, reader, who are acquainted only with the rare European cousins of these mosquitoes, will perhaps laugh, but, as an actor on this stage, I can assure you that it was one of the most unbearable scenes of my life. I was foaming at the mouth, feverish, raving. If a European were to be exposed all night without clothing to these merciless, winged blood-suckers, he would die in terrible convulsions. People refuse to believe this, yet it is not incredible to those who have been the victims of an attack.

At sunrise, our tormentors disappeared as if by magic, and we were able to breathe freely again, although our vision was partially impaired. A burst of laughter from one of us excited the curiosity of the other, who returned the laughter in good measure; it was the comic appearance of our swollen faces which gave rise to this hilarity. With our eyes almost invisible in our shapeless faces, we resembled portrait drawings by the worst of Cafre artists. Two hours later, with the help of lotions, our features were at last restored to their original state.

Our hunt, delayed by the events of the previous night, did not promise much success. Already the mirror-like calm of the water had vanished, and the surface was wrinkled by the early morning breeze. The most favourable time had passed, that early hour on which the success of the hunter's day depends. We had still to find a pathway through the rushes and venture across floating grass to take up a position secure enough to withstand the silent attack of the astute crocodile. That hideous spawn of the infernal carcass of the Styx approaches unobserved, snaps and then disappears to drown the prey he has so easily won. You, the hunter, have ears and eyes only for the hippopotamus which is about to surface in search of air. You lie in wait for him, and if your skill is equal to your ambition you will put a bullet in his brain, and he is yours. You see nothing, and believing yourself to be alone, you think only of your prey, which is not thinking of you, and does not even suspect your presence. All is calm except that, thirty paces away, near the bank, on the surface of the water, the flat top of a green head appears, a deadly green with two small eyes which are watching you. These eyes belong to a body which is nine, fifteen, twenty feet long. You must advance a little further, wade in up to your waist among the floating grasses, or you will lose several days' food supply. You must kill the hippopotamus. Your servants are there watching, silent, anxiously awaiting the outcome of your manoeuvres.

A sudden premonition flashes through your brain and hastily you retreat. You are no longer like the purple gallinule walking on the waterlily leaves; the grass is sinking beneath your feet; just a moment more and you will be safely across. Take care, danger lies all about you. Was it an eddy on the surface of the water which warned you of the movement of a crocodile? You could not say, but whether it was a presentiment or some external cause, you made the right move. You can pride yourself on having had a narrow escape. Even if it means giving up today's dinner, you console yourself with the thought that you are not the only one. While you were lying in wait for a hippopotamus, a crocodile was lying in wait for you. Had you become his victim, nature's design would have been fulfilled. All her creatures are equally dear to her and she protects them all, only sacrificing the weaker to the stronger. You cast doubt perhaps on the utility of the crocodile; perhaps you are a blindly selfish philanthropist who, in your enthusiasm, will go so far as to say that the existence of all the crocodiles, caimans and alligators in the world is not worth the death of a single man.

Having been obliged, for want of conversation, to engage in solitary debate and to discover alone the answers to a thousand whys and wherefores, I have concluded that the crocodile is more useful than is generally supposed. Various types of crocodile, all intended by nature for the same purpose, inhabit the torrid zones of the earth. They are never encountered in the more temperate climates. These tropical lands also produce animals and men in large numbers. Here we find the great carnivores which devour only a small portion of their prey and abandon the rest to the vultures. Many of the animals which are hunted by lions or wild dogs make their way exhausted, harassed, and often wounded, towards the cool of the river-beds, to quench their burning thirst. They die there and their remains, carried away by the water, are preserved for far longer than they would be on land. This is understandable, as none of the agents of destruction, such as vultures or the larvae of flies, can easily reach the corpse as it floats in the water. If there were no crocodiles, these putrefying remains would pile up at the mouth of rivers, which are often blocked by a barrier of sand, or they would be washed up on the beaches if the mouth were open. The obvious result would be that pestilences would carry off infinitely more people than all the crocodiles in the world could eat in ten years.

This explains the veneration of the ancient Egyptians for this animal as well as the superstitious beliefs of the Indous, who every year offer to the god of the river a maiden, the most beautiful of them all, adorned as for her wedding day. This god, the foul crocodile, accustomed to feeding on human corpses, and thereby purging the river, accepts the offering, disappears with her, and crocodile and Indous are satisfied.

Because of the ancient Indou custom of consigning their dead to the river, the banks of the Ganges would be uninhabitable if the river did not harbour an immense number of these animals. I would even go so far as to say that I believe the number to be insufficient. Today, Egypt is frequently ravaged by the plague, and never have there been fewer crocodiles in Egyptian rivers than at the present moment. The cholera, which seems to have originated in India, where it is now widespread, could well be caused by emanations from the million corpses annually consigned to the waters of the Ganges, for the number of crocodiles which nature has seen fit to assign to each river cannot, I believe, ever be excessive. Now, is it in the natural order of things that an immense population should make its river a refuse dump, a cemetery? I do not think so, and that is exactly why I conclude that the number of consumers being too small for the matter to be consumed, an unused surplus will result, for which other consumers must be found, otherwise the matter must deteriorate slowly through the action of heat, air and water, a slow decomposition which fills the air with a thousand noxious gases, bringing death to the human race.

I believe that these conclusions will prove to some extent the indispensability of the crocodile. This is not to say that I wish to commend him, neither do I claim to teach virtue by example, particularly as I have never been philosophical enough to lay down my arms when exposed to danger. On the contrary, each time that a flat green head with furtive eyes appeared on the surface of the water, in imitation of a rock, an irresistable instinct ensured that I never hesitated. A more or less well-aimed shot and the head disappeared, only to surface again somewhere else; Heaven knows where.

The water, which causes the bullets to ricochet, serves to protect the crocodile better than his scaly skin, the proof being that we were successful in shooting several as they lay; grey, gleaming and hideous, on a spit of land. The best opportunity of shooting them is when they appear to be having a siesta, sniffing the air and enjoying the sunshine. But whether you accompany me on a crocodile hunt, or whether you follow me in pursuit of buffalo, hippopotamus, rhinoceros or elephant, remember that the guns must be single-barrelled, of enormous calibre, and that two-tenths of the content of the bullet must be tin. This is a *sine qua non*, observed by all South African hunters. You will realise that the bullet made of pure lead flattens out on impact and cannot penetrate the hide deeply enough. Beware of using too much tin; the bullet becomes too light and brittle and breaks into pieces when it encounters the bone.

We advanced cautiously for some hours but were unable to approach closely enough to the place where our quarry was to be found. Then we came upon a wretched sort of flat crate, ten feet long and three feet wide, lying on the bank. It had obviously been constructed for the purpose of sailing out on to the waters of the lake to shoot hippopotamus at close quarters. The absence of the owner permitted us, when we had made the necessary repairs, to enjoy this facility. After draining it, we decided that the crate must be caulked, and this we did, using grass and pieces of linen taken from our own clothing. It was soon launched with three men aboard, Harding and I, accompanied by Henderick. Within ten minutes, we had discovered an enormous hippopotamus sheltering among the rushes where he seemed to be enjoying himself. His powerful head surfaced twice. We made our way slowly and silently to within six paces of him and then waited, ready to fire.

However, in spite of my intention of obeying all the rules which apply to successful hunting, I could not resist saying in a whisper, 'Mr Harding, beware of the hippopotamus surfacing; if he comes up underneath us, we will capsize' — 'Never mind' — 'Be careful not to disturb the balance, or we will ship water and sink' — 'No matter' — 'But, look here, I beg of you, we are leaking like a sieve; if we wait another minute we shall sink!' — 'Well, so what' — 'Well, do you want to find out who swims better? A crocodile or a man?' — 'No, that is not my intention' — 'Then do you want to mount the hippopotamus and be transported to land on his back?' — 'I find the idea original, but the thing is impossible' — 'Impossible, I should say so, especially as you have no spurs' — 'Yes, that's true; how singular it will be to tell the story in Europe one day, of how one bathed in company with hippopotamus and crocodiles!

This really was the thought that preoccupied my phlegmatic companion who, like me, understood perfectly well the danger of our situation: we were only two fingers above the water, and our craft was filling rapidly. It was a very close thing. On a European lake, we would simply have run the risk of a ducking, the worst that could happen would have been to lose our firearms. But here, 200 metres separated us from the land, and Heaven knows how easy it would have been for the alligators to take us as we tried to swim ashore. However that may be, Mr Harding was quite unmoved. He was deciding on the action he would take if our flat craft went down. The best procedure would have been to start bailing immediately with our hats, but neither of us dared suggest this, because it would have compromised the success of our hunt. The hippopotamus would not have shown himself. It was as well for us that we did not attempt it for the water began to heave and seethe and an astonishingly shaped, shiny wet head rose into view at the very spot we were both looking at. Two shots rang out, and the head disappeared, sinking like a stone. Then the surface of the water seemed to rise up, as a grey body appeared like an upturned canoe. Its desperate, agonised movements would have capsized us had we not been three feet away from it. Then Harding, with his small rifle, lodged a bullet in the enormous right foreleg, and the body disappeared beneath the water. We maintained our precarious position, astonished at the turmoil, and dumbfounded at the stupidity of the animal which might have done just as it pleased with us.

'Stand by to pump, Mr Harding, we're going down!'

'Pump ship, pump ship, she sinks.'[1]

It was high time, for the water was coming in over the side. Our hats saved the day as we used them to bail the wretched tub. I observed then that my phlegmatic companion had given up the idea of staging a dramatic incident simply to be able to recount it on his return. He was no more enamoured than I was of the idea of challenging the crocodiles to a regatta.

We turned back, certain of having put two bullets into the animal's head. They could not, however, have touched the brain, as death would have been instantaneous. We ate our meagre supper, drinking our coffee on the grass which served us as both carpet and sofa, while the sky overhead was our canopy. Our adventures provided us with ample matter for conversation. We were beginning to consider moving camp to avoid a repetition of the discomforts of the previous night when the breeze, instead of dropping, announced its

1 English in the original. *Translator's note*

intention of growing stronger. Our tent was at hand, ready to receive us, and without more ado we withdrew to sleep, hoping for a more peaceful night. We had earned it. But according to the old adage, 'Man proposes, God disposes', we were suddenly awakened by we knew not what and, upon looking around, believed ourselves to have been transported to we knew not where. Our surroundings were completely altered; the things which had been about us had quite disappeared. A violent gust had pulled out the pegs, broken the ropes and ripped the canvas, leaving us without a roof over our heads. The tent, our only home, had blown away without us, leaving us at the mercy of the teasing wind.

What were we to do without our house, I ask you? Just what you would have done yourself. We did without it. There was no alternative, no other way. At the time, I found the deprivation hard to bear. Later, when I had become accustomed to it, I realised that a house was rather unnecessary. Furthermore, I discovered that I slept much more peacefully in the open air.

However that may be, as soon as day broke we set off in search of our scattered possessions. Then we separated, some of us going in search of the hippopotamus, which might not have survived, the rest in quest of a few water-birds, which were fairly plentiful on the banks. I was fortunate enough to bag seven pretty little teal, *Anas madagascarensis*, a few blacksmith plovers, some waders and some little cormorants; I took care to add a number of turtle doves, for our meagre provisions were already at an end.

Later, as Harding and I were roasting some of the birds spitted on a ramrod, I informed him of my intention of sending to the bay for more substantial supplies, as much for ourselves as for our young Cafres, who were calmly squatting round the fire, staring into the flames. The little wretches were sniffing the smell of the fat as it dripped into the embers. I considered this means of subsistance poetical enough, but not very sustaining.

'Good Heavens,' said my companion, 'you are too kind to concern yourself in this way. Truly you are not made for travelling; you are too solicitous. Thank God we lack nothing, and neither do our Cafres.'

'But our Cafres have absolutely nothing. They have been with us nearly two days and, just think, they have not had a bite to eat.'

'That is true; but they have an immense advantage over us: they can spend three whole days in this way without complaining. Look, their stomachs are only flat; when they are hollow, the time will have come.'

I considered these remarks to be just and true, and at the same time very droll on the part of a European. But Mr Harding, who had been longer in Natal than I, had had the opportunity of observing their customs closely, and at that time when there was a shortage of food, the Cafres did not eat every day.

Our subsequent attempts at hunting were rewarded with little success. We lay on the bank in the dark, downwind from the hippopotamus and succeeded in wounding several, which turned and dived into the water. My friend Harding's leave of absence was almost expired and we were already on our way back, when we saw a number of vultures high up in the air, gliding and wheeling over the very spot where we had shot our first hippopotamus. To turn back was impossible for we had not the time, and were obliged to proceed on our way. The following day we had the satisfaction as well as the regret of learning that the enormous animal had been found dead among the floating grass, and had been cut up and eaten by the Cafres, much to the disappointment of the vultures who were looking on.

During the journey, Henderick the Bastaard, our driver, gave us proof of the excellence of his eyesight. We had reached a high point of land from which we were able to command a view of ravines, valleys, hillocks and mountain sides stretching away before us within a radius of twelve leagues. What seemed to *our* eyes to be close by, was in fact a long way off. Suddenly Henderick laid down the long whip, seized a gun, jumped down from the box saying 'Hold on!', and indicated a point more than 1 000 metres off, where he had seen the movement of the head of a gazelle, *Ant. mergens Burschellii.*[1] Our man headed for the steep slope, slid down to the bottom, climbed up the other side of the valley, descended the next slope, only to ascend the following one. Then, having been lost to our sight six times over, he reappeared a long way off, barely visible, walking slowly, crouched and alert. The duyker was close; a moment later we saw the puff of smoke rise, and finally the sound of the shot reached us. He had won his prize.

These people, I thought, would make the best cannoneers in the world. How had he been able to distinguish the head of a small animal lying concealed in long grass which was the same colour as its coat? This incident astonished me, although it can quite easily be explained. In the first place, among these people who live in a country where the light is much brighter than in Europe, there is a prominence of the brow bone, which means that the eyes are protected and sunken. There is thus more concentration, which results in more acute vision. And the very first thing that even the least observant visitor remarks upon, is the brightness of the black eyes which is a consequence of their being deep-set. The habit of hunting develops the faculty of sight to the highest degree, particularly as the horizon, which is ever present to the gaze, is vast, the air con-

1 Burschell's leaping antelope.

stantly pure and the light brilliant almost all the year round. Add to all this the simple life, and you will realise that the European would share some of the same advantages, were he to find himself in similar circumstances.

To see, means more than simply to look at. I have known South Africans who saw more accurately by comparing objects, judging them by their shape, proportion and movement. This is the result of long observation and is very useful in avoiding misconceptions. It is necessary to know and understand things thoroughly in order to be able to recognise them when they are barely perceptible at a great distance, and this knowledge is acquired at an early age by all the peoples of southern Africa whether they be herdsmen or hunters.

I believe that it is quite appropriate to tell at this point the story of an event which I witnessed. To them the matter is very simple; to us it is quite the contrary: you will be the judge. It concerns seeing, combined with observation.

I was exploring the Verlooren Valley at the time, and was returning from a leopard hunt with Henderick Gous and Bruyns the mulatto; we were riding beside the lake on a wide sandy path. Five hours previously, two or three thousand sheep had passed that way; not an inch of ground had escaped their footprints. Bruyns, the famous hyaena and leopard hunter, could read the tracks of animals of any species, and Bruyns had literally read what no scholar could have deciphered.

One of your sheep has strayed, said he to Henderick Gous, reining in his horse. 'You are joking,' said the master. 'Not at all,' replied the mulatto. 'He was behind among the stragglers; his tracks go off to the left without rejoining the main flock. There they are, let us follow them.'

We took these imprints as guides and hardly had we travelled 250 paces, than we found the lost animal. In the dry shifting sand, the hooves leave only small conical hollows; thus a fine degree of observation is required to identify a single track cutting across all the others which have not deviated from the path.

CHAPTER VII

Hunt at Om-Komas — Part played by Swedish naturalist Wahlberg — Dead elephant — Cafres behave like vultures — the Cafre Bob — A conversation with this man — Polygamy, the basis of Cafre society — Seduced by the beauty of the country — Migrant locusts, their ravages — Means of destroying them.

On my return to Natal I realised that this little excursion had not resulted in any very interesting additions to my collection; the best perhaps was the blacksmith plover, a shrill, mocking bird, which fell a victim to its show of aggression. After him in interest was the wattled crane, very rare in these parts; then the marabou stork, big, broad and strong, and also rare. There were some large-headed waders, godwits, Madagascan teals, Egyptian geese, ducks of various kinds, *anhingas*, cormorants, white herons. We also saw great spur-winged geese, gleaming bronze and green, known by the Dutch name of *Bastaard-makouw*,[1] but they were always a long way off and out of reach.

It was important to me to explore the country around Natal to see what it might yield, and gradually to accustom myself to hardship. Opportunities were rare, which was reason enough not to refuse them.

In spite of what I have just said of their rarity, an opportunity did soon present itself. The proposition was made to me by an Englishman, Edward Parker, a young man of captivating appearance, with blue eyes, black hair and a long beard. He was a scion of a worthy and respectable family in London, but wild, extravagant, fickle and a butcher of horses. His contribution to the expedition was his span of fourteen oxen, mine was my wagon, Mr Wahlberg contributed his tent, while Mr Gregory and others provided the horses and the provisions. No sooner said than done. With E. Parker, that was the way: resolution and execution. If things went wrong, you tried something else, without ever thinking of the losses and the disappointments of the day before; there was always tomorrow. You strange young man, with your singular ways which amazed me so, where have you been led by that mercurial restlessness of yours, which would allow you no respose? What a head you had, bursting with ideas and inspirations! The world was too small for you, distances too short, life too lacking in adventure. Your blood was hot; you needed to fight buffalo, shoot Cafres, live the hard life. Then

1 Bastard Muscovy duck.

suddenly you would seek the bosom of indolence. As a contrast you would turn towards the soft life in Graham's Town; you desired and won its prettiest girl. She was happy to be yours but you would not take her without a large fortune. With your own fine fortune squandered on horses, is it true that you coveted another man's and that you attempted to make it yours? Hapless wretch, what did you do? You, who claimed to be a gentleman, betrayed that noble word, or rather your hot head led you astray. It was not your will, but your wild passions which dominated your brain. I do not accuse you, I blame the action of the tropical sun.

In spite of what later came to pass, Parker was at that time a *gentleman rider*.[1] He had the bearing, the manners, the address of a gentleman; we were all enchanted by him and considered ourselves fortunate to be associated with him in this venture.

We set off in high spirits and full of expectation. We passed the camp and crossed the Om-Lasy river, proceeded by way of the dunes and encamped at Lofa mouth. The next day, the wagon, carrying a small boat, was obliged to make a detour in order to find a ford. The rest of the party swam the river on horseback, in ten feet of water, a fairly simple operation. On reaching the other side, we found ourselves among a great population of Cafres living in various *mouzis* or villages. In one of these villages, the chief received us very properly, in our capacity as Englishmen. He ordered curdled milk, *amas*, and we were copiously served. He presided over our meal, gravely swathed in an English *comberge*[2] and frequently repeated these words, which he emphasized with gestures, pointing and clicking his fingers: '*Amaglichman ouena moushlé kakoulou. Yasy mena ka amaboune ouena. Amaboune tchinga! tchinga amaboune! Tena tanta kakoulou Amaglichman abantu mouniama tèna!*' 'You people are English; that is good. It is easy for me to see that you are not those Dutch peasants; may they be damned, yes damned! We black men like the English very much.'

Parker was known to these people, whom he had once visited in company with Ogle, that same Ogle who later laid claims to rights and prerogatives as king of the Cafres from Port Natal to the Omzimvobo River.

Parker was English; those of us who accompanied him were for the most part born in Europe, and in the eyes of the Cafres of that time, all who came from Europe could only be English. My advice to any traveller who wishes to discover the country with the intention of sharing his experiences with his fellow countrymen, is this: you cannot do better than to take advantage of the esteem in which

1 English in the original. *Translator's note*
2 Compare *kombers* (Afrik.) — blanket. *Translator's note*

certain nations are held here, even if, in your attempts to identify yourself with one of these, you are obliged to assume an air of arrogance and impassivity.

In any case I would have wasted my time and my trouble in trying to explain that I was French. The Dutch farmers, unaware of my real name, or unable to pronounce it exactly, found it simpler to say *franscheman*. There could be no misunderstanding for the first three years, when I was the only Frenchman among them. The Cafres took it to be my real name and used it habitually. When another Frenchman arrived, he was given the same name, and therefore could only be my brother; willy-nilly, I was obliged to accept the relationship. When the new arrival made known his surname, this was assumed by the natives to be his Christian name.

Even those Cafres who knew me best, could scarcely imagine that the French were of a different tribe from the English, as Europeans to them were much alike in their tastes and general ideas, so different from those of the South African Dutch farmers. The Cafres, by a process of natural reasoning, grouped together all those who came from beyond the seas. It was a general division which allowed of no subdivision, and great would have been their astonishment, if a Dutch or a French colony had sprung up in these parts which did not establish ties of friendship with the English settlement at Port Natal, for they believe that the South African Dutch are a breakaway tribe, forced out by poverty, held in dishonour by all the other whites, inferior to the English and tossed back and forth between the whites who reject them, and the blacks who do all in their power to drive them back whence they came.

They would have been amazed if, in the course of some European war, troops had arrived who appeared to favour the South African Dutch. Their disbelief would have stemmed from the fact that the English are depicted by English missionaries and traders, who are critical of the poor emigrants from the Cape Colony, as being the only white nation, while the rest are but humble tributaries!

What would be the attitude of the Cafres today if a force of 3 000 horsemen, supported by 200 artillerymen, landed on these shores which are still innocent of European confrontation? The reply is simple for the answer is to be found in the past. Politically wise, the Cafres have once already allied themselves to the strongest side; what they did in 1842 they would do again in the same circumstances.

What part would the Boers play, those Boers who had allied themselves completely with Holland and who would have offered themselves to the pope or even the devil to avoid a return to English law, if only the pope had been able to deliver them from the yoke, or the devil had agreed to send them munitions. Their future conduct is easy to guess: the Boers would do as the snowball does, and this avalanche of men which would destroy everything that did not go along with it, would win back the good Cape Colony from the English. The support of 3 200 men here, where no comparable European force has ever appeared, would give the impetus needed and would sustain it to the end, for the enthusiasm would be general. It would be impossible for England to fortify these coasts sufficiently to repel an invasion, or even to prevent a landing by patrolling the seas with warships. This country could be invaded with complete success by any European power which cared to make the attempt. But these thoughts are alien to the habits of mind of a peaceful explorer, whose only desire is to further his knowledge. Let us then pursue our subject.

We spent one more night beside the silted river mouth and the following day about ten o'clock we reached the Om-Komas, the river of the female buffalo, which is not silted up, and where we hoped to kill hippopotamus.

Our boat, which we immediately launched, accommodated us all and bore us to within ten paces of a herd of twelve of these animals. All of the heads which had been showing above the water disappeared as they were struck virtually point-blank by our bullets. There was blood; we saw a pink stream trickling from the nostrils of some of those which came up for air. Of the seven or eight wounded, we hoped to retrieve at least three or four. But hunting has its disappointments as well as its triumphs; we waited more than an hour watching the river but not a single corpse rose to the surface. Of course we could begin again, wait again, nothing would be simpler; but the self-appointed leader of the expedition preferred to go upstream, look for a ford, cross to the west bank and hunt buffalo.

The rest of us, who were unfamiliar with the locality, were quite indifferent as to whether we stayed where we were or crossed to the other bank. There was no difficulty then in adopting the suggested plan and so some of us went by land and the others by water. In our fruitless attempts to find a short cut along the wooded river banks, we tired our horses out quite unnecessarily. Mr Wahlberg, who was in the boat, must have congratulated himself on taking the slow way, for it was he who tasted the first fruit of all that Natal had to offer. It was an astonishing prospect for a European and this is the description which he himself gave me: 'All around our fragile boat, the dripping heads of at least thirty hippopotamus appeared. To our right, on the left bank of the Om-Komas, forty buffaloes came down to drink. Our gaze travelled from one group to the other and we were just rejoicing in the fearlessness of these animals which were unaccustomed to the sight of a boat, when a loud noise attracted our attention to a point barely 200 feet away on the river bank; four elephants had come down to the river to drink and to bathe. We realised that we must take advantage of our position, formulate a plan of attack immediately, and silently communicate it to the rest of the party. Unfortunately, the sound of our whispering and the scent of our bodies reached the elephants which, without consultation, but as if by common accord, made off. This alerted the buffaloes. In a few seconds they were retreating noisily, trampling in their confusion everything that stood in their way. Only the hippopotamus remained, which we had already attacked in vain. We could do no more than feast our eyes on this sight, but what a satisfying sight it was — three of the largest species of animal to be found in Africa and all gathered within so small a space.'

Mr Wahlberg subsequently often spoke of this encounter, which in those days we considered beautiful in its rarity; but time and circumstances have brought us a long way since then. We have both witnessed scenes of nature incredible to a European, and realise that the chief merit of the spectacle at Om-Komas was its novelty.

After travelling for some hours the wagon, with a drag on two of the wheels, descended a long steep slope which led down to the ford over the river. The crossing was effected without incident, and soon we halted for the night, not far from the *mouzi* of Balène, which was situated on high ground overlooking the Om-Komas,[1] a beautiful river, steeply embanked.

As our supplies were exhausted, and the hunt had unfortunately failed to provide us with sustenance, we were forced to find some other source of food supply. We were discussing the matter when Parker arrived and took it upon himself to decide that we must sacrifice one of our draught oxen. The deed was postponed until the next day when the ox was chosen and killed and provided sufficient food to satisfy our needs for several days. Hunters are ashamed to have recourse to this, the worst of solutions, but under the circumstances there was no choice. Yes, of course there is shame in telling of such an expedient, but the day will come when I will tell not of disappointment, but of success beyond my wildest dreams. This success is still a long way off but, Reader, if you choose to travel with me, it is only fitting that you should share with me in the delays, the tedium, the fatigues, the dangers and the disappointments before we arrive at last within sight of those delights which only the hunter and the explorer can truly comprehend.

The day before we had been visited by an English deserter from Graham's Town. This was Robert Joice, who for about seven years had been living in these parts among the natives. He provided us with

1 The female buffalo.

73

some information on buffalo hunting, and elaborated at some length on the recent death of an elephant which had been killed by Cafres armed with guns. He had just come from the spot only a few leagues away where, expecting to discover an enormous corpse, he had been astonished to see that a wild lion had already taken possession of the dead animal. The narrator's air of credibility guaranteed his tale, and we all decided immediately to visit the elephant carcass. Meanwhile, even though we had not at our disposal sufficient horses for all who wished to take part, Parker said to me, 'You have only to express the wish and it will be granted. Leave everything to me.'

And indeed, the next morning, we found ourselves well mounted. The plan was seemingly to go and hunt buffalo in the south-west. Our trackers set off ahead of us in that direction. Meanwhile we had engaged the services of a Cafre who knew all the paths, and who would be able to lead us directly to the true object of our curiosity which was the elephant. The way to the elephant lay in the opposite direction from the buffalo and we had to change course gradually over a distance of four leagues.

But such pestilential emanations reached us while we were yet a kilometre away, that we were obliged to hold our noses. We were at that time still innocent of the killings in which I was to participate two years later. The odour of a dead animal disgusts all except his killer; every successful hunter is soon persuaded of this truth.

We approached cautiously upwind for the lion might have returned. Instead a confusion of voices reached us; beyond any doubt the place was occupied by Cafres. The sight that met our eyes deserved to be captured by the brush of a master painter. The most hideous, disgusting, repulsive scene imaginable lay before us. Picture fifteen naked Cafres, their bodies shining with grease. Ten of them were crouched down to eat, surrounded by guns, assegais and shields, while four others were carving, with admirable skill, steaks that were three feet wide, four feet long, and an inch thick. These wretches were knee-deep in larvae and swarming flies, foul contagion which would have turned the stomach of a veteran campaigner of the Old Guard. One alone tended the fire which he stoked continually, for the abundance of flesh and grease threatened to extinguish it. It was unbelievable how they sliced, grilled and ate, while the ammoniacal gases stung our eyes till the tears flowed.

I found the place unbearable, particularly as Parker, pointing out a superb grilled steak, defied me to eat it. I admit to having expressed an earlier wish to do so, but that was before we encountered the reality, and the recollection in the face of this filth, was too much for me. I moved upwind and contemplated the remains of the elephant; he was large, even immense, each tusk weighing fifty pounds.

He must have been a superb specimen. Certainly, had I been there from the first, I would have attempted to get possession of the skeleton, an amazing piece, twelve feet high, of the sort that our principal museums still lack. And who had succeeded in killing such an animal? I hastened to enquire. The Cafre was there; I sent for him. There soon arrived a contorted looking man who was virtually inarticulate. The puniest of the whole troupe, he seemed weighed down by his *bawians-bout*.[1] If I recall correctly, his name was Bob. He lived either at Lofa[2] or at Omzinnto.[3] However that may be, my astonishment was boundless as I compared, on the one hand, the feeble broken man, armed with an inferior gun, and on the other, the monstrous animal which he had brought down. I examined him closely and I observed that his head was in a horrible state, furrowed in every direction. His face was covered with scars, one cheek-bone was broken, as was his jaw, and the lower lid of one eye hung down to his cheek. He gave a brief explanation of the accident of which he had been the victim.

'Master, I was a child. I accompanied the men to the hunt and I was sleeping beside them, hidden in the bush. A hyaena seized me by the face and was carrying me off, when the men, aroused by my cries, leapt up. The hyaena took fright, released his hold on me and ran away. Since that time I have been as you see me now. I still hunt and I kill what I can. You have the proof before your eyes.'

I could only congratulate him, for I had nothing to offer him. I enquired about his master, who was in fact Ogle, and about the reward which awaited him for the tusks of the dead animal, 'One tusk is his,' he told me, 'the other belongs to me, but he alone reserves the right to decide the price, which is generally represented by one cow.' 'Are you satisfied with that price?' 'Yes master, but I would prefer two cows to one.' 'What do you do with these cows? Is it for their milk that you prize them so highly?' 'Master, it is for the milk, and for the calves which they give; and then, when the number is sufficient, I use them to buy wives.' 'Women or girls?' 'I do not buy those who are already women, but girls whom I make into women.' 'You have several already?' and as I said this I considered the sorry state of my man. 'I have four, master, and I would like more.' 'Why, have you not enough already?' 'Master, just consider: is it possible to have too many wives? We black men, the more we have, the greater we are.' 'Why great? Is it then the number of

1 *Monkey ham* — nickname given by the Hottentots to a gimcrack English musket.
2 A little river in the western (*sic*) part of Port Natal which flows into the Indian Ocean not far from Om-Las.
3 River to the West of Om-komas.

your wives which distinguishes you?' 'Not only wives, master, but also cows.' 'How can this be?' 'Ah! master, you know as well as I; there are but two things which we prize absolutely, cows and women.' 'You astonish me. What is the connection?' 'Master, with the first we buy[1] the second, who render us a thousand services, and procure for us an ease which we would not otherwise know.' 'And is that all?' 'No, not yet; you know that our wives give us daughters, who are in their turn bought by other men the way their mothers were.'

This short conversation immediately enlightened me about the social system of the Cafres. Herds take the place of money, women represent great revenue, and are the equivalent of those luxuries which we of an older civilization value. To preach monogamy to the Cafres is the equivalent of preaching to us about equality of wealth. Will this system of equality ever be practised among us? Let us give the matter some thought.

I hazard the guess that no European religion will prove acceptable to the Cafres, in spite of all the efforts of the English government. Even though in the attempt the Cafres were to be decimated or transplanted, success would be doubtful. Consider for a moment the Malay people who have not altered their ways although they have lived so long at the Cape of Good Hope. Polygamy offers many advantages to those who practise it, and the Cafres understand it perfectly.

I have had every opportunity of observing and studying their way of life, and I have never found a Cafre who complained of his wives, or a woman who was dissatisfied with the head of the house. I believed at first that jealousy must sometimes enter their hearts, but I was completely mistaken. This terrible passion is unknown in the land of the Cafres, and far from entertaining it, every first wife redoubles her efforts in order to make her husband rich enough to marry again. Once married, the second wife is united to the first by bonds which we in our language lack words to describe. These women are infinitely closer and more intimate than two sisters. There is sometimes rivalry between sisters, and even jealousy, but between these wives this is never the case. Marriage to them means contributing to the wealth of the community. The children of one belong also to the other. I could never discover from one of my Cafres the identify of his natural mother. His father had five wives; he pointed them all out to me and said, 'Here are my five mothers', and each one in turn embraced the tall young man with a warmth which I found incredible.

It is a fact that the more numerous the community, the greater

1 The Cafre word *tinga* is not accurately translated as 'buy' but infinitely better by 'exchange'.

the general prosperity. The work of each woman provides a surplus and as more wives are acquired so the surplus is increased. Each community has only one great consumer: the man, the chief.

There are many other reasons why the Cafres are not at all disposed to abandon polygamy. I will take the liberty of mentioning the matter of health. When a woman becomes a mother, and is suckling her child, nature imposes almost sacred duties upon her. Throughout this long period the wife has no thought for her husband, who nevertheless continues to regard her with tender affection. He is the chief, he has his rights, or rather he had them, for it is in vain that he solicits the least favour.

One single wife is thus insufficient, and I have seen cases of this kind where ten or fifteen were not enough. I knew Masjlébé, one of Panda's headmen, who lived in the northern part of Om-Schlatousse; he had sixty wives and each had from him one or more children. The noble Tonglas from north of the Touguela[1] was in a similar situation. Not to mention Panda, who allowed me the sight of a group of eighty of his wives. He had nearly 400 when I left, and I should not be in the least surprised if one day I hear that each of them has become a mother, for he already had a great number of heirs.

The sun is warm in these lands, men are born strong and well formed, education is purely physical, excesses are unknown; when he is an adult, a young man seeks a wife. Sterility is so rare that I have seen only one case of it, and that was among the Makatisses near the Vaal River,[2] where the people are dirty, wretched, and of no account, inferior in every way to those of the littoral.

However, it would be absurd to imagine that I contemplate the possibility of polygamy among *us*; as many obstacles oppose it as would stand in the way of its dissolution among the Cafres. But generally speaking, taking into consideration all points of view, from all over the world, with its great number of polygamous peoples, it would seem that this persuasion predominates, and that it approximates most closely to the natural condition.

Consider nature herself, this great teacher, and you will realise that monogamy results from the designs of civilization. Consider the effects of this system and you will be obliged to admit that where it exists, the masses have degenerated to the point where they are no longer as nature originally intended them.

Among the Cafres you see no crooked spines, no bow legs, no birth deformities, no freaks of nature.[3] In contrast, look about you

1 Fisher river.   2 The 'yellow' river flows into the Groote Rivier.
3 Some have had the effrontery to say that these would have been disposed of. This is a calumny for no such deed was ever contemplated.

at home. I shall not use as an example the town of Arras, where I am at the moment writing these lines; that would be lacking in generosity, and the terrain would be too advantageous to my theory; but choose any town you like in old Europe, visit it yourself and then decide whether I am wrong. These reflections, however simple they may be, are worth recording; they may perhaps serve to persuade someone to my way of thinking that the abstinence of Cafre men during the lactation period is responsible for the well-being of the new-born child.

I lost no time in taking leave of the Cafre Bob. On our return to camp, my companions and I were of one mind, which is to say that the stench had robbed us of our appetites.

The following day, in order to comply with the wishes of Parker's changeable disposition, we turned our backs on Om-Komas, and stationed ourselves on the little Om-Schlango,[1] river where the rain prevented us from hunting the small buck which are found there, and which are known to the Dutch by the name of *orbitje* or *orby*, and which the naturalists call *Redunca scoparia*. Two days later, when the weather had cleared, Piet killed one of them at daybreak; a single bullet fired at 150 paces penetrated the femur, the abdomen and the humerus, so that there were six holes in the pelt. In spite of this, the dogs had no easy task in getting hold of it.

From Om-Schlango we moved on to camp at Om-Zinto, where, becoming out of humour because the hunt had yielded so little, we resolved to return to the bay. Nobody offered any opposition, which was hardly surprising, as our supplies were by now exhausted.

However, I shall not proceed without mentioning a place which I discovered lying between Om-Schlango and Om-Zinto. It was a knoll, 500 feet high, surrounded on three sides by a deep stony gully, where I found, collected in the hollow rocks, the purest water. Beyond stretched rich, green grasslands, and further away still there were sand dunes covered with those thick protective bushes which prevent the wind from blowing the sand away. To left and right grew isolated mimosa bushes while in the valleys there were wild bananas. Here and there the earth offered up patches of stone or sand, gravel, clay or marshland. Silence reigned over the whole perfect scene. Wherever one looked, a picturesque sight met the eye; steep slopes or gracefully curved contours, bare rock or thickly wooded hillside. The place was crying out for an owner and for a few moments I thought that that owner must be me. France lay far away in the past. The great clear horizon, marking the meeting place of sea and sky, the immensity of the landscape, the peace which was enthroned there like a queen, all conspired to form an obstacle in

1 River of rushes.

the path of my return. How could I fail to realise my dearest wish!

I was resolved; I would stay and live life in my own way; I was happy. The sacrifice of motherland, family, society was nothing; I gave no thought to my friends, those dear old friends whom I love so much. While I hesitated still, a thought struck me, quick and sharp as an arrow: 'Wretch, are you mad enough to contemplate leading an abnormal life in these solitudes? You, a single individual, alone of your sex, will find only emptiness.' I realised the truth of this, and bade farewell to the unclaimed acres which could have been mine simply for the asking.

Poor knoll, whose wild beauty I found so enticing! You put stony ground like an obstacle beneath my feet; you hindered my progress with thorny trees which clutched at my clothing and tore at my flesh; you lured me on like a wanton maid. More than once I hesitated, panting. My strength failed me, but not my courage. I forced my way through, and while the goal was still before me, I felt no fatigue, no pain, no danger, and I reached it at last.

Ah, I pity you. Other feet than mine will tread upon you. The pick, the shovel and the axe, those first tools of civilization, will rob you of your most beautiful ornaments. Convenient, doubtless, but sad is the country which is traversed by roads, like long serpents along which all the vices of civilization are peddled. A country into which European civilization is introduced is immediately sullied; nature is violated. Look at her the next day and ask yourself: has she not lost her character, her unique appeal, those distinguishing features which awakened the admiration of the European observer who came to look dispassionately upon the work of the creator?

But that is not all: cleared and settled by man, she acquires in his eyes a greater value. She becomes an object of envy, which eventually leads to bloodshed and strife. He who tilled the land loses his life for it. He gives back his body and his blood to the earth which nurtured him. And then the conqueror is himself dispossessed by others who establish a stronger dominion. Time passes over these scenes of carnage, levelling all but the resistant rocks which continue to stand like tombstones, the witnesses of past sorrow.

One cannot travel far in any civilized land without encountering evidence of man's ferocity. Each landscape which fills the heart with joy, each vista which lulls the senses with voluptuous delight, all these places can testify to the violent death of a man. Today you may discover there the delirious joy which makes you oblivious of the miseries of earthly life, but yesterday it was otherwise. You are standing upon the very spot which witnessed man's fury against man, the gnashing of teeth and the death rattle. Yet you stand there, daring to grasp at the fleeting, frivolous joys of life! Just think of the past; conjure up the scenes played out on this very ground, and then tell me whether your foot does not draw back trembling as it touches the bloodsoaked earth! Do you blame me then for loving virgin lands? Unfortunately, these are what Europeans covet most. God forbid that I should wish civilization to come to these lands. The natives were happier before the arrival of the whites, and Djacka, for all his cruelty, was perhaps a lesser scourge.

On our way back from Om-Zinto we crossed the Om-Komas, where we saw for the first time innumerable swarms of locusts, which settled on the green pastures and on every variety of tree, whose appearance they altered completely so that the trees seemed more luxuriant than usual, and the dull green of their foliage now appeared purplish with gleams of silver and mother-of-pearl. To the observer, the colours were admirable, although the beat of thousands of glazed wings made an oppressively loud noise. At our approach, these destructive insects rose into the air in huge drifts to reveal the denuded skeletons of abandoned trees, while all about us fresh swarms darkened the sun and made so much noise for half a league around that we were unable to exchange a word.

These countless multitudes are finally driven off by a strong breeze which carries them away and scatters them, exhausted, over lands which they have already ravaged or where the grass is no longer green. More numerous than all the blades of grass in the whole of the land, they soon fall to the ground where, for the want of food, and unable to fly, they die and are burnt by the sun, which dries them out and bakes them. Then the sheep, cattle and horses graze on them. But their numbers are so great that they fill the air with noxious gases, which give rise to pestilential maladies. This is why at least once a year, all over Cafre land, care is taken to burn the dry grass. The fire destroys an immense quantity of the eggs and larvae of these insects, and by this simple means the crops are protected from complete devastation.

I have heard from a Dutch farmer of another method used by those colonists who happen to discover the place where the locusts have just hatched. Swarming over an area, 200, 300 or 400 feet square, their wings not yet competely formed, their feet unsteady, they hop about feebly. Nothing could be simpler. A flock of 500 to 1 000 sheep is brought along. If these animals are hungry, they will try to eat the clumsy insects, and in the crush their feet will trample most of them. After the sheep, comes the turn of the kites and the crows, which will feast on this easy prey crawling on the ground.

When a swarm of locusts several miles wide is moving in the direction of their gardens, all the Cafres, whatever their age, come out of the *mouzi* to protect the harvest. Men, women, children, uttering discordant cries, and armed with *tongas*[1] or long sticks, beat the air and sometimes the branches, to drive the destructive insects away, or to prevent them from settling. In spite of all the noise there is always some damage done, but at least all is not lost.

This method is always used when an attack threatens. It is certainly effective, but it requires too many people to be of much use to the colonists, who have only their families to help them. However, even if it is possible to preserve a part of the harvest, it is not possible to defend the pasture lands which are so vital to the South African farmer, who owns numerous flocks and herds.

When an entire area is devastated, there is nothing for it but to travel twenty or thirty leagues in search of grazing. It is principally because they destroy the grazing that the locusts are so much feared by colonists and Cafre alike, but for the Boschjesman, who owns nothing, their arrival is an occasion for joy. He collects them, stuffs them into skin bags, and uses them for food when hunting is bad. I have seen Cafre children roasting locusts threaded on a stick over the fire. The cooking was quickly done, the wings and the head were discarded and the rest was eaten. Curious to discover why they were considered a delicacy, I tasted some without any sort of seasoning, and found them neither pleasant nor disagreeable. The dish had practically no taste at all, yet it was not completely tasteless. It was neither appetising nor quite insipid. I was reminded of our snail-eaters in France, and I concluded that we would also have many enthusiastic locust-eaters if these insects happened to leave Africa and visit our country.

These swarms of locusts were virtually the only interesting thing I observed during the fourteen day excursion. A few gazelles had been shot, as well as some bustard, partridges, ducks, Egyptian geese and violet storks, known to naturalists as *Ciconia umbellata*. I also gathered a hundred or so dried plants. Such were the poor results of my excursion; it was time ill-spent. Mr Wahlberg, on the other hand, found an enormous boa-python near the mouth of a little river; I very much envied him at the time. I subsequently found a good number of them at the bay itself where they were not so rare.

I took up my usual occupations with renewed enthusiasm in order to regain the time lost, but various circumstances occurred which for a long time preoccupied the inhabitants of Natal. As isolation was impossible I did what everybody else was doing and played my part in the events which were to influence the fortunes of the country.

1 A little club with a knob on the end.

CHAPTER VIII

Panda takes refuge in the territory of the Boers and entreats their co-operation against Dingaan — The causes of his flight — Commission to discover his intentions — I am part of this — Our arrival at Om-Tougate — A visit to the prince — His manner of receiving us — An intimate scene — Portrait of the king — Exchange of treaties of alliance — A bloody episode — War dance — An accident — Return to Natal.

On 20 September 1839, we heard mention for the first time of Panda, a man of distinction among the Amazoulous. Half brother to Dingaan, who was king at that time, and full brother of Djacka, whom Dingaan had assassinated in order to come to power, Panda had, according to the Cafres, incontestable rights to the throne. Although he led an indolent life, surrounded by his numerous wives, and could not be accused of plotting to overthrow the reigning prince, Panda continued to be an object of suspicion in Dingaan's eyes.

The despot had expressed in the presence of his principal counsellors of death, a desire to be rid of Panda, whom he considered, he said, to be a worthless warrior. This was due, he said, to the fact that Panda's heart was like a woman's; and as nothing remains secret, even at the court of a Cafre king, these rumours reached Panda and put him on his guard.

At that time he lived like a prince on the banks of the Om-Matagoulou, not far north of the Touguela. Dingaan sent out an order that all the people living between the Touguela and the Om-Schlatousse should unite, and commanded that Panda should come and settle with them to the north of Omphilos-Om-Schlopu.

Immediately Panda took counsel with the elders and the distinguished warriors. They were unanimous in interpreting the order as a ruse on the part of Dingaan who intended to isolate Panda's adherents with the object of disposing of them. Almost all of his counsellors, in spite of their terror at the very name of Dingaan, advised Panda not to comply with this order. Reassured of the loyalty of his people, and taking no heed of a second summons, Panda sent out directives to prepare for departure and, followed by 17 000 souls of all ages, he crossed the Touguela, which is the southern limit of the Amazoulou country and the northern boundary of Natal.

Here he encountered Hans Delange, who was hunting hippopotamus, and delivered over to him a herd of 130 oxen and cows to be given back to the white people from whom, according to him, they originally came. Then Panda, who had less to fear from the whites than from the forces of Dingaan, came and settled ten leagues away from the bay of Natal, just south of the little Om-Tougate river. Meanwhile the whites, fearful of this proximity, raised a great outcry. They would not believe that Panda was a fugitive, and in their eyes the deliberate step which he had taken was nothing but a subterfuge, authorizing the entry of Dingaan's army into their territory, Dingaan who was their sworn enemy, who had refused payment of his acknowledged debt, and whose deceitful intentions had been clearly revealed. They mistrusted Panda as much as they did Dingaan himself.

One more step and the advice of the women would prevail, for the African Dutch women have strong opinions and do not hesitate to make them known. The husbands do as their wives bid them. The plan was to attack the refugees unawares, to butcher some of them in order to compel the rest to return from whence they came. Death was to confront the poor devils as relentlessly as it pursued them, for among the Amazoulous deserters are shown no mercy. Such is the strange and cruel policy of the despot that, had his warriors succeeded in surrounding them, not one of the 17 000 refugees would have been spared.

It is regrettable to have to say so, but the white inhabitants of Natal were less concerned to preserve themselves from danger than to take possession of the 25 000 cattle which Panda had brought with him. It was in order to acquire these animals that they racked their brains to find a plausible excuse for killing Panda's people. I did as the others were doing and boldly expressed my opinion, which was not applauded. I was convinced that Panda had been obliged to flee in the face of imminent danger and I tried to persuade the others of this but they chose not to believe me.

However, when the whites began to consider that they were numerically too weak to execute the projected butchery and when they began to see that they could not carry enough bullets to destroy so many people, even if there were no resistance at all, they were obliged to consider other measures. Finally it was agreed to send a special commission. This was the suggestion of Mr Roos, Landroost of Conguela; it was my opinion also and that of every man who hated bloodshed.

But men had to be found to take part in this mission, which was certainly not without danger, and the memory of the recent murder of Retief was a deterrent. There were no volunteers and no means of compelling those men who would have been most suitable. They opposed the thing and put impediments in the way of the procedure which had been agreed upon. Finally Mr Roos, a resolute and determined old man, Mr Breda, who was no less so, and a few others, including myself, set the example of dedication to duty. Our energetic determination, reinforced by a scornful challenge, goaded the undecided into joining us without more ado. The core of the party was thus formed, and seemed likely to grow. We settled on a departure date and the news was conveyed to Panda.

This decision was soon known to the English on the shore, and Captain Jarvis did his utmost to dissuade the farmers from sending a delegation which might share in the fate of Pieter Retief. These were humane sentiments, but it must be confessed that the real intention of this intervention was to prevent an alliance between the farmers and Panda, which would probably have resulted in the overthrow of Dingaan, who had recently agreed to consider overtures from agents of Britain. A good understanding had been established between them, and the king's downfall would mean that other approaches would have to be made which might not be crowned with success. Our resolution stood firm, however, and dawn on 21 October 1839 saw us setting out with 13 wagons and 28 men, dressed as if for hunting. The force was not sufficient to resist an attack, but as we were going to mingle with Panda's people, our numbers were not important. We were at his mercy in any event.

We crossed the Om-Guinée and outspanned for the night on the banks of Om-Schlango, the river of reeds, where I found some iron-ore while climbing a slope intent on private business. We set off again next day and by three o'clock were looking down upon a great stretch of country, seamed with rivers, and rich with the greenest of pastures, where thickly wooded hills contrasted with bare slopes, and the horizon was edged by distant blue mountains. Everywhere we looked, there were huge herds of oxen and cows peacefully grazing. These were Panda's cattle, taken from Dingaan as he fled. They filled the plain; never before had I seen so many. We were amazed by their numbers and marvelled at their beautiful condition. Indeed we all agreed that Panda's idea had been an excellent one: in saving his own life he had wounded the tyrant in his most tender spot.

It was not long before we came in sight of a *mouzi*, the improvised residence of the chief, built upon a perfect vantage point. Many men were making their way towards it. We chose this moment to unfurl the flag of the young republic at the rear of the principal wagon, somewhat in the manner of a ship's flag. We discharged our arms in a salute, which was echoed by a great sound of approbation. It was the voice of the black people, swarming down below, who thus expressed their faith in us.

We were soon passing along the rows of huts which were arranged to form a wide enclosure. Warriors, women, children, all came running out to see us. Many of them had never before approached a white man. Their curiosity was so great that the crowds which pressed about us rendered our progress impossible. The long whips cracked above their heads, exciting their astonishment to no small degree. But as they soon realised that the whiplash touched no one, they crowded back again in such numbers that the progress of our oxen was impeded once more. Next upon the scene came several Cafre headmen, heralds-at-arms or policemen who, armed with *tongas*, struck out at those who did not move fast enough. Blows rained down, but the storm was of short duration. As our way was now cleared, we proceeded 100 paces and laagered[1] our oxen.

Our first concern was to pay our respects to Panda who, in accordance with Cafre etiquette, had not left his hut to welcome us in spite of his great desire to see us arrive. His hut was situated, as is customary, in a special precinct at the upper end of the great oval enclosure. Nearby, and in the same segment, were the dwellings of his wives, his mothers, his daughters, all the females of his household.

We went in on all fours and took his hand in the most cordial manner, to which he murmured an acknowledgement. Then, squatting or sitting on our heels according to the Cafre custom, we spoke of the purpose of our visit, and Panda expressed his great satisfaction at our coming. His eyes, shining like black diamonds, first caught my attention, and I observed him closely. I then turned to examining his dwelling, and was astonished to observe only the strictest simplicity, apart from the brilliant gleam of the floor of beaten clay in which objects were reflected as in an artificial horizon.

Crouched in uncomfortable attitudes with the heat becoming unbearable, we suggested that Panda should come out and inspect the gifts we had brought him in token of friendship. Slowly and gravely, Panda arose, and in princely fashion he followed us, accompanied by a group of his favourites. His numerous subjects fell back as he passed, opening a pathway before him, calling after him their acclamation and expressions of their satisfaction mingled with requests and petitions. I was able to distinguish the word *ignama*, *ignama*,[2] which means meat. The people were not sufficiently replete, although that very day sixteen oxen had been consumed. Nevertheless, Panda was shown the greatest respect that might be shown to

---

1 A.D. has invented a French verb *larguer* but in explaining that this means 'to unharness' he seems to have missed the significance of what was essentially a defensive manoeuvre. *Translator's note*

2 John Bird in his *Annals of Natal*, p. 557, translating from Delegorgue, says in a footnote 'It is probable that knowledge of the language has failed the author in this instance. The cry was almost certainly "*Wena 'mnyama* (thou black one)", the favourite and usual phrase of salutation to the chief of a black race. The people would not have ventured to be importunate for meat.' A more probable interpretation is that the word used was *ngonyama*, i.e. lion, which was a commonly used praise-name for the king. *Translator's note*

any man, and I doubt that any European emperor or prince receives as much.

The ceremony of the gifts took place without further ado. Panda seemed very pleased with the makeshift wool-muslin cloaks, and a naval dagger which I had the honour to beg him to accept; he regretted, however, that the curved dagger had only one cutting edge.

It remained for him to thank us personally. A herald arrived to receive his orders and two oxen, wonderfully fat, were immediately brought and killed to satisfy our needs and those of our servants.

'For twenty-eight men,' I said to my neighbour, 'it seems to me that this is prodigious extravagance, a monstrous meal.'

'Say nothing,' said he, 'for fear of altering an admirable custom practised among the Amazoulous. It is not too much. If you travel among them in their country, and ask to stay at the kraal of a great chief, each evening a heifer will be brought you for supper. If the man in charge is not a great chief, or if it is materially impossible for him to satisfy these requirements, he will come to you very politely, express his regrets, and assure you of his good intentions.'

At the time I did not believe him. This gentlemanly hospitality seemed an unlikely story and my farmer friend a shameless braggart, but I now admit to his credit that he did not exaggerate and that later, when hunting among the Amazoulous, I had on more than one occasion the opportunity of experiencing the happy manifestations of this patriarchal system. A refusal under these circumstances would have been regarded as an affront. It goes without saying that in return for these tactful attentions it is as well to offer the donor some appropriate gift; necklaces of glass beads or woollen blankets, by which they set great store. I never failed to do this, although Cafre etiquette does not require that any gift at all should be sent in return.

And these naked men, barbarians in the Roman sense, we presume to call savages! To think that we are so simple-minded or so cruel as to send agents of civilization among them. What matter for thought!

The night passed peacefully enough although some of our party, fearful for their safety, were unable to close their eyes. Lying on their guns, with their bridles over their arms, a false alarm would have sent them flying. Had our mission not been so serious, such a practical joke would certainly have been played on them.

We were all up and doing before dawn, for among the Cafres business is attended to early, and generally before they break their fast. We were intending to request Panda to come to us, when we decided that it would be more gracious if we ourselves were to be present at his levee. I was twenty paces in advance of the others and when I presented myself at the enclosure, the *om-douna*[1] on

---

1 Chief of the *mouzi* — a title equivalent to that of officer.

guard, who had received no orders concerning us, allowed me to pass. I approached the hut and lay down flat upon the ground. Supporting myself on my hands, I crawled head first through the low opening and squatted on my heels the way I had done the day before. When my eyes grew accustomed to the gloom, I became aware of the most picturesque sight. I rubbed my eyes to assure myself that this was not a vision, that it was indeed reality.

Upon mats spread out on the ground, lay ten young girls, their naked bodies firmly rounded and soft as velvet. The limbs of at least six of them were entwined with those of the king. One supported his head upon her body, a living pillow whose breathing induced opium dreams; another bore up his right arm; a third had hold of his left hand and laid her temple upon the broad chest of the brother of Djacka; yet another held his right leg, while the left leg cradled the last one of all.

All were asleep and I, the only watcher, was intending to stay and observe, so that I might describe for you my reader, this charming, dimly-lit scene, this picture of the night of an Amazoulou chief, when my companions, the farmers, appeared at the entrance of the hut, demanding audience. I withdrew and told them that Panda was still asleep and that it would be better to wait so as not to upset him.

One of them impatiently thrust his head in through the entrance and was able to glimpse something of the delightful laocoonism which I have just attempted to describe. The loud remarks which ensued gave the alarm: only then did Panda disengage himself from the embraces of his wives to proceed to the examination of more serious matters. With this man there was no embarrassment, no time wasted in dressing; his night attire served equally well as a council robe; an ample cloak in the Roman style, with which he draped himself in an eminently noble fashion, enhanced the features in which the habit of command was boldly traced. The comparison which I was at leisure to make, was to the complete disadvantage of the farmers who surrounded him: great, gangling, long-limbed fellows, with clumsy gestures, awkward bearing, dull faces, faltering speech, gaping mouths, men made to drive oxen and to hold converse with them. Panda was quite different: the large, well-shaped, brilliant black eyes were over-shadowed by a jutting brow, surmounted by a high, square forehead on which a few early wrinkles were beginning to show; the nose was not unusual, except for the flaring well-defined nostrils, the mouth was wide with a ready smile expressive of quick comprehension, and the square chin was indicative of strength; in all it was a well-shaped head borne upon a superb body, shining and stout. His bearing was so noble, the limbs so obedient to the will, the gestures so formal, that a Parisian might well have believed that Panda had frequented royal palaces in his youth. A missionary who was asked his opinion of Panda replied, *'I know Panda; he is a Caffir gentleman.'*[1] Although the description is a happy one, in my opinion it falls short of the truth.

Panda was soon seated in our midst in a long tent which had been erected for the purpose of serving as a council chamber. The interpreter, Klaas Pommer, made our intentions known to him, our plans for the future, based on a common goal which was none other than the overthrow of Dingaan. Various secret clauses were adopted, to be executed in the event of a successful outcome, clauses of the greatest importance to the farmers, the cession of the bay of Saint Lucia for example.

Responsible men were to be nominated to guarantee the execution of the treaty in case of Panda's death. Dingaan had set a price of a thousand cattle on Panda's head which could prove a temptation to many people and which required that all sorts of precautions should be taken.

Mr Roos requested him to send for his three principal headmen, who would be answerable to us for his life in the event of assassination; that is to say that they would be held accountable, in order to avoid conspiracies, as well as to establish an active surveillance. They would together maintain the existing order until the will of the farmers was made known. It was also agreed that all their efforts should be devoted to the implementation of the principal objective of the treaty. Panda sent for two of the headmen and then, after some hesitation, named the third. The resolution was read to them to which they agreed.

Satisfied, we parted company and the new ministers, pleased with us and with the confidence which the king had placed in them, went down into the plain to make known to the people gathered there the decisions of the white men concerning not only themselves but the nation as a whole.

Some of us, including Dr Krauss and myself, who had not yet recovered from the fatigues of the previous day, went off to lie down and rest in the wagons. Only minutes later we were roused by an indescribable clamour. I jumped down and went to where the farmers were gathered, to discover the cause of the uproar.

At the bottom of the hill, 150 paces away, the black mass was moving restlessly, swaying, murmuring, shouting Cafre cries, warcries that were terrifying, strange and barbarous to our ears. A thousand conflicting demands rent the air and went unanswered. I felt that I was being pursued by a bad dream, I rubbed my eyes, but it was indeed reality in all its frightening ugliness.

All those Cafres who had previously been silent listeners, now

1 English in the original. *Translator's note*

took an active part in the bloody altercations. A long undulating serpent of men coiled its way towards a particular spot, where all the fighting sticks were struck downwards and when raised again were tinged with blood. The crowd which clustered about the scene of action was uttering loud confused cries as if to stifle those of the victim and conceal the hideous sight.

It was a man whom they were bludgeoning to death and the man was Panga Zoaga, the third of Panda's great headmen, the one who had just accepted responsibility for the life of the chief. 'He was a great rascal, a wizard, *Om-Tagaty*,' the Amazoulous told us, 'who, under Dingaan, had caused many men to be put to death; now reinstated to power under Panda, his past conduct filled us with fear for the future. The people, as you see, have just performed an act of justice.'

But this explanation did not satisfy us; the sight of blood filled us with fear for our own safety. It was possible that these people, excited by scenes of carnage, would fall upon us next and make short work of our little band, who would have been no match for them. It was at that moment that the old man, Mr Roos, overly cautious perhaps, circulated the order to take up arms. I was aware of the danger of such a demonstration, and opposed it as strongly as I could. The Amazoulous would believe that we were afraid; we must avoid that at all costs, and put them off the scent by trying to divert their attention elsewhere.

Panda was sent for to explain to us the reason for this scene, which we regretted having been obliged to witness. He came, feigning anger; 4 000 warriors formed a circle about him and he glared with apparent menace at the perpetrators of the murder.

In our eyes, Panda had absolved himself of the crime; his eloquence convinced us of his innocence and only several days later did we learn that this had been his first act of authority: the moment we recognised him as chief of his tribe, a man had to die by his orders, and the blood of this same man was to be used to anoint his limbs at night while the heart, roasted, was to be presented to him to eat, so that it might fortify his body and quicken his courage.

Such are the superstitions which prevail among the Amazoulou Cafres. I know that several people with whom I was acquainted in Natal would not admit that this was so, but as I am the only one to have lived nearly ten months in the heart of their country, I have been too well informed to continue to doubt. Never before had I seen so great a number of men gathered together. The eloquence of the orators, the exaggerated rapidity of their movements, their impassioned speeches, the profusion of their words, the quick, bold gestures, unfamiliar to us Europeans, gestures which were more eloquent than words, all this struck me most particularly.

But I had observed enough at close quarters, and now I wished to survey the scene from a distance. I moved off and took up my position at the top of a hill. From this vantage point, I could see what looked like an enormous brown crescent, between the two horns of which I was able to distinguish the council of headmen presided over by Panda, and here and there, singly or gathered together in groups, stood the tall farmers, some interested, others more or less indifferent to the proceedings.

I could not dispel from my mind thoughts of the danger of our situation, now that we had put ourselves at the mercy of the capricious Panda. The heated discussion initiated by us in consequence of the shocking murder of Panga Zoaka, had inflamed those hardened skulls, and it was possible that we might become the victims of the fiery emotions we had aroused. Continually before my mind was the memory of Dingaan's treachery when Retief and fifty-nine men, the pick of the farmers, had been killed in so pitiable and infamous a manner.

I was absorbed in the painful recollection of these dismal scenes, when suddenly a thousand shrill whistles rent the air, loud enough to split even a Cafre's head. All the warriors had begun running at great speed, fanning out in every direction. When they were 300 paces from the centre, they suddenly spun around as one man; then, chanting their war-cry, these warriors who all looked like devils to me, began to charge.

We're done for, I thought; those stupid peasants must have committed some indiscretion; neither they, nor I, nor any one of us, will escape. I cannot adequately express the regret I felt, not for the loss of my life for that was not a consideration, but because I was going to be struck down without firing a shot from the gun which was lying in my wagon, the gun which I would have put to such good use before I was stabbed to death.

This is the dream which has haunted me throughout so many restless nights, the dream in which I am faced by numerous enemies and find myself without a gun, or discover that my bullets are designed for a gun of another calibre; in desperation, I fire short of the mark and am put to flight by the thousand nameless terrors so often encountered in dreams; I experience the resentment of the man who is willing to lose his life only on condition that those he has killed should accompany him into eternity. And yet, in dreams, is not flight itself impossible? Are you not surrounded by watching eyes? Do your legs not refuse to assist you? You wish to flee but you cannot move; what anguish you suffer! Death awaits you and you cannot offer any resistance, cannot take your revenge, cannot live to see your enemies expire at your feet! What a fearful situation! Your regrets, your last regrets are so bitter; and you fear they will pursue you forever into the life beyond. Have you not experienced all these sensations when a heavy black nightmare has settled pitilessly upon your terrified breast? You too have shared my terror, my anguish, my despair. But you were dreaming and I was not. However, whether dream or reality, the sensations are the same, and I am sure you will understand mine.

I do not comprehend my puzzling behaviour but whatever my fears might have been, I never for a moment thought of escape and particularly not of escaping alone. I began to run as fast as I could towards the warriors and was soon behind them. When I noticed a break in their ranks, I dashed through. I reached the wagons, snatched up my gun, loaded it, and only then did I take time to draw breath.

But imagine my astonishment when I saw that only half of the assembled farmers were armed. I had completely misunderstood the situation and I had been the more easily misled because I did not know the Amazoulou customs. This simulated anger, this sudden advance, this wild stamping, accompanied by the most horrible hissing, was the prelude to a war-dance, for Panda felt it necessary to divert our attention from the painful emotions we had recently experienced.

The circle formed in the most orderly manner; Panda sat in the centre upon his great armchair, carved all of a piece; gathered about him we stood watching, our guns loaded for a general salute. The warriors intoned warlike chants which were accompanied by the heavy rhythmical stamping of feet and the raising and lowering of the inevitable *tonga*. Deep-throated sounds reached our ears, reminiscent of the ventriloquist's art, which must have required great efforts to produce. The wonderful effect of these voices chanting in unison is beyond my powers to describe. The expression on the faces of the warriors as they chanted was particularly arresting. These people must have a deep appreciation of music for it appears to affect them to a very high degree. The only music on this occasion was that of the human voice, repeatedly chanting warlike words, but the effect produced was that each man seemed to put aside his habitual expression in order to assume the face of battle. The black eye became fiery, the movements of the body more energetic, the features more forbidding, the stature seemed taller, the chest broader. A sort of martial fervour seemed to fill every individual and if the chant had not remained constantly solemn, one might have detected some frenzy in the gestures. The seething, repressed passion was comparable to the excitement which is stirred in us by the sound of drums, bugles and patriotic songs.

As an interlude after the first act, we had a sort of pantomine which we found very amusing, but which the Cafres took very seriously, and to which they attached an importance which we did not understand. A man left the ranks and ran right round the enclosure from one end to the other, imitating a gazelle pursued by a hunter, leaping over bushes and disappearing behind them. After giving a display of outstanding speed and an amazing imitation of the animal, he resumed his place.

Then it was the turn of another, who came darting forward. Snakes seemed everywhere beneath his feet, nowhere was he able to tread; horror was painted upon his face, his muscles were excessively contracted, he made unbelievable efforts. His act completed, he returned to his place, while the spectators all pointed at him with the index finger, which is the equivalent of our applause. A third man was transformed into a leopard, and his success in a difficult interpretation earned him high praise.

But now why this applause? Why are the index fingers already pointing? Here comes one who is applauded in advance. He is a lion, a real lion with all its gestures. See him leap, crouch, roar, and with the tail of his *motgeas*[1] swish his flanks, then pounce, sit and flex his claws. The acclamation increases twofold as he displays even greater shows of strength and agility. Talking volubly, the spectators all point at him and finally Panda, impassive until that moment, rises and also points his index finger in the direction of the performer.

This mark of attention was not accorded because of the difficulty of the performance, but because this man was a warrior, well known for having put to death numerous enemies single-handed. He had just proved that his body was still strong and supple, and accepted the respect due to him, for Panda, in deigning to rise, seemed to be saying, 'You are amongst the bravest of them all; I depend upon you.'

Others, no less interesting than the first, appeared and during the performance, an orator, standing a few paces away from the king, spoke extempore and with extreme volubility. In his interminable praises, he compared Panda to the sun, giving life to all things; to the boundless ocean, to all that is great, powerful and beautiful. This poor devil had a difficult task, only a Cafre could be born so long-winded. Panda paid no attention; it was obvious that he was bored, but the demands of etiquette must be complied with in their society as in ours. Let us take consolation then for we are not the only ones who are obliged to conform.

Behind us a group of women were singing as they stamped their feet and clapped their hands to a rhythmic beat. Almost all of them had beautiful teeth and many had attractive enough faces, but all of them, without exception, were too plump. This was not surprising

1 Garment made of strips of fur intended to secure the penis cap in front, while behind these are five or seven floating tails.

when one learnt that they all belonged to the family of Panda and consequently enjoyed the title of *inkoskazy* (princess) and the privilege attached to it which was to live in complete idleness.

Our turn also came to take part in the display. At a given signal our shots rang out in salute. This show of confidence was, I believed, a great imprudence with several thousand Cafres surrounding us only twenty-five paces away. If they had had the least intention of harming us, they were in a position to strike us down without losing a man, for we could have done nothing in our own defence. But I saved one of my two shots with the intention of blowing off Panda's head if his people had shown any signs of hostility.

One salvo was apparently not enough; the command for a second was given which almost ended in disaster, due to an unfortunate accident which nobody could have foreseen. Mr Morewood, my neighbour on the right, was two paces behind Panda when his magazine caught fire. The force of the explosion, added to the shock, sent him reeling. Thanks to the immediate assistance which was rendered, this accident had no unfortunate consequences. But how differently things might have turned out for us if one of the flying splinters had wounded Panda! These people with their ignorance of arms might well have imagined the worst. They could not fail to attribute the incident to deliberate intention on our part. Certainly not one of us would have come out of the enclosure alive. It was only later that we realised the imminence of the danger which had surrounded us; only later did our hair stand on end.

When the dance was over, everything returned to normal. A heavy rain was falling, which contributed not a little to calming the spirits. In the evening, I visited a number of huts where men and women were all crowded together, roasting and eating large quantities of meat. In vain I enquired about the bloody affair of the morning; I found no one indiscreet enough to give me an honest answer.

The next day, which was a Sunday, the farmers celebrated divine service in their own fashion. They were very particular not to set forth without fulfilling this duty upon which, according to them, the success of our mission depended. I took advantage of the opportunity to visit the *mouzi* and its inhabitants once more. I was strolling about, as though I were in the Palais Royal, when one of the wives of a headman called to me for some snuff of which they are all, without exception, passionately fond.

In order to gratify her I went in, intending to examine in detail the furnishings of the hut, but once inside, I had eyes only for her. In the features of this woman there was something so refined, in her expression so much to interest, in her manner an air of such good breeding, that I was charmed. All about her hung that particular Cafre fragrance which belongs only to people of distinction, and which I had at last learned to find attractive. Upon my honour, this woman could make me forget many another.

I took her necklace made of round beads in exchange for one of my gilt buttons, with which she adorned her bosom. This trinket gave her some pleasure, but it was my silk necktie that she most desired. I was prepared to exchange this only for her belt of plaited bark, but she refused. I gave her a pretty, multicoloured handkerchief, which she gladly accepted, but she would not consent to give up her belt. This ornament, which serves to distinguish married women, is not an object of beauty. It is generally worn on the abdomen above the folded edge of the *om-gobo*.[1]

Two other women then appeared in quest of tobacco. Then came the husband who, like all the others, raised the palm of his hand to his nose and sniffed loudly to indicate what he wanted. I made friends with all these people without any difficulty, at least for the moment, and we conversed comfortably. It was a matter of interest to me to discover just how far the complacency of an Amazoulou husband would extend, and after several attempts to explain myself, I eventually said: 'These are your three wives; the first and the second are yours, you can keep them; but as for the third, I declare that she is my favourite. She is mine, you understand? *Yebo, yebo, baba*, 'Yes, yes, master,' he said to me, laughing. His wives laughed a great deal also, and I thought that the one I had chosen seemed flattered.

However, do not jump to any conclusions. An hour later we were setting off for Natal. That 'yes, yes, master', was a feigned submission which disguised the most complete denial. It was simply good manners, a pleasantry accepted as such. His wife had understood perfectly; her role also had been well played.

What a striking similarity with Europe! Had I remained longer, had the crack of the whips announcing our departure not obliged me to leave the improvised ambush, my snuffbox would have been literally cleaned out and nothing in return! How fortunate that the time for departure came just as I was allowing myself to be seduced.

Each nation has its weakness; in Tahiti it was iron, among the Hottentots it was grease or brandy; the Cafres could not resist glass beads and tobacco, whilst with us it is cashmere and gold. However, I must say in defence of the honour of the Cafre ladies, that it is very rarely that they allow themselves to be seduced by the attractions even of glass beads, which are what they most desire. If some behave differently, it is because they no longer conform to the community. If they are liberated by the death of a husband, they

1 Woman's garment which performs the function of a dress during the day and a blanket at night.

94

become part of a neutral category, which is neither that of the married woman, nor that of the young girl. They no longer have their maidenhood to cherish, they no longer have any duties to fulfil; they are free, and consequently compliant, free, although not to meet a man of distinction who already has forty or fifty wives, they could have no pretensions to such an honour, but an *Om-Phogazane*, a simple Cafre, a common man who, too poor to acquire a first wife, eagerly grasps at the opportunity which is offered him.

Upon our departure, I learnt that Panda was displeased with us because the old headman with the glass eyes, Mr F. Roos, had not wanted to accept all the gifts which had been offered to us. In refusing, Mr Roos had intended to act with genteel modesty, but one should have no considerations of this sort when dealing with unsophisticated people who will be affronted by a refusal.

We slept the next night at Om-Guinée and the following day arrived early at Conguela. The most accute anxiety reigned there on our account; they had thought that they would never see us again.

It was then November 1839. The week after our return to Conguela, several messages were received from Panda. One of the envoys delegated to address Mr Roos on behalf of the king said to him, 'I am very sorry that the old chief with the glass eyes no longer wishes to be my father.'

At about the same time, an envoy of Dingaan, expressing the opinion of his master before the council at Pieter's Mauritz Burg, then known as *Boschjesmans Rand*, said in speaking of Panda: 'He is not a man; he has turned away his face; he is a woman. He was useless to Dingaan his master, and he will be of no use to you. Do not trust him, for his face may turn again'. These expressive metaphors are common among the Cafres. I have known some that were very beautiful, as well as those that were trivial to our way of thinking. When they occur more frequently in this narrative, I shall comment about them at greater length.

CHAPTER IX

Boschismans or Boschjesmans Rand. A stockaded camp becomes the capital of Pieter Mauritz Burg — The surrounding forests — Departure of the English occupational forces — War is decided upon against Dingaan, king of the Amazoulous.

I spent part of the months of November and December at Pieters Mauritz Burg which was at that time only a stockaded camp, simply a collection of crude shanties made of wood and rushes and plastered with cow-dung. These wretched shelters swarmed with bugs and remarkably vigorous rats, which each night ate our candles and carried off our handkerchiefs and stockings. Frequently, when we awoke in the morning even our shoes were missing because the rats had dragged them to the far corners of the room or even next door.

Outside there was yet another scourge. A mass of dogs, twenty times more numerous than the population itself, rendered the thoroughfares impassable. These animals were never still. They barked and fought incessantly. Had they only attacked each other, the evil would not have been so great, but several times, generally at night, they fell upon passersby whom they flung to the ground, tearing at their clothes and ripping their flesh.

The heat, which is not alleviated by cool breezes as it is at the bay, is so intense during these two months, that neither I nor my companions were able to go out of doors after nine o'clock in the morning. My hunting expeditions were not very productive; the surrounding country of flat land and marshes yielded only snipe, crab-eaters, the bald ibis and various kinds of widow-bird, among which the redshouldered widow-bird was without doubt the most beautiful.

Pieters Mauritz Burg at that time was still called Boschjesmans Rand, because of the neighbouring mountains of that name. It was only when the council decided to lay out the plan of a town, that the leager[1] of Boschjesmans Rand chose a name compounded of those of two prominent emigrants: Pieter Retief and Gert Mauritz or Maritz.

The only animals which I saw were *rhée-booken*[2] on the mountain slopes, and river rats, *Aulacaudus* on the banks of the little river which today borders the town, and which was then called Klein

1 Leager means camp.
2 Antelopes. The *rhée-book* is the *Redunca capreolus*.

96

Boschjesmans Rivier.[1] There were also a few hares to be found near the *rhée-booken*, but really nothing to encourage the hunter.

In the distance, one can see dark green crevices cutting deeply into the lighter green of the mountain grasslands when they are in their prime, and this dark green is even more pronounced when the grazing reaches maturity. All over the valleys, the eye is drawn to particular hillsides where this green appears to grow darker as one approaches and objects increase in size until they take on colossal proportions. Eventually one becomes aware that these are forests of huge trees: *out-bosch*, timber forests. These trees are principally *geele-out*,[2] *stinck-out*,[3] *hyster-out*.[4] Most of the *geele-out* grow to 100 or 120 feet high, and from the root to the first branches form a fine straight column, unblemished by any knot. It is therefore a simple matter to cut perfect pieces sixty feet long by three feet wide. Unfortunately this wood is only suitable for permanent, sheltered constructions. I have heard it said by those who know that it is quite useless for naval construction.

The *stinck-out* is particularly hard and resistant, but it does not provide such fine long pieces. Its whole life is one of suffering. It is contorted beneath its burden of hanging moss, which adorns it like an immense beard and, while I am well acquainted with the parasite, I am ignorant of the shape of the tree's own leaves. The bark is always damp because of the moss, and it is often coated with earth. This poor plant seems to have no life of its own. Its appearance, although picturesque, is rather gloomy; the birds themselves shun it. However, in Natal, it is valued for its use in the manufacture of gun butts. *Hyster-out* is an excellent wood used to make axles for wagons.

These *out-bosch* are composed only of a limited variety of trees and are therefore not rich in bird life. Parrots, touracos, green pigeons, francolins and a few small birds, shrikes and warblers, were all that I encountered there; furthermore, the height of the trees is an obstacle to hunting in the European fashion. I have made the same experiment twenty times over, with the same result: the shot is too scattered and retains too little of its force to bring down these birds from the top of yellowwoods which are 100 or 110 feet high. It goes without saying that I refer to a double-barrelled gun, for with long guns, my servants did not meet with the same disappointment.

These forests once sheltered the larger animals. Elephants were found there and even today buffalo still live in some parts. In

1 The word *caffer* is understood to come after Boschjesmans.
2 Yellowwood.
3 Stinkwood.
4 Ironwood.

Djacka's time the last of the Natal Cafres, in an attempt to escape his notice, established their *mouzis* in the heart of the forests and the animals disappeared. In order to ensnare the game, as well as to avoid being trodden on during the night, the Cafres, called *Boschjesmans-Caffers*,[1] dug deep ditches, lined them with sharp stakes and cleverly covered them over. I saw many of these ditches which had been partially uncovered and which, as a result, I was easily able to avoid. Unfortunately not all of them are yet discovered, and several Dutch hunters have paid with their lives for their desire to bring down a buffalo. The son of Mr Meyer of Meyer Howek was found impaled in one of these traps.

I was beginning to feel quite sufficiently acquainted with Pieters Mauritz Burg and its environs, when the order came recalling the English troops who were occupying Port Natal. Their departure was to be effected forthwith aboard the *Vectis* which had just arrived and which incidentally brought letters for me from the Cape as well as from Europe. Several rather strange rumours were circulating as to the reasons for this sudden departure. According to one version, England found herself obliged to rally her forces. Another claimed that Sir George Napier, Governor of the Cape Colony, had been blamed for the measures he had taken in Natal. He was, it was claimed, condemned to pay the enormous costs of the occupation which had been pronounced to be completely futile. Every attempt was made to conceal the real reason, which was as follows. Having been called upon to withdraw his forces by a certain date, Captain Jarvis had requested reinforcements which the Governor of the Cape had found it impossible to send him and, in order not to expose to certain death the handful of soldiers who were determined to resist attack, it was decided to put a ship at their disposal to transport them and their equipment back to the Cape.

The redcoats[2] weighed anchor, and hardly were they under way when a tricolor flag was hoisted to the top of the selfsame mast where, until so recently, their own flag had flown; a number of cannon shots was fired, not as a message of farewell to wish them 'Bon voyage, may your trip be a happy one; come back soon!' but rather, 'You are relieving us of your unwelcome presence; may you go far, far away and never come back.' The cannon spoke to the echoes, which repeated the message, but the self-satisfied English

---

1 These are the Cafres after whom the Boers have chosen to name various places, mountains or rivers. The abbreviation being the accepted form, and only the name Boschjesmans remaining, one might well believe that this referred to the real Boschjesmans, but such was not the intention of the Boers and never was a true Boschjesman seen in the land of Natal from the mountains of Quathlambène to the sea.

2 Name given by the Boers to the English troops.

chose to make a diametrically opposed interpretation. This ironic demonstration was seen by them as expressing regret and suggested to their imagination gentle melancholy birds bearing fond messages to those who were leaving from those who stayed behind. Following in the vessel's wake the echoes of the cannon shots became embodied in the dark-plumed petrels, those celestial spirits of sea and air, whose plaintive cry breaks the sad heart of the traveller as he bids farewell to the land and the memories he leaves far behind.

The Boers, relieved of a presence which restricted their freedom of action, and liberated from all intervention on the part of the English, decided to take immediate advantage of the favourable circumstances which now arose.

Dingaan was delaying payment of the war debt which had already been agreed upon. Panda, when he defected, had been joined by various influential chiefs and warriors who all shared one common goal, the overthrow of Dingaan. The king could doubtless depend upon loyal men among his troops, but there were also many malcontents who were silenced only by the fear of death.

A commando was resolved upon: this is what the Arabs would call a *razzia*. No other name will do for this sort of warfare which owes nothing to European tactics. Panda was to send in his warriors on one flank, the Boers were to engage the other. Caught between two bodies of enemy troops, Dingaan would find it impossible to divide his forces, particularly as he had numerous herds to protect, and so he must inevitably succumb.

As soon as the official order went out to prepare for war, I began making my own preparations, although I could have taken advantage of my status as a foreigner to exempt myself. I was overjoyed at the prospect of visiting with impunity the land of the Amazoulous.

My head was already full of a thousand glorious speculations upon the nature of this country where no Frenchman had ever set foot before. Perhaps I would have the rare opportunity of seeing two armies of black men, like the Romans of yore, fighting hand to hand, protected by their white shields and armed with their *om-kondos*,[1] that terrible sharp-pointed weapon which inflicts a deep, four-lipped wound. In imagination I saw them, advancing on each other like brave black lions, obedient to their master's command. Then I pictured how we white men would appear, our horses snorting and pawing the ground, and put the enemy warriors to flight, assisted in the pursuit by our fortunate allies, drumming on their shields. I saw myself ahead of all the rest, carried in hot pursuit by my fiery steed, separated from my comrades and surrounded by fugitives who were determined to isolate me. I made amazing use of

1 Assegai: a javelin which the Cafres throw from 100 paces.

my gun; every one of my shots hit the mark and their *om-kondos*, whistling past my ears, fell harmlessly to the ground. Oh! my fears for my horse were acute but for myself I feared nothing! My body was like an empty vessel, while my soul floated above it. Such are the fancies born of excited anticipation. Everything in prospect appears attractive, even the ugly face of war; but confronted with reality, one loses consciousness of oneself. For a second the heart remembers those who are dear, and then one plunges into the fray.

Death is all about you, you take no heed of it, but are you truly in possession of your senses? No. You have become a war machine, dealing death to all around you. And when the storm is past, when peace is restored, your feet stumble upon a corpse. Then it is that you experience an irresistable feeling of horror, for the man who lies there dead is a victim of war, a fallen fruit, a broken reed, and it is sad to think that a dead man is of no use at all.

CHAPTER X

A six week campaign into Dingaan's country

It was 13 January 1840, and the Boer commando was already making its way from Pieters Mauritz Burg towards the Touguela river. In spite of my wish to leave Port Natal a few days earlier, I had been obliged to await my opportunity, which eventually came when Edward Parker placed several of his horses at my disposal. We set off at about eleven o'clock, and arrived that evening at the little camp at Om-Las which was at the time occupied by Hans Delange. The following day, after three hours riding, we arrived at Pieters Mauritz Burg, where we learnt that the last wagons were on the point of departure. I took advantage of the opportunity to transfer my small quantity of baggage which consisted chiefly of munitions and my scientific equipment, for I hoped to use any leisure time to gather natural history specimens.

I left Pieters Mauritz Burg on the 15th in the company of three other horsemen. We climbed the ridge of mountains called Boschjesmans Rand, crossed the Om-Guinée, and then allowed our horses to graze for an hour beside its limpid waters. The day was particuarly hot, I was drenched with sweat and covered in dust; the river, clear, cool and deep, was flowing invitingly over the rocks. I had the time and I had no reason to resist so strong a temptation. Throwing off my clothes, I plunged with delight into the water. A cold bathe in these hot lands is an indescribable pleasure; all fatigue seems to disappear in an instant. One risks paying dearly, however, for one's innocent pleasures if I judge by my own experience, for I almost died as a result and suffered agonies for fifteen long months.

About half past ten in the evening we met up with our wagon, half way between Om-Guinée and Mooi Rivier.[1] Wrapped up in our woollen blankets, we chose to spend the night in the open on a mattress of long grass which was preferable to the congestion inside the wagon.

On the 16th the oxen were harnessed before daybreak. The dew had been heavy, the air was almost cold. The countryside, which was superb, offered rich pasturage and the only trees we could see were in the *kloofs*.[2] By about ten o'clock, we were looking down on the

1 Beautiful river.
2 Valleys.

graceful and charming Mooi Rivier, which held the hillside in its sinuous embrace. From the mountain top, it resembled a river of quicksilver, endeavouring to find obstacles in its path in order to delay the progress of its waters, as if it feared the oblivion which awaited it in the sea. This river must be beautiful indeed, for the Boers, who gave it its name, are in general quite unmoved by natural beauty, and often pass without a glance those things which most excite our admiration.

We had just set off on the morning of the 17th, when five eland (*Boselaphus oreas*) appeared on our left. The best horseman among us immediately started out in their direction, but they quickly made off along the stony hillside, reached the top and disappeared, leaving us nothing but the memory of having seen them.

At about eleven o'clock, our wagons, at the risk of complete disintegration, began the difficult descent down a detestable track, which is the only means of reaching the Boschjesmans Rivier ford. To prevent certain disaster, we had to steady the wagons and control their speed, and to this end straps were tied to the projection at the end of the ladders. It is true that two or three men suffice to perform this balancing manoeuvre, but it is tiring and success is by no means certain, as the men have difficulty in keeping their footing while they are being dragged along by the weight of the wagon down the steep rough slope. The Boschjesmans Rivier, remarkable for its hard stone bed, was soon behind us, but not without much cracking of the long powerful whips and much shouting on the part of our drivers. It is an unpleasant river which, without any warning, can become a raging torrent, capable of carrying off wagon and oxen alike, which is why the Boer drivers regard it as one of the worst.

We had outspanned and were resting by the side of the road, when we saw coming towards us a man, driving two oxen harnessed to a forked branch upon which a chest had been fixed. This primitive sledge interested me and, asking the man the reason for its construction, I learnt that his son had just been dragged by a galloping horse, until eventually his foot had freed itself from the stirrup. As he had been incapable of proceeding, they had carried him to the nearest dwelling, and for the transport of his goods, they had constructed this simple vehicle. I did not forget this, and later used it myself while hunting to transport the heavier game. It was also useful when the trees were too dense or the valleys too deep to bring in a wagon.

The pasture lands here were of better quality than those at Mooi Rivier. The valleys were full of mimosas, a sign of the sweetness of the *Zoet-gras*. The plains were turning to gold and the sun was already drying out the grass, which was all to be burnt in a month or six weeks time, so that the new grass might sprout and grow.

As we travelled northwards, our gaze was continually drawn towards the tall range of the Draaken's Berg, 15 or 20 leagues away to the left. The mountains stood out blue against the horizon, their precipitous, unscaled flanks supported by rocky buttresses, whose angle of incline seemed to approach the perpendicular. They extended as far as the eye could see. The southern stretches, particularly, stirred my imagination, for I knew that no white man had ever set foot there. But the time had not yet come to explore these mountains, and when, later, I was able to climb them, it was in pursuit of an objective which would admit of no delay. That same day we crossed a little river and, as night was falling, we made our camp and lit our fires just north of it.

On the 18th at about midday, after having made a brief stop at Doorn-Kop,[1] we reached the banks of the Touguela, which were teeming with men, horses and wagons. The confused and noisy shouts of the Boers were mingled with the cracking of the whips, the rumble of wagon wheels on the stones and the swirling sound of the river which was clogged with oxen, wagons, horses and men. This turmoil was repeated by the echoes on the opposite bank, producing an uproar which would have done justice to a retreating army of 20 000 men — and yet there were only 308 armed men, 60 Hottentot and 400 Cafre servants, possibly 600 horses, 700 oxen and 50 wagons.

I must mention that there was a commandant nominally in charge, who was expected to command without any right to inflict punishment, with the result that each man obeyed only when he felt inclined to do so. The crossing took several hours, after which we set up camp on a bend half a mile further down the river. Certain grasses in the vicinity gave off a strong scent of roses; the Boers called them *stinck-gras*.

We spent the 19th and the 20th at this place awaiting the arrival of a number of colonists who lived to the west of the Draaken's Berg. I spent both these long days trying to gather plants and insects, but I was already suffering from the results of my imprudence at Om-Guinée. I was harassed by a hacking cough, accompanied by a fever which drained me of all my strength. I was obliged to give up my work; I was seriously ill without recourse to the least medication, and without food congenial to a European stomach. I lived for the forty-one days of the expedition on nothing but pieces of quiveringly raw beef which had been grilled, without salt, on the point of a ramrod, and not the shadow of a slice of bread. I had to a certain extent brought it on myself. Severely afflicted from the outset, I had been unable to conceal my condition and several people advised me to take advantage of the return of Stephanus Maritz's wagon. I would

1 Hill of the mimosas.

gladly have accepted this suggestion had I not been fearful of what people would say. As the only Frenchman among them, my retreat would have been generally remarked upon and, although necessitated by the want of a field hospital, it would certainly have been attributed to cowardice. Nevertheless, I had almost decided to take no account of this opinion, when I realised that perhaps I might never again have an opportunity to visit the Amazoulou country, and so I decided to stay.

Instead of employing these two days of enforced delay in drawing up a plan of campaign, and far from anticipating unforeseen circumstances and considering what precautions could be taken, the Boers spent their time reading the Bible and singing hymns, while the huge quantities of meat roasting over the fires almost extinguished the flames. In their moments of leisure the young men, who were of rather limited intelligence, indulged in trifling games or engaged each other in scuffling matches or attempted to be witty by telling the coarsest of jokes. As they were accustomed to living in the bosom of their isolated families, this great gathering of men was an occasion for merry-making, particularly as the meat was fat and the daily ration for each man not less than ten pounds.

For these South African Dutch, the ideal existence consists in eating great quantities of grilled meat, drinking hourly cups of coffee and having a woman for the night. It means gazing, for daily recreation, upon the great, shiny, fat herds which adorn their green pastures and engaging, from time to time, in the diversions of the hunt to restore their strength. This is their idea of comfort; what they call *lekker leeven*.[1]

Many of them considered this war which we were about to engage in against the Amazoulous as no more than a simple, although very profitable, hunting expedition. Several of them saw in it the means of establishing a fortune and increasing their legitimate share of the spoils by stealing additional cattle. This was generally accepted and could conveniently be described as a perquisite. In addition, it was permissible to take back for domestic service three or four young Cafres, boys or girls, forcibly removed from their parents, who would, to avoid any suggestion of slavery, be described as apprentices. The farmers would dispute among themselves the ownership of the young people and barter them for horses or cattle, and then, as if ashamed, they would say: 'If it was up to me, I would not have them at all, but what will my wife say if I do not take some home? It is difficult to find servants in Natal!'

On the evening of the second day, I had the opportunity to feast my eyes upon a wonderful sight. A bright light enabled one to dis-

1 To live well.

tinguish objects a long way off. It was produced by a grass fire to the north which, in a line two miles wide, was coming down the mountainside like a river of flame, and seemed to engulf everything in its path. Towards midnight this destructive fire, for want of fuel, died out on the banks of a stream, which put an end to its ravages. I began to realise how simple a matter it would have been to destroy a certain Boer encampment, lately established in the long dry grass, and of how, if the enemy Cafres had resorted to this irresistable means of attack and had taken advantage of the breeze, a quarter of an hour would have sufficed to destroy the wagons which serve as a refuge in this kind of warfare. However, although this was recognised as an elementary means of attack, no measures were ever taken to withstand it. This example of negligence, which must be attributed to extreme heedlessness, was not the only one which I observed. There were many others which I shall refer to when the occasion arises.

We struck camp on the 21st and soon afterwards the wagons, in single file, crossed Klip Rivier, a wretched river, full of stones. We were now without any doubt in Amazoulou country, enemy territory; but this was not judged to be sufficient reason to proceed more cautiously. A distance of four miles separated the first wagons from the last. Distributed over so long a line, what sort of a force was 300 or 400 men, even though armed with guns, if they were attacked by 15 000 or 20 000 Cafres? Certainly, resistance would not have been possible. But Commandant-General Pretorius had his own tactics which is to say he had no tactics at all.

After an unbroken journey of some seven hours in very hot, dry weather, we took up our position on a beautiful plain dotted with mimosas. These trees provided me with gum, the only natural medicament capable of calming the increasingly acute irritation from which I had suffered for some time.

The following day we waited for the stragglers who might yet arrive; if we did not stay to welcome them, the fear of making the journey alone would probably have inclined them to turn back. At about ten o'clock, there was an alarm which sent us scrambling for our guns. I was as capable of action as the next man, if not required to shift my position; what is more, I felt better immediately, because I was about to experience the excitement for which I had waited so long. We soon realised it was a false alarm. About 400 Cafres, carrying their shields, had been seen by a patrol, but these Cafres were visitors, a troop of Matouana's men who came to offer us their services in a combined attack against Dingaan. In answer to a request by Pretorius, they lined up and executed the *sina* or war dance accompanied by various battle hymns, whose effect was most picturesque and impressive. All these warriors wore round their heads a pad

105

of otter fur in the manner of a turban, designed to w..
single long feather of the Numidian crane was attached tc
a perpendicular position and swayed in the wind. From th..
hung rows of ox tails, like a sort of loose garment, protecting
upper part of the body; from the waist to the knee, following the
curve of the hips and the buttocks, hung the elegant *symba*[1] made of
400 strips of genet fur, twisted into spirals and sewn in imitation of
monkey tails. Ornamental garters were made from black or white ox
tails, the tuft protecting the front of the leg from thorns; similar
tails, shortened and tied above the ankle, covered the upper part of
the foot for the same purpose. The arms also were adorned at three
different points with these floating tufts, which swayed gracefully
with the movement of the body. The first was placed three inches
below the shoulder, the second two inches below the elbow, the
third at the wrist. The shield was five feet high, the weapon was the
om-kondo (assegai). Their leader wore a similar, though richer
costume. On his head were tufts of turaco feathers some red, some
blue, which also adorned the front of his body, although here the
colours were mixed. The bustard, the Angolan roller, the Natal
parrot, the wood pigeon, the widowbird, all had paid the price of
these various ornaments.

To our way of thinking, these are trifling things which may
easily be obtained in the country where these people live; but if you
think about it, you will realise that, as the Cafres have no efficient
means of catching birds, they must gather feathers which have
dropped to the ground, and then you will understand how long it
takes to collect a complete outfit. This is the reason why they are so
much prized. For example a *symba* costs at least ten cows, which is
more than a trapper earns in a year.

I share the opinion of all those who have seen this garment and
cannot too much praise its beauty, grace and elegance. To attempt
to convey in words all its attractions would be impossible, because
the eyes of Europeans have never seen anything comparable. *Our*
clothes are kept constantly buttoned up; *theirs* alternatively reveal
and conceal their bodies as they move; in rapid action, their floating
tails, their widowbird plumes, stream out behind them, suggesting
that the individual who wears them is imbued with the spirit of long-
maned horses and the courage of lions. *We* have nothing of this sort.

In battle, their songs and their movements combine with their
appearance to produce an effect so terrifying that even the bravest
are momentarily filled with fear. In order to convey to you something of this impression, I will confess that I likened these black men

---

1 A military kilt called *symba* after the genet whose skin is used in its manufacture.

106

on more than one occasion, to the fearful devils with which the good Fathers of Saint-Acheul endeavoured to terrify my adolescence. There was, however, always this difference; there is nothing repellent about these warriors; on the contrary, they are the finest soldiers imaginable.

On the 23rd we travelled through countryside where mimosa grew in profusion. Later, we entered a great bare plain, where we drew up our wagons into a circle within sight of the mountain, two or three leagues distant, on which stood the various *mouzis* of Matouana. Some of our young men went hunting, although we already had an abundance of food. One of them brought back the hindquarters of a female *Boselaphus oreas*,[1] the flesh of which was pronounced to be delicious.

The intolerable bellowing of men and oxen at the camp combined to give me a splitting headache, and so I generally went a little distance off, to amuse myself by watching insects and other living things. On one particular occasion, I had the idea of making a rough sketch of some Cafres in order to record their dress.

A man came and stood before me. He was tall, strong, well-built and confident of bearing. His features were broad and pronounced, not without some nobility, but expressive of the high opinion which he had of himself. It was Pretorius, commander in chief of the expedition. 'You are able to draw,' he said to me. 'I have learnt this from various people, and now that I find you at work, allow me,' and taking up some crumpled papers upon which I had been scribbling on my lap, he began to run his eye over them with the affectation of a connoisseur. I pointed out to him that the things were of no consequence at all, adding that these few lines were of interest only to me, and were intended as no more than aids to memory; that with time and opportunity, it would be a simple matter to capture a better likeness.

'I am pleased to hear it,' he then said. 'Since you admit that it would not be impossible for you to reproduce faithfully what you see, I hope that you will have the goodness to make my portrait.' Then he added, 'For you will understand that the dangerous life which I lead may not last very long. I have already been thrown to the ground by a Cafre from whom I had this wound on my hand, and I owe my life to the quick action of one of my companions, who killed him just as he was about to kill me. Each day may be my last, and once I am dead, the memory of my features will rapidly fade in the minds of my dear ones and of my numerous friends. Even at the Cape there are people who, without knowing me, have vowed friendship; I mean people who have never seen me, but have

1 *Canna* which the Boers call eland.

only read reports of me in the newspapers; these people have asked me to send them my likeness, but as we have no artists among us, I have not until now been able to satisfy their wishes. You will not take it amiss that I wish to profit by your skill.'

I was about to find some pretext for avoiding the unpleasant task, for I was convinced that I would never succeed in flattering him sufficiently to make the portrait acceptable, when he pursued the conversation in an attempt to impress upon me the urgency of the matter, particularly as statues and busts of all Napoleon's generals, and even of Napoleon himself, were to be seen everywhere. Apparently, in his own estimation, he ranked as a conqueror, with a place amongst the famous, or rather, forgive me, alongside Napoleon, of whom he chose to speak as of his youngest brother. Poor man!

I had great difficulty in controlling a desire to laugh. I was about to burst out, when I succeeded in diverting my thoughts, and suggested that the work be put off until our return. Pretorius thanked me in anticipation of this, and then left to answer the call of duty. As soon as he was sufficiently far off, I was at liberty to give free expression to my feelings.

I must say immediately, before I am asked for the sketch of the hero, that since that time, Pretorius and I never had occasion to meet and so I was never reminded of my promise. Up until that time, I would not have been averse to sketching the man. He had as yet shown himself to be only ignorant and cowardly, although lucky in war; but since then, in handling the Natal affair with the English, his conduct has been that of a shameful traitor. His compatriots had given him a mandate; they entrusted him with their honour and the care of their future prospects; he betrayed that trust in return for permission to retain all his own lands.

That evening we had rain for the first time since setting out. It fell in torrents, thunderclaps rent the air and it seemed that we were their target. The noise was so loud, so sustained and so continuous, that all conversation became impossible. The Boers attempted to make their voices heard above the storm by singing monotonous, mournful hymns. I found the remedy more disagreeable than the complaint.

By the 24th, the crumbling soft earth on which we were camped had become so waterlogged by the torrential rain of the previous day that it was impossible to move the wagons. From early morning, great billows of smoke had been rising from Matouana's mountain; he was burning his *mouzis*, either as a signal of departure for war or to deceive the spies of Dingaan.

On the 25th and the 26th we still had not moved and were waiting for the weather to clear. We were expecting a reinforcement of several men who finally arrived, exhausted by the continual rain. On the

27th, with infinite difficulty, we were able to move four leagues, the wheels of our wagons heavy with mud. We had only five pairs of oxen to draw each wagon, having decided on the size of the spans to avoid congestion, but they were not powerful enough under these conditions. We made our camp just south of two adjoining mountains, the more westerly one of which was flat-topped, while the one towards the east was irregular in shape; both were visible from a great distance off. We were visited here by Cafre scouts, sent by Nonglas, who was in command of Panda's forces. These men were charged with informing the latter, who was travelling with our party, that the two opposing armies had met up with each other, and had probably at that moment already joined battle. We knew that the number of warriors on either side was equally matched; that the morale of Panda's troops was high, while the fire of Dingaan's troops had cooled, for they had two foes to conquer, first Panda's army and then ours. It is unlikely that they faced this prospect with hope in their hearts.

On the 28th we left the mountains behind us to the right. The way was long and difficult; I rode two or three miles ahead of the convoy to explore the land, and saw several antelope, *canna*, fleeter of foot than any horse.

A league beyond the mountains, and five or six miles before reaching Zand Rivier, I crossed a dry river bed where a layer of fossilised coal, two feet thick and eight feet deep had been exposed. Two years later, samples which I collected were given to Mr Fowler, an English officer, who was returning to London, and who proposed having them examined by a scientific society. A young farmer brought back the skin of an animal which the Boers did not recognise. I was later able to identify it as a *bastaard Guyms-book*, *Aigoceros equina*.

That day we crossed Zand Rivier and set up camp a short distance beyond it. On the 29th we crossed Om-Sinyate, the river of buffaloes, whose steep banks confronted us with great difficulties. In spite of the fact that several wagons overturned and that some were damaged, we all reached the slopes of a nearby mountain, where we made our camp.

On this spot we discovered a large number of whitened bones and many Cafre skulls lying scattered in the long grass. This was where the memorable Sunday battle had taken place, in which twenty-five Cafre regiments of 1 000 men each, attacking in waves, had overrun a camp of 800 to 900 Boers and in retreating had left behind 3 200 dead. This bloody affair took place on 16 September 1838, and as a result the little river which runs near there has been called Bloed Rivier, the river of blood.

Some of the farmers have told me that numbers of wounded

Cafres, who were unable to escape, had taken refuge in the rushes, others who were in deeper water, remained submerged except for their noses, exactly like the hippopotamus, and by this clever and patient ruse, these wretches hoped that under cover of darkness, they would be able to drag themselves to safety. But as soon as the subterfuge was discovered, the little river was inspected and searched with the utmost attention, and soon the semi-stagnant waters were tinged with blood; all the fugitives were mercilessly shot dead by the Boers who made a sport of picking off their helpless prey.

There is something in this barbaric conduct that turns the stomach of the European, but I shall return to this subject later. However, I do not intend to accuse these Boers of infamous behaviour before I have given an account of the immigration. Their chosen men had recently been treacherously cut down by Dingaan who, twelve or fifteen days later, massacred 317 women and children, left without protection on the banks of the Boschjesmans Rivier by the men, who were confident that the treaties had been made in good faith. Did not the Amazoulous give evidence of their love of carnage by this vile and disgusting act? Did they not delight in stabbing the corpses through and through, stripping them naked, slashing open the bellies of all the women whom they believed to be with child, snatching out the unborn infant, and dashing its head against the iron rim of the wagon wheel? It was these selfsame men who subsequently came under fire from the Boers. It was these same fiery black warriors, tainted with the blood of white women, whose bones we had found. They who had been without mercy, asked for none. Once discovered, they knew that death was inevitable but, obeying the irresistable instinct of self-preservation, they dived underwater, and remained concealed until, for want of air, they were forced to the surface, where their heads were immediately shattered by the avenging bullets of the Boers. As far as one could see this was a deserted spot; the earth was unmarked by wagon ruts, and we needed to send out patrols in order to discover the easiest route to follow.

On the 30th, at about five o'clock, a Cafre carrying a white flag came from Nonglas to tell us that Dingaan's last resort was to try to join forces with Massilicatzi, but that in order to do this, he would have to pass through the country of the Knop-nuys-Caffers the knob-nosed people, who were also called Makazanes, from whom he had much to fear. To avoid this danger he would have to bear more to the west, in which case he would find himself in the midst of the Ama-Souasis, who were implacable foes. And so, whichever way he turned, he faced dangers so certain that he must inevitably perish. The messenger added that Dingaan, fearing for his life, had taken refuge in a cave, not far from his town, to await an opportunity to make his escape towards the north.

110

On the morning of the 31st, a council of war was called. It was held out of doors which was, I suppose, the reason why the judges wore their hats. I say 'judges', because this council was made up only of judges, apart from one reporter. There was no counsel for the defence to answer the prosecutor; it would have been ill-advised to provide assistance for the men whom they all wished to see condemned to death and shot. I have said 'judges', because these men played the part of judges, although they did not resemble judges in either appearance, intelligence or judgment. I have said 'judges' although, for fear of debasing the title, I would have preferred to call them by another name. If you are determined to have an accurate idea of this council, composed of stupid and cruel men, then picture a revolutionary tribunal at the time of the Terror.

The business of this tribunal was to pronounce sentence of capital punishment to be carried out immediately upon the court's rising. Before these white men, with their undistinguished faces, there appeared two black men, manacled together, the right wrist of one attached to the left wrist of the other. They were called Tamboussa and Combezena; their faces showed no emotion. Who were these men, and how had they come to be at the mercy of the Boers? I am going to tell you, so that you will know how the Boers interpret the rights of man.

Tamboussa had for a long time occupied a position of great power among the Amazoulous. After the despot Dingaan, Tamboussa and then Schlala came next in importance. They were, at one and the same time, his ministers and his counsellors. But in spite of their great position which permitted them to live in luxury equal only to that of the king, when they were in the presence of their master, they appeared as mere slaves. However important they might seem in the eyes of the common people, a great gulf separated them from Dingaan.

As a delicate mission carried out under difficult circumstances can only be perfectly fulfilled by one who has had a share in formulating the details and who thus understands them thoroughly, so had Dingaan, in adopting Tamboussa's plan, entrusted him to go to Pieters Mauritz Burg, bearing words of peace to the farmers, along with 200 superb head of cattle, a present by means of which Dingaan proposed to renew asurances of his good intentions and to gain time to pay his acknowledged debt of 19 000 cattle: oxen, cows and calves. 'Go,' he said, 'speak for me and may success go with you.'

Men went on their knees before Tamboussa, but Tamboussa was humble before Dingaan and, as a faithful servant prepared to die in the service of his master, he set forth followed by Combezena, in spite of rumours of war. He soon stood before the council of farmers.

Dingaan's actions were judged to be delaying tactics, disguising hostile intentions. The cattle were hastily accepted, not as a gift, but in part payment of a debt. Tamboussa pleaded, at length and eloquently, the cause which he had come to defend. But arrangements had already been made, orders had been given. Each day's delay increased the possibility of an adverse change in circumstances and so action must be taken. Tamboussa's eloquence was not rewarded with success. On the contrary, it proved to be his downfall, and for the following reasons.

Panda, whose presence was required to furnish the necessary details, found himself admitted to a seat on the council. Tamboussa, who sought to win favour for the views of his master, spoke too much in support of Dingaan. Panda had great difficulty in disguising his resentment. Furious, he arose and attacked Tamboussa ruthlessly, accusing him of having instigated the massacres of UngunKuncklove[1] and of Boschjesmans Rivier, promising to provide a thousand proofs of these accusations if required to do so.

Tamboussa countered his adversary's fury with cold impassivity. 'I do not see it as my duty to reply to such an accusation. Dingaan, my master, has charged me with a commission which it is my first duty to fulfil. I would not neglect my master's business to attend to my own.' They did not take into account the dignity of his reply or the nobility of his silence. Neither did they respect his office as envoy, whatever Tamboussa himself was, or might have been.

Without more ado, he and his assistant were clapped in irons. Tied together in a state of complete nakedness, they were relegated to a dank place, whence they were brought only when the commando moved on. Then great was their joy when they saw the sun again, that star which naked men love for its warmth. They walked under escort although Tamboussa would not have attempted to escape: he was too great, too noble a man to resort to such paltry means.

When the torrential rains came and the cold set in, their shelter was beneath a wagon. It is true that I myself had no other, but I was dressed in woollen clothes. Poor devils, their only protection was the skin which their creator had given them. The wind lashed their ribs, they shivered continually, their teeth chattered, their limbs stiffened, but they bore their torture nobly, and no word of complaint escaped their lips.

It was in this condition that they appeared, not to be judged but to hear sentence passed against them. It will suffice here to quote the words of Paul Zietsman, who acted as secretary to Pretorius. The latter could not write, so the former had been charged with keeping the journal of the expedition.

1 The great elephant, name of Dingaan's capital.

On 31 January 1840, the resolution was taken to decide the fate of the prisoner Tamboussa, former counsellor of Dingaan, and of a lesser chief called Combezena, also a prisoner. A council was convened, before which Panda and other headmen were called to give evidence. All stated that they had previously resided in the vicinity of the Amazoulou capital at the time that Tamboussa was in power; that they had witnessed his deeds; that they could swear a solemn oath before the omniscient God of the white man, before the sun, before the present assembly, and before the whole world, that all the bloody deeds of Dingaan were perpetrated with the concurrence, and on the advice, of Tamboussa; that upon the flimsiest of pretexts, he had incited the monster to destroy this or that *mouzi*, not sparing even the women and children; that it was also due to his influence that Retief and his companions had been assassinated; that it was this same influence which had determined the subsequent massacre of the emigrants' women and children, who had been left defenceless.

Panda added that, as a result of the intriguing of the prisoner he himself had been seized and dragged to the place of execution, where he was to have been put to death, and that he had been saved only by the intercession of his influential mother, the stepmother of Dingaan.

The prisoner, called upon to defend himself, admitted to the truth of all these accusations, as well as to the justice of the fate which awaited him; nobly adding that, although he was prepared to pay with his life for his numerous crimes, Combezena, his companion in captivity, was innocent and did not deserve to die. Panda, however, hastened to counter these words by saying that Combezena had been a principal instigator in the atrocities committed by Dingaan, and had communicated false reports with the object of winning the king's favour.

The commander-in-chief, on the advice of the court martial, then saw fit to pass the terrible sentence of death on the two prisoners. He impressed upon them the two-fold dread of their situation, for after having suffered earthly sentence, they would appear before another judge, but that they could avoid eternal suffering if they would confess their crimes before him, and humbly beg his pardon. A few hours later, the prisoners were led away, and the justice of man was satisfied.[1]

I was present at this trial, and I must add that, although pressed to do so, Tamboussa had nothing to say in his own defence. He

1 *Natal*, a reprint by John Centlivres Chase, Graham's-Town 1853.

spoke only to confirm the innocence of his companion — a proof of selflessness and admirable disinterest at such a moment. When Pretorius spoke to him of God, *Kos-Pezou*, the Master in heaven, and the eternal suffering which he could avoid by taking action hitherto unknown to him, Tamboussa replied that he had only one master, that his duty was to remain faithful to him and that the Master in heaven, if there were one, could not fail to be grateful to him for having performed this duty.

When the two prisoners arrived at the place of execution, they were still tied together. Two farmers who had been delegated to form a firing squad stood sixty paces away. When the shots went off, both prisoners fell. Combezena died instantly but Tamboussa was only wounded in the body. Then, as calmly as ever, and in spite of his suffering, he arose and stood steadfastly facing the guns, until the second round of shots rang out and he fell to the ground. These men know how to die, I thought, and I went away full of admiration, but a prey to a thousand regrets, for this act of Boer justice seemed to me despicable.

That same day, we crossed the Omphilos-Omschlopu, the white river. Dingaan's capital stood some distance to the east of the point at which we crossed. This river meets the Omphilos-Mouniama, the black river, eighteen leagues from the sea and, now called the Omphilozie, they flow together towards the Bay of Saint Lucia. On naval maps, the Omphilozie of the Amazoulous is shown as the Saint Lucia river. These rivers, Omschlopu and Mouniama, after rising in the mountains of Quathlambène, water a vast stretch of barren country and then, half way to the sea, they enter a wooded region which abounds in game of all kinds. Their course now meanders round the many obstacles which stand in their way. I spent part of 1841 and 1842 near the confluence in the forests, hunting big game, principally elephant, which I shall refer to more fully at a later stage.

Omphilos-Omschlopu has a distinctive sandy bed from which it derives the name white river. In contrast, the bed of Omphilos-Mouniama, although only a short distance away, is strewn in many places with round blackish stones, which give the impression of darkening the colour of the water, thus explaining the name black river.

Along the way, our patrols encountered a dozen Cafres who were not wearing the identifying marks of the partisans of Panda, which consisted of two thongs of white skin, suspended from the neck and hanging down over the back and the chest. The Boers asked no questions and showed no mercy.

We set up camp in a pretty valley, where we were beseiged all night long by a heavy storm. On 1 February we resumed our journey.

114

At eleven o'clock that morning we received information that a great number of cattle, herded by Cafres, had been discovered in the neighbourhood. A hundred and fifty horsemen were immediately despatched to seize the cattle, and we set up camp on the spot. Shortly afterwards we learnt of the rout of Dingaan's forces, one whole regiment of which had been completely destroyed. Schlala had been run through with an assegai. As we wished to be quite certain of the good news, we sent out a man to confirm it. Isaac Niewkerk was entrusted with the commission. He accepted all the more willingly as a couple of bottles of brandy had been secretly slipped into his saddle bags.

The 2nd of February was spent in acts of piety: the Bible was read and hymns were sung. But this religious sound was soon augmented by a much more agreeable one, a noise which is irresistably attractive to the South African ear; the lowing of 3 000 oxen and cows. Need I tell you that the voice of the preacher went unheard, that the hymn-singing stopped as if by magic? Elbowing each other out of the way as they abandoned their overturned Bibles, the pious congregation rushed to welcome the new arrivals, the true objects of their veneration.

They were tireless in their admiration of the plump and shiny beasts whose combined mass offered us the spectacle of a delightful medley of variegated colours — white, blue, black, yellow and red. And I, fresh from Europe, mocked at these men with their predilection, their affinity, their love, their passion even, for these beasts. I searched for an explanation, but failing to find one, I chose to attribute the attraction to similarity of character. Perhaps I was not entirely mistaken, but I now admit that I was not entirely right either.

Later, when we had travelled many miles together, I came to know these oxen better and then I too shared with the South Africans their love for these obedient, patient, devoted companions. Lonely as I was, and surrounded by men of uncertain temperament, my true friends, my most faithful servants, were my oxen.

And so when the epidemic of the Sogoupana mountains, or some say it was the flies, took them from me, down to the very last one; when Bloem, who had eaten from my hand, breathed his last, when Holland and Bister-Weld lay down, never to rise again, these my two favourite lead oxen, the most careful, intelligent, surefooted of all the bovine race; then my heart broke and I wept bitter tears. And it was not, as you might believe, from selfish concern at the loss of their services, or the prospect of three months forced imprisonment in the desert; it was their going, their pitiful end which filled my heart with sadness, and I would willingly have forfeited my collections and even my projected expeditions to have had it otherwise.

Although I had for some time been a critical observer of this susceptibility on the part of the Boers, I can nevertheless recall an occasion on which I was moved to pity by the plight of a farmer whose wife was seriously ill. He had come a long way and had been delayed with his wagon and oxen for two hours in front of a shop. 'My wife is ill,' he said in answer to queries. 'Very ill, it is true; perhaps she will even die, although she does not want for care. But just look at my oxen, Mister, my poor oxen; it is their sorry state, their thinness, their wretched condition, which concerns me most. They have worked so hard, they are so good, so disciplined, so brave!' 'That's right,' came the reply, 'they have not the guile to deceive you, that is why you love them and even prefer them.' 'That's just it, Mister, you have spoken a true word,' said the farmer with tears in his eyes.

And if I was at that time foolish enough to shrug my shoulders contemptuously, it was because I did not yet know the qualities of the ox or of the South African Dutch woman. My God what oxen! Alas! what women! The first deserve to be much more highly praised, the second much less so.

We soon received confirmation of the news of Dingaan's defeat from the spies of Job, our ally. There was evidence that, as he fled, the despot had been stopped in his tracks by a swollen river. Niewkerk returned that same evening; he had come upon the enemy forces resting after their exertions on the other side of a ravine; he had even almost stumbled into Schlala's camp. But although Dingaan's forces had not yet conceded defeat, they were nevertheless in no condition to fight with any expectation of victory. One thousand of his warriors had fallen and, although the advantage was clearly Panda's, Isaac Niewkerk observed no fewer than 1 200 wounded men in the camp of Nonglas, whose full complement was reckoned at 5 000 men at arms.

On the 3rd the commandant gave out the order that every man who was still in possession of a horse should make preparations for departure, which was fixed for seven o'clock. This meant that, had we not lost any horses, every man would have taken part in the expedition -- unbelievable tactics and further evidence of Pretorius' strange conception of strategy!

Accordingly, 210 men set forth. Although I was expected to remain behind because of the state of my health, I tried several times to bribe some horseman to lend me his mount so that I might take his place in the expeditionary force. My proposition, to my great regret, was repeatedly rejected for every man feared losing his share of the anticipated booty.

What a strange sight these men made, setting off in the greatest confusion, riding up the hills in disorderly fashion, their long guns

116

slung clumsily over one shoulder. No distinction was made between the dress of commandant or veld-cornet, corporal or simple horseman, and there was no formality in the execution of orders — orders which no one was inclined to issue because no one bothered to obey.

When they had ridden for an hour, a spy came to inform the Boers that their arrival had sent a contingent of Amazoulous scurrying from a hilltop where they had taken up their position.

Commandant Lombaart immediately set off in pursuit at the head of a troop of 25 men mounted on fast horses, while the rest followed as rapidly as the difficult terrain would allow. Fortunately for the enemy who, as they were on foot, would soon have been overtaken, a thick mist came down over the surrounding mountains and gorges, which enabled them to escape unseen and to hide between the rocks and in the caves which characterise this part of the mountain. Although several Boers approached closely enough to hear them calling to each other, the detachment of twenty-five returned that evening after a fruitless search.

On the 4th they continued to move in a north-easterly direction. This day was not distinguished by any incident. On the 5th, our 250 men rode all day until nightfall, in the hope of overtaking the fleeing enemy. They encountered nothing but difficulty in negotiating the country, which was littered with rocky outcrops and intersected by the valleys of a thousand meandering streams. They camped at the foot of a mountain on muddy ground, taking the precaution of forming a circle about them with their saddled horses in case of a surprise attack.

At sunrise on the 6th the journey was resumed and continued in the same direction for some distance until, finding no trace of the enemy, our men turned towards the east and soon afterwards received information that a party of Amazoulous had entrenched themselves at the top of a steep and inaccessible mountain. The place was surrounded and the commander-in-chief announced through an interpreter to those who had sought refuge in the mountain caves, that their lives would be spared if they gave up their arms and surrendered. However, as there was no response, Commandant Lombaard, in charge of twenty-five men, received orders to advance on the natural fortress and to shoot all the men but to spare the women and children. The order to advance was courageously carried out in spite of difficulties caused by the boulders which blocked the approaches. Three of the leading Amazoulous have been shot dead, the rest cried out for mercy. Immediately the firing ceased, and the men came out bringing with them fifty women and a number of children, who were all taken and kindly treated. But two hours later when, with one accord the warriors attempted to escape to the

117

nearby caves, they were shot down, more rapidly than they could ever have anticipated.

The manner in which the Boers behaved on this occasion intrigued their Amazoulou allies who were both admiring and disapproving. More than one spoke scornfully of the style of warfare practised by the white man. 'What?' said Nonglas, 'after forcing them to abandon such a difficult position, you spare their lives. This is not war, this is not profiting by your advantages. In war one must kill many, all if possible.'

At about three o'clock heavy rain, which seemed likely to set in, forced the Boers to make a halt. An abandoned kraal served to shelter them, the open grain pits providing an abundance of maize on which they feasted and amply satisfied their hunger.

It was here that Nonglas, with two Amazoulous, awaited the arrival of Commandant Pretorius in order to intercede on behalf of two chiefs called Kouana and Maputa who were described as being senior headmen of Dingaan. It was said that they had for some time been determined to rebel but that no opportunity had arisen until the recent battle between Dingaan and Panda. Their present wish was to join forces with the white man.

Pretorius, in his reply, assured Kouana and Maputa that he was sympathetic to their wishes; however, he charged them to appear in person the following day and to surrender themselves formally. In order that they might understand something of the ways of the white man, the envoys were invited to enquire of Panda himself the manner of his treatment, to which the chief replied by describing in flattering terms the advantages which he enjoyed in his present situation, a state which contrasted singularly with the servility in which he had lived under Dingaan, whom he could approach only by crawling like a dog.

On the 8th the party reached the Om-Pongola[1] river, the banks of which were covered with mimosa trees. From the top of a steep rock, it is possible, with the aid of a telescope, to follow the course of the river. To the south, the country is excessively furrowed by ravines and covered in rough, steep, ironstone hillocks. To the north, in contrast, the land appears to extend in an open plain for as far as twelve miles beyond the banks of the river.

No precise information could be obtained concerning Dingaan. It was learned that he had crossed the Om-Pongola five days previously with some of his wives and a few herdsmen; there was no doubt that he had fled the country. Some said that he had with him no more than a hundred men capable of bearing arms; that his cowardly flight had so incensed his people that even those who had

1 River of the gnu.

once been his most faithful followers, had sworn to tear him to pieces if ever he chanced to fall into their hands.

Reassured that the forces of Dingaan had been dispersed, and concerned about the ravages of sickness among the horses, the Boers decided to turn back. Pretorius, on leaving Nonglas to watch over the banks of the Om-Pongola, made him promise to send the swiftest of his runners in the event of his hearing any news of Dingaan, adding that, should the occasion arise, he Pretorius, would immediately dispatch a hundred horsemen with the intention of taking alive, if possible, the monster whose capture would be the occasion of so much rejoicing. Once these measures had been taken, the commando set out for Om-Philos-Mouniama, driving before them a herd of 10 000 oxen and cows.

They arrived back at the camp on the evening of the 9th. It was a Sunday but, because of the incessant rain which had been falling since the 5th, it was not possible to congregate in any numbers for divine service. However, several tents were transformed into places of worship and thanks were offered up to the Almighty for the successes which had been won.

On the 10th Pretorius complimented Panda on his conduct throughout the campaign. He congratulated him warmly on the victories of the valiant Nonglas; he endeavoured to persuade the Cafre king and his assembled officers that the white men did not attribute the successful outcome of the war to their own strength alone but to the higher providence of which they had merely been the instrument used to punish Dingaan for his infamous deeds.

Turning to Panda once more, he told him that he recognised the justice of his claims to the seat of power left vacant by the flight of Dingaan; that in consequence, he designated and recognised Panda as chief of the Amazoulou people and that he acted by virtue of the authority conferred on him by the council of the people sitting at Pieters Mauritz Burg; that henceforth Panda would be considered their principal ally; that his enemies would be treated as though they were also the enemies of the Boers but that he would not be permitted to wage war on other tribes without having previously asked and obtained permission, a request which should be accompanied by a statement of underlying causes; that in the event of his claims proving to be just, an adequate force composed of mounted Boers, would be put at his disposal.

Panda did not hesitate to accept the proposals of the council and replied in fitting terms: 'I solemnly swear,' said he, 'by all that exists, that I will forever remain loyal to you and to your government and that, should it come to my knowledge that you have been attacked, I engage to put at your disposal immediately all my forces which, in the interests of your cause, will be sacrificed to the last man, if you so require.'

At that time Panda was reckoned to have a force of 10 000 chosen warriors but I beg to query that number for I was subsequently in a position to establish with greater accuracy the number of able bodied men capable of bearing arms, either in attack or in defence. Forty thousand warriors, including the *abafanas*, young men under eighteen, made up the total of the Amazoulou forces. Only 20 000 would be available to go into the field, the rest being required to protect the women and children as well as the herds which, because of their great numbers, required the attention of half the active population.

On the 11th, two messengers arrived from Nonglas to report that he had found it impossible to discover any news of Dingaan and, as there were no herds in the area under his observation, he asked permission to leave. His request was received just as we were resolving to hasten our return to Pieters Mauritz Burg because of the sickness which daily claimed numerous victims among our horses.

On the 12th, a young Hottentot boy was deliberately shot dead by another child of his own age. As the council did not deem itself competent to judge the accused, the latter was simply sent back under escort to the authorities at Pieters Mauritz Burg.

On the 14th, the commander-in-chief, having ordered the colours of the young republic to be shown, instructed that a public proclamation should be read, announcing the extension of the territory's boundaries to the north. The strip of land thus annexed stretched from the Touguela to the Om-Philos-Mouniama, with the added inclusion of the Bay of Saint Lucia. He tried every means of drawing attention to this acquistion of land, but little interest was aroused. Nobody applauded it and nobody contested it because it was, at least for the moment, one of those inoffensive moves which, in themselves, are neither good nor bad. In any case, the Boers were doing no more than imitating what the English had done.

May I question the justice of such procedures? Each time that they discovered a land hitherto unknown to them, European navigators unhesitatingly took possession of it in the name of their sovereign, secure in the knowledge of the military superiority of the nation which they represented over the newly-discovered people. The principal objective of this precautionary measure was to avoid the rival claims of any other sovereign and, taking no thought of the likelihood of colonization, these pretenders baptized the newly acquired territory which, from that time forth, formed part of the crown lands. By what right did the newcomers seize the inhabited country? The right of might and nothing more. When one attempted to explain these motives to the natives, they simply laughed. Unable to take the matter seriously, they laughed at the foolishness of the Europeans. They laughed as we would laugh if a Chinese junk arrived to take possession of France in the name of the Celestial Emperor; we would consider it a matter for great mirth, and this is just what the natives did.

The situation here was exactly similar. The land was not virgin, it was inhabited by a numerous population and the Boers had not the strength of numbers to occupy and defend a territory of this extent when they already had a vast land which they did not know how to use. Far from needing to provide for superfluous numbers of people, their difficulties lay in too sparse a population, for Natal, as it was originally delineated, could support 8 million inhabitants, while the actual number of both blacks and whites together totalled barely 45 000, scattered over the entire area.

Not only was it unjust to take possession of this land, which in any case Panda had no right to dispose of in favour of the Boers, but there was no need to do so. Furthermore, the annexation placed an unnecessary additional burden on the Boers; and finally the measure was simply bad politics which gave a wrong example to the Cafres who saw in it the triumph of greed and covetousness. In fact, however, no occupation was ever attempted; a wise decision which quite justly made a mockery of the famous proclamation of Pretorius.

The man who had been appointed to keep the journal of the expedition took great care to record the text of this document and had no trepidation in noting with complete gravity: 'Afterwards, a salute was fired in honour of the council of the people; and a great cheer went up from the entire army; then all the men cried with one voice: "Thanks be to God by whose grace the victory has been given".' Can you picture this army composed of 436 men; can you imagine the voice of such an army, and the victory which such an army might win, even with the help of God? I must have facts if I am to be convinced, but I can find none here to suggest a victory worthy of a *Te Deum*. I can only humbly say that I took part in this war which ended without a single battle having been fought at which white men were present.

On the 15th, rain delayed us all day and in order to pass the time, I occupied myself in writing down a few notes and observations. I was employed in this manner when a farmer interrupted me to enquire bluntly what my intentions were. When I answered him sharply but honestly, he continued, 'But have you permission from the commandant? I doubt that he would give it you, because only one man should be permitted to write down what is happening. If there are two, one will describe as white what the other calls black, and this cannot fail to do harm to our community.'

I advised my friend to lodge a complaint against me if he wished, but he did not do so; if he had done, I would not have been much surprised to have been forbidden to take up my pen again. A singular conception of freedom! In the main, the Boers have not the sense of justice required to comprehend the word *liberty* as we understand it in Europe.

On the 16th, despite the fact that it was a Sunday, we struck camp at about 11 o'clock after the performance of religious observances. I was due to travel that day in the wagon of an Englishman called Hamilton, who had celebrated Saturday evening in the company of two bottles of brandy which alas, were empty on the sabbath. His servants, who had been chastised in proportion to his alcoholic irritation, had made off, and both domestics and oxen failed to answer the roll-call prior to departure.

Although we were obviously in difficulties, the entire commando set off without offering us any assistance. We had been waiting for two hours, lonely and abandoned in our wagon without any oxen when, to complete our despair, torrential rain began to fall. When it finally began to clear, we noticed numerous Amazoulou Cafres coming down the mountainsides and emerging from the bushes where they had been hiding. These men were converging from all directions and were on their way back to their *mouzis* to discover how much damage the Boers had inflicted. Some of them began rounding up the herds which had been carelessly abandoned in the open plains by our patrols. Our position was certainly not a happy one; they had reason to be most ill-disposed towards us and we had much to fear from their approach. Hamilton, not wishing to forsake his property under these circumstances, talked of settling down to spend the night, a proposition diametrically opposed to my wishes since, weak and unwell as I was, I had already resolved to set off on foot and overtake the rest of the commando, however far they had gone.

Fortunately our oxen were returned to us by a passing patrol and our difficult situation was relieved. We travelled on in a desultory fashion until nightfall when we discovered that for more than an hour we had been going in the wrong direction. We eventually found our way back to join the Boers by following the smoke from their fires.

Along the way we found lying on the ground a number of Cafres who had been killed by our people. I very much wanted to collect their heads, but the reluctance of my companion to accommodate such luggage in his wagon, added to the distaste which I myself felt for such work, prevented me from taking advantage of a rare opportunity.

Early on the 17th, a council of war was called to judge the conduct of the principal Cafre chiefs in our employ. Nonglas came first. It was agreed that he had behaved with discernment, prudence and courage; he was highly praised for his loyalty and his devotion. Job's son and Matouana next presented themselves. They were accused of having misappropriated a great number of cattle. Witnesses gave evidence in support of these allegations and added that these two chiefs, encountering opposition among some Makatisses, had seized them and had released them only after cutting off their lips and their noses. As a consequence, the two chiefs were to be put in irons and taken to Pieters Mauritz Burg where their fate would be decided.

The son of Job, on hearing this decision, immediately hastened to address a request to his father to send back several thousand head of stolen cattle. The request being fulfilled a few days later, the Boers were persuaded to annul the decision of the council and set the two chiefs free.

That same day, we left Tamboussa Rivier on the banks of which the chief of that name had been shot, and we went on to camp for the night at Bloed Rivier. The incessant rains had made the roads muddy and difficult for the wagons to negotiate. When we learned that the Om-Siniaty was swollen and giving cause for alarm, we hastened our departure.

The next day, which was the 18th, at eight in the morning, we arrived at the ford on the banks of the river where the fast-flowing waters were five feet deep. There was general hesitation; most preferred not to attempt the crossing. But it had to be done, and for the first and last time, Commandant Pretorius set the example, driving with the aid of a great whip. It was gratifying to watch this bold venture. The lead oxen, firmly guided by horsemen to keep them from faltering, flung themselves into the stream, their heads alone appearing above the water; the wagon followed, bumping noisily over the stones. The noise ceased abruptly and the wagon disappeared except for two and a half feet of canvas tent; and then finally there was only the sound of the foaming current swirling about the bodies of the snorting oxen, the sharp crack of the whip and the terrifying yells which, according to the farmers will encourage even the most water-shy ox. On our side of the river, we were all watching anxiously. There was a certain bravado about the scene; the lives of the oxen were endangered; and if the first wagon failed, the rest of us were going to be obliged to wait until the water subsided, which might take a week or perhaps even as much as twelve. And so we prayed more for this wagon than for those that were to follow. By good fortune, the sound of its wheels rang out once more as they touched the stony river bed on the other side; it climbed, or rather scaled, the steep slope and took up its position proudly on the high ground, inviting us to follow suit.

The other wagons accepted the challenge, some successfully, while others were not so fortunate. Three wagons, whose teams had drowned, obstructed the main ford and instead of first clearing the passage, eight wagons, including the one in which I was travelling, were caught up in midstream. There was indeed great difficulty in effecting a crossing in five feet of water. The oxen were forced to swim as they dragged the wagon over the river bed. We lost about sixty oxen, our munitions and our dry provisions but in spite of everything, the operation was a success. I lost most of my goods including some collections which I particularly regretted.

On the 19th, we crossed the little river where I had found a deposit of coal. The weather was growing appreciably cooler and made us apprehensive of the following day's journey which was to take us a long way over the muddy mountains sometimes called Waater Berg or Moeder Berg, water mountain, muddy mountain, because of the water and the mud which are encountered there, or else are known by the happier name Honing Berg, mountains of honey.

On the 20th, we began the ascent into these mountains, where we were faced with obstacles which would have deterred all but the South African wagon driver. The journey was slow, long and painful. The cold was intense and, although we were clothed, we suffered acutely; what then must have been the suffering of the young Cafre apprentices who were naked? Four of them died that day and yet there was no snow, although the wind, which was from the south-east, was bitingly cold.

On the 21st, we crossed yet another river in the bed of which a layer of coal was evident, and when I pointed this out to a companion, he informed me that there was copper to be found not far from the mountain we had crossed the previous day, but I cannot confirm this.

On the 22nd, we reached Klip Rivier where several of our Cafres were beaten with the *chambock*.[1] In order to avoid serious accident, they were advised to lie flat so that, as the blows were dealt, the tip of the terrible eight-foot long lash would bite into the ground, otherwise this fine extremity, which was as thick as a finger and as flexible as a rope, would penetrate deeply into the flesh as it flicked around the body, or would split open the stomach, even if the blows were not particularly heavy.

Each man received his dozen cuts, writhing and twisting like an eel in a frying pan and then stood up, his forehead bathed in sweat, without complaining too much about the weight of the blows. I realised that these naked bodies are much more capable than ours of withstanding suffering and that, while we grit our teeth with pain,

---

1 Lash made of hippopotamus hide three metres long and used to punish the hindmost oxen.

they in similar circumstances simply laugh.

On the 23rd we learnt that the Touguela was swollen by the rains and that the crossing would present great difficulties. A horseman coming from Pieters Mauritz Burg with dispatches had almost drowned, along with his horse. However, as the level of the water was rapidly subsiding we were able to cross on the evening of the 21st.

On the 25th, as a result of communications with people from the capital, a few loaves of bread made their appearance to gladden our eyes. I accepted a piece out of curiosity and did not waste time in looking at it; but although the slice was very thin, my stomach would not accept it. I found it too dry, too bitter and too difficult to digest and to my great surprise, I experienced acute stomach pains which caused me to suffer all day long.

On the 26th, 27th, 28th and 29th we journeyed on towards Pieters Mauritz Burg without any untoward incident. On the 30th, weary of my companion's slow pace and reckoning that I could reach the capital on foot that same day, I left the wagon at half past six taking as provisions only a slice of grilled meat. Six leagues separated me from the Om-Guinée and from there it was six leagues further to Pieters Mauritz Burg. For an invalid, unable to stomach food, the way was long, but I had so strong a desire to reach a town where I could find the things I needed for my condition, that I took no heed of advice or remonstrance.

When I had been walking for a while, I encountered some of Job's Cafres who were taking beer to their master. This Job was a rather powerful Cafre, and I could pass as powerful too, with a little deception. Did I not belong to that section of South African society which crowns kings? On this occasion, goaded on by thirst, I resorted to moral pressure, and soon the precious little pot of beer was laid at my feet. I did with it what you would have done in my place; neither hunger nor thirst will spare the elements which can satisfy them; I would have drunk water if these Cafres had been carrying it.

However, when the thing was done, the Cafre who was in charge of the brew, said to me, 'Do you know, master, that you have just drunk the beer of Job, my master?' To which I simply replied, 'It is true and I know it. Job is your master and this beer is his; but are we whites not the masters of Job, your master? If Job had been in my place and feeling thirsty, he would have drunk this beer; but he was not; it is I who was here, and what he would have done, I have done; he could not take it amiss.'

Then this Cafre demanded further explanations, and to be rid of him I said, 'You will tell your master that a white man who loves him well has drunk his beer, firstly because this white man loves Job and secondly because he loves Job's beer.' And after delivering so persuasive a speech, I went on my way, very pleased with my Cafre-like eloquence, which I had probably discovered at the bottom of the beer pot.

At about midday, I reached the upper ford on the Om-Guinée, a mile or two from the beautiful waterfall and made the crossing in water three and a half feet deep, flowing over the large boulders which are the terror of wagon drivers. On reaching the other side, I found several wagons with the oxen unyoked. I was received like a pariah and considered myself fortunate to be given permission to dip .into the enormous cooking-pot for a copious portion of that delicious broth which the Boers throw away when they have eaten the meat, a South African custom which the French cannot comprehend; but which at the time I was too grateful to criticise.

Immediately after leaving my ferocious looking hosts, I began the ascent, which was to last several hours, of the mountain range which separates the Om-Guinée from Pieters Mauritz Burg. Although the heat was intense, there was nothing for it but to press on. Eventually I came to a fork in the road, the two branches of which were equally rutted; I hesitated at first and then made up my mind to take the road to the right; this was the wrong decision.

However, as this road was bound to lead somewhere, I was not unduly worried until, after I had been walking for an hour, the sky which had been burning hot, suddenly clouded over in less than ten minutes. The change was rapid and I welcomed the first raindrops with joy. The thunder rumbled and rolled, the lightning played over the nearby mountaintops; the explosive and liquid elements brought me exquisite pleasure. I had been very hot up there in the mountains where water is only to be found at the bottom of deep gorges. Had I gone down to find it, my thirst would certainly have doubled by the time I had climbed out again. And so naturally, I was pleased to see the rain, but my happiness was of short duration and I soon passed from one extreme of emotion to the other. A few minutes of rain were enough to soak me to the skin and then I longed for the sun to dry me again. We human beings, with our feeble constitutions, must have moderation in all things.

I was obliged, because of the wet slippery ground, to remove my boots and to walk in the grass which grew beside the road. For half an hour I had been deafened by the thunder which crackled around me, accompanied by a rapid succession of lightning flashes. Trees were being struck down before my very eyes; and this was beginning to cause me some alarm, when suddenly I found myself hurled to the ground, probably as a result of a thunderbolt which struck the earth fifteen paces away. I felt nothing and got to my feet immediately, but the moment I tried to walk, my left leg refused to move, the back of the knee had stiffened and the muscles appeared to have shortened. It was only with much difficulty that I was able to hobble on my way, although an hour later the limb had returned to normal. The rain was falling in torrents and I could discover nothing of my surroundings except the road in front of me which appeared to have narrowed and which showed absolutely no trace of wheel ruts, leading me to believe that I had gone astray. At last, just as I realised that I was on the brow of a hill, with the land dropping away steeply to left and to right, a breeze sprang up and cleared the air, revealing a most picturesque landscape down below. Against a background of forest, stood the *mouzis* of the Boschjesmans-Cafres, composed of hemispherical huts arranged in a circle in the manner of all Cafre huts, while farther off was a cluster of square houses belonging to the whites; it was Duplessis' camp. Once I was certain of this, I had no difficulty in establishing in which direction Pieters Mauritz Burg lay and I arrived there shortly before nightfall.

Although the place was, at that time, very wretched, I was overjoyed to find myself there once more. For, to tell the truth, I had been in such poor health during the first fortnight of the commando that several of the Boers believed that I would perish during the course of the expedition. One of these farmers was even kind enough to console me: 'If you die here my friend,' he said to me, 'rest assured that the nearest mountain or river will bear your name; it will be Franchemans Berg or Franchemans Rivier.' As I was, at that time, the only Frenchman in the territory of Natal, no one enquired my real name. I was simply known everywhere as the Frenchman. I consider myself fortunate today that not one mountain or hill, not one river or stream, is named after me.

Two days after my return to Pieters Mauritz Burg, every man who had taken part in the commando was requested to present himself at a given place to receive his part of the booty. Being ill, I cared but little and I delegated to represent me, a man whom I believed to be of good faith. This man, on my behalf, collected the cattle which were mine by right, but cunning like all the Boers, he made off with them and I never saw so much as their horns. It is true that I attached no value to them, but I could have wished them put to better use, and I regretted that a scoundrel had made off with what might have been of use to some poor devil. Twenty head of cattle at that time were worth only £20 sterling, or 250 francs, but they could have provided some family with a measure of comfort.

CHAPTER XI

I find a temporary lodging at the bay of Port Natal — The *rooye-book* — Some observations on the habitat of animals of different species — Habits of the *rooye-book* — Snakes — Boa pythons — Poisonous varieties

Some days later I returned to the bay where I had the opportunity of acquiring a pleasant dwelling, perfectly situated for the work in which I was engaged. My health, however, showed no signs of improvement and the situation of my dwelling was more harmful than beneficial. I tried not to be deterred by this and continued to pursue my researches into natural history although this was sometimes simply a matter of routine in which there was often an element of distaste. However, I was never discouraged; I continued tenacious and steadfast, perhaps for the first time in my life.

Hunting for small game close to my cottage had its attractions; there were birds and often, among them, species which I had never seen before. There were monkeys swinging from branch to branch, which in their audacity seemed to be taunting me in full view of the workroom where I was busy skinning their fellows. There were *rooye-booken*, *Cephalopus natalensis*, timid antelopes, which in their ignorance, came to sniff around my kitchen. There were *addidas*, *Ibis addidas*,[1] filling the air with their cries in the early morning and at twilight, and there were the calaos, *Buceros buccinator*, imitating the sound of the trumpet and looking like carnival characters.

More graceful, light and gay were the *Souimangas*, the amethyst sunbirds, like feathered butterflies, dipping their tongues into the calyx of the flowers of the *Caffer-Boom*, or of the wild hemp; then there were the butterflies themselves with their rich, bright colours, and the beetles of every shape and size. I was happy among all these living creatures and although I was alone, time passed all too quickly. Surrounded by these beautiful things how could I feel one moment of boredom? Was all this not a fruitful source of meditation? Was it not the life I had dreamed of since my earliest years? The *rooye-booken*, which I preferred to all other game, supplied me with meat, although I was first introduced to them by way of my scientific research. I wrote down what I was able to learn of their ways and I can do no better here than to transcribe what I noted at

1 *Addidas*: name given to this type of ibis because of its cry.

the end of June 1840.

But first of all let me digress. I do not know whether any other traveller has made the observation that I had occasion to make every time that I hunted in Africa, and which I shall elaborate upon here: I refer to the preference shown by every herbivorous animal for those localities which are rich in natural objects whose colouring perfectly matches the animals themselves. It is obvious that this instinctive precaution is intended to confuse their enemies and, in particular, man who hunts by sight alone.

As these objects such as tree trunks, or mounds of earth, or stone, cannot have been put there to serve the animals, apparently it is the animals which have chosen their surroundings. I conclude that certain antelope, considered today as creatures of the woods, could live equally well in the plains, if the plains had provided them with comparable means of concealing themselves.

In the woods frequented by the *Cephalopus natalensis* the earth puts forth a red clay which is carried by termites to the trunks of fallen trees to build their nests, and which matches the colour of the little animal's skin. I have frequently fired at the trunk of a tree, mistaking it for a *rooye-book*; I have often hesitated and allowed the *rooye-book* to escape because I mistook him for a tree trunk. Sometimes I was more fortunate and happened to kill the animal without being in any way sure that it was one.

In the plains or on the hills inhabited by the *Riet-Book, Reduncaeleotragus*,[1] at intervals of a hundred paces or so stand hemispherical mounds of earth made by large ants. These mounds have exactly the height, the shape and the colour of the recumbent *riet-book* so that the animal is distinguished only by its movements. One needs a good eye or even a spy glass if one wishes to avoid those errors which are so disappointing to the hunter and which I myself made on more than one occasion. After crawling on my stomach for 300 paces, my eyes were swimming in perspiration and I was panting but happy; I was nearly there, barely sixty paces separated me from my quarry. But when I raised my head, what did I find? A mound of grey earth, nothing more. It is this sort of hoax played by nature that one takes care not to recount to one's hunting companions, for their mocking laughter, though deserved, can sometimes be embarrassing.

In the land of the Amazoulous where elephants abound in the mimosa thickets, on the banks of the Om-philos-Mouniama and the Om-Schlopu, round black and grey stones, the size of an elephant,

1 *Riet-book*: antelope which frequents those places where long reeds grow. It is worth mentioning that the Boers on one hand and the Amazoulou Cafres on the other have given it exactly the same name, reed buck; *omschlango* in Amazoulou.

are often clustered together like a troop and from the hilltops we mistook them ten times over for the animals we were seeking. In the land of Massilicatzi, beyond the Makali mountains, on the banks of the Oury or Limpopo, we saw a number of giraffe; the first we saw were standing quite still and we mistook them for split trees, twenty feet high. At other times we mistook the broken trees, which are common in these parts, for giraffe, their height, colour and shape all conspiring to convince us. The elephant, the rhinoceros and the wild boar, all wallowing to their heart's content in the clayey drinking holes which are to be found everywhere in the forests, take on the local colour, with the result that one passes them by without realising that they are there.

It is true that those animals which are fleet of foot — the *Equus Burschellii*, the *Gazella albifrons*, the *Gazella euchore*, the *Catoblepas gnou*, the *Catoblepas gorgon*, the *Ant. melampus* — all live on the open plains which are bare of deceptive rocks and trees, for these animals need the open spaces where they can more easily take flight and the exception which they make to my theory does not disprove it.

I thought that it might be of interest to draw attention to the resourcefulness of nature, which protects one species at the expense of another. The *rooye-book* brought this to mind; let us return to him. In about June, the mating season of these antelope comes to an end; they begin to shed their hair and are more and more rarely seen together in pairs. This *Cephalopus* is to be found only in the forests which line the coasts of Natal from which it derives the name *natalensis*. It is not found in places where mimosas grow. The most common of the Natal gazelles, it is graceful and fleet of foot and very timid, with a highly developed sense of hearing. It is constantly on the alert and is thus rarely taken unawares in the depths of the forests. The thud of its hoofs is often heard, and the cracking of twigs as it passes, as well as the peculiar whistling of its nostrils. This whistling sound which belongs also to the *Coerulea*, seems to be a particular feature of the species;[1] it is a certain indication that the animal is fleeing, or is about to do so.

If it should happen that the hunter sees the buck before he himself is seen, he must take advantage of that moment of hesitation which I attribute to astonishment on the part of the animal, for after the first leap all is lost; the buck will instinctively put obstacles between itself and the hunter.

The most favourable time for hunting is when the sun is ten or fifteen degrees above the horizon; that is to say in the early morning or in the evening, when the animal breaks cover and can be found

---

1 The *riet-book* and various other species also make a slightly resonant sound through the nostrils, but I could not describe this as a nasal whistle.

grazing on the outskirts of the forest, most frequently within a radius of fifteen paces. It is recognisable from afar by its particular movements and its red colouring; the difficulty is to approach it, which can only be done by lying flat on the ground and dragging oneself along under protection of some isolated bush, always bearing in mind to keep down wind.

When he is hit, but not brought down by a shot, the *rooye-book* leaps ten paces, stops, gazes at the hunter as if he had not heard the shot or felt the wound. If he is mortally wounded he tries to defend himself with his sharp little horns and one must be on one's guard for he can use them to good effect. When he knows he is dying, he makes a plaintive little sound, like a cry for mercy; some say that he weeps. Rarely are both his horns intact; frequently one is broken and sometimes both; the damage is done when he is fleeing at great speed through the dense bush. Both sexes have horns. A single young is produced and the female is able to give birth once a year.

These animals live in isolation. The coat is fiery red in the adult, while in the younger animal the colour is deeper and mixed with brown. The skin is comparatively thick and the flesh, which is white, is delicious. These *rooye-booken*, which are a good deal hunted, have become quite rare over a period of four years. When I first arrived, I observed ten or fifteen in the area between Berea and Conguela, a distance of two miles, but by the time I left, there were only one or two; sometimes I saw none at all. The South Africans have a method of stalking these buck which I too have used to advantage and which it might be appropriate to mention here, although our European hunters will be sure to be amused.

When a serious hunter sets out to stalk an animal, *be kruyppen* the Dutch call it, he first of all removes his shoes and his trousers because the hardened soles of the shoes make a sharp sound on the dead branches, and the trousers pick up too many thorns; then he lies flat on the ground and creeps towards his prey. If he uses this method and exercises patience, his endeavours will be crowned with success.

As I was always ferreting about in the bush, it was not long before I made the acquaintance of those characters whom everybody would prefer to keep at a distance; I mean those famous pythons whose fearsome qualities are so much exaggerated by travellers.

It is true that all animals have an innate fear of even the smallest snake; instinct tells them that these hideous creatures, in spite of their insignificant size, are often mortally dangerous. Even man himself leaps aside when he sees one, before he has had time to think. But this does not mean that the non-poisonous varieties, whose only defence is their strength, should be greatly feared by man.

It is well known, or at least I imagine it is, that in general snakes do not attack man. All the poisonous as well as the non-poisonous varieties in southern Africa disappear as soon as a man approaches and one hears them slithering off through the dry grass. This happens at virtually every step along the way and it is a well known thing.

But there exist among the venomous snakes several species which move so slowly that they continually risk being trodden upon. To avoid this they often take shelter close to a bush, usually a thorn bush. If the snake is out of his hole looking for rats or some other little quadrupeds to eat, and he hears footsteps approaching, his first concern is to stiffen his muscles, to rise up, to puff out his neck, to open his mouth slightly, to flicker his forked tongue and to hiss, producing the sort of sound that a man might make expelling air from his throat and passing it over his palate.

Now the snake is ready to strike, and woe betide the careless passer-by, however innocent his intentions might be. The snake's body, which is all of a piece, without joint or limb, is a weapon — a bow, a rope, a poisoned arrow. Coiled in a spiral it becomes a powerful spring; the head flashes out, the mouth is opened wide and it bites — without much force it is true, but sinking the hollow, backward-sloping teeth into its victim This breed is truly dangerous.

The pythons are a very different matter. Nature has denied them poison but she has endowed them with bodies that are muscular, strong and agile and, even if their strength is excessive for the crushing of their habitual prey, the Natal python has never used this strength, as far as I know, to do harm to man. These reptiles feed chiefly on large moles, rock rabbits, river rats and birds. Their greatest crime is that they find their way into barns where there are sitting hens; they swallow the hen, or even the goose, or the muscovy duck and remain sitting on the eggs while they digest their prey, which is very unpleasant for the poultry farmer.

It sometimes happens that they find their way into a house, unbeknown to the inhabitants, settle down in the loft, and peacefully spend several days there, waiting for good fortune to send some rats or even a cat. I witnessed a surprising incident of this sort which took place in Mr Ferreira's house at Conguela. He had climbed up a ladder to search on top of the rush ceiling for some object which he knew to be there. The ladder was not high enough for him to be able to see what he was doing and so he groped about until his hand came in contact with something cold. He groped further and then he gave a sudden shudder. He jumped down crying, 'Snake'. It was a python eight or nine feet long which was quickly rendered harmless by a few blows with a stick. Mr and Mrs Ferreira had spent several nights under the strangest canopy imaginable.

This snake had certainly had every opportunity to do harm, but since he had not done so, one can assume that there is no danger in his proximity. The Cafres know this and they never kill him. In fact they regard him as a messenger from their 'dead brother',[1] and when one of these reptiles is seen in the *mouzi*, they believe that they must kill a cow to please this dead brother, whose body lies in the ground, even if they never had a brother at all.

It is a mistake then to fear the Natal pythons; one must simply remember that they are not venomous, that their bite is not mortal as their teeth are very fragile, and that the only real danger would be in their embrace, if one were careless enough to become ensnared in their coils. It is possible even to be quite bold when approaching them. This is what happened to me on two separate occasions.

It was 15 July 1840 at about ten o'clock in the morning. It was winter time; the days were fine and clear; the heat was no longer intense, men welcomed the sun's rays with pleasure and snakes were basking their cold bodies in the beneficent warmth, the only innocent pleasure at their disposal. I was busy following a bird and had to cross a sort of glade where *weld-calebasses-boom*[2] grew and where there were numerous ant-bear[3] holes. The bare earth was tufted with dry or burnt grass. Fifty paces away, near one of the ant-bear holes, under a tree, I saw something move; I took it to be a civet;[4] I moved rapidly towards it, just in time to see the tail of an enormous snake disappearing underground; and then, almost immediately afterwards, a second head appeared and followed after the disappearing tail; it was another python, no less large, which was also attempting to escape. My gun was loaded with double zero buckshot and I hit him a third of the way along his body. A leap brought me alongside him but I saw my hopes disappearing down the hole with his tail. In spite of the strong repugnance I have always felt in touching a live snake, I did not hesitate to seize him and to pit my weight against his strength. I held on without too much effort, considering all the while what I should do, and I thought I could succeed if I used some ingenuity. So I repeated my jerking of the tail. The animal held on tight inside his sandy hole. I was perspiring heavily but I did not intend to lose the fruit of my labours. I must have looked a comical sight as I tugged away in this ludicrous situation. Suddenly the scene changed; the sand fell inwards; the animal, deprived of its hold, shot out of the hole and I fell on my back. Can you picture me flat on the ground? Can you picture this snake,

---

1 The *dead brother* of the Amazoulous is a mythical being upon whom several superstitious beliefs are based. There is further mention of him in a later chapter on the customs of these people. This brother is nothing but an evil spirit invented by the *iniangas*, i.e. Cafre wizards — *inianga* means moon — who require this sacrifice to be made.
2 The wild calabash tree, *Strychnos spinosus*, which will be referred to again later.
3 Animals which live on ants and larvae.
4 Quadruped of a family closely related to the mongoose and the skunk.

thirteen foot long and twenty inches in circumference, bringing his head round to meet his tail to which I was holding fast, and with his mouth wide open, hissing at me and demanding that I let it go? But I got nimbly to my feet and dragging my reptile by the tail, I forced him to straighten out his body.

A stick which I found lying on the ground, helped me out of a difficult situation. I dropped the tail and picked up the stick. The python raised his head threateningly. With a blow I forced it down. I put my foot on the head and victoriously grasped my adversary by the neck. Then I dragged him along, trying to avoid the tail which was writhing about in an attempt to coil itself round my body. During this operation, I managed to undo my necktie with my left hand and knot it around the snake's neck; then, after fixing the other end to a strong low-hanging branch, I stood back and contemplated what some would call a monster, and what I too began to realise was an enormous animal; it was a full grown female weighing more than 150 pounds.

A few days later, I again had dealings with one of these creatures, and this is what I wrote down that day: On 24 July 1840, at about two o'clock in the afternoon, I was lying ill in bed when the two young Cafre servants of a half-caste neighbour came to inform me that their master had discovered a very large snake, and that he was watching over it until I should arrive. I took my gun and set off at a run to my neighbour's place. There I found two men gazing upwards at the top of a little tree, fifteen feet high and entwined with creepers, some of which were thorny. I had to look very hard to make out the body of the snake whose head they claimed to see. In fact all that I could see was a round dark shape.

Armed with a long pole, I tried to prod it and so dislodge it, for it was not possible to beat it. My attempts were in vain. I was just about to shoot it to save time, when I had the idea of climbing into a neighbouring tree. I managed this without any difficulty and had them pass me the pole which was unfortunately too long and heavy for my purpose; then I ventured on to a strong horizontal branch which led me to within two arms' length of the reptile, lying coiled and motionless. After reassuring myself that I could aim my blows at it without falling, I set to work beating it with the long pole, intending to make it move off. It raised its head, thrusting its neck forward, trying to get at me. Unable to fire at it because of its proximity, I succeeded in thrusting into its pink and white mouth the end of my stick which it grasped, but released again when it realised that the object was insensitive to the effects of its rage. I took advantage of this moment to withdraw, and as the snake advanced once more, some well aimed blows forced it back to its original position. I climbed down the tree without having gained the

134

least advantage, and with the assistance of my servants, I pelted the creature with bits of wood and wild fruit.

After half an hour of this activity, which tried the animal as much as it did us, the python raised its head, stretched itself out, grasped the tip of the branch which had supported me and coiled itself around it. A young Cafre armed with an axe climbed into the tree and in less than three minutes we heard the cracking of the branch which was as thick as two men and very long and horizontal. I calculated where it should fall to the earth so that I might seize the reptile before it realised what was happening and I was in such haste to reach the spot that the branch almost fell on my head. In spite of the difficulties, all went well; the surprised animal was pulled out alive and I seized it by the neck, to the great astonishment of my bastaards, who kept their distance; only one of them would consent, albeit reluctantly, to help me tie the animal to a piece of wood which served to transport it to the hut. 'Master,' he said to me, 'I would rather kill a lion than take hold of one of these gentleman alive, as you have just done; because even if they are dead, when you touch them, a shiver runs all over your body, right down to your bones.'

Preoccupied as I was with pythons, I did not expect to become immediately acquainted with the baser variety of reptile. Unfortunately for me, the next morning when I awoke, I became aware that I had been bitten on the right knee by a poisonous snake. Could it have happened the previous evening as I was walking through the thorn bush, without paying particular attention, or was it during the night in my bedroom? I could not say; the fact was that a black spot pinpointed the pain which soon became very intense. The swelling had increased the circumference of my right knee by four inches and seemed likely to burst the skin. As the fever reached its peak, there was a repetition of the pain in the groin; then came delirium during which I said some strange things. The worst of it was that I was absolutely alone, two miles from the nearest habitation, and I had been without servants for several days.

From time to time, I was visited by a German called Schulz, who claimed to be a doctor, but what is the use of a doctor without medicines? We discussed the matter at some length but this brought me no relief at all. I needed leeches and would have applied a hundred all at once but, as always happens when the need is greatest, the leeches were not to be found, for the high wind kept them out of reach at the bottom of the water. I would recommend to every traveller who intends venturing into a land where snakes are to be found, to provide himself with a pneumatic pump; this is simple to use and may prove to be of great advantage.

After nine days of atrocious and undiminished suffering suddenly, within two hours, the sickness left me as if by magic. The swelling subsided, leaving behind folds of wrinkled flesh. I had used no alkali, there was none to be had in Natal; I had at my disposal only pumpkin poultices which produced almost no effect whatsoever. I have often observed that, whatever the treatment in these cases, the duration of the affliction is always nine or ten days, the only difference being that, when volatile alkali is used, the swelling and the pain are considerably reduced. I believe I am right in attributing my wound to the *nacht-adder*[1] which is related to the *poff-adder*, although it is smaller; both belong to the family of vipers.

This experience confirmed me in my belief that only the poisonous varieties of snake deserve their terrible reputation, and that this terror is largely based on the fact that the pain they inflict is excessive, and that death would certainly ensue if the bite were to affect a vital part of the body, like the abdomen, the chest or the throat, particularly if the attack occurred during the mating season when the animal is at its most vigorous. I also began to think how unfortunate is was that the bad reputation, which is well deserved by some varieties, has led to all snakes being considered as undesirable. The result of this is that man ruthlessly kills every snake which he encounters, in spite of the fact that some species are very beautiful, very gentle, very interesting and perform services which are useful to him. I will mention just one of these, the one the Cafres call *ischlouzély*, which often lives in the hedge of thorns that surrounds the *mouzi*. It makes its way into the huts, nests in the household pots or baskets and spends the night under the same blanket, so to speak, as the naked people themselves, while not even the children, those little creatures who often take pleasure in doing cruel things, attempt to harm it. Because it hunts the rats which eat their grain, the people like to see the little snake about the house and regard it as a friend. The first one that I encountered ran the risk of being treated like all the others. Guessing my intentions, a black man explained to me that one did not kill that kind of snake. 'He will not run away', he said to me, 'go up to him and you will see.' Indeed, the snake moved only when I tried to touch him on the head; he made no attempt to bite or to escape. He was two and a half feet long and his colour was a mixture of yellow, brown and green.

The most dangerous reptiles, whose scientific names I do not know, are the *ring-hals-slange*, the necklace snake, the *spouwer slange*, the spitting snake, called *phesy* by the Cafres, endowed with the rare gift of spitting its venom from a distance of four paces into the enemy's eye which, according to the Cafres, swells up and finally bursts into glassy fragments; the *nacht-adder*, the snake of the night, the *poff-adder*, called *bloulou* by the Cafres, which is short,

1 Night adder.

stocky and slow and which jerks strongly backwards when it intends to strike; the *geele-slange* or *kooper-kaapel*, the yellow or hooded snake, with its rapid movements and acrid venom, fortunately a very rare species; the *boom-slange* or tree snake, which hypnotizes the birds, is grey-green in colour and nine feet long, an agile snake which seldom bothers man; and finally the one the Amazoulous call *memba* which has not yet been given a name by the Dutch and which is a metallic grey-brown in colour, between eleven and thirteen feet long, very slim and so agile that once, when my Cafre Boulandje and I were pursued by one of them, it moved as fast as we did, and would have caught us had we not thrown ourselves sideways into the grass which impeded its movements and slowed it down. This is the one that the Cafres most fear; they say that it does not attack the Achilles tendon or the knee like other snakes, but that it leaps up to reach the neck or the back. According to them, there is no hope of saving its victim.

CHAPTER XII

Since arriving in Natal, I had taken no part in any important
hunting expedition; to have done so would have required a considerable financial outlay on my part; I would have needed my own
servants and transport for thirty leagues into the interior. A hunting
expedition is no easy undertaking in a country where, if you want a
thing well done, you do it yourself. However, circumstances arose
which removed the major difficulties.

My neighbours, the bastaards, Elias and Piet Kotze, were preparing
to hunt hippopotamus in the Touguela. They had a wagon and two
teams but they lacked ammunition. Their only interest in hunting
these animals was to obtain the fat. I had a wagon and ammunition
but no oxen, no driver, no servants. My only interest was in the heads
and the skins. We needed each other and so it was a simple matter
to come to an agreement. In return for a payment of 50 rixdollars,[1]
they agreed to use their teams and to drive them, but as they were
also to help in the preparation of my specimens, I agreed to pay them
a fee of 25 rixdollars for each hippopotamus hide which we loaded
on to the wagons. It was further agreed that I would provide the
ammunition and that they were to have all the fat.

Satisfied with these conditions, which were very much to their
advantage, they promised me repeatedly that the expedition would
be successful. They said that, to please me, they would kill the
oldest hippopotamus, the grand old man of the river.

And so on 27 August 1840, at about four o'clock in the afternoon,
we set off with two wagons and were soon facing the difficult climb
up the Berea. Right at the start, we stuck fast in the sand, with the
oxen unable to pull us out and, in spite of my loud expressions of
displeasure, we were obliged to wait there until morning. The oxen

1 The Cape rixdollar is worth 1F 35c.

were tired, and the proof of this was that the next day, they pulled us out without any difficulty.

On the 30th we crossed the Om-Vooty[1] and had just passed some Cafres out hunting buffalo, when my wagon began to roll too rapidly down a slope, and my left-hand wheel ox broke his traces. The two wheels on the left side passed over his body so that we feared for his life, but to our great astonishment, when we were able to turn and look back, we saw him get up and attempt to follow us.

The weather was cold, it was raining, and the ground was wet and slippery; in spite of these difficulties, my companions, who were keen to reach the Touguela, insisted that we press on. We harnessed our oxen and began making our way painfully up the clayey slope. We were almost at the top when Elias' wagon, which was in the lead, swerved sharply and overturned, blocking the way.

To complete our wretchedness, a rain squall came up just as we were beginning the operation of righting the wagon and settling everything back into place. The work in the driving rain went on for two hours, during which time I noticed that one of the Cafres, who was called Om-Kopo, was nowhere to be seen; I discovered him at last, flattened out like a toad, under my wagon. His eyes were blood-shot and starting from his head, his black skin was turning dirty white and then ashen and his teeth were chattering so much that he was unable to speak. The only answer that he could make to my enquiries was a great shuddering of the head, which was sufficient indication of his complaint.

In fact the diagnosis was not difficult; Om-Kopo's only garment was his *motgeas*[2] which was composed of nothing more than five or six leather thongs so arranged as to preserve his modesty, and these had become saturated by the rain.

On this particular occasion I was travelling like a colonial governor; I had brought with me Cape wines and French brandy, thanks to which luxuries Om-Kopo was able to gulp down half a bottle of fortifying liquid which cheered him immensely.

How many times thereafter did I not receive expressions of his gratitude for the pleasurable inner warmth produced by the *tchouala ka aba loungo*,[3] how many times did he not call me *om-tagaty* for having poured new strength into him, just as his own was abandoning him and leaving him to die. This man must surely have been pardoned had he become a drunkard; his devotion to Bacchus would have resulted from sheer gratitude. Fortunately for Om-Kopo, superior forces denied him the opportunity to express this gratitude as he would have wished.

1 River twenty leagues north-north-east of Port Natal.
2 Garment worn by Cafre men for the sake of modesty.
3 Beer, or fermented drink, of the white men.

On 1 September we made our way over trackless country, and on the 2nd we outspanned on high ground within an hour and a half's walk of the river. We found a few farmers already there; they had come by another route, but their objectives were the same as ours. Together we walked down through the mimosa bushes, crossing pretty streams of running water on the way. We made our way easily along the well-worn tortuous hippopotamus paths. New green leaves were just appearing on the trees and the thousand little natural noises were taken up and repeated by the echoes. All about us, the creatures of nature were alive and free because as yet these parts were uninhabited by man. And we had come to shatter their peace and cloud their joy with the thunder of our guns. A sense of real regret came over me but I stifled it, for there are two things which are quite incompatible — the sentiments of the poet and those of the hunter.

When the sound of rushing water announced the proximity of the river, we dispersed to take up the positions which we felt were most advantageous, and shortly afterwards the rocky walls of the opposite bank echoed to the sound of our gunfire. Many shots were fired that day but only one, well aimed by our neighbours, claimed its victim, a female hippopotamus.

It was not possible for two different parties to occupy the same vantage point without poaching upon each other's preserves. Conflict must ensue and to avoid this, I suggested we look for another place. My companions agreed and the next day we moved two leagues down the river. Even there, we had to leave the wagons on high ground, 1000 feet above the water, as the sharp rocks and the steep slope made a closer approach impossible.

On 4 September we set off before dawn, leaving the wagons guarded by a young Cafre. Our intention was to take advantage of the still water of the early morning. Three quarters of an hour later we heard the hippopotamuses blowing. The sound was prolonged, which led us to believe that the animals were peaceful and would soon surface. Elias asked permission to fire the first shot. This privilege is generally accorded to the finest marksman. In deference to his age, however, I agreed to let him do it.

He went off, took up his position, shouldered his gun, aimed carefully and fired. From the sound of the shot, I reckoned that it had hit the water and rebounded on to the rocks on the opposite bank. I felt annoyance at his lack of skill as I saw him returning, making excuses for missing his aim. I hastened to take up my position, and soon several heads appeared on the surface of the water; they rose and then disappeared again without giving me time to take careful aim. I fired off a few shots, two of which hit their mark, for I saw blood spurting from two of the heads, the two I had particularly aimed for. My eyes were still fixed on these heads when a great clamour broke out on the opposite bank and distracted my attention.

Two large grey-black bodies were trotting along, one behind the other. Nimbly they negotiated the slope and splashed through the shallows into the deep water, where their heads soon appeared, completely exposed, on the surface. These two hippopotamuses which had been startled by the ricochet of my bullet, were unwittingly making their way towards me and, to profit by my advantage, I took cover behind a bank of reeds. When they reappeared, fifteen paces away, I put a ball through the head of one of them, six inches from the eye. The wound was not mortal, although the animal lost a lot of blood and was forced to surface more frequently than is usual.

At about three in the afternoon, our servants returned with un-favourable reports. We decided to put an end to our wounded hippo-potamuses. My companions agreed with my proposal to single out one of the animals upon which we would concentrate all our fire. We fired twenty-seven shots at him; there were already six in his head, but none in his cranium. Elias had shattered his olfactory canal and water was entering through the wound. The animal submerged and his movements led us to believe that he intended climbing up the bank and making for the bush to escape our attacks. His struggles were titanic; he rose and fell back again into the turbulent water and then surged up once more; he was in fact moving towards us and we hastily reloaded our guns.

His body came up and he raised his broad snout as if to pick up our scent. He was so close that we could make out the bullet furrows on his hideous face; we waited, lying flat on the ground so that he would not see us. But the moment had come; to delay any longer would have meant to risk being crushed. Pieter and I raised our guns simultaneously and our shots, which hit him at ten paces, put an end to him. Elias, who had witnessed the final round said, 'That's it master, I saw yours hit, he is dead. The sun is setting, let us go.'

The next day, which was a Sunday, was not observed by our men, although they prided themselves on being devout. They were obliged to set to work, as we were dependent for food supplies on the flesh of the animal we had killed the day before. And so, before the sun had time to look down into the Touguela Valley, my bastaards had already discovered our hippopotamus which had been carried by the current 400 paces downstream, where fortunately some large stones had prevented it from drifting any further. It was a female, riddled with bullets. My men had judged it to be unsuited to my purposes and so, armed with sharp knives, they were busy cutting it up.

As I had not their urgent reasons to hurry to the spot, I arrived only at about eight o'clock. Billowing smoke, drifting up the rock face near a bend in the river, led me to where they were, as did also the presence of vultures, wheeling high in the sky, or perched in the tree-tops. Shortly afterwards I heard voices and then I saw the enormous red body alongside of which the black skins of several Cafres formed a striking contrast.

As I drew nearer, the air was heavy with emanations from the corpse, an equine odour which I found very disagreeable. And then I saw that the trees and the bushes all around were hung with strips of the pink and white meat which is so prized by South Africans. Om-Kopo's fire was about to be extinguished beneath the weight of the meat intended for his own consumption, and this was apparently his fourth meal that day. I do not exaggerate when I tell you that he had consumed more than fifteen pounds of fat meat.

I forgave him his gluttony when I tasted the meat which was white, succulent and tender; it has something of both pork and veal, but is much superior to either. When it is grilled in this way over the coals, I prefer the lean meat; the fat requires longer and slower cooking. However I must say that the melted fat, like that of the rhinoceros, is the most wholesome and delicious that I have ever tasted;

The Dutch colonists are well acquainted with it and prefer it to butter, olive oil or lard in the making of stews; in addition, it is considered to have rare properties which contribute to the destruction of internal infections and it is swallowed for this purpose by the spoonful. I tried this remedy and was soon convinced of its beneficial effects.

The rest of the day was spent in transferring the precious meat to the wagon. Some was salted, while the rest was exposed to the air to dry; the smell, carried on the wind, attracted several hyenas as well as a lion which arrived roaring and then decided to withdraw.

On Monday the 6th, I took care to be at my post early. My men joined me there, but as they considered the position to be ill-judged, they preferred to go off and explore while I remained alone, waiting for a head to appear on the water. An hour went by; I fired three shots and two heads appeared, oozing blood through their wounds. I was preparing to fire my fourth shot, when something grey rose to the surface. It could not be the head of a crocodile, because the shape was rounded instead of oblong. I hesitated, I waited and then to satisfy my curiosity, I climbed up on to higher ground.

From this vantage point, I could clearly see that there was a large body under the water, but I hesitated to form a positive opinion as to what it was. Several minutes went by and the body continued to rise. I had been convinced that the first hippopotamus I had shot, had died instantly. In fact it was this selfsame animal which was returning to the surface; I could not be mistaken.

But all alone as I was, I could do nothing; I needed the assistance of my men. To tell the truth I did not know where they had gone. As we had not agreed on a signal, I resorted to using my double-barrelled gun from which I fired eight successive shots at regular intervals. The echo was so loud that it was impossible I should not be heard. An hour went by and no one came. The time seemed long to me; I fretted and fumed, and to relieve my ill humour, as well as to chivvy my men, I decided to go in search of them. As usually happens in these cases, I met nobody, but on my way back I came upon my bastaards who had passed me in the bush, without my seeing them. They had been sleeping in the shade, the good-for-nothings, hoping in this way to escape the chore which awaited them, for I intended to prepare the animal as a specimen.

I roundly accused them of the sin of sloth; one of them objected that the hippopotamus was in the middle of the river, surrounded by crocodiles and that, as neither Coudou's Cafres nor Coudou himself had arrived, it would be impossible for them to do anything about pulling the animal out. I was quick to reply that since they feared for their swarthy skins, I would take it upon myself to perform the task, intending to prove that they were cowards.

This pleased them very much; they believed themselves exempted from a chore which presented some measure of danger. I was aware of this and dispatched the oldest of them to the wagons to bring back all the *os-riem*, or leather thongs. At the same time, I put the others to collecting the big dry branches which were lying on the ground, and to encourage them by example, I set to work, considering all the while how to proceed.

I was asked several times, 'Master, what are you going to do?' I took care not to reply, and when all the materials were assembled, I constructed my raft. Intending that my venture should fail so that he might make fun of me, Pieter had brought me spongey wood which would float for only a short while. I flung it back at him. A quarter of an hour later, I had the wood I needed.

Immersed up to my armpits in the water in defiance of the crocodiles which my companions so much feared, I needed only ten minutes to complete the simple construction. I had a mooring rope, I made a gaff and I found a means of stowing my gun clear of the water, while I placed an axe ready to hand in case a crocodile should attempt to attack. My men were astonished at my determination, my industry and the degree of my success. I wanted Piet to come with me to make the hippopotamus fast, for it was essential that we should not float past it on the current.

He found the suggestion very disagreeable; however he finally made a pretence of obedience, but when I pushed off, he leapt backwards on to the land which was his element, he said, but upon which he was no braver than he was elsewhere. I punted out to the middle of the stream, and then let myself drift; but to tell the truth, my raft was absorbing water and beginning to sink. I was immersed up to my waist, but this was my only discomfort, as the crocodiles kept out of my way.

Without too much difficulty, I succeeded in negotioting the current. Without even having to use my gaff, I seized the hippopotamus by the tail and tied a couple of hitch-knots round it, attaching the other end of the rope to the raft. Then I cut across the current and headed back to the bank. My men, who did not understand my methods, expected to see me dragging my enormous animal along with my hands, by the foot or by the tail. Anticipating my defeat, they burst out laughing. They were enjoying the prospect of my discomfiture, when suddenly there I was, stepping confidently ashore, holding the end of the rope by means of which I was slowly towing in my hippopotamus. Then they stopped laughing and gaped in stunned silence. I shall not repeat the words I used to force them into the water, because these form part only of the African Dutch vocabulary. Having gained in authority by the superiority I had just proved, I felt I had every right to make them do as I wanted, which was to roll my amphibious animal out of the water, like a barrel. Following this, I performed the principal incisions, and in less than an hour, with the encouragement of a few stimulating words to which my insolent bastaards could find no reply, we removed the skin.

The animal was a large female in perfect condition, although the skin presented us with some problems. Two sorts of parasite had attached themselves to it; ticks in the ears and leeches around the anus; and it was so heavy that six men had great difficulty in heaving in only ten paces from the edge of the water.

On Tuesday the 7th, I needed the assistance of all my men as we had previously agreed. But it would have been a pity not to have given them time to salt the fat which was their share. Elias and Piet said that they were ill; only old David, a half-caste of Malay origin, agreed to help me; a young Cafre joined us and although we worked all day, we were not able to remove all the adhering muscle. Fortunately Coudou's Cafres arrived and I employed them to carry the skin twenty paces off to some large rocks where I intended to spread it out to dry.

On the succeeding days I was so engrossed in my difficult task that I could not find the time to continue to hunt hippopotamus. In any case, they had left the nearest *Zee-Koe-Gat*, (hippopotamus pool) probably due to the fact that I was making fires at night to protect the skin from hyaenas.

I had treated with alum the side of the skin which I particularly desired to preserve intact; I believed that success was certain, but as a result of a terrible rainstorm, the skin produced nodules in several places and I had to redouble my efforts to preserve it.

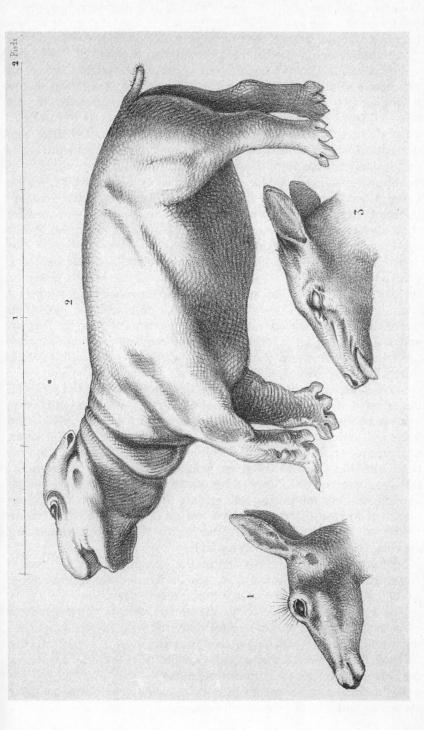

2 Pieds.

1. REDUNCA LALANDII   2. HIPPOPOTAMUS AMPHIBIUS (Fœtus)   3. CEPHALOPUS NATALENSIS

During this nocturnal deluge, which it is beyond my powers to describe, our only shelter was the canvas of my tent hastily spread over a horizontal branch, and beneath which we took shelter, sitting like Brahmins wrapped in burnous, hoping that it would soon be over.

But it was not soon over; the rain continued to fall in a deluge. In less than a minute everything was soaked through, our canvas shelter having formed a tunnel which directed the water in upon us. Our fire was extinguished; the least little mountain stream was transformed into a raging torrent which swept our things into the river and threatened to carry us off as well. To complete our wretchedness, we found that our guns were filled with water right up to the muzzle.

Moments later, the deluge was reinforced by fiery flashes from the heavens and explosions of thunder which made our hearts leap. An enormous tree, 120 paces off was struck by lightning and we who were sheltering at the foot of another tree just as large, felt that it too might come crashing down upon us.

The great carnivores take advantage of these battles of the elements; it is to their advantage to fish, as it were, in troubled waters. Profiting by the general confusion and the fear which roots every herbivore trembling to the spot, they approach with impunity and seize their distracted prey. They are now at their boldest; the lion, the leopard and the hyaena join in chorus with the roar of the thunder; with temerity they disregard man and often succeed in seizing his beasts, even when they are still tied to the wheels of the wagon.

All night long we heard the terrible refrain of their voices to which our guns were incapable of response. Fifty paces away the base hyaena howled; beyond him the leopard coughed and only fifteen paces off, twenty crocodiles tore at the corpse, while in the intervals of calm, we could hear them plopping back into the water. Had we been armed in the usual way, we would not have been concerned at the proximity of these beasts, but on this occasion we were forced to recognise our inferiority, having only our pocket knives to defend ourselves in case of attack, which was no defence at all. The storm might well have had fatal consequences for us, but as it turned out, we escaped with no more than a soaking.

At last, a wan light appearing in the east announced the dawn. Although the rain had not stopped, and the leopard was still coughing, we hoped that the coming of day would relieve the situation.

The sun soon appeared above the horizon and the untimely heat of its rays promised another storm that afternoon, as well as increasing my fears for that precious object upon which all my attention was focused. The skin was drying as well as might be expected, considering that I had no control over the temperature.

I was obliged to accept all of Fortune's gifts, whether welcome or otherwise and, thank Heaven, there seemed lately to be more of the

146

former. My men, who were constantly engaged in burning up my powder and shot, finally killed a hippopotamus which they abandoned to the Cafres because it was too thin. The next day they were more fortunate; Elias put a bullet into the head of an enormous old male, probably the grand old man of the river, but, on the pretext that my first project was not yet complete, and that he considered me incapable of transporting two animals at once, he violated his promise, and, giving me no warning, he allowed the body to be cut up immediately. Three days later, as the sex and the size of the animal had been concealed from me, I went to the place where it was lying to make enquiries and was astonished to find the skull lying on the ground, perfectly clean of all muscle. It was the biggest I had yet seen. I immediately enquired of Elias himself what he intended to do with it, and I learnt to my astonishment, that it was destined for a collector at Port Natal. These rascals were quite clearly in competition with me. Not content with what I had offered them, they intended to enter the field of natural history with specimens which were mine by right. To cut the matter short, I pointed out to them that they were in the wrong, and made my dissatisfaction perfectly plain. Elias accepted my argument but Piet would not, and as I found further dissension with them repugnant, I took possession of the precious head, making it quite understood that my final argument would be at the point of a gun.

I regret to have to say so, but with people like this, there is no other way. I had said I would do it and I would have done it, and the council at Pieter's Mauritz Burg would not have felt itself competent to pronounce judgment on me for an act of this kind which had been committed such a long way off. One did not apply to this ill-constituted tribunal with any expectation that justice would be done. One was therefore obliged to carry out sentence oneself, however unacceptable this might have been to one's conscience.

On the 14th the half-dried skin had to be carried back to the place where we had left the wagons. The task was not an easy one. The distance was barely two miles, but we had to climb more than 1000 feet over rocks and through trees which barred the way. I would not consider allowing my men to carry the skin, and I could not make use of the rear axle of my wagon which was too broad, so finally I sent for a team of twelve oxen and had the skin attached to the upper branches of a mimosa tree, felled for the purpose. This improvised sled was made fast by a chain to the main shaft. All was now in readiness and awaiting the crack of the whip, but once again the bastaards began objecting. The trees, they said, would get in the way; it would be dark before we reached the top. I did not care how long it took, for I was determined to succeed.

I gave orders for trees to be cut down if they obstructed the way.

147

My bastaards were stationed behind the oxen to drive them and I posted myself behind my bastaards with the same objective as the Russian sergeants who encourage their troops from behind with a cane. I was armed with the strength of my will and the loaded gun which, by constant use, had become almost part of me. Finally, after six hours of unrelenting effort, the operation was successfully accomplished. Both oxen and men were tired out and I allowed them to take the rest they needed.

Shortly before we had set out, some Amazoulou Cafres, living on the far side of the river, had crossed over to us by way of the stones. There were seven or eight of them, including several women. Their bodies were emaciated, livid black and repulsive to behold. They told us that, having heard our shots from afar, they had come in the hope of finding the debris of our hunt. Gnawing hunger alone had induced them to approach us. At the time of the war their silos (*nogoty*) had been emptied and so, deprived of every necessity, they were reduced to seeking food in the woods. In coming to us, they had hoped to find nourishment which would restore their strength. I would like to have given them a hundred pounds of the meat which my men had packed. Unfortunately I had no right to it and I found myself in the difficult position of having nothing to offer them.

They then enquired as to where they could find the carcasses of our four hippopotamuses. We pointed out the spot and they took some of our fire to light their way. They found only a few shreds of meat adhering to the bones which the hyenas had already picked almost bare. Here and there in the mud, trodden by the vultures and littered with their droppings, were scattered bits of the flesh which my men had cut off. The vultures, having gorged their fill, made way for man as the Cafres rushed eagerly towards this disgusting sight. They scarcely paused to wash the shredded remains before they grilled them and devoured them; they made bundles of the bones, loaded them on their shoulders and carried them back to the *mouzi* to extract the marrow. For their sakes and for mine, I would have welcomed their visit twelve days earlier, for they would have fallen upon a time of plenty and I could have made good use of their services.

So much superior are their constitutions to ours, that after only four days of this food, their thin bodies would undoubtedly have been restored. I have witnessed several cases where after only three or four days, Cafres who were thin to the point of exhaustion, were restored to a condition of perfect plumpness simply by eating substantial food. I do not, however, claim to be a judge of these matters; I write only of what I have seen.

On the 16th we took up our position a little further downstream, at a spot commonly known as *Zee-Koe-Gat*. Because the river was much wider here and a strong breeze was rippling the surface, we had no success that day, which proved to be uneventful in every way, except for the sighting of a leopard on the opposite bank. Startled from its lair by the whistle of a bullet, it leapt up and then disappeared rapidly behind the reeds.

On the 18th we moved still further downstream. The day was too advanced to shoot hippopotamus, so we hunted *riet-booken* instead. Only three of them appeared, but as they were very timid, I was unable to get a shot at them. My men had no better luck than I.

The next day, the 19th, was equally unsuccessful. I wounded, but did not kill, two hippopotamuses, while my men wounded several others. We were convinced that this was not because our aim was faulty, but because our bullets were not strong enough. I decided to sacrifice my eating utensils which were in fact made of tin although I claimed earlier to be travelling like a colonial governor.

While exploring along the bank we discovered a dead hippopotamus in the water, lodged up against a barrier of stones; it was young and fat and had been dead for two days. There was a bullet wound near the eye. We were uncertain as to whether it was one of ours so we handed it over to Coudou who lost no time in sending word to his *mouzi*, which was close by. In less than no time, twenty women arrived and set to work cutting up the meat, while the men severed the limbs with their assegais. The work was completed in less than an hour, whereupon the animal set off for the *mouzi*, not on his own feet, but cut up into pieces, wrapped in leaves and transported on the heads of these sturdy women.

On the 20th we rested. On the 21st I aimed my second shot of the day at a hippopotamus which, having drifted away from the herd, presented a favorable target. The bullet struck near the eye and blood bubbled up. I aimed several more shots at him, which forced him to seek shelter and, shortly afterwards, I saw him retreating into a creek near the opposite bank where he remained in hiding. He had either to be dislodged from his retreat or even better, stealthily approached in his hiding place and attacked there. This would be possible only if we could cross the river with our guns.

All the while I was thinking of Coudou, a man of superb physique, Herculean strength, and legendary courage. I had heard much of this noble Cafre and was curious to see him in action. This was my opportunity to make use of his services and to admire him at the same time. I sent for him and spoke to him in his language, pointing towards the hippopotamus which I had wounded: 'Go across the river and drive him towards us. You will not be afraid?' 'No,' he replied, 'I have killed many others.' 'It is not necessary to kill him,' I said. 'We will see,' he coldly replied. 'Go then and my eyes will follow you and watch how you proceed.' And he went without further ado and took up two great assegais as if they had been lances made of laurel. He examined the blades which he plunged several times into the water and then into the sand as if to remove a speck of rust. Then he called to one of his men to follow him, bringing two spare assegais. He set off, confident in his strength and his skill, and, to see his expressive face now devoid of emotion, one would have thought he was off to kill a sheep.

A quarter of an hour later he had reached the opposite bank. Studying the animal's movements, he took advantage of the moment when it submerged to test the depth of the water which varied greatly. Within a few minutes he had found a rock only half a foot beneath the surface; he climbed upon it and waited for the head of the hippopotamus to reappear. Silently, we watched and waited, but not for long. Suddenly Coudou brandished the assegai in the air and then hurled it at the black body which recoiled with a great start and began to thrash about. The second assegai also struck its mark and the animal's struggles produced further churning of the water. Then it swung about and, swimming under water, joined the rest of the herd which apparently would not accept it, for it remained among them only a short time, while Coudou retrieved his assegais which were drifting with the current, proclaiming loudly all the while that he feared nothing from the presence of the many crocodiles.

The wounded animal then took shelter under a bank of reeds where it was difficult for a man, and particularly a naked man, to reach it. Coudou followed it and we watched as he parted the reeds, as one might part the curtains of a bed. He was face to face now with the hippopotamus which was oozing blood through several apertures. Two assegais were implanted in rapid succession into the body of the monster which recoiled suddenly, spraying its attacker with water. Undeterred, Coudou took up his third weapon, a great stabbing assegai and, keeping hold of the shaft, he thrust the blade deep, as one does into a whale. In vain the animal attempted to shake him off; the powerful movements would have dislodged three ordinary men. When the animal's struggles became too violent, he momentarily let go of the shaft, only to take hold of it again and to thrust it more deeply into the wound. His skill was such that I was tempted to cry 'Bravo'.

My admiration was particularly excited by the fact that Coudou had chosen to position himself on a spot from which retreat was impossible should the animal have attempted to climb ashore. Finally, unable to withstand further harassment, it made an effort to retreat. Whereupon I saw our valiant Cafre, with a triumphant air, withdraw his bloody assegai.

The hippopotamus, unable to remain in the water, made its way towards the bank where it lay in wait. It was within twenty feet of us with its head completely exposed, for the water was very shallow at this point. Piet and I, who were waiting for it, fired two bullets simultaneously into its head. But it was not dead yet; it turned, spun around twice, and then repeated the manoeuvre. This gave us time to reload our guns and to drop down flat on the ground, thus making way for the animal to climb the bank, which it easily did and, once it was on level ground, it set off at a ponderous trot to seek refuge in the bush. Aware that I was unequal to overtaking it, I fired from thirty paces and had the great good luck to hit it in the shoulder; it stumbled and this gave Piet, at fifteen paces, the opportunity to get it between the eye and the ear. It died instantly, its short legs collapsing before its eyes had had time to close.

My men were still reluctant to approach it and in order to encourage them, I straddled the animal's back. 'You would be very surprised,' they said, 'if he got up and galloped back to the river.' 'Of course,' I replied, 'we would all find that very amusing.'

Coudou, who had observed from a distance all that had passed, now drew near, reproaching himself for his failure, for he had hoped to accomplish the task unaided. His skill, his strength and his courage had excited my imagination, and now his modesty compelled my respect.

Near the place where we were hunting hippopotamus the bush, interspersed with mimosa trees, sheltered a good number of crowned guinea-fowl which, when pursued by our dogs, chose to evade them by running away rather than by flying. The flesh of this bird is delicious; but this alone would not be sufficient reason to mention them here. Not far from Om-Guinée, in the great forests which border the coasts, lives another species, the crested guinea-fowl, which is more beautiful and which does not often feature in collections; it bears a tuft of feathers on its head and seems more delicate than the crowned variety, to judge from the futile attempts which have been made to breed this bird in captivity.

We encountered also, in great abundance, the leaping gazelle, different in several respects from the Cape variety which is known by the name of *Cephalopus mergens Burschellii*. The coat is a pale grey rather than tawny, and the Natal animal is smaller; nevertheless the two varieties share similar characteristics. We continued hunting until the 22nd and, with our tally now standing at nine hippopotamuses, we decided to make our way back to Natal on the 23rd. We killed several *riet-booken* on the way. On the 27th, at about eleven in the morning, we reached Berea and were looking down over the bay when, to our surprise, we saw an elephant disappearing into the trees only a hundred paces away.

On my return, I made a summary of all the information I had gathered about the hippopotamus, and although the subject has been dealt with by many other travellers, I nevertheless believe it worthwhile to report on my own findings. This animal which the ancients compared to the horse, a likeness probably suggested by the upper part of the head which is all that appears on the surface of the water, has been dubbed *zee-koe* by the Dutch in South Africa.

These compound names such as river-horse and sea-cow are deceptive and do not conjure up a picture of the hippopotamus. The whites, it seems to me, have not done as well in this respect as those we commonly call savages. The Amazoulous have given the hippopotamus a name of its own which is not suggestive of the horse, the cow, the rhinoceros or the pig. They say *om-vobu*, which is the name of the hippopotamus alone and which does not deceive by false comparisons those who have never seen the animal.

According to the findings of Monsieur Duvernoy, whose researches into comparative anatomy have recently been much acclaimed, it would appear that the species which inhabits southern Africa differs in several respects from the one found in Senegal and Abyssinia. These differences, which have been discovered by studying only the skeleton, are probably hardly apparent when one observes the animal in its natural state. Before pronouncing a positive opinion, it would be necessary to study the different species, each in its own environment. This I have not done and so I shall limit myself to referring to the southern African variety.

Although the hippopotamus is one of the most important animals in the world as far as size is concerned, the hunter should not expect to be greatly surprised when he encounters one. Because of the natural habitat of his quarry, the hunter finds himself rather in the position of the fisherman; he must have all the patience required for line fishing; he must stand as still as a heron, conceal himself like a bittern, possess the cunning of the crocodile and the speed of lightning, in both hand and eye, so that when the animal comes up he may strike unerringly in the small space between ear and eye.

But whether you call it hunting or fishing, it is very diverting to shoot hippopotamus; you experience intense satisfaction when your bullet hits the target — a difficult task because, from the time the water bubbles up and the huge black head appears, you have only three seconds before it disappears again. At seventy to a hundred and ten paces, your target is only six inches square, for although the hippopotamus's head is huge, the bony cavity which protects the brain is so small that it is more difficult than one might imagine to kill a hippopotamus in the water. I fired twenty-seven shots at my first animal, seven of which penetrated the head, before I mortally wounded him. During another day's hunting, my men and I wounded twenty-seven hippopotamuses in half an hour, all in the head; that evening we pulled only one out of the water but he was not among those we had wounded that day.

There are two methods of hunting the hippopotamus, the first of which is to stalk him at night. The hunter lies in wait for him at the river mouth, where he will emerge to eat reeds, or else he seeks him out in the plains where he goes to graze. But to aim accurately by moonlight is almost impossible and the long wait becomes painful if the hunter is attacked by millions of mosquitoes. Hunting at night is therefore not much practised for it is unfruitful and is only for the truly intrepid with their suntanned faces and their dreams of *zee-koe-spek*. The alternative is to hunt the hippopotamus during the day when he is in the water and comes up for air. We have already seen the difficulties of this method and to avoid some of these, one generally goes out during those few hours which are most favourable to the hunter.

He must already have taken up his position by early dawn when the half light enables him to see objects a hundred paces off. At that hour the breeze has not yet sprung up and the water is as smooth as glass with the hideous black heads floating on the surface. The hippopotamus appears to be resting after the fatigues of the night; he seems to be asleep. Quiet now! Raise your gun to your shoulder and line up your sights; take careful aim at the head with the red ears; calculate the distance between ear and eye. 'Marksman, fire!' The shot rings out, all the heads disappear; an enormous body leaps up, half out of the water, suggesting colossal proportions beneath. The great gun's ringing shot is echoed by the granite rocks of the river bank, which pass it on to the far-away mountains of the escarpment where it is taken up and repeated by multiple reverberations so that the vibrations produced by a small quantity of gunpowder rumble around the mountain gorges like thunder in the pure air.

But the wily hippopotamuses are not unduly upset; they are familiar with the electrically charged atmosphere, the smell of gunpowder. They know about the proximity of man, and they adapt their movements to the dangers of the situation. The heads re-appear, one by one or several at a time. They seem to come up in turn, each one takes a breath, blows out bubbles and then disappears again. There is little time to take aim, but the area they expose is large enough to encourage hopes of a successful shot. The bullets rain down and already several heads re-appear, with blood bubbling through the nostrils or seeping from wounds. This happens when they are hit between the eyes. Animals which are wounded in this way are forced to come up more frequently for air, but they are more cautious and reveal very little of themselves. The others follow their example and soon, hunter, you will have to be satisfied with firing at their snouts. It is perhaps a good idea at this point to give up, for one uses so much ammunition and circumstances rarely favour the hunter! In order to kill a hippopotamus which exposes only its nostrils, it would be necessary for the bullet to travel up the olfactory canal and to penetrate the cranium, a very rare thing which cannot possibly be depended upon.

The hunter might perhaps try settling down patiently and waiting for the hippopotamus to yawn. The animal, which appears to feel the necessity of doing this rather frequently, opens his mouth in a positively frightening manner, his jaws forming a right angle. It is very difficult to fire at the critical moment, but if the bullet hits the roof of the mouth, death is instantaneous.

It is as well to give up all attempts to fire horizontally because the bullets ricochet and are lost. It is preferable to position oneself on high ground so that the shots are fired almost vertically at the top of the animal's head; but if there are no natural advantages of the terrain, one must try to dislodge the hippopotamuses from their holes.

A boat is excellent for a manoeuvre of this kind as it will carry the hunter in among the herd. Strong assegais, fixed to long poles, are used to sound the depths of the water and to prod the animals which, astonished to find themselves attacked in their holes, will be sure to move off. At this point, one must take care that the boat is not caught in the turbulence churned up by the agitated movements of the amphibians. Sometimes they overturn the boat and wreck it; sometimes they take hold of the boards in their teeth and crunch them; one runs the risk of having to swim to safety, abandoning one's guns, which is an infinitely regrettable thing to have to do, and almost as bad as being taken by a crocodile, that secret observer of all activity on the surface of the water. Even though his boat has just been wrecked, the hunter need fear no further danger from the hippopotamus which, as far as I know, will not attack a man as he swims for the shore.

As there is not always a boat at one's disposal, one makes do with a hastily constructed raft which, more often than not, sinks because it is made of absorbent wood and is in any case so difficult to manoeuvre that it is of little or no use. In some cases, one manages to use the rocks, even those covered by water, which permit the hunter to approach his quarry more closely and which offer him, at the same time, a firm footing; but rocks are not always available and even when they are, one is obliged to sound the depths of the water as well as taking the usual precautions against crocodiles. In short, the hunter is rarely successful in dislodging the hippopotamus from his hole, as these animals, in spite of their stupid appearance, will always have chosen a position that will suit them to greatest advantage.

I should perhaps explain why I talk of holes in relation to animals which live in rivers. Every river in South Africa, in spite of the majestic abundance of its waters during the rainy season, is destined to play a sadly depleted role during the winter or the dry season. The noble river owes its greatness to its tributaries and prospers when they too are affluent. Then come the lean times; the little tributaries can contribute no longer and the noble river declines from its state of opulence to one of penury and may dry up completely. I have known the Om-Philos-Om-Schlopu to be so dry that twenty-four leagues from its mouth, where it is sometimes seventy feet wide and ten feet deep, water was to be found only by digging eighteen inches down into the sand of the river bed.

The biggest rivers, which have many tributaries, are not reduced to quite this state of impoverishment. Touguela and Oury for example, draw their water from numerous and often distant sources, but this does not prevent their having insufficient water to cover the bodies of the amphibious inhabitants. The hippopotamuses know this better even than the crocodiles which have the ability to live a long time without food and are able to bury themselves under the sand for weeks on end. The instinct of the hippopotamus, which prefers to remain near its pastures, leads it to excavate the river bed in certain places, thus ensuring for itself at least eight or nine feet of water. The Boers call these *zee-koe-gat*. It is difficult to estimate the size of these holes, or pools, when the river is full, but having had the opportunity, near the Tropic of Capricorn, 150 leagues from the coast, of seeing the Oury or Limpopo river in the dry season, when numerous hippopotamus pools were revealed, I am able, without contradiction, to give details of their proportions. They were generally fifteen feet long by fifteen feet wide and eight or nine feet deep. They were capable of accommodating twelve hippopotamuses or even more, for these animals huddle together closely in their pools, a fact confirmed by the proximity of the heads on the surface. There is sometimes communication between the pools by means of furrows and the rivers often have a longitudinal furrow running down the centre of the bed, which serves as a corridor for the hippopotamuses. This was the case with the Om-Lalas where this furrow made the crossing very difficult for our wagons; the water at the ford was generally three or four feet deep in any case, and when the wagons sank even deeper into the furrow, much unfortunate damage was incurred.

If one makes one's way up a river which is inhabited by hippopotamus and which is as yet untroubled by man's presence, one will encounter these holes or pools everywhere, even near the source. Where the water is plentiful, so will the hippopotamus be plentiful too. During the dry season it is only in the deep lakes, which have constant water, and near the wide mouths of rivers, that one sees the amphibians. Each year, as they become aware of the water level going down, they set off to follow the current downstream; thus they are very numerous on the shore where a network of their tracks can often be seen.

Every year then, the hippopotamuses are forced to quit the interior even when they are not harassed by man. I must have observed this seasonal migration at a time when these parts were still innocent of contact with the white man, for shortly afterwards the animals, which are so vulnerable to attack where the river is narrow and shallow in the upper reaches, realised their disadvantage and set off to find the wider stretches of water down near the sea where they can still be found to this day.

Their numbers in the territory have sadly diminished, hardly a tenth remaining of those that were there when I arrived in 1839. Near the Touguela mouth, the last time I was there, towards the end of 1842, I estimated that there were about a hundred, spread over a space of three leagues. This number was sufficient to encourage the expectations of the hunter, but the animals were so distrustful, keeping their distance from the bank, and their movements were so different from those I had known during the first years, that it was a waste of time to try to hunt them.

To convey some idea of the decline in numbers, I can do no better than to quote the figures which I collected during my long stay in south-eastern Africa. In 1839 three men hunting for a month killed from thirty to thirty-six hippopotamuses on the Touguela; in 1840 it was between twenty and twenty-three; in 1841 it was ten; in 1842, four; in 1843, one or two and sometimes none at all.

The species which was common in the Cape Colony at the time of Levaillant, and which was particularly abundant at Berg Rivier, is now reduced to two old males which I saw in 1838 on the farm belonging to Mr Melck, the famous horse breeder, who considered them to be his own property and who afforded them every protection. The oldest Hottentots in the district claimed to have known them for sixty years.

It is not difficult to predict that the species will disappear completely from the country of Natal, as it has done from every other place where the white man has settled. Without a doubt, it is the first animal which is destined to become extinct because the resources with which nature has provided it are insufficient to protect it from man.

The fully grown male is broad and heavy. He is four and a half to five feet tall, ten to eleven feet long, with legs one and a half feet high. His speed on flat ground is equivalent to that of a man; it is less on an upward slope and more on the downward, but never enough to carry him out of danger. His only defence, which the Cafres have no difficulty in penetrating, is the thickness of his skin which is stretched over a layer of fat, covering wide flat ribs that are easily broken. Added to this he has a peaceful temperament and even in the water, his natural element, he will not harm a man. Hunting accidents sometimes happen; but only on land and in exceptional circumstances. The English lieutenant Harding, in whose company I made my first hippopotamus hunt, told me of an isolated incident near the Fish Rivier, when one of his Hottentots was bitten, but this is the only account to have reached my ears.

The shores of lakes are often covered in reeds which are rooted in the mud. The amphibians come up through these reeds each night and return the same way in the morning. The pathways which they trample are only about eighteen inches wide on the ground, but form a wide round tunnel, about a metre high, which opens up as the animal passes through and closes again behind him. I frequently ventured into these tunnels, in spite of the mud which made progress difficult, hoping for a face to face encounter with a hippopotamus. Mr Harding, who was more experienced than I, accused me of what he called temerity and assured me that it was in just that sort of covered pathway that one of his best Hottentots had been bitten and then crushed underfoot by a hippopotamus whose path he had crossed when it was intent on returning to the water.

Fear is enough to make this, the mildest of animals, behave in an aggressive manner. He attempts to protect himself in this way for he has no other means of defence, but this does not mean that he is aggressive by nature. He will never initiate an attack on a man; on the contrary, he will usually run away. He makes little effort to defend himself when the Cafres riddle him with their *om-kondos* in an attempt to chase him from their gardens where he goes to graze at night.

Koudou of Touguela, the very model of strength, agility and bravery had no difficulty in killing hippopotamuses with his sharp weapons. I have seen him at work in broad daylight, in situations of great danger, on land or in the water; he attacked the hippopotamus wherever he could find him, even amongst the crocodiles, and the wounds which he inflicted were so deep and so wide, that I could scarcely believe my eyes. Koudou did not regard this as a great feat as he did not consider the hippopotamus a vindictive animal.

Certain travellers, surprised no doubt at the unusual nature of the animal's teeth, mistakenly believed that he feeds on fish. To disprove this, one need only look at the excrement which he drops on the rocks near the river as he emerges from the water. This is composed of grass, young reeds and sometimes shoots although never fruit or roots. The matter is so poorly masticated that the remains of the digested reeds resemble toothpicks. The odour of the excrement is equine, similar to that of elephant droppings, but less peppery than the odour of the dung of the rhinoceros, whether *Simus* or *Bicornis*. The hippopotamus leaves his droppings in a heap which is to say that he does not trample them, as the rhinoceros does. He is entirely herbivorous, but he is no more a ruminant than the other pachyderms.

The female has two teats and produces a single young. She is distinguished from all other quadrupeds, pachyderms, solipeds and fissipeds, except possibly for the tapir, in that she carries her young on her back when in the water. When the herd comes up for air, it is easy to distinguish among them the females with very young calves. Right behind the huge head of the mother, a little head comes to the surface; the two heads take in air at the same moment and submerge again simultaneously. The baby must at that moment be astride the mother's neck, which is the narrowest part of her body. Her intention must be to spare her offspring from fatigue as well as to teach him not to expose himself to the danger of the hunter's bullet. I believe that this maternal concern does not last for more than a few months, certainly no more than a year, as the young heads I saw were very small.

The flesh of an old hippopotamus is too tough to be eaten grilled. It needs to be stewed for a good while before producing an agreeable flavour. The flesh of the young animal is white and tender and similar to pork or veal, but infinitely more succulent; when it is eaten fresh it has laxative properties. The fat is composed of spongy vesicles which, during the cooking process, produce the most delicious dripping, well known to the Dutch Boers in Natal by the name of *zee-koe-spek*, at the very mention of which, every hippopotamus hunter breaks into an appreciative smile.

It was to obtain this prized *zee-koe-spek* that every one of these hunters, at least once a year, set off for the hippopotamus country. These expeditions became the most pleasurable social occasions for the Boers. There would be a month of feasting and much fat would be consumed. Without exaggeration, I can say that on their return a great alteration could be observed in the appearance of all the members of the party. However thin they might have been when they set out, all of them, whites, Cafres and dogs, returned home plump and filled out. The Cafres, in particular, glowed, and the dogs had become so fat and lazy that they had difficulty moving about. The Boers preferred to shoot the *rooye-kop*, or red-headed hippopotamus, those whose ears were transparent and flesh-coloured, a certain sign that they were young and fat.

Although in general the Amazoulous consider that no self-respecting man should eat the flesh of the hippopotamus, those who live at the coast are not bound by this rule, particularly those who live at the kraals of Noboka and Om-Kodouka, where not only the fat and the flesh are prized, but also the skin which they eat after it has been boiled for a long time and which even I myself found to be quite palatable.

The skin of the hippopotamus is grey-black on the upper part of the body but lighter on the lower parts. The stomach is grey-white to flesh coloured. A farmer by the name of Combring one day killed a hippopotamus whose flanks were as light coloured as its stomach and which he immediately named *wit-zee-koe*, the white hippopotamus. This was a rare exception which reminded me of the white elephant of the king of Siam. In spite of the thickness of the skin, parasites attach themselves to it. All the animals killed on the coasts of Natal had ticks in their ears and I saw several with a large number of little leeches around the anus.

When the hippopotamus grazes, he crops the grass right down to the roots. One lone animal is capable of causing enormous damage during the course of a single night's grazing in the Cafre gardens. Not only does he devour the maize and the sugar cane, but he tramples the new shoots flat. However, all that is needed to keep him out is a flimsy, low fence. Those animals which live at Om-Nonnoty in Natal and at Om-Lalas in the Amazoulou country are reputed to be the fattest and the finest, due to the quality of the pasturage.

In spite of his weight and his short legs, the hippopotamus often ranges ten or twelve miles away from the river in the course of the night and will climb to a height of 1000 or 1500 feet to reach his favourite pasture grounds. He will venture up steep, narrow paths which are difficult even for a man to climb. Sometimes his nocturnal wanderings are prolonged well into the morning.

The following story was recounted to me by an intrepid South African hunter. This man once surprised a hippopotamus in among steep, sharp rocks on a bank overlooking a river. Reckoning that his retreat was cut off, the animal did not hesitate to leap forty feet from the steep embankment into the water which was fortunately deep at that point. I knew that the hippopotamus, when frightened and wishing to escape as fast as possible, was capable of diving ten or even fifteen feet, and I would not have believed the hunter's story, had his probity not been beyond doubt.

This behaviour of the hippopotamus must be well known to the Amazoulous of Noboka at St Lucia Bay because their method of hunting is based on such knowledge. On the banks of the Touguela they dig deep wide ditches which they line with sharp stakes and then cover with branches. When the animals emerge from the water they are driven towards these ditches along passageways constructed for the purpose which allow of no deviation. But the amphibians soon learn to recognise these traps and to avoid them Noboka's Cafres then go one better; they implant sharp pointed stakes just beneath the surface of the water. They are careful to locate these at the foot of a steep embankment, twelve or fifteen feet high where the hippopotamus paths lead to the river. During the night, when the hippopotamuses are grazing, the Cafres seek them out and drive them with flaming torches, loud cries and the beating of shields towards the prepared traps. Many of the frightened animals leap into the water and are impaled on the invisible stakes. All that remains to be done is to retrieve the floating bodies when the sun comes up. The noise which the hippopotamus makes when he rises to the surface in the evening, sounds something like the neighing of a horse; it also bears some resemblance to a grunt, but it is probably best likened to a powerful snore.

The famous Buffon was mistaken when he claimed that the canine tooth of the hippopotamus could weigh as much as twelve or thirteen pounds; the biggest I ever saw did not exceed five, and I doubt that they ever weigh more than six pounds.

The fertile imagination of the ancients invented the fable that the hippopotamus belches forth fire; it cannot be that steel causes the sparks to fly from his teeth, but rather, or so it seems to me, because he blows water through his nostrils, and when there is a strong breeze, the water is dispersed in the form of a vapour which resembles smoke.

Levaillant assures us that the speed of the hippopotamus under water equals the speed of the horse on land. Permit me to say that this is an exaggeration and that the speed is more or less equal to that of a man. I believe that I am quite correct in saying this, for it is based on observations I made of an animal which was being harassed by my men. In an attempt to escape his pursuers, he set off for the river, with an assegai embedded in his side. The shaft was visible above the water, which enabled me to estimate his speed with great accuracy.

I have heard it said that the hippopotamus, when he feels the need to sleep during the night, takes hold with his canines of a rocky protuberance, or the branch of a tree, to support the weight of his enormous head above the water. I can state quite categorically that this claim is completely without foundation, because the canines show no evidence of such action. Furthermore, the animal spends the hours of daylight in the water where he rests, rising to the surface to breathe even while he sleeps. He is active during the hours of darkness, a period which is frequently insufficient for him to consume an adequate amount of nourishment. I say this without fear of contradiction, for I have seen him grazing in the marshy plains in those areas where he is undisturbed by man, at three o'clock in the afternoon.

It has also been claimed, and the theory is supported particularly by hunters, that when the hippopotamus is mortally wounded, he dives to the bottom of the river and takes hold of a root or a stone between his canines. Shortly afterwards he dies, with his teeth clamped around this object, which serves as an anchor. Three quarters of an hour after firing what he believes to be an excellent shot, the hunter anticipates seeing the body of the amphibian rise to the surface, but nothing happens, and he is in despair. I hesitate to destroy the theory, as it serves to excuse an inaccurate shot but, as science requires accurate information, it is my duty once more to reveal the truth. The lower canines, which are the only ones with commercial value, particularly in the manufacture of dentures, are of the thickest, whitest ivory known, although they are far from equalling in strength those of the carnivores. I have seen a hippopotamus grasp in his jaws a raft made from wagon boards, on which three hunters were floating. The shock of the impact was great; raft and hunters were on the point of disappearing under the water, when the animal suddenly abandoned his hold, which surprised the hunters greatly, until they noticed, embedded in the raft, a broken canine, four inches long.

The explorer Bruce claims to have seen on the lake of Tzane in Abyssinia, hippopotamuses eighteen to twenty feet long; permit me to suggest that he only thought he saw them.

Levaillant must certainly have encountered hippopotamus; I mean it would have been a simple matter for him to have encountered them, for at the time when he was venturing twenty-four leagues beyond Cape Town, many were to be found at Berg Rivier, but the ingenious scholar tells us little of the habits of this interesting species. He has a poor opinion of the drawings which had been published up until that time, but his own are no great improvement; he has exaggerated the lips which cover the great canines, he makes the body too massive, and most remarkable of all, his hippopotamuses have claws on their feet. However it is possible that the fault lies with the draughtsmen.

I have already mentioned how the farmers, armed with their heavy guns, would wait downwind for the hippopotamus to emerge from the water, whereupon they would attempt to wound him by aiming at the vulnerable spot on the shoulder. As great patience is required, both in lying in wait for the quarry and in supporting the onslaughts of the mosquitoes, the farmers sometimes prefer to set up a loaded gun, with a taut string attached to the trigger. When the hippopotamus starts off along the narrow path, he steps on the string, which is stretched across his way, thus releasing the shot. Unfortunately, it is impossible with these guns to achieve the necessary precision and only the strength of a blunderbuss would be equal to the task. As the Dutch have complete faith in their guns, which they load with heavy strong shot, they have invented no ingenious device for the capture of the hippopotamus, although elephant hunting has produced some new ideas which have occasionally been put into practice, but which are not often used because of the expense. I intend to discuss these later.

Mention has been made of the appearance of the hippopotamus in bays and open roadsteads. There is nothing unusual in this. Although he prefers the rivers, the presence of man on the river banks forces him to migrate and the hippopotamus takes to the sea, in order to travel from one river mouth to the next. He will sometimes spend the day in the peaceful waters of the bay for it matters little to him whether they be salty or sweet.

The hippopotamus is comparable to the pig in that every part of his body can be used by man; the skin which is two or three fingers thick, is used to make all sorts of canes, crops and whips. It can also be turned into gelatine. The whole of the flesh and the entrails provide wholesome nourishment, which is however disdained by the Boers who, because of the abundance of meat available to them, tend to be wasteful; they prize only the fat and discard the lean.

The bones, which are similar to those of the rhinoceros and the elephant in that there is no single medullary canal, are spongy and contain a fine marrowy fat which the Cafres extract by boiling after they have crushed them. Sometimes even, after the hunt, they will suck the raw bones as we would a sugar lump dipped in liqueur. Curious to discover the attraction, I imitated them and concluded that they were justified in their appreciation. The lower canines have a fairly high commercial value, and all the teeth are capable of yielding ivory-black, which could be used in industry, but this has not yet been tried.

On my return from this first expedition, I busied myself quietly with investigations of less consequence, which nevertheless brought me great satisfaction. I will mention only one of these; the acquisition of a new species of lark, the most beautiful of its kind.

The 7th July 1841 was a memorable day in my career as a naturalist, for a beautiful bird, the most brightly coloured of the species, came into my possession: this was a lark which rose suddenly into the air fifteen feet ahead of me, displaying its pink abdomen. I fired and succeeded in bringing it down immediately. Its total length was seven inches seven lines,[1] and its wingspan eleven inches six lines. The upper part of the body resembled that of the sentinel lark. The two outer feathers of the tail were completely white while the others were black for more than half of their length, but tipped with white. The remainder of the feathers were black, trimmed with fawny-white. The feathers of the wings were similarly edged. The front of the throat was adorned with pink feathers. Between this collar and the breast, the feathers were brownish-black and fawn. On the whole of the breast and the abdomen, the pink shade was repeated. A fleck

1 A line measured a twelfth of an inch. *Translator's note*

of white appeared on top of the wings. Pink was also present in the fold of the wing, colouring the fine tips of the little feathers. The eyes were brown, the upper part of the beak darker brown and the lower one paler. This lark is rare at Port Natal. I was the first naturalist to obtain one. Two years later Mr Wahlberg acquired several in the Amazoulou country, on the banks of the Om-Lalas, where they are more frequently encountered.

Rather than name the bird for some friend, I have decided that I cannot do better than retain its native name, which will help other explorers to identify it: I shall therefore call it *Alauda hamgazy*.[1]

1 Compare the Zulu *Angazi*: I do not know. *Translator's note*

CHAPTER XIII

Journey to the Amazoulou country — The locust bird — The cattle egret — A Cafre hut — Oum-Matagoulou — Om-Lalas — Om-Schlatousse — The missionary Grout — Arrival at Om-Landelle — Inkoskazis — Arrival at Souzouana's — A Cafre doctor — Unbearable heat — Botany — Omphilos-Omschlopu — Monkeys

The state of my health, following the hunt which I have just described, was so poor that I had begun making arrangements to leave Natal and to return overland to the Cape of Good Hope, when I found myself involved in yet another, and larger, expedition to the Amazoulou country. A farmer, by the name of Combring, had just returned from those parts and was loud in his praises of the natural beauty, and of the abundance of game, which he encountered there. His account, supported by tangible proof, excited the enthusiasm of my driver, Henning Dafel, and awakened my interest to such an extent that I changed my plans. In consequence, I acquired a team of excellent oxen; I inspected my weapons, to which I added a great 600 calibre rifled elephant gun, and I began looking about for suitable men to make up my party. I had soon found seven men, whom I provided with arms; in addition I took on two young Cafres to lead the oxen. Henning, who drove from the box, was the only white to accompany me. Our party numbered eleven in all, with every man a novice at big game hunting, but full of confidence and hope.

Doctor Poortman of Pieters Mauritz Burg, hearing of my departure, came down to join the party with the intention of travelling as far as Om-Inioné, the river of birds, where he proposed making a collection of aquatics. Grateful for his company, I welcomed him gladly and although the sun was already low in the heavens we set out, planning to spend the night at Om-Guinée. It was 15 October 1841. On the 16th, we went no further than Om-Schlange where we beat the woods in the hope of finding elephant, but we found only spoor that was two weeks old, and a buffalo which we wounded. The next day was wasted on useless exploration for we found only a *Cephalopus natalensis*.

On the 18th, we were near Om-Schlouty where my men, who were beginning to suffer the pangs of hunger, went out to hunt for the pot.

It was on this occasion that Boulandje was bitten by a puff-adder. We tried all the means at our disposal: ligature, cross-shaped incision, ammonia, internal and external cauterization with powder, application

164

of the *slange-steen* and of the pneumatic pump. In spite of all these remedies, which were promptly applied, the man suffered agonies for ten days, just as I had done after a similar bite.

This was the first opportunity I had had to observe the action of the famous *slange-steen*, the snakestone, whose wonderful properties have been so much vaunted. It is reputed to come from the Boschjesmans, who obtain it by killing the snake which bears the stone on its head. This would seem to confirm the old saying that the remedy is to be found near the cause but I must seriously question this belief, which is given credence by the Boers. I have never seen a snake with a stone on its head and besides, upon examination, the *slange-steen* turned out to be nothing but a pumice stone, smoothed by the water. It is oblong in shape, rounded and flattened, grey in colour, light and porous. It is one and a half inches long and an inch wide. It must be plunged into hot water before being applied to the swollen wound, whereupon it soon turns brown as a result of the blood which it has absorbed. Before saturation point is reached, it adheres firmly to the wound, but when saturation is complete, it detaches itself. Before it is reapplied it must be thoroughly washed, until it returns to its original colour. We repeated this operation on our patient several times. I had thus every opportunity of studying the action of the stone, and I am obliged to admit that some of the claims are justified. However, there are others which I cannot confirm because the necessary ingredients in the treatment were not to hand.

I had been told that in order to ascertain how long the application should be continued, the patient must be made to drink warm milk, preferably fresh from the cow. Because of the acidity of the poison which has permeated the blood of the patient, the milk immediately turns sour, and is vomited up in curds. This treatment must be repeated until there is evidence that the patient's stomach is able to tolerate the fresh milk. Many claim to have witnessed this but, although I have often been present at such an accident, I have never been able, at the time, to procure fresh milk.

If no *slange-steen* is available, the Boers take a live fowl and pluck the feathers from the pectoral muscles, where an incision is made. The exposed flesh is then placed on the wound which has been previously opened to receive it. The throbbing flesh of the bird absorbs sufficient poison to cause its death, while the patient experiences great relief.

The Boschjesmans prefer to suck up the venom with their lips and spit it out; but it is essential that the mucous membranes should not be exposed to the danger. They are even bold enough to drink the venom contained in the vesicles and experience no ill effect, thus proving that it is only active when it enters the blood.

The Amazoulous, who are so much exposed to snakebite, have no treatment other than the ashes of the spinal column of the snake itself. These ashes are applied externally and taken internally at the same time, but I doubt that their alkaline properties are strong enough to have any effect. This is a remedy which, like so many others, makes more impression on the mind than on the body. They have in their country a little cotton tree, the roots of which they could put to good use, but their knowledge of medicinal plants is rather limited; the Hottentots are superior in this respect.

On the day of the accident we camped at Wolf Gat; on the 19th at Om-Schlala; on the 20th at Om-Nonnoty, where I wounded a buffalo, as a consequence of seeing a little white heron. But let me explain: this bird is a species of heron related to the egrets which he resembles in that his feathers are snowy white, although he has a slight reddish tint in the crest. He lives in flocks several hundred strong and perches in the trees. He is indiscriminate in frequenting either the shores or the open plains, or even the bush. He feeds principally on the ticks which attach themselves to animals and on grasshoppers which are plentiful in the grasslands. The Boers call him the *Spring-Haan-Voogel*, the locust bird. Naturalists know him as *Ardea bubulcus*.

His habits vary according to time and place. I noticed him on several occasions on the banks of a lake, like the other herons, and to my great astonishment, I came upon him frequently, standing only three feet away from the line of flames when the dry grass was being burnt. He had no fear of fire, but waited on the ground to seize the dazed grasshoppers as they fled the smoke, while the kite hovered above, waiting to catch in its claws those that tried to fly away. In the plains, he is to be found among the cattle and walks about among them, searching for the ticks, swollen with blood, which have fallen to the ground. In the bush, he rides on the back of the buffaloes, picking off the ticks with his beak. The unconcerned buffalo moves about as he grazes, but our heron is not at all disconcerted. You will now understand that it is a simple matter to detect the presence of a buffalo when, from a distance, something white can be seen travelling along above the tall grass. While there is a bird which reveals the buffalo to the hunter, there is unfortunately also a bird which warns the buffalo of the hunter's approach; these are the cattle egrets, two species of which exist in Natal. The buffalo allows these birds to roam all over his back and sides; like the woodpecker, they attach themselves by means of their tail feathers, and move all over the animal in search of ticks. The buffalo grazes in peace when he is accompanied by such guardians, for he relies on them to keep watch.

In fact, the hunter is often fifty or sixty paces off when these tickbirds rise into the air with an unattractive squawk, which is their cry of alarm, and their clumsy host immediately sets off. They render a similar service to the *Boselaphus oreas* and to the rhinoceros. There are no other birds in the world which I have cursed as much as I have these.

At three o'clock on the afternoon of the 21st, we stood on the banks of the Touguela, which I intended to cross without delay. A high wind was blowing and the shifting sands at the ford were under three feet of water. The Amazoulou country on the other side of the river wore a dreary aspect due to the approaching storm. Poortman, who was not going beyond the Om-Inioné, a few leagues further on, was afraid to put the Touguela behind him, as the waters threatened at any moment to become impassable. Poortman knew not the first thing about travel. He had a wife in Pieters Mauritz Burg, and this anchor allowed him to drift no further than a cable's length.

Poortman was a spectator of our crossing and a witness to our difficulties when the shaft came close to breaking. The wheels sank into the sand and, had we not been blessed with a good driver and excellent oxen to pull us out, the expedition would have ended then and there, for by the next day the water would have come down in spate and carried everything away.

There was however some damage and loss; we hung out our wet things to dry in the wind, which exacted heavy payment for its services. It stole away a whole set of my clothing and although I ran in pursuit, I was not fast enough. Not a single thorn-bush put out its arms with their hooked claws to assist me. Fearful of the wind, they turned cowering away and, grateful to be spared, they made no attempt to rescue my clothes.

The reader, sitting by his fireside, will probably find some amusement in this account of how the wind ill-treated a poor devil who, far from any shop, was unable to replace his lost belongings. I too can laugh about it today, but at the time I was not amused by the ludicrous scene. My reader will understand that, as I was entering a hot country, I was not fearful of the cold, but of the action of the sun which raises blisters on those parts of the body that are exposed to its rays. In the circumstances, however, I had to accept my lot and go on my way.

Hurriedly, we bundled back all the things which had come adrift from the wagon, and painfully climbed the steep hillside towards the *mouzi* of Nonglass, which stood at the top. The climb took us two hours and I considered that we were fortunate to reach our destination for there was no proper road and the wind was excessively strong. We were detained here on the 22nd by the incessant rain and spent the night in the principal hut of Nonglass to which we were invited by his wives.

As it was rather cold, the fire was being constantly refuelled, which resulted in more smoke than heat. All other occupation being impossible, I smoked my pipe as I chatted and observed my confined surroundings. The external and the internal aspects of all Cafre huts are alike; the furnishing is similar in them all, but, as is the case among all peoples, the dwellings of the great are distinguished by luxury, whether in the choice of materials, or in their workmanship.

Nonglass's hut, a hemisphere constructed from 3000 curved intersecting wooden poles, was twenty feet in diameter and eight feet high. In the centre of the hut three principal poles, blackened columns polished by the smoke, supported a heavy transverse beam upon which eight other beams rested. In the floor, between the first and the third poles, was a circular cavity with a flattened raised edge; this was the hearth upon which stood the great earthenware pot in which the food was cooking. Around the hearth, the men were squatting or lying on mats, engaged in leather work or basket-making, talking or resting.

Opposite the hemispherical door, which was eighteen inches to two feet high, and the only way out for both people and smoke, stood a sort of rack which held the great pots for *ombyla*, *mabèle* or *tchouala*, maize, Cafre corn or beer, to be drawn from the *nogoty* for immediate needs. Here and there, hanging on the walls or lying on the floor, were the spades and the picks, the baskets, the *ischlouzo-ka-tchouala* — beer strainers of admirable workmanship, the *sitébè* — mats to hold the meat, the *tounga* — wooden pots for milking.[1] Suspended in bundles were assegais with a few hunting shields; for the military shields are kept in a hut raised on stakes, as a protection against rats. The floor, made from the earth of ant-heaps compressed with cowdung, was polished to a dark mirror-like brilliance and shone like a piece of marble. I was immediately struck by its cleanliness.

That evening, I expressed a desire to write some notes, although I did not think it would be possible to obtain sufficient illumination to do so. I had underestimated my hosts' inventiveness. I was provided with a torch made from a long blade of *tambouki-gras*, the sort from which Boschjesmans make their arrows, thick as a reed, and which burnt with a clear steady flame. My candleholder was a willing Cafre who held the grass in one hand while in the other, he held a reserve supply.

When I wished to rest, mats were unrolled and I was given a pretty little wooden pillow, which my bad European habits led me to pad with a scarf in order to cushion more comfortably a head that was still too tender.

On the morning of the 23rd, the rain was still falling but, noticing

1 In all of southern Africa, milking is done by the men; a woman would feel dishonoured if it were said that she milked cows.

that the skies were about to clear, I distributed some little gifts in payment of my debt. Furthermore, to demonstrate to the ladies of Nonglass that I was grateful for their kind welcome, I patted their children. Some of them smiled back at me, but the favourite, the one whom Nonglass intended as his principal heir, could not look at me. However much I tried, neither caresses nor presents could bring him round; his young imagination viewed me with the same horror as our little white children feel at the sight of a negro.

Let me not be told that the Caucasian race is the most beautiful of all, and that it is universally pleasing. Each race has its own standards of beauty. The clothing with which the whites cover themselves, has more charm in the eyes of the natives, than their bodies, which are never seen unclothed. Were they to see the naked white body, the natives would realise that they themselves were infinitely more beautiful, with their well-fleshed muscles and their firm rounded curves. There have doubtless, at some time, been finer specimens among us than there are at present. At the moment, our bodies are so misshapen by our clothing, that our health is in danger and our sculptors in despair. I would recommend to them that they discover the beauty of the naked Cafre.

At about ten o'clock, we drew up on the banks of the Oum-Matagoulou where we fired a few shots at the hippopotamuses; but in view of the abundance of *riet-booken*, we turned our attention to these antelopes. Henning made the first killing; one of my Cafres, Mâhléy only wounded his victim which, in attempting to escape, jumped into a little stream where it was seized by a crocodile and dragged under the water. My man, seeing the object of his desire taken from beneath his nose by this filthy creature, was so astonished that he cursed all the crocodiles on earth. He began by calling them *Om-Tagaty*, (wizards), indicating by his rapid and expressive gestures that the first crocodile he came upon, warming itself in the sun, would pay dearly for this deed; then his expressions of regret at having lost his prize were mingled with tears which were followed by laughter that clearly said: 'Tomorrow, *riet-booken* and crocodiles, tomorrow, just you wait and see.'

However, we had succeeded in bringing back one *riet-book* to satisfy our hunger, and in a short while nothing remained of it. The conversation was animated and joyous, for this was the first occasion upon which my men had eaten anything since Om-Schlango. Om-Matagoulou was a good place to revictual, but I was impatient to reach Omphilos as quickly as possible, and so I decided to set off on the 25th.

Towards evening, we camped on a hill to the north of which was a great plain extending as far as the Om-Gohey mountains which spanned our horizon from west to north-east. In the east we could

169

see the sea, the Indian Ocean, immense and blue, which appeared to melt into the sky. In spite of the dusk coming on, my driver and I went into the dunes to hunt, and each of us brought back a *riet-book*. The time of plenty had returned; my men were no longer anxious and began to anticipate all sorts of wonderful things.

On the 26th we travelled all day, and on the 27th we were able to outspan at Om-Lalas where the water over the ford rises and falls with the tide. This river, as it crosses the dunes, forms elbow-like bends where we saw a number of hippopotamuses. We killed one the first day.

We discovered here the strange mimosa which produces the enormous fruit already known to the inhabitants of the colony at the Cape of Good Hope. The sea had often cast up near Cape Town, on the shores of Table Bay or False Bay, a flattened, hard, brown fruit. The Dutch called them *Zee-Bontjes*, sea beans, because they did not know their origin, and these so-called beans were always found without their pod. Near Om-Lalas, we came across a number of these fruit, hanging from the tops of trees which grew on the banks of the little tributaries. My men found pods that were three feet long and contained fourteen to seventeen seeds, each seed being large and strong enough to make an excellent snuffbox. Since my return, I have been able to compare these fruit from the land of the Amazoulous, with those brought back from India, which are produced by the *Endata Pursoetha, mimosa scandens*. It seems that this plant exists in Oceania, perhaps even in South America; an English naval captain gave me some of the seeds which he had picked up on the shores of the Pacific Ocean, near Guayaquil. Apparently this fruit, when it is consigned to the waves, travels enormous distances, carried by the currents.

Three or four miles from the river mouth, the sea was breaking on to a sandbank, which seemed to extend for some distance. I decided to remain at this place until the 31st, so that we might cut up our hippopotamus; I wished also to have time to prepare some specimens. The day before, three wagons had arrived, bringing the men whose names I had included in my request to the council for permission to hunt in Zoulou-land. The new arrivals were David Stellar, the most famous hippopotamus hunter in Natal, Richard King, and Douglas.

They had brought with them a fine little dinghy, to facilitate hunting the amphibious animals. This boat served to transport me and my effects to the other side of the Om-Lalas; without it I would not have been able to cross the river because of the hippopotamus path which increased the depth of the water from three foot to four and a half or five. The boat carried all my things over in two trips, and I had only to reload them on the other side and to thank my companions for their assistance. On 1 November, we set up camp together on the southern shore of the lake of Om-Schlatousse. On the 2nd, because of the wind, we crossed to the northern shore where, in spite of our numbers and the skill of our marksmen, we were unable to do more than wound the hippopotamuses which we then lost sight of, for they hid themselves away to die under the floating grasses. On the 3rd, we crossed the Om-Schlatousse and climbed the steep sandy bank with a combined span of twenty-four oxen to draw my wagon. At about midday we arrived at the dwelling of the American missionary Grout.

Richard King, who had been commissioned to bring out a small quantity of goods for this missionary, went with his companions to greet him. I, who did not know the man, and had no reason to make his acquaintance, continued working on my specimens. Hardly had my companions concluded their visit, when a very precisely worded letter came for me from Mr Grout, to this effect:

> Sir, I was most displeased, a short while since, to have been obliged to have your oxen driven from my garden where I found them eating the young wheat which I recently planted, and doing damage detrimental to my property. If you behave on my property with this sort of negligence, I have reason to believe that, when you are in the Amazoulou country, you will have no scruple in allowing your oxen to enter the gardens of the Cafres. Allow me sir to caution you in order to spare you any possible unpleasantness. I am etc.

It is true that some of the oxen, in the absence of their herdsman, had permitted their sacrilegious tongues to touch a few shoots of the young wheat sown by Mr Grout. Mr Grout had had to expel them because, contrary to Cafre custom, his garden was not enclosed by a continuous fence; far from it, there was no fence at all. But as these oxen were not mine, he ought to have addressed himself to their master. And what is more, he should have been content simply to state the facts, without the addition of insulting remarks. He addressed himself to the wrong man for, in matters of this sort, I have little patience, and without enquiring whether any oxen other than mine had entered his field, without deigning even to take up my pen, I gave a verbal reply to the messenger of the *om-phondiss*:

> If there is damage, let your master inform me of the cost; I wish to pay. I wish also that the *om-phondiss* would hold his tongue, for he speaks to me as a master and he is not my master; he is master of none here. Neither white nor black, but only his servants owe him obedience. Panda alone is master of all those who are in this country, whether they be white or black. All, including the *om-phondiss*, must obey his orders. You have heard my message, now go!

I intended spending some time in their country, and I was determined that the Cafres should not believe that I was in any way dependent on a missionary who had no credit with Panda. Moreover, I was angered by the tone of his approach which was indicative of the worldly power he had had the effrontery to assume. Whether he accepted that he was wrong, or whether he realised that I was not to be addressed like a South African farmer, the reverend doctor did not reply. I kept his letter and reread it often, experiencing each time the same degree of irritation.

Since I have come to speak of European missionaries in southern Africa, I beg my reader's permission to allow me, in passing, to express my opinion of them. A declaration of good faith on my part would perhaps be appropriate, otherwise it might be imagined that I were the sworn enemy of the spread of civilization among the Cafres. This is not the case and I am simply expressing my own views of the matter.

We Europeans are very civilized; according to many people, the Cafres are not. It is said that they are savages. Nevertheless, they are civilized in their own way; only one important condition is missing; I mean the knowledge and use of writing to express and transmit their ideas. I say that they are civilized, because they live together in societies governed by laws which, even if they are not written down, are at least known to all, laws which the chief in his high position infringes, it is true, but which, emanating from the great laws of nature, are understood by every man. I say that they are civilized, because these laws constrain them to respect each other, even when their customs already teach them to help each other, for hospitality is one of their virtues. We call them savages, but they are in fact civilized men. There is no real difference between them and us except in the degree of civilization, and in order to destroy this false idea of barbarity which is so mistakenly applied to the Cafres, I hasten to add that savages *do* exist in southern Africa and they are the Boschjesmans who live in isolated family groups, sustaining their vagrant existence by hunting and plundering, just as the leopards do, and killing without fear or remorse the traveller who comes within range of their arrows. The Cafres are diametrically different from these people.

As far as I know them, the Cafres are beyond reproach. Individually, they are good, and if collectively they are cruel, let this surprise no one for they are dominated and activated by the whim of the chief. Then let us not criticise them, but their despotic system of government, the only system in truth which can be applied to illiterate people.

I consider it indispensable that they should learn to read. I would prescribe that, instead of a European religion, whatever it might be, a simply morality without accompaniment of dogma or of cult should be preached amongst them, a morality which would serve to stimulate the introduction of books and the teaching of reading and writing. I would prefer this to the preaching of our Christian religion which attacks polygamy, the basis of the social order of these people, because polygamy is good, useful and necessary to the Cafres who in no way practise it as the Orientals do, for the Turks and the Asiatics debase woman by restricting her personal liberty and curtailing her activity while the Cafres assign to woman her proper place in society. Another reason why I would prefer this system of simple morality is because the Cafres, who are men of judgment, do not accept the mystical forms which veil our religion and which constitute the principal reason for their rejection of it, and their scorn of us. Furthermore the reason why they call our missionaries liars, is that they preach what is incredible and unacceptable, and finally, because this mysticism, which has been so long disputed in Europe and especially in France, has regrettably produced only evils from which we must try to spare these people.

The system which we Europeans are at present attempting to impose on them is that of excessive civilization, which does not suit the Cafres at all, for they are in no way prepared for it. Some compromise would be preferable. If I dared to compare the advantages and the disadvantages of the state of excessive civilization which prevails in our own country, with the advantages and disadvantages of the simple condition in which the Cafres live, I would not hesitate to pronounce in favour of the view that these latter are infinitely less miserable, both mentally and physically, than are our own people. Allow me to make an observation; over there, a man need not toil relentlessly in order to support his existence. This man lives well, but not luxuriously. In our society, men must toil to the furthest limits of their strength and endurance. The working man has difficulty in simply keeping alive. The food which he earns by his labour, is dissipated in the energy which he expends in performing that labour. If he does not work, he cannot earn. He cannot hunt for food in the woods, and if he attempts to steal, the law which protects property will get him. It is true that the man may receive benefits but this does not apply in every case, and it is never sufficient to sustain him. So, in weariness and deprivation, he languishes and dies like an expiring flame.

At one end of the scale then is the Cafre, the so-called savage, at the other end the civilized man. As far as his moral faculties are concerned, I say that the Cafre has feelings; he knows suffering and anxiety; since he is a rational man, it cannot be otherwise, but I am convinced that five-sixths of our people suffer more than he does. You will hasten to say, 'But the Cafres, having a smaller sum of unhappiness, must consequently have a smaller sum of happiness

173

than we have.'

I am no philosopher, but I believe that it is only unhappiness which leaves its mark. I believe that the absence of unhappiness is happiness, and that even the least amount of it must benefit a nation just as it does an individual. Besides, real happiness is to be found in nature and not in the thousand pleasures invented by civilization.

> It may be compared to the fire whose soft glow
> Secretly permeates all other elements,
> It descends into the rocks, rises to the clouds,
> It will redden the coral within the sea sand,
> And live in the icicles which winter freezes.

We passed the *mouzi* of Magalébé on the 3rd, and a short while later, we began making our way up the most difficult of mountain passes to negotiate which we were obliged to travel for 200 paces along the edge of a very steep ridge, supporting the wagons by means of thongs made fast behind. We then made a sharp downward turn, with the heavy wagons threatening to overtake and crush the teams, although we had put drags on the right back and the left front wheels as is the custom in southern Africa. A hundred foot descent lay before us, and had it not been for the soft ground between the loose stones, which enabled our locked wheels to plough into the earth and provided the friction denied by the harder ground, a number of our oxen would have been crushed. This slope reminded me of the Russian mountains.

On this occasion, as on a thousand others, I had the opportunity of observing that the Boers are the finest wagon drivers in the world. Their boldness in the management of their teams is exceptional; many times have I seen them perform wonderful feats of strength, while negotiating mountain passes. They will frequently drive their teams along a ridge bordering on a precipitous drop of perhaps 1200 feet, where a single unexpected stone could send wagon and oxen crashing to destruction in the depths below. They make light of these dangers, which fill me with trepidation. I take pleasure in doing them the justice of recognising their excellence in this difficult exercise.

I believe that they owe this contempt of danger partly to their descent from the nucleus of sailors of the Dutch East India Company, who first settled at the Cape. I recognised in the manufacture of their harness, their yokes, their strops, their whips, something of the sailor, rather than of the European peasant farmer. These men, conditioned by the unrelenting difficulties of life at sea, would not be deterred by the challenges of the land. Once surmounted, these difficulties became simply a matter of routine, a routine which I observed on many occasions.

On the 4th, we entered a sparsely wooded area, watered by a

small river called the Sélène. In the trees on its banks I saw grey crested touracos, *Coliphymus concolor*, perched in the highest branches. We were made aware of their presence by their cries, which are as unattractive as their plumage. This was our first encounter with these birds, and I can vouch for the curious fact that they are never seen further south. Buffaloes appeared several times during the course of the day. A herd of these animals came to a sudden halt eighty paces in front of us, as if astonished to see us. A shot was fired which killed one of them and dispersed the rest.

The next day, we continued on our way through the bush, often having to cut a path through the trees with our axes. As our progress was slow, it was evening before we reached the *mouzi* of Om-Landelle, situated in the midst of fine pastures, but in a dry area, with virtually no water. I was particularly struck by the excellent condition of the cattle at this *mouzi*; they ranged freely and frolicked like gnus; they came running, agile and fleet of foot and stopped to stare at our toiling oxen as we passed by, then they spun around and galloped away, with a flash of glowing colour on their rounded hind-quarters, which the Boers call the *breeches*.

The first man to approach us was a headman of Panda, sent by his master to greet us and to solicit goods for barter. This man's name was Om-Phinieri. He was a true Cafre gentleman, whose aspect was as pleasing as his name; his manners were those of a courtier; there was something more than mere politeness in his demeanour, something exquisitely engaging, acquired in keeping company with great men, for Om-Phinieri was a sort of private secretary to Panda, continually at his side to receive and transmit orders, as aides-de-camp do. His appearance charmed me so that I formed a very favourable impression of the man, and in all my subsequent dealings with him I had no reason to change my mind.

Om-Landelle, into whose principal hut we were received, was a man of the first importance in Amazoulou society; he had thirty or forty wives, among whom were three of Panda's sisters. Unfortunately, Om-Landelle was away, and it was Om-Phinieri who undertook to introduce us into the presence of the three *inkoskazis* (princesses).

I had admired the astonishing plumpness of the master's oxen, but I was even more impressed by the remarkable *embonpoint* of these ladies of quality. They were former acquaintances of mine; we had met at Om-Tougate at the time of Panda's desertion, but they had been less impressive then, as they were fatigued by arduous travel. Here at home, it was a different matter. The *inkoskazis* congratulated me on my delightful idea of paying them a visit, adding that they had not fogotten my beard or my tobacco which they 'loved to tears'; then came the compliments, half Dutch, half Cafre: '*Mooi, mooi Oum-Longo, mouschlé kakoulou ouena!*' There followed the sniffing of the palm, too obvious an intimation for me to delay the offering of *gouaye*.

The taking of snuff is a serious business among these people. First of all, before squatting in a circle, they blow their noses and then, according to the taste or the quality of the individual, the tobacco is inhaled from the hand, or carried to the nostrils on a little ivory spoon. At this point there is a pause while the nail of the right thumb is rubbed across the forehead; tears fill the eyes and overflow. There is another pause followed by prolonged weeping, for this is the moment of exquisite pleasure. No one laughs, there is complete silence, broken finally by a sneeze, which is followed by another, then two, three sneezes, until everybody is sneezing, like a burst of gunfire, and he who is not stimulated by tobacco to produce sneezes, induces them by tickling his nostrils with a straw. The ritual ends, as it does in every land where snuff is taken, with the use of the hand-kerchief; there is however one difference; the handkerchief which the Cafre uses can never be lost! A Cafre who is taking snuff is like a dog which is gnawing a bone; neither wants to be disturbed. To interrupt their pleasure is an impoliteness so great as to be considered an affront.

When my *inkoskazis* had savoured at their leisure the delights of my rose and bergamot snuff, I felt compelled to return their compliments by improvising my own, in the Cafre style. My discourse was liberally sprinkled with the attributes '*Mouschlé kakoulou, mafouta kakoulou,*' to preface their title of *inkoskazi*. 'Most beautiful and most fat princesses', I said to them. These expressions pleased them so much that one of them proceeded to demonstrate to me that my praises fell short of the truth and that they, princesses of the blood, were even fatter than my words had suggested; she revealed her leg, a real pillar of Notre Dame, on which it was difficult to detect the presence of an ankle. Observing my astonishment, and with the intention of increasing it to the utmost, she drew aside her blue shawl, and with her left hand beat her breast and her abdomen several times as if to say, 'Have you ever seen princesses as fat as we are?' 'Never, never,' I replied, opening my eyes wide, and adding to myself, 'May Heaven preserve me!'

Richard King, Douglas and David Stellar were witnesses to this scene, which later gave rise to much mirth. Shortly after this, we received several great pots filled with *amas* (curdled sour milk) sent by our princesses. The gift being in proportion to the size of the donors, there was sufficient for fifty men. In addition to this, Om-Phinieri on behalf of Panda presented us with a cow as a gift.

On the 6th, to the great regret of these ladies, we took our departure and set off in the direction of the *mouzi* of Souzouana a league away, where we camped under some large trees. These trees, although they

176

are not woody, attain the height and strength of our oaks; they were the *norsh-doorn-boom* or the *kooker-boom*, the quiver tree.

I was setting out to find Souzouana to whom I wished to pay my respects, when I came upon two men squatting on their heels facing each other, their bodies streaming with sweat, alternately repeating the same words a thousand times over. One was the *inianga*, or doctor, the other was a man of the common people who was trying to discover the cause of his son's illness, for he despaired of his life and sought the means to cure him.

When he had repeated the question a thousand times; when he had heard a thousand identical replies; when fatigue finally overcame him, the *inianga* fell into a state of meditation, pressed his forehead with his left hand, pointed the index finger of his right hand to the ground and pronounced his diagnosis, to the great satisfaction of his petitioner who paid close attention. 'It is the spirit of the grandfather,' he said, 'which has returned to torment your son. The spirit of the grandfather desires a cow; he will not leave the child in peace until his wish is granted.'

It is incredible that such oracular advice, and such a remedy, should require so lengthy a preamble. This does not imply that the man was not completely satisfied. I saw him pay the *inianga* in glass beads and then go off to prepare the sacrifice which had been demanded. Poor man, I had no wish to destroy his faith; I was reflecting with pity on his stupidity, and on the stupidity of all these simple people, whose superstitious beliefs were so blatantly exploited, when suddenly a vivid recollection flashed before my mind; the memory of the alms-box dedicated to the saints or the virgin; the candles that are lighted in their name; the vows, the pilgrimages, the rosaries, the medals, the scapulars. At that moment I realised that this ordinary man was no different from any other ordinary man in all the countries of the earth.

Then, when I was least expecting to see him, a little thin old man came towards me, his left hand covering his mouth as a sign of respect and astonishment. His fine head suggested unusual intelligence and spirit; this was Souzouana, old Souzouana, whom later, I was indiscreet enough to address as *Omdala* (old), intending the epithet as a mark of respect. He turned almost white with anger, and stiffening his sinews, he said, 'You call me old do you? You call me old do you? How can you have that opinion of me? Do you not know that this hand has killed many elephants and many men too. Do you doubt that it is still capable of doing so? Ah! let the opportunity arise and you will see that Souzouana can still lead the attack against the elephant; you will see how his muscles respond; you will see how deep his *omkondo* can bite, and you call him *Omdala*! *Omdala*! Let war come, and you will see Souzouana fighting alongside the young men; you will see him repel the enemy attack with his shield; you will see his *tonga* covered in blood, for his heart is great, the heart of Souzouana! *Omdala! Omdala!* Is it possible? Is your heart beautiful, is your heart white, when you call me *Omdala*? You wish to rank Souzouana among the incapable, the infirm, the insane; Souzouana who is still a match for the bravest in the field. Fie upon you, child with a long beard! *Omdala*, I would prefer to believe that you intended some other name.' And circling about in front of me he spluttered, '*Omdala, Omdala*'. He would have repeated the word until the sun went down[1] had I not explained to him that this epithet was a term of respect among the whites, such as one might commonly use to one's old father. He had the intelligence to admit that his customs and mine in this respect might differ, just as they did in our mode of living and of dressing. Later, as a result of long acquaintance, I came to realise that Souzouana was a most worthy man. I received from him a thousand services which I attempted to repay to the best of my ability by presenting him with the sort of trinket which white men bring. I never suspected that he would later be accused of the crime of too great a fondness for me; I never guessed that this attachment would cost him his life. But I must not anticipate events; too soon, alas would come the fatal time when I would be robbed of the friendship of a fine old man whose noble qualities had so captivated me.

The first day's hunting yielded a buffalo and a quagga, which I skinned. On the 7th I returned to camp at about midday under a blazing sun and discovered that the brackish water, which was all that was available at the *mouzi*, provided little relief. At about two o'clock the sun was infernally hot and, in order to protect myself from its rays, I took the strange but effective precaution of putting on a woollen shirt and a seaman's coat, just as if the weather had been cold. To begin with, my companions laughed at my homoeopathic measures which had the effect of producing a heavy perspiration, but I persevered and towards evening I felt appreciably more comfortable. The others, stretched out in their wagons, gasping and incapable even of conversation, did not experience the calm relaxation I felt, which was brought about by fatigue. The heat kept them awake, for even the night was hot and still, without a breath of air; nature itself seemed to be baking. Overcome by the effects of this exceptional heat, King, Stellar and Douglas discussed a plan to yoke up their oxen and set off for the river, where at least the water was

1 All the blacks I knew shared this habit; they did not attempt to vary their ideas or their words; they repeated as rapidly and as often as possible the expressions which they considered to be the strongest and the most insulting. I can recall seeing negroes begin a quarrel at the Lézard river and continue it the whole way to Pointe-à-Pitre — an excercise in perseverance.

drinkable, big trees cooled the air and one could escape the heat by spending part of the day lying in the river. They would have put their plan into action immediately, had the heat from which they were suffering not drained them of all strength and courage.

Near the place where Souzouana's *mouzi* stood, there grew some trees, the fruit of which attracted my attention. One of these trees, which stood no more than eighteen feet high and which was not at all beautiful, bore great numbers of these oval shaped fruit which were wider near the stalk, more conical near the tip and characterised by sharp protuberances. They were as green as the unopened bud of a poppy. The Amazoulous have no use for these fruit.

Another tree amused us by its strange appearance; it was hung all over with cylindrical, round-ended fruit which reminded us of the appetising display in a pork-butcher's window. In order to complete the illusion, only the brown colouring was lacking to transform our green vegetables into sausages. The tree is known by the name of *Tripinnaria tenacium*. The Amazoulous described as *mouty* the fruit of this tree, as well as that of the tree mentioned above, which is not to say that the trees were poisonous, but only that the monkeys would not eat the fruit. It is well known that man, lacking the instincts which guide the animals in their choice of food, profits by their example, particularly by that of the quadrumanes.

The following day, the temperature had lost nothing of its intensity, until at about three o'clock in the afternoon, the breeze came up in the east, and my companions took advantage of the change to take their departure. I would like to have followed them, but various reasons determined that I should remain.

When I complained to Souzouana of the excessive heat which affects even the Cafres themselves, he said to me, 'The north wind is very hot here; what you have just experienced is nothing, but if you remain you will find that when it penetrates the mouth and the nostrils, it intoxicates a man, dazes him, dries his eyes and makes him fall to the ground.' I repeat his very words but I hasten to add that I never witnessed such disastrous effects, although I was often subsequently exposed to these conditions. It is true that I felt dazed and bewildered, but only for a short while.

We remained here until the 11th, adding a few buffaloes and kudus to our trophies of the hunt. We then went down to the Om-Philos-Om-Schlopu, four or five miles away, where we met up again with our hunters who, in the space of three days, had killed three rhinoceros, four buffaloes and an elephant. They told us wonderful stories of these hideous rhinoceroses, which they killed for the sole purpose of having them out of the way. These were the rhinoceros *simus* of which, in their ignorance, they made no use at all. The Amazoulou Cafres have certain prejudices in regard to this animal which they passed on to us, so that the hyaenas and the vultures found themselves the only guests at the immense and delicious feast which took place every time we killed one.

But, before closing this chapter, let us say a word about a delectable fruit which we found after leaving the *mouzi* of Souzouana. As we passed alongside a rocky ridge grown here and there with various species of trees and shrubs, we saw a movement in the branches of a tree which was laden with fruit. It was a troop of monkeys, *Ama-Kaho*, which, alarmed at our approach, were swinging away from branch to branch to escape us. When we arrived beneath the tree, we shook down a quantity of the fruit which we broke open and ate. This fruit belongs to a tree which the botanists call *Strychnos*, but this *Strychnos* differs from the *S. spinosus* which is so common on the sandy plains around the bay of Natal. It is smaller, the woody outer covering and the flesh are yellow, it is sweeter and less acid, and its smell and flavour are not at all the same. If this *Strychnos* is not quite identical to the one from Nossi-Bé, it must be closely related.

The monkeys appeared to have eaten a large quantity of the fruit to judge from the debris which cluttered the ground. My Cafres followed suit and I must admit that, in my turn, I imitated my Cafres as I found the fruit very palatable in that it was less acid than most of the wild fruit which grows in this part of Africa. The tree is also found in the great woods surrounding Port Natal, as it favours the density of the forest, while the *Strychnos spinosus* is more at home in open glades and on the dry plains. This is perhaps the reason why it is less common.

When they arrived at the bay of Natal, the Boers gave the name *wild-kalabas-boom* to the *Strychnos spinosus*, and the one that resembles the *Strychnos* of Nossi-Bé, they called the *klein-wild-kalabas-boom* or *geèle wild-kalabas-boom*. The fruit of the *Strychnos spinosus*, when it is ripe, has a very strong smell and is well known for its refreshing qualities. Indeed, the flesh may quench a man's thirst, but it has certain disagreeable properties also. On one occasion, when I was in the company of Mr Wahlberg of Stockholm, and various other people, we all consumed several of these fruit, for there was no water available. This produced vomiting among some of us, and the reverse effect in others. For my part, I felt no ill-effects; the Cafres insist that the fruit is good medicine for those who are in need of its properties, but that it has no effect on those whose stomachs do not require it. It forms the staple diet of the monkeys which inhabit the bush of Port Natal. They have discovered how to hasten the ripening process of the fruit which is normally very slow; they detach the biggest of the green fruit and leave it to lie on the sand, exposed to the sun and the dew. When we needed the fruit for our own use, we looked for it not in the trees, but on the ground.

CHAPTER XIV

We camped among some tambooty trees on the south bank of the
Om-Philos-Omschlopu, three hours walk from the confluence of the
two Omphilos rivers. This place offered two great advantages to the
hunter offset by certain disadvantages, which we only discovered
later. Frequently we sighted, on the slopes across the river, herds of
wild animals which were peacefully grazing, unaware of our proximity;
there were buffalo, alone or in groups of up to fifteen, kudus, varying
from seven to eighteen in number, *cannas*, from eight to forty at
different times, and from three to as many as eight quaggas. Sometimes there was a white rhinoceros[1] or some elephants which were
attracted by the fruit of the giant fig-trees. To reach them, all we had
to do was to cross the river, which was always fordable in the dry
season, and to walk a few hundred paces, taking cover behind trees
or bushes. The proximity of these animals meant that our cooking
pots were always well supplied, and the custom was to waste in
proportion to the abundance which was available. The trees afforded
us some shade and this was a considerable advantage. The river had
usually enough water for bathing; we were camped close to it but in
a sufficiently elevated position to have no fears of humidity or
flooding or even mosquitoes. But in exchange for the enjoyment of
these little advantages, we were exposed to real danger. As we were
camped near their pathway to the river, elephants might well come in
the night, upset our tents, huts and wagons, and trample us underfoot.

In spite of my remonstrances, we had surrounded our camp with
heaps of debris, negligently cast away too close to the huts. As a
result, I found that all the rats in the country appeared to have
arranged to meet at my place. Slithering after them came the snakes;
every hole was inhabited, the hollow of every tambooty tree sheltered
one or several, and very soon these dangerous neighbours became our
guests; not a day passed that we did not kill one. In this respect
almost any other campsite would have been preferable.

Neither were we in a position open enough to enjoy a wide ex-

---

1   The white rhinoceros is the *Rhinoceros simus*, the second species of African
    bicorn, unknown to Levaillant.

panse of view, and a further disadvantage was that the Cafres assured us that the locality was unhealthy both for man and beast. I doubted that it was unhealthy for man but as for the cattle, that was a different matter; within three days I was obliged to send mine back to Souzouana's *mouzi*, because those of King and Stellar were already passing blood through the urethral canal. In addition, we had been misguided enough to set up our camp under the trees, which could be dangerous in a storm. Apart from this, these tambooty trees apparently contain in their wood, their bark and their leaves an element which is anything but harmless.

However, since it was the most advantageous position from which to pursue our principal objective, we ignored the dangers which posed no immediate threat, accepted the proximity of the snakes, and endured not only cohabitation with them under the same roof, but also their presence in the same bed, even under the same blanket, and I can assure you, for I have experienced it, that almost anything is preferable to the icy shudder which this intimacy produces. It is a case of saying with the poet, *Horresco referens*! The muscles react quite differently from the way they do in performing feats of strength, and seem to ossify; the body no longer obeys the mind, the mind appears to hesitate and cannot take any decision because it is convinced that immense danger threatens the body to which it is attached. However, as there is no possibility of changing one's position in a futile attempt to alleviate the situation, one remains rigid and finally sees one's resolution crowned with success.

On the 14th, in an attempt to clean up the approaches to the camp, I set fire to the grass which, to avoid engulfing my hut, I intended to burn in sections. But the negligence of one of my servants proved almost fatal. There was an imminent risk of all my goods going up in flames; the line of the blaze was approaching rapidly and had reached to within twenty paces of my hut, when I flung off my coat and, ordering my Cafres to make use of their woollen blankets, together we succeeded in beating out the fire.

On the 15th, Boulandje, although he was one of the least adept of my hunters, brought down a large female white rhinoceros, which he hit behind the shoulder, hardly seven inches above the sternum; she could only have taken five steps before staggering to a halt and then falling on to her right side. This was the first of the species to be killed by my men and I hastened to congratulate Boulandje who, while admitting his inferiority, complacently anticipated the fortune he could make with his gun, for although I paid each of my Cafres at the rate of one or even several cows per annum, I granted them as a bonus one cow for every elephant killed, taking it as understood that each elephant could only be killed by one man.

On the 16th, I took seven men with me and arrived early at the place where our female was lying; I had taken care to arm myself with some small sharp knives with which to remove the skin, although my Cafres tried to persuade me of the impossibility of doing so. Henning, my driver, had orders to bring my team of twelve oxen at about three o'clock in the afternoon to drag the remains along the two and a half leagues which separated us from the camp. The sight of the dead animal made me think that my men might well be right. Not only would we have great difficulty in skinning it, but I foresaw further problems in transporting the hide, and even greater ones in its preservation. In spite of the risk of having to abandon the project in the face of insurmountable difficulties, I set about making the principal incisions. My men watched me doubtfully, and I read in their eyes the thought: 'We are beginning a task which we can never finish.'

I completed the preliminary incisions while my servants looked on, astonished at the effectiveness of my sharp little knives. I then assigned to each man a portion of the labour, reserving for myself the most difficult share, and in less than an hour we had completed the work on one side. It was at this point that we encountered our first obstacle; we had to turn the animal over. There were eight of us, which was not sufficient for the task. We bent to our labours but the enormous beast would not yield; we redoubled our efforts, but were unable even to raise the legs sufficiently to tip the body over. Finally, I resorted to using thongs fixed to the feet and passed round the nearest tree. This allowed us to use all our combined strength to pull, first on the front part of the body, and then on the back. In this way we would be able to rest after the first exertions and recoup our strength for the final effort. However, to my great disappointment, my plan did not succeed. At the first attempt, I had noticed some slackness among my helpers, which I attributed to ill-will and rebelliousness. I meted out a few unexpected rewards in the shape of kicks, punches and cuffs of every sort, as a result of which the blood flowed more rapidly in their veins and their vigour was restored.

As I had, in my impatience, infused some additional strength into them, I needed now to give it direction. So that we might co-ordinate our efforts and heave together in unison, I began to intone an old sea-shanty, the rhythm of which they responded to so well that we soon had the rhinoceros lying on its other side.

Several of the men began complaining about the light shower of blows which had fallen on their naked bodies. I explained to them that I bore them no ill-will, that those means which I had employed were the only effective ones, that they were always used by the whites in charge on board naval vessels, and that I myself had been subjected to them for the two and a half years I spent at sea.

When they had listened to my explanation, one of them spoke up:

Indao ka ama Loungo, Indao Imbu, aki indao ka abanto mouniama.
'This is a bad custom of the white man; there is nothing of this kind in the customs of the black man.'

Perhaps the Cafre was not altogether wrong, but I reckoned that I was justified in employing such innocent means to achieve my purpose. I made it understood that there were no hard feelings on my part; that I was still on the best of terms with them; this became so apparent that finally they understood, and a little later even those who had complained the most were laughing at my original method of injecting strength into a man.

I removed the skull to facilitate loading the heavy skin on to a tree which had been felled for the purpose. The loading took us only half an hour, but my oxen found it hard work to drag the skin along, supported on its tree and protected by the branches from scraping along the ground. Seven or eight times we watched our load overturn, dragging the tree over with it, which meant that the journey cost us a great deal of time and trouble. Night had already fallen when we finally reached the camp, worn out, hungry and thirsty. We had triumphed over our difficulties, and I was gratified by my own achievement and satisfied with the co-operation of my servants. I treated them liberally to coffee, generously sweetened, into which I poured a half bottle of French brandy. In less than an hour, their fatigue had been replaced by noisy good cheer which kept them awake almost all the night.

The following three days were spent in trying to reduce the weight of the skin; each evening I carefully covered it with a layer of alum and crushed salt, and placed thorny branches on top of it to prevent the damage which hyaenas might cause, even though I slept only fifteen paces away in the wagon. On the evening of the third day, as the weight of the skin had been reduced by half, I decided to dry it out further by suspending it by the back legs from a large strong tree. The weight, in spite of the reduction, was such that it broke a branch two feet in circumference.

From early morning on the 21st the sun beat down and so we sat around discussing the herd of buffalo which, during the night, had come close to our tents and huts but had done no serious damage. As we were talking, we noticed, grazing 500 paces off, a huge *Rhinoceros simus*. Unfortunately, in our eagerness to reach him, we positioned ourselves upwind, which meant that he got scent of us and disappeared into the bush so completely that a four hour search uncovered no trace of him.

The day before, one of my Cafre hunters, Mahlé, had unwittingly fallen among *manghetjannes*, *Cynhyaena venatica*, wild dogs. Without pausing to calculate the outcome, he fired a shot and wounded one of the animals which returned to the attack, followed by five or six others. Mahlé, whose gun was now empty, had just the time to scramble into a low tree, where he hung his gun on a branch. At this vantage point he was inaccessible, although surrounded by the snarling animals which bared their long sharp canines, intending to make an excellent meal of my hunter.

But, secure in the knowledge that his powder-horn was half full, that his leather pouch contained twenty bullets, and that he handled his gun with admirable skill, Mahlé, as I was saying, simply laughed at the fury of these carnivores which are perhaps the most destructive of them all. He took time to load his gun and to aim carefully before firing at his first victim, then at a second and a third. The wild dogs were not easily routed and, although two were already lying dead, others were still prowling around at a distance. Mahlé kept up his fire in the hope of discouraging them completely and, judging it unwise to attempt to cross through the pack, he made up his mind to spend the next two hours perched in his tree.

After this long interval, he climbed down, loaded the finer specimen of the two dead animals on his back, and brought it to me. I found it even more filthy than the hyaena, but it was of some value to me. I expressed my gratitude to Mahlé, and not only in *galogo* (brandy), for that evening he was able to distribute among his friends a large ration of leaf tobacco which, crushed and mixed with ashes of aloe, provided them with a fertile source of enjoyment for a whole week.

The striking thing about the wild dog is its astonishing likeness to the hyaena, although many of its characteristics are those of the domestic dog; it can be situated exactly between the two. The naturalist who invented the name 'cynhyaena', describes the animal perfectly. The features which the cynhyaena has in common with the Cape hyaena (*crocuta*) are the roundness of the head, the wide, thick, pricked ears which are almost bald on the outside, although they are furry inside. The shape of the nose and the eye are similar, as are the thickness of the neck and the hair. There are two glands near the anus which secrete an oil which is thinner and lighter and even more repulsive than that of the hyaena, for there is a suggestion of garlic which turns the stomach of the observer, however brief his inspection of the parts. The wild dog is smaller, narrower, lighter and less strong than the hyaena, but much more fleet of foot; the hindquarters are less sloping and better formed; in fact he is shaped more like the domestic dog. His four upper canines and two lower ones have edges so sharp that he has no difficulty in severing the hocks of the antelope which he pursues.

His colouring is variegated; grey-white, tawny-yellow, and blackish-brown. The white patches can be seen on the chest, under the neck, on the legs and the tip of the tail; everywhere else the hair is tawny and brown, with patches of indistinct colour. Only on the tail are

185

these colours clearly defined; tawny at the root, brown-black in the middle, and white at the tip. His total length is four feet four inches; the tail measuring one foot two inches; his height is two feet two inches. In his habits, he differs essentially from the hyaena. He lives in packs and hunts during the day, obedient to the accepted leader of the troop. He is bold and brave, more destructive and more voracious than any other animal. It is said that he lives only by hunting, never on prey that is already dead, unless it has just been killed by the hunter.

A Dutch farmer told me of an incident which illustrates the voracity of these animals and which will also serve to give some idea of their cleverness. A wounded eland (*Boselaphus oreas*), in an attempt to shake off his pursuer, had left the hunter 2000 paces behind. The hunter was following after him at an easy gait, when suddenly forty wild dogs, having picked up the scent of the blood-trail, fell unexpectedly upon the exhausted animal. Hearing the noisy clamour they made, the farmer realised that he was about to be deprived of his trophy. He put his horse at the gallop and, with shouting and gunshots, he forced the marauders to retreat. As he searched for his victim, great was his astonishment to discover only a little heap of bones on the spot where, five minutes earlier, an entire eland had stood! Baffled and bewildered, he followed the pack of carnivores, intending to wreak his revenge. The dogs, realising that they were being hotly pursued, attempted to increase their mobility by disgorging enormous pieces of meat which littered the ground over an area of 500 to 600 paces, and which they doubtless intended to retrieve later.

I have mentioned *Hyaena crocuta*, or the spotted hyaena. I would like to say a few words about him for there are few animals which have given rise to so many myths and so many misconceptions among the uninitiated.

The Ancients believed that the hyaena was both male and female because of the presence of an orifice situated near the two glands which secrete an oily liquid, an orifice whose function they could not comprehend. The extreme voracity and the enormous strength of the jaws of the hyaena gave rise to the belief that it was a most formidable animal. The mournful sound which it makes at night, and the fact that it devours human corpses, have given rise to superstitious beliefs among certain peoples and have filled most of us with a great horror of this disgusting creature.

The hyaena (*Hyaena crocuta*) is more timid than bold; more voracious than destructive; more likely to inspire disgust than fear. As it possesses none of the speed of the *Cynhyaena venatica*, it has no success in hunting the fleet-footed animals. As it does not stalk its prey in imitation of the cat family, it is incapable of springing upon the back of its victim; its hindquarters are so weak and so ill-made that it cannot easily leap. Its physical disadvantages dictate that it should be active at night rather than during the day. These disadvantages also determine that it should feed on the leavings of the lion and the leopard. Indeed the hyaena performs by night those functions which the vulture performs by day.

But in those parts of the country where man keeps domestic animals, these docile creatures become the hyaena's prey, particularly where there are no lions in the vicinity. I tend to think that when he behaves agressively, the hyaena is acting contrary to his own natural inclinations and to nature's intentions for him. I am convinced that the hyaena is not a beast of prey because, in a country swarming with animals of all kinds, he will return night after night to the great elephant carcasses; even long after he has devoured the flesh, he feeds on the bones which contain a greasy marrow. Furthermore, he will eat the earth which is impregnated with this grease, as a result of which the excrement which he always deposits in the vicinity, within an area of 50 square paces, is hard and white as chalk and remains intact for years.

Yet the hyaena will not hesitate to attack and devour wild animals which have been hurt or wounded by the hunter, for he is not averse to taking action which does not require speed or courage; and although he will never dare to attack a man who is awake and on his guard, he will not hesitate to attack a sleeping man, whom he will almost always take hold of by the face.

As an indication of the great voracity of the hyaena, it has been said that he will eat even one of his own kind, which has been wounded by the hunter. This is a myth for, in an area where there was not much to eat, as an experiment, I left the remains of a hyaena exposed for three weeks. Each night, two members of the pack came prowling around these remains, but refrained from touching them. The hyaena gives evidence of a great deal of discretion in keeping out of danger, while attempting at the same time to satisfy the demands of his enormous appetite. On many occasions I have observed that he acted with the greatest prudence, and apparently only after calculating the danger of the situation. I have often observed that the quantity of rhinoceros flesh which a single hyaena was able to devour in one night, equalled his own weight. He therefore has an appetite which can only be satisfied by consuming an astonishing quantity of meat.

One stormy night my oxen were attached to the wheels of my wagon while I lay asleep inside with my servants underneath. My driver had forgotten to gather up the ox-hide traces, the wooden yokes and the thongs which were also made of hide. A hyaena came along and bit off my thongs, one by one, from the wood to which they were secured. He had come up close behind my oxen but had not dared touch them, however great the temptation might have been;

he preferred to be satisfied with the very little which he could obtain without difficulty or danger.

The hyaena is clever at making holes in the ground, either to hollow out a burrow for himself, to make his way into an enclosure by digging under the fence, or to escape from a trap in which he is caught. The Boer children derive much amusement from their *Wolf Huis* (wolf house). This is their name for the traps which they construct for the capture of live hyaenas. I have seen some made of stones, but I prefer those which are portable like a cage, strongly made of wood and which are about four feet high and eight feet long; they are triangular in shape and closed at one end, while at the other end there is a door which lifts up and is supported by a collapsible peg. The bait is attached to this peg by a string. The animal, whether it be a hyaena, a panther or a leopard, enters the cage and seizes the bait, thus causing the trap-door to close behind him.

This kind of trap is the least harmful, the surest, the best that may be employed; the use of the spring trap, on the other hand, often results in the trapper being left with only the foot while the rest of the animal has chosen to go free without it. The gun trap is very dangerous, not only for domestic animals and humans who are unaware of its existence, but also for the trapper himself. Its positioning varies according to the size of the animal for which it is set and, without extreme precision in the placing, there can be no hope of success.

The spotted hyaena is to be found all over southern Africa, but it is more common in wooded country. It is inactive during the day, hiding away in the thick bush or in burrows or rocky caves. Soon after sunset, it emerges from cover and goes to find water. At about nine o'clock, it gives three successive calls, the last of which is prolonged. This whimpering sound which is repeated at intervals, always made my Cafres laugh. But in special circumstances, the hyaena modifies the call. Sometimes it gives a shrill, infernal laugh. I am told that on other occasions, it will imitate the cries of a young animal, a lamb, a kid or a calf, in order to deceive the mother and draw her away from the herd. As I never had she-goats or ewes or cows with young, I was not able to verify this.

The Amazoulous admit that this animal is useful to them in that it eats their dead, whom they do not take the trouble to bury, and for this reason they profess great repugnance towards it, going so far as to refuse even to touch the skin. One day I was preparing a hyaena specimen and I asked one of my Cafres, who was usually very willing, to help me in my task. 'No, master,' this man said, 'I cannot consent to touch such a filthy animal. It is not that I am afraid of him, or that I believe he will return to haunt me, but if my wife knew of it, she would certainly refuse to have me.'

The hyaena flees from man's approach and although the dogs easily overtake it, they dare not attack it for they seem to know of the astonishing strength of its jaws and its neck. When it is on the watch it appears to be sitting, because the hind quarters are very low and weak, compared with the rest of the body. The hyaena is called *Wolf* by the Boers, and sometimes *Tiger-Wolf*. The Amazoulous call it *Empiss* or *Empissy*.

But let us now leave the hyaenas, and continue with our story. On the 20th, realising that the rainy season was now upon us and that my ever-increasing stock of skins could no longer be accomodated in my tent and wagon, I decided to construct what the Dutch variously call: *Pack-huys*, *Pondock*, *Haart-Beest-Huis*, a sort of house, 20 feet long, comprising a single roof over a sort of passageway. As this work was performed concurrently with the preparation of specimens, it took twelve days to complete. I could then boast of having a little home of my own, on the virgin banks of the Omphilos.

As there were no elephants to be found, my companions had set off in search of hippopotamuses near the bay of Saint Lucia and I was left alone in the company of my servants, whom I had taught to be obedient only to my commands. I was as free as any man could wish to be. The hunting was plentiful; not a day went by that we did not kill several buffalo, eland, kudu and wild boar, but yet I was not satisfied. I wanted elephants, and to this end I would send my Cafres out in search of them. On the 23rd, Kotchobana and Boulandje had set off early, but by nine in the evening they had not returned. The roar of a lion could be heard coming from the direction which they had taken that morning, whence also they were expected to return. In the ignorance of my inexperience, I was anxious on their account. At about eleven I began to consider the possibility that, having heard the roars, they had prudently decided to seek some sort of shelter for the night. Sleep finally overcame me, temporarily dispelling all anxiety, which however assailed me anew when I awoke.

The day was spent in conjecture and then at last, when night came, my two hunters returned, dissatisfied at the outcome of their mission; they had covered a great distance and had discovered only old evidence of the presence of elephants. They had ventured too far the first day to be able to return before dark, and as they had come upon a *mouzi*, they had decided to take advantage of the shelter which it afforded.

On the 25th, when I returned from a hunting foray in the neighbourhood, having killed a number of Egyptian geese, ducks, Madagascan teal, water hens and francolins, I found awaiting me a messenger from Panda. The king sent to request glass necklaces which he wished to present to his wives and his headmen. I was neither a merchant nor a second-hand dealer, but I had provided myself with these trinkets to use as money and to distribute where I wished to make friends. I gave Panda's messenger a quantity of the beads which were too heavy for him to carry with ease and so I was obliged to offer him the help of my two most reliable Cafres, Kotchobana and Boulandje, friends who would not be parted.

Although the goods had been requested as objects of barter and not as gifts, I took care not to fix the price, leaving Panda to respond in a manner which he considered fitting. On the 29th Panda's messenger reappeared, simply to thank me in his master's name. It is unbelievable that a man should be sent forty leagues on so unimportant a mission, unless one knows that the highly-born Amazoulou sets great store by the observation of proper etiquette.

It was December before Kotchobana returned with a further request from Panda. Pleased with the necklaces, he wanted more of them and stipulated the colours which he preferred; *om-bonvo hamgazy*, *om-luloana*, blood-red and flame-red. He was anxious that Kotchobana should bring them in person, adding that, in return, he would send me some elephant tusks when the moon had waned; '*Pambylé inyanga fylé*,' he said.

CHAPTER XV

I was growing tired of preparing specimens, and the feeling that I needed a few days' holiday, added to my desire to see Panda at his royal home, prompted my sudden decision to accompany the men who were to carry the goods. However, when I inspected my wardrobe, which had been bundled unceremoniously into a bag, I almost abandoned the project. I had not a pair of shoes I could wear in the presence of a barefoot prince and, what was worse, not a pair in good enough condition to protect my feet from the mimosa thorns along the way.

Fortunately, the morning of the 4th dawned pouring with rain and we were obliged to delay our departure. My driver Henning, a resourceful man as are all the Boers, put the time to profitable use and artfully manufactured for me a very fine pair of *veld-schoen*.

On the 5th when the sun was up I set out, followed by the three bearers. We soon passed the principal *mouzi* of Souzouana, and at about ten o'clock we reached this chief's second *mouzi*, four leagues further on, which commanded a view from a height of 400 feet over an immense wooded plain, chequered here and there by clearings, which was known to all the Cafres as Om-Schlaty-Om-Koulou, which means great forest. Ahead of us lay the prospect of travelling nine leagues to the first little Cafre village where we could spend the night. I reckoned that by forcing the pace, we should arrive there before nightfall. We were on the point of setting off when the rain began falling again as heavily as it had done the day before. I was reluctantly obliged to heed the chief's warning that it was impossible to cover the distance without running the risk of having to spend the night in the bush, where lions prowled after dark. He might have been right, but I was quite aware of the fact that some self-interest prompted him to insist that I remain. Hardly had I agreed to delay my departure, when his headmen came to me and begged me to send out Kotchobana and Boulandje to hunt buffalo or *canna* in order to provide a treat for all the inhabitants of the *mouzi*. I agreed to this request, but left my hunters free to do as they chose. They were perfectly willing to exhibit their superior skills, and they set out immediately in the driving rain which soon soaked their bodies and drenched their guns, while the game made off to find shelter in the depths of the bush. The unfavourable conditions soon cooled the ardour of my Cafres, who returned complaining of the weather, although they were in some measure consoled by the fact that the Amazoulous gave them credit for their good intentions.

We did not want for *amas* (sour, curdled milk) because they provided us with enough for twenty men. This was not merely a gesture of politeness, but an encouragement to us to turn our powder to greater advantage than we had yet done.

By the 6th, the weather had cleared completely, the sky was a cloudless blue and the sun which was warm at first, grew progressively hotter. We left the *mouzi* before dawn, accompanied by more than forty men, and crossed the Om-Schlaty-Om-Koulou, heading in the direction of Om-Philos-Om-Schlopu towards a mountain which resembled a pyramid and which was called Om-Grooty.

The men who accompanied us were relying heavily on the likelihood of encountering game which such a journey offered, and it was their opinion that we should put our arms to good use by bringing down some large animal. It is true that Om-Schlaty-Om-Koulou abounded in buffaloes and *cannas*, but it was not my intention to spend time searching for them. However, I agreed to a quarter of an hour's delay while my hunters attempted to approach a herd of more than a hundred *cannas*. They were unsuccessful, but I managed to wound one of the animals, although at the time I was armed only with a pistol.[1]

Great was the disappointment of the interested parties when they saw their dinner disappearing from beneath their very eyes, and all because, at that moment, I had no heavy gun to hand. I got off with a few consoling words, upon which they left us and turned back. Soon white Om-Philos was flowing at our feet, or rather between our legs. Gently laughing, she tried to tempt us to stay in the cool waters of her sunny, sandy bed. Caressing and soothing, she encircled our feet, draining them of all resolution, while she silently seemed to say, 'Stay, do not leave me.' She showed us Om-Grooty rising on the left, proud, harsh, unkind Om-Grooty, whose craggy heights we must conquer, and she seemed to say, 'If you leave me, you will go to her. Oh, then I shall pity you, pity your tongues and your feet. Go if you must but you will not forget Om-Philos.' We were enthralled by her; we could have remained with her in comfort forever, yet in spite of our inclinations and our desires, we turned our backs on Om-Philos, the temptress, freshly bejewelled each day and girdled with green rushes. From the bed where she dallied, she watched us with a pitying eye as we struggled up the craggy ridges of Om-Grooty the

1 A.D. uses *canne-fusil*, literally 'stickgun'. *Webster's New International Dictionary*, 1920, p.203, gives 'stick' as a familiar word for pistol. *Translator's note*

traitress, she who had bowed her head beneath the foot of the cruellest tyrant ever to walk this earth, Dingaan, at the very sound of whose name men tremble.

The slope was so steep and the weather so hot that it took us more than forty minutes to complete the climb. I had to deal with a spitting snake, which I shattered with a pistol shot at twenty paces; this was the kind of snake which the Amazoulou Cafres call *iphesy*. Standing on its tail, holding its body in a vertical position, it carried its head horizontally on its flattened neck which was puffed out to three times the width of the body. I had first mistaken it for a lizard and had recognised it only by the rather silent, prolonged, hissing sound that it made, similar to that of the puff-adder.

At last, panting and streaming with perspiration, we reached the top of Om-Grooty, where we sat down on seats of rough stone, the selfsame which had once served Dingaan and his court during the course of those elephant hunts over which the despot had presided while keeping well beyond the reach of danger. We had made our ascent by the southern slope which is the most difficult climb of all, although it is the shortest.

Once I had rested, I was able to judge the excellence of Dingaan's choice of vantage point; Om-Schlaty-Om-Koulou was a place favoured by the elephants, where they were frequently to be found. He had chosen this as the place where they would be hunted down and killed by his people, who were armed simply with the *om-kondo*. In order to facilitate the manoeuvres, as well as to observe his regiments more closely, Dingaan had had clearings made in the forest. From the heights where vultures fly, he could look down far beneath him to where the elephants, those colossi of earthly creation, appeared as small as insects, and his fifteen or twenty regiments, numbering 1000 men each, were reduced to the size of ants. From time to time, he amused himself by taking a closer look at the fray through a telescope which had been a present from Gardiner. He watched the conduct of his men, particularly the headmen, and described the more remarkable exploits to the courtiers who were squatting at his feet. Having closely observed all that passed before the messengers could arrive bearing reports, he dazzled his entourage with his prescience, so that they called him great wizard, *om-tagaty-om-koulou*.

I too had a spy-glass, but I preferred to use my eyes to scan this wooded country, where ten herds of buffalo, matched by as many of *cannas*, grazed side by side. In vain I searched for elephants; there were none to be seen. Eight leagues of mimosa-covered country stretched ahead, encircled to left and right by mountains, which appeared to converge in the distance. I could see Om-Schlaty-Om-Koulou merge with the forests of Om-Schlatousse in the south, and in the north-east with those of Om-Philos-Mouniama, extending as far as the source of the Mona.

What beautiful and curious things did these hidden valleys conceal? What fearful animals sheltered beneath the giant fig trees? What multitudes of living creatures had their being in these vast expanses, this naturalist's treasure-trove? The spectacle of this great landscape held me rooted to the spot, from where I could look down upon it all. I believe I would have remained gazing there until the sun went down, had my men not reminded me that we must travel another three leagues before nightfall.

That evening we came to a small *mouzi* which was under the headmanship of Djock, and situated close by this chief's own *mouzi*. On the 7th, before the sun was up, we had taken leave of our hosts, and were able to reach Panda's kraal by midday, after crossing a great plain covered in pasturage.

From afar, this royal *mouzi*, which was called Sképèle, appeared to crown the entire top of a hill, rising 250 feet above the waters of the Om-Schlopu. We presented ourselves at the main entrance where we were received by the officers on duty who hastened to send word to Panda and soon led us to him. We advanced 400 paces into the *mouzi*, before being introduced into several open-air antechambers whose walls of thorns, artistically arranged, served to conceal and defend the royal residence.

We had not long to wait before Panda arrived, accompanied by Om-Phinieri, his chief *om-douna*; he seemed pleased; he touched my hand and expressed his pleasure at the honour I did him in paying this visit. Then came the questions and the compliments which form so important a part of that courtly conversation which is peculiar to the Cafre, and so flattering to the stranger. These men, with much art, are able to convey astonishment or admiration as they speak, simply by placing the hand half over the chin, half over the open mouth.

When I wished to show him the new glass necklaces which I had brought at his request, Panda would not consent to the packets being opened in his presence. He seemed to suggest that these trifles were as nothing to him compared with the pleasure he felt at seeing me and that he would not tolerate distractions of this nature. The *om-douna* received orders to take them away so that no further mention could be made of them.

After more than an hour and a half had been spent in polite exchanges, I began to fear that to prolong the conversation would fatigue Panda, and begged his permission to retire. When he desired an explanation of my wish to withdraw, I replied that, in my anxiety to see him, I had made the journey with such speed that I had not had the leisure to enjoy smoking a single pipe, and that in consequence I would be delighted if he would allow me to be alone for a

194

short while. Panda accepted my request with a smile, accompanied by a *'Yebo omgâne'*. I thereupon withdrew to a hut which had been put at my disposal. Hardly had I settled down, when an enormous round pot of beer arrived with Panda's compliments. It contained the equivalent of about fifty bottles, and the sight of it brought smiles of joy to the faces of my followers.

This beer, which is known to the Amazoulous as *tchouala*, is made from a kind of millet they call *mabélé*, and which the Boers call kaffir corn. To make the beer, they first of all ferment the grain by sprinkling it with water and then putting it in the sun; next the grain is crushed, mixed with water and boiled in great pots. The following day, when the liquor is bubbling like champagne, the people gather round in numbers sufficient to drain the brew to the last drop, for it rapidly turns sour and within a day becomes undrinkable.

Beer made in this manner is delicious to the taste; it is very refreshing, nourishing and healthy and, in addition, is astonishingly fattening. Unfortunately, with the intention of obtaining a stronger brew which has a bite that inflames the gullet, many Cafres add the crushed root of a particular wild plant. This induces violent headaches of which I had on several occasions reason to complain, much to the amusement of the Cafres who, unlike me, consider themselves fortunate to suffer from this particular affliction. Panda's beer, however, did not contain these harmful ingredients. It was beer fit for a prince, which I would not hesitate to rank above the best champagne, for it is as agreeable to the palate as it is innocuous.

And so, I was the guest of a prince, a king, an autocrat with the power of life and death over his subjects, and a force of 30 000 to 40 000 warriors obedient to his command. His power was unlimited, his wishes were commands and this man treated me as his friend; he was pleased to tell me so and gave me ample proof of it; in accordance with the requirements of etiquette, I feigned to believe him.

But in spite of all his greatness, he could not give me what he did not have to give; the bed he offered me was, in every respect, just like his own, a mat of rushes spread on the hardened earth, a pillow of wood to rest my head upon; at my feet, a fire instead of blankets, to keep me warm; such is the Amazoulou conception of comfort. Fortunately, in knowing no better, they are content with little, and their bodies which are always in contact with hard surfaces and rough textures, acquire a firmness which is unknown to us.

I was growing accustomed to their ways, and I slept wonderfully well. When I awoke I paid a visit to the king. 'You do well to come early,' he said to me; 'this is a great day, the dancing is about to begin (the *sina* or war dance). Today you will see the *abafanas* (young men), tomorrow the *amadounas* (the headmen), and the third day you will see me take part myself. It will be beautiful, very beautiful. I am delighted that you have come to see me at such an auspicious moment. Panda is great, very great; his people, the Amazoulous are as numerous as the locusts. You, white man, you will see all this; your eyes will open in astonishment and your mouth will repeat what your eyes have seen. The heart of Panda is glad to have a witness to his greatness, the heart of Panda loves you and thanks you.'

I was taken completely unawares for I had had no intention of wasting so much valuable time simply in order to witness these dances or military exercises, one hour of which would surely suffice to surfeit me. I would like to have found some good reason for excusing myself, but I had not sufficient knowledge of his language to express myself with subtlety. I therefore replied simply, imitating his turn of phrase; 'Panda, my heart loves you; my white heart is pleased that your heart seems white also; my heart is full of this happiness; my eyes would wish to see you dancing in the midst of your warriors who are as numerous as the locusts; you who are so beautiful and so great; if only it were possible for me to wait until that day.'

Clumsily I paused, unable to continue. Then came the reply to which I could offer no objection: 'You will be able to do so; I shall send you a cow which you will kill to feed yourself and your servants.' This was tantamount to an order, and I was bound to obey. In my eyes, Panda was a lion, and I knew very well that one does not play the monkey within reach of the claws of such an animal, except perhaps from the top of a tree. I was not at that moment sitting on a branch out of reach, and so I agreed to stay.

By about eight o'clock in the morning I was seated on the ground at the right hand of Panda, who was enthroned on an enormous wooden armchair, carved all of a piece. He was completely engrossed in the prospect of the festivities and in the expectation of seeing his warriors parade before him. His conversation was only of them, their costume, their dance, their songs. He was waiting to receive the salute of the regiments of the *abafanas* whom, for the last ten minutes, I had been expecting to see arrive from the place where they had assembled.

Then suddenly, from 1500 paces away, an immense cry arose, a cry which is unique to the throats of Cafres gathered together in great numbers. Our eyes were drawn to the place from whence it came, to the slopes of the opposite hill, and we became aware of great black masses of *abafanas*, 6000 of them divided into six groups. They were preparing to advance, each regiment leading off in turn. Some minutes elapsed and then, suddenly they were before us, only 200 paces off, each regiment arranged in ranks of 100 men, ten ranks deep. Another great cry arose, accompanied this time by shrill whistling. The cry was sustained as they charged in a confused mêlée of men and shields, which surged forward like a great wave, and finally crashed at our feet as a breaker crashes on the shore. It was a fine disorder such as I could not have imagined, which suddenly resolved itself once more into the most perfect order.

As the first battle-cry rang out, the dancers leapt up and, repeating the cry, they began to dance, a rhythmical, leaping dance which stirred the spirit to combat; then they proceeded with slow stamping, until the earth rang beneath their feet, and trembled under their weight. From time to time, several *abafanas* would emerge from the ranks to salute the prince by leaping in the air and striking their shields with both feet at once.

This display of gymnastics made a fine show, and I began to appreciate its qualities of grace and originality. Suddenly, without warning, the dancers all spun about, and converged upon us as they had previously done; then, coming to a sudden halt within twenty paces of us they formed themselves into a snake, which wound its way before Panda. Each man went by at a slow trot, contorting his features and acknowledging the king in tones of seeming anger, gesticulating with the *tonga* in a threatening manner, until all had passed in salute and the next regiment heralded its approach with a ringing call.

On the first day, only six of these regiments appeared, each with its own particular song and dance which I found very entertaining; but the ones which made me laugh most were the *Tchi-tchi-tchi*, who leaped continually into the air, their feet held together and their knees joined and, in so doing, assuming such a ludicrous character that Panda laughed as much as I did.

Finding that my eyes were becoming fatigued by gazing intently at the unaccustomed movement, I left Panda's side and withdrew into my hut, where I learned that the promised cow had not yet arrived. The previous night, my supper had consisted of Cafre beer and the smoke from my pipe. In the morning, Panda's mother had sent me only *amas*, curdled sour milk. This diet did not agree with me, particularly as I had had nothing better during the journey, and so in spite of my promise to Panda, in spite of my pleasure in the strange, unusual and sometimes grotesque dancing, I decided to send Kotchobana to the king to inform him of my imminent departure which had become necessary because I feared the possible onset of illness.

'How is this?' he cried. 'The *Om-Longo* wishes to leave already! Oh no! he does not know what awaits him. He must stay. His eyes will see and his heart will be pleased. Let him stay. I like him very much this *Oum-Longo*. It pleases me that he should stay.'

This discouraging reply was immediately reported to me and I was on the point of going to thank Panda for his kindness, while assuring him at the same time that my stomach was very unhappy and that it was impossible . . . when the eagerly-awaited cow arrived. So I stayed, and the following day I was able to watch the war dances with greater ease and enjoyment.

I began to feel the necessity of thanking Panda for his hospitality. I went in person to do so, and had already passed through one of his open-air antechambers, when I was stopped by the *om-douna* on guard, who had orders not to allow anybody to pass. Fortunately, the king was not far off and, having heard me explain my business, came himself to reverse the order in my favour.

He was busy now with matters very different from his *abafanas*. A group of his wives, eighty perhaps, the cream of Amazoulou beauty, was gathered before him, rehearsing a dance. 'Come here,' he said to me, 'look and judge.' I had heard so much of the excessive jealousy of polygamous husbands that I hardly dared to obey. I was fearful of wounding the king's feelings and thereby creating an unfortunate incident, which I would prefer to avoid at all costs.

'Well,' he said, 'what do you think of them?' Privately, I thought a great deal. I was all eyes for these plump beauties with their soft, velvety skin, their rounded curves, their graceful bearing. Much of their bodies was revealed, but little of their faces, which were concealed by fringes of beads, a circumstance which only contributed to increasing my admiration. Realising that frank wonder would be simpler for me to express and that it could not fail to flatter, I had no difficulty in finding a few words to convey my great admiration. I observed that he appeared to be aware of the intended compliment when I said, 'Panda, no *Oum-Longo* possesses what you have here.' It was only the truth. 'I really believe it,' he said simply, with an air of the most complete satisfaction. Then he explained to me in minutest detail the finer points of their dress. This appeared to consist principally of shawls of bright red wool muslin folded in a square, of which he said he required further supplies and, crossed over the breast, necklaces of pink glass beads which he continually praised as being superior to anything he had yet seen.

I was so preoccupied in gazing at these choice beauties who, divided into groups of four, were moving rhythmically about the courtyard, their bodies dipping and swaying, their arms and their hands with fists closed, gesturing gracefully, as all the while they hummed some hymn of praise in honour of their lord and master; as I say, I was so preoccupied that I completely forgot the reason for my visit; Panda was not, I fear, thanked for the cow, while on the other hand he received ample expressions of gratitude for the particular favour which he had just accorded me. I returned to my hut, my head full of seductive memories which continued to inflame my imagination as I lay awake all night, until eventually I resented Panda's having revealed to me some of the mysteries of his private life.

On the 9th, twenty-five regiments passed in salute before the king, following the same procedures as on the previous day. The celebrations had taken on a more impressive character; each regiment was distinguished by its shields which stood four feet six inches high and were made of ox-hide of various colours; some were white, some black, others red, blue or yellow, or white with red or black markings; the colours were uniform for each regiment. The elite regiments were distinguished by the *symba*, a sort of kilt which hung from the waist to the knees and which was made of 300 to 400 strips of genet fur; these tassels parted gracefully and closed again to allow the free movement of the body. The head was encircled with a padded strip of otter fur from which there arose a long Numidian crane feather.

Several hours later, when all the regiments had passed in salute before the king, the massed warriors formed a circle and began chanting warlike songs with such perfect comprehension of musical sound, such faultless precision, such accuracy of note, that I was greatly astonished. When the singing was over, the distinguished orators came forward from the ranks and, taking up a position fifteen paces before the king, they improvised speeches of which the principal characteristic was extreme volubility. At a given signal the crowd, which had remained standing until that moment, squatted on the ground so that they might attend in greater comfort. After the principal orators came others who dealt particularly with the affairs of the country and matters of general interest, while Panda on his throne weighed up and considered all that was said so that he might reply to the requests of his people.

The eloquence of these men had the most extraordinary effect upon me. The rapid fluency with which they expressed themselves suggested that they were speaking extempore. I was incapable of following their words but their gestures were so expressive that I was able to comprehend all that passed.

They punctuated their phrases with sweeping movements of the right hand which was armed with the flexible *tonga*. When emphasis became necessary, when the words flowed thick and fast, when the audience needed to be forcefully convinced, the *tonga* whistled through the air; it was lowered, then raised up again immediately, it whirled about, describing circles, whose meaning could not be misconstrued, while the orator talked on and on, never hesitating for a word. There was an occasional pause, but this merely served to emphasise the import of what was to follow.

There are some fine moments in this sort of eloquence when one is amazed at the extreme ease of elocution, reinforced by the ex-

199

pressiveness of gesture; towards the end, when the orator wishes to make the final point, his features contract with apparent conviction; he becomes a leaping devil threatening to pierce with his *omkondo* whoever does not agree with him. It is the most tiring labour in the world to judge by the bodies streaming with sweat, and had I not witnessed it, I could never have believed that any man could hold forth in this manner for an hour on end.

At this point, I must express my regret at being incapable of describing adequately my impressions of that time for, although certain things might be simple enough to comprehend, they are virtually impossible to communicate. On the morning of the 10th, it was raining, but the king must dance, custom demanded that it should be so, and for this reason no one had yet departed. At about two o'clock the people began to gather, and soon the earth was trembling beneath the rhythmical stamping of powerful feet, while the air rang as with one great voice, from the throats of 25 000 warriors.

At four o'clock I was still at Panda's side, wearied and deafened by the noise, when suddenly the king arose to return to his hut. He went to exchange his purple cloak for his warrior's dress and he delegated one of his headmen to inform me that he wished me to keep his place for him until he returned.

There was no possibility of refusal; 'Sit where the king was sitting', the *om-douna* said to me, and I dared not hesitate, although I obeyed with reluctance. For the first time in my life I was sitting on a throne, thankful that it would also be the last time and that my reign would be only of short duration, in fact just as long as it took Panda to slip on a shirt, or rather, since a Cafre king does not wear one, as long as it took him to get into his battle regalia.

I was ill at ease upon my royal throne, obliged to endure the stares of so many eyes, all curious to see how I would aquit myself; I felt the leaden weight of the royal mantle fall about my shoulders and while my head was forced to endure the restriction of that iron yoke which is otherwise known as a crown, I longed for the comfort of my Phrygian cap.[1]

Although newly arrived upon the throne and a king by chance, I nevertheless had time to observe the defiance written upon the features of those who, for the space of a quarter of an hour, were to be my subjects; this must be the fate which awaits every upstart. Already my brow was furrowed with care, my glance was gloomy, my eyes were hollow; my body hunched, I sat deep in abstracted thought while the seconds dragged by like hours. Suddenly all eyes turned towards the left. My eyes too were drawn in that direction, I

1 The cap of liberty. *Translator's note*

200

immediately relinquished my throne and the nightmares that went with it; I became a man again just as before.

Panda had made his appearance. He seemed much altered. He was beautiful, superb, magnificent, imposing; his bearing had become that of a warrior and he wore his insignia with a martial grace which I had not believed he possessed. In his left hand he held four light assegais, artfully fashioned, and a great white shield patterned in black, which stood four and a half feet high, while in his right hand the tip of an iron assegai protruded from a band of monkey tails, as a lion's claw protrudes from its furry paw. His brow was adorned with a circlet of otter fur from which square lappets of purple silk plush descended to his shoulders. A feather, two or three feet long, was attached at the top of the head in front and swayed gracefully in the air. From high up at the back of the head, where the Cafre crown was placed, rose a tuft of two touraco feathers (*Corythaix porphyreolopha*) the upper one of which was red and the lower blue.

Suspended from his neck, front and back, were tassels of red and green wool which were overlaid upon oxtails dyed red, and thrown into relief by an under-layer of monkey tails, admirably arranged. Fastened at the waist and hanging down to cover the knees, was an astonishing number of strips of genet fur, 400 or 500 at least, giving the impression of a kilt, but more elegant that the kilt of antiquity. The front of the leg was protected by a white tail in the shape of a garter from which the tufted hair hung down to cover the shin. The ankles were adorned with cuffs of red and green wool. The left arm was encircled with a single row of tails above the elbow, but the right arm, the arm of action, bore three such rows, at the wrist, above the elbow, and four inches below the shoulder.

In this costume, which beggars all description, Panda was a wonderful sight to behold. He was a true warrior, a true king; his movements, his gestures, his bearing all seemed borrowed from the lion. Was the effect studied or did it come naturally to him? I have often asked myself the question, but I have not found the answer.

My servants, eager to have a better view of the dance of the king, had just gathered about me when a herald sent by Panda came up and indicated the place where I should sit. The king took up his position at the centre of a line 6000 to 8000 strong, which stood facing a line of equal numbers formed up behind me and, giving the signal to start the singing, he directed it himself like the conductor of an immense orchestra.

As he sang, he beat time by stamping rhythmically with one foot and then the other, gesturing all the while with his right arm and pointing with his assegai, raising it, lowering it, bringing it across to the right and then back to the left again, while his gestures, his words, his movements were imitated by all his followers. Our most highly trained troops could not have moved with greater precision; not one hand was raised above another, not one *tonga* broke the perfect symmetry of the line. There was not a moment's delay in the execution of each movement, no error could be perceived; this was uniformity unparalled and I, who did not understand their chant, was lost in admiration of the choir composed of between 12 000 and 16 000 voices.

Singing and dancing all the while, the column which was led by Panda, slowly and relentlessly converged upon us where we sat, and met up with the other column, giving the impression of two horns curving inward to form a circle. Only thirty paces separated us from these warriors, when a herald dashed out from Panda's side and as he passed within six feet of me, he pronounced the chilling word *om-tagaty*, a sinister expression, the implications of which I understood very well but, feigning ignorance, I asked Kotchobana, my black guardian angel, to explain its meaning. There was no reply and his silence, rendered more dramatic by his look of inexpressible unease, confirmed my worst suspicions. I questioned all my men, one after the other, but not one would reply although each man perfectly understood.

In critical moments of this sort, people are often virtually paralysed by the imminence of inevitable danger. I was still asking my unanswered questions when Panda himself advanced upon me, brandishing his iron assegai.

In that instant, an infinite number of fleeting ideas crossed my mind; I am as good as dead, I thought, escape is impossible. And as my eye unwittingly fixed itself upon his eye, anticipating his movements, my right hand, armed only with a light switch, was preparing to parry the blow, while my left hand was unfastening the buckle of the belt from which hung my great Catalonian knife. It is in vain, I thought, I shall be killed, but at least before his men arrive to help him, I shall have stabbed him ten times with my weapon, for he is not expecting retaliation; he believes that I must be an easy target as I have no shield.

But the assegai did not leave his hand. I must be mistaken then, I thought; I was wrong to suspect him of evil intent; I was ashamed that I had allowed myself to harbour such puerile fears, that I had insulted Panda by doubting him. Meanwhile without turning, he took five steps backwards, only to advance again seven paces at a run, brandishing his weapon which seemed to tremble with impatience to penetrate my breast, at which it was directed. Just make one move and I will take my revenge! Grant me one moment of vengeance before I die! This was my prayer.

But the iron seemed to adhere to his hand, in spite of the intentions which were apparent in the eyes and the movements of the king; and once again I lived on borrowed time. Retreating five steps as before and again charging seven steps forward, brandishing his weapon and threatening me with its sharp point, his intention seemed unaltered and I began to think that before he stabbed me, this man wanted me to suffer the fear of death, a greater torture than death itself.

I did not lose my composure; I would parry the blow; I could not fail, my eye was fixed on his eye, my concentration was so completely focused on his movements that, I believed, his point could not touch me; once again the blow did not fall. I was growing weary in antici- pation and he appeared to be tiring of his repeated threats, for he turned away and went back to his place among his troops. I remained where I was, pondering the meaning of this pantomime of which I was the unwitting target. I was only to find out later, when the military exercises were over.

With threatening manner, firm step and eyes shining like black diamonds, Panda took up his position at the head of the column which moved off rapidly, singing loudly. After passing close by me he made a pretence of pouncing upon the lines opposite. Simulating the terror which the approach of the chief of the Amazoulous inspired in them, they put up their shields and retreated in indescribable disorder. The column following behind the king, which was composed of 100 lines of 70 men abreast, broke ranks to avoid trampling us under foot; this was thanks largely to the heralds at arms who generously distributed blows with the *tonga* upon all those who, carried away by their enthusiasm, failed to step aside quickly enough.

When all the warriors had streamed past, we found ourselves out- side the great circle. We all drew a deep breath of relief for we had just experienced a terrible fear. Because of the noise, and my neigh- bours' reluctance to speak, I had been unable to obtain the slightest explanation of what had happened. I felt only half reassured by the absence of Panda who, thank Heavens, no longer stood over me with his arm held high and the threatening gleam of his assegai reflected in his eye.

CHAPTER XVI

Continuation of the dancing — Departure from Sképèle — The journey —
Om-Grooty — Om-Schlaty-Om-Koulou — Sight of elephants — Return to
Om-Philos-Om-Schlopu

A few minutes later, the circle re-formed around us as before, the
only difference being that this time the warriors were silent behind
their great shields, above which their heads appeared, surmounted
by tall feathers.

Suddenly a very different sound arose; the singing of voices to
which my ear was unaccustomed. The circle of warriors parted to
reveal the most picturesque sight; that sacred group, the Cafre
sultan's harem, had appeared. The front row comprised twenty
women flanked by six young girls, with two similarly constituted
rows following behind. Singing and gracefully moving their arms,
they stamped their feet, advancing two inches with each rhythmic
beat. Each woman was dressed in the great *om-gobu* made from cow-
skin which had been so well worked that it resembled broadcloth.
This garment, the upper edge of which is rolled to rest on the hips, is
opened down the front and hangs to the ground. It is always black
and is perfumed when worn by women of distinction. The upper part
of these skirts was sewn with clusters of little copper balls, pierced
and arranged in threes. The breasts and the backs of these women were
ornamented by necklaces of glass beads, crossed over the shoulders
and under the arms. The left arm also was laden with beads, while
the right was adorned with a copper band which extended from the
wrist to the elbow. The neck was encircled by four copper rings. The
women appeared so much restricted by these that they were unable
to turn their heads freely. I admit that I found this fashion ridiculous
— beautiful, perhaps, but even less useful than a copper collar on a
dog. Their heads were encircled with a band of purple silk plush and
a network of glass beads hung down over the face to cover the nose.
Attached above each ear and sloping backwards, was an elegant
cluster of black widowbird feathers.

The young girls were dressed only in a girdle which was no more
than one or two fingers deep, and made from bark which had been
artistically fringed. This girdle seemed designed to conceal, but in
fact it favoured the curious eye and left to the admirably chaste
movements of the girls themselves the task of baffling indiscreet
glances. Indeed this is one of the most interesting observations that I

204

AMAZOULOU SINA

made; the bearing of the Amazoulou girl is so natural, or perhaps cultivated with such art, that I would defy the most rigid moralist, the severest of men, to find in their nudity anything to offend. This was my independant observation, but I do not claim to be unique in making it as it is apparent to every European upon his arrival in Natal.

Eight of the women were distinguished from the others by a square of purple silk plush worn across the shoulders in the manner of a shawl. After singing for some while, the women divided into groups of four which made their way round the inside of the enclosure, performing various movements which required them to weave past each other but never to touch. Then, when the eyes of the spectators had gazed their fill, the dancers regrouped as before, singing all the while, and made their way out of the arena, while the circle of men opened up to allow them to pass and closed again behind them. Once more Panda's voice arose to lead the chant which was echoed by all about him. When the voices had died down, he was encircled by his headmen and escorted back to his quarters.

Panda then ordered that an enormous quantity of beer should be circulated among the 3000 headmen and chosen warriors. He returned to preside again from his great armchair, dressed once more in his original costume. He waited for his *abafanas* to bring before him a bull chosen from among the strongest of the royal herd, so that he might see it for himself before he presented it to the young men over whose festivities he was to preside. The animal was furious; he had already knocked down several of the most determined of his captors and, to avoid further accident, the *abafanas* despatched one of their number to inform Panda of this and to request permission to kill the animal without the usual formalities.

Panda was displeased by these precautionary measures and annoyed because so insignificant a problem had not been immediately overcome by his *abafanas* who numbered about 6000. He received the envoy with great displeasure and, in answer to the request, would condescend only to pronounce in a loud voice the word '*bamba*', which means both 'seize him' and 'hold him fast'.

As soon as they received this order the young men in a body surrounded the animal, which continued to struggle frantically, until, pressed from all sides and grasped at by a thousand hands, the bull, in spite of its anger and its strength, was forced to yield to the weight of numbers and allow itself virtually to be carried before the king. Satisfied at last, Panda pronounced the expected sentence: '*Inkonnzy boulala*,' 'Let the bull be killed.' The *abafanas*, who had no weapon other than their *tongas*, were about to wring its neck and fell it on the spot, when Panda, realising their intention, leapt to his feet and informed them that the animal must not be put to death right there before his eyes, but in his private enclosure. The bull was immediately

206

picked up and transported to this place where before very long it had been cut up into little pieces and roasted; hardly was there enough to give each *abafana* even a mouthful. There was just enough for each to taste, but too little to satisfy the appetite. It was a formality and nothing more.

I had still not found the key to the cruel enigma, the memory of which, like a nightmare, weighed heavily upon me. To this end I questioned several Amazoulous who informed me that every great king bore the title of *om-tagaty*, to justify which he must ensure that during his reign the sun never set without witnessing the death of a man. Djacka and Dingaan had been *om-tagaty-om-koulou*. I was assured that the demonstration which had caused me such suffering has been innocent of hostile intent, but had been the means whereby Panda had intended to make me aware of the power which he held over me, that my life was in his hands, and that I should have given recognition of this superior power by simulating fear and taking flight. 'This is what Cafre etiquette requires', they explained, 'and the fact that Panda was not angered by your failure to conform, simply indicates that he was aware of your ignorance of the ways of the black man.'

Let this account not be considered simply as a diverting tale. Some other traveller might one day be fortunate enough to be present at these three days of festivities, the only ones in the whole of the Amazoulou year, a sort of festival of Ceres to celebrate the ripening of the maize, before which celebration it is forbidden to touch a single ear.[1] I would beg such a traveller to recall that this behaviour on the part of the chief is completely innocent, however terrifying it may appear to be. My discomfiture of that time will at least have served to put him at his ease, and I will have rendered him no small service in warning him. As for myself, I tremble still when I recall Panda's glittering gaze. Can any more desperate position be imagined than that in which an assassin stands before one, his weapon poised ready to strike, his fiery eye flashing, while there is no possibility of retaliation or flight. Where both parties are equally armed, neither combatant envisages the possibility of death, for each, in attacking his adversary, defends his own life; but for me it was quite different. I must inevitabley receive the first blow from an adversary who was an all-powerful king surrounded by his own people. And what good would it have done me to kill him, apart from the immense satisfaction of the moment? Was I not hedged about by the king's warriors who stood ready to immolate me with a thousand thrusts of their *tongas*? Had I been more fearful, I would perhaps not have hesitated to open my great dagger-knife and attack Panda, for despair, inspired by fear,

1 Any Cafre convicted of a violation of this rule is pitilessly put to death.

gives rise to bold acts. I leave you to decide whether such an act should have proved to be ill-judged. I consider that I was fortunate to have been sufficiently self-possessed not to have betrayed my thoughts.

My Cafre, Kotchobana, the only one accustomed to interpreting any alteration in my expression, said to me later, 'Master, you seemed very angry when Panda pretended to stab you with his *omkondo*.' 'Certainly I was very angry,' I replied, 'because of the fact that, although he intended to fight with me, he had not provided me with a great shield and an iron assegai.'

He began to laugh, 'Do the whites give arms to their opponents?'

'Undoubtedly,' I replied, 'so that the contest might be equal; otherwise, he who kills an unarmed adversary is a murderer, and in every country of the world murderers are hanged.' He laughed louder still and remarked, 'So if Panda were in your country, the whites would hang him? How could that be? He is an *om-tagaty*, an *om-tagaty-omkoulou*,' The titles *kos-omkoulou*, great master, great king and *om-tagaty-omkoulou*, great wizard, great marksman, great assassin, are synonymous among the Amazoulous, and are used indiscriminately in addressing the chief whose ears are flattened by the description, for he reigns by terror and prides himself on this fact.

The dance over and my curiosity satisfied, I was nevertheless left feeling uneasy. If this were the accepted ritual of the war dance, I thought that Panda ought to have had enough good sense and sufficient nicety to warn me of the pantomime he was intending to enact. Inwardly I was perturbed, and I resolved to take my departure the very next morning. In consequence, I despatched one of my men to the king to inform him of my plans, but by way of response he sent word that, as I had not been able fully to appreciate the brilliant spectacle of the dance due to the inclement weather, he had for my benefit given orders to his people not to leave, as the dance would begin again the next day. When I received his message I stormed impatiently and swore and raved, for the dance had been a terrible torture to me in spite of its unique character. Nevertheless, I was obliged to submit to the king's wishes and accept my lot; I was his guest and I must acquiesce in all his whims and even smile at the thought of what was most disagreeable to me.

At about one o'clock in the morning the dancing began again by the light of fires made from resinous wood. Not a man remained behind in the huts. Left all alone, I struggled against sleep, which was, however, soon put to flight by the infernal din and the quaking of the earth which jolted my head from its wooden pillow. I went outside to be met by an unbelievable sight; I was witnessing the dance of the devils. The fire, the black bodies, the noise, the movement, all conspired to make me believe that I was dreaming after the fatigues of three long days spent watching and listening. Intoxi-cated with noise, my head aching, I sat down, the better to endure the strain and, succumbing to the demands of nature, I fell asleep.

It was daylight when I awoke, the dancing and the singing had stopped. Many people were moving about; nobody asked me why I was there, and certainly such a question would have proved embar-rassing.

Soon afterwards, Omphinieri came to me to discover how it was possible that I had slept while so curious a dance was being performed. 'You are ill then,' he said to me. 'No, not ill. This is how it happened. My eyes were unable to support the bright light of the fires and the continual movement of the black forms dancing back and forth. I found it necessary to shut them. In addition, the rhythmic stamping of feet, added to the lateness of the hour, made it impossible for me to keep my eyes open. I am sure you will understand.' Omphinieri, the perfect diplomat, replied that he completely understood; it was only that I should have made an effort to overcome my drowsiness if I had wished to see a really fine sight; but that, on the other hand, I was perfectly justified in sleeping, if such had been my inclination. I thought to myself that the inclination must have been very strong indeed to have permitted me to sleep deeply, sitting upright with my head between my knees, in the open air amidst an unprecedented uproar.

The day passed in every respect exactly like its predecessor; the weather was perfect. I believe that I observed more animation among the people for the heat has a very marked influence upon them. Matters of national interest were discussed at length and I found that, without making any particular effort and assisted only by the eloquence of the gestures, I followed perfectly the history of the Amazoulous, narrated by an orator who would have been considered a distinguished man in any society.

Also of great interest to me was Maniousse. He was a headman of the first rank, intelligent, valiant in battle and particularly remarkable for his height, which was six feet eight inches, and for the admirable perfection of his form. My eyes were constantly fixed upon him as he stood at the head of his regiment, addressing Panda; His men appeared dwarf-like by comparison. Maniousse, to whom it had been reported that I was desirous of seeing him at close quarters, detached himself from his regiment as soon as he was able to do so, and came over to talk to me. In order to converse, I was obliged to raise my head while he bent forward, as when one talks to a child. Never in my life have I seen so gigantic a man built in such perfect proportions.

The sun was about to set and once again, as on the previous day, I sent one of my Cafres to Panda to inform him of my departure. As soon as the king had understood what I proposed, he cried, 'Leave!

The *oumlongo* wishes to leave tomorrow! So soon? But I like the *oumlongo* very much. I wish him to be good enough to stay several days more.' I had provided my Cafre with such irrefutable arguments that Panda was eventually obliged to let me go, insisting only on presenting me with two superb elephant tusks which weighed fifty pounds each.

I made my preparations and when dawn broke on 12 December, I finally left the royal *mouzi* of Sképèle[1] accompanied, in addition to my own servants, by those whom Panda had instructed to carry the tusks, as well as by some twenty warriors who had come from the banks of the two Om-Philos to be present at the festivities.

By ten o'clock, we had reached the kraal of Djock, an old warrior who, in spite of his obesity, retained his reputation as a great captain. He was also held in high esteem because of the large number of his herds. This worthy man received us warmly and expressed his regret at having only one small pot of beer available to offer us, for he was a great headman and generally had beer in plenty. Instead, he offered us an enormous quantity of sour curdled milk which was welcomed by all my companions with the exception of those who carried the elephant tusks.

These men, who were more fatigued than the rest of us, must have felt a greater need to restore their strength, and yet they took no part in the meal, but simply watched as we refreshed ourselves. I questioned them as to the reason for this, and one of them replied that, as they were members of Panda's special corps, they were permitted to partake only of meat, kaffircorn, maize, beer, fruit and roots. To them, the chosen warriors, milk was a food suitable only for women and children. We travelled a day and a half together, and as they were unable to obtain any food other than milk, they sustained themselves during all that time only on some extremely sour wild fruit which they gathered along the way.

We were delayed for three hours in taking leave of Djock because of the rain; when the sun came out again, we set out and travelled on until dark, spending the night at a small *mouzi* which consisted of only a few huts. On the 13th, we were making our way along a valley west of Om-Grooty at about nine o'clock in the morning, when an old male buffalo appeared on the slopes above us. I felt obliged to gratify the wishes of our companions, and to allow Kotchobana and Boulandje to go off and hunt the animal. A quarter of an hour later the deed was done and the buffalo, which turned out to be one of the largest of its kind, had fallen victim to their guns. Within another quarter of an hour, the place where it lay was transformed into a butchery, a kitchen and a restaurant all rolled into one, with each

1 Sképèle with a click on the k.

210

man choosing the cut which he preferred. Souzana, who ranked highest among them, claimed the heart; Kotchobana and Boulandje, the front part of the breast, and I, who had to some extent adopted Dutch South African tastes, settled for the two shin-bones, those famous marrow-bones which are so much prized by the Boers that the very mention of the name *merg-been* brings a smile to their faces. As for the others, they arranged matters among themselves; there were several scuffles which were short-lived however because of the pressing demands of hunger. In their eagerness, they were inclined to slash about rather wildly with their *omkondos*, which sometimes resulted in the slicing of the finger, the hand or the foot of some other equally determined carver. These accidents occur on every such occasion and cannot fail to do so, since the Cafres cluster and jostle about the fallen beast just like vultures. Nevertheless, the only advisable course of action when one is in command of such men, is to leave them free to do as they please. To begin with, I attempted to persuade them to proceed methodically, which would have meant an economy of time for my part and an absence of accident for theirs; but one of these savages said to me, '*Indao ka abantou mouniama, hyasy abantou mouniama, hyasy kakoulou*, which means, 'The black men have their own ways, the black men know what they must do.'

During the hour which we spent at that place, one third of the beast was eaten or wasted, a second third packed up in branches for transport and the last third hung in the forks of trees, well covered with leaves and thorns, for my ivory bearers were anticipating the return journey and intended providing themselves with a larder, if the leopards and the vultures did not succeed in helping themselves first.

It was one o'clock before we reached the top of Om-Grooty. We stopped there once more, and scanned the woods as we had done previously. We soon became aware of four elephants making their way slowly along the side of a clearing just beneath the place where we were standing. To one side of them, a herd of more than sixty buffalo was grazing, and on the other side we could see a large number of eland (*Boselaphus oreas*) interspersed among herds of other animals. The harder we looked, the more we discovered, until eventually we counted 400 to 500. Unfortunately, our ammunition was depleted and we had to content ourselves with simply observing.

When I gave the signal to move on, Souzouana pointed out to me that the elephants were heading in our direction and would be likely to cut us off. I took no heed of his warning. We started down the hill and, as nobody seemed inclined to take the lead, I was obliged to do so myself. But as it turned out, we did not meet up with the enormous animals, an encounter which, under different circumstances, would have given me great pleasure; on this occasion, I contemplated the possibility almost fearfully.

That same evening, an hour after sunset, I arrived back at my camp at last, accompanied by only one of my Cafres, the others having been unable to keep up the pace. I felt something akin to the joy of homecoming as I saw my camp once more. Henning was growing impatient for my return; he had a letter for me and he wanted to tell me of the acquisition of an interesting new animal, apart from a thousand other matters which he wished to communicate. And so the coffee drinking was prolonged beyond midnight and my companionable pipe required filling ten times over.

CHAPTER XVII

Houahouaho — The reasons for his coming — His story — Various hunting parties

Richard King once again told me of the presence of a large species of antelope previously unknown to him, which he had encountered near Saint Lucia Bay. At the same time Henning showed me the skin of a female of this species which was of particular interest to me because of the long hair which adorned the neck in the manner of a lion's mane, and the semi-circle of white hair, two inches wide, round the hind-quarters. For our own convenience we baptised the species with three different names, one of which we finally settled upon after I had been fortunate enough to kill a male: *leeauw-book*, lion-buck, *waater-book*, water-buck, and *eezel-book*, donkey-buck, all of which names are appropriate enough in describing the female, but as the male does not have the singular distinction of long hair around his neck, and as he has less the look of a donkey than does the female, we were obliged to abandon the first and the last names and settle for the second, because of the habit these animals have of lying in the shallow river beds during the heat of the day, just as the buffaloes do in the Om-Philos rivers. It was only later that I discovered that this species had already been described by Burschell as *Kobus ellipsiprymnus*.

Henning, observing my pleasure in the possession of a hitherto unknown specimen, hastened to take advantage of the fact that I was well-disposed towards him. 'This is not all that we have acquired,' he said, 'there is something else.' 'And what is that if you please?' 'We are short of labour as you know; we cannot have too many hands for the work we are engaged in; a Cafre, an Amazoulou, came asking for work and I thought it as well to take him on provisionally until you came back.' 'If he is here let me see him.' 'Houahouaho! Houahouaho!' cried Henning.

Along came a young man of seventeen or eighteen, handsome of face and fine of figure, with brilliant dark deep-set eyes, modest of bearing and shy of manner. 'What is your name?' 'Houahouaho.' 'What brings you here?' 'Master, Henning knows the reason; Henning can tell you; Henning must have told you.' 'It is you who must speak. I am waiting for you to tell me. Speak.' 'Master, I was a prisoner, bound and on the eve of execution, when Om-Kondo (assegai) the agent of Hans Delange, passed through the *mouzi* where

213

I was being held. Om-Kondo, when acquainted with what was going on, used his influence to obtain my release, but as no one dared compromise himself, he was obliged to cut my bonds himself, advising me that my only salvation was to come here to you. To do this meant to journey for ten hours under the hot sun, which I did without pause to rest. You were with Panda. I found Henning who said: "Stay until the master returns." Master, you have returned. If you will not have me, I hope that you will not send me back to Panda.' 'Houahouaho, for what reason did Panda wish to have you assegaied?' 'Master, I loved an *intombu*, a young girl, the daughter of a headman who lived in a *mouzi* not far from mine. She loved me too. You know what happens when one is in love. We loved each other so much! It happened, and we were discovered. The headman, in his anger, lodged a complaint; I was seized and bound and I have told you the rest.' 'How can this be? Is it the custom here to put to death a man who has had intercourse with a girl?' 'Ah certainly, when complaint is lodged by the parents of the *intombu* and when the *imphana*, the young man, is an *om-phogazane*[1] who has no cows to pay for the offence he has committed; he must then pay with his life. I am an *imphana*, an *om-phogazane*; no cows; that is why I was going to be put to death.' 'Houahouaho, I do not know if you speak the truth, for I have heard it said that *schlobonka* was the accepted practice here in the country of the Amazoulous, as it is in Natal.' 'You are right, master; but while I agree that what you say is true, allow me to point out to you that you have confused the matter.'

Then Houahouaho, using four fingers in illustration, explained to me that *schlabonka* with interposition was a violation of established custom, while superposition, on the contrary, was a legal act, for it was their belief that there could be no consequences. This is the only condition upon which a man possessed of only one wife, will be received by her during lactation. I doubt that anyone can find this precaution unacceptable, for in no country in the world are the children better formed or more thriving, nowhere are they less plaintive and sickly than among the fine Amazoulou people.

They say that the traveller should tell the whole truth. For my part, I have been hard put to it to describe this custom without saying too much. Many will complain that I have not gone far enough, but I am not concerned with making myself intelligible to those who are slow to comprehend; the important thing to me is to be accurate in telling the facts, while taking care not to wound the sensibilities of chaste ears.

I agreed to allow Houahouaho to stay, while impressing upon him that it would be impossible for me to protect him if Panda should

1 Expression which means 'peasant', 'poor devil'.

send for him, but if that were to happen, I would use all my influence with the king to obtain his pardon, and I added that I hoped to bring matters to a happy conclusion.

Houahouaho thanked me simply, almost coldly, as the Cafres do, but by his conduct and his willingness to serve me for as long as this state of uncertainty lasted, I could see that he was endeavouring to render himself indispensable to me. He was well behaved, and obliging towards his new comrades whose tasks he sought to alleviate; when I put a gun into his hands, he learnt within two days to shoot as skilfully as any man.

On 14 December I sent two of my men to Omschlaty-Omkoulou to look for elephants and to drive them in our direction if possible. I would like to have gone myself, but engaged as I was in the preparation of numerous specimens, I was obliged to sacrifice the pleasures of the hunting party.

On the 20th my men returned after having travelled more than fifty leagues; they had crossed the Omschlopu near the upper part of Omschlaty-Omkoulou; they had moved across to the Mouniama and then had travelled downstream for some distance and had come upon a troop of forty elephants. My Cafres had not dared attack them, believing that in great numbers these animals are more dangerous than when isolated. This was a misconception, but at that time neither my servants nor I knew much about elephant-hunting. As for the buffaloes, the *cannas*, kudus, small antelopes of various sorts, wild boars and quaggas, our successes far exceeded our expectations. We supplied the neighbouring *mouzis* with meat and, thanks to us, several hundred people lived in circumstances of plenty hitherto unknown to them. In return for these services, which cost us no more than powder and shot, we frequently received milk, beer and the assistance of willing hands.

However great the Cafre's appetite for the delicious meat of the buffalo and the *canna*, I could see the time coming when there would be a shortage of porters because the people were sated. We would often return to camp in the evening, after hunting separately all day, to find that we had collectively bagged from eight to twelve of the larger animals, such as buffaloes and *cannas* whose combined weight sometimes exceeded 15 000 pounds, and was sometimes as high as 20 000. Obviously a hundredth part of this would have sufficed amply to meet our needs, but man is essentially destructive. We often killed with the sole object of proving our skill, or simply to obtain marrow-bones or perhaps only a tail. Once the animal had fallen, the hunter would produce some frivolous excuse for killing it.

To prevent this was not in my power, for I was always the first to set a bad example. The hyaenas and the vultures reaped the benefit of our folly as did sometimes even the lions whom I had always believed too proud to devour what the hunter had already killed. Here is how we discovered this fact. On one occasion there were four hours of daylight left when Henning went out hunting and, without giving the matter much thought, killed a buffalo, a quagga and a *canna*. After skinning the quagga, he thought that I might be pleased to have the *canna*, but as he had not the time to complete the task of skinning it, he decided to cover the animal with thorny mimosa branches and to hang his hat on a stick alongside it, convinced that, at the sight of such a scarecrow with the odour of man about it, no hyaena, fox, leopard, lion or vulture would dare to approach.

To tell the truth, I was inclined to share this opinion. Confidently we made our way next morning to the place where our *canna* was lying. 'Look at those vultures,' Henning said to me, 'perched on the top of those round mimosas; that's just where our animal is lying.'

We were on the spot in an instant. We found the branches scattered in disorder, the grass trodden and torn to reveal the sandy earth, marked with the footprints of a lion, while the stones were blackened with the blood of the *canna*, nothing of which remained but the head, lying 20 paces away in thick bush and recognisable only by the horns.

'And what about my hat!' said Henning, mystified. 'What, is it gone also?' 'Completely gone; that devil of a lion must be wearing it.' 'This is a real loss to you, since you have no other.' 'Yes, a loss that I will soon feel in this sun. There's only one thing left for me to do.' 'What's that?' 'To cut myself out a hat with powder and shot from that fellow's hide.' 'Henning, be careful not to make a mistake; I do not think you have the right culprit. Consider a moment and you will agree that a lion is too noble a gentleman to allow you to use his stomach as a wardrobe.' 'You mean that it was those snivelling hyaenas?' 'Yes, and I suspect no other; animals which, for a taste of rancid grease, are happy to gnaw at old bones, are quite capable of playing this trick on you.' 'Well, I agree, but the one to whose lot it fell must have had a very light supper.' 'Not so light, Henning; you have been wearing that felt hat for a long time now.' 'Not so long, two years at the most.' 'Two years is time enough for a felt hat to grow greasy. Do not be too upset by the loss; I am happy to be able to offer you a replacement without delay.'

My proposition failed to restore Henning to his accustomed cheerfulness; he was mourning the loss of an old friend. However much we Europeans may grow attached to insignificant things which have been of use to us, we nevertheless willingly discard the old for the new; in the eyes of those to whom fashion is unknown this has the appearance of ingratitude.

Judging by the fact that the imprints of the lion were covered over by those of the hyaena, it became apparent that the former had been the first to attack our *canna*; the hyaenas had only approached after the masters had withdrawn. Others who arrived when all had been eaten, were obliged to be satisfied with the felt hat, which must have been knocked to the ground in the turmoil.

This was the first of several occasions on which I was able to confirm that, in his natural state, the lion does not live solely by hunting; dead animals are quite acceptable to him, but they must be fresh and intact. If the game is abundant and easily come by, the lion eats as much as he sees fit, and then goes off. If, on the other hand, the hunt has proved tiring and difficult and the profits meagre, the lion, after satisfying his immediate appetite, remains concealed in a bush nearby. From this vantage point he defends his prey night and day from the approach of every other carnivore. He has little difficulty with the quadrupeds which, recognising his superior strength, instinctively stand back and watch from twenty-five, thirty or forty paces off for the opportunity to present themselves when the lord and master, ready to depart, abandons the remains of his royal feast and goes off with firm and measured tread. Those predators which trouble him most are the vultures, which swoop down and make off with some morsel or other, in defiance of the king of the forests and his formidable paws.

CHAPTER XVIII

Excursion to the bay of Saint Lucia — Noboka — A hippopotamus hunt — The first elephant falls — How the Cafres go about hippopotamus hunting — The Cafres of Makazane

For some time now, Henning had been wanting to press on as far as Saint Lucia Bay which lay between twenty and twenty-five leagues to the east of us. I had not considered it proper to seem to accede to his request, as I myself also wished to visit those parts. However, the time had now arrived to implement this simple project and I informed Henning that the day of our departure was set for 27 December.

The 26th was spent in preparations, particularly in the cleaning and checking of our firearms, and the following day when dawn broke we were already on our way, without benefit of map or guide. I knew the approximate situation of the bay in relation to our point of departure, and to keep us on the right course I had only a simple pocket compass, no bigger than an ordinary watch.

My Cafres were greatly intrigued that I should claim to be able to lead them across a stretch of country which I myself had never previously explored, and to bring them directly to the bay of Saint Lucia, which they call by the corrupted name of Om-Sonndouss. My men watched in fascination as the needle of the compass moved when I took a bearing and always returned again to the same position. They could only attribute to the supernatural what they were quite incapable of comprehending. They said it was sorcery and, in order to avoid further attempts at explanation, I agreed that it was an instrument of *om-tagaty* which was, however, quite incapable of doing any harm.

After travelling for two hours in an east-south-easterly direction, a route which we were bound to follow because of the detours of the Om-Pholozie, we noticed a mass of vultures rising from a point not far away, where a great *Rhinoceros simus* was lying dead. It had been killed twelve days previously with two bullets fired by the worst of my hunters, Wilhelm and Nanana. About midday I killed an enormous buffalo. The very next moment Henning killed another. Soon the unbearable heat and the lack of water forced us to return to the banks of the Om-Pholozie. Not far from the river, we sought shelter at a *mouzi* of fairly considerable size, which belonged to a headman who, although impoverished, was a leader of the first rank and among whose wives was one of the numerous sisters of Panda,

218

the most beautiful of them all.

We hastened to make a gift to our hosts of the two buffalo, simply indicating to them where they lay, and expecting to obtain in return *tchouala, amas, mabélé, ombyla*; anything that they might have to offer. Unfortunately, in an excess of discretion, I had forbidden my men to ask for refreshment, preferring to wait for the offer of what would be so acceptable to our burning, parched throats; but nothing was forthcoming. Our need was great and I was obliged to break my rule of conduct. I made the request, and some rather paltry provisions appeared, a disturbing foreboding of the chief's humour.

Having behaved handsomely towards him, I had expected to be treated in kind, and so I sent for him and explained to him clearly and briefly how I had reason to be dissatisfied with the welcome I had received. The man heard my remarks in stony silence. Then, as I was quite convinced that his behaviour was calculated, I assured him that I would have a word to say about him when I next visited Panda, and that this word could have unpleasant consequences for him, particularly as it was the king's will that a proper reception should be accorded me throughout his domain.

Although he must have been secretly convinced of the truth of what I said, the fellow took no heed and had it not been for the obligingness of some of the men of the community, we would probably have gone without. Kotchobana, who was of Amazoulou origin and who well knew the customs and the practices of these people, did not look kindly upon my restrained and gentle manner in dealing with them. According to him, we should have demanded or taken all that we required. 'The whites,' he said, 'defeated the Amazoulous in war. The reason why they did not kill them all to the last man, is that they wanted some to remain. Well, those who remain today are the humble servants of the whites.' According to this worthy fellow's opinion, I should have conducted myself like a conqueror.

In spite of his persuasive logic, I paid him no heed, for these methods filled me with aversion, and, anyway, I knew that by practising them, one inspires hatred and then, in the end, one is invariably beaten to death. For me discretion was the better part of valour.

An hour before sunset, Henning and I went out to inspect the surrounding countryside. Our expedition led us to a ridge which culminated in a steep drop from which we were able to admire one of the most picturesque and impressive of views. Eleven coils of the Om-Pholozie river, like snakes of gleaming water, *Iniouka* as the Amazoulous say, meandered across the landscape. The river immediately beneath us was invisible because of the steep drop; beyond was a beautiful luxuriant forest, while in the distance stretched a vast green plain, where numerous herds of buffalo and *cannas* peacefully grazed. Such a scene, which recalled the earliest days of creation, can today only be chanced upon where men are few and the innocent echoes repeat no sound of gunfire.

On the 28th, without having to deviate too much from our path, we turned off towards the left to look at a lake which was inhabited by a herd of thirty hippopotamus. The site was not promising, for where the approaches were accessible, the quarry was out of reach of our gunfire, and where the approaches were closer to the animals, they offered no foothold, for the reeds were too thick and tall, the water too deep, or covered in floating grass which would not have supported the weight of a man. We fired a few shots, however, as a token to our companions of our goodwill, and left the place. Three hours later we arrived on the banks of another lake which was elongated in shape and which seemed to me to be formed by the waters of the Sélène river. There we wounded two hippopotamus and when sufficient time had elapsed and nothing had come to the surface, we left the banks so that we might make a detour before nightfall, which would enable us to cross a flat sandy part of the valley covered with tall reeds.

It was rather late and we were tired out when we came upon a wretched *mouzi* where, in spite of its miserable appearance, we were warmly welcomed. The people were poor, but they shared with us all they had, which included the offer of their most comfortable hut. That night I found it impossible to close my eyes as a multitude of insects immediately set about devouring me, inflicting a vast number of unbearably uncomfortable bites. I was stung a thousand times over by small creatures, which I later discovered to be red ants, whose acquaintance I had not previously had occasion to make.

My patience exhausted, I left the hut, and went to lie down outside, but I soon discovered that I had exchanged Charybdis for Scylla. I had expected that this change would be for the better, but I was mistaken; the millions of mosquitoes, those aerial buglers which sound the attack before they charge, almost persuaded me that the invasion of the army of red ants was preferable. There was only one solution: my pipe. I crouched on the ground, completely enveloped in a woollen blanket, puffing smoke through the smallest possible aperture, and awaited the coming of day, which is the signal for these vast hordes to retreat. As soon as it was light, I fell asleep, crouched upon the ground. At about eight o'clock, with the sun's rays burning my face, I awakened with a start; all the others were ready, and we bid farewell to the good people whose hospitality we were determined never to accept again.

We set off for Noboka's place which, although it was eight or nine miles off, was the closest of all the *mouzis* to the bay of Saint Lucia.

We arrived an hour before sunset after a tiring journey. All along the way, at the bottom of every little valley, we had had to cross marshes of black peat-like earth, two to three feet deep, where leeches abounded and attached themselves to our legs as we waded across. To start with, I took my clothes off each time, but as the marshes began to occur too frequently, I decided that it would be more convenient to have my men carry me across. They found these repeated baths delightfully refreshing.

When we were within a few hours of our destination, we came upon some sandy plains where sour grass was growing, of the type found near the bay of Port Natal. The vegetation was no longer that of Om-Philos; in these plains there was virtually nothing growing but palm trees and stunted bushes; they were called by the Boers *wild-klaapper-noot*, wild coconut; *wild-dattle-boom*, wild date palm; then there were dwarf palms, *lataniers*, and various wild bananas.

Everything appeared more tropical, this was truly Africa; the style of the huts reflected the warmer climate; they appeared designed to protect against the heat rather than the cold. In the upper part of Om-Philos, twenty-five leagues away, the maize was just beginning to grow, while at Saint Lucia Bay it had been ripe for some time. My men and I were given a large quantity of this maize which we feasted upon. As soon as we arrived, I made my way to Noboka's hut, which was easily identified because of its great size. Noboka was one of Panda's principal headmen; he was rich in wives, but poor in cattle; poor through excess of patriotism: he had put all that he possessed at the disposal of the Amazoulous who had taken refuge with Panda in Natal and he had received no recompense; no beast had ever been returned to him as Panda, in spite of his 50 000 head of cattle, declared that he had not the means to settle his debt.

I waited upon Noboka outside his hut. He very soon appeared. He was a man of average height, but of a corpulence such as I have never seen before. He acknowledged my greetings with a yawn; Noboka had just risen from a long siesta and, without deigning to utter a word, he turned his back on me and, followed by his *omdouna*, he left the *mouzi* by a private path. Never before had I been received with such ill-mannered indifference, for I can describe this unseemly conduct in no other terms, and I gained the impression that Noboka considered himself as too great and powerful a chief to be bothered with me. This was a consoling thought, as it implied that there had been no intention on his part to insult me personally. Let me hasten to add, however, that I realised that very evening, how mistaken I had been in thinking that any impoliteness had been intended; I had taken Noboka unawares; he had been still asleep when we were introduced; he made his excuses to me personally, conversed wittily, showed himself to be extremely affable and offered to lend me his men when I went hunting.

221

At daybreak on 30 December 1841, I prepared to take advantage of his offer. Hippopotamus were to be found in plenty in a lake six miles away, but it was important to get there early. To judge by the fine description I had been given of the approaches to the lake, I reckoned that we would be very unfortunate indeed if we failed to bring back at least one hippopotamus. A single one of these animals which weigh 4000 pounds, would not provide an excessive amount of meat for all these people; in fact there would be just sufficient for one meal. For my part, I was the more determined to succeed, as Noboka appeared to set great store by our success. To encourage me in my endeavours he had had the foresight to instruct his beer porters to follow me about everywhere, so that thirst should not be the cause of failure. 'Water,' he informed me, 'makes the stomach weak and sickly; beer gives strength and courage; drink it, do not spare it, and you will succeed.' Noboka was right, and I thank him from the bottom of my heart, for I confess that my subsequent successes had their beginnings that day in Noboka's pot of beer.

Half an hour's walk brought us to a damp forest composed, in part, of trees which were quite unknown to me and which reminded me of the trees of Europe. There was a large number of snails there which I had neither the time not the facilities to collect and transport. This was the first time since my arrival in Africa that I had encountered these creatures. The humidity was certainly the determining cause of their great numbers. I ought to have gathered at least a few, but when there are great things to be done, the lesser are neglected or indeed rejected. What! Should I, the great hunter, condescend to collect these insignificant objects of creation? I allowed myself to be persuaded by my own foolishness, and the snails went peacefully on their way.

For more than an hour we followed a pretty path running alongside a narrow lake which resembled a river. The sea lay two miles off on our right hand side, separated from us by well-wooded dunes. One of the scouts came back to warn us to keep absolutely silent. 'Master,' he said, 'over there, not far away, eighty or a hundred hippopotamuses are lying, partly exposed, in the shallows.'

I ordered all the men who could not be useful to me to remain where they were, and took with me only my hunters and the ammunition bearers. Soon we had reached the bank directly opposite the place where the monsters were gathered. We could but gaze at them in astonishment. Kotchobana and Boulandje were delighted; Cafres though they were, they had seen no sight to touch this one. They gazed, round eyed and open-mouthed. Which of you can truly say that he too has seen so numerous a herd gathered in so confined a space, so exposed and so accessible (110 paces)? Such a sight is only to be seen on Lake Omsonndous.

Can you conceive of a hundred of these animals, heavy, round and massive, with grey bodies, small, transparent, flesh-coloured ears, enormous round snouts, so closely gathered together that they occupied a space of only thirty-five to forty paces? An old male, disturbed during his siesta in the sun by the movements of a neighbour, protested with a resounding *hon-hon*; another raised his snout to test the air for the presence of enemies.

A moment passed; the water rippled out in widening circles from a central point thirty paces from the recumbent herd; a grey head appeared, misshapen and hideous: it was the old man of the river. Gradually his body emerged from the water and on short legs which disappeared into the sand he made his way to rejoin his companions. In spite of his age, nobody moved to accommodate him. He found a small space and collapsed heavily into it, brushing against a young animal which arose in displeasure and went off to look for another place. Kotchobana was as new to this sort of spectacle as I was, and probably enjoyed it as much, but it was not enough simply to stare. Henning was also present, and for him 10 pounds of *zee-koe-spek* in the pot was worth more than a hundred hippopotamuses in the river. He invariably reasoned this way and, for my part, I could not blame him.

'Come along, let us take up our positions, guns in the brackets, make ready to fire.' *Vlan! vlan! vlan!* The first shot is mine. 'Careful! All set? Yes.' *Badoum, oum, oum* went the echoes, and *fla, fla, fla . . . ouf, là . . . roum, roum . . . hon, hon . . . Padadouff* went the monsters as they fled into the water. Nowhere in the world could sudden fright have caused more of a stampede, more congestion, more confusion. Our bathers, in spite of their weight, were trampling upon each other in their frantic attempts to escape. We expected soon to find the smaller ones crushed by the larger in the rout. Certainly there would be some ribs broken, apart from the damage done by our four shots which had found their target. The water displaced by the animals as they dived lapped up in waves against the bank, much as if a ship of 200 tons had been launched. Amidst the swirling water, astonished heads appeared here and there, coming towards us in an attempt to reach deep water and to escape from the fearful attack.

'Come on lads, get ready to reload; jump to it' . . . and the shot rained down on the heads. One disappeared; another came up along-side and ducked down again immediately beneath our fire. In less than two minutes, eight heads were blowing blood.

The sound of our incessant fire, repeated by the echoes, soon scattered the monsters over a wide area, and each of us took up a new vantage point. During the first half hour I counted seven animals

223

which I had wounded with direct hits below the eye, shots which, although not fatal, irritated the animals and forced them to surface more frequently and for longer periods, thereby offering us a greater opportunity of success.

But dare I confess it? In spite of the fact that our shot weighed a twelfth of a pound and was made of lead mixed with two parts in ten of tin, in spite of our skill in marksmanship, in spite of the fact that we struck more than twenty hippopotamuses in the head, not one floated up to the surface, although we waited until half past three. I was almost ready to believe the story told me by a Boer, that the hippopotamus, when wounded, takes hold in his canines of some root or rock on the river bed and remains attached to it after his death. I knew that my aim had been accurate; ill-luck alone could be accountable for my lack of success and, vexed at adverse fortune, I took my two Cafres and went off to make better use of my day by inspecting the bay of Saint Lucia of which I intended to make a sketch.

And so I abandoned the hunt and with it my hopeful intention of obliging my hosts. Hardly had we left the shores of the lake when I saw Henning coming towards us; Henning from whom we had not heard a shot for several hours. Without informing me, he had gone off to inspect the bay of Saint Lucia which he described as a nasty little hole, hardly a quarter of the diameter of the bay of Port Natal, with a sand bar at the entrance which could not be navigated by the smallest of ships, perhaps not even by a ship's boat. Twenty minutes separated us from the bay; Henning showed the path he had taken.

Before us lay a plain, a mile or a mile and a half long. Although dry at the time, it must have been flooded during the rainy season, for it was covered with reeds, sword grass and wild gladiolus, all plants which favour marshy ground. There were forests to our right where the concentration of trees was dense at the centre, becoming more sparse towards the outskirts; beyond were dunes of white sand which commanded a view of the sea some way off, while a mile away on the left hand side, the waters of the Om-Pholozie flowed down to the false bay of Saint Lucia.

In my disappointment, I regretted all the bullets we had fired in vain; my pride also suffered, for the skill which we had proved to our own satisfaction had produced no material evidence to offer to Noboka's people. Dissatisfied, I was walking along in silence, when one of the Zoulous suddenly stopped and pointed out a black shape standing alone in the plain. *Uncklove*! Elephant! The black shape was easily visible but it was not possible to distinguish its parts. Our observer was greeted with the unanimous response: *Ka uncklove*! *inyaty*! 'Not an elephant, but a buffalo!' The animal stood right in our way. We walked on for a hundred and fifty paces and then stopped. 'It is an elephant, by Dingaan!' said a Zoulou, 'I saw his trunk move.' And everybody agreed; 'It is true.' All eyes were fixed upon him, and the movement had escaped no one. This certainty having been established, I could hardly contain my delight; I danced about in eager anticipation of the pleasure that was to come. 'Well, Kotchobana, I hope that this will make up for the hippopotamuses. Come now, is your gun loaded? Are you sure of your priming? Let me see.' And I ran an appraising eye over the weapon. As for Boulandje, I did not bother taking the precaution to examine his gun, for I depended so little on his skill. 'Careful now; if we proceed with caution and composure we cannot fail. *Imphana*, pass us the beer.' We drank deep and the empty calabash rolled on the ground. 'The rest of you *imphanas*, you who carry the ammunition, you will follow us into the forest and you will remain there. But you must make no sound; do not tread upon dry branches. By Dingaan, if you frighten the elephant off, I shall put a bullet into you. Is that understood? Let us go then.'

We entered the forest and made our way along the inside edge, the better to conceal our progress. Kotchobana had always accompanied me when I went hunting, for I relied on him to read the wind and to pick up trails. We white men would need to study for a great many years to become good trackers and besides, our eyesight is not as sharp as that of the Cafre. They are able virtually to read from the tracks the species, the size and even the sex of the animal, and what is more, they are able to identify the time at which the animal passed by, whether it was days or merely hours before; and rarely are they mistaken. On this occasion once again, it was Kotchobana who was to guide us, but he was not himself, his spirit was troubled, probably because of the feverish excitement which he and I both felt, I mean that mixture of fear and pleasure which sets the heart thudding against the ribs, that delicious anxiety, seasoned with indescribable anguish, which one experiences in anticipation of a great event such as this, when one's life, housed in its frail shell, is to be thrown into the game of chance against the life of a colossus. These emotions, which are so difficult to describe, had certainly upset Kotchobana's spirit, for as we came abreast of the animal 'Let us go now, it is time,' he said. With our heads virtually between our knees, we approached the elephant. When we were sixty paces out of the forest, we were obliged to pause.

Panting, we stopped to take breath, for this manner of walking doubled-up restricts the respiration; but this was not the only reason; the elephant had raised his trunk to its fullest extent above his head, curling the end like a weather vane, sniffing the wind, and making use of his sense of smell to detect the presence of enemies in the vicinity; his immense ears arose from where they had lain flat on his shoulders and stood straight up, extended to receive the slightest sound.

'Good Heavens,' I thought, 'What fine senses! At 300 paces he has wind of us. Devil take him; he is downwind from us,' and moistening my finger in my mouth, I held it up to the air. 'Kotchobana, miserable dog that you are, where is your nose today? We have the wind behind us. Look, the elephant is moving away. *Pannzy*, lie flat, lie flat,' I hissed, beside myself with anger, and I forced him down with the barrel of my gun applied to the nape of his neck.

A quarter of a minute later, I raised my head to see the elephant grazing as peacefully as before. He was quite unaware of us. Taking more care this time, we retreated into the woods, crawling along flat on our stomachs. We paused to take breath and I gave Kotchobana brief instructions. This time I would be the guide; I would take the first shot; he and Boulandje had only to follow me. It took us more than a quarter of an hour to get downwind of the elephant, which it was possible for us to do, because the shape of the forest favoured this manoeuvre. Without revealing ourselves we were able to get close enough to see the colossus busily pulling up tufts of grass with his trunk as he walked about peacefully, like an animal in his pasture. He was coming towards us without suspecting our presence, for he could rely only on his ears and his eyes to alert him of danger. His sense of smell, the most acute of his senses, was of no use to him now, for we were downwind of him and he could get no scent of us.

The moment he lowered his head we moved twenty paces to hide behind a straggling bush which stood isolated in the bare plain; Kotchobana, Boulandje and a Zoulou with a double-barrelled gun, followed after me. We got behind our bush, from where we could hope to see the animal pass within thirty paces of us if we waited. Forty paces further on there was a clump of sword grass three feet high, big enough to conceal us, and easy enough to move to for a closer look at the elephant if he moved to the left. Kotchobana had immediately perceived the advantages of this move and, without waiting for my instructions, 'Over there, over there,' he said, and shot off as soon as the elephant put his head down again.

Although we were as quick as gazelles, we had hardly got behind the grass, when the animal raised his head, but it was apparent that he had noticed nothing. We crouched down in an attempt to make ourselves as small as possible, very well aware that the distance which separated us from the animal was no more than sixty paces. We were able to exchange a few words in low voices. 'What a stupid elephant, eh Kotchobana? To have such a long nose and not smell us, such good eyes and not see us and such huge ears and not hear us! We are indeed fortunate.'

Our guns were cocked in order to avoid the click of the catch which might have given the alarm at such close quarters and would have lost us those five seconds which precede the shot, seconds which are essential if one is to lodge a bullet in the elephant's brain, for his cranium, relative to his body, is very small. 'Well, Kotchobana, here we are at last; now we will see; at thirty-five paces I will give you a signal, then all together we will stand and take careful aim; take your time and do not be afraid, I am with you.'

But while reminding him that I was with him, I realised that he was with me; for had I been all alone, I would probably not have dared to contemplate attacking such a great mass. I alone kept watch. 'Stand up!' and all three of us rose up boldly like devils out of the earth. Five seconds passed and then: boom boom! Two shots went off. Kotchobana thought he heard a crunching sound and took to his heels. I could not see for smoke and I staggered blindly after him. Boulandje, with his ancient but incomparably sturdy weapon, still stood at the ready and then, firing his shot just as I crossed in front of him, he blew off my beard. This was not the moment to demand an explanation; I believed the elephant to be at our heels and had rapidly sprinted twenty paces, when those who had stayed behind in the wood yelled to us at the top of their voices: *Uncklove fyle, uncklove fyle*! 'The elephant is dead.'

We stopped, Kotchobana and I, looked at each other, burst out laughing and then reloaded our guns, for a fallen elephant is not necessarily a dead elephant. 'Are you ready? Let's go.' I was almost delirious with the joy of my first success. 'Come on,' I said to my men, 'five inches above the right eye; you will see the hole made by my bullet; if you do not, you may consider the elephant as yours.' But I was confident that I had seen the shot hit its mark.

We approached cautiously, parting the reeds which hid the fallen giant from our view; we were within five or six paces when a dull sound, like the rumble of distant thunder, escaped from the body; it was the air trapped in the large intestines which was breaking. In the belief that the elephant was still alive and challenging us, we were about to retreat, when I came upon our prey, lying quite still on his right flank, stone dead.

But as there was a sobbing noise such as would come from a living animal, I fired a bullet into his chest; Kotchobana and Boulandje, to make sure that he was dead, followed suit: it was, they said, to make sure that the elephant would not *kotlissa* them (treacherously betray them). Immediately thereafter, I took possession of the animal by jumping on his right flank where I had plenty of room to walk about much as one does on board ship, for the body alone was more than ten and a half feet long.

Every hunter will understand how I feasted my eyes on the enormous beast which a moment earlier could so easily have crushed us all. He lay there, robbed of his life by a bullet, such a tiny thing compared with his own size, which had penetrated fourteen inches into his skull. My gun, which I contemplated with pride, was no bigger than a matchstick when compared with his body, but what an impact it had made. As proof, the animal lay there beneath my feet and I walked upon his great flank.

It could all have been a dream. As we examined the elephant and the wound which had brought about his downfall what strange and astonishing remarks my Cafres made! They had seen it all; our efforts had so soon been crowned with success that it seemed to them they could henceforth easily kill more elephants, many elephants, upon whose tusks they were already founding their future fortunes. Nothing succeeds like success, and had we not given proof of our exceeding boldness? Was it not apparent that we had the temerity to attack what was much stronger and larger than ourselves? No retreat had been possible; the furious animal, if it had charged us, would have seized us before we had had time to take refuge in the forest.

It had been a duel to the death; but our presence of mind had been our saving grace in what might have become the most critical of situations. Only young hunters such as we were would have accepted the challenge. But had I not sworn by Saint Hubert to conduct myself in a worthy manner at my first encounter with an elephant, and in return for my devotion was it not he who had been pleased to guide my bullet? Let us give honour where honour is due, and Saint Hubert shall be honoured. I, who have reaped the benefits of his intervention, admit that I owe him a thousand favours. With difficulty I tore myself away from the object which delighted my eyes and engaged my every thought; the sun was sinking rapidly and we had three leagues to go before reaching the *mouzi* of Noboka.

Kotchobana and Boulandje were wild with joy, particularly as I had just rewarded them each with a cow in recognition of their having risked their lives to accompany me. They each carried a piece of the elephant — the tail, symbol of conquest, and the ears, whose size had excited my admiration. In half and hour we were back on the shores of the lake where Henning, shortly before, had fired a few shots at the hippopotamuses; soon we could hear him talking loudly to a group of Cafres whose raised voices and rapid speech led me to believe that they had been successful, for I well knew how loquacious these people are when the news is good.

'Henning, Henning' — 'Hallooh!' — 'Well, what?' — 'We have a hippopotamus' — 'That's good' — 'You have come from the bay, did you see it?' — 'Yes; no' — 'Why no?' . . . In spite of the thick bush, we had succeeded in reaching the party on the shore. 'What's that?' Henning asked, his eyes round with astonishment, as he touched the elephant's tail. 'Where did you find that? Did you perhaps find a dead elephant?' 'Not at all! Do you not see that this tail is still bleeding? We killed him down there in the flat country which you have just crossed, at the most twenty minutes after we saw you.' 'Who killed him?' 'I did.' 'The devil you did!' he said, astonished and a little envious, 'I do not have such luck.' 'Bah! it is nothing, you just have to find them; shooting them is nothing. This one went down like a ton of bricks. We have heard too many hunters' tales of elephants; he is an animal which is easier to kill than a buffalo. Just try it when you have the chance and you will see if I am wrong.'

By making light of the difficulties, I believed that I would encourage him to greater efforts. Henning fell into my trap; spurred on by his hunter's pride as well as by his love of gain, he tried, succeeded and became the greatest elephant hunter in Natal, second only after me.

On returning to the *mouzi*, I was expected to accept offerings of maize which arrived from all sides, accompanied by a great many compliments. I was now known as *Kos-Omkoulou, Omdoda, Manschla, Kakoulou*, which is to say great master, man of strength. And it was our success which had earned us these privileges. The next day was a day of plenty, spent in feasting. They owed it all to me and they were grateful.

Noboka was busy sitting in judgment and could not come to me, but he took the trouble to send me a pot of excellent beer which I imbibed in the company of my pipe, while my servants roasted their maize. Sleep eluded me and it was very late when I eventually succeeded in drifting off. Added to my inflamed imagination, the mosquitoes played their part in keeping me awake. Tired out at last, I sank to the ground and dreamed that I was surrounded by herds of elephants. To describe these would be beyond my powers and in any case, my reader would not wish to be plunged into the poetic land of dreams.

This was certainly the most beautiful night of my life. Happy in the dreams which are so dear to the heart of the elephant hunter, newly admitted though I was to that fraternity, I would have prolonged my sleep, had not Noboka himself arrived to awaken me in order to compliment me. Not realising that it was he, and not troubling to open my eyes, I heartily sent him to the devil. Kotchobana, who was close by, made every effort to warn me: 'It is Noboka, Noboka who is speaking to you!' I had more need of sleep than of compliments, but Noboka offered them with such generosity and believed that he was doing me such pleasure by addressing his *koluma* (speeches) to me, that I made a great effort to open my eyes and my ears to receive them. Once awake, I lost no time in sending some men to remove the elephant's tusks, while another party went out to cut up the hippopotamus, reserving for ourselves only a few pounds of the fat for use on the return journey. As for me, I was so stiff from the fatigues of the previous day, that it was more than I could do at that moment to consider going out again to hunt.

I learnt from Noboka that a troop of elephants had been seen in the tall reeds not far from the site of our triumph, but that the access was difficult and dangerous. A few days previously, David Stellar, Richard King, Douglas, Parkins and their famous Cafre, Ho, had been pursued at that very spot by some of the females and in spite of their powerful weapons they had had to abandon their projected expedition.

When I told him of the hippopotamus hunt and of how we had wasted so much ammunition in vain, Noboka said to me: 'It is true that you did not have luck, but some of the animals will surely die of their wounds. Every morning I will have the surface of the lake inspected and my people will find them, you may be sure, for although the Amazoulous of Upper Om-Philos disdain the flesh, my people and I have for a long time been accustomed to it and prize it greatly. We eat much less frequently of the flesh of the elephant. My men have always had the reputation of being the bravest and the most fortunate of the hunters of elephant and hippopotamus. On one occasion a few years ago, in Dingaan's time, my men killed thirteen elephants in half a day.' 'How can this be possible with assegais?' 'Yes it is possible with assegais, but they were big and strong and heavy, made on purpose for the hunt.'

Noboka went on to explain to me how a single man would crawl towards the elephant and, when he was almost at point blank range, would throw an assegai with a metal tip, more rounded than is usual; the blade thrown horizontally would cut into the animal's hock and hamstring him. As it was now impossible for him to flee, the elephant would remain where he was and the band of warriors would do the rest.

However incredible it seemed to me that one could hunt elephant with cold steel, I had to admit that it was possible, for Dingaan had no other means of obtaining the tusks. I once threw an ordinary fighting assegai at a dead elephant and it did not penetrate beyond four or six inches; I was standing only six paces away and I had had some experience of throwing this sort of weapon; I had already done so to advantage in the case of old wounded buffaloes which were on their feet and able to move. The principal difficulty in the case of the elephant consists in the slackness of the wrinkled skin and not in the thickness of the tissue; as a proof of this, let me mention the rhinoceros *Africanus bicornis* and *R. simus*, and the hippopotamus, whose skins, taut with the fullness of their flesh, allow the metal tip of the weapon to penetrate without resistance, although the skin is much thicker and more dense. To be convinced of this, one has only to inspect the powerful and formidable horsewhips used by the Dutch drivers, which are made from these skins and which are known all over southern Africa by the name of *chambocks*.

Noboka went on to tell me of the method used by his people to hunt hippopotamus. I had already guessed something of this as I walked beside the lake and noticed wooden stakes near the bank, which protruded just above the water. My curiosity led me to ask questions. 'You know,' the chief replied, 'that the hippopotamus, however stupid he may appear to be, has an ability to observe and to remember, which serve him well in avoiding the traps set by men. Covered ditches are, I know, commonly employed near Touguela and in other of the principal districts but, in addition to requiring a great deal of preparation and presenting a constant danger to men, they are soon known to these animals, which avoid them, either by going back on their tracks or by making a detour. They are all the more recognisable in that they are invariably surrounded by dead mimosa branches, which are intended to guide the animal towards the trap like a funnel, and because there is no grass growing on the thin layer of earth which is spread on top. For some time, my people have depended on another system which, although it requires greater effort, ensures the capture of at least one of the animals when the hunt is made at the proper season.'

'This is our method,' went on Noboka, 'it is our custom at certain times to burn the grass at various points along the banks of the lake. The grass soon grows again, green and tender, and is very attractive to the hippopotamuses, almost all of which will then frequent the places where it is to be found. Once we are assured that they will be attracted to such and such a place, we wait for the wind to blow off the lake so that the amphibians will emerge with the wind behind them. The trackers arrange to gather at night at a particular spot, while during the preceding day, two or three stakes have been implanted at the mouth of each outlet, within the radius of the area to be surrounded. According to the positions which they have occupied during the day, the hippopotamuses emerge by different paths which are rarely the same as those they will be forced to take on their return.'

'You will easily comprehend how, at a given signal, between eleven o'clock and midnight, the semi-circle of men closing in upon them constrains the great beasts to congregate in one place, and that at another signal, the sound of 200 men shouting and beating their shields induces a panic which precipitates a hasty retreat. Instinctively, in their fear, the hippopotamuses head for the lake, taking the first pathway they can find, where they run heavily into the sharp pointed stakes which pierce them and render them incapable of reaching the water. Having achieved this much, the trackers rest and wait for the coming of day, when there is a rush to retrieve the animals which have been impaled, and to put an end to the disabled.'

I readily understood the advantages of such a hunt, and I endeavoured to persuade Noboka to organise one in which my hunters and I could take part; we would have liked nothing better, in spite of the clouds of mosquitoes which we would inevitably encounter, but he replied that the time was not propitious, and that he required many men to protect his gardens from the nocturnal visits of kudu and and wild boar; and so I refrained from further requests.

That same day, I was fortunate to meet one of Makazane's Cafres who lived at Noboka's kraal among the people there. His tribe lives in the upper parts of Om-Pongola on the right bank of the river, in the direction of Delagoa Bay. This tribe is subject to the Amazoulous without ever mixing with them, as the latter believe themselves superior. Certain indelible characteristics, rather than prejudice, tend to perpetuate the difference and prohibit a fusion. The Makazanes do not have the wide hole in the ear used by the Amazoulous to carry their snuff in a container of Spanish reed. For their part, the Makazanes have a series of incisions running from the top of the forehead to the end of the nose, which resemble tattooing in relief and which inspired the Boers of Triechard's expedition to name these people *Knoopneus-Kaffers*, Cafres with button noses. They are not capable of waging war against the Amazoulous; their numerical inferiority is acknowledged. Individually, they have less courage and less physical strength, probably due to the unhealthy climate of their country, which has witnessed the death of all the whites who have tried to cross it, with the exception of John King who succeeded in doing so fifteen years ago. The commercial expedition of Mr Norden and Co. from the Cape, a well-funded enterprise which was intended to collect ivory before heading for Delagoa Bay, came to nothing. After some initial success the wagons were abandoned three days journey from the Portuguese settlement. Every member of the expedition, whites, Hottentots and Cafres succumbed to sickness, except for a Mozambiquan negro called Swart-Hendrick who, although he nearly died, had sufficient strength of character to survive. I met this man at Natal.

The expedition of the English doctors Cowie and Green, although it was speedily accomplished, was not rapid enough to save their lives: one died upon arrival at Delagoa; the other a few days later on board ship as he was attempting to make his way back. Of the Triechard expedition, comprising seventy-five persons, the ship *Mazeppa* brought back only seventeen: there were two of Triechard's sons, only three or four young men in all; the remainder was made up of women and young children; all the men over thirty had died: the old men had gone first; the survivors were all pale and livid with black rings around their sunken eyes; their stomachs were unnaturally distended, particularly those of the children, who had difficulty in bending down. Two years later the state of their health had not improved.

Four men sent from Pieters Mauritz Burg to Delagoa to contact Smellekaamp of the Dutch ship *Bresilia*, made the journey on horseback in 1843. They wanted for nothing, but in spite of all their careful preparations, two of their number were struck down by the sickness within a few days. Smellekaamp lost his entire crew. Mr Azevedo, son-in-law of the governor of Quilimane, whom I saw when he called at Natal, said to me one day, referring to the maladies which carry off Europeans on the east coast of Africa; 'Monsieur, you see in me the last of the survivors of a hundred Portuguese who came out directly from Lisbon. One year spent in Mozambique, Quilimane and Sofala was enough to carry them all off.'

In addition to the insurmountable dangers to the health of explorers in the Makazane country, must be added the treachery of these Cafres, whose reputation as poisoners in known far and wide and appears to be deserved. 'Beware,' Houahouaho had said to me, before my departure for Saint Lucia Bay, 'do not touch a pot of beer or milk before the one who gave it you has tasted from it in your presence, for in that country you will not be far from the poisoners.' It is true that even among the Amazoulous, custom requires that this tasting should be done and the writer himself will always put a drink to his lips before offering it, in order to inspire confidence by proving that no poison is present, although when I observe that such a demonstration is about to be made for my own benefit, I always prevent the taster from performing his office; my servants considered my conduct to be most imprudent.

The Makazanes from the shores of Delagoa Bay know at least how to manage a boat. It appears that they have succeeded in building dug-out canoes and they dare to use them for transport and for fishing. In this way, they differ essentially from the Amazoulous who have never invented a means of crossing rivers, not even a rough raft. When the rivers come down in flood they form natural barriers and intercept all communication, for it is rare to find a Zoulou who is able to swim although they bathe frequently. The probable reason for this inability is the lack of deep water in their rivers during the greater part of the year and then, when the rivers come down in flood, there is the presence of crocodiles, those hideous living skeletons which hide away unseen, then suddenly surge up to snatch their victim before they disappear once more, stifling his cries beneath the water.

The reason why one does not encounter the rudiments of nautical science among them, is that the Amazoulous are a people who have come from the source of the Om-Philos. *Ama* indicates the plural and *Zoulou* means *from the high places*.[1] They ask for nothing from the sea; fish is not considered to be food fit for human consumption; they have a horror of it. The flesh of a fish they say is no different from the flesh of a snake: *Ignama ka iniouka*. As they find no temptation in the produce of the sea, they see no reason to venture upon its waters; this applies equally to rivers.

1 A French traveller has just published some information on the Amazoulous, which is sometimes true and often false, and which he had from a deserter who intended blackening the name of the tribe he left behind. This traveller interprets the word Zoulou figuratively. According to him, the Amazoulous refer to themselves as *celestial* beings which I believe is quite erroneous as they do not attach any idea of superiority to that which comes from the heavens. As it is my principal concern to inform my readers, and as there are hosts of grave errors in the account of the investigator of whom I speak, errors intentionally committed, stories of man-eaters and of Tom Thumb, as if to turn the bright light of European civilization on the people of the south-east, I shall point out that a little further on, the narrator, still speaking of the Amazoulous, says they are also called *Amazizis* — the people from down below — what nonsense!

234

CHAPTER XIX

The opportunity of hunting hippopotamus might well have tempted me to stay longer at the *mouzi* of Noboka, but the heat during the day was extreme and at night the relentless attacks of the mosquitoes allowed us no rest. Moreover we were already beginning to suffer from the effects of the noxious mist which spread each evening, like a grey cloak over the vast expanse of reeds extending for twelve or fifteen leagues around the bay of Saint Lucia.

I discussed the matter with my men who agreed with me that we should stay no longer and so, without further delay, I fixed our departure for the very next day, 1 January 1842. By forcing the pace, we covered the twenty-three leagues of the return journey back to our camp in a day and a half.

As I emerged from the bush a hundred paces from my improvised dwelling, I was not a little surprised to notice a number of vultures perched in the trees which overhung my tent, while others were quarrelling over something lying on the ground. Of the three men I had left behind, two were to hunt for food, while the third was to remain in camp to guard my things; these had been my orders, but the presence of the vultures led me to believe that my orders had not been carried out. Annoyed at this disregard of my authority, I approached one of the huts, looking very displeased.

But how quickly my expression changed, how cruel was my surprise on seeing my Cafre, Mahlé, lying bathed in his own blood, his skin torn and flayed and his right leg prodigiously swollen, the calf held together by laths, with the raw flesh protruding between them. The bold, swollen flies were buzzing all about him ready to deposit their larvae within the wounds of the man who already seemed to them no better than a corpse.

'What is it, Mahlé? What dreadful thing has befallen you?' and the poor devil, exhausted with crying out in pain, his features contorted with suffering, gazed at me and succeeded at last in pronouncing the words, *'Iniaty boulala mèna, omkos.* A buffalo has injured me, master.' 'What did you do poor wretch?' 'Ah! I saw him, I shot him, he fell to the ground, and without reloading my gun, I approached him. Wilhelm was with me. The buffalo leapt up and bore down upon me, his horns lowered. He picked me up and forced me against a thorn bush, thrusting at me with his horns which I grasped and held fast. Wilhelm! ho! Wilhelm! I was counting on him; I called out to him. Wilhelm had gone — Wilhelm! ho Wilhelm! Wilhelm! Wilhelm was far away. My strength left me, the horns slipped from my grasp and the buffalo, shaking free with a butt of his head, slit my calf from ankle to thigh, cutting through the muscles; then he made off. I dragged myself along the ground, calling for Wilhelm all the while, and assuring him that the buffalo had gone.' 'What was Wilhelm doing all this time? Where had he gone, the scoundrel?' 'Ah, up a tree.' 'Leave it to me, Mahlé. Wilhelm will pay for this, the coward, the heartless wretch to suffer his friend to be attacked while he himself carried a loaded gun! The coward, where is he?' 'He and Nanana have gone off to look for my gun which was left behind and perhaps broken by the buffalo.'

The accident had taken place three days previously, on 30 December, the very day of the hunt at Saint Lucia Bay, the unluckiest date in all my experience as a hunter; for three consecutive years this day was to be marred by terrible accidents or setbacks which it was impossible for me either to avoid or to rectify.

It was not an easy task for me to attend to the gaping, hideous wound, to sponge it and to gather up the severed muscles which were hanging down six inches below the heel. I had not the least idea of how to proceed in such a case. If I had known, what bitter regrets I might have spared myself: what a service I might have rendered, and what satisfaction I would have derived from doing so! But I knew nothing, and the thought of sewing up the edges of the wound never occurred to me. In spite of my care, two and a half years later, the wound which was only partly healed, was still gaping and not yet covered over with skin where the muscles had been torn, while my man was still incapable of walking as other men do.

Each day the wound needed to be bathed, poulticed and bandaged, to which end I sacrificed my shirts. But, suffering more perhaps from our attentions than if we had left him to nature, Mahlé would remove the dressings while we were engrossed in our work, and expose his wound to the sun. I warned him that the flies would be bound to deposit their larvae on it. He took no heed of my warning however, and only two days later, the worms were already swarming in the folds of his flesh and causing him atrocious suffering.

What was to be done? I was at my wit's end. To remove the worms was not possible by ordinary means: gangrene might set in; this would mean cutting off the leg. Never had I even seen such an operation performed; how could I dare to attempt it, if it were necessary to do so. I, who hesitate even to bleed a patient, racked my brains for a solution. I had to hand arsenic, bichloride of mercury, nux vomica. I decided to take a chance and settled for the vegetable poison of which I prepared a decoction. The wound was bathed in this liquid only once, and the worms disappeared. But it was not until six weeks later that Mahlé ceased crying night and day; *Ahé mâmé, ahé mâmé*. The poor devil will bear for the rest of his days the sad reminder of our hunting trip.

He was the most faithful of all my servants, the most intelligent in making himself useful, and the most skilful of my hunters. The accident deprived him of his hopes and expectations, just as our prospects were beginning to look bright. When I returned I did for him what I could, but all that and ten times more could not compensate him for his leg; for among warlike people, a man's physical condition determines the respect in which he is held. An invalid is relegated to the *mouzi*, where he is of less use than an old woman, and often a burden upon his neighbours. This is the most wretched fate which may befall a man.

Two days later two more men were out of action: Houahouaho and Nanana. Both had been bitten by a snake as they slept. They recovered in nine or ten days, after suffering excruciating pain. What astonished me most was that this was the first incident of snakebite since we had been at Om-Philos, for a day never went by without our killing several of these hideous reptiles. There was the occasion when one escaped from the mattress which I was unrolling, while shortly afterwards another slithered from the pocket of my hunting coat which I had dropped on the ground. But, if one were to recount all the thousands of incidents involving snakes which take place during a hunting trip of several months duration, what traveller who had read them would be bold enough to venture forth and see for himself?

It was fruit season at that time; one day when the heat was excessive, my hunters picked some long green fruit which oozed a white milky fluid. I watched them as they ate the fruit in an attempt to quench their burning thirst and in my ignorance I asked if I might taste some. Boulandje was quick to satisfy my request. My Cafres watched curiously as I ate, and a burst of laughter greeted the grimace which I made at the excessively bitter taste. I spat the fruit out, but in spite of rinsing my mouth and drinking continually, two hours later I had not rid myself of the bitter taste which remained with me until the evening. Certainly it could not have been for pleasure that my men had eaten twelve or fifteen of the fruit. I am prepared to believe that the salivary glands might benefit, but it is probable that the Amazoulous attribute some medicinal properties to these fruit, for they do not always wait until a malady manifests itself before employing suitable medicaments to combat it. They believe that sickness may often be prevented by the consumption of the fruit, roots and medicinal plants which are commonly administered to those who are already ill. The enduring bitterness of this

237

fruit is in my opinion equal to that of sulphate of quinine, and could well be effective in reducing fever. The plant which produces the fruit entwines itself around a nearby tree; it is milky and so soft that it has need of support.

During the period until 10 January, we killed a good number of buffaloes and *cannas* and while hunting in the mountains, we bagged a rather beautiful antelope of medium size, which the Amazoulous call *nala*; the colonists *roye-rhée-book*, and the naturalists *Redunca lalandii*. It gave me some pleasure to acquire this animal; it was the first of its kind to come my way, and it is fairly rare in these latitudes. It is closely related to the *Redunca capreolus* and the *Eleotragus*. On that day, I had gone out hunting with the intention of finding some diversion from my usual occupations. I had begun by wounding a buffalo. For more than an hour I followed its tracks, which led me to the river and then disappeared. I needed to find something else to think about, and so I walked on until I came upon a bend in the Om-Philos which I had not seen before.

There, on a hill-slope strewn with stones and dotted with mimosas, I saw a *canna* and tried to get it to turn so that it would present a better target. I climbed to the top of the hill, from where I was able to command a view of the river down below on my left hand side. I glanced down and saw a hippopotamus peacefully grazing on the opposite bank.

However, as my *canna* could not be far off now, I continued to follow after it until it re-appeared 200 paces ahead. While making a detour, crawling flat on my stomach, I caught a glimpse of an animal barely sixty paces away which I took at first to be a kudu female. A few seconds later, I could see more clearly, and I perfectly recognised a female *ipiva*, *Kobus ellipsiprymnus*. I concealed myself and prepared to wait and watch, for I had no interest in killing the animal, as I already had one specimen in my collection, after Sképelé.

I had not long to wait; something soon moved eighty paces off; a pair of very long horns appeared, then a head; it was a male *ipiva*! I should perhaps have attempted to get closer to him, but the fear that he would escape compelled me to act fast: I aimed for his neck, and the shot went through his throat.

At the same moment, two females dashed past me only ten paces away. I was busy reloading, when along came Boulandje, ferreting about, attracted by the presence of the two antelope. We set off together in pursuit of the wounded animal, which we could hear not far off, breathing heavily and beating his horns against the branches, as if to vent his fury upon them. There might have been some danger in approaching too close; I was on my guard. He was staggering about and when he turned his blood-stained muzzle in my direction, I aimed for the upper part of the right hindquarters and brought him down once and for all. Joyfully I took hold of his horns, which he brandished about feebly as he expired.

By now Wilhelm had joined us. His arrival was timely, because to protect this fine specimen, I had already decided to spend the night on the spot. But now the task of skinning was quickly performed and the sun was just going down when we set off, laden with the precious remains.

Unfortunately, neither my men nor I had remembered that the night would be dark for, as the Cafres say, the moon was dead. Wilhelm, upon whom I had heaped all the heavy chores since the affair of Mahlé and the buffalo, was carrying the heaviest load, the skin, the head and the horns. Thus burdened, he had to walk three and a half leagues in the dark, feeling his way, taking cautious steps through the cruel thorns, over the sharp hard stones, through the treacherous marshes and gullies which lay in wait to swallow up the unsuspecting traveller. It was a formidable task, which required a thorough knowledge of the area, unbroken concentration, great strength, and the eyesight of a cat.

We had walked for four hours; always conscious of the risk of being trodden underfoot by buffalo or rhinoceros, when finally we reached the hilltop from which, in daylight, our camp could be seen three miles distant. It was probably then about ten o'clock and the lions, those great lords of the nocturnal woods, were roaring so noisily that the whole of nature trembled; it was like a monstrous concert at which the herbivores took great care not to applaud as they lay hidden and constantly on the alert.

Our situation, while not giving cause for real alarm, was nevertheless not a happy one; I was struck by the thought of man's disability in the dark, for he can see nothing and is consequently unable to use his weapons. As much to enable us to rest as to send out a call for assistance, we laid down our burdens. From the vantage point of the hilltop where we stood, I fired four resounding shots. I listened intently; no reply. Once more I sent out the signal; again there was no reply, save for the lion's roar. 'Everyone is asleep at the camp; let us press on.'

The darkness became more intense, the bush more dense, the terrain more difficult. 'Courage boys! Come on, Wilhelm, carefully; Watch out! Walk straight! We are nearly there.' He did not lack the will to succeed; in any case, he had an interest in the successful outcome of the enterprise and, better than Boulandje could ever have done, he guided us wonderfully well, for he had very often searched for honey in these parts.

The thorny branches which grew across the narrow paths tore at our faces, although our eyes escaped unharmed. We were progressing slowly but surely when suddenly Wilhelm, who was two paces ahead of me, disappeared completely. 'Wilhelm, where are you?' — 'Ah,' and his plaintive voice arose from somewhere down below. He had mistaken a thirty-feet-deep ravine for the path. Fortunately, the steep slope was covered with thorn bushes which had given way beneath his weight but which had nevertheless broken his fall although they had torn his skin. Boulandje and I had to find an easier way down and disentangle the poor devil, a task which took us more than a quarter of an hour. This done, we continued on our way, and it was midnight before we reached our camp. Everybody was fast asleep.

The neck hair in the *ipiva* male *Kobus ellipsiprymnus*, is not as long as that of the female; his pelt is sometimes slightly darker, the grey less mixed with fawn, his horns are similar to those of the *riet-book* in their shape and annulations; the nature of the horn, black inside and white with a greenish tinge outside, is exactly opposite to that of the kudu, which is black on the exterior and white in the interior. Not infrequently, one comes across horns which are three feet in length, measured along the curve.

This species is distinguished from the rest by a white band, two or three fingers deep, which rings the rump in the shape of a semi-circle. Like the kudu, it has a white stripe behind and above the eye. Its ears do not equal in dimension those of the kudu, either in width or in length; they are of more normal proportions, are reddish-fawn in colour and stand out boldly against the grey background of the rest of the coat.

As for its size, it ranks among the larger species; its strength assures its pre-eminence, for its legs are not slender, it is heavy and broad-backed, and not adapted to running. It would make a good draught animal. Its skin which is thicker than that of the other antelopes of comparable size, is firm and suitable for leatherwork. It has two types of hair, the first of which is long and sparse and reminiscent of the bristles of the wild boar; beneath these the epidermis is covered with another type of very short hair, thick and velvety, which may be likened to the down of aquatic birds.

This unusual feature seemed remarkable to me and is probably the reason why the *ipiva* frequents rivers, and lies in the water for most of the day, a habit which has earned it the name of *waater book* among the South African Dutch hunters. It is a very clean animal, but I could not say why ticks do not attach themselves to its coat.

As it bears a resemblance to the *aigoceres* on one hand and the *Strepsiceros kudu* and the *Redunca eleotragus* on the other, naturalists have created for it the genus *Kobus*, of which it remains today the sole representative. This species lives in herds of six to eight in the Amazoulou country, and from twenty-five to thirty in the land of Massilicatzi. It frequents rocky mountain slopes near rivers. The flesh is not delicate; I found it similar to that of the gnu. The Cafres value it little or not at all. They claim that the flesh of the male has a strong, disagreeable odour, but I have not been aware of this.

The next morning when I awoke, Henning, who later admitted to having heard, decided not to take the trouble to answer my call or to send the men to me. I made up my mind that prohibiting all hunting for a week would give him time to reflect upon his heedlessness and to consider what his behaviour ought to have been. For him, the intrepid, indefatigable hunter, a week thus spent without firing a shot, was punishment indeed. At any other time, I would have been the first to suffer from this inaction, but the intense heat which brought about rapid putrefaction, had rendered the preparation of specimens impossible. I mention this to explain how we were forced into the wastefulness which I shall now describe.

It was the beginning of January. One morning some of my hunters went out to replenish our food supplies; two buffaloes fell; one was an old male, the other a young female; fifty to seventy pounds of meat were taken from the female alone. Towards evening the meat, which had been fresh that morning, was already so much advanced in decay, that we were certain not to be able to use it next morning. My men asked to go out and kill again before sunset. Once more, two buffaloes were shot, one of which was judged to be very suitable. It was late; the buffaloes were left where they fell, without any incisions having been made. The next morning, my men set our to bring back the meat. At the first incision, such a stench arose from the flesh, which was already turning green, that we were obliged to kill again. An old male was the first to fall, but he was worse than useless. Next came the turn of a young male, which was hardly more suitable; finally a young female was brought down, which meant that we had killed seven buffaloes in two days to feed ten or twelve men. In fact, all we needed was a hundred pounds of meat and the approximate combined weight of the animals we had killed was 9000 pounds.

It is therefore not surprising that during a period of eight or nine months, we killed, either for ourselves or for our neighbours, more than 500 buffaloes, 60 *cannas*, 18 kudus, 2 *ipiva*, 2 quaggas, 4 hippopotamuses, 4 rhinoceroses, 200 wild boar and small antelope such as *duyker*, *bleek-steen-book*, *rooye-rhée-book*, *riet-book* and 43 elephants.

In Massilicatzi's country, which I will have occasion to mention later, we killed, over a period of eight months, a great number of animals, the list of which I have lost, but of those destined for the pot, I can recall 300 buffaloes, 56 rhinoceros, *simus* and *Bicornis africanus*. I estimate that the minimum weight of the flesh of all these together was about 1 572 000 pounds and would equal the entire cargo of a ship of 786 tons burden.

CHAPTER XX

On the 14th, having completed certain tasks, I made plans to go hunting again the next day for more *ipivas*. That evening, observing that the sun was setting in a clear sky, I warned Kotchobana, Boulandje, Wilhelm, Nanana, Houahouaho and Djantje to be ready to set out early.

On 15 January, a day of glorious memory, I arose at first light. I ate sparingly and drank my coffee like a sluggard who wishes to clear his brain; then I set out with my trusty single-barrelled twelve bore shot-gun, while one of my men carried my spare weapon, a double-barrelled sixteen bore shot-gun, a saw and a bag of salt and alum. My Cafre, Kotchobana, had his own gun and so did Boulandje but the others were without arms. My intention was that they should carry home the game. I saw three kudu a short way off, but I had no interest in killing them, as I had still a long way to go.

We walked on to Kos Berg, thus named because it had served us as a larder. Up until this point we had discovered nothing except a few honeycombs. We made a detour, leaving Kos Berg behind us to the south, and directed our steps towards the point where I had previously killed an *ipiva*. We had been walking for more than two and a half hours in single file along a gamepath. I was at the head of the column, a difficult position but one which I had chosen because I wished to lead the way, and also because I wanted to spare my Cafre's feet from the thorns.

242

Suddenly, I froze in my tracks as three lions jumped out of a bush ten paces ahead of me. In an instant we had shouldered our guns. The male lion, which had been the last to jump, was not thirty paces away and watching us intently as if he were waiting for us to pass before he returned to his lair. He was yellow and his head appeared enormous.

I was about to open fire on him; I could hardly resist the temptation, he made such a fine target! But realising that not all my Cafres were armed and that I would expose them to danger, that if some accident occurred they would be justified in blaming me, and that among them there was already a man maimed by buffaloes, I decided to drop down to a crouching position and simply to observe, an inspection which lasted only a moment, for the lion went off almost immediately. He made a great leap, landing heavily on his paws, and in a series of bounds, he disappeared completely from our sight. I estimated his size to be equal to that of a quagga.

I have been told that a lion does not fear a man who is standing, but that he will retreat as soon as the man crouches down; I have heard that the Boschjesmans, who are aware of this, plan their attack accordingly. This incident when added to subsequent events seemed to confirm the story.

We went on our way, my Cafres congratulating me on the manner in which I had acted, for if I had fired and only wounded the lion, he might, according to them, have killed us all without exception. Three-quarters of an hour later, Houahouaho, who formed part of the rearguard, pointed out an elephant. I decided to approach him. We walked for more than half an hour through the bush to reach him; cautiously, we made our way to within twenty paces. He was behind a round mimosa tree which hid him from sight; we moved closer until the tree alone separated us. He made a movement which warned me that he was about to change his position. I cast a quick glance behind me and noticed that my men were already taking aim.

As he broke cover my shot rang out, followed by three other shots. The animal, which had been struck, veered around into the wind, stretched out his trunk, beat the air with it, and moved fifty paces off while we sprinted away to get downwind. I turned round as I ran to see what he was doing, and my hat hooked on to a mimosa tree; fortunately it was not my beard, for I would doubtless have had to leave it behind, along with my skin.

Coming to a halt at a spot a hundred metres from the point where we had first fired, we reloaded our guns. I needed more time for this than my Cafres did, for I had two guns to load. Kotchobana shouted to me to come for he could see the animal standing quite still a short way off, but in spite of my haste, when I arrived, the elephant had already moved away. We followed the tracks for more than an hour before we were close enough to see that it was a female, accompanied by her calf; she was enormous. I was growing impatient and longing to meet up with her when I caught sight of a wild boar which I lost no time in killing as my men and I were hungry.

Immediately my shot rang out, my men heard the elephant trumpet and move off. They blamed me for my thoughtless action and I admitted my mistake; I had believed the animal to be some distance away but it was in fact only a hundred paces off. I put them to work cutting up our miserable wild boar, the quarters of which we grilled and ate on the spot.

Meanwhile, Kotchobana emerged from the thick bush to tell us that he had just seen, a mile away, the huge rounded backs of thirty or forty elephants. They were gathered at the confluence of the Om-Philos-Mouniama and the Om-Philos-Om-Schlopu. I was about to set off in this direction, when one of my men said to me, 'You see, master, there are so many elephants and you would not allow us to bring our guns.' 'It is true, but I myself did not expect so many, for I too left my heavy gun behind. It is a pity but I can do nothing about it.' 'Well, master, I will just have to stay here and watch them; it is sad.'

Seeing that he was so much disposed to hunt, I gave him Kotchobana's gun and handed my own gun to my favourite hunter, along with powder and shot. Now there were three of them adequately armed. 'Go on,' I said to them, 'and do your best. Try to prove yourselves without me, since you are so brave.' I had already given proof of my own abilities and I was not sorry that an opportunity had arisen to test theirs. I was particularly interested to discover whether, without me, they would find sufficient reckless courage to bring the adventure to a successful conclusion, and in order to make this observation, I had not hesitated to sacrifice my great opportunity of playing a leading role on this huge stage, although this had been the cherished dream which had brought me 3 000 leagues from home.

They set off and I remained behind, standing on a knoll from where I was able to follow their progress with the help of my spyglass. They moved downwind. Meanwhile, the elephants were approaching rapidly in my direction. Soon the animals were between my hunters and me, and much nearer to where I was standing, while my Cafres were a good distance beyond them. What did this change of position signify? There was no doubt that my men were afraid because they had allowed the elephants to pass by them without firing a shot; that at least is what I thought at the time, and what I subsequently discovered to be true.

The herd was approaching me downwind, which is exactly what I did not want. I began to run, cutting across their path, and took up

244

my position on top of a rock on the bank a hundred feet above the river. From this vantage point I was able to see much better than before. I must admit that few men can boast of having witnessed such a sight.

The steep rockface, on top of which I was sitting, was accessible to the animals from behind, although quite impregnable from the river which flowed down below. The granite slope was covered with thorny trees: mimosa, aloes and *kooker-booms*, or *na-booms*.[1] On the other side of the Om-Philos, the bush was dotted with mimosas and there were immense wild fig trees on the banks while reeds grew here and there in the sand. They were in greatest abundance near a bend in the river at the foot of a steep triangular mountain, gashed by a landslide of red earth. Among these reeds stood twelve or fifteen elephants. I had with me only one Cafre, my spy-glass and a double-barrelled shotgun which was good, but alas, not good enough for there was not any ammunition. I had no hesitation in choosing to remain a spectator, a contemplator of the great scene.

I had been at my vantage point upon the rock for fully ten minutes without hearing a single shot fired, cursing all the while my unfortunate decision to give my twelve-bore gun to one of my men. I had all the more reason to regret my action when a great noise arose behind us; there was a loud crashing and breaking of trees, and blowing and shrill trumpeting from the elephants which had been agitated by the smoke from our fire. This herd of giants was flattening the trees as a boar might flatten the grass in passing.

I was suddenly startled by a noise like ten water mills and was momentarily at a loss to understand the cause, when I noticed, crossing the river and walking along the opposite bank, five females each followed by a calf, with a single male bringing up the rear. I was looking down upon them; I could not have been better placed to fire on them. How I regretted the sixteen-bore shotgun which I had left behind at the camp. I gave a wry smile as I looked at the excellent small gun which I had with me. No hunter was more to be pitied than I. Laugh if you like, but I cannot help thinking that a six-pounder would have produced excellent results and would not have proved excessive in raking this line of giants.

A moment later, the noise was repeated, but more loudly this time, and I saw another herd of forty or fifty elephants, coming along the bank on our side, with their feet in the water; then a lone elephant crossed from one bank to the other, walking through the shifting sand and sinking down at each step. With his unsteady gait he made me think at first that he was the one we had wounded. From my double-barrelled gun I aimed two shots at his back, but it was quite

1 Quiver trees.

useless; he did not even suspect that the bullets were intended for him.

For more than half an hour, wherever I looked I saw elephants appearing and disappearing, each herd being replaced or followed by another. I saw more than two hundred of them, which I imagine was but a third of all those in the vicinity, for the forests and the gorges concealed many from my sight. It is probable that more than six hundred elephants were gathered within an area only three miles in diameter, and that we were standing right in the middle of a sort of elephant park.

At last, impatient at the inactivity, and anxious and displeased at hearing nothing from my men, I decided to return to the place where we had made our fire. In order to do this, we had to make our way past several herds. When we arrived at the spot, we found that Houahouaho, whom I had left behind there, had disappeared. Fearing that he might have been crushed by the elephants, we searched for him, calling loudly. The *long noses* answered us back, which prevented him from revealing himself. Later, he came down from the tree where he had been hiding in a state of terror.

The elephants, he told us, had come in great numbers, blowing and trumpeting round our fire and naturally, he had been obliged to flee. Just then three gunshots rang out. A minute went by, and I realised that the animal which was being fired at could not have fallen, for the guns were silent. Four minutes later there were two more shots, then silence once more; five minutes later a single shot rang out, followed by two others, one after the other, and then the dying cry of the elephant. Barely 400 paces separated me from the place. I set off in leaps and bounds. There were four more shots fired at regular intervals to ensure that the animal was dead. When I arrived, I saw a large female lying on the ground, shot dead by Kotchobana. She was not less than ten feet high, and measured twenty-five to twenty-eight feet from the end of the trunk to the tip of the tail. I learnt from my men that they had let the first herd go by, as they were moving too fast. Then they had shot at three elephants, two of which had got away while the third was mortally wounded. By following the bloody tracks, they had come upon the female. Kotchobana had aimed from a position eighteen inches or two feet above the ground and had struck the leg-bone. Wounded, the animal was forced to slow down. Then Kotchobana had reloaded in such haste that he forgot the ramrod in the barrel and had fired bullet and ramrod together into the right front leg, about the middle of the humerus.

The animal was about to fall, her leg broken in two places, when Wilhelm arrived and fired a shot into her throat which finally brought her to the ground. Running down a steep slope, Wilhelm had been unable to stop until he was barely six paces from the animal. When he discharged his gun his proximity was such that he was almost buried beneath the giant as it fell lifeless to the ground. I immediately inspected the tracks of the wounded animal which had fled and I saw that it had been bleeding profusely. According to my men, it would die. We abandoned the female after cutting off the tail as proof of possession and, as three hours of daylight remained, we set off once more.

We had been walking for more than half an hour with the wind behind us and the sun in our eyes when, suddenly, two of my Cafres, who were ahead, leapt to the left of the path and fled. I was three paces behind them with the rest of my Cafres following 200 paces in the rear discussing the outcome of the day's hunting. Mechanically, I raised my gun to my shoulder, thinking all the while of how thirsty I was and of how happy I would be to quench that thirst.

My first thought was that an elephant had got wind of us and was pursuing us, intending to attack us; I spun round rapidly and retreated ten paces. There was a loud noise of tearing bushes. 'This is it then,' I thought as I ran, 'it is an elephant; I cannot escape; he is going to kill me; it would be best to stand and wait for him.' Swinging round again even more rapidly than the first time, I dropped on to my right knee and prepared to take aim at my enemy. I saw, emerging from the thick bush fifteen paces ahead and coming between the sun and me, an enormous black body with a long head and a long horn on the nose. Suddenly, and apparently as a result of my action, the animal wheeled about and bore down on one of my men. Then, furious and indignant at this behaviour, I fired at his hindquarters, which made him wheel round again and probably saved the life of my Cafre, Nanana, for it was he whom the rhinoceros was pursuing.

I must confess that at that moment I experienced a fear which was all the more terrible in that I had not expected to find myself in close proximity to such a beast — stupid, wild, heavy and brutal, a creature which is easily irritated and which attacks first for fear of being himself attacked. He is like an enormous pig, all of whose senses are dulled, possibly without an olfactory sense at all, since he was only aware of our presence when we were ten paces off, although we were upwind.

The sun had set an hour before we reached camp. Henning had supper waiting and Heaven knows, I did justice to his culinary skills. I lost no time telling him of the adventures of the day and as a result his head was filled with a thousand projects which kept him awake all night.

The next morning at daybreak he wanted to be off elephant hunting, but his period of detention was not yet over and, however much he pleaded, I remained inflexible although it was contrary to my own interests to be so. However I gave him a day's grace and on the 18th, he was free to go out. I refused to lend him the big gun as I was persuaded that his own would suffice to bring down an elephant if he aimed for the head.

Driven on by the desire to do better than his predecessors, Henning succeeded, before evening on the first day, in tracking down a herd of elephants and killing two of them. The next day Souzouana, who always wished to please me, brought me back the two tails. Kotchobana and Boulandje had meanwhile gone off to reconnoitre in the opposite direction from Omschlaty-Omkoulou where Henning was hunting. I had kept behind with me only two men and a young Cafre, to hunt for the pot. When we had nothing better to do in the morning, we followed the dipping flight of the honey-guide,[1] which summoned us in sharp impatient tones; we called back to him when he paused, so that we would not lose him, until finally he led us to a wild bees' nest.

In the opinion of the hunter, the search for honey is not very diverting; for the observer, it does not lack a certain interest, but for those who love the finer things in nature, the interest is great. My men were always ready for this other sort of hunt, which has its own kind of danger; one of them would take his gun, his powder horn and a pouch full of shot, as much to defend us from wild animals as to make a fire when we discovered the precious deposit; the other, armed with an axe, would devote all his attention to the flight of the little traitor which indicated its position by means of sharp cries.

Sometimes, the search became exhausting; to follow the bird, we had to negotiate more than a league of deep ravines, thorn bush and sharp rocks, as steep as ramparts. As the bird was unable to comprehend that man is deterred by these obstacles, it would grow impatient, and we lost sight of it; its *chir, chir, chir, chir* fading away into the distance, along with our hopes of finding the honey.

But when the distance was not too great, it became an easy matter to follow. When the bird settled in a tree and refused to fly any further we knew the honey could not be far away. We then began searching the area listening intently for the buzzing of a honey-bee. When one came into sight we followed it with our eyes. The bee, which was returning to its hive, would make for a hole, either in a tree or in the ground or among the rocks. Once we had found the hole it was a simple matter to enlarge the aperture and extract the combs, if the bees seemed not to be angry. If, on the contrary, they were angry, the gun provided the spark and we set fire to some dry straw which we covered over with green grass. In this way we smoked out the workers which enabled us the more easily to rob them of their treasure.

---

1 A.D. calls this bird the 'informer cuckoo'. *Translator's note*

The combs are arranged vertically to prevent leakage of the honey. The wax varies in colour, appearing to turn brown with time; the texture and the colour of the honey also vary according to the flowering season. Thus, when a certain plant is flowering in the greatest profusion, the honey will bear that particular flavour; a few days later the flavour will be different, because other flowers will by then have become more numerous. In certain localities, I have tasted honey which was very bitter and disagreeable because the bees had frequented some big trees nearby, which were covered in violet flowers; in other areas the honey was highly laxative and was therefore unacceptable. But all over the Doorn-Veld, when the mimosas are in flower, the honey has an exquisite taste and is very healthy and much sought after.

The honey seekers often find only dry combs, particularly at the end of summer and at the beginning of spring. The combs should be full or 'rich' as they say; but this is never completely the case. When there is no honey, the Cafres are in the habit of eating the larvae along with the wax which surrounds them. Once I had acquired the taste, I found these sweet, milky combs perfectly acceptable.

Depending on the locality November, December or January are the best months for robbing the hives. The Cafres immediately eat what they find, the Boers save the honey and use it all the year round when there is no sugar to sweeten their tea and coffee, the bastaards make beer from it which is intoxicating in the highest degree because of the presence of the roots of the *mour-Boschis*, used to activate the fermentation. When this pernicious root is not used, honey beer is very pleasant and healthy; I often made it myself and, when I was short of time, I mixed curdled sour milk with the honey which I drank after only three days of fermentation. Out here in the bush during long hunting expeditions, it was a delicious thing which combined sufficient amounts of acid and sugar to please every palate.

Hives are principally to be found in three localities; inaccessible rock faces, hollow tree-trunks or ant heaps. The latter, when broken open by the iron bands of our wagon wheels, revealed their treasures to us while the bees escaped. It is imprudent to draw up the wagons too close to the hives, for the smell of the dogs and the horses irritates the bees which then sting the oxen and may cause serious accidents.

When the nest is situated in a hollow tree, care must be taken not to plunge one's arm through the narrow aperture if one wishes to avoid imminent death, or atrocious suffering at the very least. Various types of poisonous snakes make their homes in these trees, particularly the *kooper-kaapel* as the colonists call it. It is to these reptiles that one must attribute all the accidents for which the Boers insist on blaming the innocent sphinx, *atropos*, the death's head moth, which they call *groot-honing-bye*. This hawkmoth, more plentiful in southern Africa than in Europe, loves honey and will venture right into the hive, but most frequently one finds it fixed to the bark, a few inches from the aperture; all those which I collected were found in this position.

The Boers fear it as much as they do a snake. They imagine that the proboscis is a conductor of poison, and great was the stupefaction among them, when they saw me handle one of these moths without fear and even put it into my mouth to prove its innocence; they were so convinced of its noxiousness, that they believed I intended to take my life. These prejudices were so ingrained in them that it was in vain I attempted to persuade them to imitate me.

A number of travellers have described the characteristics of the honey-guide and maintain that it is spared by the hunter because of its usefulness to man. Somebody has said, and Buffon has repeated it, that there is danger in following this bird as it will often lead the hunter into the clutches of wild animals, such as lions and leopards. At first, when I had studied the honey-guide only in the Amazoulou country, I was tempted to reject this theory as a fable for in those parts the bird appeared to have no instinct other than the one to which it owes its name; it led us to the hives and only to the hives; and so we had no reason to mistrust it. But later, beyond Makalis-Berg, I watched my men set out on numerous fruitless searches in answer to the bird's call; after ten or fifteen vain attempts, I heard them cursing the *om-schlanvo*; one of them had twice been led to a rhinoceros skeleton, another to a dead buffalo and a third to the bones of a *canna*. Henning himself, who loved honey, had been deceived on four occasions; each time he had been led to a skeleton and twice the hyaenas had fled at his approach.

One must not conclude from these facts that the cuckoo has an understanding with the great carnivores to bring them men to eat, but rather that, feeding on insects, this fragile bird has the need of the assistance of man to move the bones beneath which swarm beetles and other insects, and which the cuckoo is unable to reach while they are hidden. Is it only just and fair that, when he cannot himself obtain the food which is necessary for his existence, this bird will ask assistance of man whom he has already helped to procure the sweets concealed by nature.[1]

1 I believe that the reader will thank me for pointing out an error committed by Monsieur Lesson in his *Manuel d'Ornithologie*, when he refers to the instincts of the honey-guide. Monsieur Lesson says, 'There is no foundation to the belief that these birds guide the Hottentots to the hive in order to collect their share of the booty. These latter, having learnt to understand the behaviour of the birds, follow them quite naturally.' Monsieur Lesson

Three species of honey guide are to be found in Natal; they are so well known that it is not necessary to give a detailed description of them.

On the 19th, Henning came back two hours before sunset. His first outing had been successful; he estimated the number of elephant he had seen at more than 500; it was probably the same herd that I had seen on the 15th, for in all the Amazoulou country from Touguela as far as Om-Pongola, there are not in my opinion, more than 1 500 elephants, for each of the great herds requires a large amount of territory.

That evening, as we were eating our supper in the *pondock*,[1] a rustling of dry leaves prompted me to say to Henning: 'Look behind you; there must be something there; there certainly is something.' 'Bah!' he said. 'It is probably a toad,' 'Well, go and look anyway.' He turned round in his seat and there, writhing on the ground, barely a foot away from him, was a horrible *iphesy* (spitting snake).

One must not even pretend to be brave when dealing with enemies like these which fill even the largest animals with fear and trembling; so we leapt up hurriedly to arm ourselves with spades and sticks. When we returned, the *iphesy* had disappeared. We were looking for it when a cry arose from one of the huts situated twenty paces off; my Cafres had seen the reptile making its way into the dry branches of the roof. It was too dark to try to find it, and with the intention of chasing it away, they burnt a quantity of horn, persuaded that the snake would flee from the smell, or be asphyxiated by the smoke. They did not quite achieve the desired effect for we found it immobilised the following day. A gunshot finished it off, to the great satisfaction of my men who considered themselves delivered from yet another sword of Damocles. I took advantage of the situation to make enquiries about the habits of this strange animal which is feared by Cafres, Boers and Hottentots alike and this is what I learnt.

It is endowed with the terrible ability to spit its poison into the eyes of a man, a dog or any other animal which approaches within three or four paces. The action of the poison brings about loss of vision due to the prodigious swelling of the eyeball. The contact of the poison upon the skin of the face produces a burning effect, with swelling and suppuration. The Amazoulous say that men die of it,

did not know that the honey-guide will continue to harass man with its cries until it sees that it is being followed and that it will persist, with the obvious intention of obtaining help. When, unaware of the proximity of man, the bird does not of its own accord approach him, those who are searching for honey will call it by striking the trunks of trees; the energetic reply, *chir-chir-chir*, will soon be heard.
1 Sort of barn.

but Henning, who had witnessed an accident of this kind, said that the skin suppurated for a long time and gave the appearance of an ugly disease; that the individual suffered very much but that he did not die, which would probably have been the case had the poison entered the eyes.

Shortly afterwards Mr Wahlberg confirmed this information. He was carrying out his investigations among the rocks when, suddenly, something passed close to his eyes. He then noticed the perpetrator of the intended attack, a spitting snake, taking refuge under the stones.

I cannot tell how the venom is ejected, but I would think that it might be explained this way; a muscle putting pressure on the vesicle would produce an ejaculation of the poison through the hooked fangs, and at the same time would adapt the projection of the poison to the required distance. I believe that the anatomist would be able to discover, quite simply, the mechanics of this operation. For my part, I must repeat what I have said before; I am concerned only with the facts as I saw them.

Towards dusk on the 23rd my Cafres came back; they were silent, and I had no need to ask about the hunt, for I guessed only too well; six days of relentless searching and nothing to show for it. Their excuse was that the elephants had been too agressive and could not be approached. I pretended to believe them, while remarking however that only the most incompetent hunter could fail to approach within firing distance.

On the 24th, Henning went off armed with the big gun and hoping to perform wonders. I sent out some men to find Kotchobana's elephant with orders to bring back the tusks and to hang the skull and the lower jaw in a tree if they were still intact, for I reckoned that they were interesting enough for a collection of comparative anatomy. When my men returned they told me that there had been no difficulty in detaching the tusks, which had been dragged off by vultures and were already lying two or three paces away from the head. This explanation seemed too strange to be true, but I pondered over it for a long time and came to the conclusion that the vultures had banded together to enable them to extract the tusks from their sockets with the intention of reaching the marrow inside. The tusks bore no trace of hyaena teeth; if any hyaena had been responsible, he would not have failed to damage all the softer parts; to tell the truth each tusk, having been emptied of all muscle as a result of putrefaction wrought by larvae, would require a force of only thirty pounds to move it, which was well within the capacity of the vultures. Their numbers provided further confirmation.

In the case of a large animal, it is not just a few vultures which come to share the feast, but 500 to 1 000. No more curious sight awaits the hunter than that of the feathered mass, rising up into the air at his approach and hovering above his head like an immense mobile canopy darkening the rays of the sun and casting a shadow upon the earth. As these birds instinctively congregate together, so might they act in concert when the general interest demands; what one bird alone is unable to do, ten, twenty or a hundred will easily perform. This is the only explanation I can offer.

On the 25th Souzouana came to seek assistance. Hoping to be able to comply with his request, I went to his kraal. The problem was a leopard which, in order to attack a dog, had not hesitated to leap a hedge fifteen feet high. This had taken place the night before and the dead dog, partially dismembered, had been found hidden in a bush. Souzouana, confident of the powers which I had at my disposal, suggested that a snare would be sufficient to deal with the marauder; and so I sent for one of my own traps which I was busy setting when Henning came along on his way back from a hunt, having wounded four male elephants and killed a female.

Two hours later I was back at home again. Henning, who had gone home by another way, continued telling me his story of a wounded elephant whose tusks, he said, could not have measured less than six to seven feet. Suddenly, my Cafres snatched up their guns and came running to tell me that they had seen elephants moving about, 1 200 paces away. I picked up my gun, Henning picked up his, and together we all set off.

After walking for twenty minutes we caught sight of the elephants 100 paces ahead; there were four females, each accompanied by a calf, and a single large old male. The animals became aware of us, and withdrew 200 paces into the open. However, there could be no hesitation, and we followed after them. As usual, I led the way. On this occasion there were seven of us, each intending to claim at least one victim.

Unfortunately, as always happens on these occasions, someone or other is bound to make a noise; everyone relies too much on his neighbour, and the one to whom it has fallen to fire the first shot is in too much of a hurry for fear that he will be pre-empted, or that there will be complaints of delay. And so, when we were sixty paces off, the animals were already watching us with their great ears spread wide.

What was to be done now? Should we be bold and approach closer still by crawling through the longish grass and then rising up at the first suggestion of a move on the part of the elephants? This was the course I chose. I fired, and hit the big one on the forehead; I heard the bullet strike; Kotchobana aimed for the chest, as was his custom; three delayed shots struck the elephant as he turned and two others failed to find their target. Piercing cries rang out as all the animals disappeared into the bush. Determined but cautious, we followed for as long as we could until, when night fell, we were obliged to find our bearings again and make our way back to the camp. It was our misfortune that day to have all our hopes dashed. So many other days were to follow this pattern that, were I to describe them all, I would deter my readers from ever becoming elephant hunters.

What distances we walked back and forth in the pursuit of our objective, often without water under the burning sun! How many nights we spent in the bush where lions roared and leopards growled, where thunderstorms shattered the trees which were our only shelter! This occurred so frequently that I grew accustomed to it and accepted as quite normal a way of life which I now find difficulty in describing.

If anyone should question this difficulty, he has only to tell me of his doubts and I will not need the assistance of long phrases to explain. All I need do is to ask him to describe the taste of bread, as he eats it every day; the difficulty he will experience in answering me will amply explain my meaning.

We spent a sleepless night. At first the elephants were trumpeting about, only 1 000 paces from the camp; a little later, we could hear them breaking trees much closer by. They were coming nearer, there was no doubt of it, but I could not make up my mind to chase them off with shouts and gunshots, for I hoped to be able to find them again when daylight came. If they went as far as to advance on the camp, each man was armed and the guns were at the ready. The strong wind bid fair to blow down our frail shelters and to tear to shreds my tent which fortunately was protected by the five tambooty trees supporting it.

At daybreak we were on the point of setting out when Souzouana again appeared to request my assistance in protecting his gardens which had been devastated during the night by elephants in search of sugar cane. As there was more that he wanted to say to me, I sent my men out with instructions regarding the direction they should take.

Souzouana's communication, like that of many men of importance, or those who wish to appear so, could be summed up in two words; but in order to convince me of the great service which he claimed to be doing me he spun it out endlessly. The worthy old man wasted my entire morning in telling me that, if only I would come and settle with his people, I would have great quantities of milk and beer to drink every day and large numbers of willing elephants to shoot at night. Happy black man, child of nature, he imagined that a white man could see as well as he could in the dark, well enough to aim a gun, and that my endeavours would surely be crowned with success. I agreed that this might be possible in bright moonlight, but did not clouds sometimes obscure the moon,

254

thus rendering hunting extremely dangerous? For the flash of the gun, which is very visible in the dark, attracts the attention of the wounded animal which then knows precisely where to attack and does not fail to pursue his advantage.

Souzouana was very insistent; it was in his own interest, and that of his people, to be so, for although his guards had beaten their shields the elephants continued to eat the maize and the sugar cane. When his guards had resorted to throwing assegais, these weapons had barely penetrated the skin of the giants, and had left them quite undeterred. As for me, I had enough to do during the day and could not sacrifice my nights to lying in wait, an interesting enough occupation, no doubt, but one which would take too much time in return for too little reward. I refused.

Souzouana changed the conversation; he spoke to me at length of Ingheta-Om-Schlopu, great forests situated beyond Om-Pholozi, which he described as being full of elephants and where I could not possibly fail, as nobody had ever hunted there before. According to his description these forests of great trees were so luxuriant that the rays of the sun never penetrated there, the resultant half-light and the cool dampness attracted the *long noses* in the heat of the summer. The only paths were those beaten by the elephants, and the thorns were more cruel there than anywhere else. But nowhere were the elephants less agressive, nowhere were they less afraid of the approach of man; they were so bold that one of them had removed a bundle of green maize off the top of the head of a woman from one of the nearby kraals.

I smiled as I listened to these stories, and immediately planned to visit the mysterious forest of Ingheta-Om-Schlopu at the first possible opportunity. In return for this information, I regaled Souzouana on rice and sugared milk which he pronounced to be delicious. My Cafres returned from their venture to Om-Philos-Mouniama, where the tracks of the animals had led them, and confessed their regret at not having followed my instructions, for on their way back they had discovered that our rowdy nocturnal visitors had spent the first hours of the day beside the river, a quarter of a league from the camp.

I spent the whole of the 27th searching for elephants. At about midday, I killed a buffalo to provide the evening meal and, although the bullet struck him in the heart, he remained on his feet for more than twenty minutes, bellowing and circling around before he fell. The animal was on the other side of the river. After going over to remove what meat we required, we returned to sit under the huge wild fig trees and cook our food over the great fires which were already blazing. Hardly had we settled down when, in spite of our proximity, a mass of vultures battened on to the dead buffalo.

They arrived from all sides and fought bitterly over the best places; the later arrivals flew down on to the backs of the first-comers, forcing them to make way. There was a great deal of pecking but those attacked paid no heed to their wounds in their determination to get their share of the spoils. There must have been more than 500 of them. The body was completely obscured and on all sides there were queues of impatient latecomers, attempting to expel those which had already gorged and to push aside the weaker ones.

No doubt there was more than one unjust operator, more than one oppressor, among this throng, with their sharp beaks and their appearance of having rolled up their sleeves, but all were equal in their voracity. As I watched them I had an uncontrollable desire to discipline the bloody rabble; I aimed straight at the mound of vultures 110 paces away; my shot rang out, and seven of them were either pierced or grazed by a bullet. Certainly I was wrong to have done such a thing, for innocent and guilty alike lay in a confused heap and, to tell the truth, my only object was curiosity to determine the effect of a shot upon a gathering of this sort. It was unnecessary destruction and blameworthy, in that these vultures render an important service by clearing away remains, which otherwise would produce noxious emanations.

That day, we encountered only animals which held no interest for us and, as one must never be distracted from one's goal if one is seriously hunting elephant, we passed by without firing a shot.

On the 28th, Henning had just set off for Om-Philos-Mouniama to find the tusks of the elephant he had killed. He had taken the big gun. I was near my tent gathering insects from newly-fallen branches. I glanced up at a clump of reeds, bowing their heads before the wind and saw something black, slightly tinged with reddish-brown, which had appeared above the green, 500 paces away. I guessed that it was a body; a moment later a trunk was raised and I saw that it was an elephant. I called Kotchobana and the other men who came running immediately. The animal's position did not favour an attack: realising the difficulties which the reeds presented, the great space they occupied, and their height of ten or twelve feet, we decided against trying to drive the animal out with gunfire.

We waited for more than an hour, but he did not change his position. Kotchobana went off to try to turn him but the elephant started moving deeper into the rushes. As he turned to the right before disappearing into the bush, I was able to confirm that he was a male of the finest proportions.

I would immediately have gone after him, had I been able to see my Cafre, or had I known where he was but for fear of putting the animal between us, I was obliged to watch and wait. A quarter of an hour dragged by, then I heard a sharp vexatious noise — the most disagreeable sound to the hunter's ear — the bursting of a pod. The elephant moved off again. My men followed; an hour later, crawling on their stomachs, they caught up with him, and directed their fire straight at him. The animal turned and fled. My men lost sight of him and returned empty-handed.

On the 29th, I encountered neither the elephants nor the *ipivas* I was looking for. On the other hand, with two shots I killed two different kinds of wild boar: the one called *uncklove-doane*, or little elephant, by the Amazoulous, is no other than the masked or large-snouted boar, *Sus phacochoerus*; the other, called by the Cafres *inglobu*, is the *Sus larvatus*. The first is known among the Boers by the name of *vlaackt-vaark*, pig of the plains, the second is called *bosch-vaark*, bush pig.

The *bosch-vaark* hardly ever leaves the forest. The *vlaackt-vaark* is sometimes found in the open plains, but is as common in the bush as the bush pig itself. The bush pig is very shaggy with black, tawny and white hairs in his coat; he has two caruncles between the eye and the nose; his head has much in common with the ordinary pig; his tusks are very short, his flesh is unpleasant to eat and is even considered inedible by the Cafres. The *vlaackt-vaark*, on the other hand, is not very shaggy, he has only a simple mane composed of very long hair, he is of uniform colour, dirty black; he has four very pronounced caruncles between the eye and the nose; his head, below the nose, is unusually broad and is different from that of the other pigs and boars; his tusks are enormous and his flesh excellent.

These two species are somewhat inferior in size to the European boar but, like them, will turn upon the hunter who has wounded them. The *bosch-vaark* which I killed that day had indicated this intention, and to escape from his charge, I could do no other than jump over his back. The animal ran under my legs, his charge frustrated, and tumbled to the ground behind me, wounded by my shot. We took hold of him immediately and, grasping him between our knees, we bled him through the throat.

One side of his body was covered with a thick layer of hardened mud which looked like cement. My men pointed this out to me, but I paid no attention, particularly as the animal had come from muddy ground when I shot him. It semed to me quite natural that he should be more dirty on one flank than the other. 'He is a fine mess,' said a Cafre who, with the point of a ramrod, was attempting to remove the crust which resembled a breast-plate; he showed me four deep scars which ran from the shoulder to the hindquarters — the flesh had been mauled by the four claws of a lion, from which the boar had escaped; he had been well on the way to recovery when I found him. Instinctively, he had spent part of his days lying on his wounded side in the mud, the soft warmth of which had performed the duty of a poultice, at the same time as it prevented the flies from depositing their larvae, the principal cause of death among wounded animals, for in a few days the worms are swarming in the wound eating the victim alive.

On the 30th, Henning returned at dusk, bringing back the tusks of his elephant. He had been fortunate enough to kill two others on the way and in the bed of the Om-Philos-Mouniama he had come upon the body of an elephant which we had wounded and which had gone there to die. Unfortunately, the essential thing was missing; alligators had removed and carried off the head and, when Henning and his hunters had waded into the water to look for it, the thieves had indicated by their manoeuvres that they were quite capable of attacking men too. My huntsmen, who did not much care to follow in the wake of the elephant's head, were careful not to carry their investigations too far and the *pop-eyes*, as the crocodiles are called, watched with regret as they retreated to the land.

That same day I came across a monstrous nest, covered by a kind of thick roof, with a hole in the north side. The shape of the hole was not round, as one might expect, but quadrangular. This nest was more than six feet in diameter, and was built in the fork of a mimosa tree, sixteen or eighteen feet above the ground, from an immense quantity of dry twigs, some of which were as thick as a little finger. On my return, Henning assured me that he knew these nests very well; the bird which builds them is called *hamer-kop*[1] by the colonists, or *Ardea ombretta* by the naturalists. To confirm this there was a little lake nearby and the smallness of the hole conformed perfectly to a bird of this size. In proportion to the size of the occupant this is the biggest nest of all.

On 1 February, finding myself free of all other occupation, I set out eagerly, accompanied by my usual Cafres, to take my turn at hunting. We intended to cross the river a league below the confluence of the two Om-Philos. There we found a few *ipivas* and, for the first time, some *Ingogoné*, known to the Boers as *blauw-wild-beest*, *Catoblepas gorgon* (*seu taurina*).

I had never seen these animals before and I was astonished at their colouring which changed from black to blue and then to glossy white according to the light. Although cloven-hoofed like all the antelopes, their gait and speed so much resembled the horse that at first I believed them to be of a similar species. The mane, the tail, the rounded hindquarters, all contributed strongly to suggest this relationship. This species is close to the genus *Catoblepas* and is not far removed from the *gnu*. Although rare in the Amazoulou country, it is common beyond the Makalis-Berg, in the land of Massilicatzi.

1 Hammer head.

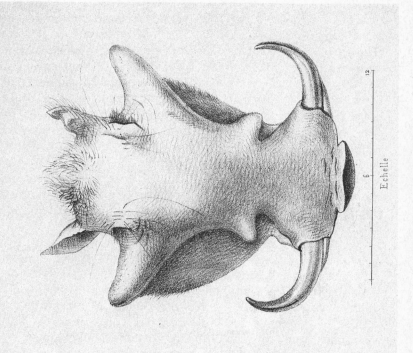

SUS PHACOCHŒRUS

Echelle

RHINOCEROS AFRICANUS BICORNIS

This is where I found it and for that reason I shall discuss it more fully later.

After a hard day's march we came to a *mouzi* where we spent the night. On the 2nd rain delayed us until midday. I made use of the time to discover what our hosts knew of Ingheta-Om-Schlopu; we were much closer to it than we had been at Souzouana's *mouzi*; but the people whom we questioned repeatedly claimed that they knew nothing of Ingheta-Om-Schlopu, that they had never even heard mention of the name. That evening, after travelling for half the day, we came to another *mouzi*; I repeated my questions without seeming to attach too much importance to the matter; but no one paid any attention and seemed not to have heard.

I was disappointed at being unable to obtain any information about a place which could not be far away and which interested me greatly, particularly as Souzouana had taken care to tell me of the numbers of elephants which were to be found there.

I had an idea and, whether it was a good one or not, I had no difficulty in putting it into practice; I tried it out immediately, attaching myself to a small group of men who were standing apart from the rest. 'Have you killed any *ignamazane* (game) today?' an elderly man asked me, — 'No *Om-Gâane*, I saw nothing, killed nothing' — 'From which direction did you come?' — 'Who, us? We came from the direction of Ingheta-Om-Schlopu' — 'From Ingheta-Om-Schlopu? There are many buffaloes up there, many, many; I am surprised that you did not see any.' I continued in this fashion until I had learnt all that I wanted to know about Ingheta-Om-Schlopu.

Unfortunately I found that this man's description coincided in more than one particular with Souzouana's and for this reason I found myself having to accept the rest of his allegations which could not have been more contrary to my aspirations. In fact my informant, a man of sense, told me that Ingheta-Om-Schlopu was the unhealthiest part of the country whose climate was as dangerous as that of the Makazanes, that to spend only a few hours there was to contract fever and dysentery, maladies to which even the black man was susceptible.

It is probably because the Cafres were aware of these dangers that they pretended to be ignorant of the place, for they knew I was thinking only of the elephants and would have chosen as my guides those who admitted to knowing the way. Although I was deterred by the thought of the sickness which surely awaited us, I was not wholly convinced. I decided to consult my men and to be guided by their opinion.

'No, no,' said Kotchobana and Boulandje. 'For a long time now we have heard talk of Ingheta-Om-Schlopu, of its elephants, its sickness and its dark forests. You know that the big animals do not frighten us and that we have followed you everywhere. We will follow you there too if you wish, but unwillingly, for we are not wizards and cannot protect ourselves from dysentery; not a single Zoulou will accompany us. Look here, master, there are elephants in other places. Trust us and do not go there.' I accepted their advice and with difficulty thrust from my mind the beautiful plans I had made for Ingheta-Om-Schlopu before I knew that it was a harbourer of pestilence, feared by the Cafres.

On the 3rd, as our path took us right away from Ingheta, every one wished to accompany us. Our guides led us up to the green mountain pastures which look down upon the wooded basin of the Om-Philos-Mouniama, whose sinuous course we later followed. When we made our first halt, each man minutely scanned the ravines, the glades, the undergrowth, the riverbed and the banks where the rushes grew. While my men and I were searching for the backs of elephants the others had eyes only for buffaloes; they pointed them out to us here and there and each time they did so I shook my head saying, *Uncklove upi na*? 'Where are the elephants?'

An hour's close scrutiny was sufficient to enable us to catch sight of any elephants which might have been there. When this period of time had elapsed, I set off towards a nearby herd of buffaloes and killed a female, as much for our own immediate use as a token of gratitude to the strangers for their help in guiding us.

Two of them, knowing that we intended spending the night at the *mouzi* of Om-Ghetjanne, remained with us. Their cooperation was very useful, for while we knew only the direction and not the distance, they were able to lead us by the shortest route. We continued along the high ground with the forest on our left. In this way we were able to keep a watch on anything that moved. In addition we were at liberty to talk without fear of frightening off the game. I was glad of this for I was able to converse with the strangers and to discover things which my own Cafres did not know.

I learnt something which I would never have suspected when one of the guides happened to remark, 'Master, can you smell the *makanos*? Here is some shade, let us stop here.' More interested in resting than in tasting the *makanos*, I sat down under one of the trees. Everybody was collecting the fruit which was lying about on the ground and which had quite a pleasant smell. 'Are they good then, your *makanos*?' I asked, as I searched about in the grass. 'Certainly, master, the elephant eats them and likes them very much.' 'But if he likes them a lot, he can never have enough of them to eat. What is one *makano*, what are a thousand *makanos* to an elephant?' 'He does not need so many to get drunk.' 'What did you say? Tell me about this.'

There followed an explanation which was no doubt simple but which was of great interest to me and which proved a similarity in the tastes and habits of man and elephant, a sort of shrewdness on the part of the elephant which distinguishes him from all the other beasts. When this animal comes upon *makanos* trees laden with well-grown fruit, his first instinct is to pull them all down with his trunk. A few days suffice not only to ripen the fallen fruit, but to ferment them as well. The elephant returns to find his fruit, gathers them up and eats them.

Woe to the ignorant hunter whose scent has been carried by the wind in the direction of the feasting giant. Even at a distance of as much as 600 paces, the charge is immediate and decisive. The elephant pursues the man in a blind fury which has been aroused and sustained by the intoxication of the fermented fruit. The hunter's only escape is to head downwind by way of the thick undergrowth or to take refuge among steep rocks if they are to hand.

Initially I believed that this was simply a tall story but imagine my surprise when I witnessed personally the effect of the *makano* fruit on the elephant and even experienced it myself.

The skin of the fruit gives off a smell of turpentine like the American mango; it is green on the tree, turning to apple green when it falls, ripe, to the ground. The flesh is white and transparent like *spermaceti*. Inside is a stone which the teeth of a man cannot crack open. The pulp which surrounds the stone is very acid; it puts the teeth on edge. The fruit is flattened and almost oval in shape. Not more than ten *makanos* are sufficient to produce a state of intoxication in man. It is thus not surprising that the elephant, after having eaten bushels of them, exchanges his habitual serious demeanour for one of irrational fury.

To distract ourselves on the long journey, we made facetious remarks, each one more amusing than the last, whenever our guide spoke. One of our party expressed the wish that we might encounter a herd of elephants so intoxicated that their trunks would be linked to support each other; another said that he would cut off their tails. We tried to outdo each other in imagining all the abominable tricks which we would play on the *long noses*, going so far even as to propose cutting off their most distinguishing feature. Everybody laughed at this stream of witticisms which, as it flowed thick and fast produced louder and louder laughter; the *makano* was already going to their heads!

'Elephants, elephants! Down there,' said the man at the head of the column in a low voice, pointing to the mouth of a deep gorge down below. The laughter suddenly ceased; each face assumed a grave look as when, amidst the laughter which follows upon a jest, someone challenges you to a duel.

Down in the valley three of the biggest and most impressive fellows I had ever seen were grazing on a yellow-green carpet of tall strong grass, the sort of grass which would hinder the progress of the hunter and give the elephants the advantage. Immediately, I resolved upon my plan of action. The wind was favourable and we needed to make very few detours; even though the trees and bushes were scanty, the tall grass would serve our purpose equally well. 'Go easy boys! Let us climb down this way; and watch out — no rolling stones!'

We slithered slowly and carefully down the steep narrow path, one behind the other, and almost lost our elephants from view. Although we could not see them, we took our bearings from a nearby mountain and this enabled us to approach them directly, crawling along on our stomachs through the long grass. They were barely 500 paces away now and we got ourselves into single file, with Kotchobana just ahead of me. From time to time we stopped to take a deep breath.

At forty paces, Kotchobana, who was an arm's length in front of me suddenly stopped. I gave him a questioning look and he signalled with his left hand, pointing out a hare which was crouching in the grass, barely six inches from his foot. I thought it very stupid to pay attention to a hare in such circumstances. I conveyed this to him with a sign. Without moving, Kotchobana gave me a look as if to say, 'Don't you see!' and indicated with a glance a spot fifteen paces ahead.

The deuce! Confound it! Two elands (*Ant. canna*) stood there grazing and quite unaware of our presence. Only then did I realise what he was trying to tell me: the hare would leap away; not realising where the noise came from, the *cannas* would be bound to move off, and the elephants would follow their example, Curse the hare! I would have killed it with a stick if I had had one to hand. I hesitated a moment, but I was powerless. 'Go on,' I said to Kotchobana. The hare jumped, the *cannas* bolted, and the elephants disappeared. 'Go on, we'll catch up with them.'

And indeed, after crawling 150 or 200 paces, we caught sight of them again; redoubling our precautions, we approached to within thirty-five paces of them. The biggest of them was enormous; an animal of medium size was standing between him and us, and the third one was behind. 'Leave that one; get the big one, Kotchobana; ready Boulandje.' Three shots rang out simultaneously, and the elephant turned and headed off. 'I hit him! What about you, Kotchobana?' 'Me too' — 'And you, Boulandje?' — 'So did I.'

We reloaded and followed the pachyderms; two minutes later we saw that all three had stopped; only the big one was waving his trunk, curling it up towards his head. 'At least, these fellows are standing still, Kotchobana; they did not run very far.' We were about to fire our second round, when they saw us and moved away. As the big one turned, we all three hit him at sixty paces. 'Come on, boys, courage! They are making for the mountain which they do not intend to climb; they will come back this way at least once more.' We followed in their tracks which described almost a complete circle and came upon them looking as peaceful as when we had first seen them.

Boulandje and I aimed at the big one; Kotchobana, preferring to be independent, aimed at one of the others. Only two shots rang out, mine failed to go off. When Kotchobana saw that his shot had broken his elephant's humerus, he cried out, *Inkoniana bambylé*, 'the calf is caught', which meant that the little elephant was unable to escape. But Kotchobana was mistaken in calling it a calf; in spite of being ten feet tall it looked like one compared with the big elephant.

I ran up to within ten paces to try and get a shot above the eye, but the animal, as if it guessed my intention, began wheeling about on its hind legs, thus depriving me of the opportunity to take careful aim. Unconsciously obeying a powerful instinct, I continued to advance, until it dawned on me that in falling he might crush me. I stepped back, the animal paused for a moment, and I fired the fatal shot. He fell lifeless to the ground.

Each tusk weighed more than thirty pounds, which suggested that those of the big male would probably weigh between ninety and a hundred pounds. As I hastily reloaded I saw him walking away briskly in an attempt to reach the bush. 'Come on, Kotchobana, this is the one we want; quick, after him!' But the young mimosa trees which were hidden in the grass, tore at our legs and so hindered our progress that the elephant was soon out of sight. We followed until there was just enough sunlight left for us to reach the *mouzi* of Om-Ghet-Janne before nightfall.

The reception which we received from the chief was as generous as the gifts which we offered our hosts. All that they had was put at our disposal with an open-handedness which I found very pleasing. Om-Ghet-Janne squatted down by my side as close as he could get and, listening intently to my conversation, interjected with admiring observations.

By the next day these good people had accepted us as part of the family and they gathered closely around to inspect us. The men examined our guns which were a mystery to them, although they pretended to understand the mechanism; the women gazed wide-eyed and open-mouthed at the colour of my skin and the quality and length of my hair and beard. I sat like a log in the centre of the curious throng, allowing the young girls to run their fingers through my beard; some thought that it was a garment made from the tail of an animal found in the land of the white men. This garment they believed, was worn with the intention of protecting my face, just as I wore clothes to protect the rest of my body. Others were of the opinion that it was natural and that white men were covered with hair, not only on their chins, but all over their bodies, like baboons.

You may easily imagine that I felt obliged to defend the honour of the white man. Nothing could have been simpler; where all the bodies were naked, there was no impropriety in uncovering my chest. This had the immediate effect of convincing them that whites really were men, and to judge by the remarks, fine men at that, and not monkeys. I find this curiosity perfectly natural, since similar sentiments are manifested among our own people; consider the interest shown in the Hottentot Venus who was all the rage in Paris and whom everyone wished to scrutinize from head to foot.

The 4th was a day of rest for us, while half of the *mouzi* went off to cut up the elephant. At that time the sugar cane was ripening and we received many bunches as gifts. Sucking the pith became our constant occupation.

On the 5th, when we left, sixty men accompanied us, hoping to profit by our hunting. Unfortunately for them I was interested in nothing but elephants; the only one we saw was on the other side of the river and it moved away at our approach. As our scouts had nothing to report, we continued on our way. I killed a *canna* and towards dusk we came to a royal *mouzi* called Nogoty, which means 'the hole', and where there lived an *inkoskazi*, one of Panda's sisters.

I was not well received here, for I brought no cloth, no bead necklaces, to offer the princess who ruled over the *mouzi* which comprised 200 to 300 people. But I did not care whether she was hospitable or not; the weather was fine and so we asked no further favours. Making our fire out in the open, we grilled some excellent *canna* steaks, and lay down to sleep beside the embers.

At dawn we were setting off without bidding farewell to the mistress of the house, when a trapper came by and gave us warning of a herd of elephants which he had seen a league further on. This was not the direction that we had intended to take, but for so good a reason a detour would cost us nothing: and so we went, quite prepared for some lively hunting.

We soon reached high ground from where we were able to look down upon the herd. Smoke from a neighbouring fire was blowing almost imperceptibly from right to left; the breeze was uncertain and I allowed myself to be guided by this slight indication of its direction. 'Come on, my black friends, we will go round to the left. It is further, but that does not matter, look at the wind.' We headed off towards the left, but in spite of our haste, we took nearly three-quarters of an hour, during which time luck was against us for the breeze changed direction. Besides the fact that we were almost sure to fail, we were running into certain danger.

Unfortunately, we had by now come too close to consider attacking the herd from the other side; particularly as a line of bush stretched out before us, with elephants scattered about everywhere. 'The wind is behind us', said Kotchobana. 'Do you know that, master?' 'Yes — too bad; the breeze deceived us at the beginning. Another time we will do better. Come on, choose a big one.'

We moved another sixty paces forward until we were only fifteen paces from the edge of the bush where the backs, ears and tusks of elephants stood out here and there. We chose our victim, but the animal was in an unfavourable position and, while we were waiting for it to turn, a young elephant, seven feet high, thrust his head out of the foliage close beside us, just as a traveller might thrust his head out of the window of a stage coach. The sight of this head appearing was so comical that I burst out laughing. The head disappeared and the mother elephant, alerted by her calf, made off noisily. In spite of all the commotion, another fine specimen continued peacefully grazing, sixty paces away, his flank most invitingly turned towards us. Certain that he would not remain long in that position, we ran towards him, preparing to fire at him as he retreated. But he did not retreat. Twenty paces still separated us, when the elephant, raising his trunk, began advancing on us with a determined air. The raised trunk protected his forehead. He lowered it for a moment and in that short time he was struck by four bullets. The elephant, in a fury, began to charge, uprooting trees which stood in his path, and bearing down upon us with intent to kill.

But man's instinct of self-preservation lends strength to his legs, and we sprinted back 300 paces, swift as gazelles. We changed direction to put the elephant off our tracks. He spun around and went to rejoin the retreating herd, which comprised 150 to 200 animals. Shortly afterwards, we saw them in two long files, making their way up a huge gorge which led to Om-Schlaty-Om-Koulou, six leagues away.

We believed that that is where we would find them, and even though we would have to devote the whole day to the pursuit, and spend the night in the forest, we followed the great tracks which had the appearance of a road opening up before us. Three hours later we were forced to abandon the pursuit, for the tracks led to the west and we needed to head south to reach Om-Schlaty.

An hour later, four elephants were spotted 600 paces off. All were outstanding specimens, very evenly matched, but they were on the move, and however fast we went after them, we were unable to catch up with them and cut them off.

We could see the bony flanks of Om-Grooty not far way, standing

266

out like the sides of a pyramid. We reached it, we climbed it, and once again we saw from the top more than eighty elephants, gathered beyond the Om-Philos-Om-Schlopu beside the dried-up marshes. The descent presented no difficulty, although on the way down we lost Wilhelm the dawdler, who seemed to be dreaming of other things. An hour later, we had reached the marsh which was bordered on the southern side by a rocky hill-slope.

I was beginning to think that we had already passed by the group of elephants which must have been standing so still that we had not seen them, when Houahouaho signalled that he had just caught sight of a trunk near the top of the marsh, forty paces away and twelve feet below where we were standing. Kotchobana had also seen something move and, after a brief hesitation, he began to run towards it. I ran after him and as I ran, I loaded my gun.

There was the elephant, twenty paces away on our right, climbing up the steep slope, his body slanted at an angle and about to straighten out again. We raised our guns and took aim and when his whole head came into view, right across our path, we fired and my bullet, striking him in the left temple, brought him down. Kotchobana had aimed at the vulnerable point in the shoulder. We could find no trace of his shot which, in any case, could not possibly have been the cause of so rapid a death.

We had left behind us the main body of elephants which, disturbed by our gunfire, had raised such a dense cloud of dust as they retreated, that they were obscured from our view, although we could barely hear each other speak above the din made by the tusks as they crashed together in a confusion which could be likened to the rout of a great army. The sound of trumpeting, the shrill cries and the crack and thud of falling trees conveyed some impression of the terrible strength of these giants, while they, the monsters of creation, fled for fear of us puny but intelligent human beings. I understood at that moment the great power with which man is endowed, and I was filled with wonder.

A quarter of an hour after we had claimed our victim, we were surprised to hear a gunshot, 200 paces off. The next moment, a voice called out *Houetou*[1] *upi na*? It was Wilhelm the late-comer who, having heard our gunfire, had made haste to join us, but as the herd of elephants was by then between him and us, Wilhelm, to his dismay had found himself cut off and had been forced to use his weapon. He was quite beside himself with excitement, a mixture of fear, recently overcome, and glowing pride, for Wilhelm had just seen his elephant fall to the ground.

'Come on! Come on,' he cried, foaming at the mouth, 'he is right

1 Abbreviation of *abantu*, plural of *montou* — a man or person.

near here, I left him on the ground; come and finish him off or he will get up and go away.' We set off at a run, but he had already gone. In spite of Wilhelm's protestations that he had wounded the animal, we could find no trace of it, although we were convinced that elephants had in fact been there at the time that we supposed them to be a great distance away. It was fortunate for us that the elephants had not chosen to retreat towards the spot where we had been standing about chatting a short while before. It is doubtful whether we could have turned them back in time and they might well have trampled us underfoot. We tried to catch up with the herd but our efforts were in vain and we arrived rather late at the *mouzi* of Baye-Bang.

On the 7th, my men went to collect the tusks. That evening I returned alone to the camp. We had travelled no less than sixty leagues in the course of only a few days.

While on the subject of elephant hunting, I feel it is as well at this point to set down some of the details I have learnt about the habits of these zoological giants. I may sometimes repeat what I have previously said, but the necessity of presenting here a complete picture of the prince of quadrupeds may well require some repetition of facts already mentioned.

In the eyes of the South African hunter, the elephant is the most important of all animals, the object of all his desires. The *canna* (*Boselaphus oreas*), the buffalo, the hippopotamus, the rhinoceros, the giraffe, all form part of the common run of hunting, and hunters who have killed none but these have not known real success. They are still unaware of the indescribable excitement which is in store for them when a gigantic quadruped falls victim to their bullets. But, I hasten to add, elephant hunting is no child's play. Very few, even among the best of marksmen, dare attempt it and once thwarted, many are disheartened and will make no further attempt. The task is very laborious and great resolution is required to succeed.

Elephant hunting has much in common with duelling. It very often happens that even the female will not wait for the first shot to be fired, but will charge furiously at the man who has disturbed her tranquility and threatened her young. The elephant has very long legs, while man has short ones; a man may easily be seized in the trunk, crushed by the tusks, thrown in the air, trampled underfoot; this sad fate discourages the most intrepid. All the elephant hunters I have known, have been men whose strength of character set them apart from the masses and to prove my point, I quote the names Christian Muller, Hans Delange, Gert Roedolph, men who are well-known in Natal for their acts of rare courage.

One cannot hope to find the great herds, those which yield the most valuable rewards, within reach of the dwelling places of white men. The elephant will frequently appear in the midst of the most populous Cafre settlements, while he will avoid those places where even a few white families are established. The effects of gunfire are well-known to him and he prudently avoids the danger which he fears.

And so the hunter must go beyond the frontiers; he must go and settle among distant tribes whose character he cannot always depend upon. He must become accustomed to their language, their way of life; he must win their confidence in order to obtain the precious information he needs and the co-operation of a great number of men, without whose assistance his chances of success are negligible.

These preliminary measures present a great number of difficulties and expose him to dangers which cannot always be overcome at the crucial moment. In addition to all this, what elephant hunters refer to as a hunt, takes as much time as a European would spend on a voyage to Brazil and back, with a stopover of two months. Three months is the usual duration of the successful elephant hunt, but if there are difficulties the return could be delayed by as much as six months; not everyone can take such long leave of absence. The temporary widowhood of their wives is an obstacle to many. And so, to become a first-rate elephant hunter, the prime essential is to be a bachelor.

The animals are not easy to find. One may actually live in a part of the country which they frequent and where there is evidence of their presence, and yet not come across a single one of them. One must wait for the rainy season, when the thunder rumbles, when the vegetation is luxuriant and the fruit have followed the flowers; it is then that the elephants come out in great numbers, almost as if they were emerging from beneath the earth. Where in fact do they come from? Since they can be found all year round, they obviously do not emigrate. But why, at this season, is the usual number multiplied by twenty? This question has never been satisfactorily answered, although I know for certain that they could only come down from the north where richer lands have sustained them during the dry season. When the hunter locates an isolated elephant, the first precaution he takes is to make sure of the direction of the wind which, if a safe and easy approach is to be ensured, must be blowing away from the animal.

Once this condition is fulfilled, he must next inspect his guns to avoid the danger of misfiring; this inspection increases the confidence of the hunter as he will then aim with greater accuracy, which in turn increases his courage, that indispensable ingredient of success; he is now ready to begin his approach.

In the bush, nothing could be easier; each man keeps in line and watches his feet. The trees, the hanging branches, the bushes, all offer sufficient protection to make it unnecessary for the hunter to crouch, although he must frequently do so if he wishes to be able to see ahead. In the open plains, which afford no protection but the grass, the approach may be difficult, but it can also often be quite easy; it is easy when the grass is two and a half metres high, but difficult when it is no more than a metre.

It is under these latter circumstances that crawling along on the stomach, *by-kruipen*, is useful; the Boschjesman practises this art to perfection. Whatever one's aptitude, one must attempt to practise it too, for the elephant is worth the effort; even if one must sacrifice the last shred of one's clothing, the long white tusks are a rich reward for the painful exercise. Three hunters lie flat on the ground, one behind the other, their bodies imitating the coils of a snake, their hands supporting their nether regions, their feet and knees taking it in turn to provide the locomotion, while the gun is dragged along step by step in the right hand.

After covering fifty metres in this fashion it becomes necessary to rest, and you all roll over on your backs to allow the lungs more freedom to breathe; with your nose to the ground, breathing becomes difficult because of the condensation of heat. After resting for a minute, the man snake turns on to its stomach once more and slithers away through the grass. But it is possible that it has not adhered strictly to its course, or perhaps the elephant might have moved; a glance would settle the matter but take care! Your head must not show above the grass!

In this crawling position, the man's head is nearest to the animal he is stalking. If he wishes to snatch a hurried glance, he must wriggle about and raise himself up, bit by bit, to a crouching position which allows him the best opportunity of ducking if the elephant offers the least sign of making investigations.

At last the elephant is at close quarters. Mercifully, he will be peaceful, for the condition of the crawlers is pitiful; their hands, having performed the function of feet, are cut to pieces by the sharp grass; their foreheads are drenched in sweat which is pouring into their eyes, while their reddened hands attempt in vain to stem the flow; their clothes are sodden, their lungs cry out for air, their limbs tremble with exhaustion; they turn on to their backs again for a moment and, if they are lucky, this cessation of physical agitation will not give way to mental agitation brought on by the consciousness of the proximity of danger.

A minute and a half go by during which time a rumbling noise, like distant thunder, reaches the men's ears; the animal's intestines disgorge. The time has come, the last two crawlers have caught up with the first, and take up their position by his side, their feet outstretched towards the elephant; each man glances up to confirm the animal's position.

Thirty to thirty-five paces is the most effective distance; the animal stands exposed to the hunters facing almost broadside on. 'This is it! Follow me! Stand up!' Where do these men come from, who seem to surge out of the earth so close to the giant? Their sudden appearance is something to be wondered at, their audacity is frightening. Their guns thunder and the bullet seeks out the concave place above the eye. The smoke billows out, the hunters retreat, the massive animal staggers and falls . . . Bang! bang! bang! Only now does the sound reach your ears, for you, the observer of all this courage, the onlooker at this scene of a giant being attacked by pygmies, you have stood apart and have kept your distance.

The sight of so much good fortune makes you tremble with desire. How easy it is to shoot and to kill! You will of course never forget the axe they use to slit open the sockets and extract the tusks. But take care, do not be deceived, for if success were always so certain, women would hunt elephants while their husbands rested, and if that were to happen, my gun would lie idle and rust! Unhappily for those whose fortunes are made from ivory, and luckily for the race of *long noses*, the coincidence of favourable circumstances is exceptional.

Most commonly elephants are encountered in herds which may number three, seven, fifteen, thirty, fifty, eighty or even several hundred. I will not claim that these animals have the intelligence to post sentries but, among the herd, one individual or another is bound to notice the approach of the hunter. He will trumpet noisily and warn the herd, which will then retreat, abandoning its position at the slightest suggestion of danger. At this point, hope deserts the hunter unless he is mounted on an excellent horse.

But it is possible that the herd will behave quite differently and hold its ground, while one individual spreads wide its great ears, raises its trunk in a threatening manner and advances on the hunter who is not in a position to take aim at the vulnerable spot. To fire at the chest is a simple expedient which cannot be relied upon, but which must nevertheless be attempted. The weapon must be fired, the bullet must wound the animal in an attempt to arrest its progress. There is little hope for the man who does not fire, for he must put all his trust in his legs. It sometimes happens that he is seized by the elephant, which is unrelenting in its fury, even when the man has not wounded it but has simply been guilty of approaching too close to the giant, who values his solitude; nothing can resist the onslaught of the furious colossus.

Many Cafres, men and women alike, have paid with their lives for approaching, albeit unbeknown, too close to an elephant; how much more dangerous then is the position of the hunter who, with his furtive, purposeful approach, disturbs the wily animal. You must remain calm, control your emotions, master your fears; stand and wait for the elephant to charge; remind yourself that this time you fire only to defend yourself, that your life depends on the accuracy of your aim . . . but your gun misfires! Good God! The percussion cap has not gone off. Then reload! Take aim again. The elephant is upon you. You feel the rush of air as his trunk, that elastic nose, is raised ready to lash you. Bang! The shot goes off this time. You turn and run and just as he thought he had you, he realises that he is wounded. Ashamed, he turns and trots off to join his companions who have been disturbed by the sound of the shot . . . And what about your ivory? The elephant is taking it away with him! You are in despair! But stop for a moment and consider . . . Three more steps and you would have been crushed! Let that thought be a consolation to you; let that pour balm upon your regrets.

You will not always be disappointed. You will see elephants making off when your fire has been misdirected or ineffectual; but then you yourself will also sometimes run away, which is wise; for as the South Africans say, the wounded animal will always return to sniff the powder at the place where it was ignited. But while you are retreating as fast as your legs can carry you, you may suddenly come upon a temple with a hundred grey arches and two hundred rounded columns, with an astonishing sound of organs emanating from it; beware of seeking refuge beneath these arches, for the columns will move off, bearing the whole edifice along with them, and woe be to him who finds himself in its way! Blessed are those animals which have long legs or which live in holes, for they can escape danger, while man has nothing but his cool head, which may very well fail him, and the use of his weapons, which must be powerful to be effective.

The army of elephants advances to the sound of the trumpet; the animals jostle to find a place in the front row and the masses press from behind. Tusks, those terrible weapons, crash together with the rich sound of ivory. Dust rises in impenetrable clouds, the undergrowth is trampled underfoot, the squadron of elephants flattens all in its path; trees three feet in circumference are twisted, uprooted, broken and their top branches frequently dumped far away. And when the ponderous march of the cohort of latter-day titans is opposed by the hoary giants of the vegetable kingdom, these latter, however great their size and their strength, give way beneath the weight, although their branches in falling, could well crush the perpetrators of the sacrilege. I have seen healthy strong trees, sixty feet high, and nine feet in circumference snapped like a cane across a man's knee. This was the work of only one or two elephants; imagine then what their collective force must be.

Mere words cannot convey the picture of destruction left in the wake of a hastily retreating herd of elephants. Even a whirlwind does not leave behind such devastation. Ten and even twenty years later, nature will not yet have repaired all the damage; tree trunks, which are all bending in the same direction, give evidence of the passage of the batallion of monsters, and trees which were young at the time, still bear traces of having been bent to the ground. They suggest to the imagination a long procession of plant invalids climbing the mountainside and setting off on a pilgrimage across the plains.

In spite of all this, the man who wants ivory must not let his imagination exaggerate the dangers to such an extent that they appear insurmountable. The elephant is big and strong; he is fast, canny, wise and implacable. Man is small, weak and slow; but man is intelligent, and his intelligence has provided him with terrible weapons. If he has courage man will emerge the victor from an encounter in which at first his insignificant stature appears pitiful, and the elephant is aware of this for on countless occasions it has been apparent that he does not underestimate man.

In fact, if fifty elephants in rows of ten should burst into a clearing to find one single man, standing there defying them with a gun or even beating upon a shield, the entire herd will come to a standstill and almost always it will retreat; if it turns aside and by-passes the man, it is because other men are coming in pursuit.

The behaviour of these animals can most easily be observed when they are cornered in the long valleys dotted with bushes, furrowed by ravines and bordered by steep escarpments. Tracked down and surrounded here they are held prisoner. When the grass is long and dry, man will often use fire to form a barrier across the entrance to the valley, or else a line of men will defend the passage with shields which they use as drums to make a great noise and force the *long noses*[1] to climb into the narrow gorges. In the upper reaches, one man alone is sufficient deterrent, and on the steep sides of the slope, like spectators of long ago at the shows in ancient Rome, warriors stand about in groups, their duty simply being to talk loudly and to beat their shields when necessary.

When they want the elephants to leave the wider and less well-guarded part of the valley, to move into the narrower section, the men begin shouting and beating their shields behind the animals, while silence reigns in the confines to which they are being driven. The elephants obey as meekly as domesticated beasts. Then the hunters mingle with the herds, shooting one here, driving off another there, retreating, returning to the attack, slithering down into a ravine, or scrambling hurriedly up a slope, while the trunks threaten

1 *Om-pondo-om-koulou* — nickname given to the elephant by the Amazoulous.

and beat the air, ready to crush the man who ventures too close for, as everyone knows, such a man is doomed.

In this improvised arena, like a gladiator in ancient Rome, more than once I proved myself before an audience of 600 trackers. These combats, during which our strength was soon exhausted by a thousand leaps and circumlocutions, never lasted less than two hours and, the giants, overcome by the intense heat, were obliged to have recourse to a unique means of refreshment. The first time I witnessed this strange sight, water was a long way off; my tongue was burning and, perched on top of a rock from where I was studying the movements of the herds down below, I began to think that I was being lured by a tempting dream.

Beneath the rock I sat on grew clusters of round-topped mimosas, their luxuriant green foliage enriched with bright golden buds. The grey or red-brown backs of elephants stood out like enormous stones and from among these backs, or these stones, rose a stream of water which fell again in fine rain. The mere sight of water gives so much pleasure to the man who is parched with thirst and I truly believed that I was about to quench mine. I continued to gaze, and this time a spurt of water sparkled like diamonds in the air and then took on all the colours of the rainbow. I was about to surrender to the charm of this illusion, when my Cafres suddenly started yelling and making such a din that they disturbed the elephants which, I later found out, crowd together when they are overcome with heat, so that all might benefit from the water which one of them presses from a pocket in his stomach and squirts into the air with his trunk.

In spite of the apparent resignation of the elephants, who as a last resort, huddle in a mass, taking advantage of the protection of the trees and interlock their heads so as to present only their less vulnerable hindquarters, they are finally driven to impatience and despair by the incessant gunfire and, with a common accord, they charge the barrier and make a wide breach in it. On more than one occasion, we found our men trapped there under fallen trees.

It was a fine thing to see the intelligence of the females and the maternal instinct which was increased by the threat of danger. The little ones, which normally trot at their mother's heels, were invisible in these attempts to escape, when the feet of the adult animals, in the confusion, might unavoidably have crushed the frail young. Between the four feet of the female, beneath the maternal dome, ran the calf, its stumbling steps guided by the mother, who passed her trunk down under her chest, took hold of the trunk of her offspring and led it along as a human mother guides the uncertain footsteps of her child. However fast the bullets fell, the mother with her body protected the body of the little elephant; for him her anxious concern was greater than it was for herself, and it

274

was only when they had left the danger far behind that she allowed him to return to his normal place at her heels.

When the groups separated it became apparent that some were composed only of old males, and others only of females, each followed by a calf, with a large male bringing up the rear, as if detailed to protect the retreat. The females without young would gather in isolated herds, unaccompanied by any male; their smaller size made them recognisable from afar. Their tusks, which never exceded thirty pounds in weight and were more often less than fifteen pounds, were quite sufficient to protect them from attack.

Obviously, any hunter of conscience will direct his attentions only to the large old males, while sparing the young ones and the females, unless the tusks of the latter rival those of the average-sized male. Besides, to stalk and attack the male is easier, so the advantages are twofold.

The males are solemn; they are philosophers with cool, restrained emotions. They do not show much evidence of vivacity or light-heartedness and appear to make decisions only after long reflection. The females are more emotional, their passions are warmer; they fear for their young. The sight of man irritates them exessively; they charge instantly and with great determination. Among all wild animals the females are more irascible of character than the males. However, although in general the males are peaceful enough, the hunter must not neglect to take precautions, for they too are capable of charging furiously and with as much determination as the female.

The elephant has in common with man a predilection for a gentle warming of the brain induced by fruit which have been fermented by the action of the sun: the *omkouschlouâne* and the *makano* of the Amazoulous. These wild fruit, which he brings down with his trunk, within a few days of lying on the earth, develop the qualities he is seeking, and it is when the elephant is caught unawares eating the fruit that the hunter is in the greatest danger. The Cafres are emphatic that there is no salvation possible in such cases and that the man, whoever he may be, must resign himself to his sad fate. As a result of this intoxication, the males become as dangerous as the females. Some individuals are more to be feared than others, although their appearance might give quite the opposite impression — I mean those whom nature has not provided with tusks. Their behaviour is like that of the coward who attempts to intimidate his adversary. The South African Dutch apply the vulgar name *poes-kop* to all those animals which have been denied horns as the result of an abnormality of nature; this nickname is also used to describe the elephants I have just mentioned. They are particularly feared by hunters whom they charge with lowered head, intending to ensure that their privacy is respected. I killed one of these when it charged me: it was a female. I saw about fifteen of them in the course of my hunting trips and to judge by their size, all seemed to be females.

The one I killed pleased the Cafres enormously because of the large quantity of fat in the intestines. A few days later when I went back to inspect the skeleton, I noticed that the head seemed small in proportion to the strength of the animal's body. I began to suspect that among these animals the size of the head is not necessarily related to the size of the body, but to the weight of the tusks, since I have killed males of the same size as this female which had heavy tusks and whose heads were almost double the size.

The head of my *poes-kop* elephant was very much like that of a young animal whose tusks are just beginning to come through. The sockets were closed and the head itself did not weigh very much although this was an adult female with a calf. It is said that in India and Ceylon, where some of the species have been introduced into the service of man, elephants without tusks are common. Levaillant assures us that there, the number of elephants with tusks is as limited as the number of *poes-kop* elephants in Africa.

As it is certain that all animals degenerate under the influence of man, because in the domesticated condition they have less need to protect themselves or to find food, it follows that their tusks will be less well developed and may be totally absent without inconvenience to the animal. Perhaps this is the explanation.

But many people believe that these animals lose their tusks as the stag loses his horns. It is hardly worth refuting this error, for it becomes apparent upon the most superficial inspection of an elephant's head. However, it has its origins in the density and pattern of growth of the tusk, which it is important to understand.

The socket is formed before the existence of the tooth itself. A fatty transparent substance, not unlike bone marrow, occupies the hollow cylinder from which the tusk is to grow. This matter soon thickens near the mouth of the socket; it thickens and hardens into a sort of hollow cone. To this first layer, a second is soon added from within, then a third, and so on, until eventually there are a thousand others. The cone grows longer and broader each day until the point pushes its way through and appears on the surface in the shape of a white button.

The tusk then grows from within as the layers are superimposed; each of these layers, if it were detached, would present the appearance of a cone slightly curved towards the tip; to give an exact idea by a comparison which everyone may understand, let me say that one must try to imagine a number of paper cornets inserted one into another — such is the disposition of the layers. For a tusk to reach its greatest length requires a great deal of time; for it to attain its greatest weight will take the whole of the animal's life. The ivory is thus very dense, but not all dense matter is equally strong. The strength depends upon the manner in which the molecules or the conglomerates of molecules are joined; frequently a tusk is broken in the effort which the elephant makes to uproot a tree; hence the probable origin of the fable immortalised by the authors of old. What I have just said concerning the formation of the tooth is further proved by the manner in which it is destroyed. I have found in the bush, a great number of tusks which have lain there for forty years, exposed to the action of air, heat and water.

These tusks bore longitudinal fissures, such as those which appear in a fallen tree which has been stripped of its bark; apart from this, the rough surface reveals a great number of superimposed layers, detached at the base and standing up almost like the tips of thatch on a rustic roof. Each of these layers may be considered as a splinter off the base of the cone and, the more closely I inpsected them, the more convinced of this I became.

The presence of these elephant's teeth, which are encountered in large quantities in the heart of the bush, requires an explanation which would be misplaced if it were intended only for scholars, but which I include for the interest of the layman.

Let me explain: at one time there were numerous Cafres living in these parts, who were much given to hunting the great pachyderms. The tusks were collected together at a central *mouzi*; but, following a disastrous war, the remnants of the tribe moved to another part of the country. The conqueror, a keeper of herds, razed the villages to the ground but neglected to remove the ivory. And so there it remained. Its existence probably gave rise to the story of the eleph-ants' graveyard which, according to the oriental poets, is where all the elephants go to die.

But if I am required to explain how another fable has found some credibility, the one where the hunter has sawn through nine-tenths of the tree against which the elephant will lean while he sleeps, then I declare that I withdraw in the face of such improbability.

The elephant has no difficulty in getting to his feet; in fact he rises with the greatest of ease from the mud puddles in the forest, where he has been sprawling, and where he leaves his huge footprints behind. There is no doubt that if the animal feared falling he would never be seen sliding down steep sandy inclines, eighty feet high, with his legs thrust stiffly out before him and his feet digging a wide furrow like a wagon going downhill with a drag on the wheels.

Tusks are the only teeth which provide ivory. All are not equally curved; some are very straight but sometimes the two tusks, when joined together, will form a perfect circle; and so I am inclined to believe that the curvature cannot be taken as a distinctive character-istic. The length varies according to the age and the sex; the longest

I have seen were seven foot, measured along the curve, and weighed 120 pounds each. Levaillant mentions one of 160 pounds, and if I give credit to the story told me by a bastaard, an old hunter whom I came across in Natal, the Norden expedition to the Massilicatzi country, of which he was a member, is reputed to have brought back the biggest and heaviest tusks in all of southern Africa. In the Amazoulou country, long heavy tusks are rare. Although my hunting trips accounted for forty-three elephants, only two pairs of tusks measured as much as six feet and weighed seventy pounds. The ivory from the female is more highly prized than that of the male. It is thicker and does not turn yellow as readily.

Where the tusks are to be removed, the operation is sometimes undertaken immediately; the flesh and the skin adhering to the socket is cut away from the outside to free the tusks, but it often happens that, to save a lot of trouble, the hunter, among the Amazoulous at least, simply cuts off the tail as evidence of ownership and after nine or ten days when the larvae and all the agents of destruction have loosened the muscles, the tusks may be withdrawn without effort, and will bear no trace of the axe. But this method is not without disadvantages; the tusk, which does not deteriorate while the animal is alive although it is in constant contact with the air, now produces long cracks brought about by the action of the sun, which proves that in spite of its density the tusk never ceases to absorb a certain amount of moisture.

Consequently, the dry tusk no longer has the same weight; I knew a famour hunter Hans Delange who, to avoid reducing his price at the sales, took care to treat his tusks with the object of restoring their fullness, if not their freshness; a few days in advance he sprinkled them with sea-salt, which he then watered. When the water had been completely absorbed and the cracks had closed up, this man took his tusks to the market place where the purchaser, finding no faults, paid dearly for them, beyond the value of their real weight.

Along all the coasts of Africa, the demand for ivory by European traders has encouraged the natives to hunt for it. Those who understand the use of guns hunt elephant with them. But the Amazoulous, possessing no weapons of this sort, must of necessity use their own methods however ineffectual they may be. Their system is simple, but it requires great presence of mind, skill and strength.

Forty men in single file approach to within fifty paces of an elephant. The leader, armed with an *omkondo* (assegai) with a broad sharp blade, moves ahead of the rest and advances to within ten paces of the animal, or even nearer if he sees fit; from this position, with a flourish, he hurls his javelin horizontally at the animal's hock. Thus the animal is rendered incapable of escaping and his attackers shower him with their *omkondos* whose quivering shafts penetrate his body until, exhausted from the loss of blood, and overcome by frustrated anger, the animal falls to the ground never to rise again.

Covered ditches bristling with sharpened stakes, into which the herds are driven, can be used only once; their preparation requires a great deal of time; their position being unknown to strangers, they are the cause of numerous terrible accidents; for these reasons they have today been almost completely abandoned.

Stakes planted along the banks of rivers, in the manner of *chevaux de frise*,[1] at the bottom of steep slopes used by the animals as path-ways to the water, have proved unsatisfactory and are no longer used. There remained then, as a last resort, only their sharp weapons and this is how the Zoulou kings like Djaka and Dingaan procured the ivory they needed. Panda still uses this method to this day.

A week before the time fixed upon for the great hunt, heralds-at-arms travel throughout the land, from the banks of the Om-Pongola to the Touguela and from the seashore to the mountains of Quathlambéne, ordering all warriors to prepare their arms and to foregather at Om-Philos-Om-Schlopu, at the pyramid mountain of Om-Grooty.

From early morning on the eve of the appointed day, 20 000 men begin gathering from fifty leagues around; a seething black mass congregates on the green and red-brown crest of the 800-foot-high pyramid mountain, while the council of headmen, squatting on their heels, listen intently to the instructions of the chief as he sits in his great chair carved from a single piece of wood.

Dingaan commands the regiments, numbering 1 000 men each, to go out and form a vast network to round up the elephants and drive them in towards the foot of Om-Grooty. The order is immediately executed and files of black men wind their way down the steep sides of the mountain.

Om-Grooty, at other times completely deserted, now sees its bare summit metamorphosed into a town, without houses or tents it is true, but inhabited by naked men bearing an assortment of shields which conceal bundles of shining *omkondos*. The clear blue sky is the only roof these men require, although the despot has had his hut transported to the place, along with twenty or thirty of his four hundred wives and a few choice cattle to gladden his eyes.

The beaters, scattered for twelve leagues around, drive the herds of elephants towards Om-Schlaty-Om-Koulou. The scouts on Om-Grooty and Dingaan himself, armed with his telescope, a present from Gardiner, watch as the great herds are driven in, amidst clouds of dust. Then, putting his plan into action, Dingaan commands one herd to be brought forward by a thousand men, while the next is

1 Iron spikes used to repel a cavalry charge. *Translator's note*

pushed back by another thousand men; some animals are to be cornered while others are to be pursued. And all the while, seated on the heights from where he gazes down like an eagle, Dingaan the tyrant, with his will of iron, amuses himself by imagining the elephants as vile insects, his brave and intelligent people as a society of ants, and himself, in realisation of whose whim the whole scene has been enacted, as a god, if he has any idea of what a god might be.

This Om-Grooty which appealed to me so much, has something about it of the truly magical; towards the north it forms a long narrow spur, while it assumes in the south the aspect of a pyramid with its base standing in the waters of the Om-Philos, and its head high in the sky, where the vultures fly. From here the eye plunges into the depths of the forests, discovering all their secrets, and then runs over the steep mountain slopes, across the gorges and the precipices, taking in ten leagues at a glance as easily as if they were drawn on a map. Suffice it to say that from the top of Om-Grooty everything is revealed in miniature until imagination becomes illusion's fool.

When a reasonable number of elephants has been gathered together in Om-Schlaty-Om-Koulou, Dingaan and his captains count the isolated herds, discounting those composed only of females, and indicate to the heads of the regiments the groups of males which they are to attack, specifying the tactics they are to deploy in case of a change of position on the part of the elephants. However, whatever happens, the regiments must unite to form an immense circle in the centre of which the animals are to be contained, for to surround is the basis of all Amazoulou strategy, whether in hunting or in war.

Soon, every regiment has taken up its position and the elephants begin to grow restive because of the proximity of the warriors; only then is the purple cloak of the king hoisted to the top of a mast and the war-cry echoes out from the heights of Om-Grooty as a signal for the hunt to begin.

All at once, the mass of men rushes towards the mass of elephants. Blades gleam, men's voices rend the air and rise in a dull, rhythmic terrifying roar, but more piercing still is the sound which the elephants produce on their trumpets and which dominates all other sounds, so that it seems that the men must be doomed.

The animals, surprised by so many enemies, break their ranks and as soon as some large male is isolated from the herd, the warriors surround him and thrust at him a thousand times. Furious, the beast spins around and charges, overturning men and throwing shields and javelins into the air. Bold and intrepid, the men come on; ten, twenty, a hundred men sometimes, are subjected to this treatment. But in spite of his courage, his energy, his fury, the elephant finally succumbs to the force of numbers; the attack ceases for a moment. A man is crawling behind the animal; he is close upon its heels, while at its head other warriors divert its attention with harassment; the elephant's concentration is centred on them, for it is from this quarter that all his torment comes, and so he pays little attention to the man who is taking hold of his tail, who clings to it and then cuts it off. This done, the man rushes rapidly away to deposit at the feet of the despot the bloody trophy cut from the living victim.

Dingaan smiles at the offering. 'It is good,' he says, 'my people are brave! If it is my wish, my people can do anything! O Amazoulous! You are the masters of the earth! More numerous than the locusts, more courageous than lions, stronger than elephants, what nations of the earth can resist you? Have you not killed all other men, taken all their herds? Yes, you are the masters! It is good; let the elephant be killed now since I hold his tail. My heart is white! Go now.'

'It is good,' Dingaan repeats, rising from his seat and pointing with his index finger as a sign of the highest approbation, at the brave warrior who hastens away to execute the command.

The elephant, his anger draining away with his life-blood, is harassed once more. He falls to the ground, the muscles of his trunk are cut and the swarm of warriors settles on him like a cloud of vultures upon their prey. It is thus that the will of the despot triumphs over obstacles which are seemingly insurmountable, particularly when one considers the ineffectiveness of the weapons employed. But remember also that a people united is a strong people. Moreover, when the possibility of death is before him, the warrior does not try to evade it, for inevitable death is behind him, the ignominious death which the chief reserves for every coward, and which must be avoided at all costs.

As a result, the Amazoulou performs prodigious feats which are unheard of in the history of all other nations; an example of this being the occasion when Dingaan conceived the strange whim of re-enacting one of his dreams, and commanded his warriors to bring back alive a wild elephant. A thousand hands took hold, restrained and led the animal before the king. Consider that these men are naked and that their resources are as nothing compared with ours. But the fear of death is strong and endows them with strength sufficient to subdue even the elephant.

Now, if you consider the immense deployment of forces required for an Amazoulou royal hunt, and the meagre resources employed by the Boschjesmans to achieve the same ends, the advantage as to the excellence of method must indubitably rest with the latter. Indeed what could be simpler or more courageous?

This little man crawls along the ground, looking very much like an earth-coloured lizard. His head bristles with little poisoned arrows fixed in his hair, points uppermost. On his back is a quiver, roughly made from the skin of the gnu, and a bow seventy centimetres long; these are his usual weapons. But for elephant hunting, the Boschjesman carries a special weapon made for the purpose. This is a stick, thirty-five centimetres long with, at one end, a little triangular flat piece of iron lightly fixed into a notch from which it detaches itself at the slightest movement of withdrawal. This iron head is almost entirely covered in a thick layer of black poison, which melts in the heat like pitch. The man crawls on towards the elephant; from time to time he stops to listen; when he is a few paces off, he waits patiently for the animal to present his hindquarters. The animal moves, the man crawls closer, until he can touch the huge heels. The Boschjesman stands up, extends his arm and thrusts his weapon into the elephant's stomach, into the groin, or simply into the leg. A single drop of blood spurts out and death becomes inevitable. The elephant has felt almost nothing. He moves off only when he hears the sound of his attacker's retreating footsteps; but his blood begins to coagulate and a few hours later he dies.

And so the Boschjesman, all alone and without witnesses, performs with terrible dexterity, the work of a thousand Amazoulous who have no resource but their strength.

The South African Dutch have also invented a method aimed at preventing the animal from escaping. I have never witnessed the use of this method, but its effectiveness is attested to by various reports which leave me in no doubt that it has been put into practice.

When a Boer lives close to wooded country where there is a network of elephant paths, this is his method of proceeding. The first thing he does is to forge about forty harpoon heads which, together with the shaft, will measure forty-five centimetres. Next, he will choose some trees whose circumference is slightly larger than an elephant's foot. These trees provide him with stumps, forty centimetres high, in the centre of which the shaft of the harpoon will be firmly implanted. These preparations made, there remains only to discover the path which the elephants habitually use, and the rest of the business can be attended to, during daylight hours, by one man alone. In fact, all that has to be done, is to dig holes in the centre of the narrow pathway, which are capable of accommodating the harpoon sockets and, when these are in position, to cover them with grass and then with earth, which is carefully levelled.

These animals walk in single file and if the leader is fortunate enough to avoid stepping on the invisible spikes, one of the next in line will inevitably find himself nailed, while his misadventure will not even serve as a warning to those beind. The animal finds himself attached to a heel which is forty centimetres higher than his other feet. The efforts which he makes with his trunk to remove the obstacle are in vain, and serve only to augment the pain; as a result, he is finally forced to abandon the futile attempt. He is now in the position of being unable to escape because of the inequality of the length of his legs. The hunter, arriving the next day, finds the imprints of the wooden shoe, follows them and comes upon the animal which is in no position to avoid the fatal shot.

The people of southern Africa have never considered the possibility of capturing elephants live, taming them and putting them to serve man's interests. The needs of the natives are too elementary to necessitate the use of such monstrous animals and the whites of Dutch and French origin are determined to follow in the footsteps of their forefathers and never to deviate by introducing new methods. They are also too stupid to understand the advantages of such as innovation and too indolent to make the attempt.

Many of the whites know that in India the elephant serves man meekly and intelligently, but they offer the objection that the African variety is resistant to discipline and has a love of liberty which cannot successfully be overcome.

The story of an attempt of this nature has come to my ears. An elephant, captured very young, grew up tractable and docile at first, but soon became ill-natured and cantankerous. After persevering for seven years, his master was obliged to put him down, as he threatened to kill all those who approached him. But were all the necessary steps taken to educate him? I have my doubts.

There is today, living in the menagerie of the Jardin des Plantes, an African elephant which is perhaps even more docile than its Asiatic neighbour; this proves that the animal is capable of altering its character. However, the example of an animal which is supervised continually and which is in constant contact with man, does not provide conclusive proof; for even the lion himself has been trained to pull a cart, although the species is far from being capable of living subservient to the will of man.

However, when animal-loving societies turn their attention to the African elephant, this beautiful animal which is superior to the Asiatic variety in its grace, its height and its fearful tusks, they might consider experimenting on young animals separated from their mothers. If their efforts are not rewarded with success, they must never consider imitating the Indians by attempting to train adult animals. Only when the education of the young animal has been put to the test can definite conclusions be drawn with regard to the African species.

Perhaps it will be of some interest if I recount here what I know about the capture of a little elephant, no more than one metre high and which had not yet left its mother. I do not know whether any other traveller has described the simple method by which the young elephant quickly learns to follow the hunter.

When a herd of females is frightened and runs away, it frequently happens that the mother, concerned only with her own safety, forgets to look after her calf; the little one in his anxiety, searches for her in vain, turning this way and that in the hope of finding his way. The hunters quickly cut the little elephant off from the retreating herd. One of them stops him; the little animal charges and often tumbles the man over. But the man quickly wipes his hand over his forehead, which is wet with sweat, seizes the end of the elephant's trunk and rubs his hand over the double orifice. From that moment, peace is declared and, his anger forgotten, the young animal follows after the man as if he were his mother. Deceived by the smell, he attaches himself to his particular man and ruthlessly charges any other whose smell he does not know.

On three different occasions, my driver Henning succeeded, with the greatest of ease, in persuading a young elephant to follow him. On the first two of these occasions, the young animals were extremely petulant; they staved in the huts of the *mouzi* where we were to spend the night, sent the inhabitants sprawling, broke pots, sucked up water from the tanks and squirted it into the faces of passers-by, until I was obliged to consent reluctantly to their being put down. On the third occasion the outcome was no more fortunate. Fearing that the herd to which the little elephant belonged would return during the night and capsize my wagon, trample my men, and generally wreak havoc, I had him tied up 150 paces away at the foot of a steep precipice which was difficult of access. He was bound by a number of thongs and unable to move, but the rain came down and the little elephant made desperate attempts to escape; the knots tightened in such a manner that they strangled him.

Cow's milk, according to the Boers, does not at all agree with young elephants; they will drink it, but they will die within three weeks of being on this diet. If no other food is available, the milk can be mixed with an equal quantity of water; the healthiest food that one can give them is the water in which beef has been boiled.

When they are very young, these animals can justly be described as pretty. Their bodies are covered with hair which, by human standards, seems rough, but which to an elephant is soft down. Their movements are agile and their gait rapid. They are as capricious as children and take pleasure in turning men upside down one after another. Then suddenly abandoning this game, they turn to some other occupation, testing their strength by demolishing everything within reach. They are indefatigable and the only means of ensuring a moment's peace is to hitch up their forelegs.

The ancients were not the only ones to have found a certain

284

similarity between man and elephant. The Cafres share these ideas. *Uncklove montou omkoulou kakoulou* — 'The elephant is a very big man,' is how they describe him. The sight of the skeleton inspires this comparison. The position of the sexual parts and the udder of the female elephant, as well as their astonishing shape, lends substance to the comparison. The sensitive groping trunk further enhances the idea and, if one examines closely the qualities of the elephant, everything tends to bear out the comparison. The delicacy of his taste in the choice of food, his intelligence, his wisdom, are comparable to those of man. He even possesses modesty, that emotion which is considered to be exclusively human and which distinguishes man from beast. The elephant is a hundred times more refined than the Boschjesman. This is what ensures his place alongside man, morally speaking. But scientific classification does not take behaviour into account, it considers only the shape of the skeleton, and for this reason the noble beast is relegated to an unworthy position among the animals of low intelligence; for it is common knowledge that the other pachyderms have been provided with a meagre supply of intelligence and even less refinement.

However, it is a mistake to believe that the elephant owes the intelligence he possesses to the formation of his elevated brow which slightly resembles that of man. His brain is far from having the volume which it is commonly believed to possess. The brainpan is very small and between its upper surface and the top of the head there is a large space filled only with bony lamella; the brain, then, is covered over by two arches and one cannot in any way judge the interior by the shape and size of the exterior.

To state precisely the age which an African elephant may attain is not possible; as yet there has been no means of calculating the age of the wild elephant. One can only hazard a guess, which I am not prepared to do. The period of gestation is equally unknown. It must be the same as that of the Asiatic species, which it would be a simple matter to discover.

As for the method of copulation, this can only be surmised; presumably the female kneels down; this would seem necessary, although no one has seen it. A hunter from Natal called Molemann assured me that, not far from Om-Schlango, he and his son had come upon two elephants in this situation. He would have stayed to assure himself of how they were positioned, had not the male charged him furiously and come within an ace of hoisting him into the air with his trunk. His powers of recollection had been somewhat confused by fear, but nevertheless he believed that he was not wrong in saying that such was the position of the female.

The flesh of the elephant bears some resemblance to veal. All the parts are good, but the feet in particular provide a delicious meal.

The flesh of the adult or old elephant is the coarsest meat I know, the least of its fibres being as thick as a quill. It is too tough to be grilled, but requires at least eight hours cooking in water, the resultant broth being delicious and more particularly so when served with pieces of the trunk. The internal parts are similar to those of the pig, but of a firmer texture. The fat from the intestines is most sought after. When cold it resembles ant eggs or congealed olive oil.

The bones of the elephant, like those of the other great pachyderms, do not have a medullary canal running through the centre. A fine oily substance circulates in the cells, which are as porous as pumice stone. This grease may easily be extracted by crushing the bones and boiling them. It is the finest fat of any wild animal; the Cafres prize it highly and use it to anoint their skins.

The Amazoulous, whose prejudices are almost as binding as laws, will no more eat elephant flesh than they will that of the *Rhinoceros simus* or various other animals; whoever violates this rule is an *om-phogazane* (a worthless man). They prize only the fat and use it to anoint their skins before the dance; they also use it to soften their skin cloaks.

The Makatisse Cafres, the circumcised race from the interior, do not practise the same abstinence. To them, the elephant is regarded as a source of food, as are the two kinds of rhinoceros, the hippopotamus, the gnu, the quagga and even the spotted hyaena, that most ignoble and disgusting of animals whose task it is to dispose of the corpses of men.

The skin of the elephant is similar to that of the rhinoceros and the hippopotamus, but it is inferior to these; first of all because it is not as thick, and secondly because it is not smooth, but falls in a thousand wrinkles. These are the reasons why it is not in demand for the manufacture of *chambocks*, a sort of horse-whip nine feet long, designed to chastise the rear oxen. It is even less sought after, as its texture is not particuarly strong.

The elephant takes great care of his wrinkled skin which, however, provides him with no protection from the sting of certain winged insects. When he is in the forests, he wallows in mud puddles so that the clay covers his back and sides. To detach the old layers of skin, he rubs against the great trees; and when the heat becomes oppressive at about three o'clock in the afternoon he looks for a river where the water is about two feet deep and running over clean sand; picking up the wet sand he throws it all over his body which then cools off in the air; he follows this by spraying himself with water; in fact he pays as much attention to his toilet as a 'fashionable-type'.

Looking at the sad African elephant in the Jardin des Plantes, encrusted with the residue of old skin, no one would guess at the excessive cleanliness of the wild elephant, which every hunter has commented upon. But can one not make yet a further comparison with man himself? Consider the prisoner, does he not differ from the free man because of the filth of his skin? His disgust with life in a state of captivity is certainly the cause of this difference. It is to this same cause also that must be attributed the puny development of the bodies of these captured animals, which grow to only two-thirds of the size of those which are free. And so, had I encountered the female of the Jardin des Plantes on a hunting trip, she would have been safe from my bullet, for her appearance is insignificant and wretched indeed.

END OF THE FIRST VOLUME

NATURAL HISTORY INDEX

Like any other index, this one provides a guide to the information in the book: it enables the reader to turn quickly to the people, plants and animals mentioned by the author. It goes much further than most other book indexes, however, for it contains much supplementary information which, it is hoped, will be both useful and entertaining for the general reader, as well as the specialist in biology. Thus, besides pointing to material in the text, entries include factual information and, wherever possible, discussion or comment enabling the non-specialist to put facts into a wider biological context, as well as into social and historical perspective.

The index includes:

(a) Brief notes on the lives and the contributions to biological science made by scientists and travellers mentioned in the text, from Aristotle to some of Delegorgue's contemporaries. Special attention is given to those who appear to have had the greatest influence on Delegorgue as a naturalist, and also those whose work influenced, for good or ill, the study of the South African flora and fauna.

(b) Discussions of topics of scientific and medical interest raised or suggested by the text, e.g., the prevalence of some diseases and 19th century methods of treatment; the occurrence of, and attempts to control, certain pests; the preservation of natural history specimens.

(c) The identification and a brief classification of every animal and plant mentioned in the text. The entry word is the name first given by Delegorgue, whether this be a scientific, common, Dutch or vernacular name, and each is given precisely as Delegorgue gives it, with his often idiosyncratic, inconsistent or French phonetic spelling, his punctuation, his italicisation and his sometimes casual observance of nomenclatural conventions. Delegorgue's alternative names are given in each entry, and explained where necessary; all forms are appropriately cross-referenced, as are useful modern common names. (And, for the sake of uniformity, common names are without initial capitals. This is appropriate to a work of natural history, whereas it might be unacceptable in a specialist text on, say, ornithology.) Because many of the scientific names and usages given by Delegorgue are now outmoded – and some are confused or downright wrong – identification has at times had to be based on deduction or educated guesswork. Where this has occurred, lines of reasoning are summarised, and where exact identification has been impossible (as with some plants), the merits of various possibilites are argued.

Identification proceeds as far as species whenever possible, and generic and specific names are italicised and abbreviated in the accepted fashion, e.g., *Antidorcas marsupialis* (abbreviated *A. marsupialis*). To include authorities would, it was decided, be unnecessarily pedantic and these are as a rule omitted. For each plant the name of the family is given in brackets, e.g., (Poaceae). Animal classification is more complex, and two taxonomic subdivisions are usually supplied, and the following abbreviations are used, listed in descending order: P. ~ Phylum; S.P. ~ Subphylum; C. ~ Class; O. ~ Order; S.O. ~ Suborder; I.O. ~ Infraorder; F. ~ Family; S.F. ~ Subfamily. While biologists may wish for greater detail here, the taxonomic groups have been chosen with an eye to combining accessibility with ease of reading. Most of the animals listed are vertebrates of the three great classes Reptilia (reptiles), Aves (birds) and Mammalia (mammals) (all Phylum Chordata). Delegorgue gives less prominence (wrongly, some will consider) to invertebrates, and their identification and classification are therefore given simply and economically, without the sometimes cumbersome invertebrate names and terms that might dismay the lay-reader.

Delegorgue's use of metric and imperial measures is unpredictable. Generally, but not always, he uses the metric system for small measures and the imperial for large. In the index these measurements have been expressed in forms likely to be readily appreciated by the general reader rather than the scientist. It is, for example, easier to picture centimetres than millimetres. Also, some imperial measures, especially those based on human body proportions, such as the foot and the inch, remain convenient and are included after the metric version.

S.J. Alexander

Aarde vark also ant-bear, earth pig, *orycterope* ~ 44, 133
    Orycteropus afer, the antbear (sole survivor of O. Tubulidentata, F. Orycteropodidae). The Afrikaans name, *erdvark* ('aardvark' is not correct), means 'earth pig' as A.D. notes (44), and the animal is superficially piglike, though the head seems equine, with large, donkey-like ears. It is nocturnal, emerging from its extensive burrow to forage for ants or termites, digging into nests and inserting the long snout and very long, tubular tongue.
    O. afer is widely distributed in Africa, occurring in all habitats except dense forest, from Ethiopia to the Cape.
Acacia ~ *see* Mimosa
Addidas ~ *see Ibis addidas*
African fish eagle ~ *see under* Eagle
Africanus bicornis ~ *see* Rhinoceros
Aigoceres, Aigoceros equina ~ *see Bastaard guyms-book*
Ailments, human ~ *see under* Illness
Alauda hamgazy ~ *see under* Lark
Albatross *also Mouton du Cap* ~ 9
    Large marine birds (O. Procellariiformes, F. Diomedeidae). The com-

monest albatross off the south west coast of Africa is *Diomedea melanophris*, the blackbrowed albatross. A.D.'s *'mouton du Cap'* indicates his identification of *D. excelans*, the wandering albatross, once known as the 'Cape sheep'. (c.f. 'mutton-bird', old name for some petrels (q.v.) e.g. *Pterodroma lessonii*, the whiteheaded petrel).
Alkali ~ *see under* Snakebite
Alligator ~ *see under* Crocodile
Aloe ~ 245
    Possibly the bottlebrush aloe, *Aloe rupestris*, or *A. spectabilis*, the Natal aloe. Both are substantial, unbranched plants which would stand out on a hillside (Liliaceae).
    Although A.D. had noted very large aloes (see *Kooker-boom*) and must certainly have seen many others, he makes but this single reference to aloes *as* aloes.
Alum, as preservative *also* Salt and alum ~ 144, 184, 242
    Excellent results for taxidermy were achieved by rubbing a mixture of burnt alum and saltpetre into mammal skins. Burnt alum is a white, porous mass produced by heating

(Alum, *cont.*)

potash-alum (potassium aluminium sulphate) to 200°C; saltpetre is potassium nitrate (KNO_3).

Although saltpetre would have been in regular use (for pickling meat, and for some medicines), and therefore readily available, A.D. seems instead to have carried common salt (sodium chloride: NaCl) with him, probably in the form of rock salt as it had to be crushed (184). His method worked well – he produced some fine skins – but alum alone was not, apparently, successful in the rainy spring weather.

Amakaho ~ *see* Monkey

Amaryllis ~ 32

Amaryllis itself must be excluded from this charming picture, for it does not occur in the area.

Possibilities are *Ammocharis, Nerine, Brunsvigea* or (perhaps most satisfactorily 'pink and white', and enchanting to see) *Crinum* (Amaryllidaceae).

Amethyst sunbird ~ *see Souimanga*

Ammonia ~ *see under* Snakebite

Amphibian/amphibious animal

Words used generally in zoology, then and now, for any animal making its living both on land and in water. A.D. thus correctly applies them to the hippopotamus (q.v.).

Anas madagascariensis ~ *see* Teal

Angolan roller ~ *see* Roller, Angolan

Anhinga ~ *see* Snake bird

Animalcules ~ 46

Very small animals – in this case, the macroscopic faunal component of marine surface plankton. The marine biologist and student of invertebrate zoology will find this vague and all-embracing reference frustrating.

Ant. ~

A.D.'s abbreviation for the genus *Antilope*, no longer in use for any southern African antelope.

Ant. Canna ~ *see* Eland

Ant. melampus ~ 130

The impala, *Aepyceros melampus* (F. Bovidae, S.F. Aepycerotinae): *Antilope melampus* is a former name.

The impala is graceful, with a shiny, reddish coat and long, slender legs. It is still plentiful in north-east Natal, but, strangely, A.D. mentions it only once.

Ant. mergens Burschellii ~ *see* Duyker

Antbear ~ *see Aarde vark*

Ants ~ 133, 220

It is remarkable that A.D. was so long in South Africa before making the painful acquaintance of ants (220). Many species of brownish to reddish ants are indigenous to the region, and a number of these will sting if the nest is disturbed. Possibly the hut in which A.D. tried to sleep had been untenanted for some while, during which the ants had made their nest. The antbear (see *Aarde vark*) will take ants as well as termites, (q.v.). (Insects: O. Hymenoptera, F. Formicidae).

Ants, white ~ *see* Termites

Apiaster ~ *see* Bee-eaters

Arachnids, tracheal ~ *see* Ticks

Arago, Jacques Étienne Victor ~ 19–21

At 18, J.E.V. Arago, the third of four variously celebrated brothers, was a member of L.C. de S. Freycinet's *Uranie* voyage of exploration (1817–1821). Following this he turned to journalism and the drama – perhaps appropriately, for his writings on South Africa seem to have been fanciful and highly coloured.

Arago travelled again later, but not to Africa: he died in Brazil. It has not been possible to learn more of the 'famous lion hunt' (21) or to trace Arago's hunting companion, Rouvières.

Ardea bubulcus also Cattle egret, Locust bird, *Spring-Haan-Voogel*, Tickbird ~ 53, 166–7

Bubulcus ibis, the cattle egret or tickbird (O. Ciconiiformes, F. Ardeidae: herons, egrets, bitterns). Widespread in southern Africa. It often, as A.D. records, perches on the backs of large mammals and feeds on their ticks (q.v.), but ticks form a relatively small part of the diet, which consists mainly of insects and other small animals disturbed by the movements of the mammals. A.D. seems to be describing *B. ibis* in its breeding plumage (166), and seasonal plumage variation may account for apparent textual blurring among the herons and egrets. A.D. seems also – perhaps through faulty notes or memory – to have confused the feeding behaviour of *B. ibis* with that of the oxpecker (166; *see Buphaga*).

A.D. errs in applying 'Locustbird' to

(Ardea bubulcus, cont.)

B. *ibis*. The name was given, as *Spring-haans Vogel* (c.f. Afrikaans: *Sprinkaan voël*) to *Ciconia ciconia*, the white stork (*see* Stork), and (as *Klein Springhaan Vogel*) to both the wattled starling (*Creatophora cinerea*) and the blackwinged pratincole (*Glareola nordmanni*). These birds are reported to gather – sometimes to flock – round locust swarms and, with starlings and kestrels, to follow veld fires for insects. *See also* Heron; Stork

Ardea ombretta ~ *see* Umbretta

Aristotle (384–322 BC) ~ 23–5

A pupil of Plato; later, tutor to Alexander the Great. Justly called the father of science, he founded mechanics, physiology and natural history. His *Historia animalium* is keenly observed and often startlingly accurate.

Reverence for Aristotle, however, caused stagnation in the biological sciences – and indeed, in science as a whole – for a very long time. A.D. shows a 19th century residue of this, with a tendency to distort or muddle new information so as to fit or match it to some Aristotelian comment or description. While every scientist of the early 19th century would have been conscious of Aristotle's towering presence it is probable that his genius and his contribution to science have not, even now, been given their true perspective and their proper value.

Atropos ~ *see* Sphinx

Aulacaudus ~ *see* Rat, river

Baboon ~ 14, 22

The chacma baboon, *Papio ursinus* (S.O. Anthropoidea, F. Cercopithecidae), was originally described from the Cape of Good Hope. It was common and widespread, as is clear from many place names (22). It had already begun to disappear from some localities (e.g. Table Mountain, 14) and A.D. reports only one actual sighting (22).

It is curious that A.D. does not use '*chacma*', for Cuvier (q.v.) had used it as a colloquial name in French in 1819.

Bald ibis ~ *see* Ibis, bald

Banana, wild ~ 78, 221

The Natal strelitzia, *Strelitzia nicolai* (Strelitziaceae). This tall, coastal plant is known as the Natal wild banana, for it does resemble the true bananas (Musaceae) in being fleshy, with large, rectangular, tattered leaves, glossy green above and greyish below. The true wild banana, *Ensete ventricosum*, has its natural distribution in South Africa restricted to a small area of the northern Transvaal.

Barbet ~ 54

Small- to medium-sized birds, with typically heavy bill (O. Piciformes, F. Capitonidae). Several different species are common residents of the Natal coastal forest, including *Lybius torquatus* (blackcollared barbet), *Pogoniulus pusillus* (redfronted tinker barbet), *P. bilineatus* (goldenrumped tinker barbet) and *Trachyphonus vaillantii* (crested barbet).

Bastaard guyms-book also Aigoceres, Aigoceros equina ~ 109, 240

The roan antelope (Afrikaans: *bastergemsbok*), *Hippotragus equinus* (F. Bovidae, S.F. Hippotraginae). A large antelope with a coat so distinctive that A.D. easily recognised it from a skin (240): brown, with a slight strawberry tinge in certain lights. The relatively short, ridged and recurved horns of both sexes were the source of a number of 19th century spelling variations on a generic name meaning 'goat-horned': *Egocerus, Aegocera, Aigocerus, Oegocerus, Aegocerus* and *Aegocoerus*. A.D. adds his own variants. Roan were once plentiful, but distribution is now patchy.

Bastaard-makouw, Bastard muscovy duck ~ *see* Goose

Bastergemsbok ~ *see* Bastaard *guymsbook*

Bateleur ~ *see under* Eagle

Bee-eaters *also* Apiaster, *berg-swaluwe* ~ 31, 32, 54

Merops apiaster, the European bee-eater, common and widespread in southern Africa, where it winters and breeds, inhabiting woodland, savannah and scrubby grassland. Flocks circle high in the air and roost in tall trees. (O. Apodiformes, F. Meropidae).

The old name, *berg-swaluwe* (= mountain swallows) is evocative of

(Bee-eaters, *cont.*)
the swallow-like diurnal habit: they
feed and migrate by day. Prey, including a wide range of insects besides
wild and hive bees, is caught on the
wing.
Bees ~ 242, 248–9
Apis mellifica, the honey bee, a familiar social insect and one whose
honey-laden nests seem to have been
commonplace discoveries for A.D. and
his men (242). Several races or varieties of *A. mellifica* occur in Africa (O.
Hymenoptera, F. Apidae).
Belon, Pierre ~ 23–4
16th Century French naturalist who
founded two botanic gardens over 100
years before the creation of the *Jardin
des Plantes*. After travelling widely in
the Middle East he wrote treatises on
plants, birds and fishes. He is still
revered by French zoologists as one of
the first to establish vertebrate
skeletal homologies. Cuvier (q.v.) will
surely have owed a great debt to
Belon.
Berg-swaluwe ~ *see* Bee-eaters
Bicornis, Bicornis africanus ~ *see* Rhinoceros
Bird of heaven ~ *see* Phaeton
'Birds of Satan' ~ *see* Petrel
Bittern ~ 28, 152
For A.D. the bittern epitomises
camouflage or concealment. Indeed,
Botaurus stellaris (called the
Eurasian bittern, but fairly wide-
spread in Africa, also) is adept at
concealment. This shy, solitary marsh
bird adopts the defensive 'bittern
posture' among the reeds, with head
and neck upthrust so that the
vertically streaked plumage blends
with the background (O. Ciconii-
formes, F. Ardeidae).
Black mamba ~ *see under Memba*
Black rhinoceros ~ *see under* Rhinoceros
Black wildebeest ~ *see* Gnu
Blackbird ~ *see* White-breasted blackbird
Blacksmith plover ~ *see* Plover
Blauw-wild-beest ~ *see Catoblepas gorgon*
Bleek-steen-book ~ *see Steen-book*
Blesbok ~ *see Gazella albifrons*
Bloulou ~ *see Poff-adder*
Blouwildebees, blue wildebeest ~ *see
Catoblepas gorgon*
Boa-python ~ *see* Python
Boar, wild ~ *see* Bushpig; Warthog
Bonte-book also Gazella pygarga ~ 43
Damaliscus dorcas dorcas, the bonte-

bok (F. Bovidae, S.F. Alcelaphinae).
The common name of this medium-
sized antelope refers to the coat which
includes besides white, several shades
of brown, in parts glossed purple (Afrikaans *bont*: many coloured).
In addition to the protection noted
by A.D., farmers had, in 1837, begun
to set aside land as reserves for bontebok, without which they might have
become extinct, for today they are the
least common of the southern African
antelope. A former name is *Antilope
pygarga*: A.D. seems at times to use
Gazella and *Antilope* interchangeably
(*see* Gazelle).
Another former name is *A. albifrons*, referring to the white blaze
from forehead to nostrils. However,
A.D. almost certainly applies *Gazella
albifrons* (q.v.) to the closely related
blesbok.
Boom-slange also Tree snake ~ 137
Dispholidus typus, the *boomslang*
(Afrikaans: tree snake) is one of many
tree-dwelling snakes. The male is
green, the female usually light- or
darkbrown. The body is slender and
agile, but A.D. exaggerates the length,
which is 120–155 cm. (4–5 ft). The
snake rests on a branch, coiled, un-
moving and so well camouflaged that
birds may perch on it. A.D. believes
the 'hypnotizing' myth, which may
have arisen from the boomslang's
habit of holding prey immobile in its
jaws while venom trickles down the
grooved fangs into the wound. The
venom is potent: 0.0002 mg is sufficient to kill a pigeon (S.O. Serpentes,
F. Colubridae).
Bos cafer ~ *see* Buffalo
Bosch-luys ~ *see* Ticks and mites
Bosch touw boom ~ *see* Fig tree
Bosch-vaark ~ *see* Bushpig
Boselaphus oreas ~ *see* Eland
Botterklapper ~ *see Strychnos*, edible
Brindled gnu ~ *see under Catoblepas gorgon*
Brown hyaena ~ *see* Hyaena
*Buceros abyssinicus, Buceros buc-
cinator* ~ *see* hornbill
Buffalo *also Bos cafer, Iniaty* ~ xii, 20–1,
72, 73, 74, 97–8, 164, 166, 175, 178,
179, 181, 184, 189, 192, 193, 210–11,
215–16, 218–19, 220, 235–6, 238–9,
241, 255–6, 260, 261, 268
Syncerus caffer (formerly *Bos caffer*),
the Cape buffalo (F. Bovidae, S.F.

293

(Buffalo *cont.*)

Bovinae). This is a large, ox-like animal, dark in colour and heavily built, with massive horns swinging out and down from bulky bosses on the forehead. Once, huge herds of buffalo (211) roamed widely in South Africa; now, it is confined to the Transvaal south to the Swaziland border and to the Natal game reserves.

S. caffer is a very dangerous animal and, as A.D. comments, is unlikely to have been domesticated (19–21). Herds may charge in panic, and a single agitated animal may fearfully injure a victim by goring and trampling, as A.D. discovered (235–7).

'*Iniaty*' is from the Zulu for buffalo: *inyathi*, hence '*Om-Sinyate*': *Umsinyathi* – river of buffaloes.

Buffon, Georges Louis Leclerc, Compte de (1707–88) ~ 23–4, 28n, 160, 250

18th century French naturalist and author of the massive *Histoire naturelle* (44 vols, the last eight completed posthumously by Lacépède). Buffon took brilliant first steps on the long path of evolutionary thinking by setting up anatomical evidence for animal relationships and suggesting, for example, that an ape might be an imperfect man. Buffon is respected, even today, especially by French zoologists, though the present reaction against unquestioning veneration does help reduce the kinds of distortions A.D. and Buffon himself (24) introduced when evaluating new information in the light of older work. A.D.'s glee at disproving Buffon in even a minor matter (160) is refreshing.

Bugs ~ 96

A.D. probably refers to the bedbug, *Cimex* sp: *C. lectularius*, perhaps, or *C. rotundatus* (insects: O. Hemiptera). Improved building methods, cleanliness and the development of insecticides now help control these insects, but where hygiene is poor – in Pietermaritzburg and elsewhere – they still flourish. They produce a characteristic smell and their bites are irritating, but they transmit no disease.

See also Insects, biting and sucking.

Buphaga ~ 53, 166

Oxpeckers: *Buphagus africanus* and *B. erythrorhynchus* – the yellowbilled and redbilled oxpecker (O. Passeri-formes, F. Buphagidae). These birds feed on the ticks (q.v.) and other ectoparasites of big game, domestic cattle, etc., and both species clamber about on the host mammal, clinging on with curved claws and using the stiff tail as a prop and for balance. Although A.D. saw both species in Natal, their distribution is now very restricted because of cattle dipping and because of diminished ranges of big game: *B. africanus* is no longer recorded in Natal and *B. erythrorhynchus* comes no further south than northern Zululand. *See also Ardea bubulcus*

Burchell, W.J. ~ (xi), 213

Renowned traveller and naturalist. Author of *Travels in the Interior of South Africa*, in two volumes, published in London in 1822 and 1824.

A.D. invariably spells his name 'Burschell', (e.g. 213) which is surprising, for he would surely have been well-known and already (as A.D. indicated) had had his name attached to various animals he had discovered, described or named. He remains an inextricable part of South African vertebrate zoology in, for example, *Pterocles burchelli* (Aves), and *Equus burchelli* (Mamm.); also as an authority, e.g. *Connochaetes taurinus* Burchell.

Burschell's leaping antelope ~ *see* Duyker

Bush lice ~ *see* Ticks and mites

Bushpig *also Bosch-vaark, inglobu, sus larvatus* ~ 130, 189, 215, 232, 241, 244, 257–8

Most of A.D.s references to 'wild boar' are doubtless to the bushpig (Afrikaans: *bosvark*), formerly *Sus larvatus*, now *Potamochoerus porcus* (O. Artiodactyla, F. Suidae), although he does not distinguish *P. porcus* from the warthog (q.v.) until the final chapter (257) and it is impossible to be certain.

Bushpigs are gregarious, living in groups (sounders) of up to 12. They forage in damper places than do warthog, rooting up bulbs, tubers, rhizomes and soil-dwelling invertebrates. Males may reach 80 kg and, if cornered, become dangerous and slash with their sharp lower canines. A.D.'s '*inglobu*' is from Zulu, *ingulube*: pig.

Bustard ~ xii, 36, 81, 106

Ground-dwelling birds of chicken- to

(Bustard *cont.*)
turkey-size, occurring in open country.

In the Cape A.D. may have seen the kori bustard (*Ardeotis kori*), Stanley's bustard (*Neotis denhami*), Ludwig's bustard (*N. ludwigii*) or the karoo korhaan (*Eupodotis vigorsii*). The feathers used in Zulu ceremonial dress (106) may have been those of *N. denhami*, *E. ruficrista* (redcrested korhaan) or *E. melanogaster* (black-bellied korhaan) (O. Gruiformes, F. Otididae).

Caama ~ 109
The red hartebeest, *Alcelaphus buselaphus* (F. Bovidae, S.F. Alcelaphinae). The vernacular (probably Khoi) name, *caama*, is retained and distinguishes the extant *A.b. caama* from the extinct north African *A.b. buselaphus*. The ungainly appearance of this large antelope is deceiving, for it is fleet of foot. The body colour varies from red-brown to yellowish fawn, with lighter rump, blackish or plum-coloured legs and other dark markings on the face and shoulders.

The red hartebeest is gregarious, occurring in herds of about 20 which coalesce with others to form aggregations of 300 or more. It is surprising that A.D. mentions this animal only once, for at that time it would have been one of the commonest antelope. It might, possibly, be that he mistook herds with the paler colouration for some other large antelope, e.g. eland (q.v.).

The animal is now confined to the north west in southern Africa.

Caffer-Boom ~ 128
Probably the coast erythrina, *Erythrina caffra*, once known as the kaffirboom; otherwise, the common coral tree, *E. lysistemon*. The former has orange flowers, while the coral tree's flowers are a beautiful clear scarlet (Fabaceae).

Caiman ~ *see under* Crocodile
Calabash tree ~ *see Weld-calebasses-boom*
Calao ~ *see* Hornbill
Canadian otter ~ *see Lutra canadensis*
Candle bush ~ *see Kaarsh-boschjes*
Cane rat ~ *see* Rat, river
Canna ~ *see* Eland

Cape cobra ~ *see under Geele-slange*
Cape fox ~ *see* Fox
Cape hyaena ~ *see under* Hyaena
Cape jerboa ~ *see Spring has*
Cape penguin *also* Penguin ~ 25, 27
Flightless marine birds (O. Sphenisciformes, F. Spheniscidae). The body is plump and the wings are flattened to form flippers for swimming. A.D. probably refers to *Spheniscus demersus*, the jackass penguin, the most common penguin on the southern African coast.
Cape petrel ~ *see under* Petrel
Carapaces ~ *see under* Crustaceans
Cardan ~ 28n
French version of the name of Girolamo Cardano (1501–1576), Italian mathematician, physician and astrologer. The only one of the quartet of authorities quoted by Buffon (q.v.) to have been readily traceable. It is likely that the others (Charleton, Rondelet and Wormius) were later disciples of Cardan, a remarkable – indeed prophetic – thinker, whose *De Varietate Rerum* (1557) dwelt upon 'progressive development' in the natural world. Animals were not created for human use, he said: they exist for their own sakes.

Cardan may have been factually inaccurate but his insights will certainly have provided a foundation for Buffon's own zoological thinking. Buffon may therefore have placed reliance on Cardan's every word.
Carée-Boom, Carrée-Hout-Boom ~ 33, 36
The karee bush or tree. Several species of *Rhus* (Anacardiaceae) have this common name, but A.D. probably refers to *R. lancea*, a small to medium sized (8m approx.) evergreen tree, characteristic of riverine fringe thicket and plentiful in the south western Cape.

'Karee' is the Khoi name for the plant, whose many branches provide wood too twisted for planks, but useful for fenceposts and implement handles. Such usefulness apparently made one tree noteworthy enough for its name to have been given to a homestead (36).
Caruncular Coot ~ *see* Coot
Catoblepas gnou ~ *see* Gnu
Catoblepas gorgon also Blauw-wild-beest, Ingogoné, taurina ~ 130, 258–60
Connochaetes taurinus, the blue

(Catoblepas gorgon cont.)
wildebeest or brindled gnu (Afrikaans: *blouwildebees*) (F. Bovidae, S.F. Alcelaphinae). In the former name, *Catoblepas gorgon*, '*gorgon*' is a corruption of the Zulu name *inkonkoni*, rendered phonetically by A.D. as *Ingogoné*. Some authorities still give kongoni as an accepted common name. His '*seu taurina*' (*see Seu* for explanation) indicates that *taurina* was an acceptable alternative as specific name, retained now as *taurinus*. Although *C. taurinus* is no longer to be found where A.D. saw it, it is still plentiful north of the Orange River, and is common in the Umfolozi and Hluhluwe game reserves. *C. taurinus* travels in herds of from a dozen to several hundred individuals.

Cattle egret ~ *see under Ardea bubulcus*
Cattle sickness ~ 182
Probably redwater fever. Red blood cells are destroyed and haemoglobin is excreted, colouring the urine as A.D. describes. This leaves animals anaemic, with enlarged spleens. Presently capillaries, including those of the brain, become blocked. The disease organism, *Babesia bovis,* is transmitted by ticks (*see* Ticks and mites).

Cayman ~ *see under* Crocodile
Centipede ~ 55
Swift-running, carnivorous terrestrial arthropods, with long, sinuous and flattened segmented bodies and many pairs of legs. Centipedes are unlikely to be the preferred food of hornbills (q.v.). The ground hornbill does not, reportedly, take myriapods at all, while the crowned hornbill takes the slower, non-poisonous, and herbivorous millipedes. In these the long, segmented body is often cylindrical and the paired legs are shorter and more numerous than those of centipedes (both S.P. Myriapoda). *See also* Woodlouse

Cephalopus mergens Burschellii ~ *see* Duyker
Cephalopus natalensis ~ *see Rooye-booken*
Cetaceans ~ 45
The Order Cetacea includes those marine mammals that have a superficially fish-shaped body, with fins and a fluked tail. *See* Dolphin; Whales and whaling.

Chamois ~ *see Rhee-book*

Charleton ~ *see under* Cardan
Cheetah ~ 34
Acinonyx jubatus (F. Felidae, S.F. Felinae). The fastest animals on earth over short distances. Elegant cats with beautifully spotted coats which have always been prized. Still widely distributed in South Africa but almost completely absent from the Cape Province.

Cholera ~ 63
An acute bacterial infection (*Vibrio cholerae*) contracted from food and drinking water contaminated by human faeces. Thus, the drinking of unboiled, faecally contaminated stream or pondwater may be directly related to the incidence of cholera. As severe cramps and diarrhoea are cholera symptoms, cholera could have been one of the diseases once grouped as 'dysentery' (q.v.).

Cholera cannot, of course, be contracted simply by inhaling malodorous gases released as corpses decompose. A.D.'s oft-iterated belief in this notion serves only to illustrate the paucity of epidemiological information available in his time. *See also* 256; Crocodile; Locusts

Ciconia umbellata ~ *see under* Stork
Civet ~ 133
The African civet, *Civettictis civetta*, is small, sleek, somewhat doglike and patterned in grey, black and white. That a python (q.v.) might, briefly, be taken for a civet is quite possible (F. Viverridae, S.F. Viverrinae: civets and genets). Even more snakelike, however, is the striped weasel, *Poecilogale albinucha* (Afrikaans: *Slangmuishond*), lowslung, longbodied and slender (3–4cm/1.5" diam.) (F. Mustelidae, S.F. Mustelinae). *See* Mongoose; Skunk

Cobra, Cape ~ *see under Geele-slange*
Cobra, Egyptian ~ *see Geele-slange*
Cobra, spitting ~ *see Spouwer-slange*
Coconut, ~ *see Wild-klaapper-noot*
Coerulea ~ *see Riet-Book*
Colds ~ 12
It is highly unlikely that sudden climatic change would give everyone at the Cape a viral infection on the same day. No doubt 'cold in the head' means a simple runny nose – reaction by the sinus cavities to change of temperature, humidity and air pressure. It is interesting to note in this connection

(Colds *cont.*)

that the strong south-easterly wind so familiar to all who have been to Cape Town has long been known as 'The Cape doctor'.

Coliphymus concolor ~ see under Touraco/ Turaco

Coot *also* Caruncular coot ~ 22, 25

Water birds (O. Gruiformes, F. Rallidae: rails, crakes, gallinules, moorhens, coots etc.). *Fulica cristata*, the redknobbed (A.D.'s 'caruncular') coot, inhabits almost all southern African inland waters.

Cormorant *also* Little cormorant, river cormorant ~ 25, 66, 69

Medium to large birds of marine and inland waters (O. Pelicaniformes, F. Phalacrocoracidae). A.D. probably refers to the smallest of the southern African cormorants, *Phalacrocorax africanus*, the reed cormorant, which is restricted to inland waters.

He would surely also have seen *P. carbo*, the whitebreasted cormorant, and *P. capensis*, the Cape cormorant.

Corythaix porphyreolopha ~ see under Touraco/Turaco

Cotton tree ~ 166

Possibly *Ipomoea albivenia* (Convolvulaceae), the climbing kapok or wild cotton. The large, tuberous roots are eaten, and water in which they have been cooked is given as a bland, nutritious food to newborn babies in Zimbabwe. Their use in cases of snakebite (q.v.) is not recorded and it may simply be that they were given, as wholesome and digestible, to any invalid.

Less likely is the milk bush or wild cotton, *Xysmalobium undulatum* (Asclepiadaceae), a stout, herbaceous perennial of 1.8m. Although many asclepiads have useful roots, in this species it is not the roots but the leaves that are used, as spinach.

The true cotton plant was not available – it was introduced into Natal in the 1850s. Several of its relatives (*Hibiscus* spp: Malvaceae) produce usable fibre and many remedies, but there is no record of use for snakebite.

Crab eater ~ 96

Probably a kingfisher (O. Alcediniformes, F. Alcedinidae). Several species take river crabs, including (appropriate to the locality), the giant kingfisher (*Ceryle maxima*) the halfcollared kingfisher (*Alcedo semitorquata*) and the brownhooded kingfisher (*Halcyon albiventris*).

Crane *including* Numidian and wattled crane ~ 69, 106, 199, 201

Very large, long-legged birds (O. Gruiformes, F. Gruidae). A.D.'s 'Numidian crane' is probably *Balearica regulorum*, the crowned crane (which occurs as far north as Kenya and Uganda: hence, possibly, 'Numidian') – a very large and handsomely crested and coloured bird which may have been the source of the long crane feathers used in Zulu ceremonial dress (106, 199, 201).

The wattled crane, *Grus carunculata* (69) is elegant and heronlike and prefers midland to highland marshes, vleis and moist grassland. Whitish wattles hang under the chin.

Crocodile *also* Alligator, caiman, cayman ~ 45–6, 60, 62–5, 142–6, 150, 152, 154, 155, 157

Crocodylus niloticus, the Nile crocodile (O. Crocodilia, F. Crocodylidae), widely distributed in Africa and once very plentiful in southern African rivers – as witness many river and place-names: no wonder A.D. writes reprovingly in this connection of Le Vaillant (*see* Levaillant; 45–6). These large and ancient reptiles spend much time basking on river banks or motionless in the water. They are watchful and can produce a sudden and startling turn of speed in pursuit of prey (mammals and birds). This, and the narrow eyes in the long, flattened skull, gives them an air of cunning (152, 154). The Boers apparently used 'crocodile' and 'caiman' or 'cayman' interchangeably and A.D. often does the same, including 'alligator' for good measure although he probably knew better (62). Briefly, alligators and caiman (both F. Alligatoridae) do not occur in Africa: they are New World reptiles, although there is one group of alligators in China.

C. niloticus was venerated by the ancient Egyptians (63), who worshipped also two crocodile gods. The Egyptians valued everything related to the seasonal rise and fall of the Nile (*see also* Ibis, sacred). A.D. errs, however, in likening the role or status of crocodiles in Egypt to that of the

(Crocodile *cont.*)

Indian crocodile (the gharial or gavial, *Gavialis gangeticus*: F. Gavialidae). Hindu (A.D.s 'Indou') reverence for the gharial arose partly by association (the Ganges and some other rivers are sacred), partly from fear, but there is apparently no crocodilian god and A.D.'s story of human sacrifice, if true, is more likely to have come from the near or middle east than from India. The gavial does feed on human corpses consigned to rivers and might, by so doing, help in a very small way to control the spread of disease, but not – as A.D. suggests – merely by eliminating the effluvia of decay (*see also* Cholera; Dysentery; Pestilence; Plague).

Crow *also Ourigourap*, white crow, *witte-kraai* ~ 36–7, 45, 80

A.D.'s white crow/*witte-kraai*/*ourigourap* (*ouri*, San: white) (37) is probably the pied crow, *Corvus albus*. Later references could be to *C. albus*, *C. capensis* (the black crow) or *C. albicollis* (the whitenecked raven) all of which would take locusts (q.v.) when available (80) (O. Passeriformes, F. Corvidae).

Crowned crane ~ *see under* Crane

Crowned guinea-fowl ~ *see under* Guinea-fowl

Crowned hornbill ~ *see under* Hornbill

Crustaceans ~ 23–4

A group of primarily aquatic arthropods especially numerous in the sea. A.D. probably refers to large forms, such as crabs, crayfish and lobsters. He misuses 'carapace' to refer to the whole body of the animal. Strictly, the word applies only to the cuticular shield over head and thorax. *See also* Hyaena

Cuckoo *includes* Diderick, golden-green and Klaas cuckoo ~ 54

A.D. records the presence of three species of *Chrysococcyx* in forest near Port Natal (O. Cuculiformes, F. Cuculidae: cuckoos, coucals etc.).

The 'Diderick' cuckoo is *C. caprius*, the Diederik or Didric cuckoo: small, with metallic green above, bronze reflections and a white stripe on eyebrow and midcrown. This is the most widespread and abundant of the golden cuckoos. The name derives from the plaintive call: *dee-dee-deederik*, and was given to it by

Le Vaillant (*see* Levaillant).

The 'golden-green' cuckoo is *C. cupreus*, the emerald cuckoo: small; the male bright metallic green with chrome yellow belly; common in many parts of Natal and found throughout Africa. 'Klaas' cuckoo is *C. klaas*, Klaas's cuckoo, named by Le Vaillant after his faithful Hottentot servant, Klaas. It is small; the male is bright metallic green above and on the sides of the chest; there is a small white patch behind the eye.

C. klaas has a range similar to that of *C. cupreus*, though it is more active and has been recorded further south. Evergreen and riverine forests are favourite haunts of all three species.

Cuckoo, informer ~ *see* Honey-guide

Cuvier, Georges L.C.F. Dagobert, *Baron* (1769–1832) ~ 21

As would any French naturalist of the period, A.D. refers respectfully to Cuvier as the 'father of modern science'. Indeed, Cuvier had been led by his studies of the marine fauna of Normandy to develop the principles of comparative anatomy: thus emerged a new line of zoological thought now taken for granted as fundamental. Further, Cuvier founded the science of vertebrate palaeontology via a study of fossil elephants, and devised his own system of classification of the animal kingdom. He dominated 19th Century thinking in zoology and it is not surprising that, having weightier matters on his mind, this prolific author should have perpetuated errors handed down from less well-informed times. Cuvier held several posts of academic and scientific eminence during his life.

He is best known for his five-volume *Leçons d'Anatomie comparée* (1800–05), and for *Le Regne Animal* in four volumes (1817, revised 1829). *See also* Cardan; Duvernoy, Georges Louis.

Cynhyaena venatica ~ *see* Wild dog

'Damned souls' ~ *see* Petrel

Dassie ~ *see* Rock rabbits

Date palm, ~ *see Wild-dattle-boom*

Death's head moth ~ *see* Sphinx

Diderick cuckoo, Diederick cuckoo ~ *see under* Cuckoo

Diseases, animal ~ *see* Cattle sickness (redwater fever), *Paerde sickt* (equine influenza)*; see also* Ticks and mites
Diseases, human ~ *see* Illnesses
Dog, wild ~ *see* Wild dog
Dolphin ~ 4
So many different genera and species of dolphin, porpoise, killer and false killer whale occur along the Atlantic seaboard of southern Africa that it is impossible to guess at the identity of those caught on A.D.'s voyage (marine mammals of O. Cetacea, F. Delphinidae). *See also* Cetaceans
Donkey-buck ~ *see* Water-buck
Doorn-veld ~ *see* Mimosa
Dove *also* turtle dove ~ 21, 26, 66
A.D.'s description of the repetitive call (21) is vague enough to fit the calls of many dove species common in the western Cape (O. Columbiformes, F. Columbidae: doves and pigeons).

Doves often seem sleepy or sluggish – perhaps that was why A.D. elected, parched and weary, to use one of these easy-to-kill birds to slake his thirst (26).

The 'turtle dove' (66) is doubtless *Streptopelia capicola*, the Cape turtle dove: it frequents riverine bush throughout southern Africa.
Duck ~ 22, 25, 28, 69, 81, 189
Several species of these familiar waterbirds are common throughout southern Africa (O. Anseriformes, F. Anatidae: ducks, geese, swans).
Duiker, grey ~ *see* Duyker
Duiker, red ~ *see* Rooye-booken
Duvernoy, Georges Louis ~ 152
Like many natural history scholars of the 18th and 19th Centuries, Duvernoy began as a medical man: he was doctor to the Army of the Alps. Later he helped Cuvier (q.v.) in the preparation of *Leçons d'Anatomie Comparée*, and A.D. knew him as a comparative anatomist. However, the deductions made by Duvernoy based on skeletal material are incorrect as quoted. Duvernoy held a chair of Natural History for 10 years and in 1837 was a successor to Cuvier at the College de France.
Duyker *also Ant. mergens Burschellii, Cephalopus mergens Burschellii*, Burschell's leaping antelope ~ 22, 67, 151, 241
Sylvicapra grimmia, the common or grey duiker (Afrikaans: diver), a small

antelope with short simple horns (F. Bovidae, S.F. Cephalophinae). It makes characteristic plunging or diving leaps. Some former names from the 19th century, when several species and sub-species (since discarded) were recognised, are: *Antilope burchellii, A. mergens* and *Cephalophus grimmii*. This early taxonomic splitting arose because of the colour variation exhibited by *S. grimmia*. It ranges from greyish-buff (151) to reddish yellow, and A.D. apparently saw both extremes, for he records that one duiker in Natal was the same colour as the long grass – probably a deep gold or fawn (67). He does not confuse the grey duiker with the tiny red duiker, *Cephalophus natalensis* (*see Rooye-booken*).
Dwarf palm ~ 221
The shortstemmed swamp-dwelling palm tree, *Raphia australis*, should probably be excluded: it was unlikely to have occurred as far south as St. Lucia. It is unlikely, too, that A.D. would have mistaken young palms for 'dwarfs' unless he was deceived by the recurved tips of recumbent *Phoenix reclinata* stems (*see Wild-dattleboom*).

Perhaps his 'dwarf' was not a palm at all, but merely palmlike in appearance. The most attractive possibility is the diminutive fanpalm-like sedge, *Prionium serratum* (Juncaceae: called the rush tree, palmita or *palmiet*), though the locality may be too far north for its natural occurrence. Almost as attractive would be cycads (*Encephalartos* spp: Zamiaceae) or the superficially similar tree ferns (Cyathaceae), although the former are not usually found at the coast. Finally, *Dracaena hookerana* (Agavaceae) is a small tree with terminal rosettes of straplike leaves, convincingly palmlike, especially in young specimens.
Dysentery ~ 260–1
A.D. probably uses this term in its original sense of severe colonic irritation, with pain and diarrhoea, perhaps with blood and mucus.

These are, of course, symptoms of a number of diseases, and it seems unlikely that those now specifically called dysentery would have been a serious problem at the time. These,

(Dysentery *cont.*)

contracted via faecal contamination of food or drinking water, are amoebic dysentery (infection with the protozoan parasite *Entamoeba histolytica*) and bacillary dysentery (caused by the *Shigella* bacillus). The link with 'fevers' (260, and q.v.) may, however, signify 'malarial dysentery', in which malaria is aggravated by the bacillary infection (*see* Malaria). Otherwise dysentery in its general sense may have been caused by a range of bacteria, protozoans, parasitic worms and flukes. *See also* Cholera

Eagle *includes* African fish eagle, bateleur ~ 14, 58

Large raptors, the diurnal birds of prey (O. Falconiformes, F. Accipitridae: eagles, hawks, vultures etc.).

The African fish eagle, *Haliaeetus vocifer* (58) is the most handsome of the African eagles, with black, white and chestnut coloration. Its musical, yelping call is known as 'the voice of Africa'. The nest is a large pile of sticks with a lined bowl, usually in the fork of a tree near water.

The bateleur (58), *Terathopius ecaudatus*, is a longwinged, scavenging harrier-eagle, which builds a large, lined nesting platform of sticks, usually in the forest canopy or on the horizontal fork of a large tree.

The dearth of eagles at Table Mountain (14), together with the absence of vultures (q.v.), may indicate that suitable prey had already begun to disappear from that locality.

Earth pig ~ *see Aarde vark*

Eezel-book ~ *see* Water-buck

Egret ~ *see Ardea bubulcus*; Little egret; *see also* Heron

Egyptian cobra ~ *see Geele-slange*

Egyptian goose ~ *see* Goose

Eland *also Ant. canna, Boselaphus oreas, canna* ~ 20, 22, 102, 107n, 166, 181, 186, 189, 192, 193, 211, 215–17, 220, 241, 263, 265, 268

Taurotragus oryx, the eland, is the largest of the African antelope (F. Bovidae, S.F. Bovinae). It is heavy and ox-like, with spiral horns and a short mane on the neck and shoulders. Eland distribution was once very

wide: Van Riebeeck recorded them at Hout Bay and they were common along the Liesbeeck and Salt rivers. Today they are restricted to the northern, central and north-eastern parts of southern Africa: their former presence is reflected in innumerable place-names.

A.D.'s use of '*Boselaphus oreas*' (e.g. 20) is at first confusing. Although *T. oryx* was formerly *Capra oreas*, the distantly related red hartebeest, *Alcelaphus buselaphus*, seemed also to be a possibility (*see* Caama). However, A.D. eventually (102) identifies '*B. oreas*' as the eland.

'*Canna*' seems to have been a vernacular (Khoi or San) name for the eland. A.D. uses it mainly as a common name, occasionally as a scientific one (e.g. 263: *Ant. canna*, i.e. *Antilope canna*). The name did in fact briefly find its way into scientific nomenclature as *Damalis canna*.

Eleotragus ~ *see Riet-book*

Elephant *also* 'Long noses', *om-pomalo om-koulou, uncklove* ~ xii, 51, 73, 74–5, 97, 129–30, 151, 164, 179, 181, 187, 189, 211, 215, 224–30, 241, 243–87

The African elephant *Loxodonta africana*, the largest of the terrestrial mammals (O. Proboscidea, F. Elephantidae), known in Zulu as *indhlovu* or *indlovu*: elephant (A.D.'s '*uncklove*'). The nickname 'long nose' obviously refers to the trunk: '*om-pomalo*' is *impumulo*: nose, and '*om-koulou*' is *inkhulu*: big, great.

Elephants were once widespread in southern Africa but their wholesale slaughter for ivory was already under way in the 17th century, a process which accelerated in the 18th and 19th centuries. They were recorded as extinct in Natal by 1860: the final chapter of this book gives insight into the 19th century attitudes that were the cause of this, for Boers and Europeans and their firearms eventually destroyed tribal hunting traditions of Zulu (277–81) and Bushman (281–2), and replaced these modest, almost ritualistic killings with mass slaughter.

However, elephants continue to move into northern Zululand from southern Mozambique, and there is now a resident population in Tongaland. And, although elephants

(Elephants *cont.*)
will never again roam over the Durban Berea (151), conservation methods in South Africa have been successful and public concern is alive and increasing, especially with the impetus from heightened international awareness of the threat to *L. africana* throughout the African continent.

While the 19th century attitude often seems both cold and brutal, A.D.'s final chapter does, paradoxically, also convey a sense of respect and admiration for the elephant. It contains a number of biological observations some of which the modern reader, replete with elephant lore, will find unremarkable, while others may readily be confirmed or otherwise with the aid of a good textbook. However, A.D.'s description of a means of body cooling, using water expelled from 'a pocket' of the stomach (274) is valuable and requires comment.

Elephants, like some other pachydermatous mammals, have few or no sweat glands, so that evaporative body cooling, for them, must occur via the evaporation of water applied to the skin externally. Free water – from a river or water hole or, rarely, bored for with a tusk tip – may be drawn up by the trunk (4–10 litres in an adult 'trunkful') and sprayed over the head and shoulders. When free water is lacking similar use may, as A.D. indicates, be made of water from the stomach.

This relates to the fact that elephants drink large volumes (up to 50 gal., i.e., 225 litres, in one day, has been recorded), so that the stomach contents are often aqueous – and, incidentally, not ill-smelling – as hunters in dry regions have long known and relied upon. Animals foraging or travelling some distance from water can, apparently, regurgitate a quantity of this stomach water (there is no 'pocket'), either into the mouth cavity or, possibly, into the large naso-pharyngeal sac. It is then withdrawn by the trunk tip and sprayed as A.D. describes. This cooling device may be a temporary adjunct to the heat radiation from relatively thin-skinned areas such as the ears

during conditions of extreme drought. The stomach water of adults may also cool and even sustain calves when distances between water holes are great. A.D.'s description, which suggests that adults cluster together to share the cooling effects of water spraying, seems to add substance to a picture which, for mammals so large and well-known, is surprisingly vague. The physiological basis for water retention in the stomach – for at least several hours – and for its inoffen-sive, even potable, condition, appears not to have been investigated.

The Asian elephant (283), *Elephas*, is smaller than *L. africana*, with a shorter, deeper skull, smaller ears, and short, straight tusks, which often do not occur in females. Although *L. africana* females do grow tusks, these are smaller than those of the males because their growth almost ceases at puberty, and sometimes they atrophy. As A.D. records (e.g. 276), tuskless individuals are not uncommon. These are reportedly more aggressive than animals with tusks.

Elephant, little ~ *see* Warthog

Emerald cuckoo ~ *see under* Cuckoo

Empiss / Empissy ~ *see* Hyaena

Endata Pursoetha ~ *see Zee-Bontjes*

Equine influenza ~ *see Paerde sickt*

Equus Burschellii ~ 130
Burchell's zebra, *Equus burchelli* (O. Perissodactyla, F. Equidae), is named for W. J. Burchell (q.v.) the great traveller and naturalist, who brought the original specimen from South Africa and presented it to the British Museum.

Erdvark ~ see Aarde vark

Euchore ~ see Spring-booken

Euphorbias ~ 33n
A.D. refers to low-growing, succulent plants, fleshy in appearance and probably greyish in hue. Not all of these will have been *Euphorbia* spp – though many must, for this is a huge genus with many succulent South African species (Euphorbiaceae).

For larger, tree-sized euphorbias ~ *see Norsh-doorn-boom.*

Fever ~ 2, 38, 238, 260–1
The 'tenacious fever' A.D. contracted in Guadeloupe (2) cannot be identified, but if it was, as is likely, malaria (q.v.) the superb constitution which brought him through that disease in South Africa is much to be admired.

There may be some truth in his deduction (38) that stagnant brackish water is more wholesome than stagnant fresh water, but he was unaware that the distribution of 'fever'-producing pathogens may be governed primarily, not by water salinity, but by climatic factors. A.D.'s beliefs and deductions are products of his time. *See also* Dysentery

Fig tree *also Bosch-touw-boom*, giant fig tree, rope tree, wild fig tree ~ 55, 181, 194, 245
Many species of fig tree (*Ficus* spp: Moraceae) are indigenous to southern Africa – A.D. seems to have noticed only very large specimens.

Although some *Ficus* spp are constant in size and growth habit, others show great flexibility. The sycomore fig (*F. sycomorus*) for example, may vary in height from 5–25m, depending on environmental factors. Others may grow as normal trees and shrubs in open ground, but will, on rocky outcrops, send out roots against bare rock and into crevices. An elaboration of this tendency is seen in 'stranglers', which start growth in the branches of a host tree and send down long aerial roots which become true roots when they reach the ground: the aerial portions strangle the host to death. This explains 'rope tree' and *'bosch touw boom'* (Afrikaans: *bostou boom*) (55). While several *Ficus* spp fit A.D.'s description, a very likely 'giant fig' is the giant-leafed fig, *F. vogelii*, which grows to 25m, may be a strangler, and bears small fruit.

Finch ~ *see* Sparrows
Fish eagle ~ *see* Eagle
Fissipeds ~ 158
Animals with divided feet. A.D. clearly intends the word to mean cloven-hoofed ungulates (O. Artiodactyla: even-toed forms such as pigs and antelope). However, when the word was in current use (it is now obsolete) it was given as the name of a taxonomic grouping (S.O. Fissipedia) of the terrestrial carnivores with separate toes, i.e. dogs, cats and bears.

Flamingo ~ 26–9
Two species of flamingo, not three (27) occur in the marine and inland waters of South Africa: *Phoenicopterus ruber* and *P. minor*, the greater and lesser flamingoes (O. Phoenicopteriformes, F. Phoenicopteridae).

A.D. describes the appearance and habits of *P. ruber* with colourful accuracy. Although his phylogenetic arguments (27–8) are ill-founded, it is interesting to note that the debate concerning the relationships between flamingoes and other bird groups has gone on for so long. It continues: some authorities place them near storks, etc. (Ciconiiformes) and ducks (Anseriformes). Others ally them to the Charadriiformes (avocets and stilts).

As A.D. suggests (29) flamingoes prefer saline and brackish water.

Flies ~ 63, 74, 236–7, 258
Any two-winged insect (O. Diptera). A.D. generally includes as 'flies' only the large and (he believed) objectionable or dangerous blowflies (F. Calliphoridae, also known as bluebottles and greenbottles), e.g. *Calliphora, Lucilia, Pollenia,* etc.

Blowflies often lay eggs on decomposing meat on which the larvae (maggots or A.D.'s 'worms') feed. The contemporary belief that the flies and larvae were diseased or carried 'foul contagion' conditioned A.D.'s treatment of Mahlé (236–7; *see also* Wounds) and increased Mahlé's suffering. (For screw worm larvae of the fly *Chrysomia see* Ticks and mites.)

Flying fish ~ 4
Marine fishes (F. Exocoetidae) which jump out of the water to evade predators, and which can glide considerable distances through the air, aided by enlarged, winglike fins.

The two-winged *Exocoetus volitans* is very common and occurs in all tropical seas. *Cypselurus heterurus* has four wings and is found on both sides of the tropical Atlantic.

Fox ~ 34, 216
Vulpes chama, the Cape fox, has a beautiful, silvery coat (34). A.D. probably does not refer to *V. chama* when listing the 'fox' among scavengers in Natal (216). More likely

(Fox *cont.*)
would be the black-backed jackal, *Canis mesomelas*, or, in well-watered areas, the side-striped jackal, *C. adustus*: both will take carrion if available, though *C. mesomelas* is predominantly insectivorous and *C. adustus* is mainly vegetarian (all F. Canidae, S.F. Caninae).

Francolin ~ 57, 97, 189
The 'staccato, urgent' call (57) identifies this bird as *Francolinus levaillanti*, the redwing francolin, which roosts on the ground and calls in the early morning and evening (O. Galliformes, F. Phasianidae: francolins, quail, pheasants etc).

Fruit, long, green, bitter ~ 237–8
The climbing habit of the plant, its milky latex and the shape and colour of the fruit suggest *Sarcostemma viminale*, the caustic vine (Afrikaans: *melkbos*). This produces a long follicle which, when young and green, is eaten, both raw and cooked, as a relish (Asclepiadaceae). A.D.'s men ate several fruit to his one, and laughed at his reaction: perhaps there was something they hadn't told him – about discarding bitter rind or seeds, for example.

Fruit, oval, green, with protuberances ~ 179
The height of the plant given excludes several whose fruit matches A.D.'s description (e.g. *Datura stramonium*). A strong possibility is *Ricinus communis*, the castor oil plant (Euphorbiaceae), not indigenous but now cosmopolitan. The unripe fruit are bright green and the seeds are poisonous.

Otherwise, there are climbing cucurbits which might have grown several metres up a tree or shrub, so confusing the casual observer. For example, the unripe fruit of *Cucumis africanus*, oval and covered with stout, blunt spines, are green (Cucurbitaceae). The fruit is bitter and is ignored by the indigenous people except in time of famine.

Fruit, sausage-shaped ~ *see Tripinnaria tenacium*

G. acharus ~ *see* Ticks and mites
Gallinule, purple ~ 62
Porphyrio porphyrio, the purple gallinule, (also known as the swamp hen or king reed hen) is widely distributed in southern Africa and elsewhere. Reedbeds are the preferred habitat of this handsome bird which, concealing itself by day, emerges at dawn and dusk and sometimes forages in open shallows, clambering about the vegetation with its large, red feet (O. Gruiformes, F. Rallidae: rails, crakes, gallinules etc.)

Gazella albifrons ~ 130
Probably the blesbok, *Damaliscus dorcas phillipsi*, formerly *Antilope albifrons* (*albifrons* describing the white face blaze) (F. Bovidae, S.F. Alcelaphinae). The blesbok, unlike *D.d. dorcas*, the bontebok (*see Bontebook*), still occurs marginally in Natal, and is lighter in colour than the bontebok. Both have the white blaze, so that the old name supplied by A.D. is not conclusive on its own. Fortunately, here, the locality tends to confirm identity.

Gazella euchore ~ *see Spring-booken*
Gazella pygarga ~ *see Bonte-book*
Gazelle ~
A word used loosely to refer to especially dainty or graceful antelope: the Zulu dance in imitation of the gazelle (92) must have had these qualities. For typical general usage of 'gazelle' *see* e.g. 67, 81, 151, 226.

Gazella as generic name no longer applies to any southern African antelope. There are 10 species of true gazelle, *Gazella* spp, but these occur in North and East Africa and in Asia only.

Geele-out also Yellowwood ~ 97
Although A.D. does not mention seeing yellowwood (Afrikaans: *geelhout*) trees before reaching Pietermaritzburg he must have encountered several species in the Cape. In Natal he may have seen *Podocarpus falcatus* (Outeniqua yellowwood), *P. henkelli* (Henkel's yellowwood) and *P. latifolius*, the 'real' yellowwood, which yields fine timber (Podocarpaceae).

Geele-slange also Kooper-kaapel, yellow snake, hooded snake ~ 132, 137, 249–50
Despite the names implying a yellow or coppery colour this snake is

(Geele-slange cont.)
probably not the yellow or Cape cobra, *Naja nivea*, which is absent from subtropical regions. It is more likely to be *Naja haje annulifera*, the Egyptian cobra or *bosveld kapel* (*kapel*, Afrikaans: cobra), often a uniform light brown in colour. It favours grassland, where it is common, and may use abandoned termite nests for retreat (132; the unnamed snake is obviously a cobra). It is unlikely, however, that the snake found in hollow trees near the coast would be a cobra (249–50). More probably the *'kooper-kaapel'* in this instance was a green mamba (see *Memba*). (S.O. Serpentes, F. Elapidae).

Geèle wild-kalabas-boom ~ see *Strychnos*, edible

Genet *also Symba* ~ 34, 106n, 199, 201
The small-spotted or feline genet, *Genetta genetta*, and the large-spotted or blotched genet, *G. tigrina*, are both decoratively spotted and banded. It is interesting that the Zulu name for the animal, *insimba* (A.D.'s *symba*) should have been transferred to the military skirt of genet fur (106) which still forms part of ceremonial dress. (O. Carnivora, F. Viverridae).

Giant fig tree ~ see Fig tree

Giraffe ~ 130, 268
Giraffa camelopardalis (= big as a camel, spotted like a leopard). No longer present naturally in Natal. A.D. must surely have seen giraffes there – and elsewhere in South Africa – and it is curious that the only sighting he describes is one that took place much later, near the Limpopo (130). Otherwise he merely mentions them in passing (O. Artiodactyla, F. Giraffidae).

Gladiolus ~ 224
It is impossible to identify this St. Lucia plant precisely. *Gladiolus* spp are erect herbs with sword-shaped leaves and the inflorescence a spike. *G. dalenii* (formerly *G. natalensis*) is a possibility, but other species – and other related genera of similar appearance – cannot be excluded (Iridaceae).

Gnu *also Catoblepas gnou* ~ 118, 130, 258, 282, 286
Connochaetes gnou, the black wildebeest or white-tailed gnu (F. Bovidae, S.F. Alcelaphinae). These are rather cowlike, with the head carried on a short, thick neck. There is a tuft of long hair on the muzzle, a throat fringe and a mane. Distribution is now very limited and, as they occur only in southern Africa, they were for a while under threat of extinction. Although conservation methods have been highly successful, it is hard to believe that they once ranged in hundreds of thousands in all four provinces of South Africa.
Catoblepas and also *Catablepas* are former generic names. 'Gnu' and *gnou* derive from the characteristic loud vocalisation: 'ge-nu'. (For the brindled gnu or blue wildebeest *see Catoblepas gorgon*)

Godwit ~ 25, 69
Probably the bartailed godwit, *Limosa lapponica*, a large and long-legged wader with distribution wide enough to have been recorded by A.D. in both the western Cape and Natal (O. Charadriiformes, F. Scolopacidae).

Golden-green cuckoo ~ see under Cuckoo

Goose *includes* Egyptian goose and spurwinged goose or *Bastaard-makouw* ~ 28, 69, 81, 189
A.D. mentions two geese common in southern African inland waters (O. Anseriformes, F. Anatidae: ducks, geese, swans). The Egyptian goose, *Alopochen aegyptiacus* (69, 81, 189) is ubiquitous, while the larger, darker and more handsome spurwinged goose (69), *Plectropterus gambensis*, is absent from the dry west. A.D. gives *Bastaard-makouw* or bastard Muscovy duck as a vernacular name for this bird, now known in Afrikaans as *wildemakou*.

Grasshoppers ~ 55, 166
A.D. seems to use 'grasshoppers' and 'locusts' (q.v.) synonymously and indeed, non-flying 'hoppers' occurring in swarms are juvenile locusts. 'Grasshopper', though, is a more general term which also includes nonlocustan forms: small, non-gregarious insects all distinguished by the possession of large hind legs for jumping (insects: O. Saltatoria, formerly Orthoptera).

Grebe ~ see Horned grebe
Green mamba ~ see Memba
Green pigeon ~ see Pigeon
Grey, crested touraco ~ see under Touraco/ Turaco

Grey heron ~ *see* Heron
Groenklapper ~ *see Weld-calebasses-boom*
Groot-honing-bye ~ *see* Sphinx
Ground hornbill ~ *see under* Hornbill
Guinea-fowl *includes* Crested, *and*
Crowned guinea-fowl ~ 151
Numida meleagris, the helmeted guineafowl (A.D.'s 'crowned') is very common in all but the dry west of southern Africa. It prefers open grassland, vleis, savannah etc., and may be found in large flocks of several hundred. It has been widely introduced as a semi-domesticated bird and now breeds in many parts of the world.

Guttera pucherani, the crested guineafowl, is confined to the north east of southern Africa and prefers matted thickets at the edge of lowland evergreen forest, bushveld etc. It may occur in small flocks of 10–30. (Both O. Galliformes, F. Numididae).

Hadeda ibis ~ *see Ibis addidas*
Hamer-kop, Hammer head ~ *see* Umbretta
Hare ~ (viii), 36, 97, 263
In the west and south west Cape (36) A.D. may have encountered *Lepus capensis*, the Cape hare, which is almost completely restricted to this region. It is more likely, however, that all of his sightings, in the Cape and in Natal, will have been of the scrub hare, *L. saxatilis*, one of the commoner small mammals and very widely distributed. (O. Lagomorpha, F. Leporidae)
Hartebeest, red ~ *see Caama*
Hawfinch ~ *see* Sparrows
Hawkmoth ~ *see* Sphinx
Hemp, wild ~ 128
Probably *Leonotis leonurus*, wild hemp or wild dagga, which, like all *Leonotis* spp, has tubular flowers with nectar attractive to birds. (Lamiaceae)
Heron *includes* Grey, night, purple, and white herons ~ 25, 28, 69, 152
Wading birds which stand, long-legged, silent and motionless in shallow water, waiting for their prey (152). Though the long, slender beak is held down and at rest, the head and neck are poised ready to strike (O. Ciconiiformes, F. Ardeidae: herons,

egrets, bitterns).
Grey heron (25): *Ardea cinerea*, whose pearly grey-and-white plumage is touched with black.
Night heron (25): the French indicates small size, so that the bird is probably *Gorsachius leuconotus*, the white backed night heron, rather than the larger (but more common) black-crowned night heron, *Nycticorax nycticorax*.
Purple heron (25): *Ardea purpurea*, called the purple heron, even though the general body colour is more slaty than purple; neck and upper breast are pale rufous striped with black, shading down to dark maroon.
White heron (69): possibly *Egretta garzetta* (*see* Little egret). The 'white heron' mentioned later (166–7) is obviously the cattle egret, *Bubulcus ibis* (*see Ardea bubulcus*)
Hippopotamus *also Om-vobu*, river-horse, sea cow, *zee-koe* ~ (viii), 43, 53, 60, 62, 64–7, 72, 73, 82, 138–62, *145*, 169–71, 189, 220, 222–5, 230–2, 235, 238, 241, 286
Hippopotamus amphibius (O. Artiodactyla, F. Hippopotamidae): very large mammals of amphibious habit. *H. amphibius* was once widespread in southern Africa, and Van Riebeeck recorded its presence in the swamp that is now Church Square, Cape Town. They have been hunted for their meat and fat and their hides and teeth, and, as they are close-cropping grass eaters, have routinely been eradicated in agricultural areas. Remaining animals are concentrated mainly in the northern and eastern Transvaal, and marginally into Natal and Zululand.

Nineteenth century attitudes are clear from A.D.'s approach to hippopotamus hunting (138–62): his comment on declining numbers (156) seems particuarly naive in the light of this.

Of the various common names, neither 'river horse' nor 'sea cow' (Dutch: *zee koe*, Afrikaans: *seekoei*) is truly apt. The Zulu, *imvubu* ('*omvobu*') simply means hippopotamus; hence, Umzimvubu River. The illustration (*145*) is of a dead juvenile, or perhaps foetal, specimen and is drawn from an angle that is singularly uninformative.

Honey bees ~ *see* Bees

Honey-guide *also* Informer cuckoo, *om-schlanvo* ~ 248–51

The greater honeyguide, *Indicator indicator*, obviously made a vivid impression on A.D., whose account of it was clear enough for incorporation in Stark and Sclater (1903) as *I. sparrmani*, Sparrman's honeyguide.

I. indicator does guide human beings (but not, apparently, other mammals) to bees' nests, as also does *I. variegatus*, the scalythroated honeyguide. Both of these feed on bees and their wax, as does the lesser honeyguide, *I. minor*, which does not exhibit the guiding behaviour. These three species of *Indicator* probably constitute the trio A.D. mentions. Perhaps he missed the less common sharpbilled honeyguide, *Protodiscus regulus*, which hawks insects in flight and does not guide.

There seems, sadly, to be no later substantiation of A.D.'s attractive suggestion (250) that guiding behaviour is an adaptation giving birds access to any otherwise unavailable insects. If guiding behaviour is released by the presence of a bees' nest and a human being, it does seem logical that the birds should seek access to any other concentration of edible insects in the same way. Honey hunters could, in that case, be lured to maggoty carrion or beetle-infested bones, and so be endangered by non-human scavengers.

A.D.'s 'informer cuckoo' is apt. Like cuckoos, honeyguides are brood parasitic, and barbets (q.v.) are especially subject to this parasitism – their own young are killed by the honeyguide chick.

The Zulu *inhlava* ('*om-schlanvo*') is a general word applied to the several species.

Hooded snake ~ *see Geele-slange*

Hooklipped rhinoceros ~ *see under* Rhinoceros

Hornbill *also* Calao; *includes Buceros abyssinicus, B. buccinator* ~ 55–7, 128

'*Buceros buccinator*' is obviously the trumpeter hornbill, *Bycanistes bucinator* – and what a lively description of it A.D. gives! '*B. abyssinicus*' is probably the very large, turkeylike ground hornbill, *Bucorvus leadbea-*

teri, which is entirely carnivorous (55) and forages on the ground, digging with the bill and walking with a rolling gait. Another, less likely, possibility, is *Tockus alboterminatus*, the crowned hornbill, whose food preferences do not completely match A.D.'s description (all O. Coraciiformes, F. Bucerotidae).

The great bill and casque are not hollow, but are filled with light honeycombed or spongelike bone: they cannot unbalance the bird in flight and no special buoyancy mechanisms are necessary. In particular, A.D.'s suggested pneumatic mechanism (based, perhaps, on a rather limited understanding of avian air sacs) involves two fallacies (56). The first is that birds are able to fill a subcutaneous space (if, indeed, such a space exists) with air, and this they cannot do. The second is that inflation with air makes a body more buoyant in air. An air-filled balloon or bladder, as A.D. surely knew, does not float up in air. It will only be buoyant in a denser medium, e.g. water.

Horned grebe ~ 25

Grebes are aquatic birds, ducklike, but differing in the possession of lobed toes, pointed bills, erect, slender necks and practically no tails. (O. Podicipediformes, F. Podicipedidae). 'Horned' doubtless refers to the conspicuous crest of the great crested grebe, *Podiceps cristatus*, which frequents larger pans, vleis and dams in southern Africa, usually those with emergent aquatic vegetation.

Horse sickness ~ *see Paerde sickt*

Hubert, Saint ~ 228

The French patron saint of hunters and trappers, though originally revered only in the great forest area of Ardenne, where the historical Hubert, a missionary, lived. He died in 727. During the next 700 years there became attached to him a legend first associated with the much earlier St. Eustace: he was believed to have hunted in the forest on a Good Friday and been converted to holiness by the sight of a stag with a crucifix between its antlers. St. Hubert's emblem is a stag.

Hyaena *also* Cape hyaena, *Empiss/empissy, Hyaena crocuta, Hyaena fusca*, spotted hyaena, *strand-wolf*, tiger-

(Hyaena cont.)
   wolf, wolf ~ 22–5, 43, 75, 142, 144,
   146, 180, 184–9, 215–17, 250, 252,
   286
   A.D.'s 'Hyaena fusca' is H. brunnea,
   the brown hyaena, known in Afrikaans as the strandwolf because of its
   habit in some areas of frequenting
   beaches in search of carrion (as here –
   23). 'H. crocuta' is Crocuta crocuta,
   the spotted hyaena: 'tiger-wolf' and
   'wolf' are descriptive (both F. Hyaeni-
   dae, S.F. Hyaeninae). A.D.'s 'Empiss'
   and 'Empissy' (189) are from Zulu
   impisi: hyaena.
   The distributional ranges of both
   have shrunk since the end of the 18th
   century. Then, H. brunnea could be
   seen on the shores of Table Bay. At the
   end of the 19th century it still occurred at Malmesbury and Beaufort
   West, but now it is more or less restricted to Namibia and regions north
   of the Orange River. It is predominantly nocturnal, foraging and scavenging.
   C. crocuta was almost absent from
   the Cape Province by 1870 and is now
   rare in southern Africa. It scavenges
   and preys on zebra and some
   antelope – a recent finding dispelling
   the almost legendary belief that it fed
   only on carrion. The wolfish appearance is belied by its behaviour, of
   which A.D. gives a lively account
   (186–89). The habit of crunching and
   swallowing bones (187), but probably
   not soil, produces hard white scats
   which may take months to disin-
   tegrate. Quaint tales about imitative
   abilities of hyaenas (e.g. 188) obviously arise from the animal's
   remarkable range of vocalizations,
   including whoops, laughs, giggles and
   grunts. C. crocuta will indeed include
   human corpses as part of the carrion
   component of its diet (186, 286) and
   may disinter them if too shallowly
   buried.
Hyrax ~ see Rock rabbits
Hyster-out also Ironwood ~ 97
   The ironwood (Afrikaans: ysterhout)
   tree occurs coastally from the western
   Cape to northern Natal, in bush, littoral scrub and evergreen forest. Olea
   capensis has three subspecies, of
   which O.c. macrocarpa produces fine
   timber (Oleaceae). Besides wagon axles it has been used for railway

sleepers, flooring blocks and for bridge
construction – also, beautiful furniture, though ironwood is difficult to
work.

Ibis addidas also Ibis of the bush ~ 57–8,
128
   'Addidas' is A.D.'s French phonetic
   rendering of 'hadeda', the onomato-
   poeic common name of Bostrychia
   hagedash. The loud, raucous call (128)
   of the hadeda ibis – now a boldly urban bird – is well-known to Natalians,
   and much loved. It feeds on insects,
   other small invertebrates (see Woodlouse) and small reptiles. The nest is
   not on the ground (58), but is a flimsy,
   lined platform of sticks on a horizontal
   tree branch 1–12m up (O. Ciconiiformes, F. Plataleidae: ibises and spoon-
   bills).
Ibis, bald ~ 58, 96
   Geronticus calvus, the bald ibis, has
   the crown of the head naked, domed
   and bright red in colour. It builds nest
   platforms on cliff ledges, waterfall
   faces and on the sides of mountains
   and river gorges (O. Ciconiiformes, F.
   Plataleidae).
Ibis of the bush ~ see Ibis addidas
Ibis, sacred ~ 58
   To the ancient Egyptians Threskior-
   nis aethiopicus was sacred, because
   its annual arrival and breeding coincided with the mystical and lifegiving
   rising and flooding of the Nile. They
   believed it to represent Thoth, the
   ibis-headed moon deity, scribe of the
   gods, and subject also to cyclical movements and fluctuations. They rev-
   erently mummified many specimens
   and placed them in human tombs.
   Cuvier (q.v.) was the first naturalist to
   make the match between the T. aethiopicus of science and the sacred bird of
   the ancients.
   Despite A.D.'s assumption to the
   contrary, the bird is more likely to
   nest in bushes or trees than on the
   ground. (O. Ciconiiformes, F. Plataleidae).
Ignicolor ~ see Sparrows
Ilala palm ~ see Wild-klaapper-noot
Illnesses ~ see Cholera; Colds; Dysentery;
   Fever; Malaria; Pestilence; Plague;
   Port-natal-sickt; Snakebite; Wounds.
   The illness from which A.D. suffered

(Illnesses *cont.*)
for many months was probably malaria (q.v.).

Impala ~ *see Ant. melampus*

Indou ~
A.D.'s French phonetic version of Hindu. *See under* Crocodile

Informer cuckoo ~ *see* Honey-guide

Inglobu ~ *see* Bushpig

Iniaty ~ *see* Buffalo

Ingogoné ~ *see Catoblepas gorgon*

Insects, biting and sucking ~ 26
It was probably not mosquitoes which attacked A.D. with such ferocity at Lange Valley, for he is explicit about these later. The only clue is from the bloodstains on his underclothing – indicative of fleas (whose faeces after a blood meal are blood red) or of blood-engorged bedbugs crushed in the course of the restless night. A.D.'s 'myriads' gives the modern reader a repellent picture of the domestic hygiene of the period in parts of South Africa. *See also* Bugs.

Iphesy ~ *see Spouwer-slange*

Ipiva ~ *see* Water-buck

Ironwood ~ *see Hyster-out*

Ischlouzély ~ 136
Probably the aurora snake, *Lamprophis aurora* (O. Serpentes, F. Colubridae), one of South Africa's prettiest snakes. It is green above, yellow below, and has a distinctive browny-orange vertebral stripe. *L. aurora* is a nocturnal constrictor of quiet disposition. It preys on rodents and is often found near human habitation.

The vernacular name is mysterious.

Jackal ~ *see* Fox

Jerboa, Cape ~ *see Spring has*

Kaarsh-boschjes also Candle bush ~ 43–4
Probably the waxberry or the candleberry (Afrikaans: *kersbessie*, perhaps formerly *kersbossie*, candlebush), *Myrica cordifolia* (Myricaceae).

It is not the fruit pulp which is rich in fat and 'berry wax', but the fruit coat – and also the surfaces of leaves and stems. Perhaps A.D. saw the fruit being peeled and did not realise that the coat, and not the pulp, was to be retained for the extraction of the wax in boiling water. So productive is the plant that the wax, besides being used for candlemaking locally, was also exported until the practice ceased to be economically worthwhile.

Karee bush ~ *see Carée-Boom*

Kersbossie, kersbessie ~ *see Kaarshboschjes*

Kingfisher ~ *see* Crab eater

Kite ~ 80, 166
Smallish to medium sized and slender diurnal birds of prey (O. Falconiformes, F. Accipitridae: eagles, hawks, kites, etc.) Probably *Elanus caeruleus*, the blackshouldered kite. This takes mainly rodents but would certainly avail itself of locusts and grasshoppers (q.q.v.) and any other insects that were plentiful and easy to catch. Kites prefer open country and are both hunters and scavengers.

Klaas cuckoo ~ *see under* Cuckoo

Klein wild-kalabas-boom ~ *see Strychnos, edible*

Klip-dassen ~ *see* Rock rabbits

Klip-springer ~ 22
Oreotragus oreotragus (F. Bovidae, S.F. Antilopinae): small, agile antelope which characteristically bound from rock to rock and up the sides of steep rock-faces – hence Afrikaans, *klipspringer*: rock jumper. Distribution is wide, but patchy because of the preferred rocky habitat. They are most commonly found in pairs or in small family groups.

Kobus ellipsiprymnus ~ *see* Water-buck

Kooker-boom *also* Kokerboom, quiver tree ~ 176–7, 245
A.D. twice, and puzzlingly, indicates that the '*kokerboom*' or 'quiver tree' and the very different-looking *noorsdoring boom* are one and the same (*see Norsh-doorn-boom*).

The quiver tree, *Aloe dichotoma* (Liliaceae), a large branching aloe, was first recorded in 1685 by Simon van der Stel, who noted that Bushmen made quivers for their arrows from its hollowed-out branches.

As *A. dichotoma* occurs in the dry west of southern Africa A.D. may have been applying the common name to the larger true tree aloe, *A. bainesii* in Natal (in dense bush); otherwise he may have referred to the smaller krantz aloe, *A. arborescens*.

Kooper-kaapel ~ *see Geele-slange*

Kraus ~ 47, 88

Ferdinand Krauss (1812–1890) was born in Stuttgart and practised as a pharmacist or apothecary before studying at Tübingen and Heidelberg. He arrived at Cape Town in May 1838, having travelled with the family of Baron von Ludwig: Ludwig was probably his patron and the financial backer for his collecting.

Krauss trekked east to Port Elizabeth in November 1838, and arrived in April 1839. Meanwhile, A.D. boarded the *Mazeppa* at Cape Town (5 May) and arrived four days later. So it was that he and Krauss (and Wahlberg q.v.) were companions when the *Mazeppa* continued her journey, arriving at Port Natal on June 10.

A.D. does not say how much time he and Krauss spent together before Krauss left South Africa – he was back in Stuttgart by August 1840. Krauss seems to have been independent, lodging at Umlazi or Congella Trekker encampments between collecting expeditions and, like A.D., accompanying trekkers on hunting trips.

Krauss travelled to Mpande's homestead independently of A.D. in October 1839: A.D. joined him there. He was back at Congella on the 28th, after an absence of four days.

Krauss kept a travel journal – as was almost *de rigeur* at the time – which was published under the title *Cape to Zululand: Observations by a collector and naturalist*, 1838–40.

Krauss' other, exclusively scientific publications have all the hallmarks of the formal scientific training A.D. lacked. He was relatively unusual among biologists travelling in South Africa at the time in being more interested in invertebrates (particularly Crustacea and Coelenterata) than in big game or birds. It was Krauss who, perhaps while A.D. was finding fault with Pietermaritzburg and its environs, first described the river crab whose type locality is Boesmansrand: '*Ich fand sie nur einem Wasserfalle am Boschmannsrandgebirge in die Nähe von Pietermauritzburg in Natal . . .*' (Krauss, 1843). This crab is now known as *Potamonautes (Orthopotamonautes) depressus depressus* (Krauss 1843).

While Krauss did not apparently transmit his passion for invertebrates (other than insects) to A.D., he did exert a certain influence on him and on the way his work was presented.

Carcinologists are not the only biologists who remember Krauss. His name has entered botanical nomenclature in, for example, *Acacia kraussiana*.

Kudu *also Strepsiceros kudu* ~ 179, 181, 189, 215, 232, 240, 241, 242

Tragelaphus strepsiceros, the kudu, a large antelope noted for the handsome corkscrew horns of the male and, in both sexes, the broad, spoonshaped ears (F. Bovidae, S.F. Bovinae).

The kudu is one of the more resilient of large southern African mammals.

Lala palm ~ *see Wild-klaapper-noot*
Large-headed wader ~ *see* Wader
Large-snouted boar ~ *see* Warthog
Lark *includes Alauda hamgazy*, Sentinel lark ~ 53, 162–3

While A.D. may well have encountered larks (53) (O. Passeriformes, F. Alaudidae) his '*Alauda hamgazy*' is not a lark, but a longclaw (F. Motacillidae), as is the 'sentinel lark'.

The former is the pinkthroated longclaw, *Macronyx ameliae*, a beautifully coloured bird: A.D.'s description is lovely. It is rare in Natal. The 'sentinel lark', so called by Le Vaillant (*see* Levaillant), is the related orange-throated longclaw, *M. capensis*, far commoner than *M. ameliae* in Natal and found coastally to the south-west Cape.

A.D.'s choice of *Alauda hamgazy* (a name that never found its way into ornithological literature) is interesting. His Zulu glossary (Vol. 2) lists *Hamgâzy* as meaning 'blood', and he confirms on p. 190 of the present volume that '*hamgazy*' is incorporated to mean 'blood red' (Zulu *igazi*: blood).

However, '*Angazi*': I do not know, must have been the Zulu's answer to many a naturalist's question and has inevitably found its way into nomenclature, as with the nyala, *Tragelaphus angasii*. This particular nomenclatural oddity is not unique to South Africa. There is, for example, some uncertainty in Australia regard-

(Lark *cont.*)

ing the precise meaning of 'Kangaroo', but there are those who insist it is the Aboriginal for 'I don't know'.

Larvae ~ *see* Flies; Wounds

A.D. uses this term – correctly – for insect caterpillars in general. Mostly, however, he applies it more restrictedly to blowfly maggots.

Lataniers ~ 221

Latania, a genus of borassoid palm, does not occur in Africa: it is restricted to the Mascarene Islands, and one species is known as the Bourbon palm, named for the island of Bourbon, now Réunion.

Clearly, a traveller acquainted with the flora of French possessions would be more likely than most to make this misidentification. As the related southern African *Borassus aethiopicum* occurs naturally no further south than Mozambique, A.D. may have been misled by particuarly large specimens of *Hyphaene natalensis*, the fan-leafed ilala palm (*see Wild-Klaapper-noot*).

Latax ~ 23–5

The word used by Aristotle (q.v.) for the beaver in a discussion of amphibious mammals of the fresh (not marine) waters of Mediterranean Europe.

The link between Aristotle's *Latax*, Belon's (q.v.) sea-wolf (q.v.) and the hyaena (q.v.) of southern Africa is so tenuous as to be invisible beyond the borders of A.D.'s imagination.

Leeauw-book ~ *see* Water-buck

Leeches ~ 53, 135, 144, 159, 221

Wormlike invertebrates related to earthworms: marine, freshwater and terrestrial (P. Annelida, C. Hirudinea). Many are (usually temporary) ectoparasites, attaching to the skin of the host by means of suckers, slitting the skin and ingesting blood. Tavernier (q.v.) reported being plagued by leeches in Indian forests (53) and there is no reason to doubt him, despite A.D.'s speculations (*see* Ticks and mites). A.D. himself was easily able to distinguish between ticks and the freshwater leeches of Natal (e.g. 144, 159). He appears to have had a typically French faith in the efficacy of medicinal leeches (e.g. for snakebite, q.v.). Indeed, the French used *Hirudo medicinalis* to treat everything from

gout to madness, and in 1833 41 million leeches were imported into France from elsewhere in Europe – an interesting example of the effect of civilisation on the population of an invertebrate animal.

There is currently a return to the medical use of leeches, which can now be readily bred and reared in the laboratory.

Leopard ~ 22–3, 34, 50, 146, 149, 188, 216, 253

Panthera pardus (F. Felidae, S.F. Felinae) the largest of the African spotted cats. The leopard has a wide sub-Saharan distribution and although its numbers are now much reduced it is still plentiful in the Transvaal, parts of Natal and mountainous regions of the Cape Province. It is a predator, usually solitary, secretive and silent. It is still hunted, as it was in A.D.'s day (34), for its skin. A.D. seems to use *lèopard* and *panthère* interchangeably, but in one instance (188) both words occur together and are rendered 'leopard' and 'panther'. As 'panther' is usually applied to the black variety of *P. pardus* found mainly in tropical rain forest it may be that A.D. actually saw a rare black specimen on this occasion.

Lesson, René Primivère ~ 250n.

19th century French ornithologist.

In 1830 he published *Centurie Zoologique*, with many plates representing birds. The '*Manuel d'Ornithologie*' quoted by A.D. is probably the 1831 work in two volumes entitled *Traité d'Ornithologie*, which was an exhaustive taxonomic survey of the C. Aves.

While Lesson's work has left little mark on southern African ornithology, his name persists here and there, e.g. *Pterodroma lessonii* (the white-headed petrel).

Leucadendron argenteum ~ *see Protea argentea*

Leucogaster ~ *see* White-breasted blackbird

Levaillant ~ (x), 2, 3, 14, 41, 44, 45–6, 156, 160, 161, 181n, 276, 278

Francois Le Vaillant (1753–1824) was born in Dutch Guiana of French parents. He was educated in Germany and Lorraine and, having inherited a

(Levaillant *cont.*)
ornithology and for travel from his father, determined to travel abroad collecting natural history specimens. He spent over three years at the Cape (1781–84).

On his return to Paris he arranged the material he had collected and wrote his account of his travels. In 1793 he was imprisoned by the Jacobins, but the overthrow of Robespierre enabled him to regain his freedom and cheat the guillotine. He died at the age of 71, having spent his last 30 years at La Nové near Sezanne, 70 miles east of Paris.

Le Vaillant's South African sojourn is recorded in five volumes. The first two (*Travels into the interior parts of Africa by way of the Cape of Good Hope . . .*) were published in 1790; the remaining three (*New travels . . .*) in 1795. English translations were soon available, as were versions in German and Dutch.

The works were, it seems, ghost-written – or at least, edited – by others (probably one Casimir Varon; also, perhaps, the Abbé Philippo and Legrand d'Aussi). The reason may have been that Le Vaillant's French, because of his early childhood, was unpolished and inadequate to the task.

Whatever the precise details of authorship, the obviously readable and entertaining *Travels* of Le Vaillant are crowded with inaccuracies, chronological, geographical, social, zoological, botanical. Some errors were, it is suggested, deliberate, for reasons of vainglory or concealment; some were careless; some were pure romantic fiction. One cannot help sympathising with A.D.'s repeated disillusionment as he finds one part after another of the great man's colourful and inspiring reminiscences to be false or mistaken.

But, for all that, Le Vaillant is not to be belittled or discarded. His magnificently produced series, *Histoire Naturelle des Oiseaux d'Afrique* (1796–1808) contains much of value. He will always be honoured for it – even though his credulity and desire for approbation misled him into dubious realms of invention and misrepresentation only a hairsbreadth away from blatant deceit. His name will continue to resound through southern African zoology, especially ornithology, as an important authority, and in nomenclature, e.g. *Trachyphonus vaillantii* (crested barbet); *Clamator levaillantii* (striped cuckoo); *Francolinus levaillantii, F. levaillantoides* (redwing and Orange River francolins)

Lion ~ 20, 63, 74, 142, 146, 189, 215–17, 239, 243

Panthera leo (F. Felidae, S.F. Felinae): the largest of the African carnivores. The once very wide distributional range had, as A.D. comments (20), long begun to shrink. Lions had disappeared from most of the Cape Colony by the 1860s, and from the greater part of Natal, excluding the north-east, shortly thereafter. References to the habits of *P. leo* are scattered throughout A.D.'s narrative. The beast was clearly regarded highly by him, and by the Zulu people (*see also* 281 and 283).

Lion-buck ~ *see* Water-buck

Little cormorant ~ *see* Cormorant

Little egret ~ 25

Egretta garzetta, a cosmopolitan wading bird, pure white in colour: sometimes known as the great white heron (O. Ciconiiformes, F. Ardeidae). A.D.'s use in French of '*aigrette*' is a reminder that many egrets are distinguished by the fine, lacelike plumes or 'aigrettes' of the males in the breeding season. It is possible that the 'white heron' (69) is also *E. garzetta. See also* Heron.

Little elephant ~ *see* Warthog

Locust ~ 34, 80–1

Name given loosely to any large tropical or subtropical grasshopper (q.v.); properly applied to those whose numbers occasionally build up to form huge migrating swarms. A.D.'s first passing comment suggests that he had seen or heard of a minor outbreak of the brown locust of the Karroo, *Locusta pardalina* (34). He certainly witnessed – for his account is vivid – a small Natal outbreak of *Nomadacris septemfasciata*, one of the three most important 'plague' locusts of Africa, and whose southernmost limit is Natal. Several such small outbreaks may have preceded the major one that occurred in Natal during 1847–54.

The simple control measures listed

(Locust *cont.*)

by A.D. (80–81) would make almost no impression on even a small outbreak, and even now satisfactory control methods are still being sought. The insects are a nutritious food source (81) but tend, for various historical and cultural reasons, to be avoided unless other protein food is unavailable. They have a reportedly 'grassy' flavour. (O. Saltatoria, formerly Orthoptera)

The gregarious, swarming phase in the locust life history was used to picturesque effect in Zulu speech, symbolising great numbers (196, 281).
See also Pestilence

Locust bird ~ *see Ardea bubulcus*

Long nose ~ *see* Elephant

Longclaw ~ *see* Lark

Lourie, loury ~ *see* Touraco/Turaco

Lutra canadensis also Canadian otter ~ 23–5

The Canadian otter is very similar to the European otter, *L. lutra*: sleek, low-slung and amphibious in habit (F. Mustelidae, S.F. Lutrinae). *See also* Otter, South African.

Madagascan teal ~ *see Teal*

Makano ~ 261–2, 275

The Marula or cider tree, *Sclerocarya birrea caffra* (Anacardiaceae), which fruits prolifically. A.D.'s *'makano'* for the fruit is from Zulu: *amaganu* (the tree is *umganu*). His description of the fruit and its properties is vivid, and the elephant's liking for the fermented fruit is well known and well documented. The fruits are enjoyed also by baboons, monkeys, bushpigs and cattle. They ripen on the ground and are collected and used by indigenous people, unfermented, in porridge or, after a few days' fermentation, made into beer. The nuts are hard, but contain edible and nutritious kernels.

Maggots ~ *see* Flies; Wounds

Malaria ~ 101–5, 107, 116, 125–8, 134, 137, 164, 232–33

On 19 January 1840 A.D. succumbed to an unnamed illness from which he suffered 'agonies for fifteen long months'. While the sudden plunge into a cold river on a hot day (101) may have precipitated the onset of a disease already incubating, it cannot have been the direct cause. The symptoms – headache, cough, fever, nausea and stomach pain – indicate malaria. Even stronger evidence is the apparently cyclic course of the disease in which bouts of illness alternated with returns to robust normality. A.D. would have been bitten by the malarial mosquito (q.v.), *Anopheles*, some 5–12 days before the symptoms appeared. This would have occurred early in January at Port Natal, to which he had returned after spending November and December in Pietermaritzburg. The symptoms were those of 'benign tertian' malaria, which is caused by the protozoan parasite *Plasmodium vivax*. This most widespread form is not fatal, though it may persist and/or recur for years if untreated. It is characterised by a repeating pattern of severe feverishness alternating with normal body temperature.

Sadly, though A.D. knew of quinine sulphate as an antipyretic (238), he seems not to have known it as a preventative of or a specific for malaria, though it had been so used in Europe since early in the 17th century. He does not say *how* he used the helpful 'mimosa' gum (105): *Acacia* gums have little documented medicinal use, but some are highly nutritious and used as a form of 'iron rations' by Africans, while Zulus do make decoctions of some *Acacia* barks for, among other things, abdominal problems (*see* Mimosa).

It was almost certainly also malaria which afflicted travellers to Delagoa Bay (232–3). The pallor and distended abdomens (from enlargement of the spleen) of survivors are typical of *P. vivax* infection. Those who died may have suffered from 'malignant tertian'/'cerebral' malaria caused by *P. falciparum* – the only directly lethal form of the disease. One cannot discount, however, the possibility that benign tertian malaria in combination with other infections (e.g. dysentery, q.v.), poor nutrition, etc. may have been fatal.

Recovery from malaria brings resistance, but only to that particular strain of the parasite. Removal to

(Malaria *cont.*)

another area means exposure to another strain and a return of susceptibility. This is why A.D.'s previous infection did not immunise him, and also why Zulus travelling to Delagoa Bay succumbed. *See also* Fever

Mamba ~ *see Memba*

Manghetjannes ~ *see under* Wild dog

Mangroves ~ 58

A.D. uses the term to mean, not merely the plants collectively called mangroves, but also the environment in which they live – i.e. the mangrove swamp forest as a whole in the mud or silt of a tidal estuary. Natal coastal mangrove swamps may include a mixture of mangroves: the red mangrove, *Rhizophora mucronata*, the black mangrove, *Bruguiera gymnorrhiza*, and one or more species of onionwood, *Cassipourea* (all Rhizophoraceae), mingled with the white mangrove, *Avicennia marina* (Verbenaceae).

Marabou Stork ~ *see under* Stork

Marula ~ *see Makano*

Masked boar ~ *see* Warthog

Memba ~ 137, 249–50

Both the black mamba (*Dendroaspis polylepis*) and the green (*D. angusticeps*) occur in Natal (S.O. Serpentes, F. Elapidae). A.D.'s phonetic spelling would enable any French reader to say the word, directly from Zulu *imamba*, with perfect intonation.

The black mamba (137) is never jet black but is brownish (light or dark) over much of its range, and a uniform lead grey (A.D.'s 'metallic grey brown') in humid coastal areas. It does rear high to strike, sometimes to 5–6 ft (1.5–1.8m).

The snake sheltering in hollow trees – a danger to unwary honey-seekers – is more likely to have been a green mamba than a cobra (249–50). The cobra prefers grassland (*see Geele-slange*).

Midges ~ *see under* Mosquitoes

Millipede ~ *see* Woodlouse (for pill millipede); Centipede (for brief outline of centipede and millipede features)

Mimosa *also Doorn-veld*, thorn bushes, thorn trees, thorn veld ~ 50, 78, 102, 103, 105, 118, 129, 130, 140, 151, 167, 170, 191, 193, 216, 238, 239, 240, 242, 243, 245, 248, 249, 255, 258, 264, 274

The large (about 600 spp) genus *Mimosa* is almost completely absent from southern Africa. It is, however, an old genus in taxonomic terms (named by Linnaeus in 1753). At that time it was much larger: the 1 070 (approx.) spp of *Acacia* were given separate status in 1806 and A.D. may, perhaps, be forgiven for not being botanically up to date.

He will have encountered many species, for about 36 are indigenous to South Africa, including shrubs and trees, with and without thorns of differing length and fierceness. *Acacia* spp are widespread, but A.D. records them only from Natal, in many localities, and with many growth forms. A short list of his possible sightings and prickly encounters would include *A. caffra, A. ataxacantha, A. brevispica, A. burkei, A. gerardii, A. karroo, A. kraussiana, A. nigrescens, A. nilotica, A. schweinfurthii, A. senegal. A. sieberana* and *A. tortilis*. Landscapes may be dominated by certain *Acacia* species or groups of species – round-topped, flattopped, scrubby, very thorny, etc. – dependent on locality, terrain and climatic conditions. Also, as A.D. uses '*Mimosa*' as a synonym for *Entada* (*see Zee-Bontjes*), it is possible that he lumped other, superficially similar, plants under the '*Mimosa*' heading, such as *Albizia* spp and *Cassia* spp (Fabaceae).

Acacia gums (105) may be used as confectionary, as a concentrated food source and as adhesives (gum arabic is derived from *A. senegal*), but have little known medicinal use. *See also* Malaria

Acacia barks, however, are used medicinally. *A. caffra* bark infusions are taken as an emetic and for abdominal problems. *Acacia* bark decoctions are used in traditional Zulu medicine for snakebite – one specific A.D. did not, apparently, encounter. *See also* Snakebite

Mimosa scandens ~ *see Zee-Bontjes*

Moerbossie ~ *see Mour-Boschis*

Mole ~ 132

As prey of the python (q.v.): A.D. is particular to say 'large' moles. Perhaps he merely means 'adult'. The largest of the several golden mole species occurring in Natal grows to about 15cm (6") in total length (O. Insectivora, F. Chrysochloridae). The common molerat, *Cryptomys hotten-*

313

(Mole *cont.*)

totus, may reach about 18cm (7") (O. Rodentia, F. Bathyergidae).

Mongoose ~ 133n

A.D. may have encountered a number of genera and species, of which the banded mongoose, *Mungos mungo* and the suricate, *Suricata suricatta* bear perhaps the closest superficial resemblance to small specimens of the civet (q.v.). Both civet and mongoose are of F. Viverridae, but the former is of S.F. Viverrinae, while the latter is of S.F. Herpestinae.

Monkey *also Amakaho* ~ 128, 179, 180, 201

Probably the vervet monkey *Cercopithecus aethiops*(S.O. Anthropoidea, F. Cercopithecidae), which would have been so abundant in coastal bush – and inland – that it is surprising A.D. so seldom mentions it. His *Amakaho* (180) is from Zulu: *inkawu*, the blue, i.e. vervet, monkey (pl not *amakawu*, but *izinkawu*).

Monkey orange, black, spineless ~ *see Strychnos*, edible

Monkey orange, spiny ~ *see Weldcalebasses-boom*

Mosquitoes ~ 61, 153, 161, 181, 220, 229, 232, 235

Delicately built true flies (insects: O. Diptera) with long legs, narrow wings and mouthparts adapted for piercing and sucking: most feed on the blood of birds or mammals. Eggs are laid in water and the larvae are aquatic. An innate circadian rhythm which includes, among other things, activity at dusk, accounts for the sudden clouds of these insects over rivers and lakes at that time. There may be seasonal variation in the relative abundance of the two main mosquito groups, anophelines (*Anopheles*, etc.) and culicines (*Culex*, etc.). This is reflected in seasonal variations in the prevalence of diseases of which they are vectors. Some *Anopheles* spp carry malaria (q.v.), though malarial areas in southern Africa are now fairly limited as a result of control measures and other precautions.

Flies closely resembling mosquitoes, but harmless, are the midges (*Chironomus* spp) which also appear in clouds over water at sunset. A.D. may frequently have mistaken these for mosquitoes.

Moss ~ 42–3, 97

This is 'old man's beard' or 'Spanish moss', and is not a moss but a cosmopolitan lichen, *Usnea* spp. It is mentioned frequently by almost all early travellers in forested regions of the world for the impressively cobwebbed and spectral quality it imparts to forests and swamps. It has not been possible to confirm A.D.'s descriptions of its uses.

Mountain reedbuck ~ *see Redunca lalandii*

Mour-Boschis ~ 249

The name *moerbossie* is given to several species of *Anacampseros* (Portulacaceae), low-growing shrubs or herbs. The roots of three species, *A. albissima, A. papyracea* and *A. tomentosa*, are recorded as being used in the fermentation of beer in various parts of South Africa.

Mouse ~ xii

Some 25 genera and many species of rats and mice are indigenous to southern Africa (rodents: F. Cricetidae and F. Muridae).

Mouton du Cap ~ *see* Albatross

Mouty ~ 179

Zulu *umuthi*: medicine. In English often spelled muti.

Myriapods ~ *see* Centipede; Woodlouse

Na-boom ~ see Norsch-doorn-boom

Nacht-adder *also* Night adder, snake of the night ~ 135–6

Causus rhombeatus, the common night adder (S.O. Serpentes, F. Viperidae): a small (60–90cm; 2–3ft) snake with a dark V behind the head, followed by a series of dark, rhomboidal patches. A night adder could well have bitten A.D. and also Boulandje (164–5; *see also* Snakebite). The venom is relatively weak and symptoms (swelling, haemorrhage, fever) are not severe, even without treatment.

Although the snake puffs up and hisses if provoked, this is for show, and the nickname 'demon adder' is not deserved.

Nala ~ *see Redunca lalandii*

Natal parrot ~ *see* Parrot

Natal sores ~ *see Port-natal-sickt*

Necklace snake ~ *see Ring-hals-slange*

Night adder ~ *see Nacht-adder*

Night heron ~ *see under* Heron
Norsh-doorn-boom *also Na-boom* ~ 176–7, 245

A.D. twice indicates that the *noorsdoringboom* (*Euphorbia* spp) is identical with the quiver tree (*Aloe* spp: *see Kooker-boom*), a surprising error in one usually so observant.

'*Noorsdoringboom*' comes either from the morose (Afrikaans: *noors*) appearance of these spiny, fleshy and usually leafless plants or from the disagreeable effects of consuming honey made from the copious nectar.

In Natal the name is given to the candelabra tree, *Euphorbia ingens* and to the river *Euphorbia, E. triangularis*. The latex is irritant and may be toxic, and the name *na-boom* is from Khoi: *gnap* – powerful or energetic (Euphorbiaceae).

Numidian crane ~ *see under* Crane
Nux vomica ~ *see* Wounds; *Weld-calebasses-boom*

Omkouschlouâne ~ 275

A.D.'s French phonetic rendering of, probably, *umkhuhluwana*: the -*wana*, a diminutive, indicating that this is the little *mkhuhla* tree. The *mkhuhla* is the Natal mahogany, *Trichilia emetica* (Meliaceae), which produces pale yellow-green fruits whose flesh is edible and whose oily seeds have several uses.

If the 'little' *mkhuhla* is not a small *T. emetica*, it may be one of the monkey orange shrubs – though A.D. identifies these separately (*see Strychnos*, edible, and *Weldcalebasses-boom*). Beer has reportedly been made using monkey orange fruit. A near homophone is the *inhlokoshiyane*, i.e. *Rhus pentheri* (Anacardiaceae) which produces edible fruit.

Finally, A.D. himself identifies *omkouschlouâne* (in his Zulu glossary, Vol. 2) as a 'wild fig'. Again, he may have been confused by slight similarities in the sound of some words, e.g. *umkhonswane* (*Ficus ingens*) and *amakhiwane* (fruits of *F. capensis*).

Om-pomalo om-koulou ~ *see* Elephant
Om-Pongola ~ 118

The footnote, indicating that Om-Pongola means 'river of the gnu', is incorrect. As A.D. knew, the Zulu word for gnu is *inkonkoni* – A.D.'s version *ingogoné* – and, as he also knew, *umphongolo* or '*om-pongola*' signifies a large vessel (bucket, vat or tun, according to his Vol. 2 glossary). This seems to be a case of uncharacteristic carelessness.

Omschlango ~ *see Riet-book*
Om-schlanvo ~ *see* Honey-guide
Om-Sinyate ~ *see* Buffalo
Om-vobu ~ *see* Hippopotamus
Orbitje *also Orby, Redunca scoparia* ~ 78

The oribi, *Ourebia ourebi*, (F. Bovidae, S.F. Antilopinae).

The colloquial name is probably derived from Nama: *arab*, via San: *orabi*, to Afrikaans: *oorbietjie* and English: oribi. A former scientific name is *Ourebia scoparia*: A.D. tends to use '*Redunca*' as a taxonomic catchall when in doubt.

Although the distributional range is now much diminished, the dainty, straight-horned oribi may still be found in Natal.

Orby, Oribi ~ *see Orbitje*
Orycterope ~ *see* Aarde vark
Oryx, *Oryx capensis* ~ *see* Sparrows
Ostrich ~ xii, 21, 22, 25, 43

Struthio camelus, the largest living bird (O. Struthioniformes, F. Struthionidae). The ostrich is flightless and at times nomadic; it prefers a bushveld-desert habitat, where it feeds on low plants, seeds and berries, and small animals. This habit makes it vulnerable and it was apparently threatened quite early with over-exploitation and required protection.

Later development of farming techniques (for feathers, skin, meat etc.) has protected the ostrich, but has involved 'improvement' of stock by interbreeding the indigenous sub-species, *S.c. australis*, with *S.c. camelus* (Arabia) and *S.c. syriacus* (Syria).

Otter, Canadian ~ *see Lutra canadensis*
Otter, South African ~ 106, 199, 201

A.D. does not report seeing live otters, but it is likely that he did because he so readily identifies the fur as used in Zulu ceremonial dress. *Lutra maculicollis*, the spotted-necked otter, has soft hair with a beautiful sheen and delicate colouring. Its skin has high commercial value today (F. Mustelidae, S.F. Lutrinae).

Ourigourap ~ see Crow
Out-bosch ~ 97–8

Timber forest (literally, 'wood bush', Afrikaans *houtbos*) – a term used to describe forests containing stinkwood, ironwood and yellowwood trees – all much prized for their beautifully textured, grained and coloured timbers. *Houtbos* now applies mainly to the southern Cape coastal forests. *See also Geele-out; Hyster-out; Stinck-out*

Oxpeckers ~ *see Buphaga*

Pachyderms ~ 53, 158, 263, 277, 286

Literally, 'thick-skins', a word that might have been applied to any animal with a very tough hide, e.g. crocodile, buffalo, hippopotamus, rhinoceros or elephant (*see* 64), requiring special guns and ammunition. Usually applied only to large and relatively hairless mammals with a thick, leathery hide, especially elephant and rhino.

Paerde sickt also Horse sickness ~ 37, 120

A disease which spread fast and was lethal, with horses lost in a few weeks and a high death toll in the space of a year (37). Both the Cape and Natal (120) were affected.

This was surely equine influenza – if the crude Boer remedies described can be used as clues to symptoms: constipation and loss of appetite, fever and severe debilitation. Good nursing and a light diet would have saved many lives: the 'remedies' must have inflicted horrible suffering and hastened death. Unhygienic stabling, etc. will have helped spread the infection. (A.D.'s *Paerde sickt*: cf Afrikaans *perd siekte*: horse sickness)

Palm, dwarf ~ *see* Dwarf palm

Panther ~ *see* Leopard

Parrot *also* Natal parrot ~ 97, 106

A.D. probably saw *Poicephalus robustus* near Pietermaritzburg – the Cape parrot, no longer, sadly, called Le Vaillant's parrot as formerly. The feathers used in Zulu ceremonial dress (106) may have been those of *P. robustus* or of the more northerly brownheaded parrot, *P. cryptoxanthus*, which has bright green plumage (O. Psittaciformes, F. Psittacidae).

Partridge ~ xii, 14, 81

Although the Chukar partridge, *Alectoris chukar*, was introduced into South Africa, the experiment was unsuccessful apart from Robben Island. A.D. will therefore not have encountered true partridges at all. Either he uses 'partridge' loosely to refer to partridge- or pheasantlike game birds in general, or, misled by the Dutch *patrijs* (Afrikaans *patrys*), he means the several species of sandgrouse so named (*Pterocles* spp: O. Pterocliformes, F. Pteroclidae).

Another possibility is the greywing francolin, *Francolinus africanus*, once known as the Cape partridge (O. Galliformes, F. Phasianidae).

Pelican ~ 25, 56

Large birds of marine and inland waters (O. Pelicaniformes, F. Pelecanidae). A.D. may have seen both the white pelican (*Pelecanus onocrotalus*) and the pinkbacked pelican (*P. rufescens*) in the south west Cape.

Penguin ~ *see* Cape penguin

Pestilence ~ 63–4, 80

A.D.'s writing is rich in such words and phrases as 'pestilence', 'pestilential emanations', 'pestilential maladies', 'foul contagion', etc. They reek themselves of the dread-filled mystery which surrounded the transmission of disease until comparatively recently. For A.D. and his contemporaries decay produced gases both evil-smelling and poisonous. The very odour of corruption was dangerous, whether it emanated from corpses consigned to the Ganges (64) or from heaps of rotting locusts (80). We need to remind ourselves occasionally that we have not known and understood the ways of parasites and other parthogens for all that long. To A.D. 'influenza' must still have had its sinister connotations as a creeping 'influence' from some dark region. Again, to him, malaria (q.v.) must have betokened *mala aria*, bad air: the subtle, disease-laden miasma or (his words) 'noxious mist' hovering nightly over swamps and, specifically, the St Lucia reedbeds (235). *See also* Cholera; Crocodile; Plague

Petrel *also* 'Birds of Satan', Cape petrel, 'damned souls', *Procellaria capensis*, *Procellaria pelagica*, 'sataniques', 'shoemakers' ~ 7–9, 99

(Petrel *cont.*)

Marine birds (O. Procellariiformes) called petrels or 'St Peter's birds' from their apparent ability to walk on water. Many are gregarious, and flocks may follow ships, alert for scraps of food thrown overboard. Some species dive for food; most feed at or near the surface. A.D.'s description of their habits (7–8) is accurate, if patchy. The chequered 'Cape petrel', A.D.'s *'Procellaria capensis'*, (7–8), is the Cape pigeon or pintado petrel, *Daption capense*. His 'shoemaker' (9) is the common Cape hen or white-chinned petrel, *Procellaria aequinoctialis* (both F. Procellariidae).

'Procellaria pelagica' is the European storm petrel, a common non-breeding visitor to southern African waters: *Hydrobates pelagicus* (F. Oceanitidae).

Mariners traditionally regard petrels as harbingers of bad weather. A.D.'s 'birds of Satan' (*'sataniques'*) and 'damned souls' are echoed in the English 'devil's bird' and 'Mother Carey's chickens'. Perhaps the foul smell exuded after death in some (8) contributes to the evil reputation. A.D. would have approved the names given by old whalers and sealers to *P. aequinoctialis*: 'stinker' and 'stink-pot'.

Phaeton *also* Bird of heaven ~ 5

Large marine birds of the genus *Phaethon* (O. Pelicaniformes, F. Phaethontidae), known in English as tropicbirds. Although neither of the southern African species occurs on the Atlantic seaboard, A.D.'s French name for the bird he saw, *'paille-en-queue'*, indicates that it certainly was *a* tropicbird. His name describes the characteristic long, narrow tail-feathers as aptly as does the English common name, 'marlin-spike'.

Pig of the plains ~ *see* Warthog

Pigeon *includes* Green pigeon, wood pigeon ~ 54, 97, 106

Several pigeons occur at or near Port Natal (54) and it is not possible to tell which A.D. saw there. *Columba arquatrix*, the Rameron pigeon, is common. One can identify A.D.'s 'green pigeon' (97) as *Treron calva*, common in forest and woodland of the east of southern Africa. *T. calva* may also have been the 'wood pigeon' whose feathers were used in Zulu ceremonial dress (106), but several other species also prefer a forest or woodland habitat. (O. Columbiformes, F. Columbidae). (For Delegorgue's pigeon, *see* 'Adulphe Delegorgue: Scientist', xix).

Plague ~ 63

Presumably A.D. refers to bubonic or pneumonic plague, linking the occurrence of those diseases in Egypt to a paucity of crocodiles (q.v.) in the rivers.

Both types of plague are caused by the bacterium *Pasteurella pestis*, and both are transmitted by rat fleas – and not by contaminated water or by the gases released during decay. Besides, A.D. errs: in India human corpses are consigned to rivers – to be eaten, or not, by crocodiles – but in Egypt this is not the custom, and never could have been. The Nile's enormous seasonal fluctuations make this form of corpse disposal completely impractical.

Plover *includes* Blacksmith plover ~ 25, 66, 69

Wading birds, of which A.D. may have seen several genera and species in the western Cape and elsewhere (O. Charadriiformes, F. Charadriidae).

The blacksmith plover,*Vanellus armatus* (66, 69) has a distinctive, clinking call which, as A.D. comments (69), betrays it to the human hunter. It is common on the shorelines of dams, pans, vleis etc. throughout southern Africa.

Poff-adder also Bloulou, puff adder ~ 136–7, 164, 193

Probably the common puffadder, *Bitis arietans* (S.O. Serpentes, F. Viperidae). It is a large, sluggish-looking adder, coloured yellow to brown and with darker bars or chevrons on the back.

It is highly unlikely that A.D. (136, 137) and Boulandje (164) were bitten by puffadders, whose venom is slow and may be deadly. Even if a puffadder bite does not kill, the venom is cytotoxic and causes massive tissue destruction. Besides, *B. arietans* does not strike gratuitously and the venom is reserved for its prey unless the snake is provoked. (*See also Nacht-adder*; Snakebite)

'Bloulou' is Zulu: *ibululu* = puffadder.

Port Natal scurvy ~ *see* Port-natal-sickt

Port-natal-sickt *also* Port Natal scurvy, *Port-natal-seurven*, Port Natal sickness ~ 51–2

'Natal sores' (called 'veld sores' in other parts of South Africa) are a kind of impetigo, an itchy staphylococcal – or possibly sometimes viral – skin infection spread by scratching, and festering and becoming ulcerated if untreated, especially in hot and humid weather. A.D.'s description is of Natal sores neglected or mistreated to the extent that they qualify rather as the condition known as 'tropical ulcer': chronic open sores which can be so severe as to require skin grafting.

Any small skin lesion may provide a site for infection: a scratch (52) or insect bite, for example. Ticks and mites (q.v.) do not directly cause Natal sores, but their bite causes inflammation and itching and so encourages the spread of bacteria. Similarly, the presence or absence of ticks would have only an indirect relationship to the incidence of the condition and tick eradication (52) would have been just one facet of a general push towards improved living conditions. Personal and domestic hygiene would have been of importance, as would good nutrition. Modern treatment is highly effective and usually consists of application of an antibiotic to the affected skin.

In Afrikaans the name would be *Port Natal siekte*: French phonetic spelling would eliminate the terminal 'e'.

Pouched gazelle ~ *see Spring-booken*
Powder ~ *see under* Snakebite
Procellaria capensis ~ *see* Petrei
Procellaria pelagica ~ *see* Petrel
Pronk-book ~ *see Spring-booken*
Protea argentea ~ 14–15

The 'silver tree', *Leucadendron argenteum* (Proteaceae) indeed grows wild nowhere but on the slopes of Table Mountain. It was A. Sparrman (q.v.) who first recorded (1786) their use as firewood and their good growth when cultivated at Constantia, though A.D. does not mention this.

Puff adder ~ *see Poff-adder*
Purple gallinule ~ *see* Gallinule, purple
Purple heron ~ *see* Heron
Python *also* Boa-python ~ 81, 131–5

Python sebae natalensis, the African rock python, occurs in most parts of Africa, except for deserts (S.O. Serpentes, F. Pythonidae). It is the largest snake in southern Africa, and may grow to a length of 960cm (32ft). It takes live prey, catching it in ambush and coiling round it to prevent it from breathing. Thus, as constrictors, pythons are the Old World equivalent of the New World boas: hence A.D.'s 'boa-python' (81). His zestful account of python habits and associated myth needs no comment or amplification, though it should be noted that the prey items he lists (132) would be the preferred food of medium-sized pythons. Adults take small antelope, and large pythons can capture kudu calves and impala.

Quadrumanes ~ 179

Literally, 'four hands': an archaic term referring to those primates in which the digits of both fore-and hind-limbs are prehensile.

Quagga ~ 178, 181, 215, 216, 241, 286

Equus quagga (O. Perissodactyla, F. Equidae): extinct. The anterior half of the body was striped; posteriorly it was brown and white. Early reports (1750–1800) were of huge quagga herds as far south-west as Ceres and Swellendam. Extinction was caused by over-exploitation (for food for Hottentot servants and for sport of the most wanton kind) and by sheep overgrazing. Numbers and range had dwindled drastically by 1820. A few lingered in the Orange Free State and the Eastern Cape. The last wild quagga were shot near Aberdeen in 1858 and near Kingwilliamstown in 1861.

Quinine sulphate ~ *see under* Malaria
Quiver tree ~ *see Kooker-boom*

Rail ~ *see* Water rail
Rat, house ~ 96

Pietermaritzburg dwellings were probably infested with *Rattus rattus*, an introduced species which has spread widely wherever there are human activities. (*R. norvegicus*, the closely related brown rat, occurs in

(Rat, house *cont.*)
  ports, but seldom inland.) (O. Roden-
  tia, F. Muridae: rats and mice.)
Rat, river *also Aulacaudus* ~ 96, 132
  Thrynomys swinderianus, formerly
  Aulacodus swinderianus, the greater
  canerat (O. Rodentia, F. Thrynomyi-
  dae). A very large rodent (total length
  72cm) in reedbeds and vegetation
  fringing rivers, lakes and swamps.
  Predominantly nocturnal and solitary.
Red ants ~ *see* Ants
Red hartebeest ~ *see Caama*
Red-shouldered widow bird ~ *see* Widow
  bird
Redunca capreolus ~ *see Rhee-book*
Redunca-eleotragus ~ *see Riet-book*
*Redunca lalandii also Nala, rooye-rhée-
  book, roye-rhée-book* ~ 238, 241, *144*
  Redunca fulvorufula, the mountain
  reed buck (Zulu: *inxala*; Afrikaans:
  rooiribbok. F. Bovidae, S.F. Reduncinae). An antelope which lives on dry,
  grassy, stony slopes with trees or
  bushes for cover, though available
  water is an essential requirement.
  One former name for *R. fulvorufula*
  is *Antilope lalandia*. Another is *Cervi-
  capra eleotragus* – a fact rendering
  dubious A.D.'s ability to distinguish
  perfectly between *R. fulvorufula* and
  the rietbok, *R. arundinum*, (*see Riet-
  book* for further brief discussion). As a
  means of aiding identification the illustration (*144*, Fig.1) is useless, being without distinguishing features.
Redunca scoparia ~ *see Orbitje*
Redwater fever ~ *see* Cattle sickness
Reed buck ~ *see Riet-book*
Reedbuck, mountain ~ *see Redunca lalandii*
Reed-hen *also* Water hen ~ 25, 189
  Probably the moorhen, *Gallinula
  chloropus*, an almost cosmopolitan
  water bird which clambers about
  reeds and roosts in them or in low
  bushes. If there is a distinction between A.D.'s 'reed-hen' (25) and the
  'water hen' he shot in Natal (189), the
  latter was probably *G. angulata*, the
  lesser moorhen (O. Gruiformes, F.
  Rallidae: rails, crakes, gallinules,
  moorhens, coots etc.).
Rhebok ~ *see Rhee-book*
*Rhee-book, Rhèe-booken also Redunca
  capreolus* ~ 44, 96–7
  Pelea capreolus, the grey rhebok (Afrikaans: *vaalribbok*) (F. Bovidae, S.F.
  Peleinae).

A.D.'s footnote (44) says 'species of
Cape chamois', so he must have been
impressed with this antelope's locomotion in its preferred rocky or mon-
tane habitat. It leaps high, or, if disturbed, bounds along with legs extended in a typical 'rockinghorse' gait,
displaying the white underside of the
tail. The colouring is greyish brown
with white underparts, and the male
has short, upstanding horns.
Rhenoster ~ *see* Rhinoceros
Rhinoceros *also Africanus Bicornis, Bicornis, Bicornis Africanus, Rhenoster,
  Rhinoceros Simus, Simus,* White rhinoceros ~ 53, 130, 157–8, 166, 179,
  180–1, 182–4, 218, 230–1, 239, 241,
  247, *259*, 268, 286
Two genera of rhinoceros (Afrikaans:
renoster) occur in southern Africa. The
squarelipped or white rhinoceros
(A.D.'s *'Rhinoceros Simus'*) is *Ceratotherium simum*, while the hooklipped
or black rhinoceros, (A.D.'s *'Africanus
Bicornis'*, etc.) is *Diceros bicornis*
(both O. Perissodactyla, F. Rhinocero-
tidae). Place names (e.g. 36) indicate
that both species were once widespread, but they were much depleted
by A.D.'s time. Complete extinction
has been averted by conservation
methods and reintroduction, although
C. simum and *D. bicornis* are again
under threat in the late 20th Century.
  A.D. was able to distinguish between the two, but often failed to
mention which he observed or hunted.
D. bicornis is solitary and the male
does not defend a territory. At a distance the dark grey colouring, the
prehensile upper lip and the small,
rounded ears would be enough to
identify it. *C. simum* is lighter in
colour, has longer, almost tubular
ears and has a distinct hump behind
the head. It lives in small groups and
the bulls are territorial. The illustration of *'Rhinoceros Africanus Bicornis'*
(*259*) is more likely to have been taken
from a (juvenile or foetal) white rhinoceros, *Ceratotherium simum* if the
shape of the ear is accurate. Unfortunately the absence of most adult
features – and the fact that the
muzzle, and thus the square or hooked
lip, has been partially obliterated in
printing – makes it impossible to be
certain. The printer's insistence on

(Rhinoceros *cont.*)
symmetry has made this illustration valueless.

Rietbok ~ *see Riet-book*

Riet-Book also *Coerulea, Eleotragus, omschlango, Redunca-eleotragus,* reed buck ~ 129–30, 149, 151, 169–70, 238, 240–1
Redunca arundinum (formerly *Antilope coerulescens*) the *rietbok* or reedbuck (F. Bovidae, S.F. Reduncinae), whose Zulu name is *inhlangu* (A.D.'s *'omschlango'*). *R. arundinum* occurs only where there is open water with cover – stands of tall grass or reedbeds.
Confused nomenclature (and perhaps A.D. himself was deceived by local colour varieties or subspecies) lends doubt to precise identification. It was not *R. arundinum* that formerly bore the specific name *eleotragus*, but the mountain reedbuck, *R. fulvorufula* (A.D.'s *Redunca lalandii*, q.v.) which prefers dry, grassy slopes. The identification of both in A.D.'s text therefore requires caution.

Ring-hals-slange also Necklace snake ~ 136
The rinkals or rinkhals, *Hemachatus haemachatus* (S.O. Serpentes, F. Elapidae). It is a stout, short (61–91.5cm) relative of the cobras. Brown or black, sometimes banded, it is widespread and plentiful in southern Africa. Under provocation the rinkals will rear up and spit venom, but vigorous teasing induces it to sham dead.
Venom in the eyes may produce severe conjunctivitis, but the effects – unlike the mythical ones related by A.D. – usually pass with time.

Rinkals/rinkhals ~ *see Ring-hals-slange*

River cormorant ~ *see* Cormorant

River-horse ~ *see* Hippopotamus

River rat ~ *see* Rat, river

Roan antelope ~ *see Bastaard guyms-book*

Robben ~ *see* Seal

Rock dassie ~ *see* Rock rabbits

Rock rabbits *also Klip-dassen* ~ 22, 132
The rock dassie, a small, compact, agile and surefooted mammal, also known as hyrax, rock rabbit and stone badger (O. Hyracoidea, F. Procaviidae: *Procavia capensis*). The English 'dassie' comes from the Dutch *das*: badger. *P. capensis* is still widely distributed in all four provinces of South Africa: it occurs in colonies where there are rocky outcrops with crevices for shelter and suitable plants for food. Colony size is related to the size of the habitat.

Roller, Angolan ~ 106
Several rollers – birds of bright plumage and powerful flight – might qualify as 'Angolan', having been recorded from that large territory. The safest guess is *Coracius caudata*, the lilacbreasted roller, which has a wide distribution from South Africa to Ethiopia, and including Angola. It was possibly the bright blue wing feathers of this bird that were used in Zulu ceremonial dress (O. Coraciiformes, F. Coraciidae).

Rondelet ~ *see under* Cardan

Rooiribbok ~ *see Redunca lalandii*

Rooye-booken also *Cephalopus natalensis* ~ 128–31, *145*, 164
The red duiker, *Cephalophus natalensis* (F. Bovidae, S.F. Cephalophinae). The pelage is richly red ('*rooye*': Afrikaans: *rooi*). The type locality is in Durban, but the tiny antelope disappeared from there long ago. It is still found in Natal coastal bush, however, which is surprising considering the assiduity with which it was hunted (131). A.D.'s descriptions are useful, but the illustration (*145*, Fig.3) is of the head of an unpleasantly dead specimen which, in view of the absence of horns or other distinguishing features, is zoologically worthless.

Rooye-rhée-book ~ *see Redunca lalandii*

Rope tree ~ *see* Fig tree

Rouvières ~ *see* Arago

Roye-rhée-book ~ *see Redunca lalandii*

Sacred ibis ~ *see* Ibis, sacred

Salt and alum ~ *see* Alum

'Sataniques' ~ *see* Petrel

Sausage tree ~ *see Tripinnaria tenacium*

Sea beans ~ *see Zee-Bontjes*

Sea-cow ~ *see* Hippopotamus

Sea swallow ~ 25
This could refer to any of the following: *Hirundo cucullata*, the greater striped swallow; *H. fuligula*, the rock martin; or *Riparia paludicola*, the brownthroated or African sand martin (O. Passeriformes, F. Hirundinidae: swallows and martins).

Sea-wolf ~ 24–5

Belon's (q.v.) description of this creature is probably secondhand: his own travels were concentrated in the eastern Mediterranean and Middle East. A.D. doubts that the sea-wolf occurs in Britain, but provides no date or title for Belon's extract which thus remains inaccessible to us. All we do know is that the 16th Century naturalist set down a description which resembled that of *Hyaena brunnea* (*see* Hyaena).

Seagull ~ 25, 45

Several different species of seagull (*Larus* spp) are common on the south western and south eastern Cape coasts: detailed identification is not possible from the information given (O. Charadriiformes, F. Laridae: skuas, gulls, terns).

Seals *also* Robben ~ 35

Finfooted marine mammals (O. Pinnipedia). *Arctocephalus pusillus*, the Cape fur seal, habitually breeds on South African coasts. One of its preferred sites early gained the name Seal Island: Robben Island (A.D.'s 'Eyland') from Dutch *rob*: seal.

Secretary bird ~ 43

Sagittarius serpentarius (O. Falconiformes, F. Sagittariidae), longlegged and large (standing up to 1.5m), found throughout southern Africa. A predator – apparently valued as such and protected – on insects, amphibians, small reptiles and small mammals, especially rodents. It is the hunting habit which long ago provided the common name: *saqr-et-tair*, Arabic: hunting bird, and not the fancied resemblance of the crest to quill pens.

Seeboontjie ~ *see Zee-Bontjes*

Sentinel lark ~ *see under* Lark

Seu ~ 258

A Latin word meaning 'or'; 'also'. A.D. uses it to indicate that an animal (in this case the blue wildebeest, his '*Catoblepas gorgon*' q.v.) may have two acceptable specific names, thus, *Catoblepas gorgon*, also known as (*seu*) *Catoblepas taurina*.

Shark ~ 4–5

Marine fishes in which the skeleton is of cartilage, not bone. The seamen could have hauled in a number of different species, ranging from small dogfish to sharks of all sizes.

'Shoemakers' ~ *see under* Petrel

Shrike ~ 54, 97

Small, aggressive birds, predators on invertebrates and small vertebrates, including other birds. A.D. probably refers to *Lanius collaris*, the fiscal shrike (*fiskaal*), given this name for its 'cruelty' (it kills and then impales its prey, building up a larder) by association with the title of a stern government official. The bird was also known, especially in Natal, as the Johnny or Jackie Hangman. A.D. may also have seen the redbacked shrike, *L. collurio* (O. Passeriformes, F. Laniidae).

Sickness, Human ~ *see* Illness

'Silver tree' ~ *see Protea argentea*

Simus ~ *see* Rhinoceros

Skunk ~ 133n

Probably the striped polecat, *Ictonyx striatus* (F. Mustelidae, S.F. Mustelinae): superficially similar to the civet (q.v.), but not a close relative.

Slange-steen ~ *see* Snakebite

Snail ~ 222

If these forest snails near St. Lucia were particularly impressive (and A.D.'s love of the flamboyant suggests they may have been) perhaps they were *Achatina fulica*, the East African giant land snail (molluscs: C. Gastropoda, O. Pulmonata).

Snake bird *also Anhinga* ~ 25, 69

Anhinga melanogaster (O. Pelicaniformes, F. Anhingidae: darters) A medium-sized bird with a long, slender, pointed bill, a long neck and a long, stiff tail. It inhabits inland waters, 'spear-fishing' prey (fish, frogs etc.) on the bill by means of a specialised trigger mechanism in the neck permitting a lightning strike.

The bird often swims 'at periscope depth', with the body so low that only the head and serpentine neck are seen – hence, 'snake bird'.

Snake of the night ~ *see Nacht-adder*

Snake stone ~ *see under* Snakebite

Snakebite ~ 135–6, 164–6, 237

As puffadder bites produce severe symptoms and are often deadly (*see Poff-adder*) it is more likely that the bites recorded by A.D. were all those of either the night adder (*see Nacht-adder*) or the southern stiletto snake (*Atractaspis bibronii*, formerly known as the burrowing adder). He spares us the truly grisly details, but presents a

(Snakebite *cont.*)

picture of the typical sequence of reactions to such adder bites: localised swelling at the site followed, as the swelling spread upward, by severe groin pain, nausea, fever and delirium. Acute suffering for nine to ten days led, with or without treatment, to a recovery which seemed almost magically sudden.

Before the development of antisera (available in South Africa by 1910) treatment of snakebite was carried out in three main ways:

1. The swallowing of alkaline 'remedies' e.g. ammonia, in order to neutralise the 'acidity' of the venom. This was as useless – and almost as dangerous – as was the drinking of decoctions containing strychnine (*see also* Wounds) and/or alcohol in an attempt to restore heart and nerve function if the venom was neurotoxic. A.D. tried none of these himself, and writes scornfully of the Zulu use of snake bone ash (166) though, as bone ash is alkaline, and as he himself subscribes to beliefs about the possibility of neutralising 'acid' venom, he really has no right to do so.

2. Removal of venom from the wound site, following the swift application of a ligature (164) nearer to the body to prevent the venom from spreading. After making an incision (164) suction was applied: A.D. lists several feasible and unfeasible methods, from simple mouth suction (165) to leeches (q.v.), to a pneumatic pump or aspirator (135, 165). Included here would be use of poultices (136) and the grim (and certainly ineffectual) Boer method of using the heart and bloodvessels of a live fowl to suck up the venom (165).

The porous snakestone (165) – if A.D. actually witnessed its use – would simply have imbibed blood from the wound for as long as the anticoagulant in the snake venom prevented clotting. Once clotting ability returned the patient would be almost recovered. Thus, the snakestone was merely an indicator of progress. The same would apply to the ability to keep down warm milk (165) – or any other food, for that matter. Absence of nausea and restoration of normal digestive function indicates that the ill effects of the venom have passed.

The quaint notion that a puffadder carries a stone on its head may have arisen by association, from the snake's frequent preference for stony crevices.

3. Neutralisation or destruction of the venom at the site of the wound. Again, this required a ligature and incisions. Then came the application of the usual alkaline substances: ammonia (164) and 'alkali' or 'volatile alkali' (136) – probably *sal volatile*, an ammonium salt. 'Cauterization with powder' (164) involved laying the flesh open and flashing gun-powder in the wound: it was thought effective in destroying venom if performed within five minutes of the bite.

Of all of these techniques, ligature and simple suction would have been most effective – but only if applied immediately. Delayed, they would, like most of the other methods, have been useless and would have increased suffering and the likelihood of infection. Had Houahouaho and Nanana (237) known this they would have considered themselves fortunate: without the help – or, perhaps, torment – of A.D.'s assorted nostrums their recovery pattern from snakebite was straightforward and accomplished in the standard time (*see also* Cotton tree)

Snipe ~ 25, 96

Probably the Ethiopian snipe, *Gallinago nigripennis*, which frequents swampy ground and casual water, and has a wide range in southern Africa (O. Charadriiformes, F. Scolopacidae: godwit, snipe, curlew, sandpiper etc.).

Solipeds ~ 158

An outmoded name for horses and their relatives (O. Perissodactyla, F. Equidae): it refers to the superficially single-toed (monodactylous) character of the feet.

Souimanga also Amethyst sunbird ~ 54, 128

Rarely used, '*souimanga*' is occasionally found in French zoological and ornithological literature. It is surprising that A.D. used it (meaning sunbird) when Le Vaillant (*see* Levaillant) always used *sucrier* for these birds.

Sunbirds are small and brightly metallic-coloured, with long, slender beaks for extracting nectar from

(Souimanga cont.)
flowers (O. Passeriformes, F. Nectariniidae). These tiny, vivid creatures are both varied and plentiful, especially in the coastal vegetation of Natal, and it is surprising that A.D. mentions them only twice – and identifies only one of them (128). This, the 'amethyst sunbird' is *Nectarinia amethystina*, the black sunbird. The adult male is a soft, velvety black with a purplish shade, and the cheeks, throat and upper tail coverts are a rich, metallic violet-purple. Depending on lighting conditions the rump appears black, violet or even pink.

Sour pasturage *also* Sour grass, *suren vlaacke* ~ 43, 221
Sourveld or sourgrass veld occurs near the sea and in a high rainfall belt. It consists of several sorts of coarse grass, and provides poor grazing. Sparrman (q.v., 1786) recorded that cattle raised on sourveld chewed thongs, bones, etc. in response to the phosphate deficiency in their diet. (*See, for contrast, Zoet-gras*).

Sparrman, Andrew ~ xiv
Swedish naturalist; friend and contemporary of Thunberg (q.v.). The two arrived – but not together – at the Cape in April 1772. Sparrman, born in 1748, was 24.

He had been a botany student under the great Linnaeus himself, but later developed a passion for zoology. After seven months at the Cape, he went, as assistant to two German naturalists, on a long sea voyage (in the *Resolution* captained by James Cook), returning to the Cape in 1775. From July 1775 to April 1776 he travelled inland, going as far as the Great Fish River near Cookhouse.

Sparrman returned to Stockholm, and, duly loaded with academic honours, published his two-volume travel memoir: *A voyage to the Cape of Good Hope, towards the Antarctic polar circle, and round the world: but chiefly into the country of the Hottentots and Caffres from the year 1772 to 1776* (Swedish edition 1783; English 1786).

These volumes are the products of a keen eye and a lively mind. Sparrman may not have been a true explorer (he travelled within the limits of settlement) and his writings may be plagued by vaguenesses and inaccuracies, but on the whole they are clear and truthful and especially interesting for the recounting of agricultural practices and methods (*see* e.g., *Protea argentea*; Sour pasturage). This subject fascinated him, but he did later publish a two-volume ornithological work including South African birds, and also a fuller account of his voyage with Captain Cook.

Sparrows *includes* Finch, Hawfinch, *Ignicolor*, *Oryx capensis*, weaver birds ~ 58
For A.D. 'sparrow' seems to be a general category for any small bird with a conspicuous, well-shaped nest. He seems to use the other names interchangeably. If it is assumed that all are passerines of F. Ploceidae (bishops, sparrows, weavers etc.) then: '*Oryx capensis*', the 'yellow and black hawfinch', is probably *Euplectes capensis*, the Cape bishop or yellow-rumped widow, described in older texts as the black and yellow bishop bird.

'*Ignicolor*' (= fire-coloured) cannot have been *E. hordeaceus*, the fire-crowned bishop, which is confined in southern Africa to the extreme east of Zimbabwe and northern Mozambique. A.D. probably means *Euplectes orix*, the red bishop, distributed throughout most of South Africa.

Relatively few birds in South Africa are known as 'finches' in English, but in Afrikaans *vink* is commonly used for many small passerines: A.D. may have been influenced by the Dutch in this usage. As for weaver birds, A.D. may have seen several species of *Ploceus* nesting in reeds near Port Natal.

Sphinx *also Atropos*, death's head moth, *Groot-honing-bye*, hawkmoth ~ 250
Acherontia atropos, the death's head hawkmoth, has a skull pattern on the dorsal surface of the thorax. 'Sphinx' comes from the rearing up of the moth's stout larvae when disturbed: early entomologists saw a resemblance to the Sphinx of Egypt and actually bestowed the name, as Sphingidae, on this whole family of moths (O. Lepidoptera).

A. atropos is large and thickbodied. It often plunders beehives, drawing up the honey by means of its exten-

(Sphinx cont.)

sible proboscis. As A.D. demonstrated to the Boers (and in typical showman's fashion), the moth can neither bite nor sting.

'*Groot-honing-bye*' (large honey bee) is curious, for no sphingid could be mistaken for a bee. However, several other old names for *A. atropos* seem, now, to be quite as mysterious or inept: to early English naturalists, for example, it was the 'Bee Tyger'.

Spitting cobra, Spitting snake ~ *see Spouwer-slange*

Spotted hyaena ~ *see under* Hyaena

Spouwer-slange also iphesy, spitting snake ~ 136, 193, 251–2

The blacknecked spitting cobra, *Naja mossambica* (Zulu: *imfezi*) (S.O. Serpentes, F. Elapidae). It is primarily nocturnal, but may bask near its retreat (a rock crevice, a tree bole, under a log, an abandoned termite nest) by day.

A.D.'s graphic account is accurate, but some of the effects of the venom are exaggerated: venom in the eyes causes severe conjunctivitis and, if untreated, eyes can become ulcerated. They do not, however, undergo the macabre changes A.D. describes (251–2). His suggested explanation of the spitting mechanism is in principle correct (252).

Spring-booken also euchore, *Gazella euchore*, pouched gazelle, *pronkbook* ~ 33–4, 36, 38, 130

The springbok: a beautiful and lively antelope of medium size: *Antidorcas marsupialis*, (F. Bovidae, S.F. Antilopinae). Le Vaillant (*see* Levaillant, 1790) named it *Antilope euchore* (*euchore*, Gk: fine dancer) which matches the Afrikaans *pronkbok*. In 'pronking' the animal leaps high (up to 1m) with the body curved, legs stiff and close together and the head held low. In swift running the body is extended and kept low over the ground.

A.D.'s 'pouch' is reflected in the name *marsupialis* (from L. *marsupium*: purse or bag): a dorsal fan of long white hairs lies flat in a pouch. The fan is erected when the animal is alarmed, and shows as a flash of white. Springbok once roamed in huge herds in arid regions and on open grassland: agriculture has severely reduced their distributional range.

Spring-Haan-Voogel ~ *see under Ardea bubulcus*

Spring has also Cape jerboa ~ 44

Pedetes capensis, the springhare (Afrikaans *springhaas*), described in A.D.'s footnote as a 'leaping hare' (O. Rodentia, F. Pedetidae: *P. capensis* is the only species).

The animal bounds and hops on powerful hind legs, using the tail, kangaroo-fashion, for balance. The habit is nocturnal, which may be why A.D. did not see it in the Eastern Cape, for even now the springhare is widely distributed in southern Africa. 'Hare' (q.v.) is of course a misnomer, as is 'jerboa', the common name of a small north African and Asian rodent (F. Dipodidae).

Spurwinged goose ~ *see* Goose

Squarelipped rhinoceros ~ *see* Rhinoceros

Starling ~ *see under Ardea bubulcus*

Steen-book also Bleek-steen-book ~ 22, 241

Sometimes miscalled the *steinbok*, the steen bok, *Raphicerus campestris*, had become rare in the western Cape by the end of the 18th century, and 18th and 19th century authors were confused about its identification. As A.D., like Thunberg (q.v.) before him, uses *duyker* and *steen-book* in the same sentence (22) he could apparently distinguish between these two small antelope: he may thus indeed have seen *R. campestris*.

Bleek-steen-book (Natal, 241) were doubtless also *R. campestris*, possibly a silvery-coated subspecies of these dainty animals (F. Bovidae, S.F. Antilopinae).

Stilt ~ 25

The blackwinged stilt, *Himantopus himantopus* (O. Charadriiformes, F. Recurvirostridae). This very long-legged bird is common in shallow inland waters throughout southern Africa.

Stinck-gras ~ 103

Probably *Eragrostis cilianensis* (Poaceae), a tufted annual grass that was introduced with impure agricultural seed from the Mediterranean region. It has an aromatic scent.

Stinck-out also Stinkwood ~ 42, 97

The stinkwood (Afrikaans, *stinkhout*) tree, *Ocotea bullata* (Lauraceae) is a medium to large evergreen tree of the high south and east coastal forests.

(*Stinck-out cont.*)

The wood is beautifully coloured and textured and has long been prized for furniture (and not merely for gun butts: 97).

The strong smell of stinkwood is released only when it is freshly cut: it can surely not have been a deterrent to birds (42).

Stork *includes* Marabou stork and Violet stork/*Ciconia umbellata* ~ 28, 69, 81
The huge black and white marabou stork, *Leptoptilos crumeniferus*, is quite common in the tropical to sub-tropical east and north of southern Africa. In Natal it is a vagrant and thus rare, as A.D. observes (69).

His 'violet stork', '*Ciconia umbellata*' is less easy to identify precisely. Purple or violet glossing of plumage above is not uncommon in storks, as in *Ciconia ciconia*, the common white stork, which also has the body plumage pink-tinged. *Mycteria ibis*, the yellow-billed stork, has the white body plumage washed with rose-pink; wings and tail are black. (O. Ciconiiformes, F. Ciconiidae). *See also Ardea bubulcus.*

Strand-wolf ~ *see* Hyaena
Stripsiceros kudu ~ *see* Kudu
Strychnos, edible *also see Geèle wild-kalabas-boom, klein wild-kalabas-boom, and see weld-calebasses-boom* ~ 180
Strychnos madagascariensis, the black or spineless monkey orange (Afrikaans: *botterklapper*), a small shrubby tree common in the east of South Africa, in scrub, coastal forest and riverine fringes (Loganiaceae). The almost spherical fruit is up to 8cm in diameter, bluish green when young, yellow with brown patches when ripe, with a thick, woody shell. The pulp, sweet, acidulous and refreshing, is dried by the indigenous people and stored (some say it keeps for years) for use as porridge: the delicate flavour is reminiscent of dried apricots.

Strychnos spinosus ~ *see Weld-calebasses-boom*
Sulphate of quinine ~ *see* Malaria
Sunbird ~ *see Souimanga*
Suren vlaacke ~ *see* Sour pasturage
Sus larvatus ~ *see* Bushpig
Sus phacochoerus ~ *see* Warthog
Swift ~ 31

Several species of *Apus*, the swifts (O. Apodiformes, F. Apodidae) fly low be-fore a storm, as A.D. describes, much as do the bee-eaters (q.v.) to which they are related.

Sword grass ~ 224, 226

Possibly spear grass, *Heteropogon contortus* (Poaceae), a densely tufted, perennial sour grass of rocky places. The name comes from the shape of the sharp callus of the spikelet, which adheres to the coat of any passing mammal, aiding dispersal. Otherwise, a 'sword grass' may be any grass with long, swordshaped leaves and robust flower stems.

Symba ~ *see* Genet

Tambooty trees ~ 181, 182, 254

Spirostachys africana, the tamboti tree: medium-sized with a rounded crown (Euphorbiaceae). It occurs in the eastern parts of South Africa. A more correct spelling would be tomboti, from Zulu, *umthomboti* – a 'poison tree': the milky latex was once used to tip arrowheads and is still used as a fish poison. *S. africana* is indeed 'anything but harmless' (182).

Although A.D. deemed the trees dangerous in a storm (182) he used them to support his tent in a high gale (254). Perhaps the former indicated his apprehension of being struck by lightning: the latter simply provides confirmation of the strength and durability of tamboti wood.

Tambouki-gras ~ 168

Tambookie grass or *tambukigras*: a general name for several species of *Cymbopogon, Hyparrhenia* and *Miscanthidium*: tall, coarse grasses, some of which are used for thatching. They were once used for Bushman arrow shafts and as tapers (Poaceae).

The name derives from that of the Tambouki or Tambuki people (xv): the Amatembu tribe which took this name after absorbing a Bushman people in the region called Tambukiland (named for the latter) – the present Queenstown district.

Tapir ~ 158

Any similarities between the hippopotamus and the tapir are superficial and related to a shared amphibious

(Tapir *cont.*)

habit. They belong to different mammalian orders: the closest relatives of the hippopotamus are the pigs and antelope (O. Artiodactyla: the 'even-toed' ungulates), while the tapir's affinities are to the rhinoceros and the horses (O. Perissodactyla: the 'odd-toed' ungulates). Tapirs do not occur in Africa, but in Malaya and the New World. Some species live in the swamps and wet tropical forests of south east Asia and south and central America.

Taurina ~ *see Catoblepas gorgon; Seu*

Tavernier, Jean Baptiste ~ 53

17th century French traveller and pioneer of trade with India. His first journey to India (1638–43) was followed by four more, after which he returned to settle in affluence and to publish accounts of his journeys. A.D. had probably read *Les Six Voyages de J. B. Tavernier* (1676).

Teal *also Anas madagascarensis*, Madagascan teal ~ 66, 69, 189

Probably the small, blue-billed hottentot teal, *Anas hottentota*, whose distributional range includes Madagascar (O. Anseriformes, F. Anatidae: ducks, geese, swans etc.).

Termites *also* White ants ~ xii, 129, 133

Termites or white ants are social insects living in colonies of hundreds of thousands of individuals (O. Isoptera). Nests may be subterranean or else visible as clay mounds of varying height and shape, and of a cement-like consistency, with internal cells for the inhabitants (129). Of a number of South African species, two common termites are *Amitermes atlanticus* (Cape Province) and *Macrotermes natalensis* (Natal). Termite nests are, of course, raided by the antbear (*see Aarde vark*).

Tern ~ 45

Terns are slender, gull-like birds with narrow wings and forked tails: they hover over water picking up small fish in forceps-like bills. Several species of marine tern, *Sterna* spp, are common in the Eastern Cape (O. Charadriiformes, F. Laridae: skuas, gulls, terns).

Thorn bushes/trees/veld ~ *see* Mimosa

Thunberg, Charles Peter (Carl Pehr) ~ (x)

Swedish naturalist, friend and close contemporary of Sparrman (q.v.). The two arrived – but not together – at the Cape in April 1772. Thunberg, already with a doctorate in physics from Uppsala, was 28.

In the almost three years he spent in South Africa, Thunberg travelled far more extensively than did Sparrman. However, although he returned to Sweden before Sparrman, his travel journals were not published until after Sparrman's.

The South African travels were included with Thunberg's other expeditions, in two volumes: *Travels in Europe, Africa and Asia performed between the years 1770 and 1779* (Swedish edition 1788; English 1793 or 1795).

Like many naturalists of the period he had a fine working knowledge of numerous disciplines; like many, he often had small regard for detail that would now be considered essential. Respected in botanical circles even now as 'the father of Cape botany' he was often casual about precise localities of the great numbers of plants he lovingly described. His name remains prominent, not only as the authority for many familiar species (e.g. of *Acacia* and *Ficus*), but also in nomenclature, e.g. *Thunbergia* (Acanthaceae); *Thunbergiella* (Umbelliferae).

In view of Thunberg's prominence, and of the great usefulness of his writings to any naturalist visiting South Africa, one would expect A.D. to have known and referred to his work. In fact, A.D.'s botanical knowledge is, in some areas, so woolly that he seems to have consulted no authorities at all. Perhaps (for it is pleasant to speculate) the ebullient A.D. *did* consult Thunberg, only to discard volumes which – however sound – were filled with lamentations over the lack in South Africa of urban comforts and European landscapes.

Tick bird ~ *see under Ardea bubulcus*

Ticks and mites *also Bosch-luys*, bush lice, *G. acharus*, tracheal arachnids ~ 52–3, 144, 159, 166, 240

As A.D. records, many species of tick (Afrikaans: *bosluis*) occur in Natal, and there are many more species of the related, smaller arachnids known as mites (both O. Acarina). Indeed, the genus *Acarus* ('*G. acharus*') now pertains only to certain mites and not to ticks. It is difficult to understand why, to A.D., ticks in particular are 'tracheal' arachnids as there are few Arachnida which do not breathe by means of tracheal tubules carrying air from the body surface to the tissues.

Ticks are usually temporary, sometimes permanent, ectoparasites, clinging to a host and piercing its integument so that its body fluid can be drawn into the tick's extensible gut (I.O. Ixodides).

The tiny red ticks at Port Natal were 'pepper ticks', i.e. juveniles which, having hatched at the base of a grass stem, ascend the stem in huge numbers, so increasing their chances of being brushed off onto the skin of a passing mammal – the young individual's first host (52–3). A.D. acted as first host for many young ticks – perhaps *Hyalomma rufipes* (the red-legged tick) or *Rhipicephalus appendiculatus* (the brown ear tick). They may have caused the itching and blistering he describes – as might lesions left by burrowing mites – but although this would have aggravated 'Natal sores' ('*Port-natal-sickt*' q.v.) it would not have caused them.

The severe effects on cattle and horses (52–3) occur in summer when adult tick activity reaches a peak. Ears are infested with *Rhipicephalus appendiculatus*, while *Hyalomma rufipes* and the 'bont', i.e. coloured, tick, *Amblyomma hebraeum*, attach elsewhere. The latter two have large mouthparts and the resultant skin damage may lead to the formation of abscesses. Tissue damage may then be exacerbated by the fly *Chrysomia bezziana*, which lays eggs at the bite sites. These hatch into screw worm larvae which cause massive tissue destruction: a dreadful sequence of events that A.D. clearly witnessed (53).

Dipping would have been the only solution, with tick 'burdens' so high, but apparently the Boers at Port Natal had not yet begun using arsenic for this purpose.

It is not surprising, therefore, that cattle succumbed to such diseases as redwater fever (182: Cattle sickness q.v.), caused by the pathogen *Babesia*

bovis carried and transmitted by ticks.

The large, ornately coloured ticks A.D. noted on rhinoceros were probably the bont ticks, *Amblyomma sparsum* and *A. tholloni* (53), while those on the soft areas of hippopotamus skin and that of other big game would be *A. tholloni*, *A. hebraeum* and the glossy brown tick, *Rhipicephalus simus* (53, 144, 159).

The 'ticks' noted on birds and reptiles (53) may indeed have been ticks ('soft' ticks: I.O. Argasidae) but may also have been mites. Many mites are parasitic, penetrating the skin between feathers and scales, but a number are commensal and feed on the surface debris from skin, scales, feathers and skin secretions.

Tavernier's (53) 'leeches' were surely just that: he is highly unlikely to have been plagued by ticks in the rain forests of India, despite A.D.'s wishful speculations. *See also Ardea bubulcus; Buphaga*; Cattle sickness; Leeches; *Port-natal-sickt*

Tiger-wolf ~ *see* Hyaena

Toucan ~ 56–7

Toucans (O. Piciformes, F. Ramphastidae) resemble hornbills (q.v.) in having a huge, bizarre and brightly coloured bill, but they lack the helmet-like outgrowth of the hornbill. They are confined to tropical regions of the Americas, from Mexico to Argentina.

A.D.'s comparison of toucan and hornbill is enlightened: it would be good to know the identity of the 'famous naturalist' (56) who influenced his thinking.

Touraco/Turaco *also* Loury, *includes Coliphymus concolor*/grey, crested touraco; *Touraco porphyroelopha* / *Corythaix porphyreolopha* ~ 54, 97, 106, 175, 201

Touracos or louries are medium to large birds, often with bright plumage and a conspicuously crested head (O. Musophagiformes, F. Musophagidae). They feed mainly on fruit, seeds and buds.

'*Touraco porphyroelopha*' (54) or '*Corythaix porphyreolopha*' (201) is *Tauraco porphyreolophus*, the purple crested lourie: body mainly green, crest and wing coverts metallic purple, wings crimson. It is fairly common in the extreme east of

(Touraco *cont.*)
southern Africa, in riverine forest, evergreen thicket and woodland. The feathers would indeed have formed a colourful component of Zulu ceremonial dress (106, 201). '*Coliphymus concolor*' is the grey lourie, *Corythaixoides concolor*. As A.D. comments (175) it is absent from the south, and occurs mainly in Zululand and the Transvaal. The 'unattractive' cry is a loud, drawn-out, nasal 'Go-'way' (hence called the 'goaway' bird), although the bird also grunts, yowls and shrieks.

Tracheal arachnids ~ *see* Ticks and mites

Tree-creeper ~ xii
Salpornis spilonotus, the spotted creeper (Afrikaans: *boomkruiper*) (O. Passeriformes, F. Salpornithidae). Long-billed insectivorous birds somewhat resembling woodpeckers. They forage on tree trunks and branches, starting near the bottom and fluttering and clambering upward.

Tree snake ~ *see Boom-slange*

Tripinnaria tenacium ~ 179
The sausage tree, *Kigelia africana* (Bignoniaceae). The older '*Tripinnaria*' describes the compound leaf which often has three pairs of opposite leaflets (pinnae) and a terminal one. 'Sausages' may be 1m long and 125mm in diameter, greyish and rough. They are roasted and used to flavour beer, and seeds may be roasted and eaten. They also have many medicinal and magical uses and would be justly called muti (*see Mouty*).
A.D. notes that monkeys do not eat the fruit. Interestingly, some mammals wait for the large, red flowers to fall and eat them with apparent relish.

Tropicbird ~ *see* Phaeton

Trumpeter hornbill ~ *see* Hornbill

Turaco ~ *see* Touraco/Turaco

Turtle dove ~ *see* Dove

Umbretta *also Ardea ombretta, hamer-kop*, hammer head ~ 58, 258
Scopus umbretta, the *hamerkop* or (sometimes) hammerhead, so called because of the crest which, when erect, looks like the claw on a hammer. The bird stands about 60cm high and resembles a heavily built heron, with large eyes and a spadelike bill (O. Ciconiiformes, F. Scopidae). It frequents the banks of rivers, estuaries, swamps and marshes, and may perch on the backs of hippos.
The huge nest (58) which may be used for many seasons, is remarkable enough to have generated a rich mythology. The Xhosa people, for example, believed it to be divided into three rooms, one of them a sort of larder. This notion found its way, with quaint embellishments, into some Victorian textbooks.

Uncklove ~ see Elephant

Uncklove-doane ~ *see* Warthog

Veld sores ~ *see Port-natal-sickt*

Vegetable ivory palm ~ *see Wild-klaapper-noot*

Violet stork ~ *see under* Stork

Vlaackt-vaark ~ *see* Warthog

Volatile alkali ~ *see under* Snakebite

Vulture ~ 14, 36, 55, 63, 67, 142, 148, 180, 187, 215–7, 218, 235, 252–3, 255–6
Large diurnal birds of prey (raptors) which generally prefer – or subsist entirely upon – carrion rather than live prey. For A.D. they are almost a symbol for the scavenging habit (187) and the dearth of vultures at Table Mountain (14) may be taken as an indication of a generalised disappearance of indigenous fauna from that locality. A.D. was also impressed by the huge flocks of vultures descending on any large carcase (255–6, 281) and by the lofty heights from which they scan the ground for food.
To A.D., vultures are vultures and he notes no differences from place to place. The Cape vulture, *Gyps coprotheres*, occurs over most of South Africa. At the Natal coast, he may have seen in addition the Egyptian vulture, *Neophron percnopterus*, the whitebacked vulture, *Gyps africanus*, and the lappetfaced vulture, *Torgos tracheliotus* (O. Falconiformes, F. Accipitridae).

Waater-book ~ *see* Water-buck

Wader *also* Large-headed wader ~ 66, 69
Term commonly applied to sand-pipers, snipe and their allies (O. Cha-radriiformes, F. Scolopacidae), and several genera and species of scolopa-cid waders occur in Natal. However, the wading habit is not confined to this family and the 'large-headed' wader may have been a member of another. One strong possibility is the water dikkop, *Burhinus vermiculatus* (F. Burhinidae), a longlegged, plover-like bird with a heavy bill and large eyes giving the head a somewhat over-sized appearance.

Wahlberg, Johan August (1810–56) ~ 41, 43, 46–7, 69, 72–3, 81, 163, 180, 252
Swedish naturalist, collector, hunter and traveller, continuing in the tra-dition of his 18th century com-patriots Sparrman and Thunberg (q.q.v.). He arrived at the Cape in February 1839. When he, A.D. and Krauss (q.v.) reached Port Natal, Wahlberg stayed at the Congella trekker camp. He returned to Stock-holm in August 1845 after a number of hunting and collecting trips, some of them in the company of A.D. In 1843 he rendezvoused with A.D. at the Limpopo.

One of Wahlberg's interests – he was, like many of his contemporaries, something of a polymath – was sur-veying. It was he who surveyed and laid out Pietermaritzburg for the Trekkers.

Presumably he returned home with many specimens, especially of birds, but he did not publish for some years. In 1855 a paper in Swedish described 'new birds from Damaraland, South Africa', while 'new South African birds' appeared in German, appar-ently posthumously, in 1857. Wahl-berg remains an inextricable part of South African ornithology, e.g. in *Aquila wahlberg*i, known as Wahl-berg's eagle.

Warbler ~ 97
Several species of warbler (O. Passeri-formes, F. Sylviidae) occur in and near Pietermaritzburg. Genera include *Acrocephalus*, *Chloropeta* and *Bra-dypterus*. Warblers are usually small and often drably coloured and shy. Identification needs to be based on a number of features, including call.

Warthog *also* Large-snouted boar, little elephant, masked boar, pig of the plains, *Sus phacochoerus*, *uncklove-doane*, *vlaackt-vaark* ~ 130, 189, 215, 232, 241, 244, 257, *259*
Most of A.D.'s references to 'wild boar' are probably to bushpig (q.v.), but all are included here as he does not dis-tinguish bushpig from warthog until the final chapter (257). *Phacochoerus aethiopicus*, the warthog, formerly *Sus phacochoerus*, is indeed a 'pig of the plains' (Afrikaans: *vlakvark*), pre-ferring open grassland and not being dependent on the availability of water.

It is large and long-snouted, with males reaching 104kg – hence 'little elephant', which is the literal mean-ing of the Zulu name for the warthog, *indlovu dawane* ('*uncklove-doane*'). The warthog does seem to be 'masked': the snout is broadened by bony outgrowths of the jaw enclosing the bases of the tusk-like canines, and there are two pairs of conspicuous facial outgrowths of skin, the 'warts', one pair on the cheeks, the other antero-lateral to the eyes.

The illustration (*259*) is a frontal view of the head of *P. aethiopicus* probably taken from a preserved specimen in view of the smooth tight-ness of the skin and its relatively hairless condition.

Water-buck *also* Donkey-buck, *eezel-book*, *ipiva*, *Kobus ellipsiprymnus*, *leeauw-book*, lion-buck ~ 213, 238–41, 242, 258
Kobus ellipsiprymnus, the large, handsome waterbuck (Afrikaans: *waterbok*), so called because seldom found more than 2km from open water (F. Bovidae, S.F. Reduncinae). Easily-distinguished by the white ring round the rump.

A.D.'s suggested names (never ac-cepted by other naturalists) were logical. 'Donkey buck' or '*Eezel-book*' (cf Afrikaans, *eselbok*) would em-phasise the donkey-coloured coat and the hornlessness of females and young. 'Lion-buck' or '*leeauw-book*' (cf Afrikaans *leeubok*) would focus on the mane-like neck- and chest-hair. '*Ipi-va*' comes directly from the Zulu name for the waterbuck: *iphiva*.

K. ellipsiprymnus is one of the few names to have survived unchanged

(Water-buck *cont.*)

from A.D.'s time. Although Burchell (q.v.) may have used it, he did not bestow it (213). The species, as *Antilope ellipsiprymnus*, was established by Ogilby (1833); the genus, *Kobus*, by Smith (1840).

Distribution of waterbuck is now restricted to the northern and northeastern parts of southern Africa, though they are preserved in the Hluhluwe and Umfolozi game reserves.

Water hen ~ *see* Reed-hen

Water rail ~ 25

Probably *Rallus caerulescens*, the African rail (O. Gruiformes, F. Rallidae: rails, crakes, gallinules). It frequents reedbeds, marshes and swamps, and hides amid dense reeds.

Waterbok ~ *see* Water-buck

Wattled crane ~ *see under* Crane

Waxberry ~ *see Kaarsh-boschjes*

Waxbill ~ 54

The grey waxbill (*Estrilda perreini*) and/or the swee waxbill (*E. melanotis*) would have frequented Natal coastal forest; less likely – because of its rather different habitat preference – is the orangebreasted waxbill (*Sporaeginthus subflavus*) (O. Passeriformes, F. Estrildidae: waxbills, mannikins, twinspots, firefinches etc.).

Weaver birds ~ *see* Sparrows

Weld-calebasses-boom also Strychnos spinosus, wild calabash tree, *wildkalabas-boom* ~ 133, 180

Strychnos spinosa, the spiny or green monkey orange (Afrikaans: *Groenklapper*) a small deciduous tree which is widely distributed in open woodland and riverine fringes from the east coast to the north in South Africa (Loganiaceae). The fruit is spherical and woodyshelled, may be up to 12cm in diameter and the edible pulp is acidulous. In time of crop failure in Zulu rural areas it is an important food source. The adverse reaction to it (180) may have been not to the pulp but to inadvertently swallowed seeds, which may be irritant or possibly toxic: several species in the genus contain poisonous alkaloids – strychnine comes from seeds of the Indian *Strychnos nux-vomica*, while curare is extracted from the bark of *S. toxifera* of South America. *See also Strychnos*, edible; Wounds

Whales and whaling ~ 45

Van Riebeeck recorded 'many thousands' of whales in Table Bay, Saldanha Bay and neighbouring waters. A local whaling industry began in 1790 and it is believed that two stations operated in Table Bay, two in False Bay and one in Algoa Bay until 1859. Local and foreign (American and British) whalers so depleted the population that by 1836 the local annual catch never exceeded 10.

Almost all animals caught were *Balaena glacialis*, the southern right whale (O. Cetacea, S.O. Mysticeti, F. Balaenidae), which have long baleen plates, give a high oil yield and float after being killed: the 'right' whale to catch, obviously.

A.D. notes that 'foreigners' were prohibited from whaling round the Cape coast. Successive Dutch and British authorities at the Cape issued proclamations to this effect between 1787 and 1833.

White ants ~ *see* Termites

White-breasted blackbird *also* Blackbird, *Leucogaster* ~ 54

A.D.'s beautiful description probably applies to the plumcoloured starling, *Cinnyricinclus leucogaster* (O. Passeriformes, F. Sturnidae). The male has the upper parts, throat, breast and tail iridescent purple, varying with the angle of the light from black to rose pink. The bird would certainly have been present in riverine forest near Port Natal. A.D. apparently confused the starling with the European blackbird, *Turdus merula* (F. Turdidae), as his use of the French *'merle'* indicates.

White crow ~ *see* Crow

White heron ~ *see* Heron; Little egret. *See also Ardea bubulcus*

White rhinoceros ~ *see* Rhinoceros

Widow bird *also* Red-shouldered widow bird ~ 54, 96, 106, 204

The genus *Euplectes* (O. Passeriformes, F. Ploceidae) includes both bishops and widows, but while bishops have short tails at all times, most widow males develop long tails in the breeding season. A.D. probably saw *E. axillaris*, the red-shouldered widow, in the coastal forest (54) as well as inland (96) as other common species prefer a more open habitat.

Long black widow tail feathers

(Widow bird *cont.*)
added great elegance to Zulu ceremonial dress (106, 204) and may have been the extremely long feathers of *E. progne*, the longtailed widow.

Wild banana ~ *see* Banana, wild

Wild boar ~ *see* Bushpig; Warthog

Wild calabash tree ~ *see Weld-calebasses-boom*

Wild calabash tree, small ~ *see Strychnos, edible*

Wild coconut ~ *see Wild-klaapper-noot*

Wild date palm ~ *see Wild-dattle-boom*

Wild-dattle-boom also Wild date palm ~ 221
Phoenix reclinata, the wild date palm or *wildedadel boom* (Arecaceae). Confined to the eastern coastal and sandy regions of South Africa from the Eastern Cape to the eastern Transvaal.
, The yellow flesh of the small dates is thin, but sweet and tasty. The indigenous people eat them and use them in sweet fermented and unfermented drinks.
The name *reclinata* comes from the characteristic recumbent position of some older branches, whose growing tips are recurved vertically. If there is long grass or other undergrowth this may give the impression of a parent plant surrounded by young individuals.

Wild dog *also Cynhyaena venatica, manghetjannes* ~ 63, 184–6
Lycaon pictus, the African wild dog or Cape hunting dog (F. Canidae, SF Simocyoninae). It is a ferocious diurnal carnivore, living and hunting in packs of up to 15. It yelps, barks and growls, locates its fellows with an oboe-like call, and makes a bird-like twittering when excited. The name *pictus* (= painted) is apt: the coat is bright with patches of black, yellow and white, and no two animals are identical. Because *L. pictus* has been treated as vermin, the distributional range has shrunk drastically and it has not been recorded in Natal since 1930. A.D.'s account is both graphic and accurate, but he seems not to know that the 'naturalist who invented the name *Cynhyaena*' (185) was the great Cuvier (q.v.). Burchell (q.v.) applied the name *Hyaena venatica*.
Manghetjannes: A.D.'s interesting

French phonetic spelling of Zulu: *amankentshane* pl (from sing. *inkentshane*): wild dogs or hunting dogs.

Wildebeest, black ~ *see* Gnu

Wildebeest, blue ~ *see Catoblepas gorgon*

Wildedadel boom ~ *see Wild-dattle-boom*

Wild fig tree ~ *see* Fig tree

Wild gladiolus ~ *see* Gladiolus, wild

Wild hemp ~ *see* Hemp

Wild-kalabas-boom ~ *see Weld-calebasses-boom*

Wild-kalabas-boom, geèle, klein ~ *see Strychnos*, edible

Wild-klaapper-noot also Wild coconut ~ 231
Hyphaene natalensis, the ilala palm, also known as the vegetable ivory palm (but not as the 'wild coconut' or '*wildeklapperneut*') (Arecaceae). It is common coastally in Natal and Zululand and, being a fan palm, may have been mistaken for a *Latania* by A.D. (*see Lataniers*).
The fruit, very slow to ripen, has an edible spongy casing and a hard, bony and ivory-coloured hollow seed. The ilala palm is tapped for palm wine.

Witte-kraai ~ *see* Crow

Wolf ~ *see* Hyaena

Woodlouse ~ 58
This arthropod taken by the hadeda ibis (*see Ibis addidas*) is neither an insect nor a woodlouse: woodlice are crustaceans and terrestrial woodlice are small, usually less than 1cm. The organism in question must have been a large pill millipede, similar to a woodlouse in body form and in the ability to roll up for protection (S.P. Myriapoda, C. Diplopoda). *Sphaerotherium giganteum* (4–5cm) is a giant pill millipede still found in the coastal forest of northern Natal. (*See* Centipede for a brief account of some myriapod features).

Wood pigeon ~ *see* Pigeon

Wormius ~ *see under* Cardan

Worms ~ *see* Flies, wounds
A.D. occasionally uses this term for insect larvae, especially the larvae or maggots of blowflies. The word is more properly applied only to non-arthropodan invertebrates of vermiform appearance.

Wounds ~ 235–7
Fortunately A.D. did not apply arsenic or a mercury preparation to Mahlé's open wounds – though it may surprise modern readers to learn that

(Wounds *cont.*)

these poisons have, in very small quantities, current medicinal use and were until relatively recently available (in the form of various compounds) over the pharmacist's counter. A.D. used nux vomica ('the vegetable poison'), which, prepared from the seeds of the East Indian *Strychnos nux-vomica*, contains strychnine and was commonly taken internally as a tonic or stimulant – not used as a disinfectant wash (*see also* Snakebite; *Weld-calebasses-boom*). A.D. considered blowfly maggots dangerous (*see* Flies) and used the wash to kill them. Sadly for Mahlé, it would not be discovered until World War I that maggots eat away suppurating flesh and permit quick, clean healing: maggots would have lessened and shortened Mahlé's 'atrocious suffering', and would probably have reduced scarring.

Yellow snake ~ *see Geele-slange*
Yellowwood ~ *see Geele-out*

Zebra ~ *see Equus Burschellii*

Zee-Bontjes also Endata Pursoetha, mimosa scandens, sea beans ~ 170

Obviously a misspelled *Entada pursaetha*, the sea bean or *seeboontjie* (Fabaceae). A former name is *Mimosa entada*. A.D.'s '*scandens*' refers to the scandent or climbing habit of this large forest plant. The huge seeds, 4–6cm in diameter, are sometimes carried down rivers to the sea and may be washed up on beaches.

Zee-koe ~ *see* Hippopotamus

Zoet-gras ~ 102

Name given by A.D. to a type of grassland north of Mooi River. *Soetgras* (Afrikaans: sweet grass) is a general term for grasses affording palatable or sweet grazing for cattle. It is vague, being applied to whole mixtures of palatable grasses and, on occasion, to all *Eragrostis* spp or to all young, spring grasses (Poaceae). *See also for contrast,* Sour pasturage

GENERAL INDEX

Idiosyncratic and often inconsistent renderings of personal names, place-names, and Zulu and Dutch/Afrikaans words and phrases are a feature of Delegorgue's text. While these oddities and anomalies give to the work its own particular flavour, they also raise special problems for the indexer and annotator.

Where the text carries different spellings of the same name or word, page references are given under the orthographic form in which the name or word *first* appears, but in all such cases alternative spellings are shown alongside the main entry, thus: *Abanto also Abantou*. Where different names or words are used for the same subject, page references are given under the name or word which appears most frequently in the text, and the alternatives are shown thus: Amazoulou country *also* Zoulouland. In all such cases, cross-references are provided where appropriate. Where Delegorgue's rendering of Zulu or Dutch/Afrikaans words is likely to obstruct comprehension of the text, these terms have been included in the index together with explanatory notes.

In the annotations and in sub-entries, modern orthography is used in respect of proper nouns and Zulu and Dutch/Afrikaans words and phrases, and A.D.'s orthography is given in parentheses where this will assist the reader to identify the relevant passages in the text, thus: Bushmans (Boschjesmans) River massacres. Where there is a well-accepted alternative modern spelling of a name, as for example Mlandela and Myandeya, the variation is shown thus: Mlandela/Myandeya. Since the rendering of place-names, especially those of Zulu origin, is confusingly varied and inconsistent, the modern orthography used in the annotations and sub-entries is that which appears on recent official topographical maps.

Sub-entries are ordered alphabetically without regard to initial prepositions and conjunctions. In cross-references, sub-entries are shown in parentheses, thus: *see* Amazoulous (food and drink).

The following abbreviations are used in the annotations: A.D. ~ Adulphe Delegorgue; km ~ kilometres.

C. de B. Webb

Abafanas also Imphana, Imphanas ~ The Zulu word *umfana*, pl *abafana*, means boy or young man. ~ 195, 198, 206, 214, 215
 as beer-porters during hunt ~ 225
 and killing of the bull ~ 206–7
 in national parade ~ 196–7, 199, 202, 203, 204, 206
 regiments of ~ 196, 197, 199

singing and dancing of ~ 197, 199, 200, 201–2
 in Zulu army ~ 120
Abanto also Abantou ~ The Zulu word *abantu*, plural of *umuntu*, means people, human beings. A.D.'s *abantou mouniama*, p. 211, is his rendering of the Zulu phrase meaning black people. The statement, p. 267, that

(Amazoulous, *cont.*)

(hospitality ~ 86, 168, 176, 192, 195, 196, 197, 198, 210, 215, 219, 220, 221

hunting practices and techniques ~ 159–60, 193, 230–2, 278–81

kingship ~ 207, 208, 280

lighting (torches) ~ 168

marital relations ~ 94–5

medicinal plants, knowledge of ~ 166, 180, 237

milking practices ~ 168n.

national parade, i.e. festival linked to mid-summer *umkhosi* or 'first-fruits' ceremony ~ 195–203, 204–6, 207, 208–9

notable warriors ~ 92

nudity ~ 204–5

oratory ~ 89, 92, 95, 199–200

physical attributes and beauty ~ 87, 92, 93–4, 148, 169, 198, 204–5

and physical disability ~ 237

poisoners amongst ~ 233

polygyny ~ 77, 87, 94

poverty and hunger amongst ~ 148

praising, i.e. *ukubonga* ~ 92

regimental cries ~ 197

regimental dress and insignia ~ 199

regiments, i.e. *amabutho* ~ 193, 196, 199, 279, 280

sexual conventions ~ 213–14

sleeping arrangements ~ 168, 195

and snakebite, treatment of ~ 165–6

and snuff-taking ~ 176

superstition amongst ~ 88, 89, 133 and n, 177, 218

and whites ~ 169, 219, 264–5

wives, faithfulness of ~ 94

widows, status of ~ 94–5

see also Cafres; Cafres of Natal; Dingaan; Djacka; *Om-douna*; Panda

Amiens, Peace of ~ Treaty signed between Britain, France, Spain and Holland in 1802. It provided, *inter alia*, for the termination of Britain's war-time occupation of the Cape, and the restoration of the colony to the Dutch. ~ (ix), (xii)

Ammunition ~ *see* Firearms and ammunition

Apprentices ~ Africans captured by Boers during military campaigns, and then 'apprenticed', i.e. bound in service to white masters. ~ 124

Arago, Jacques ~ French traveller, who visited the Cape *c.* 1820, and whose observations about draught animals A.D. derides. ~ 19, 20

Aristotle ~ Greek philosopher, logician and scientist of 4th century B.C. ~ 23, 24

Arms ~ *see* Amazoulous (arms); Firearms and ammunition; *Omkondo*; Shields; *Tongas*

Assegais ~ *see Omkondo*

Azi ~ see Yasy

Balene ~ The reference may be to the Hlangwini chief, Baleni, who, after a period of wandering, settled with his following on the lower reaches of the Mkomazi River. ~ 73

ukuBamba ~ see Bambylé

Bambylé ~ A.D.'s rendering of the Zulu for 'is caught' or 'has been caught'; from the verb *ukubamba*, meaning to grasp, lay hold of, etc. ~ 264

Barrow ~ J. Barrow, author of *An account of travels into the interior of southern Africa*, 2 vols., London, 1801, 1804, and of *A Voyage to Cochinchina . . . to which is annexed on account of a journey to the . . . Bootchuana*, London, 1806. ~ (xi)

Barter ~ (ix), 175, 189–90

Bastaards ~ *see* Half-castes

Batavia ~ Dutch possession in Far East. The Dutch republic that functioned as a satellite of Revolutionary and Napoleonic France, 1795–1806, was known as the Batavian Republic. The appellation 'Batavian' is frequently attached to instances of Dutch action or manifestations of Dutch influence of that period. ~ (ix), (xi), 11n., 13

see also Dutch

Bawians Berg *also* Mountain of the Baboons ~ The modern Afrikaans orthography is Bobbejaansberg. The hill lies on the southern shore of the Verlorevlei estuary at Elands Bay. ~ 22

Baye-Bang ~ A Zulu homestead head, living close to the lower reaches of the Black Mfolozi. The name, which is not Zulu, appears to be a nickname derived from the nineteenth century equivalent of the modern Afrikaans *baie bang,* meaning 'very scared'. ~ 268

Beads ~ (ix), 94, 198

in dress of royal women ~ 204

necklaces requested by Mpande ~ 189, 190, 194

as payment for services ~ 177

Beer *also Tchouala ~ Utshwala* is a commonly used Zulu word for beer. ~ 125, 168, 195, 210, 215, 219, 222, 225, 229, 254

(Beer, *cont.*)
honey-beer made by Bastaards ~ 249
manufacture of ~ 195
at Mpande's (Panda's) homestead ~ 195, 206
amaBele ~ *see Mabèle*
Belon, Pierre ~ French naturalist of sixteenth century ~ 23, 24
Berea ~ Ridge of hills overlooking bay of Port Natal. The name, of New Testament derivation, was initially applied to the mission station which Capt. A.F. Gardiner established on the ridge in 1835. ~ 52, 138
Berg Rivier ~ The Berg River rises in the Franschhoek mountains and flows in a north-north-westerly direction, disgorging into the Atlantic at St. Helena Bay. ~ 21
hippopotamuses in ~ 43, 156, 161
Bester, *Mr* ~ Farmer living at Karamelck-Fontyn. ~ 39
Beulton ~ Biltong is the word, of South African Dutch origin, for strips of salted, sun-dried meat. Traditionally, biltong was made from game. ~ 34
iBhunu ~ *see Amaboune*
Biedow River ~ The Biedouw stream is a tributary of the Doring River, which in turn flows into the Olifants, one of the major rivers of the north-western Cape. ~ 32
Biedow Valley ~ The Biedouw valley lies to the east of the village of Clanwilliam. ~ 32
Biggarsberg ~ *see* Honing Berg
Biltong ~ *see* Beulton
Black Mfolozi/Umfolozi ~ *see* Omphilos-Mouniama
Bloed Rivier ~ The Blood or iNcome River, which flows into the Buffalo, forms part of the northern tributary system of the Tugela. On 16 December 1838 (not 16 September as stated by A.D., p.109) the forces of Dingane were defeated, with heavy losses, by an invading commando of emigrant Boers, who had encamped on the bank of the river some 15 km above its junction with the Buffalo. It is from that massacre that the name Blood River derives. ~ 123
Boer-Zulu battle, 1838 ~ 109
Bob ~ African elephant-hunter in service of H. Ogle, and living in southern Natal. ~ 75–6, 78
Bobbejaansberg ~ *see* Bawians Berg
Boers *also* African-Dutch, Farmers, Peasants ~ The persons so referred to were agriculturalists and pastoralists, either wholly or partly of European origin, who spoke a dialect of Dutch. Specific references to those living in the Cape and those living in Natal are given under separate entries. ~ (xii), 16, 17, 19
buildings and structures ~ 188
conservatism ~ 283
food ~ 126, 142, 211, 249
hunting and trapping ~ 22–3, 36, 131, 161, 188, 282–3
locust control ~ 80
and natural beauty ~ 102
pastoralism ~ 81
resourcefulness ~ 191
wagon-driving ~ 19, 123–4, 174, 231
women, dominant role of ~ 83
see also Amaboune; Farmers, Cape Colony; Emigrant Boers, Natal
Boesmansrand ~ *see* Boschjesmans Rand
ukuBonga ~ *see* Amazoulous (praising)
Boschjesmanes *also* Boschesmans, Boschjesmans ~ The San hunter-gatherer people of southern Africa were commonly designated 'Bushmen' by the intrusive whites. A.D.'s assertion, p.98n., that no Bushmen were seen in Natal is incorrect. Archaeological evidence indicates a widespread San presence to the east of the Drakensberg, and Natal colonial records show that there were San bands frequenting the Drakensberg and its foothills as late as the 1860s and early 1870s. ~ (vii), 33, 98n., 172
arrows ~ 168, 282
hunting techniques and practices ~ 243, 270, 281–2
immodesty ~ 285
and snakebite ~ 165
Boschjesmans-Caffers *also* Boschesmans-Cafres ~ Literally Bushman-Kaffirs. The reference is to Bantu-speaking Africans who had moved into the forests and fastnesses of Natal in the early decades of the nineteenth century in search of refuge from the wars of Shaka and the widespread disturbances of those years. ~ 98, 127
Boschjesmans Rand ~ The Boesmansrand is a range of hills to the west and north of Pietermaritzburg. ~ 96, 101
Boschjesmans Rivier ~ The Bushmans River in northern Natal is a southern tributary of the Tugela. On 17 February 1838 large numbers of emigrant Boers who had encamped along the banks of the lower Bushmans and

(Boschjesmans Rivier *cont.*)
   neighbouring streams were subjected to a surprise attack by the Zulu. In this encounter nearly 300 Boer men, women and children and more than 200 of their 'Coloured' servants were killed, and thousands of sheep, cattle and horses were taken by the Zulu. A.D.'s crossing of the river was probably on the middle reaches near the present-day village of Estcourt. ~ 102
massacres, 1838 ~ 40, 110, 112
Boulala ~ The Zulu word *ukubulala* means to kill. ~ 206
Boulandje *also* Boulantje ~ African in service of A.D. ~ 137, 164, 182, 189, 190, 191, 210, 211, 222, 225, 226, 227, 228, 237, 238, 242, 260, 263, 264
Brandt family ~ Occupants of farm Theefontein ~ 41
Brandy ~ 33, 122, 139
Bread ~ 125
Breda, *Mr* ~ Probably Michiel van Breda. He and his son, Servaas, were prominent personalities amongst the emigrant Boers in Natal, and both accompanied the expedition that visited Mpande near the Tongati river in 1839. ~ 83–4
Brink ~ Carl Frederik Brink served as journalist and map maker on an expedition into Great Namaqualand in 1761–2 under the leadership of Capt. H. Hop. Dutch and French versions of Brink's journal were published in Amsterdam in 1778, and a German version in Leipzig in 1779. ~ (x)
British occupation of Port Natal, 1838–9 ~ 48–50
   Boer reaction to withdrawal ~ 98–9
   reasons for occupation ~ 48
   relations between Boers and troops ~ 48, 59
   withdrawal of force ~ 98
Bruce, James ~ Author of *Travels to Discover the Source of the Nile*, 1790. ~ 161
Bruyns ~ Mulatto hunter at the Cape 68
Buffalo ~ *see Inyaty*
Buffalo River ~ *see* Om-Sinyate
Buffon ~ G-L. L., *Comte de*, eighteenth century French naturalist, remembered for his great work *Histoire naturelle, générale et particulière*, which appeared in 36 volumes between 1749 and 1788. This endeavour to synthesize previously disconnected data

about the natural world had a lasting influence, although specific aspects of his work were criticised and faulted. ~ 23, 24, 160, 250
ukuBulala ~ *see Boulala*
Burchell, W. J. *also* Burschell ~ Author of *Travels in the interior of South Africa*, 2 vols., London, 1822–24. Contrary to what is stated by Albert-Montémont in his Introduction, p.(xi), Burchell's expeditions took place in the years 1811–1815. The reference, p.213, to Burchell's description and naming of the water buck is incorrect. ~ (xi), 213
Burgher, *Mr* ~ Occupant of farm Tygerhoek in the Hantam area. ~ 33
   reward for action against Korana, 1835 ~ 33
Bushmen ~ *see* Boschjesmanes
By-kruipen also be-kruyppen ~ A.D.s rendering of the South African Dutch word *bekruip*, meaning to creep up upon or stalk. ~ 270

Cafrerie *also* Cafre Land, Land of the Cafres ~ Territories occupied by Xhosa chiefdoms to the east of the Cape Colony. ~ (vii), (viii), (ix), (x), 12n., 46, 80
Cafres ~ The name 'Kaffirs' was commonly used in the nineteenth century, often without pejorative intent, for the Bantu-speaking peoples of southern Africa, and more particularly for the Xhosa. ~ (x), (xi), 12n., 44, 76
   agriculture and crops ~ 159
   at Algoa Bay ~ 44
   in Cape Town ~ 11 and n.
   and cattle ~ 76
   and 'civilisation' ~ 172, 173
   courteousness ~ 194
   dress ~ 34 and n., 106, 139 and n.
   economic needs, low level of ~ 283
   economic system ~ 77
   educational needs ~ 172–3
   family relationships ~ 76
   food ~ 81, 240–1, 249
   hunting practices ~ 34, 106, 156, 157, 225, 278
   ivory hunting ~ 277, 278–9
   legal and governmental system ~ 172, 173
   locust control ~ 80–1
   manufactures ~ 34
   marital relationships ~ 76, 77
   milking practices ~ 168 and n.

(Cape Town, *cont.*)
    early development ~ 11 and n.
    health resort for Anglo-Indians ~
        12–13
    hippopotomuses near ~ 161
    missionary influence in ~ 13
    mixed population in ~ 11 and n.
    naming of ~ 11
    physical features ~ 11 and n., 12, 13,
        14
    social and cultural life ~ 13
Cattle ~ (viii), (ix), 19–21, 43, 115–16
    'Afrikaander' ~ 19–20
    barter with Dutch ~ 11n.
    'Bastaard-Vaaderlanders' ~ 20
    ceremonial and ritual uses ~ 206–7
    draught oxen ~ 15, 16, 18, 19, 20, 101,
        102, 103, 138, 139, 147, 148, 164, 167,
        171, 183, 184
    gifts of ~ 86, 176, 196, 197
    herds of Mlandela (Om-Landelle) ~ 175
    herds of Mpande (Panda) ~ 82, 83
    Hottentot ~ 11n, 21
    Mfengu (Fingou) purchases ~ 44
    monetary value of ~ 127
    pasturage ~ 43, 81, 102, 194
    and placating of ancestral spirits ~ 177
    'ransom' extracted by Boers, 1840
        ~ 123
    as reward ~ 98, 228
    sale of ~ 33
    scarcity because of emigration of Boers
        ~ 15, 16
    seized by Boers from Zulu, 1840 ~ 115,
        119, 127
    'Vaaderlanders' ~ 20
    wealth in ~ 75, 76, 83, 221
    and 'wife-buying' ~ 75
    'Zoulah' ~ 20, 115, 119, 120
    Zulu 'debt' to Boers ~ 82–3, 111
    Zulu herds coveted by Boers ~ 83
    Zulu royal ~ 279
Cedar Berg *also* Cedar Mountains ~
    Approached from Cape Town, the
    Cederberg range runs in a north-
    north-westerly direction some 75–80
    km inland from the Atlantic coast.
    The village of Clanwilliam is situated
    just to the west of the northern,
    Pakhuis and Krakadouwberg, exten-
    sions of the range. ~ 31
Chambock ~ A sjambok, from Malay *sam-
    boq*, is a lash or whip usually made
    from hippo hide. ~ 124, 231
Champion, *Revd* G. ~ George Champion
    served in Natal between 1835 and
    1838 as a member of the American
    Board Zulu Mission. His departure
    was occasioned by Zulu attacks on the

emigrant Boers in 1838. ~ 40
Charter, *Major*. ~ Maj. S. Charters was in
    command of a British detachment
    which occupied Port Natal in
    December 1838 in an endeavour to
    restrain conflict between the emi-
    grant Boers and the Zulu and other
    indigenous African people. Charters
    returned to the Cape in January 1839,
    leaving Capt. H. Jervis in command of
    the occupation force. ~ 48
Clanwilliam ~ Village in the western
    Cape, situated near northern extrem-
    ity of the Cederberg some 200 km
    north-north-east of Cape Town and 54
    km inland from the Atlantic
    coast. ~ 30, 31
    agriculture in surrounding district
        ~ 30, 31, 32
Cloete, *Lt.-Col.* ~ Colonel Josias Cloete
    commanded a force of British troops
    which was sent to Port Natal from the
    Cape in 1842 to relieve a garrison
    which had been besieged at the bay by
    the emigrant Boers. Cloete, without
    resort to arms, secured the submis-
    sion of the majority in the Boer Coun-
    cil, but was criticised for calling on the
    Africans living in the vicinity of the
    bay to round up, and bring in to the
    garrison, cattle and horses belonging
    to the Boers. ~ 40
Coal beds ~
    between Honing Berg and Klip Rivier
        ~ 124
    near Zand Rivier ~ 109
Coeberg ~ The Koeberg, literally 'cow
    mountain', lies some 27 km north-
    north-east of Cape Town, and 12 km
    east of the present-day village of
    Melkbosstrand. ~ 39
Combezana ~ Khambezana, emissary of
    Dingane, was executed by the emi-
    grant Boers of Natal, 1840. ~ 111,
    114
    detention and trial ~ 111, 112–14
    execution ~ 114
    mission from Dingane ~ 111
Combring ~ A.D.'s rendering of the name
    now commonly spelt Combrink. Emi-
    grant Boer at Port Natal. ~ 164
Conguela ~ Congella, from the Zulu
    Khangela, was the site of a major
    emigrant Boer encampment on the
    western shore of the bay of Port
    Natal. ~ 35, 95
    A.D. accommodated at ~ 50
    F. Roos landdrost at ~ 83
    water at ~ 52
    see also Port Natal

Djantje ~ A servant in A.D.'s employ. Jantshi in modern Zulu orthography. ~ 242

Djock ~ The reference may be to Joko, a chief of the Makoba branch of the Zungu people, who occupied land north of the White Mfolozi in the vicinity of certain of the principal Zulu royal homesteads. ~ 194, 210

inDoda ~ *see* Omdoda

Domestic animals ~ (vii*)*
see also Cattle; Horses; Sheep

Doorn-Kop ~ The hill Doornkop in northern Natal (possibly so-named because of thorny 'mimosa' trees growing on its slopes) lies some 15 km south-west of the present-day village of Colenso. ~ 103 and n.

Doorn-Rivier ~ The Doring River is a tributary of the Olifants, which flows into the Atlantic some 180 km north-north-west of Cape Town. ~ 32

Doorn-Veld ~ Thornveld: a commonly used South African name for regions of grassland which support open, often scrubby, thorn-tree forestation. ~ 249

Doring River ~ *see* Doorn-Rivier

Dorpspruit ~ *see* Klein Boschjesmans Rivier

Douglas ~ Probably John Douglas, seaman, hunter and trader, who was in Natal at the time of A.D.'s visit. ~ 170, 176, 178, 179, 230

Draaken's Berg *also* Quathlambène mountains ~ The central sector of the Drakensberg range, running roughly parallel to the south-east African coastline, separates Natal from the central plateau of southern Africa. Khahlamba, the Zulu name for the range, means, variously, a rough bony object such as a skeleton, a tall thin person, or a row of upward pointing spears. ~ 98n., 103, 279

inDuna ~ *see* Om-douna

Durban ~ *see* Port Natal

Dutch ~ (viii), (ix), 11 and n, 12n,
see also Batavia; Boers; Farmers, Cape Colony; Dutch settlers, Cape; Emigrant Boers, Natal; Holland

Dutch settlers, Cape *also* Colonists ~ The Dutch East India Company station which Van Riebeeck established on the shores of Table Bay in 1652, was opened to settlers, initially on a limited experimental basis, in 1655. From those beginnings, it became a colony of European settlement. ~ 11 and n., 12n

in Cape Town ~ 11, 13
miscegenation and intermarriage ~ 11n
relations with Hottentots ~ 11n, 12n

Edict of Nantes ~ The edict, signed in 1594 by Henry IV of France, guaranteed religious and civil liberty to French Protestants. Its revocation in 1685 was a major reason for the emigration of the Huguenots. ~ 33

Elands Berg *also* Mountain of the Cannas ~ The Elandsberg is a mountain near Elands Bay on the Cape west coast. ~ 22

Elephant River ~ *see* Olyphant's Rivier

Elephants *also* Uncklove ~ *inDlovu* is the Zulu word for elephant. ~ 51, 114, 224–5, 285
see also Hunting (elephant)

Embyla ~ *see* Maize

Emhlophe ~ *see* Om-schlopu

Emigrant Boers, Natal *also* African-Dutch, Farmers, Peasants ~ Dutch-speaking colonists who, after abandoning the Cape Colony, crossed the Drakensberg into Natal in 1837 and subsequently. ~ 59
and A.D. ~ 54–5, 71
and African allies, 1840 ~ 122–3
African attitudes towards ~ 71
alliance with Mpande (Panda) against Dingane (Dingaan), 1839–40 ~ 88, 112–13, 114, 118–19
and annexation of Zulu territory, 1840 ~ 120–1
apprenticing of African children ~ 104
at Blood River (Bloed Rivier) battle, 1838 ~ 109–10
bread made by ~ 125
campaign against Dingane (Dingaan), 1840 ~ 101–27
and cattle ~ 83, 104, 115, 116, 119, 127
cruelty ~ 110, 111
and Dambuza (Tamboussa) ~ 111–14, 121–2
deputation to Mpande (Panda), 1839 ~ 83–95
and Dingane (Dingaan) ~ 83, 95, 99, 111–12
and English ~ 59, 71–2, 98–9
fear of Zulu ~ 83–4, 86, 89
fighting style and practices ~ 116–18
food and eating habits ~ 104, 125, 158
games and pastimes ~ 104
governmental arrangements ~ 119, 147
hunting practices ~ 23, 158
individualism ~ 103

345

Ignama ~ *Inyama* is the Zulu word for meat, flesh. ~ 85, 234

Ignamazane ~ *Inyamazane* is the Zulu word for wild animal, game. ~ 260

Illovo ~ *see* Lofa

Imphana ~ *see Abafanas*

Indao ~ One of the meanings of the Zulu word *indawo* is appropriate limit or proper extent or degree of any action. ~ 184

Ingheta-Om-Schlopu ~ Forest north of the Mfolozi rivers. ~ 255, 260–1

Inianga ~ *Inyanga* is the Zulu word for doctor, herbalist, medicine-man, diviner. The word also means moon and lunar-month. ~ 133n., 177

Iniouka ~ *Inyoka* is the Zulu word for snake. ~ 219, 234

Inkoniana ~ *Inkonyana* is the Zulu word for calf or small beast. ~ 264

Inkonnzy ~ *Inkunzi* is the Zulu word for bull. ~ 206

Inkosikazy also King's wives, etc. ~ *Inkosikazi* is the Zulu word for the principal wife of a king or chief. As a courtesy title, it may be applied to other women of rank. The women described by A.D. as Mpande's wives, pp. 77 and 87, may well have been girls of the royal *isigodlo*, i.e. girls presented to the king, or taken by him, as tribute. White visitors to the Zulu kingdom commonly misidentified these girls as concubines. Their function was to attend to the king, and they were disposable by him in marriage. ~ 77, 87, 92–3, 175–6, 198, 265

at elephant hunts ~ 279

participation in dancing ~ 193, 204–6

physical appearance and dress ~ 92–3, 176, 198, 204–6

Intombu ~ *Intombi* is the Zulu word for a young girl of marriageable age. ~ 214

Inyaty also Iniaty ~ *Inyathi* is the Zulu word for buffalo. ~ 224, 235

Inyoni ~ *see* Om-Inione

Iphesy ~ *Imfezi* is the Zulu word for cobra or ringhals. ~ 251

Ischlouzo ~ The Zulu word *ihluzo* means a beer strainer. ~ 168

Ivory ~ 35, 232, 277, 278

see also Tusks

Jarvis, *Captain* ~ Capt. Henry Jervis was given the command in January 1839 of a detachment of British troops which had been sent to Port Natal from the Cape the previous December for the purpose of restraining conflict between the emigrant Boers and the Zulu and other indigenous African peoples. The occupation force withdrew in December 1839.

opposes Boer deputation to Mpande (Panda), 1839 ~ 84

relations with Dingane (Dingaan) ~ 84

success with emigrant Boers ~ 48–9

and withdrawal from Port Natal ~ 98

Job ~ The reference is probably to Jobe kaMaphitha, who was chief of the Sithole people living near Ilenge/eLenge mountain (Job's Kop) some 16 km north-north-west of the confluence of the Sundays and Tugela rivers. ~ 125

and A.D. ~ 125

and Boer campaign, 1840 ~ 116

Boers arrest son, 1840 ~ 122–3

cattle ransom for son ~ 123

Joice, Robert ~ Robert Joyce moved into the Natal–Zululand area *c.* 1837, having deserted from the 72nd Regiment in Grahamstown some five years earlier. ~ 73–4

Joko ~ *see* Djock

Jong, Cornelius ~ Dutch explorer, who visited the Cape in 1796. ~ (x)

Joyce ~ *see* Joice, Robert

Kakoulou ~ The Zulu word *kakhulu*, when used adverbially, means greatly, exceedingly, very much, and when used as an interjection means certainly, indeed. ~ 70, 175, 176, 211, 285

Karamelck-Fonteyn ~ The reference is almost certainly to the farm Karnmelks Fontein in the Malmesbury–Hopefield region of the western Cape. ~ 39

Karee Houten Boom ~ *see* Gemerkte-Caree-Hout-Boom

Karnmelks Fontein ~ *see* Karamelck-Fonteyn

Karosses ~ *see* Kros

Karroo *also* Karrou ~ Arid, sparsely vegetated regions of the Cape. The Little Karoo is bounded by the Swartberg range to the north and the Langeberg and Outeniqua mountains to the south. The Great Karoo, or Great Thirstland, extends over a large part of the central and north-western areas of the Cape. ~ (vii), 32, 33, 38

Khahlamba ~ *see* Draaken's Berg

Khambazana ~ *see* Combezana
kwaKhangela ~ *see* Conguela
Khoikhoi ~ *see* Hottentots
umKhomazi ~ *see* Om-Komas
Khombazana ~ *see* Combezana
umKhonto ~ *see Omkondo*
inKhosikazi ~ *see Inkosikazy*
inKhosi phezulu ~ *see Kos-Pezou*
umKhulu ~ *see Om-Koulou*
King, John ~ Probably a confused allusion to John Ross (alias Charles Maclean), who accompanied James S. King to Port Natal in 1825 as an apprentice on the brig *Mary*, and who is reputed to have made the overland journey from Natal to Delagoa Bay and back in 1827. ~ 232
King, Richard ~ A hunter and trader who established himself at Port Natal in the early 1830s, and subsequently earned his living as a wagon driver, transport rider and farmer. ~ 170, 171, 176, 178, 213, 230
Klein Boschjesmans Rivier ~ The Little Bushmans River, now commonly known as the Dorpspruit, bounded the original Boer village of Pietermaritzburg to the north and east. It is not to be confused with the Little Bushmans River to the south-west of present-day Ladysmith. ~ 96–7
Klip Rivier ~ The Klip River is one of the northern tributaries of the upper Tugela. The present-day village of Colenso is situated to the south-west of the confluence of the two rivers. ~ 105, 124
Klwana kaNgqengelele ~ *see* Kouana
Knop-nuys-Caffers *also* Knoopneus-Kaffers ~ A.D.'s renderings of 'knopneus-kaffers', a term used by the Boers to refer generally to the Tsonga peoples occupying the lands surrounding Delagoa Bay, and more particularly to the Magwamba offshoot of the Tsonga in the Spelonken district of the northern Transvaal. The name derives from scarification practices amongst the Magwamba which raised knob-like protruberances on the nose. A.D. is using the name in its general sense. ~ 110, 232
see also Makazanes
Koeberg ~ *see* Coeberg
Kolbe ~ P. Kolb/Kolbe/Kolber, author of *Caput Bonae Spei hodiernum, das ist vollständige Beschreibung des Afrikanischen Vorgebürges der Gutin Hoffnung*, published in 1719. ~ (ix), (x)

Koluma ~ *Inkulumo* is the Zulu word for speech or address. ~ 229
Koranas ~ The Kora consisted of remnants of the Gorachoqua and other Khoikhoi groups who had been dislodged from their territories in the western Cape by white colonisation. In the early decades of the nineteenth century they were living to the north of the middle reaches of the Orange. ~ 33
Kos-Berg. ~ A hill – possibly that known in Zulu as Ngceba – near the confluence of the White and Black Mfolozi rivers. The Dutch word *kos* means food. ~ 242
inKosikazi ~ *see Inkosikazy*
inKosi phezulu ~ *see Kos-Pezou*
Kos-Omkoulou ~ The Zulu phrase *inkhosi/inkosi inkhulu* literally means great chief or king. ~ 229
Kos-Pezou ~ The Zulu phrase *inkosi/inkhosi phezulu* literally means king on high. ~ 114
Kotchobana ~ African hunter in A.D.'s employ. ~ 189, 190, 191, 197, 202, 208, 210, 211, 219, 222, 223, 225, 226, 227, 228, 242, 243, 244, 246, 252, 253, 256, 260, 263, 264, 266
Kotze, Elias ~ A 'half-caste' living at Port Natal. ~ 138
    hunting expedition with A.D. ~ 138, 140, 141, 144, 147
Kotze, Henderick ~ Field cornet and farmer with property near Verlorevlei (Verlooren Valley). ~ 21, 30, 35
Kotze, Pieter ~ A 'half-caste' living at Port Natal. ~ 138
    hunting expedition with A.D. ~ 138, 141, 143, 144, 147, 151
Kouana ~ The reference is probably to Klwana kaNgqengelele, sometimes identified as Klwana kaKoboyela, who was a leading *induna* under Dingane. ~ 118
Koudou ~ *see* Coudou
Kraus, *Mr* ~ Dr F. Krauss, a German naturalist, travelled from Port Elizabeth to Port Natal in 1839 on board the *Mazeppa*, on which A.D. and the Swedish naturalist, Wahlberg, were journeying from Cape Town to Natal. Krauss was in Natal from 10 June 1839 to 5 February 1840, and was with A.D. on the Boer deputation to Mpande, 1839. His *Travel Journal: Cape to Zululand*, ed. by O. Spohr, was published in Cape Town in 1973. ~ 47, 88
Kros ~ A.D.'s rendering of the Dutch word

(Makatisses *cont.*)
driven off their lands in what is now the north-eastern Orange Free State at the start of disturbances (the *Difaqane, Lifaqane, Mfecane*) which affected much of south-east Africa and the central plateau in the 1820s. For a time the Tlokoa survived by raiding the resources of other chiefdoms on the highveld. By association, the name Mantatees came to be applied by whites in the 1820s and 1830s to other marauders and groups of landless refugees from the central plateau region. ~ (xii), 123

Makazanes ~ The reference is to the Mabhudu-Tsonga people living south of Delagoa Bay, who were ruled in the first half of the 19th century by a chief named Makhasane. ~ 110, 232, 233
see also Knop-nuys-Caffers

Malays ~ A commonly used, but inaccurate, generic name for slaves and political prisoners brought to the Cape from the Far East, and for their Cape Muslim descendants. ~ 11 and n., 76

Maniousse ~ Probably a reference to Manyosi kaDlekezele of the Mbatha people, who acquired fame as a warrior in Shaka's reign, and occupied important positions under the kings Dingane and Mpande. ~ 209

Manschla ~ *Amandla* is the Zulu word for strength. ~ 229

Mantatees ~ *see* Makatisses

Manyosi ~ *see* Maniousse

Maritz *also* Mauritz, Gert ~ Gerhardus (Gert) Maritz, was one of the leaders of the emigrant Boers. ~ 96

Maritz, Stephanus ~ The reference is possibly to Johannes Stephanus Maritz, elder brother of Gerhardus Maritz, and a prominent personality among the emigrant Boers in Natal. ~ 103

Masjlebe ~ possibly Madlebe kaMgedeza of the Zungu people, who was installed by Dingane as *induna* in the lower Mhlatuze area. ~ 77

Massilicatzi *also* Moselekatse ~ Mzilikazi of the Khumalo people abandoned his ancestral lands about the sources of the Black Mfolozi in the early 1820s, and by the 1830s had established a powerful state, the Ndebele kingdom, in the western reaches of what is now the Transvaal. In the face of the Trekker advance and other threats,

Mzilikazi and large numbers of his subjects withdrew from the Transvaal in the late 1830s, and after some years re-established the Ndebele kingdom in what is now commonly known as Matabeleland in south-western Zimbabwe. ~ (xii), 110, 130, 240

Matigulu/eMatikulu ~ *see* Om-Matagoulou

Matiwane ~ *see* Matouana

Matjes Fonteyn ~ The Matjiesfontein referred to by A.D. lies to the east of present-day Clanwilliam, close to the confluence of the Doring and Biedouw rivers. Not to be confused with the Karoo hamlet of the same name. ~ 32

Matouana ~ A chief who, in the records of the emigrant Boers, is variously referred to as Mattowan, Matowaan, Mataan, etc. He and his followers lived near a southern spur of the Biggarsberg in the locality now known as Matiwaanshoek. In modern Zulu orthography the name would be rendered as Matiwane. ~ 105, 107, 108, 123
Boer accusations against, 1840 ~ 123
burning of homesteads ~ 108
cattle ransom for ~ 123
hostility against Dingane (Dingaan), 1840 ~ 105, 108

Matouana's men ~ 105, 106

Matouana's mountain ~ The reference is probably to a southerly spur of the Biggarsberg where the Modder Spruit rises some 12 km north of present-day Ladysmith. The spur forms the north-westerly limits of the locality now known as Matiwaanshoek. ~ 108

umMbila ~ *see* Maize

eMdloti ~ *see* Om-Schlouty

Medicines ~ 237

Melck, *Mr* ~ Farmer with property on the Berg River. The farm which A.D. visited was probably Kersefontein some 10 km upstream from the mouth of the Berg River at St. Helena Bay. ~ 39, 43, 150

Mena ~ *Mina* is the Zulu word for I, myself, me. ~ 70

Meyer Howek ~ Presumably Meyer Hoek, a farm belonging to Mr Meyer. ~ 98

Meyer, *Mr* ~ Natal Boer. There were several bearers of the surname Meyer amongst the emigrant Boers in Natal. One with whom A.D. was associated was the field-cornet Jan Meyer, who was a member of the Boer deputation that met with Mpande in 1839. ~ 98

Mfengu ~ *see* Fingous
Mfinyeli ~ see Om-Phinieri
Mfolozi ~ *see* Omphilos
Mgeni ~ *see* Om-Guinée
Mgojane ~ *see* Om-Ghetjanne
Mgungundlovu ~ *see* Unkunglove
Mhlali ~ *see* Om-Schlala
Mhlatuze ~ *see* Om-Schlatousse
Milk ~ 210, 215, 254
   see *also* Amas; Amazoulous (food and drink)
Mina ~ *see* Mena
Mirages and optical illusions ~ 35
Miscegenation ~ 11 and n.
   see *also* Half-castes
Missionaries ~ 39, 41, 71, 172, 173
   African reactions to ~ 173
   attitude to Boers and English ~ 71
Mkomazi ~ *see* Om-Komas
Mlalazi ~ *see* Om-Lalas
Mlandela ~ *see* Om-Landelle
Mlazi ~ *see* Om-Las
Moeder Berg ~ *see* Honing Berg
Molemann ~ Natal hunter. The reference is presumably to one of the Moolman family, who were among the emigrant Boers in Natal. ~ 285
Mona ~ The Mona River is a northern tributary of the Black Mfolozi. It rises in the hills to the north-east of present-day Nongoma and flows into the Black Mfolozi some 25 km north-west of the latter's confluence with the White Mfolozi, and some 20 km north of the Ngolothi range. ~ 194
Monkeys ~ *see Ama-Kaho*
Montou ~ *see Abanto*
Mooi Rivier ~ The imPofana (literally Little Elands) River was renamed the Mooi (literally the Nice or Pretty) River by the emigrant Boers. Its head-waters are in the Drakensberg in the locality now known as Giant's Castle, and it flows in a generally north-easterly direction, disgorging into the Tugela some 30 km north of present-day Greytown. A.D.'s narrative suggests that the river was crossed somewhere in the vicinity of the present-day town of Mooi River. ~ 101, 102
Morewood, *Mr* ~ E. Morewood was a Port Natal trader. He accompanied the Boer delegation that visited Mpande at the Tongati river in 1839. ~ 93
Moselekatse ~ *see* Massilicatzi
Mosquitoes ~ 60–1
Motgeas ~ *Umutsha* is the Zulu word for loin-cover. ~ 92

Mouniama ~ A.D.'s rendering of the Zulu word *omnyama*, from the root *-nyama*, meaning black or dark. ~ 70, 211
Mouniama ~ Probably the Munyana River, a southern tributary of the White Mfolozi. The confluence of the two rivers is close to the Ngolothi range. ~ 215
Mountain of the Baboons ~ *see* Bawians Berg
Mountain of the Cannas ~ *see* Elands Berg
Mouschlé ~ The Zulu root of the word *muhle* is *-hle*, meaning good, beautiful, nice. ~ 70, 175, 176
Mouty ~ *umuThi* is the Zulu word for medicine or tree; *ubuthi* is the word for poison. ~ 179
Mouzi ~ A.D.'s rendering of the Zulu word *umuzi*, meaning homestead or cluster of huts. The typical form of an *umuzi* was a collection of domed grass huts about a central open space and enclosed within a hedge or fence. The *umuzi* of a commoner might consist of no more than one or two huts; that of a man with many wives and de-pendants of hundreds of huts. The Zulu kings maintained a number of homesteads in various parts of the kingdom, and of these some were of very considerable size since they served, also, as barracks for men of the regiments engaged in peace-time service. ~ 51, 70, 98, 107, 108, 210, 215, 218, 220, 260, and *passim*
   of Djock ~ 194
   of Noboka ~ 220, 228, 229, 235
   Nogoty royal *mouzi* ~ 265
   of Nonglass ~ 167
   of Om-Ghet-Janne ~ 264
   Sképèle, royal *mouzi* ~ 194, 210
   of Souzouana ~ 191, 260
Mpande kaSenzangakhona ~ *see* Panda
Mpangazitha kaMncumbatha ~ *see* Panga Zoaga
Msunduzi ~ *see* Om-Sonndouss
Muhle ~ *see Mouschlé*
Mulattos ~ *see* Half-castes
Munywana ~ *see* Mouniama
Mvoti ~ *see* Om-Vooty
Myandela/Myandeya ~ *see* Om-Landelle
Mzilikazi ~ *see* Massilicatzi
Mzinto ~ *see* Omzinnto
Mzinyathi ~ *see* Om-Sinyate

Namaqua ~ One of several names used to identify the Naman or Nama cluster of Khoi-Khoin clans, whose lands lay to the south and north of the lower reaches of the Orange River. ~ (xi)

Nanana ~ African hunter in A.D.'s employ. ~ 218, 236, 237, 242, 247

Nantes, Edict of ~ see Edict of Nantes

Napier, *Sir* George ~ Governor of the Cape, January 1838 – March 1844 ~ 48, 50, 98

Natal ~ The name (derived from the Portuguese 'Terra do Natal', i.e. 'land of the birth') owes its origin to the fact that a fleet, under the command of Vasco da Gama, was positioned off the south-east African coast, probably in the vicinity of present-day Port St. Johns, on Christmas day 1497. By the nineteenth century, the natural harbourage around which the modern city of Durban has developed had come to be known as Port Natal, and the name 'Natal' had come to be applied specifically to the lands between the coast and the Drakensberg to the north and south of the port. ~ (ix), (xii), 12n., 121

iNdawo ~ see *Indao*

amaNdla ~ see *Manschla*

Ndlela kaSompisi ~ see Schlala

Negroes at the Cape ~ (vii), 11 and n.

umNgeni ~ see Om-Guinée

Ngolothi ~ see Om-Grooty

oNgoye see Om-Goey

eNgqolothi ~ see Om-Grooty

iNgubo ~ see *Om-gobo*

Niewkerk, Isaac ~ Boer spy on expedition against Dingane, 1840. The reference is presumably to Izak van Niekerk. ~ 115, 116

iNkawu ~ see *Ama-kaho*

iNkonyana ~ see *Inkoniana*

iNkosikazi ~ see *Inkosikazy*

iNkosi phezulu ~ see *Kos-Pezou*

iNkunzi ~ see *Inkonnzy*

Noboka ~ Probably Nqoboka kaLanga, chief of the Sokhulu people, who occupied land close to the St. Lucia estuary. ~ 158, 159, 220, 221, 229–30

Nogoty ~ As used on p.168, the word is A.D.'s rendering of the Zulu word *umGodi*, meaning grain-pit, storage-pit, etc.; as used on p.265, it is his rendering of the name of a royal homestead in the charge of one of Mpande's sisters. ~ 168, 265

Nongalaza ~ see Nonglas *and* Tonglas

Nonglas(s) ~ Nongalaza kaNondela was one of Mpande's principal *izinduna*. He supported Mpande's secession in 1839, and was in command of Mpande's forces when, in concert with the Boers of Natal, they took to the field against Dingane in 1840.

A.D.'s visit to ~ 167–8

expedition against Dingane (Dingaan), 1840 ~ 109, 110, 116, 118, 119, 122

hospitality of ~ 168

intercedes for rebels against Dingane (Dingaan), 1840 ~ 118

relations with Boers ~ 118, 119, 122

views on warfare ~ 118

see also Tonglas

Nonoti ~ see Om-Nonnoty

Nqoboka ~ see Noboka

Nseleni ~ see Sélèni

iNtombi ~ see *Intombu*

iNtonga ~ see *Tongas*

umuNtu ~ see *Abanto*

iNyama ~ see *Ignama*

iNyamazane ~ see *Ignamazane*

iNyanga ~ see *Inianga*

iNyoka ~ see *Iniouka*

Nyoni ~ see Om-Inione

Nzobo kaSobadli ~ see Tamboussa

Ogle ~ Henry Ogle was one of the pioneer English hunters and traders who came to Port Natal in 1824. After the establishment of British rule in Natal in 1843, he settled with a large African following near the Mkomazi River in the south of the colony, where he functioned as a chief. ~ 51, 70, 75

Ohlange ~ see Om-Schlango

Olyphant's Rivier ~ Olifants River. Several rivers in southern Africa are so named. A.D.'s reference is to the river in the western Cape which disgorges into the Atlantic some 180 km north-north-west of Cape Town. ~ (vii), 31

Ombyla ~ see Maize

Omdala ~ A Zulu word, from the root *-dala*, meaning old. ~ 177, 178

Omdoda ~ *inDoda* is the Zulu word for man. ~ 229

Om-douna ~ A.D.'s rendering of *iDuna* or *inDuna*. In the Zulu kingdom, the title *iduna* (pl. *amaduna*) was reserved for men of high position close to the king. The title *induna* (pl. *izinduna*) had a wider application, being used for any man in a position of authority or command. ~ 86n., 194, 195, 198, 200

Om-Ghetjanne *also* Om-Ghet-Janne ~ The name appears to be A.D.'s rendering of Mgojane. The best-known bearer of the name was Mgojane kaSomapunga, a chief of the Ndwandwe people. The lands on which the Ndwandwe chiefdom developed lay some distance to the north of the middle reaches of the Black Mfolozi, but Shaka placed Somapunga amongst the Mkwanazi people, whose lands were just to the north of the confluence of the Black and White Mfolozis. It is, thus, possible that his son, Mgojane was living in that locality at the time of A.D.'s visit. ~ 261, 264–5

Om-gobo ~ *Ingubo* is the Zulu word for a cloak or skirt. ~ 94, 204

Om-Goey *also* Om-Gohey ~ Probably the Ngoye hills, which lie east-north-east of present-day Eshowe, between the Mhlatuze and Mlalazi rivers. ~ 40, 169

Om-Grooty ~ The context in which this name occurs suggests that A.D. is referring to a mountain or mountain range adjacent to the hunting grounds surrounding the lower reaches of the White and Black Mfolozi rivers. His rendering may be a corruption of Ngolothi (*also* Kungeloti), which is the name of a prominent mountain overlooking the north bank of the White Mfolozi some 15 km to the west of the confluence of the Mfolozi rivers. ~ 192, 193, 210, 211, 266, 279, 280

Om-Guinée *also* Omguinée ~ The Mgeni river disgorges into the Indian Ocean some six km north of the bay at Port Natal. ~ 52, 59, 84, 95, 101, 125, 126

Om-Inione ~ The context suggests that the reference may be to the Nyoni stream, a northern tributary of the lower Tugela. ~ 164

Om-Kadouka ~ The name appears to be A.D.'s rendering of Mgoduka. The best-known bearer of the name was one of Dingane's spies, who had his eyes put out for failing to locate cattle which the Zulu were seeking in the Baca country. It is unlikely that this man was the Mgoduka referred to by A.D. ~ 158

Om-Komas ~ The Mkomazi River disgorges into the Indian Ocean some 45 km south of present-day Durban. ~ 72, 73, 78, 80

Omkondo also Assegaai ~ *Umkhonto* is the Zulu word for spear. ~ 99 and n., 157, 200, 201, 202, 208, 211, 230, 278, 279

Om-Kondo ~ Man in service of Hans de Lange. ~ 213–14

Om-Kopo ~ African in employ of A.D. ~ 139, 142

Om-Koulou ~ The Zulu word *umkhulu*, from the root -*khulu*, means great, big, large, important. ~ 193, 207, 208, 229, 285

Om-Lalas ~ The Mlalazi stream rises near present-day Eshowe, and flows into the Indian Ocean just north of the village of Mtunzini. ~ 40, 155, 159, 170

hunting in vicinity of ~ 170

Om-Landelle ~ Mlandela/Myandeya ka-Mbiya, a scion of the Mthethwa chiefly house, was elevated to chiefship over the Mthethwa people by the Zulu king Shaka. His close ties with the Zulu royal house were reinforced by Shaka's successors, Dingane and Mpande. From Dingane he received as wives two high-ranking women of the royal house, Nomzinhlanga and Nomcoba, and from Mpande he received the princesses Nomqotho, Gijima and Nomaklwa. The best-known of his homesteads, kwaSemklebane, was situated in the vicinity of the Mendu hills between the Nseleni stream and the confluence of the Mfolozi rivers. ~ 175, 176

Om-Las *also* Om-Lasy ~ The Mlazi River disgorges into the Indian Ocean a short distance to the south of the bay of Port Natal. Om-Las/Umlaas was also the name of a staging-post on the Durban-Pietermaritzburg road close to the upper reaches of the river. ~ 52, 70, 75n., 101

Om-Matagoulou *also* Oum-Matagoulou ~ The Matigulu River flows into the Indian Ocean some 15 km to the north of the Tugela mouth. ~ 169

Om-Nonnoty ~ The Nonoti River flows into the Indian Ocean some 14 km to the south of the Tugela mouth. ~ 159, 166

Omnyama ~ *see Mouniama*

Omphilos *also* Omphilozie, Ompholozie ~ The White and Black Mfolozi rivers meet some 25 km west-north-west of the present-day village of Mtubatuba. East of the confluence, the river feeds into the Mfolozi swamps to the south of the St. Lucia estuary. ~ 218, 219, 224, 238, 244, 245, 258

elephants in vicinity of ~ 245–6, 251, 254, 255

(Omphilos *cont.*)

hunting in vicinity of ~ 218–20, 222, 235–6, 238–40, 241, 242–8, 251, 252, 253–4, 255–7, 258

maize-growing in river valley ~ 221

Omphilos-Mouniama ~ A.D.'s rendering of Imfolozi emnyama, which is the Zulu name for the Black Mfolozi, the more northerly of the two Mfolozi rivers which converge some 45 km west of the St. Lucia estuary. ~ 114, 119, 120, 129–30, 193, 261

elephants in vicinity of ~ 129, 266

forests in vicinity of ~ 255, 256, 258, 262–4, 265–8

hunting in vicinity of ~ 255, 256, 258, 262–4, 265–8

Omphilos-om-Schlopu ~ A.D.'s rendering of Imfolozi emhlophe, which is the Zulu name for the White Mfolozi, the more southerly of the two Mfolozi rivers which converge in the lowlands to the west of the St. Lucia estuary. Around the middle reaches of the river, in the Mahlabatini area, where the Zulu ancestral lands were located, there was a clustering of important royal homesteads. ~ 82, 114, 129, 155, 179, 181, 192, 194, 215, 279

hunting in vicinity of ~ 129–30, 179, 181–90, 215–17

Om-Phinieri ~ The references are almost certainly to Mfinyeli kaNguzalele of the Xulu people, who was one of Mpande's close personal attendants. ~ 175, 176, 194, 209

Om-phogazane ~ *Umfokazana* is the Zulu word for menial or person of no account. ~ 214, 286

Ompholozie ~ see Omphilos

Om-phondiss ~ A.D.'s rendering of *umfundisi*, the Zulu word for teacher or minister. ~ 171

Om-Pongola ~ The Pongola/Phongolo River was one of the natural features used to identify the northern margins of the Zulu kingdom. A.D.'s explanation of the meaning of the name, p.118n., is questionable. The Zulu word *umphongolo* means barrel, cask or crate. ~ 118, 119, 279

Om-Schlala ~ The Mhlali stream flows into the Indian Ocean some 55 km north-north-east of present-day Durban. ~ 166

Om-Schlango ~ The reference on p.78 is probably to the Mahlongwa River a few km south of the Mkomazi; those on pp.84 and 164 are probably to the Ohlange/Umhlanga River some 18 km north of present-day Durban; that on p.285 is indeterminate. ~ 78, 84, 164, 285

Om-Schlatousse ~ The Mhlatuze River flows into the Indian Ocean at present-day Richards Bay. ~ 40, 82, 171, 193

Om-Schlaty-Om-Koulou ~ Hlatikulu, from the Zulu noun *ihlathi*, pl. *ama-hlathi*, meaning forest, and *-khulu* meaning large, is a common locality-name. A.D.'s references appear to be to the forested area east of the Ngolo-thi range and adjacent to the White Mfolozi. ~ 191, 192, 193, 215, 248, 266, 279, 280

Om-schlopu ~ A.D.'s rendering of the Zulu word *emhlophe*, from the root *-mhlophe*, meaning white, pale, faded.

see Ingetha-Om-Schlopu; Omphilos-om-Schlopu

Om-Schlouty ~ The Mdloti River disgorges into the sea some 27 km to the north-east of present-day Durban. ~ 164

Om-Sinyate *also* Om-Siniaty ~ The Mzinyathi or Buffalo River is one of the major northern tributaries of the Tugela. ~ 109, 123

Om-Sonndouss ~ A.D. interprets Sonndouss as a Zulu corruption of St. Lucia, but his informants were probably referring to the Msunduzi, a stream in the marshy country south of the lower reaches of the Mfolozi close to the St. Lucia estuary. ~ 218

see *also* Lake Omsondouss

Om-Tagaty ~ *Umthakathi* is the Zulu word for a person who uses supernatural powers for evil purposes. ~ 89, 169, 202, 207, 208

Om-Tougate ~ The reference appears to be to the Tongati River some 35 km north of present-day Durban. ~ 83

Om-Vooty ~ The Mvoti River enters the sea some 65 km north-north-east of present-day Durban. ~ 139

Om-vubu ~ *Imvubu* is the Zulu word for hippopotamus. ~ 152

Omzinnto *also* Om-Zinto ~ The Mzinto River runs into the sea some 60 km south-south-west of present-day Durban. ~ 75, 78

Oorlogs Kloof Rivier ~ The Oorlogskloof River rises in the Hantam mountains a few miles to the west of present-day Calvinia, and forms part of the tributary system of the Doring River. ~ 33

Ostriches ~ 21

Ouena ~ Wena is the Zulu word for thou or you. ~ 70, 85n., 175

Oum-Longo ~ Umlungu, pl. *abelungu*, is the Zulu word for a white person. On p.175, the word *mooi* that precedes *Oum-Longo* is the Dutch for nice, pretty or handsome. ~ 175, 184, 197, 198, 210

Oum-Matagoulou ~ *see* Om-Matagoulou

Oury River ~ *see* Limpopo River

Out-Boom ~ *see* Gemerkte-Carrée-Hout-Boom

Owen, *Dr* ~ The reference is to the Revd F. Owen, who served as a missionary to the Zulu, 1837–8. ~ 40

Pack-Huys ~ A *pakhuys* in modern Afrikaans is a warehouse or packing shed. ~ 189

Paerde sickt see Horses (*paerde sickt*)

Panda ~ Mpande kaSenzangakhona, who succeeded to the Zulu kingship in 1840, was, contrary to A.D.'s statement, p.82, half-brother to Shaka, the founder of the kingdom, as well as to the latter's successor, Dingane. In September 1839, with a large following, Mpande seceded and established himself south of the lower Tugela near the Tongati River. Here he entered into an alliance with the Boers of Natal, and after defeating Dingane's forces at the amaQongqo hills in January 1840, he assumed the governance of the Zulu kingdom. ~ 82, 172, 175, 265

accords recognition to notable warrior ~ 92

and A.D. ~ 176, 194–9, 200, 202–3, 207, 209–10

alliance with Boers against Dingane (Dingaan), 1839 ~ 88, 119

and barter ~ 175, 190

and Boers ~ 82–3, 85, 112, 113, 119

Boer gifts to ~ 86

campaign against Dingane (Dingaan), 1840 ~ 109, 114, 116, 118, 119

cattle herds ~ 82, 83, 84, 206, 221

cession to Boers of St. Lucia Bay ~ 88

courteousness ~ 194

and Dingane (Dingaan), 1839–40 ~ 82–3, 88, 95, 99, 112, 113, 118

domestic life ~ 85, 87, 194

execution of Mpangazitha ~ 88–9, 90

extension of Boer alliance, 1840 ~ 119–20

and F. Roos ~ 95

and ivory hunting ~ 279

and missionaries ~ 40

missionary opinion of ~ 87–8

and national festival ~ 196–203, 206

and Noboka ~ 221

patronage ~ 206

physical appearance and dress ~ 85, 87, 200, 201, 206, 207

plans to overthrow Dingane (Dingaan), 1839 ~ 99

power and authority ~ 195, 196, 199, 214

and Pretorius ~ 119

reception of Boer delegation, 1839 ~ 84–6, 90–3, 95

recognised as Zulu king by Boers, 1840 ~ 119

respect shown by subjects ~ 85–6

secession, September 1839 ~ 82, 175

temporary homestead near Tongati ~ 84, 85

trial of Dambuza (Tamboussa) and Combezana ~ 112, 113

victory over Dingane (Dingaan), 1840 ~ 116, 119

women of his household ~ 77, 87, 92–3, 175–6, 198

wooden armchair or throne ~ 196, 199, 200, 206

Panga Zoaga ~ The reference is probably to Mpangazitha kaMncumbatha, one of Mpande's great *izinduna*, who was executed at the Hlawe stream near the site of present-day Tongaat village by men of the izimPohlo regiment in 1839. ~ 88–9, 90

Pannzy ~ The Zulu word *phansi* means down, on the ground. ~ 226

Parker, Edward ~ English adventurer who came to Natal *c.*1838. ~ 69, 70, 78, 106

Parkins ~ Possibly a corrupted rendering of the name Parker. ~ 228

Pastures

devasted by locusts ~ 81

near Pietermaritzburg ~ 96

near the Mooi River ~ 101, 102

sour pasture near Port Elizabeth ~ 43

sweet pasture near Bushmans River ~ 102

Paterson ~ W. Paterson, explorer and traveller, was the author of *A Narrative of Four Journeys into the Country of the Hottentots, and Caffraria*, London, 1789. ~ (x)

Peasants ~ *see* Boers

Percival ~ Eighteenth-century English traveller. ~ (xi)

Phansi ~ see *Pannzy*

Philip, *Dr* J. ~ Appointed superintendent of the London Missionary Society stations in South Africa in 1822. He was the author of *Researches in South Africa*, London, 1828, and became a figure of considerable controversy because of his philanthropic concerns. ~ (xi), 13

Phongolo ~ *see* Om-Pongola

Pieters Mauritz Burg ~ Pietermaritzburg was the seat of the governing council of the emigrant Boers of Natal. ~ 95, 96–7, 101, 125, 126

Plettenbergs Bay ~ Plettenberg Bay on the Cape south coast was named after Joachim van Plettenberg, governor of the Cape from 1774–85, who erected a beacon there. A.D.'s corrections of Le Vaillant's observations about the location of the bay are themselves incorrect. ~ 45

Poes-kop ~ Literally 'puss-head', a term used by the Boers to refer to an animal that had been dehorned or, in the case of an elephant, had lost its tusks. The modern Afrikaans rendering is *poens-kop*. ~ 275

Polygyny ~ 75–7, 94–5

Pommer, Klaas ~ Zulu interpreter with emigrant Boer deputation to Mpande, 1839. ~ 88

Pondock also Haart-Beest-Huis ~ In modern Afrikaans, *pondok* means hovel, hut, shanty. ~ 189, 251 and n.

Pongola ~ *see* Om-Pongola

Poortman ~ Bernardus Poortman came to Natal from the Netherlands and practised as a physician among the emigrant Boers. ~ 164, 167

Port Elisabeth ~ The town of Port Elizabeth developed in the early nineteenth century in proximity to the anchorage in Algoa Bay. The stone pyramid to which A.D. refers was erected by Sir Rufane Donkin, acting governor of the Cape (1820–21), in memory of his wife, Elizabeth, after whom the town was named. ~ (viii), 42, 45, 46

Port Natal ~ The name Port Natal was applied to both the natural harbour and the white settlement established on its shores in 1824. ~ 35

British occupation, 1838–9 ~ 49–50, 59
living conditions at ~ 51–2
physical features ~ 46, 48
see also Conguela

Portugal ~ (viii), 10n., 11n

Pretorius, *Commandant-general* ~ A.W.J. Pretorius, a leading figure among the emigrant Boers, was given command of the campaign against Dingane in 1840.

and annexation of Zulu territory, 1840 ~ 120
appearance and personality ~ 107–8
and Nongalaza (Nonglas) ~ 119
relations with A.D. ~ 107–8
relations with Mpande (Panda) ~ 119
treatment of deserters from Dingane (Dingaan) ~ 118
as tactician ~ 105
tries Dambuza (Tamboussa) and Khombazana (Combezana) ~ 113–14

Quathlambène ~ *see* Draaken's Berg

Redlinghuys, *Mr* ~ Farmer, freemason, and field commandant of the Hantam district in the north-western Cape. ~ 36

Republic ~ The Republic of Natalia which was formed by the emigrant Boers and whose *de facto* independence was most effective during the two and a half years between the termination of the first British occupation of Port Natal in December 1839 and the submission of the Boers to British authority in July 1842. ~ 84, 98

Retief, P. ~ Leader of the emigrant Boer advance into Natal. Retief and a party of his followers and their servants were killed at Mgungundlovu, the capital of the Zulu king, Dingane, in February 1838. ~ 40 and n., 110

legacy of fear left by murder ~ 83
naming of Pietermaritzburg ~ 96
Retief emigration ~ *see* Emigration of Boers

Rhenoster Rivier ~ The Renoster River of the Hantam mountains rises some 10 km to the north-east of the present-day village of Calvinia. ~ 36

Rice ~ 255

Riebeck Kaastel ~ Riebeek-Kasteel is a mountain some 80 km north-north-east of Cape Town. A.D.'s account of the naming of this natural feature is apocryphal. It was named in honour of Jan van Riebeeck in 1661. ~ 12n

Roos, *Mr* F. ~ F. Roos was a leading figure among the emigrant Boers in Natal. ~ 50, 83

with deputation to Mpande, 1839 ~ 83–4, 88, 89, 95

Rose, Cowper ~ Author of the work *Four Years in Southern Africa*, published in 1829. ~ (xi)

Saint Helena Fontyn ~ The farm St. Helenafontein lies on the Cape west coast almost midway between the Great Berg and Verlorevlei estuaries at St. Helena Bay and Elands Bay respectively. ~ 39

Saint-Lucia Bay ~ St. Lucia Bay lies some 250 km north-east of Port Natal. ~ 114, 221, 224

annexed by Boers, 1840 ~ 120

coveted by Boers, 1839 ~ 88

hunting in vicinity of ~ 189, 218, 222–4, 225–30

Saldanha Bay ~ The bay lies on the Atlantic coast of the Cape colony. ~ (ix)

Salt Lake ~ Probably a reference to present-day Soutpan or Wadrifsoutpan on the Langvlei-Kreefbaai estuary system. ~ 26

Salt River ~ *see* Zout-Rivier

San ~ *see* Boschjesmanes

Schlabonka ~ The Zulu word *ukuhlobonga* means external sexual intercourse. ~ 214

Schlala ~ From the context it appears probable that Schlala was a corrupted rendering of Ndlela, which was the name of one of Dingane's principal *izinduna*. ~ 116

death of ~ 115

wealth and station ~ 111

Schulz ~ A German living at Port Natal. Possibly the person referred to in some of the Boer records as Dr Schultz. ~ 135

Sea voyage, Cape Town to Port Natal ~ 41–7

Sea voyage, Europe to Cape Town ~ 3–11

Sélène ~ The Nseleni stream, close to present-day Empangeni, flows into the Nsezi River, which broadens out to form an elongated lake, before feeding into Richards Bay. ~ 175, 220

Semple ~ (xi)

Shaka ~ *see* Djacka

Sheep ~ (viii), 80

Shields, Zulu ~ 199

iShinga ~ see Tchinga

amaSi ~ see Amas

Simon's Bay ~ *see* Simon's Town

Simon's Town ~ Simonstown village lies on the western shores of False Bay. After the loss of numerous ships in Table Bay during the winter months, the Dutch East India Company in 1743 made Simonstown the official winter anchorage. ~ 15 and n.

Siswana ~ *see* Souzouana

Sitébè ~ *Isithebe* is the Zulu word for eating mat. ~ 168

Sjambok ~ *see* Chambock

Sképèle ~ One of Mpande's royal homesteads north of the middle reaches of the White Mfolozi. Probably a corrupted rendering of the name eSiklebhe/esiKlebhe, sometimes also given as eSiklebheni/esiKlebheni. ~ 194, 210

national parade at ~ 196–203, 204–7, 208–9

Slaber family ~ Original occupants of the farm Theefontein in the north-western Cape. The conventional present-day spelling of the name is Slabbert. ~ 41

Smellekaamp ~ Johan Arnold Smellekamp was a Dutch agent who established close relations with the Natal Boers in the 1840s, and eventually settled in South Africa. On the second of his missions on board the trading vessel *Brazilia* in 1843, he travelled to Delagoa Bay, where he was visited by a deputation of emigrant Boers. ~ 233

Smett family ~ Farmers in the Clanwilliam district. The spelling of the name appears to be a corrupted rendering of Smit or Smidt. ~ 31

Smith ~ Dr Andrew Smith, botanist and explorer, undertook extensive travel in the interior of southern Africa in the 1830s. His official *Report* on the expedition was published in Cape Town in 1836. ~ (xi)

Snake poison ~ 135, 237, 251–2

treatment of ~ 135–6, 164–6

Snakes ~ A.D.'s identifications are principally of better known venomous snakes. Non-venomous varieties also abound. According to Zulu belief, deceased persons (not simply 'brothers' as A.D. states, p.133n.) may assume the forms of certain non-venomous snakes (not simply pythons as A.D. suggests, *loc. cit.*) ~ 81, 131, 132, 133 and n., 134–7, 164, 193, 249, 251–2

Vienna, Treaty of ~ Peace settlement of 1815 at the end of the Napoleonic wars. The terms provided, *inter alia*, for Britain to retain the Cape, which she had occupied from 1795 to 1803, and reoccupied in 1806. ~ (ix)

Visagie family ~ Farmers in Hantam district. ~ 33

Viticulture ~ (vii), (viii), 11n., 139

imVubu ~ *see Om-vubu*

Wagons ~ 16–19
  on campaign against Dingane (Dingaan), 1840 ~ 101, 102, 103, 123
  Cape tented wagon ~ 16–18, 19
  driving of ~ 18–19, 102, 103, 123, 139, 164, 167, 174, 286
  on hunting expeditions ~ 138, 167, 174
  scarcity in Cape Town because of Boer emigration ~ 15
  travel in ~ 19

Wahlberg ~ J. G. Wahlberg was a Swedish naturalist. He travelled with A.D. from Cape Town to Natal on board the *Mazeppa*, arriving on 10 June 1839. For the next five years, until November 1844, Port Natal was the base from which he conducted his hunting and collecting expeditions, several of which were made in the company of A.D. Wahlberg published little, but his papers and collections are highly regarded scientific sources. ~ 41, 43, 46, 47, 69, 72–3, 81, 163, 180, 252

Wena ~ *see Ouena*

uWethu ~ *see Houetou*

Whaling ~ 45

White Mfolozi ~ *see* Omphilos-om-Schlopu

Wilhelm ~ Hunter in A.D.'s employ. ~ 218, 235–6, 239–40, 242, 246–7, 267–8

Wine ~ *see* Viticulture

Wolf Rivier ~ The Wolf River rises some 24 km south-west of present-day Calvinia, and forms part of the tributary system of the Doring River. ~ 32

Women ~ *see* Amazoulous (marital relations; wives, faithfulness of; widows, status of; sexual conventions); Boers (women, dominant role of); Cafres (women; family relationships; marital relations; polygyny; sexual practices); Cafres of Natal ('wife-buying'; women; polygyny; family relationships); Emigrant Boers (women, role of; sexual habits); *Inkosikazy*

Xhosa people ~ *see* Cafres

Yasy, also Hyasy ~ *Azi* is the Zulu word for know, understand, be able. ~ 70, 211

Zand Rivier ~ The reference is probably to the Zandspruit, a stream which forms part of the southern tributary system which flows into the Buffalo River some 10 km north-east of the present-day village of Dundee. ~ 109

umuZi ~ *see Mouzi*

Zietsman, Paul ~ Secretary to A.W.J. Pretorius ~ 112

emZinto ~ *see* Omzinnto

amaZizi ~ *see* Amazizi

Zoet-gras ~ Literally sweet grass ~ 102

Zoulouland *see* Amazoulou country

Zout Pan ~ A saline water hole approximately mid-way between Clanwilliam and the Hantam mountains. ~ 32

Zout Rivier ~ The lower section of the Deep River, which rises near Riebeek Kasteel and disgorges into Table Bay, is commonly known as Sout Rivier or Salt River. A tributary of the Olifants River further north on the Cape west coast bears the same name. A.D.'s reference is to the former. ~ 21

Zulu kingdom ~ *see* Amazoulou country

Zulu people ~ *see* Amazoulous